To the Three Ds
Willow and Jester

Contents

PART I

THE FUNDAMENTALS OF IMMIGRATION AND REFUGEE LAW

PART II

TEMPORARY IMMIGRATION PROGRAMS

12 Refugee and Humanitarian Resettlement Program

13 Refugee Determination System in Canada

PART VIII

LEGAL PROFESSIONALS

16 Regulating the Practice of Immigration, Refugee, and Citizenship Law 531

Preface

The first edition of *Canadian Immigration and Refugee Law for Legal Professionals*, published in 2008, was born out of frustration and hope. I began teaching immigration and refugee law at Seneca College with some practical knowledge of Canada's immigration and refugee systems, having worked for the Refugee Status Advisory Committee, Toronto Enforcement CIC, and the Immigration and Refugee Board over a number of years. I drew on statutes, regulations, rules, forms, guides, and operations manuals for my lectures. These tools all fit together like pieces of a puzzle, but trying to collect all the pieces to create a picture of the "system" was as frustrating to me as it was to my students: there was just too much information and too many places to look for it. I—we—needed a text. When I found there was no textbook geared to college students that fleshed out the complexities of the subject and concentrated on broader program descriptions, I decided to take on the project. It was my aim to write a text that would explain in plain language the complexities of the immigration and refugee systems, and that would serve as the foundation for a curriculum. But this textbook is not meant only for students; it also meets the needs of practising professionals, as a practical resource for the professional tool kit, to accompany case law and annotated statutes and regulations on immigration, refugee, and citizenship matters.

The goal for this third edition remains the same: to introduce readers to the basic principles and processes of Canadian immigration and refugee law, from eligibility criteria to decision-making, based on the most current information as possible; and, where that information is likely to be updated after publication, to provide a solid foundation on which readers can build their knowledge of professional resources to search and find it.

In the short time since the second edition was published in 2013, the Canadian government has continued to reform Canada's immigration, refugee, and citizenship systems. Instructors, students, and new professionals alike need to stay abreast of these changes—hence this new edition.

The third edition has been restructured into eight parts, with shorter chapters focusing on specific programs. The text has been enhanced with a number of features:

- keywords highlighted and defined within the text;
- new and additional illustrative scenarios;
- new and additional charts and diagrams to guide readers through application procedures and processes;
- "In the News" stories for discussion;
- updated web links that enable readers to find their way around the programs and learn how to stay up to date; and
- updated chapter review questions and new case studies.

The content in this third edition has also been updated to reflect major program and legislative changes:

- Key changes to temporary residence: the new multiple-entry visa, new study conditions for students, designated post-secondary institutions, and new rules under the Temporary Foreign Workers Program for employers and temporary workers.
- Key changes to permanent residence: new rules and caps on sponsoring parents and grandparents, and new application process requirements for the Federal Skilled Workers and Federal Skilled Trades programs under the new Express Entry system.
- The new refugee determination system, introduced by Bill C-11, the *Balanced Refugee Reform Act* (2010), and Bill C-31, the *Protecting Canada's Immigration System Act* (2012).
- The new citizenship system, introduced through amendments to the *Citizenship Act* by Bill C-24, the *Strengthening Canadian Citizenship Act* (2014).

Acknowledgments

To move from working notes to published text requires an enormous effort on the part of many. I am grateful first to my students, whose curiosity and questioning help me see more clearly what is needed to help navigate the complexities of the immigration and refugee processes—thank you for sharing my passion for Canadian immigration and refugee law. Second, I am grateful to the reviewers whose positive comments not only motivated me throughout this arduous process, but whose feedback was instructive in creating an improved edition: Subuola Awoleri, Zahra Kaderali (Sheridan College), and Jean Munn (Bow Valley College). I hope that you will be as excited as I am by the structural changes and additions to the text, and that they will work well for you in your classes.

I wish to thank Linda Pasternak and Vilma Filici (ICCRC), who teach with me at Seneca College, for keeping me up to date and for being a sounding board during this process. It is a pleasure to be working once again with Ana Rasmusson (ICCRC), who has been a part of the journey since the first edition. Her experience as a regulated immigration consultant is invaluable as the writer for the accompanying instructor's materials: muchas gracias mi amiga por todo tu trabajo!

I wish to express my deep appreciation to the supportive team at Emond Publishing: Mike Thompson, who moved up schedules to get this edition to print as quickly as possible; Heather Gough, for her patience, revisions, and guidance; Laura Bast and Jim Lyons, who coordinated production; and Sarah Gleadow, who proofread galleys. Thanks are also due to Jamie Bush and Rose Knecht, who copy-edited this edition; and Tara Wells, who designed and typeset the text.

Emond Publishing and I would also like to acknowledge the contributions made by Peter McKeracher and Lavinia Inbar to previous editions.

I am sincerely grateful for everyone's assistance and continued belief in this book. Happy reading and learning.

Lynn Fournier-Ruggles, BA, MPPAL
Summer 2015

About the Author

Lynn Fournier-Ruggles is a full-time professor in the School of Legal and Public Administration at Seneca College and teaches a variety of legal subjects to paralegal, court and tribunal, and public administration students. She has a bachelor of arts (University of Ottawa); an Excellence in Educating Adults Certificate (Seneca College); a master of arts in public policy, administration, and law (York University); and a graduate diploma in justice system administration (York University).

In addition to authoring *Canadian Immigration and Refugee Law for Legal Professionals* with Emond Publishing, Lynn has authored several academic articles: "The Cost of Getting Tough on Crime: Isn't Prevention the Policy Answer?" (2011) *Journal of Public Policy, Administration and Law*; "Establishing an Interpreter Program" (October 1996) 2:4 *Administrative Agency Practice*; and, with JO Wyspianski, "Counselling European Immigrants: Issues and Answers" in RJ Samuda & A Wolfgang, eds, *Intercultural Counselling Global Perspectives* (Toronto: CJ Hogrefe, 1985) 225–234. She also co-authored *White Paper on Quality Court Interpreter Services in Canada* for the Association of Canadian Court Administrators (2010).

Her areas of academic interest include Canadian immigration and refugee law, administrative law, court and tribunal administration, and public management and administration.

Lynn developed her knowledge of immigration and refugee law through various roles with the federal public service, including the Immigration and Refugee Board and Employment and Immigration Canada.

She has been teaching in the School of Legal and Public Administration at Seneca College since 2001.

PART I

The Fundamentals of Immigration and Refugee Law

CITIZENSHIP AND IMMIGRATION CLASSES AND PROGRAMS

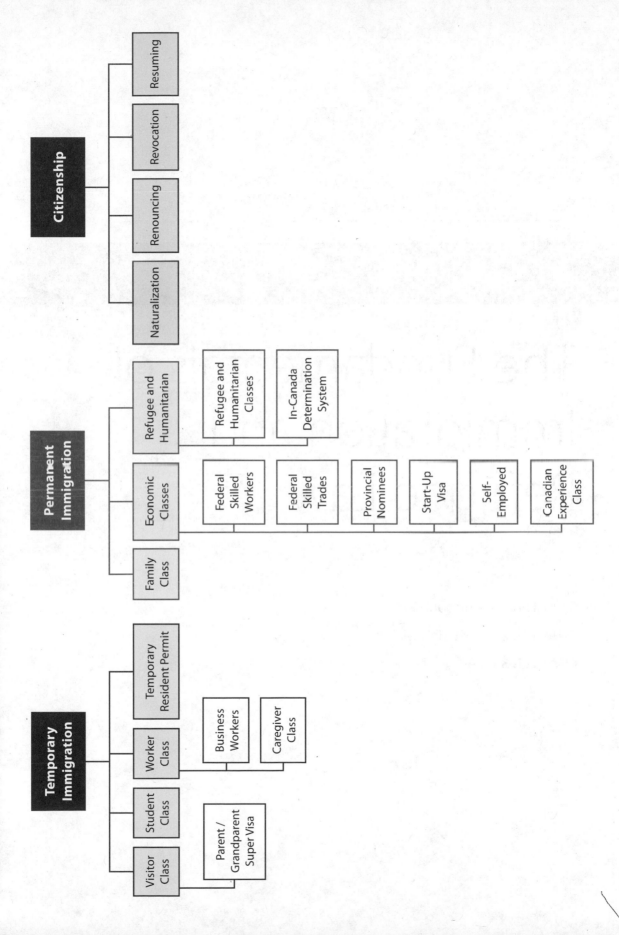

Introduction

1

LEARNING OUTCOMES

After reading this chapter, you should be able to:

- Understand the history of Canada's immigration law.

- List and describe the sources of immigration law.

- Find relevant immigration cases from the Immigration and Refugee Board, Federal Court, and Supreme Court of Canada.

- Find your way around the *Immigration and Refugee Protection Act*, the *Citizenship Act*, and their regulations.

- Search for information in policy instruments.

Introduction

Canada is a wealthy country with a highly developed social support system, a diverse population, and incredible natural resources. As a result, it is a highly attractive destination for people from around the world.

From the perspective of immigration law, an individual's status in Canada falls into one of four categories: **foreign national**, **temporary resident**, **permanent resident**, and **citizen**. Each status possesses its own set of rules and rights.

To gain entry to Canada, a foreign national requires permission from Canadian officials in the form of a **visa** (or **permit**). A foreign national with a temporary visa who is coming to Canada for a short term and is not looking for a new permanent home is a temporary resident (see Part II). Some foreign nationals, however, arrive without the proper authorization, and they may be removed immediately or may have to appear before an immigration "judge" (see Part VI), unless they have arrived in search of protection and make a refugee claim (see Part V).

A foreign national who comes to Canada to live here permanently is a permanent resident. The rights of permanent residents to enter and remain in Canada are solely determined by the *Immigration and Refugee Protection Act* (IRPA) and its regulations. This legislation provides that, under certain conditions, a permanent resident may lose that status and be forced to leave Canada (see Part III).

For policy reasons, the government also creates special immigration programs, such as the Canadian Experience Class. This class is designed to facilitate the transition from temporary to permanent residence for those immigrants who acquire Canadian education and/or work experience.

Permanent residents who follow all the rules can apply for Canadian citizenship, and when they obtain the status of citizen, they have the unqualified right to enter, leave, and remain in Canada (see Part IV). This text examines the principles and processes involved in obtaining each of these status types.

foreign national
a person from another country who is neither a Canadian citizen nor a permanent resident in Canada

temporary resident
a person who has permission to remain in Canada on a temporary basis (the main categories are students, temporary workers, and visitors)

permanent resident
a person who has been granted permanent resident status in Canada and who has not subsequently lost that status under IRPA section 46; also known as a "landed immigrant" under older legislation

citizen
a person who has the right to live in a country by virtue of birth or by legally acquiring the right

visa (or permit)
a document that permits the holder to enter Canada for a specific purpose either temporarily or permanently

Immigrant or Refugee?

The words "immigrant" and "refugee" do not mean the same thing. In the Canadian context, an *immigrant* is a person from another country who wishes to live in Canada permanently, whereas a *refugee* is a person fleeing persecution who comes to Canada to seek protection. Many refugees later choose to stay, but making Canada their permanent home is not their primary motivation for coming here. As generally used, however, the term "immigration" often refers to both immigrants and refugees.

History of Immigration Law in Canada

According to Citizenship and Immigration Canada (CIC), more than 15 million people have immigrated to Canada since Confederation in 1867. Canada's immigration scheme is founded on three pillars: economic considerations, family considerations, and refugee/humanitarian considerations. These pillars are meant to balance Canada's economic self-interests with this country's generosity and compassionate willingness to provide a safe haven to those in need from around the world.

Prior to the first *Immigration Act*, Canada's immigration rules were adapted from those of Great Britain.[1] Historically, an alien's (that is, an individual from a foreign country's) ability to enter Britain was entirely dependent on the will of the king or queen of England or on officials appointed by the monarch. The monarch's power to control immigration was gradually limited by statute law.

Prior to the federal *Immigration Act* of 1906, immigration laws in Canada were provincial; some provinces had enacted legislation primarily aimed at restricting the immigration of visible minorities.

Patterns of Immigration

Immigration to what is now Canada pre-dates the historical record. However, there are several scientific theories about the first migration to North America. One theory is that stone-age hunters followed game from Siberia into Alaska across a land bridge that once spanned what is now the Bering Strait. A second theory proposes that Asian seafarers arrived by boat. However or whenever exactly they arrived, these first migrants were probably the ancestors of Canada's First Nations peoples.

European immigration to Canada began in earnest in the early 17th century, with French settlers and fur traders. The 18th century brought a wave of British loyalists from the newly formed United States of America. In the 19th century, many immigrants came from Britain. In the 20th century, large numbers came from just about everywhere, beginning with the first huge wave from continental Europe at the beginning of the century. This 20th-century period of immigration is described as follows in CIC's publication *Forging Our Legacy: Canadian Citizenship and Immigration, 1900–1977*:

> This huge influx of people represented a watershed in Canadian immigration history. From that time until today, Canada has never received the number of immigrants that it did in 1913, when over 400,000 newcomers arrived on Canadian soil. But throughout this century immigrants did continue to choose Canada as their new country, and a second great wave (the last one to date) occurred between 1947 and 1961. Although this wave, like the first, featured newcomers from continental Europe, southern Europe, especially Italy, and central Europe became much more important sources of immigrants. By contrast, immigration from Great Britain declined substantially from the earlier period (1900–1914).[2]

Although British immigration declined, British citizens continued to receive preferential treatment over other immigrants. Various policies and laws restricted immigration from people considered to be the wrong colour or culture. Among the

---

1 For a description of the history of immigration law, see D Galloway, *Immigration Law* (Concord, Ont: Irwin Law, 1997) ch 1.

2 Citizenship and Immigration Canada, *Forging Our Legacy: Canadian Citizenship and Immigration, 1900–1977* (October 2000) ch 1, online: <http://www.cic.gc.ca/english/resources/publications/legacy/index.asp>.

best-known examples of this institutionalized racism were the Chinese head tax and the *Chinese Immigration Act* of 1923. The Act replaced the head tax, but until its repeal in 1947, this statute effectively shut down Chinese immigration.

When the Second World War erupted, anti-foreigner sentiment prevailed in Canada, and many non-British people were interned, most famously the Japanese. *Forging Our Legacy* describes the Japanese Canadian experience as follows:

> In Canada itself, probably no group of people experienced as much hardship and upheaval as the Japanese Canadians. Their ordeal began on 8 December 1941, the day after the Japanese bombed Pearl Harbor. Within hours of that attack, Ottawa ordered that fishing boats operated by Japanese-Canadian fishermen be impounded and that all Japanese aliens be registered with the Royal Canadian Mounted Police. The worst blow was delivered on 25 February 1942. On that day, Mackenzie King announced in the House of Commons that all Japanese Canadians would be forcibly removed from within a hundred-mile swath of the Pacific coast to "safeguard the defences of the Pacific Coast of Canada." Thus began the process that saw a visible minority uprooted from their homes, stripped of their property, and dispersed across Canada. Japanese Canadians, unlike their counterparts in the United States, were kept under detention until the end of the war. After the conclusion of hostilities, about 4,000 of them succumbed to pressure and left Canada for Japan under the federal government's "repatriation" scheme. Of these, more than half were Canadian-born and two-thirds were Canadian citizens.[3]

After the Second World War, the Canadian economy boomed as it had not after the First World War. This boom paved the way for more liberal immigration policies, including policies concerning displaced persons and refugees from Europe. Although these policies were more liberal, non-white immigrants were still explicitly considered undesirable, and fully a third of immigrants in the postwar wave were British.

In the mid-1960s, Canada's immigration policies finally began to change. Instead of basing the selection of immigrants on race and ethnicity, Canada adopted new selection criteria: education and skills. For the first time, significant numbers of non-British, non-European, non-white immigrants were welcomed from Africa, Asia, Latin America, and the Caribbean. These more liberal immigration policies have continued to the present day.

Today, one out of every five Canadian residents was born outside Canada. Canada accepts proportionately more immigrants than any other country in the world does, including the United States.

With respect to new permanent residents in Canada, governments generally plan for an annual immigration target of 1 percent of the country's total population. History shows, however, that this number is purely theoretical; in reality, the numbers of immigrants fluctuate in response to changes in economic, social, and labour-market factors. The highest levels of immigration—as a percentage of Canada's population—were reported between 1911 and 1913. In 1911, immigrants numbered 331,288 (representing 4.6 percent of the population) and rose in 1913 to a peak of just over

---

3   *Ibid*, ch 4.

400,000 immigrants (5.3 percent of the population). Immigration fell to one of its lowest levels (0.3 percent) in 1983–84. The *2014 Annual Report to Parliament on Immigration* states, "Canada admitted 258,953 new permanent residents in 2013, a slight increase over 2012 (257,887) and a higher level than the average number of admissions from 2009–2013 (257,000)."[4] Today, in 2015, the overall planned admission range is 260,000 to 285,000 people. The government views immigration as the primary source of Canada's net labour force growth.

Legislative History

The history of modern Canadian immigration is inextricably linked to the legislative history of immigration in this country. Currently, the two most important pieces of legislation with respect to Canadian immigration are the *Immigration and Refugee Protection Act* and the *Citizenship Act*. These two acts guide decisions about who may come to Canada and who may stay and enjoy all the rights of citizenship. In what follows, we discuss the prehistory of these statutes.

The *Immigration Act* of 1906 was a highly restrictive piece of legislation. It created a head tax for immigrants, barred many people from entering the country, and increased the government's power to deport. Its difference from earlier legislation has been described as follows:

> There had been laws since 1869 prohibiting certain kinds of immigration and since 1889 allowing designated classes of immigrants to be returned from whence they came. The 1906 Act differed in degree, significantly increasing the number of categories of prohibited immigrants and officially sanctioning the deportation of undesirable newcomers.[5]

The 1906 Act was followed by the *Immigration Act* of 1910. This Act was even more exclusionary than the 1906 Act, authorizing Cabinet to exclude "immigrants belonging to any race deemed unsuited to the climate or requirements of Canada."[6] The 1910 Act also strengthened the government's power to deport such people as anarchists, on the grounds that they would contribute to the country's political and moral instability.

These two statutes and various related laws, as well as the general approach to immigration in this country, were based, for the most part, on a policy of encouraging British and American immigration to Canada and discouraging the immigration of all other groups. An amendment to the 1906 Act sharply curtailed Asian immigration in particular. This amendment, passed in 1908, was known as the "continuous-journey regulation"; it required immigrants to Canada to travel by continuous passage from their countries of origin. This requirement was mostly designed to deter Indian

---

4 Citizenship and Immigration Canada, *2014 Annual Report to Parliament on Immigration* (Ottawa: CIC, 2014) at 11, online: <http://www.cic.gc.ca/english/resources/publications/annual -report-2014/index.asp#message>.

5 *Supra* note 2, ch 3.

6 *Ibid.*

and Japanese immigrants, for whom continuous passage to Canada was almost impossible.

Canada, however, needed cheap labour—people who were willing to work hard for low wages under harsh conditions. British and American immigrants, though more desirable from the government's point of view, were not willing to work in that way. Chinese immigrants were, as they had shown in building the Canadian Pacific Railway in the 1880s. Nonetheless, the existing laws severely restricted their entry into the country, and therefore, as *Forging Our Legacy* recounts, "Canadian industrialists ... turned increasingly towards central and southern Europe for the semi-skilled and unskilled labourers needed to supply the goods and services required by the new settlers."[7]

Immigration from Eastern, Southern, and Central Europe continued to swell Canada's population until just before the First World War. At this point, the decline of the Canadian economy increased suspicion and dislike of "foreigners" and put the brakes on the boom in immigration, as did the subsequent war. During the war, people in Canada who had originated from countries now at war with the Allies were deemed "enemy aliens" and suffered intolerance and harassment, despite the fact that most of them had settled in Canada and were contributing members of Canadian society.

Not only did many Canadians treat these "enemy aliens" badly, the government itself took hostile action against them—for example, by interning many in camps at the start of the war. The government also passed legislation, most strikingly the *Wartime Elections Act*, that penalized "enemy aliens." This Act has been described as follows:

> The *Wartime Elections Act*, invoked in the 1917 federal election, was perhaps the most extraordinary measure taken against enemy aliens. In addition to giving the federal vote to women in the armed forces and to the wives, sisters, and mothers of soldiers in active service (Canadian women as a whole had not yet won the right to vote in federal elections), the Act withdrew this right from Canadians who had been born in enemy countries and had become naturalized British subjects after 31 March 1902.[8]

These now disenfranchised, naturalized British subjects (Canadian citizenship did not yet exist) were deemed "enemy aliens," though they had fulfilled a three-year residency requirement and were hardly newcomers. The *Naturalization Act*, passed in 1914, increased the residency requirement for such immigrants to five years. British subjects (that is, immigrants to Canada who had been born in Britain) did not have to be "naturalized" in this way, and they obtained the full rights of Canadian nationals after only one year of residency.

After the First World War, the economy suffered and the fear and dislike of foreigners escalated. One of the defining events of this period of Canadian immigration

---

7   *Ibid.*

8   *Ibid*, ch 4.

history was the Winnipeg General Strike of 1919. *Forging Our Legacy* gives the following account of this event's context and significance:

> The spiralling cost of living, widespread unemployment, and disillusionment with "the system" gave rise to a wave of labour unrest that rolled across the country in 1918 and 1919, intensifying fears of an international Bolshevik conspiracy. Nothing did more to inflame anti-foreign sentiment and heighten fears of revolution than the Winnipeg General Strike of May 1919.[9]

The government's legislative reaction to the strike was again to target so-called foreigners:

> Ultimately, the decisive intervention of the federal government brought about an end to the conflict. Persuaded that enemy aliens had instigated the strike, the government succeeded in 1919 in amending the *Immigration Act*, to allow for their easy deportation. It then had ten strike leaders arrested and instituted deportation proceedings against the four who were foreign-born. When a protest parade on 21 June turned ugly, Royal North West Mounted Police charged the crowd, leaving one person dead and many others wounded. "Bloody Saturday," as it came to be called, led to the arrest and deportation of 34 foreigners and effectively broke the Winnipeg General Strike. But it would leave a long-lasting legacy of bitterness and unrest across Canada.[10]

The revised *Immigration Act* was further used to severely limit non-British immigration. Its historical significance has been described as follows:

> The revised *Immigration Act* and the Orders in Council issued under its authority signalled a dramatic shift in Canadian immigration policy. Prior to the First World War, immigration officials had chosen immigrants largely on the basis of the contribution that they could make to the Canadian economy, whereas now they attached more importance to a prospective immigrant's cultural and ideological complexion. As a result, newcomers from the white Commonwealth countries, the United States, and to a lesser extent the so-called preferred countries (that is, northwestern Europe) were welcomed, while the celebrated "stalwart peasants" of the Sifton era were not, unless, of course, their labour was in demand.[11]

In 1922, the government of Mackenzie King relaxed the *Immigration Act*'s regulations. In the following years, Mackenzie King repealed most of the legislation preventing European immigration. In 1923, however, the *Chinese Immigration Act* was enacted, preventing virtually all Chinese immigration. During the Great Depression of the 1930s, government policy and legislation were again used to close the doors to non-British immigrants and refugees, including Jewish refugees attempting to flee Nazi Germany. Many immigrants were barred from entry to Canada, and tens

---

9 *Ibid.*

10 *Ibid.*

11 *Ibid.*

of thousands who were already in Canada were deported in those years. With the outbreak of the Second World War, fear and suspicion of foreigners escalated. Many so-called foreigners were interned in camps, most notoriously those of Japanese origin, many of whom had been born in Canada.

Besides being racist, Canadian immigration laws were sexist into the mid-20th century. It has been noted that married women "did not have full authority over their national status. Classified with minors, lunatics and idiots 'under a disability,' they could not become naturalized or control their national status as independent persons, except in very special circumstances."[12]

The *Canadian Citizenship Act*—Canada's first immigration statute, which came into force in 1947—addressed some of these issues of racism and sexism. Prior to it, Canadian citizenship as we understand it today did not exist; "Canadians" were British subjects. With the passage of this Act, Canadians became citizens of their own country. The new statute also gave married women autonomy with respect to their status: the nationality of a married woman was no longer dependent on that of her husband. The significance of the *Canadian Citizenship Act* was ceremoniously acknowledged by the government, as *Forging Our Legacy* describes:

> With the enactment of this revolutionary piece of legislation, Canada became the first Commonwealth country to create its own class of citizenship separate from that of Great Britain. … In a moving and historic ceremony, staged on the evening of 3 January 1947 in the Supreme Court of Canada chamber, 26 individuals were presented with Canadian citizenship certificates. Among them were Prime Minister William Lyon Mackenzie King, who received certificate 0001, and Yousuf Karsh, the internationally acclaimed Armenian-born photographer.[13]

A new *Immigration Act* was enacted in 1952, the first such Act since 1910. Although it included provisions designed to exclude non-whites, it also provided the government with the discretion—a discretion that it proceeded to exercise—to admit large numbers of refugees and others who would otherwise have been inadmissible.

But the turning point in Canada's legislative history with respect to immigration was probably the *Immigration Act* of 1976:

> The *Immigration Act*, the cornerstone of present-day immigration policy, was enacted in 1976 and came into force in 1978. It broke new ground by spelling out the fundamental principles and objectives of Canadian immigration policy. Included among these are the promotion of Canada's demographic, economic, cultural, and social goals; family reunification; the fulfillment of Canada's international obligations in relation to the United Nations Convention (1951) and its 1967 Protocol relating to refugees, which Canada had signed in 1969; non-discrimination in immigration policy; and cooperation between all levels of government and the voluntary sector in the settlement of immigrants in Canadian society.[14]

12 *Ibid*, ch 5.

13 *Ibid*.

14 *Ibid*, ch 6.

Another important development was the creation of a new citizenship act—the *Citizenship Act*—that replaced the *Canadian Citizenship Act* and came into force in 1977. Amendments have been made to the Act over the years, and it is still in force today. The new statute addressed previous racist policies, particularly the different treatment accorded "aliens" as opposed to those originating from Britain and the British Commonwealth. (Previously, for example, British immigrants had qualified for Canadian citizenship without being called before a judge for a hearing or taking the oath of allegiance in a formal ceremony, as others were required to do.) The main thrust of the new Act has been summarized as follows:

> It was to rectify … anomalies and the unequal treatment accorded different groups of people that *An Act Respecting Citizenship* was first introduced in the House of Commons in May 1974. It received Royal Assent on 16 July 1976 and came into force, along with the *Citizenship Regulations*, on 15 February 1977. Henceforth, improved access and equal treatment of all applicants would be the guiding principles in the granting of Canadian citizenship.[15]

The new *Citizenship Act* provided equal rights and privileges, and equal obligations and duties, to all Canadians, regardless of whether they were born in Canada or whether they were born elsewhere and subsequently acquired Canadian citizenship. The Act also permitted dual citizenship, allowing Canadians to enjoy the citizenship benefits of Canada and of another country.

Planning Immigration

Under section 94 of the *Immigration and Refugee Protection Act*, the minister is required to table an annual report to Parliament that reports on the operations of the IRPA and how CIC has managed that year's immigration programs. This report includes

- information about the selection of foreign nationals, including details regarding cooperation with the provinces;
- the number of foreign nationals who became permanent residents in the previous year, and projections for the future;
- the number of persons who entered Canada in the previous year under federal–provincial agreements;
- the number of persons who were given permanent resident status in the previous year for humanitarian and compassionate reasons;
- the languages spoken by persons who became permanent residents;
- the number of times that immigration officers, having determined that doing so was justified, exercised their power to let in a person who would otherwise have been deemed inadmissible; and
- a gender-based analysis of the impact of the IRPA.

WEBLINK

A copy of the most recent annual report to Parliament on immigration can be found on the Publications and Manuals page on the CIC website at <www.cic.gc.ca/english/resources/publications/index.asp>. Under Other Publications, choose "About the Department." A list of annual reports will appear below.

---

15 *Ibid.*

The Management of Immigration and Refugee Programs

immigration
the movement of non-native people into a country in order to settle there

Canada's **immigration** management scheme is created by the IRPA, which was passed into law in 2001 and came into force on June 28, 2002, replacing the *Immigration Act* of 1976. Two departments of the federal government share responsibility for administering this statute and its regulations: (1) Citizenship and Immigration Canada (CIC) and (2) the Canada Border Services Agency (CBSA). CIC and the CBSA have discrete responsibilities in connection with the following general functions:

immigrant
a person who wishes to settle (or has settled) permanently in another country

- admitting **immigrants** (permanent residents) and temporary residents such as foreign students, visitors, and temporary workers who enhance Canada's social and economic growth;
- resettling, protecting, and providing a safe haven for **refugees** and others who are in need of protection;
- helping newcomers adapt to Canadian society and become Canadian citizens; and
- managing access to Canada to protect the security, safety, and health of Canadians and the integrity of Canadian laws.

refugee
a person who is forced to flee from persecution (as opposed to an immigrant, who chooses to move)

CIC also manages the citizenship program and, since 2008, the multiculturalism program under the *Canadian Multiculturalism Act* (1988).

Because there are many people wanting to come to Canada—on either a permanent or a temporary basis—CIC applies formal criteria to determine who will be allowed to enter. Generally, preference is given to those who are likely to make a positive contribution to the economy, or at least not burden it. Other factors, however, such as family reunification and observing Canada's commitment to providing a safe refuge for people fleeing persecution, may also be considered regardless of a person's financial circumstances.

In general, Canada supports the entry of foreign nationals who

- have valuable skills needed by Canadian employers (for example, current practice gives priority to those skilled workers who have specialized abilities and a valid job offer);
- have the means, ability, and ambition to become entrepreneurs in Canada or to extend to Canada the operation of already successful business enterprises;
- are the family members or dependants of immigrants; and
- have fled to Canada for protection from persecution by the government in their country of origin.

In general, Canada does not support the entry of foreign nationals who

- pose a threat to Canadian security;
- have a history of criminality or close connections to organized crime; or
- are likely to place a heavy burden on Canada's social support systems (for example, on the health care system) without contributing to the Canadian economy.

Sources of Immigration Law

Immigration in Canada is governed by both domestic law and international law.

Domestic law governing immigration includes the Constitution, the *Canadian Charter of Rights and Freedoms* (the Charter), federal and provincial statutes and regulations, and case law. The primary sources of immigration law are the federal *Immigration and Refugee Protection Act*, the regulations under that statute, and case law interpreting the statute and regulations. The *Citizenship Act* is another important federal statute; it sets out the procedures for obtaining Canadian citizenship. Federal–provincial agreements governing immigration to a particular province are also considered domestic law.

International law—law that is, ideally, common to all nation-states—includes multinational treaties and conventions. Canada has signed a number of international agreements that affect our immigration rules—for example, the 1951 United Nations *Convention Relating to the Status of Refugees* and the accompanying 1967 *Protocol Relating to the Status of Refugees*, as well as the *Convention on the Protection of Children and Co-operation in Respect of Inter-Country Adoption* (Hague Convention). By signing these agreements, Canada has committed to structuring our domestic law in a manner that is consistent with the legislative models in other like-minded countries.

Some of these treaties are multilateral, involving many countries. Others relate to a few specific countries—for example, the North American Free Trade Agreement (NAFTA), which contains specific provisions to facilitate temporary business entry among Canada, the United States, and Mexico.

Section 7 of the IRPA grants the minister of citizenship and immigration the power to enter into agreements with other countries or with certain international organizations. These agreements must be approved by the federal Cabinet and must be consistent with the purposes of the IRPA.

To some degree, international principles have been **codified** in our domestic law—for example, the refugee provisions of the IRPA. The IRPA is the focal point for the study of immigration law in Canada, and it is thoroughly explored in this text. Before examining the details of the IRPA and its regulations, however, we will take a step back and survey Canada's wider legal landscape, which is composed of Canada's constitutional documents, statutes and regulations, case law (judge-made law), and government policy. Each component will be discussed in turn.

codified
formalized and clarified in writing in the form of binding legislation

The Constitution

The **Constitution** is the supreme law of the land. It is the basic framework within which all other laws in Canada are created, and it establishes the basic principles to which all other laws must conform. Until 1982, Canada's Constitution and its original and defining source of law was the *British North America Act* (later renamed the *Constitution Act, 1867*), a statute of England. This statute provided the framework for Canada's democracy, but only the United Kingdom had the power to make certain constitutional amendments. The *Canada Act 1982* finally changed this; it gave Canada's Parliament the exclusive power to amend the Constitution. A truly

Constitution
the basic framework within which all other laws are created, establishing the basic principles to which all other laws must conform

Canadian constitution was created with the *Constitution Act, 1982*, which contains the *Canadian Charter of Rights and Freedoms*.

Division of Powers: Constitution Act, 1867

federal system of government
a division of law-making powers between the national (federal) and provincial governments according to subject matter

The *Constitution Act, 1867*, as Canada's supreme law, created a **federal system of government**. This division of powers between the two levels of government remains today. The federal government has jurisdiction over matters of national interest—in other words, matters that affect all Canadians from coast to coast. The provincial governments have jurisdiction over local matters within their own provinces. The federal government also has law-making jurisdiction with respect to the territories, although federal legislation has granted the territories many of the same powers that the Constitution grants the provinces.

FEDERAL POWERS

Most federal powers are set out in section 91 of the *Constitution Act, 1867*. They include the authority to regulate subjects such as naturalization and aliens, national defence, and criminal law. The basic rule governing the division of powers is that matters that require a national standard fall within the jurisdiction of the federal government. Postal service (s 91(5)), census and statistics (s 91(6)), currency and coinage (s 91(14)), and naturalization and aliens (s 91(25)), for example, are all issues of national interest; in these areas, it is important that the same legal standards are applied across the country.

residual power
power that is not otherwise delegated elsewhere; the federal government has residual power to legislate in all subject areas that are not specifically assigned to the provinces

The federal government also has **residual power** to make laws for "the peace, order, and good government" of Canada in all matters that do not come under a provincial head of power. This means that any matters not specifically delegated to the provinces are matters over which the federal government has jurisdiction.

PROVINCIAL POWERS

Most provincial powers are set out in section 92 of the *Constitution Act, 1867*, and they generally include authority over all matters of a local or private nature in the province, such as property, hospitals, schools, and child protection. (These local matters include such things as municipalities and local boards and agencies.) For example, section 92(13) assigns property and civil rights to the provincial governments. This means that labour legislation is generally under provincial law, and explains why the rules around labour vary from province to province.

In Canada, a significant degree of legislative responsibility is delegated to the provinces. This means that there are many more provincial statutes, and accompanying regulations, than there are federal ones. The areas of legislative responsibility assigned by the Constitution to the federal government and the provincial governments, respectively, are shown in the chart on page 15.

SECTION 95: CONCURRENT POWERS OF LEGISLATION

With respect to agriculture and immigration, the *Constitution Act, 1867* makes a special provision for the federal and provincial governments' sharing power. With respect to immigration, section 95 states the following:

Examples of the Law-Making Powers of the Federal and Provincial Levels of Government

Federal government law-making powers by subject matter (section 91)	Provincial government law-making powers by subject matter (section 92)
• Interprovincial/international trade • National defence • Currency • Criminal law • Naturalization and aliens • Residual powers • Peace, order, and good government	• Property laws • Civil rights (contract, tort) • Hospitals • Matters of a local nature (local trade and public works) • Municipalities • Generally, all matters of a merely local or private nature in the province

In each Province the Legislature may make Laws in relation to … Immigration into the Province; and it is hereby declared that the Parliament of Canada may from Time to Time make Laws in relation to … Immigration into all or any of the Provinces; and any Law of the Legislature of a Province relative to … Immigration shall have effect in and for the Province as long and as far only as it is not repugnant to any Act of the Parliament of Canada.

In other words, a province may make laws in relation to the immigration of people into the province, provided that those laws are not inconsistent or in conflict with any federal law. In the area of immigration, then, the two levels of government hold concurrent powers of legislation. If there is a conflict between validly enacted federal and provincial legislation, however, it is the federal legislation that prevails.

The IRPA includes various examples of provisions relating to the provinces and to the sharing of power between federal and provincial levels of government with respect to immigration:

- Section 3(1)(c) refers to the objective "to support the development of a strong and prosperous Canadian economy, in which the benefits of immigration are shared across all regions of Canada."
- Section 3(1)(j) refers to the Act's objective "to work in cooperation with the provinces to secure better recognition of the foreign credentials of permanent residents and their more rapid integration into society."
- Section 8(1) states that the federal minister of citizenship and immigration "may enter into an agreement with the government of any province for the purposes of this Act. The Minister must publish, once a year, a list of the federal–provincial agreements that are in force."
- Section 10 states that the minister "may consult with the governments of the provinces on immigration and refugee protection policies and programs, in order to facilitate cooperation and to take into consideration the effects that the implementation of this Act may have on the provinces."

IMMIGRATION AGREEMENTS

Section 8 of the IRPA provides that the minister, with the approval of the Cabinet, may enter into agreements with the provinces and territories. Each province has one or more such agreements in place, tailored to meet its specific economic, social, and labour-market needs and priorities. These agreements facilitate the exchange of information between the federal government and the provinces during the development of immigration programs and policies. For example, the Canada–Ontario Immigration Agreement, first signed in 2005, provided that the federal government would transfer $920 million to Ontario over five years to assist with the integration of new immigrants, including language training. Some of these federal–provincial agreements are comprehensive and cover a wide range of immigration issues. The agreements that the federal government now has in place with British Columbia, Alberta, Saskatchewan, Manitoba, Ontario, Quebec, Nova Scotia, Prince Edward Island, and the Yukon are comprehensive in this way.

Other agreements cover more specific issues—for example, the Provincial Nominee Program, which is relevant to British Columbia, Alberta, Saskatchewan, Manitoba, Ontario, New Brunswick, Prince Edward Island, Newfoundland and Labrador, the Northwest Territories, and the Yukon. The Provincial Nominee Program allows a province or territory to nominate people as immigrants if it believes that they will contribute to the economic growth of the province. Discussion of these provincial programs, each of which has its own criteria, is beyond the scope of this text.

CIC's most recent *Annual Report to Parliament on Immigration* is generally a good source to check for information about current federal–provincial agreements. Students who are interested in a specific federal–provincial agreement or immigration program are advised to search that province's website for specific information or to go to the CIC website and read the department's latest annual report. (See the Weblink earlier in this chapter.)

Canada–Quebec Accord

Canada and the province of Quebec have had immigration agreements since 1971. The most recent is the 1991 Canada–Quebec Accord, the most significant and comprehensive immigration agreement between Canada and a province. From Quebec's perspective, two objectives are particularly important. Objective 2 states that, among other things, the Accord strives to maintain "the preservation of Québec's demographic importance within Canada and the integration of immigrants to that province in a manner that respects the distinct identity of Québec."[16] Objective 4 states that "Québec has the rights and responsibilities set out in this Accord with respect to the number of immigrants destined to Québec and the selection, reception and integration of those immigrants."[17]

Under the Accord, Quebec has the sole responsibility for the selection of permanent residents and refugees from outside Canada who wish to settle in that province.

---

16   Citizenship and Immigration Canada, "Canada–Québec Accord Relating to Immigration and Temporary Admission of Aliens" (5 February 1991) s 2, online: <http://www.cic.gc.ca/english/department/laws-policy/agreements/quebec/can-que.asp>.

17   *Ibid*, s 4.

Because immigrants destined for Quebec must first apply to the province, most of Quebec's programs and processes involve instructions unique to that context and will not be discussed in this text. Individuals who are successfully selected by Quebec are then referred to CIC, which tests for inadmissibility on the grounds of medical risk or burden, security threat, and criminality—the same legal standards that are applied to all immigrants across the country. (The grounds of inadmissibility are discussed in Chapter 3.)

The federal government remains responsible for setting minimum national standards for the admission of all immigrants and visitors, and for the administrative function of processing applications and physical admission to Canada at ports of entry. Quebec may impose additional selection criteria for immigrants to Quebec and is responsible for integrating immigrants into the community.

The Canadian Charter of Rights and Freedoms

The *Canadian Charter of Rights and Freedoms* was designed to accomplish one of the most important constitutional functions—to express the fundamental values and principles of our society. Canada prides itself on being a free and democratic society that protects the welfare of its members. The Charter reflects that objective and provides a mechanism to balance individual freedoms with the need to protect society's more vulnerable members.

Rights and freedoms protected by the Charter include the following:

- fundamental freedoms, including freedom of expression (s 2(b)) and freedom of religion (s 2(a));
- mobility rights (s 6), such as the rights of Canadian citizens to enter, remain in, and leave Canada;
- legal rights, such as the right to life, liberty, and security of the person (s 7) and the right to an interpreter at a hearing (s 14);
- equality rights (s 15); and
- language rights, such as the right to use any one of the two official languages (English and French) in a court proceeding (s 19) or when obtaining services from the federal government (s 20(1)).

The Charter provides in section 1 that government legislation and actions cannot infringe on these rights and freedoms unless the infringement can be "demonstrably justified in a free and democratic society." Accordingly, the Charter has two important effects:

1. If any law or government policy contravenes the terms of the Charter, that law or policy may be declared unconstitutional and of no force and effect by a court or **administrative tribunal** (unless the law invokes the section 33 "notwithstanding clause").
2. Any action—by an agent or representative of any level of government—that contravenes any right or freedom protected by the Charter can be challenged in the courts by (s 24).

administrative tribunal
a specialized governmental agency established under legislation to implement legislative policy—for example, the Immigration and Refugee Board is an administrative tribunal established under the IRPA

The precise scope of the Charter's application has been a matter of debate and litigation. Although it is clear that the Charter applies to the content and effects of government law and to the nature and effects of government action, it has sometimes been difficult to define what is meant by "government" action. Many organizations and regulated industries in Canada have some connection to government, and there have been many cases argued that turn on whether the actions of a quasi-governmental organization constitute *government* action.

Unregulated private activity is not subject to the Charter. The purpose of the Charter is to establish parameters concerning what the government can do to protect minority rights in a democracy in which the majority elects the government. Because the Charter applies only to *government* activity or decisions, the protection of equality rights with respect to *non-governmental* activities has been codified in additional human rights legislation.

The purpose of human rights legislation is similar to the Charter's purpose, but the scope of such legislation extends beyond the activities and decisions of government; it regulates the actions of landlords, employers, and providers of goods and services, whether they be individuals, businesses, or private institutions. Consider, for example, the owner of an apartment building who refuses to rent to people with children. This type of discrimination would be addressed by human rights legislation.

REASONABLE LIMITS ON RIGHTS AND FREEDOMS

Section 1 of the Charter provides that all of its rights and freedoms are subject to "such reasonable limits prescribed by law as can be demonstrably justified in a free and democratic society." Each time a court considers whether a law is in violation of the Charter, it must consider whether the law imposes a "reasonable limit" on a Charter right. A law will be struck down only when both of the following conditions exist:

1. the law violates a Charter right or freedom; and
2. the law cannot be justified as a reasonable limit in a free and democratic society (the *Oakes* test).[18]

For example, freedom of expression may be curtailed by the duty of society to protect children from being exploited in pornography. In this and many other instances, the courts will conclude that although a right or freedom was violated, the violation was justifiable.

SELECTED CHARTER CASES

The reasons provided by the Supreme Court of Canada in the following four cases exemplify the Charter's power to shape the law in Canada.

18   So named because it derives from the Supreme Court of Canada's decision in *R v Oakes*, [1986] 1 SCR 103.

Andrews v Law Society of British Columbia

In the 1989 case of *Andrews*,[19] the Supreme Court first ruled on the equality provisions set out in section 15 of the Charter. The court held that this Charter right was violated by the Law Society of British Columbia's requirement that lawyers be Canadian citizens. The wording of section 15(1) is as follows:

> Every individual is equal before and under the law and has the right to the equal protection of the law without discrimination and, in particular, without discrimination based on race, national or ethnic origin, colour, religion, sex, age or mental or physical disability.

The court held that the grounds of discrimination listed in section 15 were not exhaustive, and that analogous grounds, such as "citizenship," were also covered by the Charter. The respondent, Andrews, was a British subject and permanent resident in Canada. He met all the requirements for admission to the British Columbia Bar except that of Canadian citizenship. When he was refused admission, he successfully challenged the citizenship requirement on the grounds that it violated his right to equality.

As the first section 15 case, *Andrews* laid the foundation for analyzing Charter challenges involving equality. The Supreme Court held that section 15 provides every individual a guarantee of equality before and under the law, as well as the equal protection and equal benefit of the law without discrimination. The court expanded the scope of the right to equality by rejecting the equality test—known as the "similarly situated should be similarly treated" test—that the lower court had used in the *Andrews* case for interpreting section 15. In the context of citizenship, this test resulted in unequal treatment, provided that all non-citizens were treated the same and all citizens were treated the same.

The Supreme Court held instead that discrimination is a distinction that is based on grounds relating to the personal characteristics of the individual or group and that it has the effect of imposing disadvantages not imposed on others. Distinctions based on personal characteristics that are attributed to an individual solely on the basis of his or her association with a group "will rarely escape the charge of discrimination, while those based on an individual's merits and capacities will rarely be so classed." This guarantee is not a general guarantee of equality; its focus is on the application of the law. The effect of the impugned distinction or classification on the complainant must also be considered.

The court, while noting that there may be legitimate reasons for requiring citizenship, concluded in *Andrews* that barring an entire class of persons from certain forms of employment solely on the grounds of a lack of citizenship status and without consideration of their educational and professional qualifications or their other attributes or merits infringes section 15 equality rights.

Note that although *Andrews* held that section 15 of the Charter prohibited discrimination against permanent residents, discrimination in some circumstances

---

19   *Andrews v Law Society of British Columbia*, [1989] 1 SCR 143.

will be tolerated, either because it is justifiable under section 1 of the Charter or because the Charter itself makes a distinction between citizens and non-citizens— for example, only citizens may vote in elections, and the IRPA legitimately discriminates against non-citizens with respect to the right to live in Canada permanently and not be deported.

Singh v Minister of Employment and Immigration

Singh[20] is an important case for two reasons: (1) it clarifies who is protected under the Charter, and (2) it sets out the procedural requirements for fairness. In *Singh*, the Supreme Court considered whether section 7 of the Charter applied to the adjudication of refugee claims under the *Immigration Act* of 1976 and, if so, whether those procedures denied the section 7 requirement of fundamental justice.

The wording of section 7 is as follows:

> Everyone has the right to life, liberty and security of the person and the right not to be deprived thereof except in accordance with the principles of fundamental justice.

The *Singh* case actually involved claims by six appellants, each of whom made separate and unrelated claims to "Convention refugee" status. (*Convention refugees* are people who are outside their home country or the country where they normally live, and who are unwilling to return to these countries because of a well-founded fear of persecution based on race, religion, political opinion, nationality, or membership in a particular social group   for example, women or people of a particular sexual orientation.)

Under the former refugee determination scheme, a refugee claimant was examined under oath by a senior immigration officer—a public servant in the federal Department of Employment and Immigration. Next, a transcript was made of the examination under oath and sent to the Refugee Status Advisory Committee (RSAC) for a paper review and recommendation to the minister. This was done with the six appellants in *Singh*. The minister, acting on the advice of the RSAC, determined in each case that the claimants were not Convention refugees. Each of the six appellants then applied to the Immigration Appeal Board (IAB), a quasi-judicial tribunal, for a redetermination of their claims. The IAB refused their applications on the basis that the board did not believe that there were "reasonable grounds to believe that a claim could, upon the hearing of the application, be established." On the basis of this refusal, it was decided that no hearing into their claims would be held.

Although none of the appellants were Canadian citizens, the court found that they were entitled to the protection of section 7, which applies to "every human being who is physically present in Canada and by virtue of such presence amenable to Canadian law."[21] Thus, the court extended section 7 protection to any person in Canada, regardless of whether that person has any legal right to be here.

---

20 *Singh v Minister of Employment and Immigration*, [1985] 1 SCR 177.

21 *Ibid* at para 35.

The court found that denying a refugee claimant's right, under section 55 of the *Immigration Act, 1976*, not to "be removed from Canada to a country where his life or freedom would be threatened" amounted to a deprivation of security of the person within the meaning of section 7.

The court also found that, at a minimum, the concept of fundamental justice in section 7 includes the notion of procedural fairness. The procedural scheme for refugee determinations under the former *Immigration Act* was not in accordance with fundamental justice, according to the court, because the hearings were based only on written submissions. The court held that "where a serious issue of credibility is involved, fundamental justice requires that credibility be determined on the basis of an oral hearing."[22] Only an oral hearing is adequate in such circumstances to fairly assess a refugee claimant's credibility.

The court further held that failure to provide an oral hearing was not reasonable or justifiable and therefore could not be saved under section 1. As a result of the *Singh* decision, the former refugee determination system was replaced by the current Immigration and Refugee Board (IRB), which holds quasi-judicial oral hearings for refugee claimants who are in Canada.

Canada (Minister of Employment and Immigration) v Chiarelli

Section 7 was raised again in *Chiarelli*[23] to challenge the former *Immigration Act* of 1976. This time it was raised unsuccessfully, however. In *Chiarelli*, the court ruled that non-citizens (except refugees) do not have the same unqualified right to enter and remain in Canada as Canadian citizens do. Sections 27(1)(d)(ii) and 32(2) of the *Immigration Act* of 1976 required that deportation be ordered for persons convicted of an offence carrying a maximum punishment of five years or more, without regard to the circumstances of the offence or the offender. Chiarelli, a permanent resident, immigrated with his family as an adolescent, and a decade later was declared inadmissible on the grounds of criminality and ordered deported.

Chiarelli's criminal record classified him in such a way that he was barred from admission to Canada, and the minister was authorized to issue a certificate dismissing Chiarelli's appeal. In other words, Chiarelli was not accorded the usual right to appeal, in which the deportation order would be considered in light of all of the circumstances of the case. Chiarelli argued that these provisions were contrary to the section 7 principles of fundamental justice. In response, the Supreme Court held the following:

> [I]n determining the scope of the principles of fundamental justice as they apply to this case, the Court must look to the principles and policies underlying immigration law. The most fundamental principle of immigration law is that non-citizens do not have an unqualified right to enter or remain in the country.[24]

---

22   *Ibid* at para 59.

23   *Canada (Minister of Employment and Immigration) v Chiarelli*, [1992] 1 SCR 711.

24   *Ibid* at 733.

The court noted the Charter distinction between citizens and non-citizens: only citizens are accorded the right "to enter, remain in and leave Canada" under section 6(1). The court further held that

> there has never been a universally available right of appeal from a deportation order on "all the circumstances of the case." Such an appeal has historically been a purely discretionary matter. Although it has been added as a statutory ground of appeal, the executive has always retained the power to prevent an appeal from being allowed on that ground in cases involving serious security interests.[25]

But, more to the point, with regard to the section 7 requirement of fundamental justice, the court held that

> Parliament has the right to adopt an immigration policy and to enact legislation prescribing the conditions under which non-citizens will be permitted to enter and remain in Canada. It has done so in the *Immigration Act*. ... [N]o person other than a citizen, permanent resident, Convention refugee or Indian registered under the *Indian Act* has a right to come to or remain in Canada. ... One of the conditions Parliament has imposed on a permanent resident's right to remain in Canada is that he or she not be convicted of an offence for which a term of imprisonment of five years or more may be imposed. This condition represents a legitimate, non-arbitrary choice by Parliament of a situation in which it is not in the public interest to allow a non-citizen to remain in the country. ... [T]he personal circumstances of individuals who breach this condition may vary widely. The offences ... also vary in gravity, as may the factual circumstances surrounding the commission of a particular offence. However there is one element common to all persons who fall within the class of permanent residents described in the s. 27(1)(d)(ii). They have all deliberately violated an essential condition under which they were permitted to remain in Canada. In such a situation, there is no breach of fundamental justice in giving practical effect to the termination of their right to remain in Canada. In the case of a permanent resident, deportation is the only way in which to accomplish this. There is nothing inherently unjust about a mandatory order. ... It is not necessary, in order to comply with fundamental justice, to look beyond this fact to other aggravating or mitigating circumstances.[26]

What this means, in a nutshell, is that while section 7 of the Charter does provide minimum procedural protections, it generally does not shield non-citizens from deportation.

Suresh v Canada (Minister of Citizenship and Immigration)

In *Suresh*,[27] the court again addressed the issue of deportation. This case involved an additional element: the person was a Convention refugee who faced a risk of torture

---

25 *Ibid* at 741.

26 *Ibid* at 733–34.

27 *Suresh v Canada (Minister of Citizenship and Immigration)*, 2002 SCC 1, [2002] 1 SCR 3.

if deported. In this case, the person's inadmissibility was based on his membership in a terrorist organization.

Suresh came to Canada from Sri Lanka, was recognized as a Convention refugee, and applied for landed immigrant status (now called permanent resident status). He was ordered deported on security grounds, based on the opinion of the Canadian Security Intelligence Service that he was a member and fundraiser for the Liberation Tigers of Tamil Eelam (the Tamil Tigers), an organization engaged in terrorist activity in Sri Lanka whose members were subject to torture in that country.

Section 53 of the *Immigration Act* of 1976 permitted persons who had been engaged in terrorism or who belonged to terrorist organizations, and who also posed a threat to the security of Canada, to be deported "to a country where the person's life or freedom would be threatened." The question was raised as to whether such deportation violated the procedural protection found under section 7 of the Charter.

The court held that while section 53 did not infringe the Charter, deportation to face torture is generally unconstitutional, and some of the procedures followed in Suresh's case did not meet the required constitutional standards. Therefore, according to the court, he was entitled to a new deportation hearing:

> [T]he procedural protections required by s. 7 in this case do not extend to the level of requiring the Minister to conduct a full oral hearing or a complete judicial process. However, they require more than the procedure required by the Act under s. 53(1)(b)—that is, none—and they require more than Suresh received.[28]

As to the larger question of whether to deport a refugee when doing so may subject him or her to torture, the court held that it was a matter of balancing interests:

> Canadian jurisprudence does not suggest that Canada may never deport a person to face treatment elsewhere that would be unconstitutional if imposed by Canada directly, on Canadian soil. To repeat, the appropriate approach is essentially one of balancing. The outcome will depend not only on considerations inherent in the general context but also on considerations related to the circumstances and condition of the particular person whom the government seeks to expel. On the one hand stands the state's genuine interest in combatting terrorism, preventing Canada from becoming a safe haven for terrorists, and protecting public security. On the other hand stands Canada's constitutional commitment to liberty and fair process. This said, Canadian jurisprudence suggests that this balance will usually come down against expelling a person to face torture elsewhere.[29]

So, although it would generally be a violation of the Charter to deport a refugee where there are grounds to believe that he faces a substantial risk of torture, the court left open the possibility that, in exceptional cases, such deportation might be justified.

---

28 *Ibid* at para 121.

29 *Ibid* at para 58.

WEBLINK

It is easy to access statutes and regulations online, but it is important to ensure that you are using a website that maintains regularly updated versions of the legislation. The Canadian Legal Information Institute (CanLII) website provides access to up-to-date versions of statutes and regulations for the federal, provincial, and territorial governments, as well as extensive case law. Visit CanLII at <www.canlii.org>.

Statutes and Regulations

Statutes

Statutes or legislation, such as the IRPA, are written codes of law that typically deal with a particular subject matter—for example, immigration, criminal law, child protection, or income tax. Many statutes are accompanied by **regulations**, which fill in the details regarding how the law is to be implemented.

Statutes are created by a legislature—either by the federal Parliament in Ottawa or by the provincial or territorial legislatures in each of the provinces and territories. The legislature is the elected arm of government and is accountable to the voters. Provided that doing so does not violate constitutional principles (such as those found in the Charter), a legislature can change the rules developed in case law by using clear language in a statute. Courts, for their part, may make decisions about how to interpret and apply legislation, especially when the wording in a statute is vague or ambiguous or may have changed over time. Such statutory interpretation can lead to broad changes in the operation of a law.

statute
law passed by Parliament or a provincial legislature; also called an "act"; often specifically provides for the authority to make regulations or to delegate this power; distinguished from subordinate legislation

Regulations

Many statutes, including the IRPA and the *Citizenship Act*, authorize the creation of regulations, which provide the practical details concerning the statute's implementation. Regulations are sometimes described as being "created under statutes." They are a subordinate form of legislation, often drafted by the staff of the Cabinet of the governing party. Unlike statutes, regulations need not be approved and passed by the legislature.

Regulations tend to be practical and can include lists, schedules, diagrams, forms, and charts. The information that they provide is just as important as the information in the primary legislation (the statute or act). If a statute has regulations made under it, the regulations will be found published in their own volumes, separate from the statute, and will be revised according to the same schedule as the statute itself. However, regulations cannot exist independently, without a parent statute. For a regulation to exist lawfully, it must have a parent statute that contains a provision designating regulation-making authority. If no such provision exists, no regulations may be enacted.

regulations
detailed rules, created pursuant to a statute by the governor in council, that fill in practical details regarding the statute's administration and enforcement

Case Law

Case law is judge-made law. The courts' ability to create law as well as to interpret it is considerable, as the Charter cases described above demonstrate. Case law is part of the **common law**, which has evolved from decisions of English courts going back to the Norman Conquest. Some would say that English common law began with King Henry II, who was crowned shortly after the Norman conquest and who created principles of law that were to be "common" to all free men in England. The formation

case law
interpretations of statutes and regulations created by the judgments of courts and other adjudicators; case law is part of the common law

common law
a body of legal principles and rules that can be traced back to Britain and that are found in court judgments

of common law is similar to that of **customary international law**, where customs and practice take on legal significance over time.

Common law principles still apply in Canada with respect to areas of law that are not fully codified by statute, such as contract law and tort law. As underscored by the Charter cases examined above, the common law rules of procedural fairness—developed in the common law through judicial review—play an important role in immigration law.

Case law also includes tribunal and judicial decisions that interpret the Constitution, statutes, and regulations. To achieve predictability and consistency, our courts treat similar cases in a similar manner, making decisions in accordance with **precedent**. "Rules" created by judges in legal decisions bind the decision-makers in future decisions that turn on the same or similar facts. The decisions of higher-level courts (provincial courts of appeal or the Supreme Court) must be respected and followed in lower-level courts unless the facts of the new case before the lower court differ substantially. Tribunal decisions, however, are not binding across different tribunals or even within the same tribunal. See the discussion of tribunals and the role of administrative law, below.

Policy

Policies explain the operation of legislation and regulation. Government **policy** is not law; however, it is a very important source of guidance and direction. How the law is applied in practice often evolves in response to government policy, especially where the law leaves room for discretion in administrative decision-making. Policies can be formal or informal, and they can be written or unwritten. They can also have a wide range of objectives, such as promoting fairness and determining the areas to which the government should give priority. For example, it is CIC policy to give priority to processing and finalizing within six months applications from those who are applying under the family class for spouses, common law and conjugal partners, and dependent children.[30]

The objectives and operation of government policy must be in compliance with legislation and regulations. Government policy documents are often made available to the public on government websites.

The Immigration and Refugee Protection Act: Overview

The *Immigration and Refugee Protection Act* and its regulations, especially the *Immigration and Refugee Protection Regulations*, are referred to on a regular basis throughout this text, and a brief review of their structure and content will be helpful. In contrast to many of Canada's earlier laws, the current legislative framework for immigration

customary international law
international legal customs and practices that take on the force of law over time

precedent
a court ruling on a point of law that is binding on lower courts

policy
non-binding guidelines that are created by agencies to support the administration of statutes and regulations, and that reflect the government and agency's agenda

---

30 Citizenship and Immigration Canada, "Processing Priorities" in *Operation Procedures: OP 1* (16 August 2012) s 5.14, online: <http://www.cic.gc.ca/english/resources/manuals/op/op01-eng.pdf>.

is based on non-discriminatory principles and is grounded in the values enshrined in the Charter. The IRPA came into force on June 28, 2002, replacing the *Immigration Act* of 1976. It introduced new provisions designed to increase national security and public safety, balanced with provisions intended to make it simpler for admissible persons to enter Canada.

The IRPA provides a framework for the operation of our immigration and refugee systems, setting out general rules and principles, the rights and obligations of permanent and temporary residents and protected persons, and key enforcement provisions. The regulations under it provide the specific details needed for its implementation and operation. The regulations change relatively frequently, and immigration consultants and other legal professionals must monitor information sources, such as the CIC website (<www.cic.gc.ca>), on a regular basis.

The IRPA is divided into five parts, which are further subdivided into divisions, sections, and subsections. A table of contents for the IRPA appears in the box below.

IRPA Objectives

The IRPA sets out separate objectives for the provisions regarding immigrants and the provisions regarding refugees. The objectives offer important guidance to immigration officers, the Immigration and Refugee Board of Canada (IRB), and the courts with respect to how the statute should be applied and interpreted.

IRPA Table of Contents

Sections 1 to 10: These sections set out the short title of the Act, provide definitions and objectives, and give the minister authority to appoint officers, make regulations, and set up international and provincial agreements.

Part 1: Immigration to Canada

Division 0.1: Invitation to Make an Application

Division 1: Requirements and Selection

Division 2: Examination

Division 3: Entering and Remaining in Canada

Division 4: Inadmissibility

Division 5: Loss of Status and Removal

Division 6: Detention and Release

Division 7: Right of Appeal

Division 8: Judicial Review

Division 9: Certificates and Protection of Information

Division 10: General Provisions

Part 2: Refugee Protection

Division 1: Refugee Protection, Convention Refugees, and Persons in Need of Protection

Division 2: Convention Refugees and Persons in Need of Protection

Division 3: Pre-removal Risk Assessment

Part 3: Enforcement

Part 4: Immigration and Refugee Board

Part 5: Transitional Provisions, Consequential and Related Amendments, Coordinating Amendments, Repeals and Coming into Force

Schedule: Sections E and F of Article 1 of the United Nations *Convention Relating to the Status of Refugees*

Schedule: Article 1 of the *Convention Against Torture and Other Cruel, Inhuman and Degrading Treatment or Punishment*

With respect to immigration, the objectives of the IRPA, set out in section 3(1), can be summarized as follows:

- to maximize the social, cultural, and economic benefits of immigration;
- to enrich and strengthen the social and cultural fabric of Canadian society while respecting the federal, bilingual, and multicultural character of Canada;
- to support and assist the development of minority official languages communities in Canada;
- to support the development of a strong and prosperous Canadian economy in which the benefits of immigration are shared across all regions of Canada;
- to reunite families in Canada;
- to integrate permanent residents into Canada, while recognizing mutual obligations for new immigrants and Canadian society;
- to support consistent standards and prompt processing;
- to facilitate the entry of visitors, students, and temporary workers for purposes such as trade, commerce, tourism, international understanding, and cultural, educational, and scientific activities;
- to protect the health and safety of Canadians and maintain the security of Canadian society;
- to promote international justice and security by fostering respect for human rights and by denying access to Canadian territory to persons who are criminals or who pose security risks; and
- to cooperate with the provinces to better recognize the foreign credentials of permanent residents.

With respect to refugees, the objectives of the IRPA, set out in section 3(2), can be summarized as follows:

- to recognize that the priority of the IRPA is to save lives and protect displaced and persecuted persons;
- to fulfill Canada's international legal obligations with respect to refugees and affirm its commitment to international efforts to assist with resettlement;
- to grant fair consideration to those who come to Canada claiming persecution;
- to offer a safe haven to persons with a well-founded fear of persecution based on race, religion, nationality, political opinion, or membership in a particular social group, as well as persons at risk of torture or cruel and unusual treatment or punishment;
- to establish fair and efficient procedures that will maintain the integrity of the Canadian refugee protection system, while upholding Canada's respect for the human rights and fundamental freedoms of all human beings;
- to support the self-sufficiency and the social and economic well-being of refugees by facilitating reunification with their family members in Canada;

- to protect the health and safety of Canadians and maintain the security of Canadian society; and
- to promote international justice and security by denying access to Canadian territory to persons, including refugee claimants, who are security risks or serious criminals.

The IRPA also contains a provision (s 3(3)) that directs all decision-makers to interpret and apply the IRPA in a manner that

- furthers the domestic and international interests of Canada;
- promotes accountability and transparency by enhancing public awareness of immigration and refugee programs;
- facilitates cooperation between the government of Canada, provincial governments, foreign states, international organizations, and non-governmental organizations;
- ensures that decisions made under the IRPA are consistent with the Charter, including its principles of equality and freedom from discrimination and the equality of English and French as the official languages of Canada;
- supports the government's commitment to enhancing the vitality of the English and French linguistic minority communities in Canada; and
- complies with international human rights instruments to which Canada is signatory.

The structure and mandate of the IRB—an administrative tribunal—is created by the IRPA. The IRB has four divisions: the Immigration Division, the Immigration Appeal Division, the Refugee Protection Division, and the Refugee Appeal Division. Within these divisions, members perform the following functions: hold admissibility hearings to determine whether individuals may enter or remain in Canada; hold detention reviews; hear and decide appeals on immigration matters (such as removal orders, sponsorship refusals, and residency requirements); and decide refugee claims made by individuals in Canada. IRB decisions may be subject to judicial review by the Federal Court of Canada.

The Role of Administrative Law

Administrative law is a branch of public law concerned with the legal rules and institutions used to regulate and control the exercise of state power in its relations with citizens. Much of immigration law is administrative law, because immigration law governs how government administrators and employees (that is, public servants) exercise the decision-making powers granted to them under the IRPA. Administrative decisions may be made quickly and routinely, depending on the requirements of the statute—for example, by a visa officer who issues a temporary resident visa to a foreign national. Alternatively, administrative decisions may be quasi-judicial, involving a hearing before an impartial decision-maker. Often, decisions start out as routine, but an applicant who is denied the right or the benefit being sought may challenge the decision, and it will be reheard, usually by an independent board or tribunal such as the Law Society Tribunal or the IRB.

Generally, decisions by administrative tribunals require a greater degree of procedural fairness than do routine administrative decisions made by staff. Tribunals function in a similar manner to courts, with both sides making arguments and providing evidence to the decision-maker. At the least, the person seeking a decision is entitled to be heard—that is, entitled to be given an opportunity to respond. However, this right does not necessarily extend to the right to have a full oral hearing like a trial, with the submission of evidence, an examination, the cross-examination of witnesses, and arguments. The degree of procedural fairness required in a hearing before a tribunal depends on the wording of the statute in question.

Regardless of whether a decision is administrative or quasi-judicial (that is, with a hearing before a tribunal), the decision must be fair; it must be based on the relevant criteria and made by an unbiased decision-maker. An advantage of administrative tribunals is that hearing procedures are generally much less formal than court procedures, and matters can be resolved more quickly.

Administrative decisions may be judicially reviewed by a court. On judicial review, the court considers whether the tribunal acted within its jurisdiction (that is, according to the statute and regulations), whether it exercised its discretion in an appropriate manner, and whether its procedures were fair. This is different from an appeal, which reconsiders the legal merits of the decision. On appeal, a court may overturn a decision if it finds that the decision was "wrong"—that is to say, based on an erroneous interpretation or application of the law.

Decisions of administrative tribunals may be appealed to a court only if such an appeal is expressly permitted by the statute that creates and governs the tribunal. The rationale for limiting appeals of tribunal decisions is that an appeal essentially involves replacing a tribunal's decision with a court's decision. This undermines one of the advantages of tribunals—expertise in a particular subject area. It is a principle of administrative law that courts should defer to administrative decisions made by government officials and tribunals, because these officials and tribunals possess expertise in their particular regulatory regimes, such as immigration and refugee law.

The Citizenship Act

The *Citizenship Act* does not discriminate between Canadian citizens by birth and immigrants who are born elsewhere and subsequently obtain Canadian citizenship, nor does it discriminate between men and women or between people of different nationalities or races. All citizens share the same rights and privileges, such as the right to vote and hold office, and all share the same obligations and duties. Most notably, the *Citizenship Act* permits dual citizenship, allowing Canadians to be citizens of another country as well as of Canada.

With a few exceptions, such as the children of diplomats, all persons born in Canada are Canadian citizens. Children born outside Canada who have at least one Canadian parent are automatically citizens as well.

The *Citizenship Act* is divided into eight parts, as shown in the table of contents reproduced in the box below.

Citizenship Act Table of Contents

Sections 1 and 2: These sections set out the short title and definitions.

Part I: The Right to Citizenship

Part II: Loss of Citizenship

Part III: Resumption of Citizenship

Part IV: Certificate of Citizenship

Part V: Procedure

Part V.1: Judicial Review

Part VI: Administration

Part VII: Offences

Part VIII: Status of Persons in Canada

Schedule: Oath or Affirmation of Citizenship

The *Citizenship Act* currently has two regulations: the *Citizenship Regulations* (SOR/93-246) and the *Foreign Ownership of Land Regulations* (SOR/79-416). The Act is explored in more detail in Part IV of this text.

Interpretation Tools

Immigration Regulations and Rules

Regulations under the IRPA are made by Cabinet and must be published in the *Canada Gazette* along with a regulatory impact analysis statement. These explanatory notes are helpful in determining how the regulations are to be applied, and they cover the following points:

- description of the regulation, including its purpose and function;
- alternatives to the regulation that were considered;
- benefits and costs to the public of the regulation;
- consultations that took place with interested parties and the public in the drafting of the regulation;
- compliance and enforcement issues;
- gender-based analysis of the impact of the regulation; and
- a contact person.

There are numerous regulations under the IRPA, covering a variety of subject areas. The largest is the *Immigration and Refugee Protection Regulations* (SOR/2002-227), which consists of 21 parts and provides detailed guidance regarding the application of the IRPA, including definitions of family relationships; the criteria for applying to the various permanent and temporary resident programs; definitions of classes of refugees; and procedures for detentions, release, removals, and appeals. As you study the different temporary and permanent resident programs, you will become familiar with a number of these regulations.

Examples of other regulations include the following:

- *Immigration Division Rules* (SOR/2002-229)
- *Federal Courts Citizenship, Immigration and Refugee Protection Rules* (SOR/93-22)
- *Order Designating the Minister of Citizenship and Immigration as the Minister Responsible for the Administration of That Act* (SI/2001-120);
- *Order Setting Out the Respective Responsibilities of the Minister of Citizenship and Immigration and the Minister of Public Safety and Emergency Preparedness Under the Act* (SI/2005-120); and
- *Protection of Passenger Information Regulations* (SOR/2005-346).

Citizenship Regulations

Similar to the regulations described above, the *Citizenship Regulations* set out the details for processing citizenship applications. For example, they provide specific criteria for granting, renouncing, or resuming Canadian citizenship, as well as criteria for the citizenship test. They also provide information about the oath of citizenship, procedures for citizenship ceremonies, and fees for becoming a citizen.

Policy Instruments

As noted above, policy fills in the gaps in a statute or its regulations and is intended to promote consistency, fairness, and transparency. Most policy develops and evolves over time on an informal basis, as certain procedures that work well become accepted. Policy may also be formalized through a variety of instruments that codify informal policy or create new policy. Both CIC and the IRB use a variety of policy instruments, as described below.

Consider the following types of CIC policy instruments:

1. *Policy notes.* Policy notes are memoranda used to address issues that are temporary in nature or that are limited to a specific region.
2. *Program manuals.* Citizenship and Immigration Canada publishes operational manuals to guide the activities of immigration and citizenship officers. Officers consult these manuals when applying the IRPA, the *Citizenship Act*, and their accompanying regulations; likewise, immigration practitioners should consult these documents when advising clients. The existing manuals can be found on the Reports and Statistics page on the CIC website and are as follows:
   - Citizenship Policy (CP);
   - Enforcement (ENF);

- Temporary Foreign Workers Guidelines (FW);
- Immigration Legislation (IL);
- Information Sharing (IN);
- Inland Processing (IP);
- Reference (IR);
- Overseas Processing (OP);
- Protected Persons (PP); and
- Identity Management (IM).

Note that CIC is no longer updating the manuals; instead, the department is making available Program Delivery Instructions in a modernized format.

3. *Operational bulletins (OBs).* Operational bulletins are issued to deliver urgent instructions to officers or provisional instructions to staff to be used on a one-time or temporary basis while the program and policy manuals are updated. The minister may issue a number of bulletins each month, so it is advisable to check these to see whether the processing of a given application will be affected. Both current and archived operational bulletins can be found on the Publications and Manuals page on the CIC website.

Keep in mind that although these policy instruments are important, they are merely policy and do not have the force of law. Therefore, if a manual's provision is inconsistent with the provisions of the IRPA or its regulations, it will not be valid. CIC has modified the format of its operational manuals and now combines the latest operational guidance and policy—including OBs—in one place, classifying all of them as Program Delivery Instructions.

Immigration and Refugee Board: Tribunal Rules and Policy Instruments

rules
a category of regulation that has the purpose of establishing practices and procedures for the presentation of cases

Tribunal **rules** are generally binding, like any other regulations, unless they specifically provide otherwise. The rules are authorized by section 161(1) of the IRPA and include rules of procedure for each of its divisions:

- *Adjudication Division Rules* (SOR/93-47);
- *Immigration Appeal Division Rules* (SOR/2002-230);
- *Immigration Division Rules* (SOR/2002-229);
- *Refugee Protection Division Rules* (SOR/2012-256); and
- *Refugee Appeal Division Rules* (SOR/2012-257).

Consider the following policy instruments of the IRB:

1. *Chairperson's guidelines.* The chairperson's guidelines are authorized by section 159(1)(h) of the IRPA to provide guiding principles for resolving cases and to further the government's strategic objectives. The chairperson of the

IRB is permitted to make guidelines and identify decisions as important precedents, to assist members of the IRB in carrying out their duties. Decision-makers are not required to follow the chairperson's guidelines, but are required to justify cases of non-compliance. The following guidelines existed as of February 2015:

- Guideline 1: Civilian Non-Combatants Fearing Persecution in Civil War Situations;

- Guideline 2: Detention;

- Guideline 3: Child Refugee Claimants—Procedural and Evidentiary Issues;

- Guideline 4: Women Refugee Claimants Fearing Gender-Related Persecution;

- Guideline 6: Scheduling and Changing the Date or Time of a Proceeding;

- Guideline 7: Concerning Preparation and Conduct of a Hearing in the Refugee Protection Division; and

- Guideline 8: Concerning Procedures with Respect to Vulnerable Persons Appearing Before the Immigration and Refugee Board of Canada.

The guidelines can be found on the IRB's website. Under About the Board, select "Legal and Policy References."

2. *Jurisprudential guides.* The jurisprudential guides are authorized by section 159(1)(h) of the IRPA. Their purpose is to facilitate consistency in decision-making with regard to similar cases. A jurisprudential guide reiterates the reasoning of the IRB in a specific decision so that it can be applied in similar cases. The jurisprudential guides are not mandatory, but decision-makers are required to justify non-compliance with the guides in cases with similar facts.

3. *Persuasive decisions.* Persuasive decisions are decisions identified by the head of the division, such as the head of the Refugee Protection Division, as being well reasoned. Decision-makers are encouraged to follow the same reasoning in their own decisions. However, decision-makers are not required, as they are with the jurisprudential guides, to justify their choice not to follow persuasive decisions.

4. *Policies.* Policies are formal statements explaining the details of new IRB initiatives (for example, outlining roles and responsibilities). Two examples of policies are as follows:

- Policy for Handling IRB Complaints Regarding Unauthorized, Paid Representatives (April 2008); and

- Policy on the Use of Jurisprudential Guides (March 2003), which governs the exercise of the chairperson's authority to identify a decision as a jurisprudential guide.

5. *Chairperson's instructions.* Chairperson's instructions provide formal direction to individual IRB staff. They are more narrow and specific than the policies described above.

KEY TERMS

administrative tribunal, 17

case law, 24

citizen, 4

codified, 13

common law, 24

Constitution, 13

customary international law, 25

federal system of government, 14

foreign national, 4

immigrant, 12

immigration, 12

permanent resident, 4

policy, 25

precedent, 25

refugee, 12

regulations, 24

residual power, 14

rules, 32

statute, 24

temporary resident, 4

visa (or permit), 4

REVIEW QUESTIONS

1. List and provide one historical highlight from each of Canada's immigration statutes.

2. List and provide one historical highlight from each of Canada's citizenship statutes.

3. What are the key federal statutes and regulations used in Canada for immigration, refugee, and citizenship matters?

4. Why does the federal government have responsibility for naturalization and aliens?

5. Give an example of how the federal government and the provincial governments share powers related to immigration.

6. Are permanent residents, temporary residents, and refugees protected by section 7 of the Charter? If yes, why? If no, why not?

7. Which Supreme Court decision holds that the concept of fundamental justice includes the following notion: procedural fairness requires that, where a serious issue of credibility is involved, credibility must be determined on the basis of an oral hearing?

8. Find and briefly summarize the following sections of the IRPA:

   - Section 2
   - Sections 8 and 10
   - Section 11
   - Section 12
   - Section 14
   - Section 15

   - Section 16
   - Section 18
   - Section 19

9. Which section of the IRPA requires the minister to table an annual report to Parliament?

10. What is administrative law?

11. What is a judicial review?

12. Which section of the *Citizenship Act* defines who is a Canadian citizen?

13. Which section of the *Citizenship Act* details the requirements for citizenship?

14. Where in the *Citizenship Act* does the citizenship oath appear?

EXERCISE

Find the most recent *Annual Report to Parliament on Immigration* and determine the following:

- the government's plan to admit permanent residents by category,
- the government's plan to admit temporary residents, and
- the government's plan to admit protected persons as permanent residents.

FURTHER READING

Knowles, Valerie. *Strangers at Our Gates: Canadian Immigration and Immigration Policy, 1540–1990*, revised ed (Toronto: Dundurn Press, 2007).

Malarek, Victor. *Haven's Gate: Canada's Immigration Fiasco* (Toronto: Macmillan, 1987).

Decision-Makers

2

LEARNING OUTCOMES

After reading this chapter, you should be able to:

- Identify key federal organizations involved in deciding immigration, citizenship, and refugee protection matters.

- Distinguish among the roles and functions of Citizenship and Immigration Canada (CIC), the Canada Border Services Agency (CBSA), the Immigration and Refugee Board (IRB), the Federal Court, and the Supreme Court.

- Identify the divisions of the IRB and distinguish between the jurisdiction and function of each of those divisions.

- Distinguish among the decision-making roles of the minister of CIC, the minister of Public Safety and Emergency Preparedness (PSEP), the delegates of these ministers, and decision-makers in the IRB, including the chairperson and members.

- Understand the basis in law for decision-making.

Introduction

Try searching the Internet to answer the following questions:

- Whom do you contact about how to have a client released from immigration detention?
- Do you contact Citizenship and Immigration Canada (CIC) or the Immigration and Refugee Board (IRB) if your client's sponsorship of a family member has failed?
- Which body is responsible for removing people who should not be in Canada—CIC, the IRB, or the Canada Border Services Agency (CBSA)?
- If your application to sponsor a family member is refused, do you file an appeal with the IRB, the Federal Court, or the Supreme Court?

Canadian immigration and refugee laws and related processes are complex and subject to frequent changes. A client may have a file and a client ID number with more than one organization. Therefore, determining which organization to contact depends on the issues in each case and how much progress has been made in the application and the decision-making processes.

In Chapter 1, we learned about the various sources of law governing the complexities of Canadian immigration. Now we consider the final piece of the puzzle: the role of decision-makers in immigration and refugee matters. Who makes decisions on cases? What decision-making powers do they have? Where do they get that authority? In this chapter, we look briefly at the following three levels of decision-making:

1. the ministers, including officers, for CIC and for Public Safety and Emergency Preparedness (PSEP), as well as one of the PSEP's agencies, the CBSA;
2. the four divisions of the IRB and tribunal decision-makers; and
3. the courts.

We discuss (1) who, within each of these three organizational levels, has the statutory authority to make decisions; (2) what is the source of their jurisdiction to make decisions; and (3) what relationships exist among the three levels of decision-making.

In addition to considering these three organizational levels, we look at related organizations that are involved in immigration and refugee protection matters.

Ministers Responsible for Immigration and Refugee Matters

Section 4 of the *Immigration and Refugee Protection Act* (IRPA) divides responsibility for immigration and refugee functions between two ministers:

- the minister of CIC, and
- the minister of PSEP, who is responsible for the CBSA.

Note that the Department of PSEP is now called Public Safety Canada. We use the former title in this text because that is the way it is referenced in the relevant legislation.

The following descriptions of ministerial authority relate either to the minister of CIC or to the minister of PSEP, unless otherwise specified.

Ministerial Authority and Decision-Making Powers

The minister of CIC heads the department of that name, which is responsible for general areas of immigration and citizenship, including the following:

- the development of immigration policy, including guidance to staff about how to carry out their functions and apply legislation;
- an annual plan that sets out the target numbers for immigration;
- immigration programs related to temporary and permanent immigration;
- the settlement and integration of newcomers to Canada;
- the resettlement of refugees; and
- policies related to admissibility.

The minister of PSEP heads the department of that name and takes the lead in developing policy related to immigration enforcement functions, such as those carried out by the CBSA. These functions include the management and operation of Canada's borders, in which the following are involved:

- arrests,
- detentions,
- removals, and
- port-of-entry functions.

The IRPA grants broad regulatory power to Cabinet through the **governor in council** to make rules and regulations in the form of **orders in council**. This enables the government to respond quickly to adapt the Act's broad provisions to changing circumstances. As noted in Chapter 1, regulations set out standards and criteria for selecting qualified immigration applicants and cover a broad range of definitions. For example, the regulations stipulate the amount payable by the applicant for processing the different kinds of visa applications for permanent and temporary resident visas. Regulations also identify the various categories within the economic classes of immigrants and set out specific criteria within each class. These criteria can be changed. Generally speaking, the regulations can easily be amended by an order in council. An amendment to the regulations could involve changing the amount payable for processing a visa application (s 5), or it might involve adding or repealing a class of permanent resident.

In some cases, the minister of CIC is required to table proposed regulations before each House of Parliament (the House of Commons and the Senate) so that these proposals can be referred to the appropriate committee of that House. This is required when the proposed regulations relate to provisions in the following areas:

governor in council
the governor general acting with the advice and consent of Cabinet; formal executive authority is conferred by the statutes on the governor in council

orders in council
administrative orders that serve notice of a decision taken by the executive arm of government

- examinations;
- rights and obligations of permanent and temporary residents;
- status documents;
- loss of status, and removal, detention, and release;
- examination of eligibility to refer a refugee claim;
- the principle of *non-refoulement* (that is, the principle of international law according to which refugees or asylum seekers should not be forced to return to a country in which they are liable to be subjected to persecution); and
- transportation companies (s 5(2)).

The proposed regulation need only be tabled once; it does not have to be presented to each House of Parliament again, even if it has been altered (s 5(3)). As a result, amendments can be made without further examination by Parliament.

The IRPA empowers the minister to make decisions on a variety of matters and to delegate specific powers and decisions to others.

Immigration Policy and Administrative Functions

The minister of CIC is responsible for immigration policy development and immigration processes. Did you ever wonder who decides how many immigrants Canada should accept in a given year? The minister of CIC, in consultation with the provinces, is responsible for setting the annual targets, including the number and types of foreign nationals who may come to Canada either as temporary or permanent residents.

The minister of CIC, following consultations with the provinces, must table the annual immigration report to Parliament each year on or before the first of November. At a minimum, this plan provides an estimate of the number of permanent residents to be admitted each year (see Chapter 1). The minister also determines requirements for foreign nationals, such as the minimum standards they must meet in order to qualify as permanent residents. An example of such a requirement is the "pass mark" for skilled workers discussed in Chapter 8, Economic Classes.

Under the regulations to the IRPA, each minister has administrative authority over specific areas. For example, the minister of PSEP can designate ports of entry and their dates and hours of operation.

Ministerial Discretion

In 2008, section 87.3 of the IRPA was amended to expand the discretionary powers of the minister. By means of operational bulletins (see Chapter 1), the minister of CIC has the power to issue instructions that directly affect the daily work of citizenship and immigration officers (C&I officers) and CBSA officers in their handling of cases. Section 87.3(2) states the following: "The processing of applications and requests is to be conducted in a manner that, in the opinion of the Minister, will best support the attainment of the immigration goals established by the Government of Canada."

These instructions, which reflect a change in policy and/or the regulations, are not debated in Parliament; they are published in the *Canada Gazette*. Note that instructions are added or updated, and other instructions expire, on a frequent basis. It is therefore important for legal professionals in the area of immigration to check CIC's website for updated operational bulletins concerning changes to programs, application criteria, and processing procedures. These legislative amendments authorize the minister to issue instructions to staff about the processing of applications and requests—their categorization, priority, and even their numbers (IRPA, s 87.3(3)).

Under Canadian immigration law, the minister decides whether a person is allowed to enter (is admissible) or is to be removed from Canada (see Chapter 3). The minister also has the discretionary power to grant temporary and permanent resident status to foreign nationals on humanitarian and compassionate grounds. This power may be exercised on behalf both of those who wish to come to Canada and those who are already here and wish to remain here but are inadmissible for technical, medical, or criminal reasons.

For example, you may have heard in the media about cases involving a child in need of life-saving surgery that is not available in her home country. How is it that this child may come to Canada for medical treatment if she is not healthy enough to pass the required medical examination? In such a case, the minister of CIC may exercise his discretionary powers to allow the child entry to this country. Although the child does not meet the statutory requirements for admission to Canada, the reasons for allowing her entry to Canada are compelling enough for the minister to grant temporary authorization. The minister may issue a temporary resident permit— formerly known as a "minister's permit"—that is valid for a specified and limited period of time and that can also be cancelled.

Security Certificates

In exceptional circumstances, a security certificate may be issued for the purpose of removing from Canada a permanent resident or foreign national. This may be done where there is reason to believe that this person poses a security threat and there is information that needs to be protected for security reasons. The security certificate's purpose is to ensure that the government's classified information remains confidential: it has the effect of closing the proceedings to the public and ensuring the non-disclosure of information that could seriously harm the government's ability to protect its citizens.[1]

On February 14, 2008, Bill C-3, *An Act to amend the Immigration and Refugee Protection Act (certificate and special advocate) and to make a consequential amendment to another Act* received royal assent. This Act was introduced in response to the 2007 Supreme Court ruling in *Charkaoui v Canada*[2] that additional safeguards should be incorporated into the security certificate process to enhance the protection of the rights of individuals subject to a certificate. This amendment provides that a **special advocate** must be appointed to act on behalf of such individuals.

special advocate
a person who must be appointed to act on behalf of a person who is subject to a closed security certificate hearing process to protect his or her interests

---

1   Public Safety Canada, "Security Certificates" (4 March 2014), online: <http://www.publicsafety .gc.ca/cnt/ntnl-scrt/cntr-trrrsm/scrt-crtfcts-eng.aspx>.

2   *Charkaoui v Canada (Citizenship and Immigration)*, 2007 SCC 9, [2007] 1 SCR 350.

When, in a case involving the removal of a permanent resident or foreign national, there is information that needs to be protected for security reasons and there is reason to believe that the person in question poses a security threat, both the minister of PSEP and the minister of CIC, under section 77(1) of the IRPA, must personally sign a security certificate. This power must not be delegated, because a closed process necessarily lacks transparency and public accountability.

The certificate is then referred to the Federal Court, where, in a closed security certificate hearing, a judge hears evidence, in the absence of the person named, regarding the need to protect national security or the safety of any person. The judge also hears evidence from the person named in the certificate. If the judge decides that the certificate is reasonable, then the certificate automatically becomes a removal order (IRPA, s 80).

Delegation of Authority

delegation of authority
the giving of decision-making power to someone else; for example, a minister may delegate authority to an immigration officer

designate
choose someone for a position, duty, or responsibility

officer
under section 6(1) of the IRPA, a person or class of person designated by the minister to carry out any purpose of any provision of the IRPA and given specific powers and duties

The IRPA allows certain ministerial powers, duties, requirements, and authorities to be delegated for the purposes of ensuring that Canada's immigration, refugee-protection, and citizenship programs are delivered efficiently. The minister's **delegation of authority** to others is necessary because of the sheer volume of immigration cases. Generally, whenever the word "officer" is used in the Act or its regulations with respect to a power, duty, requirement, or authority, the minister may **designate** persons to assume these responsibilities. The ministers of CIC or PSEP may both delegate their powers and may designate officers to enforce certain provisions of the Act and its regulations with regard to their respective mandates.

An **officer** is a public servant defined under section 6(1) of the IRPA. There are several types of officers, including visa officers, examining officers, immigration officers, senior immigration officers, and CBSA officers. The minister also has the authority (1) to designate certain RCMP officers to carry out immigration functions at ports of entry, and (2) to delegate to panel physicians (formerly known as "designated medical officers") the authority to carry out physical and mental examinations. The minister's delegation of authority must be made in writing and must specify the powers and duties of the designated officers (IRPA, ss 6(1), (2)).

Most of the powers that the IRPA vests in the minister in relation to the application of the law are delegated to officers through CIC's Designation of Officers and Delegation of Authority instrument, which is signed by the minister and updated regularly (see the Publications and Manuals page on the CIC website). This instrument includes a description of the duties and powers granted to officers working for CIC, the CBSA, and other agencies. It also includes a section setting out authorities that have not been delegated. For authorities under the specific mandate of the minister of PSEP—for example, authorities related to designating officers as peace officers—there is a separate designation and delegation-of-authority instrument, signed by the president of the CBSA.

Officers

As noted above, officers are public servants who, for the purposes of our discussion, work either for CIC or for the CBSA. CIC officers are responsible for the delivery of the immigration program both at Canadian missions abroad and at national, regional, and local offices across Canada. They hold a number of positions and carry out a variety of duties, including the following:

- processing applications for temporary residence (such as authorizations for visitors, students, and temporary workers), permanent residence, refugee resettlement, and citizenship;
- providing settlement and integration services for newcomers;
- conducting research;
- reporting and analyzing international trends with respect to migration, refugees, and social policy, which are used to formulate government policy; and
- developing policy and programs.

CBSA officers carry out a variety of duties related to immigration, including the following:

- examining people at ports of entry;
- detaining people who may pose a threat to Canada; and
- removing people who are inadmissible to Canada, including those involved in terrorism, organized crime, war crimes, or crimes against humanity.

Under the IRPA, officers have the power to examine people, perform searches and seizures, and exercise the powers of a **peace officer**. What follows is a general overview of officers' authorities both outside and inside Canada.

Note that officers, in their decision-making role, must follow the principles of natural justice by practising impartiality and respecting the examinee's right to be heard. Generally, it is up to the officer who is examining a person or considering an application (and examining the application's evidence and documents) to make the decision. In certain circumstances, however, one officer may read, hear, and evaluate all the pertinent information and then submit a report to another officer, who will make the decision. This exception to the rule in administrative law that "the one who hears must decide" is allowed as long as the decision-maker takes all the information into account. Subsequent chapters in this text will provide further information regarding an officer's authority to make decisions with respect to applications.

peace officer
a law enforcement officer with the power to examine people and perform searches and seizures

Before Entry: Examination on Application

Generally, a person seeking to come to Canada must apply for and obtain permission, in the form of a visa, before appearing at a port of entry. Under Canadian immigration law, this permission comes from the minister, who decides whether a person is allowed to enter (that is, "is not inadmissible"). In practice, however, the decision-making related to reviewing an application is delegated from the minister to an officer who is working outside Canada in a visa office.

A person who wishes to come to Canada must apply for temporary or permanent residence, usually before arriving. The application may be made abroad or at a port of entry, such as at the border or at an airport. It may be made orally or in writing, depending on a number of factors (described in later chapters). Some programs have been created to enable temporary residents, after their arrival in Canada, to make permanent resident applications from within Canada.

Oral applications are made when, for example, a person landing at an airport in Canada asks to make a refugee claim, or a US citizen at the Canada–US border asks to enter Canada. Written applications—for temporary or permanent residence, for example—may be made by means of forms provided by CIC. Applications are considered complete when all the instructions for completing them have been followed and all supporting documents have been submitted to the appropriate office.

Whether the person applies abroad or at a port of entry, the application must be assessed by an officer who is authorized to make a decision (IRPA, s 15(1)) about the applicant's admissibility. The officer decides whether the person qualifies under an immigration program, such as the family class or Federal Skilled Worker Program, and whether the person has the right to enter Canada. Generally, the officers who work abroad and assess applications, at visa offices or consulates, are called **visa officers**; CBSA officers working at ports of entry, such as the Canada–US border, airports, or harbours, may have titles such as "border services officer" or "enforcement officer."

visa officer
a public servant working in a Canadian consulate or visa office abroad

Visa officers typically review written applications, ensure their completeness, and evaluate the information provided. They may also interview applicants. CBSA officers typically carry out their duties orally, through examination procedures, by questioning the person and eliciting information at a port of entry—for example, about citizenship, residency, intention, employment, and length of stay.

Consider the case of Gautem Patel, a citizen of India who wishes to apply for Canadian permanent residence under the economic class, as a federal skilled worker. The process of reviewing Gautem's application and examining him in order to decide whether to grant him a permanent resident visa involves several officers, each of whom has a distinct decision-making authority. For example, one officer may review and screen Gautem's application to ensure that it is complete and meets certain minimum standards; the application will then be forwarded to a visa officer who will review it, along with additional documentation, and decide whether Gautem meets the regulatory definition of a federal skilled worker and whether there are any grounds of inadmissibility that would bar Gautem from Canada. The details of the application procedures for specific immigration programs are explored in later chapters. (See, for example, the Patel scenario under the heading "Federal Skilled Workers" in Chapter 8.)

Examination at Port of Entry

All foreign nationals are examined at the port of entry by an officer who has the authority to allow them entry and admit them as temporary or permanent residents. Section 28 of the *Immigration and Refugee Protection Regulations* provides that all persons who seek to enter Canada are deemed to be making an application and are therefore subject to an examination. Officers can compel applicants to answer questions; to provide relevant documents, photographs, and fingerprints; and to submit to medical examinations. Officers are required to act in an adjudicative capacity,

IN THE NEWS

Search and Seizure at the Borders

At the border, CBSA officers are authorized to search travellers and their belongings, including their baggage and electronic devices. They have the power to examine the contents of those devices, including personal files such as photos and email. Travellers have reduced expectations of privacy at the border, but as personal electronic devices have become more commonly used and their users' expertise has grown, many travellers have been trying to make sure that their information stays private by setting passwords and encrypting their devices.

Recently, CBSA officers' search and seizure powers were tested when a traveller from Quebec, Alain Philippon, was arrested for declining to share his BlackBerry password with customs officers. He was charged, under section 153.1 of the *Customs Act*, with hindering a customs officer, which carries a potential penalty of up to $25,000 and 12 months in prison. The case drew the attention of a legal specialist in this area:

> Rob Currie, the director of the Law and Technology Institute at the Schulich School of Law at Dalhousie University, said border agents have an established legal right to search you or your bags at the border.
>
> But he said it's not clear whether they should be able to force a traveller to reveal a smartphone password.
>
> Currie said the charge against Philippon could fall down on that point.
>
> He said a charter challenge under Section 8 could be brought at trial. That section of the Canadian Charter of Rights and Freedoms deals with unreasonable search and seizure, and by extension, the right to privacy. …
>
> Currie said the story coincides with a rising public awareness around electronic security. [He] thinks that even in the past three years, smartphones have become more deeply integrated in the lives of Canadians.
>
> "I think people really are thinking at the front of their minds about, 'What is the status of my device, and do I want the government looking into it, and what kind of rights do the government have?'" …
>
> The Supreme Court of Canada has already defined how and when police can search smartphones during a criminal investigation. Currie believes the Customs Act, which treats a smartphone the same as a suitcase, needs to be updated.
>
> "It's becoming increasingly clear that in a customs setting we're going to need some revision to accommodate the privacy interests in electronic devices, in the same way that the Supreme Court has given us revisions dealing with search and seizure, and dealing with search incident [that leads] to arrest, and that kind of thing," he said.

What do you think? Should CBSA officers be able to compel travellers to disclose their passwords? Why or why not?

Sources: Jack Julian, "Alain Philippon Phone Password Case May Meet Charter Challenge Conditions," *CBC News* (7 March 2015), online: <http://www.cbc.ca/news/canada/nova-scotia/alain-philippon-phone-password-case-may-meet-charter-challenge-conditions-1.2985694>; Office of the Privacy Commissioner of Canada, Checking In: "Your Privacy Rights at Airports and Border Crossings" (June 2014), online: <https://www.priv.gc.ca/resource/fs-fi/02_05_d_45_e.asp>.

which means that they must be unbiased in their assessments and evaluations. They render binding decisions after reviewing and considering information that is received as evidence.

SEARCH AND SEIZURE

Some officers are delegated the authority to search and seize; however, they may exercise these powers only when they have **reasonable grounds** to believe that a person who is trying to enter Canada has done any of the following (IRPA, ss 139, 140):

- concealed his or her identity;
- hidden on his or her person documents that are relevant to his or her admissibility; or
- committed, or possesses documents that may be used in the commission of, an offence listed in section 117, 118, or 122.

Section 8 of the Charter provides that all persons in Canada, including foreign nationals, have the right to be secure against unreasonable search or seizure. Therefore, officers may only exercise search and seizure powers if they have reasonable grounds to believe that one of the above criteria has been met.

Provided that there are reasonable grounds, an officer is authorized under the IRPA to conduct the following types of searches:

- search individuals, their luggage, and their personal effects (s 139(1));
- board and inspect vessels to carry out a search (s 15(3));
- seize vehicles and other items or assets used in relation to an immigration offence or to ensure compliance with the Act and its regulations (s 140); and
- seize documents that were fraudulently or improperly obtained or used, or likely to be fraudulently or improperly used, such as fraudulent passports (s 140).

Consider the following scenario—a point-of-entry examination of a traveller by officers who are exercising their authority to search and seize evidence:

> A female traveller from the United States, Martina Vidi, is stopped at the Peace Arch border crossing from Washington into British Columbia. The CBSA officer has reasonable grounds to believe that Martina is concealing her identity. The officer instructs her to pull her car into a separate lane and advises her that he wishes to conduct a search. Martina complies. The search involves an examination of all her belongings: her purse, her briefcase, two suitcases, other personal effects, and her car. The purpose of the officer's search is to detect documents or evidence that relate to Martina's identity, her admissibility, and any potential offences she may be committing under the IRPA. She is asked to empty her pockets and to remove her jacket for examination. There is no physical contact between the officer and Martina, and no force or restraint is used in the search.

reasonable grounds
a set of facts and circumstances that would satisfy an ordinarily cautious and prudent person and that are more than mere suspicion; a lower standard of proof than a balance of probabilities

In this scenario, Martina consents to the search. If a person for some reason does not consent to the search or behaves in any manner that puts the officer's safety at risk, the officer may detain the person and compel compliance with the search. Detaining the person, however, triggers his or her right to be advised of the right to counsel. Section 10 of the Charter requires that all persons being arrested or detained, including anyone submitting to an involuntary personal search, must be advised of the reason for the detention and of their right to retain and instruct counsel without delay.

After Entry: Enforcement

Certain CIC and CBSA officers—such as those bearing the titles Citizenship and Immigration (C&I) Officer, Detentions; C&I Officer, Enforcement; C&I Officer, Port of Entry; Border Services Officer; and Case Presenting Officer[3]—have the authority and powers of a peace officer to arrest and detain permanent residents or foreign nationals pursuant to section 138(1) of the IRPA. The authorization is generally given to the "title" relevant to the type of work performed.

Officers have the authority to **arrest** a permanent resident or foreign national who they believe has or may have breached the IRPA, and they may **detain** him if he poses a danger to the public, if his identity is in question, or if there is reason to believe that he will not appear for an immigration proceeding. Officers may also detain a permanent resident or foreign national at a port of entry if

arrest
to take a person into legal custody

detain
to restrict a person's liberty in any way; in the context of immigration, to keep a person in legal custody, such as in a prison or an immigration holding centre, prior to a hearing on a matter

- it is necessary to do so for the completion of an examination, and
- there are reasonable grounds to believe that the person is inadmissible for reasons of security or criminality, or for violating human or international rights.[4]

Generally, an officer must have a warrant to arrest and detain a permanent resident, foreign national, or protected person (IRPA, s 55(1)). However, the IRPA makes an exception in section 55(2) for the arrest and detention without a warrant of a foreign national

(a) who the officer has reasonable grounds to believe is inadmissible and is a danger to the public or is unlikely to appear for examination, an admissibility hearing, removal from Canada, or at a proceeding that could lead to the making of a removal order by the Minister under subsection 44(2); or

(b) if the officer is not satisfied of the identity of the foreign national in the course of any procedure under this Act.

---

3 Citizenship and Immigration Canada, "Instrument of Designation and Delegation: Immigration and Refugee Protection Act and Regulations" (6 January 2015), online: <http://www.cic.gc.ca/english/resources/manuals/il/il3-eng.pdf>.

4 For an overview of arrests and detentions, see Canada Border Services Agency, "Arrests and Detentions" (30 September 2014), online: <http://www.cbsa-asfc.gc.ca/security-securite/arr-det-eng.html>.

Return to our scenario involving Martina Vidi:

> Suppose that Martina does not agree to the search or behaves in any manner that puts her or the officer's safety at risk. The officer has the authority to detain her without a warrant, and her detention compels her to comply with the search. Of course, this is predicated on the fact that the officer has reasonable grounds to believe that Martina is concealing her identity. At this point, Martina must be advised of her right to counsel.

As peace officers, CIC and CBSA officers have the authority to apply for and obtain search warrants under the *Criminal Code*, and to execute warrants for arrest and detention. Generally, officers apply for a search warrant to obtain information that will help them establish a person's identity, locate a person wanted on an immigration arrest warrant, or obtain evidence related to an immigration investigation. An officer who wants to obtain a search warrant must make an application to a judge or justice of the peace, who will decide whether or not to issue the warrant.

Removal

After being admitted to Canada, some permanent residents and foreign nationals may do something (for example, commit a criminal act) that makes them "inadmissible"; failing to do certain things (for example, to renew a visitor's visa) may have the same consequence. (Inadmissibility matters are explored more thoroughly in Chapter 3.) When such activities come to the attention of an officer, the law allows for the removal of the individuals involved. In such a case, the officer writes an inadmissibility report to be reviewed by the minister or (as happens in practice) by the minister's delegate. The minister's delegate will review the written report and decide whether to remove the person directly or whether a hearing is required. There are three kinds of removal orders: departure orders, exclusion orders, and deportation orders (see Chapter 14). The IRPA provides the authority to issue removal orders to both the minister's delegate and members of the Immigration Division of the IRB, depending on the circumstances. The minister's delegate is given the power to issue removal orders against permanent residents only in cases where the permanent resident is inadmissible because of a failure to comply with residency obligations, and only under circumstances prescribed in the regulations.

Consider the following scenario, which illustrates the minister's authority to make decisions that could lead to a foreign national's removal from Canada. In this scenario, the minister's authority has been delegated to officers, who carry out the immigration functions.

> Jose Rodriguez comes to Canada to visit his uncle Juan, who owns a small restaurant. One of Juan's employees quits suddenly, so he asks Jose to come and work for him until he can find a replacement. Jose agrees and, over a period of several weeks, works as a waiter and bus boy, and even helps out in the kitchen. His uncle

pays him cash for his services. Jose was allowed entry to Canada as a temporary visitor but had no authorization to work. He is now considered to be in a state of non-compliance—namely, working without the proper work authorization—and is now inadmissible. Jose comes to the attention of immigration officials, and an officer writes a report against him.

In Jose's case, the minister (or, in practice, the minister's delegate) will review the officer's admissibility report and make a decision that could ultimately lead to Jose's removal from Canada. The removal process is explored in detail in Chapter 14.

Minister Responsible for Citizenship Matters

In addition to the immigration and refugee portfolios, the minister of CIC also has authority over citizenship. In the same way that the IRPA confers immigration functions on ministers, section 2(1) of the *Citizenship Act* allows for citizenship functions to be assigned to the appropriate member of Cabinet—currently, the minister of CIC. These functions include the following:

- granting Canadian citizenship to new Canadians;
- providing documentation of citizenship to citizens;
- promoting Canadian citizenship;
- making decisions on applications for renouncing or restoring Canadian citizenship; and
- revoking citizenship from a Canadian if the individual obtained her citizenship by false representation, fraud, or by knowingly concealing material circumstances.

Under section 23 of the *Citizenship Act*, the minister may delegate authority over these functions, in writing, to those responsible for applying the law. As a matter of policy, the power to determine citizenship status and to grant, retain, renounce, or resume citizenship is delegated only to those applying the law—for example, citizenship judges.[5] Citizenship judges are appointed by the governor in council upon recommendation of the minister of CIC.

The *Citizenship Act* grants broad regulatory power to Cabinet through the governor in council to make rules and regulations in the form of orders in council. The minister of CIC is required to table proposed regulations before each House of Parliament (the House of Commons and the Senate) so that they can be referred to the appropriate committee of that House.

The proposed regulation need only be tabled once, however, because it does not have to be presented to each House of Parliament again, even if it has been altered

---

5 Citizenship and Immigration Canada, "Citizenship Commission" (1 August 2014), online: <http://www.cic.gc.ca/english/department/commission/index.asp>.

(*Citizenship Act*, s 27.1(2)). As a result, amendments can be made without further examination by Parliament.

The minister has the authority to prescribe the form of citizenship applications, certificates, and other documents.

Immigration and Refugee Board

Structure

Immigration and Refugee Board (IRB)
an Independent, quasi-judicial tribunal whose mission is "to make well-reasoned decisions on immigration and refugee matters, efficiently, fairly and in accordance with the law"

Established in 1989, the **Immigration and Refugee Board (IRB)** is a federal adminis-trative tribunal that conducts admissibility hearings, detention reviews, immigration appeals, refugee protection hearings, and refugee appeals. It is sometimes referred to as "the board" or by the name of one of its four tribunals, or divisions, which are as follows:

- the Immigration Division (ID),
- the Immigration Appeal Division (IAD),
- the Refugee Protection Division (RPD), and
- the Refugee Appeal Division (RAD).

An organizational chart for the IRB and its four divisions is provided on page 49.

Each division performs specialized functions, such as adjudicating immigration matters and appeals or deciding claims for refugee protection. The IRB reports to Parliament through the minister of CIC. The minister is represented by officers from either CIC or the CBSA, who may appear before the divisions as a party to one of its proceedings. However, the board functions independently from government and, like all tribunals, is expected to exercise its role in an impartial manner.

member
the title given to a decision maker in the Refugee Protection Division, Immigration Division, or Immigration Appeal Division of the Immigration and Refugee Board

The board is composed of the following: a chairperson; numerous **members**, who preside over hearings and make decisions; and tribunal staff, who support the decision-makers and the tribunal's operations. The board has a dual accountability structure in which (1) the decision-makers are responsible to the chairperson through their respective managers—namely, a deputy chairperson, assistant deputy chairperson, and coordinating members; and (2) the public servants are responsible to separate managers—namely, the executive director, director general, regional director, and registrar. "Member" is the term used by each tribunal to denote the role of the decision-maker in immigration and refugee cases.

On June 28, 2012, Bill C-31, *Protecting Canada's Immigration System Act*, received royal assent and amended the IRPA. Some amendments came into force immediate-ly, while others came into force later. These amendments had the effect of changing the structure of the IRB (see the chart on page 49), and this involved significant changes to the appointment of decision-makers, as well as to many of the processes and timelines related to refugee matters. (See Chapter 13.)

Decision-makers are appointed by one of two processes depending on their area of specialization. They are appointed either by the governor in council process or by the merit process as public servants.

Structure of the Immigration and Refugee Board

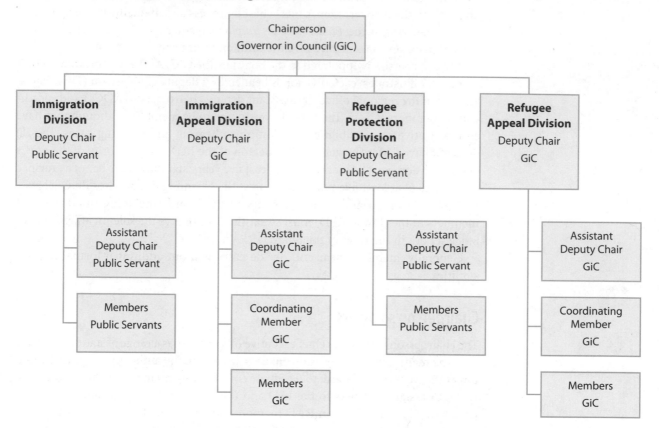

In the first process, the governor in council (GiC) appoints members to two of the board's tribunals: the IAD and the RAD.[6] The selection process for these appointments includes the review and selection of qualified candidates by the Selection Advisory Board (SAB), which is chaired by the IRB's chairperson and composed of at least seven members. The SAB makes recommendations to the minister of CIC, who recommends appointments to the GiC. The minister is responsible for managing all GiC appointments within his portfolio.

Members of the IAD and the RAD are appointed to hold office in a regional or district office of the board during good behaviour for a term not exceeding seven years, subject to removal by the GiC at any time for cause (IRPA, s 153(1)). Members may be reappointed to the same position or, in some cases—where statutory provisions allow—reappointed to another position. At least 10 percent of the members of the two divisions must be members of at least five years' standing at the bar of a province or notaries of at least five years' standing at the Chambre des notaires du Québec.

Prior to the 2012 changes to the structure of the IRB, members of the RPD were appointed through the GiC process. Now, decision-makers of both the ID and the

WEBLINK

Detailed information about the selection process for GiC appointments is available on the IRB website at <www.irb-cisr.gc.ca/Eng/BoaCom/empl/Pages/MemComSelPro.aspx>.

---

6   Prior to legislative changes, members of the RPD were also appointed by the GiC.

RPD are public servants. Public servant decision-makers apply for their positions under the federal government's merit-based process and, if qualified, are appointed in accordance with the *Public Service Employment Act* (IRPA, s 169.1(2)). Public servant decision-makers have no time limit on their terms.

The chairperson is appointed to the board by the GiC. As the organizational chart on page 49 illustrates, each division is headed by a deputy chairperson (DC), who is assisted in the regional offices by assistant deputy chairpersons (ADCs) and coordinating members (CMs). They are all considered to be members, although they have administrative responsibilities in addition to hearing and deciding cases. The ID does not have CMs. The deputy chairperson of the IAD and a majority of the ADCs of that division must be members of at least five years' standing at the bar of a province or notaries of at least five years' standing at the Chambre des notaires du Québec.

The chairperson and other members of the board (including public servant members in the ID and RPD) must swear the oath or give the solemn affirmation of office set out in the rules of the board (IRPA, s 152.1).

Generally, members hear and decide cases without additional formal responsibilities.

Chairperson's Powers

The chairperson is the IRB's chief executive officer and has a range of statutory powers over the management of decision-makers, including the authority to supervise and direct the work of the board; to designate coordinating members to the IAD and the RAD; to assign members to the IAD and the RAD; and, with the approval of the GiC, to assign an IAD or an RAD member to work in another regional or district office for up to 120 days to satisfy operational requirements (IRPA, s 159(1)(c)).

The chairperson can delegate certain powers to the deputy chairs, to the ADCs, or to other members, including CMs, only in relation to the IAD and the RAD. For example, the chairperson may delegate to an IAD member powers in relation to the RAD, and may delegate to an RAD member powers in relation to the IAD.

The chairperson's powers in relation to the RPD cannot be delegated to an ID member, and vice versa; powers in relation to the ID or the RPD may only be delegated to the DC, to the ADCs, or to other members, including CMs, of that division.

The chairperson also has the authority to issue guidelines to decision-makers and to identify any of the board's decisions as jurisprudential guides (IRPA, s 159(1)(h)). As well, the chairperson has the exclusive authority to make the rules of practice and procedure for the tribunal; these powers may not be delegated (IRPA, ss 159(2)(a), 161).

The role of the deputy chairperson is to oversee the management of decision-makers. With the exception of the power to make the rules of practice and procedure, the deputy chairperson's authority may be delegated to a board member.

Members' Powers

As noted above, decision-makers at the IRB in all divisions are called *members*. Members are selected for their expertise and for their experience in a variety of fields, including but not limited to general law, immigration and refugee law, and human rights.

Members have the powers and authority of a commissioner appointed under Part I of the *Inquiries Act*. These powers include the power to summon witnesses and to require them, on oath or affirmation, to give evidence, orally or in writing, and to produce documents. Members may do anything they consider necessary to achieve a full and proper hearing. They may also determine whether a hearing will be held in public or in private and may choose whether to conduct hearings by telephone or by video conference. Members have the authority to designate a representative for a person if he or she is a minor or a person who is unable to appreciate the nature of the proceedings.

Should a person fail to appear for his or her hearing, the member assigned to hear the case has the statutory power to determine that the hearing has been abandoned. The member may also refuse an applicant's withdrawal and make a finding of abuse of process.

The IAD is a court of record and has an official seal (IRPA, s 174(1)). It also has "all the powers, rights and privileges vested in a superior court of record" (IRPA, s 174(2)). Members in all divisions of the IRB have the power to apply the Charter and may declare a specific section of the IRPA inoperative if they find it to be in violation of a Charter right.

The Board's Four Divisions

Each of the board's four divisions has jurisdiction to hear and decide specific types of cases. Each division is supported by its own tribunal rules, which set out its practices and procedures so that those who appear before the tribunal (that is, the parties and their counsel), the members, and the tribunal staff have clear and consistent direction about how to present or process a case. What follows is a brief description of each division's decision-makers and jurisdiction. Details of their procedures are described in later chapters.

Immigration Division (ID)

Members of the ID are not bound by any legal or technical rules of evidence; they may receive and base their decisions on any evidence they consider credible and trustworthy (IRPA, s 173). Members of the ID are responsible for hearing and deciding matters regarding the following:

- admission or removal of permanent residents and foreign nationals, and
- review of immigration detentions.

Admissibility hearings determine whether a person should be allowed to enter or remain in Canada, or should be ordered removed from Canada. To return to our earlier scenario featuring Jose Rodriguez—who was caught working without a work permit—the matter will likely be referred for a hearing before a member of the ID. At the hearing, the minister, represented by a hearings officer, will argue the case against Jose. The member will hear both sides of the case and decide Jose's status in Canada.

Members review the reasons for detaining a person under the IRPA and determine whether there is sufficient reason to continue the detention or whether the person should be released. In our example, Jose can be detained if the minister's representative makes a case that there is a risk that Jose won't appear for his admissibility hearing. At the detention review, Jose will appear before a member of the ID to argue for his release, while the hearings officer will argue against his release or ask that certain conditions be imposed on a release order. ID proceedings and procedures are explored in greater detail in Chapter 14.

Immigration Appeal Division (IAD)

Members of the IAD have jurisdiction to hear and decide four types of appeals:

1. *Sponsorship appeals*—appeals from Canadian citizens and permanent residents whose applications to sponsor close family members to come to Canada have been refused;

2. *Removal order appeals*—appeals from individuals (permanent residents, foreign nationals with permanent resident visas, and protected persons) who have been ordered removed from Canada;

3. *Loss-of-permanent-residence appeals*—appeals from permanent residents regarding decisions made outside Canada on the residency obligation under section 28; and

4. *Minister's appeals*—appeals from the minister responsible for the CBSA, who may appeal a decision made by the ID at an admissibility hearing.

There are certain immigration matters for which a person has a statutory right to appeal decisions to the IAD. Section 63 of the IRPA provides appeal rights to sponsors, permanent resident visa holders, permanent residents, and protected persons, as well as to the minister (against a decision by the ID).

In hearing appeals, IAD members are not limited to reviewing findings of fact from the first hearing. Appeals are hearings *de novo* (Latin for "starting afresh," or "from the beginning"), and the IAD must receive any additional evidence that is provided and base its decision on its own assessment of the evidence—including the credibility of witnesses—even if the rules of evidence have not been strictly followed.[7] IAD hearing procedures are explored in greater detail in Chapter 15.

Let's return to our scenario concerning Juan and his nephew Jose:

> Because of all the problems that Juan, the restaurant owner, has had because of hiring his nephew Jose, he has encouraged his wife, Marie, to help out more at the restaurant. But this requires them to put their two children in daycare. As a

---

7   *Kahlon v Canada (Minister of Employment and Immigration)* (1989), 7 Imm LR (2d) 91, 97 NR 349 (FCA).

Canadian citizen, Marie decides to sponsor her mother's immigration from Mexico, with the plan that her mother will look after the children while Marie works in the restaurant. The sponsorship application is refused. What recourse does Marie have?

Permanent residents and Canadian citizens, like Marie in our scenario, have the right to appeal decisions to refuse their sponsorship applications to the IAD. A member of the IAD will hear and decide the appeal. In this example, Marie (the appellant) will present her case, and a hearings officer will represent the minister as the respondent at the appeal hearing. As noted earlier, the IAD is the only division that has "all the powers, rights and privileges vested in a superior court of record." Members may swear in and examine witnesses, and they may issue orders for the production and inspection of documents (IRPA, s 174(2)).

Refugee Protection Division (RPD)

With the coming into force of the IRPA in June 2002, the Convention Refugee Determination Division was renamed the Refugee Protection Division (RPD). Members of the RPD are responsible for hearing refugee claims made by persons in Canada and determining whether the claimants are refugees.

Refugee hearings are generally informal and non-adversarial. Members of the RPD are not bound by any legal or technical rules of evidence; they may receive and base their decision on any evidence they consider credible and trustworthy. They may inquire into any matter that they consider relevant to establishing whether a claim is well founded. Furthermore, members may take **judicial notice** of facts and of information or opinions within the division's specialized knowledge (IRPA, s 170(i)). Refugee hearings are discussed in greater detail in Chapter 13.

Refugee Appeal Division

The IRPA provides that an unsuccessful refugee claim may be appealed to the Refugee Appeal Division (RAD). This division has only recently become operative, however. When the IRPA came into force in June 2002, the sections that created the RAD (ss 110, 111) were not proclaimed into law. Now that they are law, and following amendments to the *Immigration and Refugee Protection Regulations* (IRPR) in 2012, an unsuccessful refugee claim may be appealed to the RAD by the claimant or the minister

- on a question of law, of fact, or of mixed law and fact (IRPA, s 110(1)); and
- not later than 15 working days after the day on which the person or the minister receives written reasons for the decision (IRPR, s 159.91(1)(a)).

Members of the RAD—like members of the RPD—are not bound by any legal or technical rules of evidence; they may receive and base their decision on any evidence they consider credible and trustworthy. They may inquire into any matter that they consider relevant to establishing whether a claim is well founded. Like the RPD, members of the RAD may take judicial notice of facts, information, or opinions (IRPA, s 171(b)). The RAD's procedures are explored in greater detail in Chapter 15.

judicial notice
a rule of evidence that allows a decision-maker to accept certain commonly known, indisputable, and uncontentious facts without requiring that they be proven with evidence

Courts

Matters involving the IRPA and the *Citizenship Act* may come before the courts by way of judicial review or appeal. Judicial review enables the courts to oversee administrative decisions, such as those made by the minister, by members of the IRB, and by citizenship officers. Although the courts defer to the expertise of administrative tribunals and generally accept their findings of fact, the court will determine on judicial review whether the administrative decision-making process was fair and was based on the appropriate legal considerations.

When hearing appeals from lower court decisions, courts consider whether decision-makers erred in their interpretation of the law or in their application of the law to the facts. Findings of fact, such as the credibility of a witness, are not generally reconsidered on appeal—only points of law are argued.

The federal courts have jurisdiction over the interpretation and application of the IRPA and the *Citizenship Act*. The trial court is the Federal Court, and the appeal court is the Federal Court of Appeal. If a significant legal issue is in question, decisions of the Federal Court of Appeal may be appealed to the final decision-maker in Canada—the Supreme Court of Canada.

Federal Court and Federal Court of Appeal

The Federal Court has jurisdiction to review decisions, orders, and other administrative actions of the IRB, CIC, the CBSA, and citizenship officers and judges. In this way, the courts perform a supervisory role. Judicial review may be sought by either party (the individual or the minister) provided that an application for leave to the Federal Court is made within the statutory time limit of 15 or 60 days—for matters arising in and matters arising outside Canada, respectively—after receiving the disputed decision. A Federal Court judge will either grant or deny leave for judicial review. The IRB may also refer any question of law, jurisdiction, or practice to the Federal Court at any stage of a proceeding.

Any person who wishes to challenge a decision, determination, or order under the IRPA may make an application for leave to the Federal Court. The Federal Court derives its review authority from section 18.1(3) of the *Federal Courts Act*. The grounds for review are set out in section 18.1(4) as follows:

> (4) The Federal Court may grant relief under subsection (3) if it is satisfied that the federal board, commission or other tribunal
>
>> (a) acted without jurisdiction, acted beyond its jurisdiction or refused to exercise its jurisdiction;
>>
>> (b) failed to observe a principle of natural justice, procedural fairness or other procedure that it was required by law to observe;
>>
>> (c) erred in law in making a decision or an order, whether or not the error appears on the face of the record;
>>
>> (d) based its decision or order on an erroneous finding of fact that it made in a perverse or capricious manner or without regard for the material before it;
>>
>> (e) acted, or failed to act, by reason of fraud or perjured evidence; or
>>
>> (f) acted in any other way that was contrary to law.

On judicial review of an IRB decision, the Federal Court may do any of the following:

- send the matter back for redetermination by a different member or panel,
- quash the IRB decision, or
- uphold the IRB decision.

If a party is dissatisfied with a decision of the Federal Court, leave for appeal may be sought from the Federal Court of Appeal. However, section 74(d) of the IRPA provides that an appeal may be made only if the court certifies that a serious question of general importance is involved, and states the question. The appeal then deals only with this particular question. The decision of the Federal Court is final, and no further appeals are allowed.

Non-lawyers, such as immigration consultants and paralegals, are not authorized to represent clients in Federal Court or the Federal Court of Appeal (*Federal Courts Act*, s 11; *Federal Courts Rules*, s 119). In appropriate cases, non-lawyers who are representing immigration or refugee clients should explain the judicial review process and refer their clients to an immigration lawyer. For self-represented litigants, the Federal Court provides information on court process and procedures on its website.

Supreme Court of Canada

The Supreme Court of Canada is the final court of appeal from all other Canadian courts on all subject matters. Before a case can reach the Supreme Court, all other avenues of appeal must be exhausted.

A party who is not satisfied with a Federal Court of Appeal decision has the right to seek leave to appeal to the Supreme Court, under section 40(1) of the *Supreme Court Act*. The Supreme Court may grant leave to appeal only if (1) the case involves a question of public importance, (2) it raises an important issue of law or mixed law and fact, or (3) the matter is, for any other reason, significant enough to be considered by the Supreme Court.

APPENDIX

A summary of the various decision-makers discussed in this chapter—their functions, responsibilities, and activities—is provided in the following table.

Immigration and Refugee Decision-Makers

Decision-maker(s)	Organization	Function	Responsibility or activity
Minister and designated or delegated officers	CIC	Immigration	Responsible for • immigration policy development • annual immigration plan • temporary residents immigration processes • permanent residents immigration processes • settlement and integration of newcomers to Canada • pre-removal risk assessments • most policies related to admissibility
Minister and designated or delegated officers	PSEP/CBSA	Immigration/Enforcement	Responsible for • management and operation of Canada's borders and port-of-entry functions • arrests • detentions • removals • background checks of immigration applicants
Minister only	CIC PSEP/CBSA	Enforcement	Responsible for • signing security certificates • referring security certificates to the Federal Court
Minister and designated or delegated officers	CIC	Refugee protection	Responsible for • the resettlement of refugees • admissibility of refugee claimants in Canada • determinations of eligibility
Minister and designated or delegated officers	PSEP/CBSA		Responsible for • background checks of refugee claimants • removal of refugee claimants where a "danger opinion" exists
Minister and designated or delegated officers	CIC Citizenship Commission	Citizenship	Citizenship program and policy
Member	IRB: Immigration Division	Immigration	Hears and decides • admissibility hearings for persons who are inadmissible to or removable from Canada • detention review hearings into the reasons for detention of persons under the IRPA Issues removal orders in complex cases

Decision-maker(s)	Organization	Function	Responsibility or activity
Member	IRB: Immigration Appeal Division	Immigration	Hears and decides appeals against • the minister's decision to refuse a sponsorship application (sponsorship appeal) • a removal order decision by a member of the ID or the minister from a permanent resident, foreign national with a permanent resident visa, or protected person who has been ordered removed from Canada (removal order appeal) • an immigration officer's decision that a permanent resident has lost his permanent resident status (loss-of-permanent-residence appeal) • an appeal from the minister responsible for the CBSA, who may appeal a decision made by the ID at an admissibility hearing (minister's appeal) Note: The IAD does not hear appeals against a removal order for a person who is a security threat or war criminal, has committed crimes against humanity, is involved in organized crime, or is a serious criminal, because such persons have no right of appeal.
Member	IRB: Refugee Protection Division		Hears claims made by persons in Canada and determines whether or not the claimants are refugees
Member	IRB: Refugee Appeal Division		Hears appeals from failed refugee claimants from the Refugee Protection Division
Citizenship officer or judge	Citizenship Commission		Decides citizenship applications for • grant of citizenship • retention of citizenship • renunciation of citizenship • resumption of citizenship
Judge	Federal Court		• Decides reasonableness of a security certificate • Conducts judicial review
Judges	Federal Court of Appeal		Hear appeals from the Federal Court
Judges	Supreme Court of Canada		Hear and decide an appeal only if • the case involves a question of public importance, • the case raises an important issue of law or mixed law and fact, or • the matter is, for any other reason, significant enough to be considered by the Supreme Court

KEY TERMS

arrest, 45

delegation of authority, 40

designate, 40

detain, 45

governor in council, 37

Immigration and Refugee Board (IRB), 48

judicial notice, 53

member, 48

officer, 40

orders in council, 37

peace officer, 41

reasonable grounds, 44

special advocate, 39

visa officer, 42

REVIEW QUESTIONS

1. List the ministers authorized by the IRPA to carry out immigration and refugee functions, and the responsibilities of each.

2. Provide an example of a minister's authority that cannot be delegated.

3. Provide examples of an officer's duties that are related to the examination of an application.

4. Under what circumstances can an officer exercise his or her search and seizure powers?

5. Can an officer arrest and detain an individual under the IRPA without a warrant? Explain.

6. Which minister is responsible for citizenship functions?

7. Which statute provides this authorization?

8. What are decision-makers at the IRB called?

9. Members of which divisions are appointed by the governor in council?

10. Members of which divisions are public servants?

11. In which court is a judicial review conducted?

12. If a party is not satisfied with a decision of the Federal Court, can that party appeal to the Supreme Court of Canada? Explain.

Admissibility

3

LEARNING OUTCOMES

After reading this chapter, you should be able to:

- Describe the general provisions for entering Canada.

- Describe the general provisions for applying for a visa.

- Identify the 11 grounds of inadmissibility to Canada under the *Immigration and Refugee Protection Act* and understand when exemptions to these grounds apply.

- Describe the types of decisions to which officers may refer in determining whether persons are inadmissible on certain grounds.

- Identify and distinguish among the three types of domestic crime that may make a person inadmissible to Canada: serious criminality, criminality, and organized criminality.

- Understand that different government agencies may be involved in assessing inadmissibility.

Introduction

Managing permanent and temporary immigration to Canada is a difficult balancing act. On the one hand, immigration policies aim to facilitate immigration in the interests of attracting a skilled workforce, reuniting families, encouraging students and visitors to stay on a temporary basis, and protecting refugees and persons in need of protection. On the other hand, immigration law and policy are often tied to national security, especially since 9/11, or are responsive to Canada's economic health. Consequently, rules and controls exist to exclude individuals who would place a heavy burden on health and social services in this country or pose a risk to the security and safety of Canadians.

The competing goals of immigration law and policy are reflected in the stated objectives of immigration law, particularly as set out in sections 3(1)(a) and (h) of the *Immigration and Refugee Protection Act* (IRPA):

> (a) to permit Canada to pursue the maximum social, cultural and economic benefits of immigration; ...
> (h) to protect public health and safety and to maintain the security of Canadian society.

These competing demands are also reflected in the officer's task of processing the applications of prospective temporary and permanent residents: an officer must assess a person's application to decide whether the applicant is *eligible* (that is, meets specific program criteria) and is *not inadmissible*. The officer may accept the application and issue a visa or may refuse it, thus denying the applicant access to Canada.

In this chapter, we examine the general requirements for obtaining a visa for temporary and permanent immigration. The various classes and subclasses of immigration are described in Part II (Temporary Immigration Programs) and Part III (Permanent Immigration Programs) of this text. After a foreign national has proven that he or she meets the specific criteria for a particular class of immigration, that person may nevertheless be barred from entering Canada because of **inadmissibility**. Even after being admitted, an individual may be removed from Canada should he or she become inadmissible. This chapter will outline and discuss the various grounds of inadmissibility.

Generally speaking, inadmissibility applies to all applicants in the same manner, regardless of the class or subclass under which they are requesting entry to Canada. For this reason, this text deals with inadmissibility before it deals with program eligibility requirements. In this chapter, we examine the 11 grounds of inadmissibility set out in the IRPA, which are as follows:

1. security (s 34);
2. human or international rights violations (s 35);
3. serious criminality (s 36(1));
4. criminality (s 36(2));
5. organized criminality (s 37);

inadmissibility
ineligibility for entry to Canada, on grounds such as criminality

6. health grounds (s 38);

7. financial reasons—that is, inability to provide for oneself or dependants (s 39);

8. misrepresentation (s 40);

9. cessation of refugee protection (s 40.1);

10. failure to comply with the IRPA (s 41); and

11. inadmissible family member (s 42).

General Rules

The first hurdle that a foreign national faces when applying to come to Canada is obtaining permission as either a temporary or a permanent resident. Obtaining permission involves meeting the eligibility requirements for one of the numerous classes or sub-classes under which foreign nationals may apply—for example, as visitors under temporary residence programs; as members of the family class or federal skilled worker class, under permanent residence programs; or as refugees. Note that an applicant for entry must establish eligibility under the relevant class or subclass before an officer will consider inadmissibility. This is because the background checks that are required to verify that an applicant is not inadmissible, such as police record checks, medical examinations, and other investigations, may be costly and time-consuming. Because so many applicants will fail to meet the eligibility requirements, it is more efficient to consider inadmissibility only after eligibility is confirmed.

> **What Is Your Residency Status?**
> - Canadian citizen
> - Registered under the *Indian Act*
> - Permanent resident
> - Temporary resident
> - Convention refugee
> - Protected person
> - Temporary permit holder
>
> Depending on your residency status, you have different rights and obligations.

Only Canadian citizens and registered (status) Indians have the absolute right to enter Canada and remain here. Everyone else must seek permission before they are allowed to enter Canada to live here on either a temporary or a permanent basis.

Prior to Entry: Application for a Visa

A **foreign national** is defined in section 2 of the IRPA as a person who is not a Canadian citizen or a permanent resident, and this definition includes stateless persons (that is, individuals who are not considered as a national by any state under the operation of its law). A foreign national who wishes to live temporarily or permanently in Canada must submit to an application and approval process, and must obtain either a **temporary resident visa (TRV)** (such as a visitor visa, a study permit, or a work permit) or a permanent resident visa before coming to Canada (although some foreign nationals from "visa-exempt" countries who are coming as temporary residents are excluded from this requirement).

Section 11 of the IRPA obliges all foreign nationals to apply for a visa before entering Canada. For most of them, obtaining a visa involves a formal, written application procedure to determine eligibility, and it generally includes a further assessment to

foreign national
a person, including a stateless person, who is not a Canadian citizen or a permanent resident

temporary resident visa (TRV)
a document authorizing a person to enter and remain in Canada for a period of time

determine whether the foreign national is not inadmissible. The applicant must submit to medical examinations and background checks for identity, criminality, and security. Generally, the purpose of requiring foreign nationals to obtain a visa is to stop ineligible and inadmissible persons from entering Canada before they travel. This is preferable to waiting until such persons arrive at a port of entry and then must be removed at Canada's expense.

> Before entering Canada, foreign nationals must apply to an officer for a visa or other document and satisfy the officer that they are
>
> ■ **eligible**, and
> ■ not **inadmissible** (IRPA, s 11).

eligible
in an immigration context, meeting the criteria set out in the IRPA or IRPR for the type of entry sought (temporary or permanent)

inadmissible
barred from entry to Canada for reasons that include security, criminality, and health grounds

Pursuant to section 16 of the IRPA, an applicant has a duty to tell the officer the truth and to produce any relevant evidence, including photographs and fingerprints, that the officer may reasonably require. A visa is issued only when the officer is satisfied that the applicant meets the requirements of the IRPA and its regulations—specifically, section 22 of the IRPA and related sections of the *Immigration and Refugee Protection Regulations* (IRPR), which require that the applicant has

- fulfilled certain obligations;
- met the criteria for the particular class of permanent or temporary resident that he or she has applied under; and
- shown that he or she is not inadmissible.

Obligations of Applicant
■ Answer truthfully all questions at an examination by an officer (IRPA, s 16(1)).
■ Show a visa and other documents on request (IRPA, s 16(1)).
■ Provide biometric information, such as photographic and fingerprint evidence (IRPA, s 16(2)).
■ Submit to a medical examination on request (IRPA, s 16(2)(b)).
■ Upon the request of an officer, appear for an interview with the Canadian Security Intelligence Service and answer truthfully all questions put to them during the interview (IRPA, s 16(2.1)).

Generally, an officer may refuse to issue a visa for one of two reasons:

1. the applicant does not meet the eligibility criteria for the particular class of permanent or temporary resident; or
2. the applicant (or a family member of the applicant) is inadmissible.

General Application Requirements

All applicants for any of the classes of permanent and temporary resident visas must meet certain basic criteria. A visa may be issued only if, on examination, the foreign national establishes that he or she

- has used the appropriate IRPA application documents for the particular class and subclass of resident and completed them (generally, incomplete applications are neither processed nor returned for completion);
- has applied to the appropriate office in accordance with the requirements of the IRPA;
- has paid the required processing fees and other fees, as applicable;
- holds a passport or similar document that may be used to enter the country that issued it or another country;
- meets the medical examination requirements set out in the IRPR; and
- is not inadmissible.

These criteria are considered in more detail in the chapters that follow.

Fees

Applicants are required to pay processing fees. The current processing fees for each type of application for permanent and temporary visa and permit can be found on the fee list on the CIC website, currently located at <www.cic.gc.ca/english/information/fees/fees.asp>, and in the application packages for each of the programs. Processing fees are non-refundable, even if the application is refused: the processing fee is intended to cover the costs of processing the application, regardless of the subsequent decision. Applicants should be prepared to pay additional fees, including fees to third parties for medical examinations, fees to translate documents, fees to a representative such as a lawyer or a regulated immigration consultant, and any transportation costs.

Each adult applicant for permanent residence must also include with his or her application a right-to-permanent-residence fee. This fee is refundable if the application is refused.

Medical Examinations

Medical examinations are required for applicants seeking permanent residence and their dependants, regardless of whether or not these dependants are accompanying the applicant. For applicants seeking temporary residence, there are many medical examination exemptions; these are discussed in Chapter 4. Generally, a medical examination is required for temporary residents who intend to work in occupations in which the protection of public health is essential—for example, occupations in the health services—or in occupations that require close contact with other persons. A medical examination is also required if the foreign national plans to visit for six months or longer and, during the year immediately preceding the date of applying for entry to Canada, resided, sojourned, or lived in a "designated country or territory."

Medical examinations must be performed by **panel physicians**.

panel physician
a local physician, authorized by the Canadian government; formerly known as a "designated medical practitioner"

Port-of-Entry Arrival: Examination

The events of September 11, 2001 refocused official efforts to protect the country against terrorists. At times, these efforts reduced the openness and efficiency of cross-border movement that travellers had previously enjoyed. The functions performed by the Canada Border Services Agency (CBSA) reflect these protective efforts. CBSA officers decide who is allowed to enter Canada, who should be detained under the IRPA, and who should be removed from Canada. Even when a permanent or temporary resident visa is obtained, admission to Canada is not guaranteed. Section 18(1) of the IRPA authorizes the examination of all travellers at ports of entry, including Canadian citizens, registered Indians, permanent residents, permanent resident visa holders, temporary resident visa holders, and foreign nationals. If applicants' circumstances change between the time of their acquiring a permanent resident or temporary resident visa and the time of their arrival in Canada, or if additional information about them gives rise to security concerns, they may be refused entry or have certain conditions or restrictions placed on their admission. In other words, a visa allows a person to travel to a Canadian port of entry for permanent residence or to visit, work, or study in Canada, but it does not in itself grant the visa holder admission to Canada to carry out those activities.

Ports of entry generally have two separate control points. If you have ever returned to Canada after travelling, you have experienced the interview at the first control point, known as the primary inspection line. The primary inspection line is where CBSA officers conduct the initial interview of travellers and carry out a combination of immigration and customs activities. Here, for example, they perform the basic duties of checking your identity and your immigration status, and asking about your travel and about any goods and money you may be bringing into the country.

If a traveller is a foreign national, then the examining officer must be satisfied that the traveller is not inadmissible before allowing him into Canada. CBSA officers attempt to balance their duty to prevent the entry of "problem individuals" with the goal of allowing other travellers to move easily through the checkpoint. An officer may refer a person for a secondary examination if the officer believes that a more thorough interview is required. The purpose of the secondary interview is to allow the officer to make an informed decision regarding admissibility by confirming the identity of the traveller, verifying documents such as passports and permits, and gathering information about the person's purpose in entering Canada.

Section 19(1) of IRPA states that Canadian citizens and persons registered under the *Indian Act* have an automatic right to enter and remain in Canada. Anyone else who wishes to do so must

- obtain permission to enter Canada, as either a temporary or permanent resident; and
- satisfy an officer that she is not inadmissible.

> ## Right to Enter Canada
>
> Canadian citizens and registered Indians
>
> - have an unqualified right to enter and remain in Canada (IRPA, s 19(1)).
>
> Permanent residents
>
> - must prove their status (IRPA, s 19(2)),
> - have a right to enter and remain that is subject to conditions (IRPA, ss 27, 28), and
> - may be removed if they become inadmissible.
>
> Temporary residents
>
> - are authorized to enter and stay on a temporary basis (IRPA, s 29).

Permanent Resident Visa Holders

Visa officers issue permanent resident visas for applicants (and any family members who are accompanying them) under the various categories of permanent residence as a precondition to permanent entry (IRPA, s 21). Successful applicants may travel to Canada—with confirmation of permanent residence documents or a permanent residence visa—but must undergo a further examination by an officer at the port of entry before being admitted and allowed to remain in Canada (see Chapter 6). At the point of entry, they must show a valid passport, other essential documents (for example, a list of all the household and personal items they are bringing into Canada), and proof of funds and assets.

A CBSA officer seeks to determine whether there have been any changes in the document holder's status since the issuance of the visa by the visa officer. The officer's aim in doing so is to verify that the document holder has not become inadmissible since the visa was issued. For example, the CBSA officer confirms the applicant's identity, checks that medical examinations are still valid, and verifies that the applicant has enough money to cover living expenses (such as rent, food, clothing, and transportation) for a six-month period.

If the CBSA officer is satisfied that the applicant and any accompanying family members are not inadmissible, the officer is required to allow the person entry as a permanent resident. The date on which this occurs is the day the foreign national becomes a permanent resident of Canada. Conditions may be imposed on the person, or there may be a requirement that a medical issue be monitored. Non-compliance with conditions could result in the person's future inadmissibility and removal.

Permanent Residents

When arriving at a point of entry, permanent residents must satisfy the CBSA officer that, during their absence from Canada, they have not lost their status as permanent residents or otherwise become inadmissible (IRPA, s 19(2)). Like all travellers, permanent residents returning to Canada must undergo an examination. An officer verifies the person's permanent resident card, determines whether the person has met the residency obligation (that is, to live in Canada for two years in each five-year period), and checks for other inadmissibility criteria (for example, a criminal conviction). If the officer is satisfied that the permanent resident has complied with the conditions of permanent residency and has not become inadmissible, then the officer must allow entry.

Temporary Resident Visa Holders

Foreign nationals living in certain countries require a visa to enter Canada, even on a temporary basis. Visa officers issue temporary resident visas (TRVs) in three categories: visitor, student, and temporary worker. These are described in Part II.

Like the permanent resident visa, a temporary resident visa authorizes a person to board an airplane or ship to travel to Canada; however, the final decision whether to allow a person to come into Canada is made at the port of entry (IRPA, s 22). Temporary residents must undergo an interview at the port of entry so that the officer can confirm their identity; verify their admissibility; review any visa restrictions (such as expiration of a work permit or a prohibition against work); confirm that medical examinations, if required, are still valid; and verify that they have enough money to cover living expenses for the duration of their stay. They must show the officer a valid passport and other essential documents, such as proof of funds and assets, a letter of invitation (for visitors), a letter of confirmation (for foreign students), and a return ticket. If the officer is satisfied that the foreign national and any accompanying family members are not inadmissible, then the officer is required to allow entry.

Conditions may be imposed—for example, the CBSA officer may confirm that a visitor may not work or study while in Canada and must leave Canada before the temporary resident visa has expired. Admission as a temporary resident requires compliance with any conditions imposed, and non-compliance may result in removal.

Temporary Resident Permit Holders

temporary resident permit (TRP)
a permit that may be granted in exceptional circumstances to a person who does not meet the eligibility and/or the admissibility requirements to enter or remain temporarily in Canada

It sometimes may not be possible to conduct an examination for inadmissibility immediately upon the person's arrival at the point of entry. For example, it may be too late in the day, or an interpreter may be unavailable. In such cases, an officer may issue a **temporary resident permit (TRP)** and a notice to appear, pursuant to sections 23 and 24 of the IRPA. This allows the person to enter Canada temporarily, until an examination or an admissibility hearing can be held at a later time.

A person who is issued a TRP may enter Canada but must appear for an immigration proceeding, which may be an examination or a hearing. The temporary resident is permitted to move freely within Canada; however, CIC must be notified of any change in the person's address.

In some cases, a TRP may be issued to an applicant who has been found inadmissible. This happens only where the grounds of inadmissibility are technical or medical, or where they concern the applicant's criminal history. In addition, the officer must find compelling reasons to issue the TRP, weighing them against the risks to Canada or Canadians. (This topic is discussed further in Chapter 4.)

Another situation in which a person may be issued a TRP is where there are sufficient humanitarian and compassionate grounds—for example, in the case of a child who needs to be admitted to Canada to undergo life-saving surgery. Such a child would normally be found inadmissible for medical reasons, but an exception may be made if the surgery is not available in the child's country of citizenship and if the medical bills are paid through charitable donations.

No Right of Appeal

A person whose application for either a permanent or temporary resident visa has been refused has no right to appeal to the IRB. The applicant may seek leave for a judicial review at the Federal Court (see Chapter 15). If the applicant believes that the refusal was discriminatory and without bona fide justification, the applicant may file a complaint under the *Canadian Human Rights Act*.

Grounds of Inadmissibility

As previously discussed, admissibility is assessed prior to arrival, when the foreign national applies for a visa, or it is assessed upon arrival, at the port of entry. Inadmissibility may also arise or be discovered, however, after the arrival of the foreign national or permanent resident—that is, after the person has entered the country. In such cases, inadmissibility leads to grounds for removal of the foreign national or permanent resident. Of the 11 grounds of inadmissibility set out in the IRPA, the first five (set out in ss 34–37) are the most serious. To find a person inadmissible on one of these bases—security, human or international rights violations, serious criminality, criminality, or organized criminality—an officer must have reasonable grounds to believe that the allegations against the person are true. "Reasonable grounds" is a lower standard of proof than the civil standard of proof on a **balance of probabilities**. For an officer to have "reasonable grounds" to believe an allegation, she must show a bona fide belief in a serious possibility that the allegation is true, based on credible evidence.

In the following sections, we consider the 11 grounds of inadmissibility.

balance of probabilities
the standard of proof in civil matters, determined on the basis of whether a claim or a fact as alleged is more probably true than not true

1. Security Risk (Section 34)

According to section 34(1) of the IRPA, a permanent resident or a foreign national may be found inadmissible on security grounds for

- engaging in an act of espionage that is against Canada or that is contrary to Canada's interests;
- engaging in or instigating the subversion by force of any government;
- engaging in an act of subversion against a democratic government, institution, or process (as these things are understood in Canada);
- engaging in terrorism;
- being a danger to the security of Canada;

Border Watch Line

In 2011, the federal government created a publicly accessible "wanted by the CBSA" list, which consists of the names and photographs of people who the CBSA has reasonable grounds to believe (1) are security risks; (2) have committed or were complicit in war crimes, crimes against humanity, or genocide; (3) have committed or are complicit in serious criminality or organized crimes; or (4) are wanted for removal. To view the Border Watch Line, go to <www.cbsa-asfc.gc.ca> and choose "Wanted by the CBSA."

- engaging in acts of violence that would or might endanger the lives or safety of persons in Canada; or
- being a member of an organization that there are reasonable grounds to believe engages, has engaged, or will engage in acts of espionage, subversion, or terrorism as described above.

The terms "espionage," "subversion," "democratic," and "terrorism" are not defined in either the IRPA or its regulations. However, CIC's operational manual *ENF 1: Inadmissibility* provides the following definitions:[1]

- *Espionage* is the practice of spying. It is the gathering of information in a surreptitious manner and involves secretly seeking out information, usually from a hostile country, to benefit one's own country.[2]
- *Subversion* is the practice of overturning or overthrowing; it seeks to accomplish change by illicit means or for improper purposes related to an organization.[3]
- *Democratic* refers to "government by the people, especially where the people hold the supreme political power."[4]
- *Terrorism* is defined as

    activities directed toward or in support of the threat or use of acts of violence against persons or property for the purposes of achieving a political objective; an act intended to cause death or serious bodily injury to a civilian, or to any other person not taking an active part in hostilities in a situation of armed conflict, when the purpose of such act, by its nature or context, is to intimidate a population or to compel a government or an international organization to do or to abstain from doing any act.[5]

1 Citizenship and Immigration Canada, *ENF 1: Inadmissibility* (4 September 2013) 6–9, online: <http://www.cic.gc.ca/english/resources/manuals/enf/enf01-eng.pdf>.

2 *Ibid* at 6.

3 *Ibid* at 8.

4 *Ibid*.

5 *Ibid* at 9.

Membership in an Organization That Engages in Espionage, Subversion, or Terrorism

An officer may find a person inadmissible on account of that person's own acts of espionage, subversion, or terrorism, or because the person belongs to an organization that engages in these activities. There are two types of determinations that make a person inadmissible on these grounds. They are listed in section 14 of the IRPR, as follows:

- an IRB determination, based on findings that the foreign national or permanent resident has engaged in terrorism, that the foreign national or permanent resident is a person referred to in section F of article 1 of the *Convention Relating to the Status of Refugees* (Refugee Convention)—that is, a person excluded from refugee protection for having committed crimes against peace, war crimes, or a crime against humanity; or
- a Canadian court decision under the *Criminal Code* concerning the person's commission of a terrorism offence.

In deciding whether a terrorism offence has been committed, the courts look to the *Criminal Code*'s definition of **terrorist group**.

The officer's reliance on the decisions of the IRB and the courts saves the time and expense of rehearing the issue of membership.

terrorist group
as defined under section 83.01 of the *Criminal Code*, an entity or an association of entities "that has as one of its purposes or activities facilitating or carrying out any terrorist activity"

Identifying Security Threats

Officers rely on security screening checks to identify known security threats; such checks are important tools. Also important are the many documents that an applicant must provide when applying for permanent or temporary residence. These documents provide information about the applicant's identity, relationships, financial history, work and school activities, and background.

Terrorist List

Under section 83.05 of the *Criminal Code* (created by the *Anti-terrorism Act*), the governor in council may, on the recommendation of the minister of public safety and emergency preparedness (PSEP), create a list of entities that

- have knowingly carried out, attempted to carry out, participated in, or facilitated a terrorist activity; or
- knowingly acted on behalf of, at the direction of, or in association with an entity that has knowingly carried out, attempted to carry out, participated in, or facilitated a terrorist activity.

You can find the current list of terrorist entities by going to the Public Safety Canada website at <www.publicsafety.gc.ca/cnt/ntnl-scrt/cntr-trrrsm/lstd-ntts/crrnt-lstd-ntts-eng.aspx> and choosing "Listed Terrorist Entities."

To determine whether an applicant poses a security threat, officers may also consult police and intelligence reports and, if available, records of the person's criminal convictions and previous dealings with Canadian immigration. When the identity of a person cannot be confirmed in Canada, fingerprints and photographs are taken of the person and are used not only to identify the person, but also to conduct background checks with international authorities. In cases where a security certificate has been issued against a person, this fact alone is considered conclusive proof that a person is inadmissible.

Exemptions

In rare cases, a person who is found to have engaged in one or more of the activities listed in section 34(1) may nevertheless be able to satisfy the minister that the person's being in Canada would not be detrimental to the national interest. This decision is at the discretion of the minister and may not be delegated.

2. Human or International Rights Violations (Section 35)

Permanent residents and foreign nationals who have committed violations of human or international rights outside Canada are inadmissible. Section 35 of the IRPA lists the following prohibited activities and conditions:

- committing an offence referred to in sections 4 to 7 of the *Crimes Against Humanity and War Crimes Act* while outside Canada;
- being a **prescribed senior official**; or
- being a person, other than a permanent resident, whose entry into or stay in Canada is restricted pursuant to a decision, resolution, or measure of an international organization of states, of which Canada is a member, that imposes sanctions on a country against which Canada has imposed or has agreed to impose sanctions in concert with that organization or association.

The terms "crime against humanity," "genocide," and "war crime" are defined in section 4(3) of the *Crimes Against Humanity and War Crimes Act*.

Crimes against humanity include

murder, extermination, enslavement, deportation, imprisonment, torture, sexual violence, persecution, or any other inhumane act or omission that is committed against any civilian population or any identifiable group and that, at the time and in the place of its commission, constitutes a crime against humanity according to customary international law or conventional international law or by virtue of its being criminal according to the general principles of law recognized by the community of nations, whether or not it constitutes a contravention of the law in force at the time and in the place of its commission.

Genocide is defined as

an act or omission committed with intent to destroy, in whole or in part, an identifiable group of persons, as such, that, at the time and in the place of its commission,

prescribed senior official as referenced under section 35(1)(b) of the IRPA, a senior official in the service of a government that has been designated by the minister as a perpetrator of terrorism, human rights violations, genocide, war crimes, or crimes against humanity within the meaning of sections 6(3) to (5) of the *Crimes Against Humanity and War Crimes Act*

crimes against humanity any inhumane acts or omissions that are committed against any civilian population or any identifiable group

genocide an act or omission committed with intent to destroy, in whole or in part, an identifiable group of persons

IN THE NEWS

Inadmissible on Security Grounds: The Case of Ernst Zundel

The infamous case of Ernst Zundel, a Holocaust denier, is a real-life Canadian case about a person who was found inadmissible on security grounds and removed from Canada. A German national, Zundel first came to Canada in 1958 when he was 19 years old. He lived here until 2000, never having obtained Canadian citizenship; his application was refused. During the 1980s, Zundel became well known as a Holocaust denier and disseminator of Nazi material. His company, Samisdat Publishers, produced the pamphlet "Did Six Million Really Die?" and the book *The Hitler We Loved and Why*, which led to criminal charges.

In the late 1990s, Zundel faced a complaint before the Canadian Human Rights Commission for spreading hatred against Jews on his website, but he left Canada for the United States in 2000, before the hearing was completed. Zundel returned to Canada in 2003, having been deported from the United States for overstaying his visitor's visa. Around the same time, Germany issued a warrant for his arrest on hate charges.

On May 1, 2003, the solicitor general of Canada and the minister of CIC signed a security certificate stating that Mr. Zundel was a danger to the security of Canada. Zundel was alleged to be inadmissible on the security grounds of

> engaging in acts of terrorism, being a danger to the security of Canada, engaging in acts of violence that would or might endanger the lives or safety of persons in Canada or being a member of a group that there are reasonable grounds to

believe has or will engage in acts of espionage, subversion or terrorism.[*]

Zundel was detained. As required when a security certificate is issued, the matter went before the Federal Court for approval. On February 24, 2005, Justice Blais of the Federal Court of Canada found the security certificate to be reasonable and stated in his decision,

> Mr. Zundel has associated, supported and directed members of the Movement who in one fashion or another have sought to propagate violent messages of hate and have advocated the destruction of governments and multicultural societies. Mr. Zundel's activities are not only a threat to Canada's national security but also a threat to the international community of nations. Mr. Zundel can channel the energy of members of the White Supremacist Movement from around the world, providing funding to them, bringing them together and providing them advice and direction."[†]

The security certificate issued against Zundel was conclusive proof that he was inadmissible and the removal order against him could be enforced. He had no appeal rights, because of the serious grounds of his inadmissibility. Zundel was deported to Germany where, upon his arrival, he was arrested and charged with 14 counts of inciting racial hatred. In February 2007, Zundel was sentenced to a five-year term in prison. He was released on March 1, 2010.

---

[*] *Zundel v Canada*, 2004 FCA 145, [2004] 3 FCR 638.

[†] *Zundel, Re*, 2005 FC 295 at para 112.

constitutes genocide according to customary international law or conventional international law or by virtue of its being criminal according to the general principles of law recognized by the community of nations, whether or not it constitutes a contravention of the law in force at the time and in the place of its commission.

war crime

an act or omission committed during an armed conflict that violates international laws of war

War crime is defined as

an act or omission committed during an armed conflict that, at the time and in the place of its commission, constitutes a war crime according to customary international law or conventional international law applicable to armed conflicts, whether or not it constitutes a contravention of the law in force at the time and in the place of its commission.

Section 35(1)(b) of the IRPA says that a permanent resident or foreign national is inadmissible on grounds of violating human or international rights if he or she is a prescribed senior official in the service of a government that, in the opinion of the minister of PSEP, "engages or has engaged in terrorism, systematic or gross human rights violations, or genocide, a war crime or a crime against humanity." The minister's list of governments that have engaged in these actions is revised periodically, as governments are added or removed.

Consider the following examples of governments that have been designated in this way:[6]

- the Bosnian Serb regime between March 27, 1992 and October 10, 1996;
- the Siad Barré regime in Somalia between 1969 and 1991;
- the former military governments in Haiti between 1971 and 1986, and between 1991 and 1994 (except for the period from August to December 1993);
- the former Marxist regimes of Afghanistan between 1978 and 1992;
- the governments of Ahmed Hassan al-Bakr and Saddam Hussein, in power from 1968 to May 22, 2003;
- the government of Rwanda under President Habyarimana between October 1990 and April 1994, as well as the interim government in power between April 1994 and July 1994;
- the governments of the Federal Republic of Yugoslavia and the Republic of Serbia (Milosevic) between February 28, 1998 and October 7, 2000;
- the Taliban regime in Afghanistan from September 27, 1996 to December 22, 2001; and
- the government of Ethiopia under Mengistu Haile Mariam from September 12, 1974 to May 21, 1991.

---

6 Citizenship and Immigration Canada, *ENF 2/OP 18: Evaluating Inadmissibility* (2 December 2013) s 7.4, online: <http://www.cic.gc.ca/english/resources/manuals/enf/enf02-eng.pdf>.

War Crimes Program

Canada became a signatory to the Rome Statute of the International Criminal Court on December 18, 1998 and established the War Crimes Program in 1998 to address crimes against humanity and war crimes committed during the Second World War. Today, the War Crimes Program deals with more recent cases that stem from conflicts in the former Yugoslavia, Rwanda, or Iraq and that involve not only war crimes but also crimes against humanity or genocide.

The objective of the program is to deny safe haven in Canada to persons involved in such crimes. The CBSA, CIC, the Department of Justice, and the RCMP are partners in the program, and they work together to deny visas or entry into Canada to war criminals, develop policy, investigate crimes, prosecute war criminals in Canada, and assess cases.

More information about the War Crimes Program can be found on the Department of Justice website at <www.justice.gc.ca/eng/cj-jp/wc-cdg/prog.html>.

A finding of inadmissibility under section 35 of the IRPA has far-reaching implications for an individual:

- A refugee claimant may be excluded from protection and/or have his claim suspended pending an admissibility hearing.
- The Canadian government may revoke a person's citizenship under the *Citizenship Act* for having obtained his Canadian citizenship through misrepresentation or fraud, or for knowingly concealing material circumstances.
- A fugitive may be transferred to another state under the *Extradition Act*, in a case where the Canadian government is responding to a request from a foreign state or tribunal.

Identifying Rights Violators

For the purposes of officers trying to determine whether a person (a foreign national or permanent resident) is inadmissible, three types of decisions qualify as a "conclusive finding of fact" that a person has committed human or international rights violations. These decisions are listed in section 15 of the IRPR, as follows:

- a UN-established international tribunal decision;
- an IRB determination, based on findings that the foreign national or permanent resident has committed a war crime or a crime against humanity, that the foreign national or permanent resident is a person referred to in section F of article 1 of the Refugee Convention—that is, a person excluded from refugee protection for having committed crimes against peace, war crimes, or a crime against humanity; or
- a decision by a Canadian court concerning the foreign national or permanent resident and a war crime or crime against humanity committed outside Canada under the *Criminal Code* or the *Crimes Against Humanity and War Crimes Act*.

As with the determination of security risks, reliance on the decisions of these bodies saves the time and expense of rehearing the issue. A security certificate issued against a person can also be used as conclusive proof that a person is inadmissible for violating human or international rights.

Criminality

criminality

domestic crime, as opposed to crimes against humanity or war crimes as proscribed by international law; the IRPA defines three categories of criminality: serious criminality under section 36(1), criminality under section 36(2), and organized criminality under section 37

Sections 36 and 37 deal with **criminality**.

When a person is convicted of an offence outside Canada, it is necessary to compare the elements of Canadian law with those of the foreign jurisdiction to determine whether the person is inadmissible. The particular law under which the person was convicted in the foreign country is not relevant. What matters is whether the offence committed in the foreign country is equivalent to a criminal offence in Canada. In other words, the officer must establish that the foreign offence of which the person has been convicted contains the essential elements of the equivalent offence in Canada. To accomplish this, the officer can compare foreign legal and court documents with Canadian ones, and examine the person at the admissibility hearing.

> ### Equivalency
>
> CIC's operational manual *ENF 1: Inadmissibility*, at Appendix A, instructs that the "[o]nus lies on [hearings officers] to present evidence of foreign law and necessary definitions."
>
> In *Hill v Canada (Minister of Employment and Immigration)* (1987), 1 Imm LR (2d) 1 at 9 (FCA), Urie JA wrote that
>
>> equivalency can be determined in three ways: first, by a comparison of the precise wording in each statute both through documents and, if available, through the evidence of an expert or experts in the foreign law and determining therefrom the essential ingredients of the respective offences; two, by examining the evidence adduced before the adjudicator, both oral and documentary, to ascertain whether or not that evidence was sufficient to establish that the essential ingredients of the offence in Canada had been proven in the foreign proceedings, whether precisely described in the initiating documents or in the statutory provisions in the same words or not; and three, by a combination of one and two.

Criminal charges that are dropped, or that result in a not-guilty verdict, will not cause inadmissibility. However, if a person has been charged with a crime and the trial is still under way, the person may be inadmissible pending the results of the trial.

There are three categories of criminality: serious criminality (s 36(1)), criminality (s 36(2)), and organized criminality (s 37). These are described below.

3. Serious Criminality (Section 36(1))

Serious criminality is a ground of inadmissibility for both foreign nationals and permanent residents. Generally, to qualify as a ground of inadmissibility, the offence must be punishable by a maximum of ten years' imprisonment. However, this depends on whether the offence was committed inside or outside Canada and, if outside Canada, whether the person was convicted. These three subcategories of serious criminality are described below:

- *Convicted in Canada:* The person was convicted in Canada of an offence punishable by a maximum term of imprisonment of at least ten years, or of an offence for which a term of imprisonment of more than six months was imposed (IRPA, s 36(1)(a)).
- *Convicted outside Canada:* The person was convicted of an offence that, if committed in Canada, would constitute an offence punishable by a maximum term of imprisonment of at least ten years (IRPA, s 36(1)(b)).
- *Committed an act outside Canada:* The person committed an act that is an offence in the place where it was committed and that, if committed in Canada, would constitute an offence punishable by a maximum term of imprisonment of at least ten years (IRPA, s 36(1)(c)). When it comes to determining whether a permanent resident has committed such an act, section 36(3)(d) provides an exception to the usual legal test: such a determination must be based on a balance of probabilities rather than on the reasonable grounds test.

If a permanent resident or foreign national is convicted of a serious crime while living in or visiting Canada, the court informs CIC and the CBSA of the conviction. This will lead to an allegation by the minister of inadmissibility and a referral for a hearing before the IRB. A finding of inadmissibility for reasons of serious criminality generally leads to deportation.

Exemptions

A person found inadmissible by reason of serious criminality may be exempted and permitted to enter or remain in Canada if pardoned or acquitted of the offence in question. With respect to offences committed outside Canada, the person will be exempt if he or she has been deemed to be rehabilitated or has satisfied the minister that he or she is rehabilitated.

These exemptions apply in the same way for the grounds of criminality and organized criminality. They are outlined in detail in the sections below.

4. Criminality (Section 36(2))

Whereas grounds of serious criminality apply to both foreign nationals and permanent residents, section 36(2) of IRPA provides that the grounds of criminality (a lower threshold than *serious* criminality) apply only to foreign nationals. In other words, permanent residents cannot be found inadmissible on the basis of this lower threshold of criminality.

There are four subcategories of criminality under section 36(2). Before describing these subcategories, however, we need to clarify the terminology of Canada's *Criminal Code*. The Code distinguishes among three kinds of offences:

**summary conviction
offences**

less serious offences
that carry a maximum
sentence of six months
in jail, a maximum fine
of $5,000, or both, and
that are prosecuted using
streamlined procedures

indictable offences

serious offences, such as
murder, with longer periods
of imprisonment and more
complex prosecution pro-
cedures than those for summary conviction offences

**hybrid or dual
procedure offences**

offences for which the
Crown prosecutor may
choose to proceed either
by summary conviction
or by indictment

1. **Summary conviction offences:** These are less serious offences, such as speeding, that are prosecuted using streamlined procedures in a provincial court. The *Criminal Code* sets out the general penalty rules for summary convictions in section 787(1). If convicted, a person is liable to a fine not exceeding $5,000, a term of imprisonment not exceeding six months, or both.

2. **Indictable offences:** For indictable offences, the *Criminal Code* always sets out a specific penalty, with sentences ranging from two years to life.

3. **Hybrid or dual procedure offences:** The Crown prosecutor may choose whether to proceed by summary conviction or by indictment, depending on the circumstances of the alleged offence. An example of a hybrid offence is impaired driving.

For immigration purposes, a hybrid or dual procedure offence is "deemed to be an indictable offence, even if it has been prosecuted summarily" (IRPA, s 36(3)(a)). The four subcategories of criminality set out in s 36(2) are as follows:

- *Convicted in Canada:* The person was convicted in Canada of an offence punishable by way of indictment, or of two summary conviction offences not arising out of a single occurrence.
- *Convicted outside Canada:* The person was convicted outside Canada of an offence that, if committed in Canada, would constitute an indictable offence, or of two summary conviction offences not arising out of a single occurrence that, if committed in Canada, would constitute offences.
- *Committed an act outside Canada:* The person committed an act outside Canada that is an offence in the place where it was committed and that, if committed in Canada, would constitute an indictable offence.
- *Committed an act on entering Canada:* The person committed, on entering Canada, an indictable offence prescribed by the IRPR.

Exemptions

The IRPA provides several exemptions to inadmissibility on the grounds of criminality. For example, inadmissibility does not apply if the offence was designated as a contravention under the *Contraventions Act* (IRPA, s 36(3)(e)) or if the permanent resident or foreign national was found guilty under the *Young Offenders Act* or received a youth sentence under the *Youth Criminal Justice Act*. Canada will also admit persons who have been granted a record suspension (formerly known as a pardon); have been acquitted; or, if otherwise inadmissible because of offences committed outside Canada, have either been deemed to be rehabilitated or have satisfied the minister that they are rehabilitated. Each of these exemptions is considered below:

**record suspension
(pardon)**

a grant under the *Criminal
Code* resulting in an offence
being deemed not to
have occurred; formerly
known as a pardon

1. *Record suspension (IRPA, s 36(3)(b)):* A **record suspension** may be granted under the *Criminal Code*. Issued by the federal government of Canada, this grant allows individuals who were convicted of criminal offences but have completed their sentences and demonstrated that they are law-abiding citizens to have their criminal records kept separate and apart from other

criminal records. This means that a search of the Canadian Police Information Centre (CPIC) will not disclose that the person had a criminal record or was issued a record suspension. A person who was pardoned from the offence in question is exempt from inadmissibility. A foreign pardon must be equivalent to a record suspension in Canada. This applies regardless of whether the offence occurred in or outside Canada.

2. *Acquittal (IRPA, s 36(3)(b)):* An **acquittal**, or finding of not guilty, also exempts a person from inadmissibility. This applies regardless of whether the offence in question occurred in or outside Canada.

3. *Deemed rehabilitated (IRPA, s 36(3)(c)):* A person whose conviction occurred outside Canada may be **deemed rehabilitated**. In this case, the grounds of criminal inadmissibility are removed, provided that the following criteria under section 18(2) of the IRPR are met:

    a. at least ten years have elapsed since the completion of the sentence imposed (such as probation, prison term, fines, or restitution);

    b. the conviction is not considered serious in Canada;

    c. the conviction did not involve any serious property damage, physical harm to any person, or any type of weapon; and

    d. the offence committed would be punishable in Canada by a maximum term of imprisonment of less than ten years.

    Even if ten years have passed, the person seeking entry to Canada must disclose the conviction and should provide evidence that no additional offence has occurred.

4. *Individual rehabilitation (IRPA, s 36(3)(c)):* Unlike the deeming provision described above, a person must apply to be considered for **individual rehabilitation**. To be eligible, a person must show that at least five years have passed since the completion of the sentence imposed (such as a prison term, a suspended sentence, fines, or probation) and that the conviction equates to a hybrid or indictable offence in Canada. Applications must be submitted to a Canadian visa office, where the visa officer will consider all relevant factors in determining whether to approve or refuse the application.

Consider the following case scenarios regarding exemptions to inadmissibility on the ground of criminality under section 36(2).

acquittal
a finding of not guilty

deemed rehabilitated
an exemption from criminal inadmissibility; a person who was convicted outside Canada and who meets the criteria under section 18(2) of the IRPR may be deemed rehabilitated and permitted to enter Canada

individual rehabilitation
a method of removing a ground of inadmissibility (criminality, for example) that requires the applicant to apply to a visa officer, who will then consider whether certain criteria for removal have been met

■ *Case Scenario #1:* Sovann, a Cambodian national, is interested in applying for a student permit so that he can enroll in a two-year culinary program at the University of British Columbia. Sovann is concerned that he may be inadmissible on the ground of criminality. In 1989, he was convicted in the United States of "driving while impaired." He did not serve any time in prison and he has no other convictions. In the United States, this offence may be prosecuted as a misdemeanour offence, often under a state motor vehicle law or municipal law. In Canada, however, impaired driving is a criminal offence under the *Criminal Code* and is listed as a hybrid offence.

Sovann may be deemed rehabilitated when more than ten years have elapsed since the payment of his fine in 1989. Because his offence is equivalent to a hybrid offence under Canadian law, he must apply at the Canadian visa office for individual rehabilitation at the time he submits his visa application. If his application is accepted, Sovann will be allowed to enter Canada, provided that he complies with the eligibility criteria for a student permit.

■ *Case Scenario #2:* Juanita, a Colombian national, would like to apply for a temporary resident visa to attend her sister's wedding in Canada. Juanita is concerned that she may be criminally inadmissible to Canada. She was convicted of shoplifting in April 2014 and was sentenced to one year's probation and required to attend counselling. She has no other convictions. The elements of Juanita's offence in her home country are equivalent to an offence (informally known as "theft under") in the *Criminal Code*. It is a hybrid offence that may be prosecuted either summarily or by indictment.

Unfortunately for Juanita, she is inadmissible to Canada because hybrid offences are deemed indictable for immigration purposes. Under section 36(3)(c), Juanita is eligible to apply for rehabilitation only after April 2020, five years after the completion of the imposed sentence. (Because probation is considered part of a sentence or a conviction, Juanita must count five years from the end of the probation period, which is April 2015.)

■ *Case Scenario #3:* Kelly and Alicia are friends from Trinidad and Tobago. They both want to apply for temporary resident visas to Canada. Each of them is concerned that she may be criminally inadmissible to Canada. Kelly was convicted of a crime on June 18, 2013, and received a jail sentence of three months. Alicia was convicted of driving under the influence on April 3, 2003 and had her driver's licence taken away from her for three years.

Kelly may apply for rehabilitation five years after the end of the sentence imposed. If her three-month jail sentence ended September 18, 2013, she will be eligible to apply for rehabilitation on September 18, 2018, as long as no other terms were imposed on her sentence.

Alicia's sentence ended on April 3, 2006. Because five years must elapse from the end date of the suspension or from the date her driver's licence is reinstated, Alicia became eligible to apply for rehabilitation on April 3, 2011.

Those not eligible for deemed rehabilitation or individual rehabilitation, because neither five nor ten years have elapsed since the completion of the sentence, may apply at a visa office for a TRP. A TRP will be issued only in compelling circumstances (see the discussion in Chapter 4).

An applicant may request that an officer review the details of her case and assess inadmissibility on the ground of criminality. The applicant must fill out an application for rehabilitation and check off the box "for information only." There is no fee for this type of application, although the processing usually takes several months.

5. Organized Criminality (Section 37)

Under section 37 of the IRPA, both permanent residents and foreign nationals may be found inadmissible for being members of an organized crime group under section 37 of the IRPA.

Specifically, this section applies when the permanent resident or foreign national

- is a member of an organization that is believed on reasonable grounds to be or to have been engaged in activity that is part of a pattern of criminal activity planned and organized by a number of persons acting in concert in furtherance of the commission of an indictable offence or in furtherance of the commission of an offence outside Canada that, if committed in Canada, would constitute an indictable offence, or engaging in activity that is part of such a pattern; or

- is, in the context of transnational crime, engaged in activities such as people smuggling, trafficking in persons, or money laundering.

To find a person inadmissible on these grounds, there must be proof of a pattern of criminal activity that is planned and organized by persons acting in concert, and proof of the person's membership in this organization.

According to the Enforcement manual (ENF 2/OP 18), officers typically wait for the courts to decide on the organized criminality charges before they consider inadmissibility.[7] However, in cases where local authorities are not pursuing formal charges, officers may investigate and report the person as inadmissible if organized criminal activity is uncovered.

Foreign nationals who have received a sentence of two years or more in Canada for committing a serious crime are denied access to the refugee determination system.

Amendments to the IRPA in 2012 by Bill C-31, *Protecting Canada's Immigration System Act*, now deny access to the refugee determination system to foreign nationals who have committed serious crimes in or outside Canada (IRPA, ss 101(2)(a), (b)).

Exemption

A refugee claimant whose only involvement with a criminal organization was to facilitate travel to Canada to make the refugee claim is exempt from inadmissibility. The rationale for this exemption is that it would be unfair to return a person at risk whose only involvement with a criminal organization was a necessary survival measure, and that such a person would not pose a risk of further criminality in Canada.

---

7 *Ibid* at s 5.2.

Human Smuggling and Human Trafficking

Human Smuggling

Those who are engaged in human smuggling seek material gain by facilitating the illegal entry of foreign nationals. Human smuggling is criminal when it is carried out for the purpose of profit rather than for the goal of saving lives. The government faces challenges in this regard; it is difficult to discern whether a person being smuggled is an economic migrant duped by unscrupulous agents into paying large sums of money to gain entry to Canada, or whether he is a legitimate refugee who could not have come to Canada otherwise—for example, by travelling on a commercial carrier with false documents.

Canada's anti-smuggling laws have proven to be controversial. In *R v Appulonappa* (2013 BCSC 31), the BC Supreme Court found that section 117 of the IRPA violates section 7 of the Charter because its overly broad wording criminalizes humanitarian actions undertaken to help refugees. In April 2014, the BC Court of Appeal ruled that the law is constitutional (2014 BCCA 163). Leave to appeal to the Supreme Court of Canada was granted and the appeal was heard on February 17, 2015. (The decision was pending at the time of writing).

To be charged with human smuggling, a foreign national or permanent resident must have knowingly organized, induced, aided, or abetted the entry into Canada of another person who is not in possession of a visa or passport and therefore does not have the right to enter. Human smuggling is a criminal offence in this country, with penalties increasing in accordance with the number of people smuggled. For smuggling fewer than ten persons, a smuggler may be convicted of a summary offence and ordered to pay a fine of up to $100,000 or sentenced to a term of imprisonment of not more than two years, or both. Alternatively, a smuggler of fewer than ten people may be convicted of an indictable offence and ordered to pay a fine of up to $500,000 or sentenced to a term of imprisonment of not more than ten years, or both, for a first offence. It is an indictable offence to smuggle ten or more persons, and a person who does so can be fined up to $1,000,000 or sentenced to life imprisonment, or both (IRPA, s 117).

Human Trafficking

The victims of human trafficking are not necessarily foreign nationals; trafficking has been known to occur entirely within our borders. Section 118 of IRPA provides that, to be charged with this offence, human traffickers must have knowingly "organized" (defined as recruiting, transporting, receiving, or harbouring) the entry into Canada of another person or persons, and must have done so by means of abduction, fraud, or deception, or by the use or threat of force or coercion.

With respect to either adults or children, it is an indictable offence under the *Criminal Code* to recruit, transport, transfer, receive, hold, conceal, or harbour a person, or to exercise control, direction, or influence over a person's movements for the purpose of exploiting or facilitating the exploitation of that person (s 279.01). Exploitation means

- causing a person to provide labour or a service (for example, sexual services or any kind of work, including drug trafficking and begging) by engaging in conduct that could reasonably be expected to cause the victim to believe that their safety or the safety of someone known to them would be threatened if they did not provide that labour or service (s 279.04(1)); or

■ causing a person to have an organ or tissue removed, by means of deception or the use or threat of force or of any other form of coercion (s 279.04(3)).

The IRPA sets out the aggravating factors that the court must consider in deciding penalties for human trafficking. These factors include the treatment of the victim and whether the victim was harmed or killed during the trafficking operation; whether the operation was for the benefit of or in association with a criminal organization; and the amount of profit realized (IRPA, s 121).

Inadmissible on Grounds of Organized Criminality: The Case of the Domotor Family

Consider the case of the Domotor family, which has been called Canada's largest proven human trafficking case. Twenty-two members of the extended Domotor–Kolompar human trafficking criminal organization that had operated in the Hamilton, Ontario area were convicted of human trafficking charges under the *Criminal Code*.

In April 2012, Ferenc Domotor Sr., considered to be the kingpin of the organization, was sentenced to nine years in prison after pleading guilty to charges of human trafficking, fraud, conspiracy, and organized crime before the Ontario Superior Court of Justice. He will be removed from Canada at the end of his sentence. The human trafficking ring comprised his wife, Gyongi Kolompar, and 21-year-old son, Ferenc Domotor Jr., who each received sentences ranging from time served to five years; Attila Kolompar, who pleaded guilty to two counts of conspiring to traffic humans and defrauding Hamilton's welfare system; and other extended family members. The Domotor–Kolompar family recruited as many as 19 victims from Hungary. They were brought to Canada involuntarily, had their passports taken away, were held in basements where they lived in deplorable conditions without adequate food, and were forced to work in construction jobs for little or no pay. The victims were counselled to claim refugee status and apply for social assistance.

The Domotors came to Canada from Hungary in 1998 and claimed refugee status. By 2000, they were permanent residents. As a result of their sentences, they will become inadmissible and so will face deportation after serving their sentences. Up to 20 of the 22 members of the family, including Ferenc Domotor Jr. and Attila Kolompar, were removed from Canada by May 2014; Ferenc Domotor's brother, Gyula Domotor, has not been deported because he—alone among the members of this criminal organization—has Canadian citizenship.

Sources: Canada Border Services Agency, "News Release: Minister Blaney Announces the Removal from Canada of 20 Convicted Human Traffickers" (22 July 2014), online: <http://news.gc.ca/web/article-en.do?nid=869579>; CBC News, "Hamilton Human Trafficking Kingpin Sentenced to 9 Years" (3 April 2012), online: <http://www.cbc.ca/news/canada/story/2012/04/03/hamilton-human-trafficking.html>; Department of Justice, "Human Trafficking: Legislation" (21 May 2015), online: <http://www.justice.gc.ca/eng/cj-jp/tp/legis-loi.html>.

6. Health Grounds (Section 38)

Only foreign nationals may be inadmissible for reasons of health. Permanent residents already accepted and living in Canada cannot later be found inadmissible if they develop a medical condition. In other words, once permanent resident status is granted, health concerns that arise later will not result in inadmissibility. Generally, all applicants for permanent and temporary residence must undergo a medical examination; however, the rules vary slightly for each category. For example, a temporary residence applicant must undergo a medical examination if one of the following conditions exists:

- the applicant will be working in certain occupations in Canada, such as in the health field or as a teacher or caregiver;
- the applicant plans to visit for six or more months and, in the year before entering Canada, the applicant has lived for six or more months in certain countries or territories where the risk of exposure to contagious diseases is greater than it is in Canada; or
- the applicant is applying for a Super Visa (see Chapter 4).

The requirement for a medical examination serves to protect the health and safety of Canadians and to prevent excessive demand on Canada's health and social services.

A foreign national who applies for temporary or permanent residence and who suffers from a health condition may be inadmissible under section 38(1) of the IRPA if the health condition

- is likely to be a danger to public health, such as a communicable disease (IRPA, s 38(1)(a));
- is likely to be a danger to public safety, such as a mental condition that causes unpredictable or violent behaviour (IRPA, s 38(1)(b)); or
- might reasonably be expected to cause excessive demand on health or social services, such as a condition that requires ongoing expensive medical treatment (IRPA, s 38(1)(c)).

"Excessive demand" is defined in the IRPR and generally means that the anticipated costs of the foreign national's health or social services would likely exceed the average Canadian per capita costs of such services over a period of five years, or that the foreign national would likely add to the waiting lists for such services and thereby create a delay for Canadians and permanent residents, increasing mortality and morbidity rates.

The first two conditions (ss 38(1)(a), (b)) encompass any health problem—psychological or physical—that may pose a danger to the health or safety of persons living in Canada.

Sexually transmitted viruses and diseases, such as human immunodeficiency virus (HIV) and syphilis, are seen as posing a danger to public health or safety—and therefore as grounds for inadmissibility—only where there is evidence that the person engages in high-risk behaviour, such as sharing contaminated needles or engaging in unprotected sex, and where the person is refusing to cooperate with public health authorities. Sexually transmitted viruses and diseases differ in this respect from a disease such as tuberculosis, which, if active (and contagious), is generally grounds for inadmissibility, mainly because it can be transmitted easily through coughing or sneezing. A person with inactive tuberculosis cannot transmit the disease and may be admitted into Canada, provided that regular medical follow-ups are undertaken to ensure that the disease remains inactive.

Persons who are HIV-positive may be successful with respect to the first two health considerations but be refused on the grounds of the third—that is, for being deemed to place an excessive demand on Canada's health or social services. The current guidelines for assessing HIV cases state that any applicant receiving anti-retroviral therapy is inadmissible because of excessive demand.

Medical Examination

As part of the application process, applicants for permanent residence and their dependants (whether they are coming to Canada or not) must undergo a medical examination at their own expense. Temporary residence applicants may also be required to do this, depending on factors such as their country of origin, their prospective length of stay, and the type of activity they intend to undertake in Canada, as noted above.

Furthermore, a temporary residence applicant who would normally be exempt from the medical examination may be required to submit to one if an officer suspects illness or a medical condition that could render the applicant medically inadmissible. A suspicion may be raised if the applicant appears to be sick, or if questioning by the officer reveals that the applicant was recently discharged from the hospital or is taking medication for a serious illness. The medical examination may be conducted as part of a port-of-entry examination—for example, when a temporary resident is seeking admission.

The medical examination must include the following:

- a physical and mental examination;
- a review of past medical history, laboratory tests, and diagnostic tests; and
- a medical assessment of records.

Applicants who pass their medical examinations are issued a medical certificate that is usually valid for 12 months.

Only a panel physician designated by CIC is authorized to carry out a medical assessment. The panel physician considers the following factors:

- the nature, severity, and probable duration of any health impairment from which the person is suffering;
- the danger of contagion;
- any unpredictable or unusual behaviour that may create a danger to public safety; and

- the social or health services that the person may require in Canada, and whether the use of such services would deprive Canadian nationals of these services (for example, the risk of a sudden incapacity that would require medical care).

A person who is seeking medical treatment may overcome inadmissibility and render herself admissible as a temporary resident provided that it can be shown that the medical treatment will not place excessive demand on health services.

The panel physician prepares a medical profile based on the test results and gives an opinion about whether the person is admissible, inadmissible, or requires **medical surveillance**. A designation of medical surveillance does not bar a person from admission; rather, it provides for monitoring. For example, an applicant's inactive tuberculosis must be checked periodically to ensure that it does not become active and contagious.

The panel physician's report is provided to the visa officer, who, in accordance with section 20 of the IRPR, must act based on the physician's findings. The visa officer notifies the applicant if there is a finding of inadmissibility, in order to give the applicant the opportunity to reply and provide further documentation within a reasonable period of time, before a final decision is rendered.

medical surveillance
a designation by the panel physician that provides for the monitoring of an applicant's medical condition

Exemptions

In some circumstances, foreign nationals who intend to stay in Canada for six months or longer are exempt from the requirement to submit to a medical examination. Foreign nationals in this category are the following (IRPR, s 30(1)):

- a person, such as a diplomat, who is entering Canada for the purpose of carrying out official duties, unless that person seeks to engage or continue in secondary employment in Canada;
- a family member of an accredited foreign representative (defined in section 186(b) of the IRPR), unless that family member seeks to engage or continue in employment in Canada;
- a member of the armed forces of a country that is a designated state for the purposes of the *Visiting Forces Act* who is entering or is in Canada to carry out official duties, other than a person who has been designated as a civilian component of those armed forces, unless that member seeks to engage or continue in secondary employment in Canada;
- a family member of a protected person, if the family member is not included in the protected person's application to remain in Canada as a permanent resident;
- a non-accompanying family member of a foreign national who has applied for refugee protection outside Canada; and
- a foreign national who has applied for permanent resident status and is a member of the caregiver class.

Although certain categories of foreign nationals—family class spouses, common law partners, children of sponsors, Convention refugees, and protected persons—

must undergo medical examinations for health and public safety reasons, they cannot be found inadmissible on the basis of their causing excessive demand on health or social services (IRPA, s 38(2)). Also, persons who are likely to be refused on the basis of causing excessive demand may avoid inadmissibility by having a financial arrangement that in the officer's view will satisfactorily cover the cost of the treatment and related expenses. For example, a person seeking to enter Canada for medical treatment would normally be inadmissible unless the visa officer was satisfied that the person could pay all costs associated with the medical treatment, including travel and accommodation.

7. Financial Reasons (Section 39)

A foreign national who applies for temporary or permanent residence must satisfy the visa officer of his ability both to be self-sufficient and to support any dependants in Canada, physically and legally, pursuant to section 39 of the IRPA.

At the time of processing an application abroad, the visa officer assesses the person's financial resources as well as any arrangements in place, such as job offers, and the person's potential employability. Upon the applicant's arrival in Canada, an officer verifies that the person has sufficient funds to cover the temporary stay; that adequate arrangements for care and support (not involving social assistance) are in place; or, in the case of an applicant seeking to establish permanent residence, that the person has employment or that his funds are sufficient for six months.

Exemption

Convention refugees and protected persons who apply for permanent residence in Canada are exempted by the IRPA from being found inadmissible on financial grounds.

8. Misrepresentation (Section 40)

According to section 16 of the IRPA, foreign nationals who are applying for permanent residence, or for temporary residence as visitors, students, or workers, are required to answer truthfully all questions and produce all relevant documents when examined by the officer. Failure to do so could result in inadmissibility on the grounds of **misrepresentation**.

Section 40 sets out four situations of misrepresentation. Before we examine them, however, it is worthwhile to consider the definitions of "misrepresentation" and "withholding" as set out in the Enforcement operational manual.[8] The Enforcement manual defines "misrepresentation" as "[m]isstating facts to obtain money, goods, benefits or some other thing desired by a person who might otherwise not be entitled to it. Misrepresentation may also be referred to as 'false pretences.'" **Withholding** is defined as follows:

misrepresentation
a ground of inadmissibility under the IRPA that involves misstating facts or withholding information

withholding
to hold back from doing or taking an action

---

8 *Supra* note 6, s 10.2 at 29.

To hold back from doing or taking an action; to keep (within); to refrain from granting, giving, allowing or "letting 'it' be known." A person can misrepresent themselves by being silent just as easily as a person who actively states a "mistruth." A person who refuses or declines to answer a question, preferring instead to allow outdated or false information to be accepted as current or true information, is engaging in the activity of misrepresentation.

Keeping those definitions in mind, consider the following four situations of misrepresentation:

1. A permanent resident or foreign national is inadmissible on the grounds of misrepresentation for directly or indirectly misrepresenting or withholding material facts relating to a relevant matter that induces or could induce an error in the administration of the IRPA.

    For example, a person who provides false identity documents to conceal his identity or to falsify a relationship would be found inadmissible on these grounds. Persons found inadmissible while outside Canada may be banned for five years from the date of the inadmissibility decision. Persons found inadmissible while in Canada may be banned for five years from the date that the removal order is enforced, in accordance with section 40(2)(a) of the IRPA.

    Under section 22 of the IRPR, refugee claimants are exempt from inadmissibility on these grounds if the disposition of the claim is pending, as are protected persons.

2. A permanent resident or foreign national is inadmissible on the grounds of misrepresentation if she has been sponsored by a person who is found to be inadmissible for misrepresentation.

    The consequence of this finding is a five-year ban, and the foreign national will not be permitted to apply for permanent residence for five years (IRPA, s 40(2)(3)). However, this rule does not apply unless the minister is satisfied that the facts of the case justify the inadmissibility. Also, according to section 64(3) of the IRPA, the finding may be appealed if the foreign national being sponsored is the sponsor's spouse, common law partner, or child.

3. A permanent resident or foreign national is inadmissible on the grounds of misrepresentation if a final determination is made to vacate his refugee status for fraud or misrepresentation. The Refugee Protection Division (RPD) has the authority to nullify or **vacate** a refugee determination under section 109(1) of the IRPA if it finds that the decision was obtained as a result of the permanent resident or foreign national's directly or indirectly misrepresenting or withholding material facts relating to a relevant matter in order to obtain Canada's protection. Under section 109(3), the consequence of such a finding is that the refugee claim is deemed rejected and the decision conferring refugee protection is nullified. When this occurs, the RPD provides a **notice of decision** to the refugee claimant and to the minister.

4. A permanent resident or foreign national is inadmissible on the grounds of misrepresentation on ceasing to be a citizen under section 10(1)(a) of the *Citizenship Act*, in the circumstances set out in section 10(2) of that Act.

vacate
to nullify or to void, such as may happen to a refugee determination that was obtained fraudulently

notice of decision
a written decision by the decision-maker, issued to those involved in the case

For example, if a person loses Canadian citizenship because it was obtained through misrepresentation, the officer obtains a letter confirming that the person has ceased to be a citizen from CIC, which has the responsibility for processing citizenship applications and maintaining citizenship records.

As with all other grounds of inadmissibility, a finding of misrepresentation may be made by visa officers in denying visas to applicants abroad, by port-of-entry officers in denying persons entry into Canada, and by officers in Canada in removing a person who has already been admitted to Canada.

Consider the following case scenarios.

- *Case Scenario #1:* A vehicle with four individuals arrives at a Canadian port of entry, and the driver is asked whether all the occupants in the car are Canadian citizens. The driver replies, "Yes." One of the passengers is a foreign national and remains silent.

  In this scenario, the driver misrepresented the foreign national, and the foreign national withheld material facts by remaining silent. Both are grounds for inadmissibility.

- *Case Scenario #2:* An individual appears at a Canadian port of entry to claim refugee status. The individual is using someone else's passport, but advises the officer that he used this passport for the purposes of leaving his country because his life was in danger.

  Normally, an individual who is using a false identity would be inadmissible to Canada on the basis of misrepresentation. However, the IRPA exempts persons who have claimed refugee protection if a determination of their claim is pending. This is an important exemption, justified by the fact that, without some degree of subterfuge, some refugees may not be able to escape from the countries they are fleeing.

- *Case Scenario #3:* A representative for a temporary residence applicant provides false information regarding the applicant's educational credentials. The applicant is truly unaware that the representative submitted false documentation until the officer brings this anomaly to the applicant's attention.

  Those who are unaware of a misrepresentation or whose actions or failure to act was unintentional but resulted in misrepresentation may nonetheless be found inadmissible on the grounds of misrepresentation. In the present case, the applicant is responsible for ensuring that the application is truthful and that the supporting documents are genuine. The officer could therefore find the applicant inadmissible on the grounds of misrepresentation for submitting false documents, even though the applicant was not the one who fabricated the evidence.

Exemptions

Under section 22 of the IRPR, the misrepresentation provisions do not apply to protected persons or to persons who have claimed refugee protection, provided that a disposition regarding their claim is pending. Furthermore, under section 176 of the IRPR and section 21 of the IRPA, misrepresentation provisions do not apply to those abroad who are family members of protected persons.

9. Cessation of Refugee Protection (Section 40.1)

Foreign nationals and permanent residents whose refugee protection "ceases" will become inadmissible. This generally requires the minister to make an application to the RPD of the IRB under section 108 of the Act. A determination by the RPD is considered final for these cases.

10. Failure to Comply with the IRPA (Section 41)

The grounds covered by the phrase "non-compliance with the IRPA" include contraventions of immigration law and regulations that are not captured by other grounds of inadmissibility. Section 41 of the IRPA provides for the refusal of admission, and it is especially useful for enforcing conditions or obligations that may be imposed on temporary and permanent residents. A non-compliance allegation is not a standalone allegation—it must be coupled with an allegation that the person has failed to comply with a specific requirement found elsewhere in the IRPA or IRPR.

Examples of failure to comply include the failure to do the following:[9]

- appear for an examination;
- appear for an admissibility hearing;
- obtain the written authorization of an officer to return to Canada (required by section 52(1) of the IRPA for a person who has been excluded);
- hold the relevant temporary or permanent visa in accordance with section 20 of the IRPA (for example, a visitor or student who engages in employment without a work visa);
- leave Canada by the end of the period authorized for the person's stay, as required by section 29(2) of the IRPA (for example, a person who overstays her authorized visit); or
- abide by section 29(2) of the IRPA, which provides that a temporary resident must comply with any condition set out in the Act or regulations (for example, a member of a crew under section 184 of the IRPR who does not leave Canada within 72 hours of ceasing to be a member of the crew).

The most common ground of inadmissibility is arriving at a port of entry without a valid visa, as required by section 11 of the IRPA and sections 6 and 7 of the IRPR.

---

9 These examples are taken from CIC's *ENF 2/OP 18: Evaluating Inadmissibility*, *supra* note 6 at 38–41.

11. Inadmissible Family Member (Section 42)

A person may be inadmissible as a result of having inadmissible family members, including dependants. Under section 42(1), a foreign national, other than a protected person, is inadmissible on the grounds of having an inadmissible family member if the accompanying family member or, in prescribed circumstances, the non-accompanying family member, is inadmissible. Under section 42(2), there is an exception for temporary residents and temporary resident applications:

- if the accompanying family member or, in prescribed circumstances, the non-accompanying family member, is inadmissible for the most serious reasons under section 34, 35, or 37; or
- if the foreign national is an accompanying family member of an inadmissible person who is inadmissible for the most serious reasons under section 34, 35, or 37.

Applicants for permanent and temporary residence must identify on their application forms all dependants, whether the dependants are included in the application or not. A visa officer assesses the foreign national's application, including the information it provides about the background and medical records of any dependants, to determine whether the dependants are inadmissible. If they are inadmissible, the foreign national may be inadmissible, according to section 23 of the IRPR, even if the dependants are not accompanying the foreign national to Canada. The policy reason for this provision is forward-looking: a non-accompanying dependant today could be tomorrow's sponsored applicant.

Assessing Inadmissibility

The minister of CIC is responsible for most policies related to admissibility. Visa officers who work abroad assess an applicant's admissibility. The minister of PSEP is responsible for policy regarding inadmissibility on the grounds of security, organized criminality, and violation of human or international rights. The CBSA—an agency of Public Safety Canada, formerly the Department of Public Safety and Emergency Preparedness—investigates foreign nationals and permanent residents for immigration violations, and has the authority to arrest, detain, and remove those who do not have the right to enter or stay in Canada.

Several other agencies may be involved in identifying inadmissible foreign nationals, depending on the place and circumstances. For example, the CBSA works with the Royal Canadian Mounted Police (RCMP), local police authorities, and other agencies in carrying out investigations and removals. Consider the four different processes for determining inadmissibility:

1. A CIC visa officer may refuse to issue a visa to a person who makes an application for permanent or temporary entry while outside Canada, thus barring the person from coming to Canada.

2. At a port of entry, a CBSA officer may refuse entry and issue a removal order to any of the following:

   - a returning permanent resident with a permanent resident card;
   - a new permanent resident with a confirmation of permanent resident visa;
   - a foreign national with or without a temporary resident visa; or
   - a refugee claimant.

3. A CBSA officer may find that a permanent or temporary resident who is already in Canada has become inadmissible, at which time the officer may issue a removal order or write an admissibility report to be reviewed by the minister. The minister may issue a removal order or may refer the case to the Immigration Division of the IRB.

4. The Immigration Division may hold an **admissibility hearing** for cases referred to it by the minister (usually the minister of PSEP), at which time a permanent or temporary resident may be found inadmissible and a removal order issued. The Immigration Appeal Division hears immigration appeals, including those against certain decisions on removal orders.

These processes are discussed fully in Part VI, Enforcement, and in Part VII, Appeals.

admissibility hearing
an adversarial hearing to determine whether or not an applicant is inadmissible; held at the ID when a person allegedly breaches Canadian immigration laws pursuant to IRPA section 44(1), where an officer is of the opinion that a permanent resident or foreign national is inadmissible

KEY TERMS

acquittal, 77

admissibility hearing, 90

balance of probabilities, 67

crimes against humanity, 70

criminality, 74

deemed rehabilitated, 77

eligible, 62

foreign national, 61

genocide, 70

hybrid or dual procedure offences, 76

inadmissibility, 60

inadmissible, 62

indictable offences, 76

individual rehabilitation, 77

medical surveillance, 84

misrepresentation, 85

notice of decision, 86

panel physician, 64

prescribed senior official, 70

record suspension (pardon), 76

summary conviction offences, 76

temporary resident permit (TRP), 66

temporary resident visa (TRV), 61

terrorist group, 69

vacate, 86

war crime, 72

withholding, 85

REVIEW QUESTIONS

1. List the 11 grounds of inadmissibility under the IRPA and their section numbers.

2. Provide an example of an action or condition that would render a person inadmissible under section 34(1) of the IRPA.

3. What are the differences between section 34(1) and section 35(1) of the IRPA? Give examples.

4. Which section of the IRPA deals with failure to comply with the Act? Give some examples of ways in which an individual may fail to comply. Is failing to comply with the IRPA grounds for inadmissibility?

5. Which section of the IRPA deals with inadmissible family members? In what situations will a person be inadmissible on the grounds of having an inadmissible family member?

PART II

Temporary Immigration Programs

TEMPORARY RESIDENT CLASSES

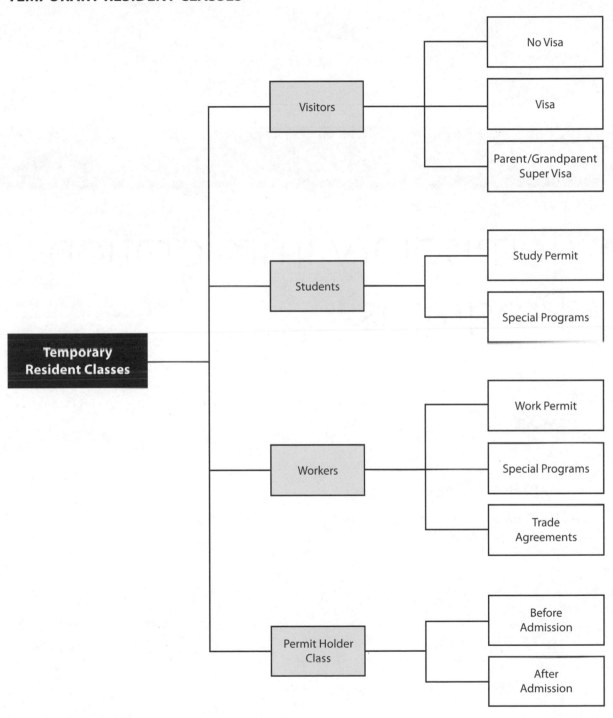

Temporary Entry

4

LEARNING OUTCOMES

After reading this chapter, you should be able to:

- Describe the general provisions for applying for a temporary resident visa.

- Understand the general obligations of temporary residents.

- Describe how temporary residents can lose, renew, or restore their status.

- Describe the general requirements for the visitor class of temporary residence.

- Describe the difference between a temporary resident visa and a temporary resident permit.

- Explain the criteria for obtaining a temporary resident permit.

Temporary Entry: General Provisions and Visitors

Temporary immigration is an important type of immigration to Canada. Each year, it allows thousands of people to visit, study, or work in Canada, which provides benefits to our economy. The government does not plan for and set quotas for temporary immigration as it does for permanent immigration; instead, it processes applications according to demand.[1] The results of this are reflected in Statistics Canada's observation that "the number of individuals admitted annually on a temporary basis has been growing faster than the number of permanent immigrants."[2]

The minister's *2014 Annual Report to Parliament on Immigration* suggests that three main groups constitute the bulk of Canada's temporary immigration: "foreign workers, important to Canada's economic growth; international students, attracted by the quality and diversity of Canada's educational system; and visitors, who come to Canada for personal or business travel."[3] Citizenship and Immigration Canada (CIC) reported that in 2013 the department received almost 2 million applications (1,889,610) from people seeking temporary resident visas as visitors, students, and workers. CIC issued 221,273 work permits to temporary foreign workers, 111,841 study permits to international students, and 687,697 visitors' visas.[4]

Temporary residence is important for family and friends, and for our economy. Imagine what would happen if people stopped coming to Canada! In the spring of 2013, visa officers (Professional Association of Foreign Service Officers [PAFSO]) initiated rotating job actions, a process that lasted six months. This resulted in a decrease in the number of temporary resident applications processed, which had an impact on the Canadian economy. Business and tourism sectors of the economy were affected, as were Canadian colleges and universities, whose international students decreased in number. Consider also the economic impact of the 2003 outbreak of SARS (severe acute respiratory syndrome), which kept not only tourists but also international students and business workers at home.

Temporary resident programs are vital to Canada's prosperity. At the same time, Canada's immigration policy recognizes that it is important to balance the need to attract foreign nationals with the need to protect Canadians by denying access to those who pose a criminal or security threat and to those who abuse our system by not leaving at the end of their permitted stay. These goals are reflected in the immigration objectives set out in section 3(1) of the *Immigration and Refugee Protection Act* (IRPA):

---

1 Citizenship and Immigration Canada, *2014 Annual Report to Parliament on Immigration* (October 2014) at 16, online: <http://www.cic.gc.ca/english/pdf/pub/annual-report-2014.pdf>.

2 Derrick Thomas, "Foreign Nationals Working Temporarily in Canada" (23 April 2014), online: Statistics Canada <http://www.statcan.gc.ca/pub/11-008-x/2010002/article/11166-eng.htm>.

3 *Supra* note 1.

4 Citizenship and Immigration Canada, *Quarterly Administrative Data Release* (20 June 2014), online: <http://www.cic.gc.ca/english/resources/statistics/data-release/2013-Q4/index.asp>.

(g) to facilitate the entry of visitors, students and temporary workers for purposes such as trade, commerce, tourism, international understanding and cultural, educational and scientific activities;

(h) to protect the health and safety of Canadians and to maintain the security of Canadian society;

(i) to promote international justice and security by fostering respect for human rights and by denying access to Canadian territory to persons who are criminals or security risks.

In this chapter, we look at the general eligibility requirements for temporary residents, some general exceptions to these requirements, and the obligations and general conditions that must be met by temporary residents after admission to Canada. We will then explore the specific requirements for the visitor class of temporary residence, including special provisions for parents and grandparents. Finally, we will consider the requirements for the permit holder class.

The specific requirements for the student and worker classes, including some special programs that lead to permanent residence for international students and workers, will be examined in Chapter 5.

> **WEBLINK**
>
> **The Importance of Keeping Informed**
> Monitor the CIC website for up-to-date information about temporary resident programs and the related application processes. The IRPR contains the details about temporary residents—including the temporary classes, eligibility criteria, and exemptions—all of which are subject to change. The minister's operational bulletins are also an important source of information about application processes and procedures. You can subscribe to media releases from CIC by signing up at <www.cic.gc.ca/english/department/media/subscription.asp> or by visiting the CIC website and choosing "Newsroom."

Temporary Resident Visas— General Provisions

There is no definition of "temporary immigration," "temporary residence," or "temporary resident" in the IRPA. The Act simply stipulates that all foreign nationals must apply for and obtain a visa before appearing at a port of entry (IRPA, s 11). Temporary residence is a prescribed category of residency, and therefore we turn to parts 9–12 of the *Immigration and Refugee Protection Regulations* (IRPR) for the requirements for each of the classes of temporary resident visas. A clear distinction is made between each class on the basis of the activity—visiting, studying, or working, for example—that the foreign national intends to undertake while temporarily in Canada.

In exceptional cases, foreign nationals may need special permission to be admitted or to be allowed to remain in Canada (for example, because they are inadmissible on health grounds). Such foreign nationals may be granted a **temporary resident permit (TRP)** and, as TRP holders, fall into a separate class of temporary residence. (See the "Permit Holder Class" section later in this chapter.)

Temporary residents (TRs) are foreign nationals who are permitted to enter and remain in Canada for a specified period of time, but who must leave by the end of the period authorized for their stay. They may re-enter Canada only if their authorization provides for re-entry; otherwise, they must reapply for permission to do so.

Generally, according to section 7 of the IRPR, a foreign national who wishes to "reside" temporarily in Canada must submit a written application subject to an approval process and obtain a temporary resident visa before coming to Canada. For those who wish to undertake a specific activity other than visiting, such as studying

temporary resident permit (TRP)
a permit that may be granted in exceptional circumstances to a person who does not meet the eligibility and/or the admissibility requirements to enter or remain temporarily in Canada

temporary resident (TR)
a foreign national who is legally allowed to be in Canada on a temporary basis, such as a tourist, student, worker, or business person

or working, a written application is required. There is an exception for some foreign nationals, who may make an oral application at a port of entry. The criteria are set out in the regulations: for example, a foreign national may be from a "visa-exempt" country or may have special status and therefore be exempt from the requirement to apply in writing before arrival (see "TRV Exemptions," below). These criteria are set out in the regulations, allowing the minister to respond quickly to changing trends by way of an order in council. This is faster and easier than having to make amendments to the Act.

An applicant has a duty to tell the truth pursuant to section 16 of the IRPA and to produce any relevant evidence requested by the officer, including photographs and fingerprints, regardless of whether the application was made orally or in writing.

Temporary Residents

A temporary resident (TR) is a foreign national who is authorized to enter and remain in Canada for a limited period.

A **temporary resident visa (TRV)** allows a foreign national to enter Canada.

A **visitor record** (IMM 1097) is issued if, upon examination, an officer decides to permit entry to a foreign national for a period of less than six months. It is a document that is attached to a foreign national's passport and includes conditions of admission and the date by which the person must leave.

---

temporary resident visa (TRV)
an official counterfoil document issued by a visa officer and placed in the applicant's passport to show that the foreign national has met the eligibility and admissibility requirements for a single entry or multiple entries to Canada as a temporary resident (e.g., as a visitor, student, or worker)

visitor record
a record of information documented by a port-of-entry officer, stapled to the holder's passport; it outlines the conditions of admission, specifies the date by which the foreign national must leave Canada, and includes other information about the foreign national and the purpose for seeking entry to Canada

A TRV is issued as a counterfoil document, or a stamped impression on a document, by an officer from a Canadian visa office such as a Canadian consulate, an embassy, a high commission, or a Visa Application Centre (VAC) outside Canada that processes immigration applications. If a foreign national is visiting Canada from a non-visa-exempt country and is coming as a tourist or to visit family or friends, a "V-1" counterfoil is used for the TRV. (See the figure on page 99.) Note that not all consulates or embassies process immigration applications, and some have different processing procedures. The TRV is placed in the applicant's passport to identify the holder as a person who may become a temporary resident upon admission to Canada.

TRVs are not always required. As discussed below, an oral application at the port of entry will suffice for those visiting Canada from visa-exempt countries; in this case, however, an officer may issue a visitor record as a means of exercising an element of control over the length of the foreign national's stay.

TRV Exemptions

The IRPR grants exceptions to the rule that all foreign nationals who seek temporary residence require a TRV before arriving at a port of entry. Some persons may be exempt on the basis of nationality, possession of certain documents, or the purpose of the entry:

- *Nationality.* Citizens of numerous countries, including Australia, France, and Britain, and citizens of a British overseas territory, do not require a TRV to enter Canada, nor do nationals or permanent residents of the United States. Section 190(1) of the IRPR provides a full list of nationality exemptions.

TRV Issued as a "V-1" Counterfoil

Source: *Temporary Residence Visa*. Reproduced with permission of Citizenship and Immigration Canada.

Visa-Exempt Country List

The minister may add countries to the nationality exemption list or remove them in response to changing trends. For example, in 1997, the Canadian government imposed visa requirements on the Czech Republic. This was in response to the rising number of Roma people from that country who travelled to Canada as visitors, then over-stayed to make refugee claims, the majority of which were refused. Ten years later, however, in October 2007, Canada lifted the visa requirements for Czech nationals who wanted to visit Canada for fewer than 90 days. In November 2013, the restrictions on all Czech visitors to Canada were lifted following a comprehensive assess-ment; the minister announced that Czech nationals no longer re-quired a TRV to visit Canada. In July 2009, in another change to the nationality exemption list, the minister imposed a visa restriction on citizens of Mexico because of an increase in refugee claims from that country.

WEBLINK

How to Find Visa-Exempt Countries
Depending on the foreign national's country of origin, a visa may not be necessary. To find out whether a foreign national needs to apply for a TRV before coming to Canada, you can consult section 190 of the IRPR. The list of countries may change at any time, so it is important to consult the most current version of the IRPR. You can also search by country on the page entitled "find out if you need a visa" on the CIC website, at <www.cic.gc.ca/english/visit/visas.asp>.

- *Documents.* Foreign nationals do not require a TRV to enter Canada if they hold certain documents, including a diplomat's passport, a passport or travel document issued by the Holy See, a national Israeli passport, or certain Hong Kong passports. Section 190(2) of the IRPR provides a full list of exemptions based on the applicant's documents.

- *Purpose of entry.* Foreign nationals may be exempt from the TRV requirement if they are members of a transportation crew, are passengers on an airplane landing in Canada for refuelling, or have come to Canada for an interview with a US consular officer regarding re-admission to the United States. Section 190(3) of the IRPR provides a full list of exemptions based on the applicant's purpose of entry.

General TRV Application Requirements

For most foreign nationals, obtaining a TRV involves a formal, written application procedure. Applicants must submit their application packages to the visa office that is responsible for serving their country. In many cases, applicants can now submit their application online for a visitor visa, study permit, or work permit, and for extensions to a visa or permit. The general temporary resident admission process is illustrated in the chart below.

Section 179 of the IRPR sets out the basic criteria that must generally be met for all classes of TRVs (that is, by all visitors, workers, and students seeking a TRV). A TRV may be issued only if an examination establishes that the foreign national

- has applied in accordance with the regulations for their particular temporary resident class;
- has applied—to the appropriate office or online—in accordance with the requirements of the IRPA;
- will leave Canada by the end of the period authorized for staying in Canada;
- has paid the required processing fees;
- holds a passport or similar document that may be used to enter the country that issued it, or another country;
- meets the medical examination requirements set out in section 30 of the IRPR;
- meets the requirements applicable to the temporary resident class; and
- is not inadmissible.

These criteria are considered in more detail below.

General Temporary Resident Admission Process

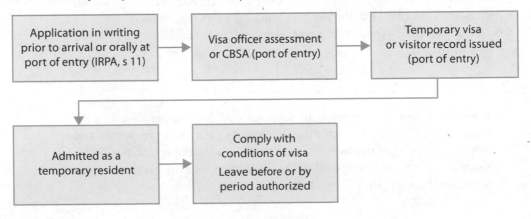

Application Documents

A foreign national is deemed to have applied for a TRV as a member of the visitor, worker, or student class by submitting a number of forms and documents that support the application. The following are examples of the forms and documentation required:

- a completed application package (see the box below);
- a valid passport or travel/identity document, unless the foreign national is exempt from passport and travel document requirements under section 52(1) of the IRPR;
- recent passport-sized photos for each family member (the name of the person should be written on the back of each photo);
- proof of custody and/or a letter of consent from the custodial parent, in a case where a child under 16 years of age is either travelling alone, is without proper identification, or is with adults other than a sole custodial parent or guardian;
- proof of current immigration status, if the foreign national is not a citizen of the country in which she is applying (see the following section);
- biometric information (photographs and fingerprints), for citizens from certain countries; and
- proof of the applicant's ability to adequately cover all reasonable expenses (both for the applicant and for any accompanying family members) to be incurred during the stay in Canada.

The Application Package

The completed application package may include the following forms:

- the appropriate visa or permit application form (for example, IMM 5257 for visitors, IMM 1294 for students, or IMM 1295 for workers);
- Family Information (IMM 5645)
- Statutory Declaration of Common-Law Union (IMM 5409), if applicable;
- Schedule 1: Application for Temporary Resident Visa (IMM 5257);
- Document Checklist (IMM 5484); and
- Use of a Representative (IMM 5476).

Fillable versions of forms are available on the CIC website and, in many cases, may be submitted electronically.

There are also cost-recovery processing fees and biometric fees (for some) that must be paid at the time of application. If the applicant is applying on paper, a fee receipt must be included showing that the fee has been paid to an approved financial institution (IMM 5401); the fees may also be paid online.

The most current instructions and forms are set out in step 2 of the applicant's Instruction Guide (IMM 5256) available on the CIC website at <http://www.cic.gc.ca/english/information/applications/guides/5256ETOC.asp>.

Applicants may also be required to provide other documents to convince the officer that they intend to return to their country of residence at the end of the period authorized for their temporary stay. For example, an applicant may be required to provide a letter from an employer in the country of residence indicating that the applicant is expected to return there.

Finally, there are specific documents required for each type of TRV, such as a letter of invitation, a **letter of acceptance**, or a genuine job offer (see the discussion later in this chapter and in Chapter 5).

letter of acceptance
a document that indicates that a foreign student has been accepted into a Canadian educational institution

Biometric Information

Applicants between the ages of 14 and 79 from certain countries are now required to present themselves to a visa application centre (VAC) for the collection of biometric information—currently fingerprints and photographs—to confirm the applicant's identity. At the time of writing, biometric information was required from applicants from 29 countries and 1 territory, including Afghanistan, Democratic Republic of Congo, Iran, Iraq, Somalia, Syria, and Sudan (see IRPR, s 12.1). Individuals must pay a fee of $85 to have this information collected. The fee for a family is $170. The CIC website states that the purpose of collecting such information is to make it more difficult for someone to forge, steal, or use the applicant's identity; resolve problems or errors that may happen if the applicant's name, date of birth, and/or place of birth are similar to those of someone else; and make it easier for the applicant to re-enter Canada the next time he applies.[5] The examining officer at the port of entry will use the biometric information to confirm the traveller's identity upon arrival in Canada.

How to Submit Applications

Online Applications

To apply online, applicants need to create a "MyCIC account." See <www.cic.gc.ca/english/my_application/apply_online.asp>.

Paper Applications

Applying outside Canada: For TRVs and study and work permits, consult the CIC website for the most up-to-date information:

- VACs: <www.cic.gc.ca/english/information/offices/vac.asp>
- Visa offices: <www.cic.gc.ca/english/information/offices/apply-where.asp>

Applying within Canada: For TRVs and study and work permits, or for change of status, extensions, and restoration of temporary status, applications are sent to the case processing centre in Vegreville, Alberta: <www.cic.gc.ca/english/information/offices/canada/vegreville.asp>. Mailing instructions are provided in the instruction guides.

---

5   Citizenship and Immigration Canada, Help Centre, "Why do I have to give my biometrics (fingerprints and photograph) when I apply for a visitor visa, study permit, or work permit?" (9 February 2015), online: <http://www.cic.gc.ca/english/helpcentre/answer.asp?q=703&t=19>.

Place of Application

Applicants outside Canada seeking a TRV as a student or worker are required by the regulations (IRPR, s 11(2)) to submit their application outside Canada to the visa office that is responsible for processing TRVs. The office must serve one of the following jurisdictions:

- the country where the applicant resides, if the applicant has been lawfully admitted to that country for at least one year; or
- the applicant's country of nationality (or, if the applicant is stateless, her country of habitual residence).

Applicants outside Canada may submit their applications electronically, through the CIC website.

Sometimes, temporary residents decide to extend their stay in Canada or wish to change their status to "student" or "worker." If already in Canada, they may submit their application electronically, through the CIC website, or they may submit it to a case processing centre (CPC), such as CPC-O in Ottawa, Ontario and CPC-V in Vegreville, Alberta. (Check the CIC website for current information about where to apply and the types of applications each CPC manages, because these are subject to change depending on the department's operational requirements.)

Consider the following scenario:

> Rose, a Colombian national, is currently working in Arizona as a live-in caregiver for the British ambassador to the United States. Rose is 32 years old, speaks fluent English, and has a university degree obtained in Colombia. After completing her education in Colombia, Rose moved to Arizona to care for the ambassador's three children. She has now worked for the ambassador for five years.
>
> The ambassador is soon moving back to London, but she has told Rose that the new Canadian ambassador would like to employ Rose in Ottawa. Rose has worked problem-free for the ambassador in Arizona, although she was never authorized to work in the United States and did not enter the United States legally. Rose would like to apply for a work permit through the Canadian consulate in Los Angeles under the Live-In Caregiver Program.

Unfortunately for Rose, she may not apply within the United States because section 11(2) of the IRPR prohibits her from doing so. Rose was not lawfully admitted to the United States at any time; therefore, she has no right to apply in Los Angeles for a work permit through the Canadian consulate. Instead, Rose must submit her application in her country of nationality, Colombia, and appear at a VAC to provide her biometric information.

On the other hand, a business person from India spending a day or two in France may apply for a Canadian TRV in Paris, as long as he was lawfully admitted to France, and a Pakistani student studying in Singapore may apply for a TRV and a study permit at the visa office there.

Section 11(2) is applicable only to persons who are physically present in the country to which they were lawfully admitted. For example, section 11(2) will not permit a Peruvian national who is physically in Peru to make a TRV application by mail to the Canadian visa office in New York City.

Consider another scenario:

> Maria is a dual citizen of Mexico and Argentina. She is currently living in the United Kingdom; she entered the United Kingdom legally but then lost her immigration status because she failed to extend her work permit. Maria would like to apply for a TRV to Canada, but she is unsure where she can submit her application.

Maria is entitled to submit her application to the Canadian visa office in either Mexico or Argentina, because Maria is a citizen of both countries. Alternatively, Maria may submit her application to the Canadian visa office in London, because she was lawfully admitted to the United Kingdom. The fact that she subsequently lost her immigration status does not disqualify her from submitting her application to the visa office in London.

Intention to Leave Canada

According to section 20(1)(b) of the IRPA, a foreign national must satisfy an officer that he will leave Canada at the end of the period authorized for his temporary stay. An officer considers certain factors in determining whether an applicant intends to remain in Canada illegally, beyond the end of his permitted stay, in order to make a refugee claim or otherwise seek to remain in the country. The officer considers

1. whether the applicant has family or economic ties to his country of residence;
2. whether the applicant has the financial capability to be self-sufficient while in Canada;
3. the applicant's immigration status in his country of residence;
4. the economic and political conditions in the applicant's country of residence; and
5. the applicant's obligations or responsibilities in his country of residence.

These factors are considered in more detail below.

1. FAMILY AND ECONOMIC TIES

The officer who reviews the application considers whether the applicant has any family living in her country of residence and whether the family will be accompanying the applicant to Canada. If the applicant does not have family in her country of residence, the applicant will be deemed not to have family ties in the country of residence. This may lead the officer to believe that the applicant is less likely to be motivated to return to her country of residence than would be the case if she did have family ties there.

The officer also examines the applicant's employment status and financial stability in her country of residence. The officer determines whether the applicant is employed and, if so, her salary. Has the applicant's employer approved a request for leave, and is the employer expecting the applicant to return to her job? This would suggest a genuine intention to return. The officer also considers whether the applicant owns any property in the country of residence and, if so, the value of the property. Significant holdings—particularly, a family home—suggest ties strong enough to indicate an intention to return.

2. FINANCIAL SELF-SUFFICIENCY

The applicant must prove that there are sufficient funds to cover living expenses for himself and for any accompanying family members for the duration of their stay while in Canada, and that there will be funds remaining to pay for the return trip home at the end of the temporary stay. The amount of money required varies according to the circumstances of the visit—for example, the length of the stay and whether the applicant will need to pay for accommodations.

The following is a list of supporting documents that could be included as evidence of an applicant's financial resources:

- bank statements or deposit books that show accumulated savings for both applicant and spouse;
- letters of employment providing the name of the employer, the applicant's position/occupation, the date that the employment commenced, and annual earnings for both applicant and spouse; and
- evidence of assets in the country of residence, such as deeds and car ownership, for both applicant and spouse.

In a case where the applicant lacks sufficient funds but a host or family member in Canada is willing to provide adequate support for the duration of the applicant's stay, the host must provide a letter of invitation (see the discussion below). The officer examines the ability of the host or family member to support the temporary resident for the duration of the TRV.

3. IMMIGRATION STATUS

The officer examines the applicant's immigration status in the country of residence. Section 11(2) of the IRPR gives TRV applicants significant flexibility to apply to come to Canada from any country, provided that they were lawfully admitted to that country and remain physically present there while their applications are processed.

Note, however, that there are situations in which applicants, despite meeting the criteria set out in section 11(2), may not be successful in their applications. This happens because they are found to lack credibility with respect to their stated intention to leave Canada at the end of the period authorized for their stay. Consider a citizen of the Bahamas who enters the United States legally but then stays beyond the authorized period. Section 11(2) permits this Bahamian applicant to apply for a Canadian TRV at a visa office in the United States, because he was lawfully admitted to the United States—even though he is no longer entitled to be there. However, the fact that he did not abide by the terms of his visa in the United States may undermine his efforts to convince the officer that he will not do the same if he is granted a Canadian TRV.

4. ECONOMIC AND POLITICAL CONDITIONS

The officer examines the economic and political situation in the applicant's country of residence. This is necessary because, even if the applicant's ties to the home country are strong, unstable economic or political conditions may cause him to reconsider returning home.

5. OTHER OBLIGATIONS AND RESPONSIBILITIES

The officer may consider any other obligations or responsibilities that the applicant has in her country of residence if they are clearly disclosed during the examination. This may include personal responsibilities, such as caring for an elderly parent, or business obligations to partners or employees.

It is important to remember that the onus to provide sufficient evidence to support the applicant's case rests on the applicant. Failure to provide supporting documentation may result in the TRV application being refused.

DUAL INTENT

dual intent
an intention to become first a temporary resident and then a permanent resident

A foreign national who intends to become a permanent resident after she becomes a temporary resident—known as having a **dual intent**—is not necessarily precluded from becoming a temporary resident. Provided that the visa officer is satisfied that the applicant has the capacity and willingness to leave Canada by the end of the period authorized for her stay, her TRV application will not, according to section 22(2) of the IRPA, necessarily be denied simply because she intends to apply for permanent status. For example, a person who has already submitted an application for permanent residence as a provincial nominee (described in Chapter 8, Economic Classes) may wish to visit Canada for the purpose of an "exploratory visit" while awaiting the processing of that application.

The foreign national must satisfy both the officer abroad and the officer at the port of entry that he has the ability and willingness to leave Canada at the end of the temporary period authorized. The fact that a foreign national has been issued a visa does not in itself guarantee admission to Canada. Under section 180 of the IRPR, the foreign national must not only meet the requirements for issuance of the visa at the time it is issued, but must be found to continue to meet those requirements at the time of the examination on entry into Canada.

Processing Fees

Applicants for TRVs and permits are required to pay processing fees. Processing fees vary depending on the type of visa or permit. There is no fee for a TRV if a work or study permit is issued at the same time. Fees and exemptions are set out in the IRPR and are subject to change. Consult the following sections for current fees and exemptions: section 296 (temporary resident visas), section 298 (temporary resident permits), section 299 (work permits), and section 300 (study permits).

Processing fees are non-refundable, even if the application is refused; the fee is for the costs of processing the application, not for the decision. In certain circumstances, however, applicants for a TRV may be exempt from paying the processing fee.

The current processing fees for each type of visa are listed on the CIC website, at <www.cic-gc.ca/english/information/fees/fees.asp>.

Passport and Travel Documents

The details of what documents are acceptable and what documents are unacceptable are set out in section 52 of the IRPR. Foreign nationals seeking to become temporary residents must hold a passport or travel document that is valid for the period authorized for their stay. Such documents, including certain passports, travel documents, identity documents, and *laissez-passers* (travel permits) from the United Nations, are listed in section 52(1) of the IRPR.

Section 52(2) provides a list of individuals who are exempt from this requirement:

(a) citizens of the United States;

(b) persons seeking to enter Canada from the United States or St. Pierre and Miquelon who have been lawfully admitted to the United States for permanent residence;

(c) residents of Greenland seeking to enter Canada from Greenland;

(d) persons seeking to enter Canada from St. Pierre and Miquelon who are citizens of France and residents of St. Pierre and Miquelon;

(e) members of the armed forces of a country that is a designated state for the purposes of the *Visiting Forces Act* who are seeking entry in order to carry out official duties, other than persons who have been designated as a civilian component of those armed forces;

(f) persons who are seeking to enter Canada as, or in order to become, members of a crew of a means of air transportation and who hold an airline flight crew licence or crew member certificate issued in accordance with International Civil Aviation Organization specifications;

(g) persons seeking to enter Canada as members of a crew who hold a seafarer's identity document issued under International Labour Organization conventions and are members of the crew of the vessel that carries them to Canada.

The validity of a TRV does not outlast the validity of a passport. Therefore, if an applicant's passport will soon expire, the applicant should renew it before applying for a TRV.

Medical Examinations

Medical examinations are required for applicants who will be working in occupations in Canada where the protection of public health is essential. Regardless of the applicant's intended period of stay in Canada, a foreign national whose prospective occupation is related to health services or requires close contact with other persons must undergo a medical examination.

Such occupations include schoolteachers, domestic workers, day nursery employees, clinical laboratory workers, medical students admitted to Canada to attend university, and physicians on short-term locums—occupations that may involve close contact with people for more than three hours per day and/or a risk of exchange of body fluids. Agricultural workers from designated countries and territories[6] are likewise required to undergo a medical examination.

A medical examination is also generally required in the following situations, regardless of the foreign national's prospective occupation in Canada (IRPR, s 30(1)):

- the foreign national is seeking entry into Canada or applying for a renewal of a work or study permit or authorization to remain in Canada, as a temporary resident for a period in excess of six consecutive months, including an actual or proposed period of absence from Canada of less than 14 days; and
- the foreign national resided or sojourned for six or more consecutive months in a designated country or territory during the one year immediately preceding the date of seeking entry to Canada.

Medical examinations must be performed by designated panel physicians. To avoid processing delays, they should be done at least two months before the expiry of the temporary resident's work or study permit.

In certain circumstances, a foreign national seeking to stay in Canada for six months or longer may be exempt from the medical examination requirement. Section 30(1) of the IRPR lists the following exempt persons:

- a person entering Canada with the purpose of carrying out official duties, unless that person seeks to engage or continue in secondary employment in Canada;
- a family member of an accredited foreign representative, as listed in section 186(b) of the IRPR, unless that family member seeks to engage or continue in employment in Canada;
- a member of the armed forces of a country that is a designated state for the purposes of the *Visiting Forces Act* who is entering or is in Canada to carry out official duties, other than a person who has been designated as a civilian component of those armed forces, unless that member seeks to engage or continue in secondary employment in Canada;
- a family member of a protected person, if the family member is not included in the protected person's application to remain in Canada as a permanent resident;
- a non-accompanying family member of a foreign national who has applied for refugee protection outside Canada; or
- a foreign national who has applied for permanent resident status and is a member of the live-in caregiver class.

---

6 Designated countries or territories are those that have been determined to have a higher incidence of serious communicable disease than Canada has. The list of designated countries/territories includes most countries, with the exception of countries in Western Europe, the United States, Australia, New Zealand, and Japan. The list of currently designated countries/territories is available on the CIC website at <http://www.cic.gc.ca/english/information/medical/dcl.asp>.

Decision on Application

A TRV is issued only when the officer is satisfied that the applicant meets the requirements of the IRPA and its regulations (IRPA, s 22; IRPR, s 179)—namely, that the applicant has

- fulfilled certain application obligations;
- met the criteria for the particular class of temporary resident that he has applied under; and
- shown that he is not inadmissible.

Applications for a TRV may be refused for any of the following reasons:

- the applicant does not meet the eligibility criteria for the particular class of temporary resident;
- the applicant (or any family member) is inadmissible on the grounds of security risk, human or international rights violations, serious criminality, criminality, organized criminality, health risk, financial reasons, misrepresentation, or non-compliance with the IRPA, or because of an inadmissible family member; or
- the officer is not satisfied that the applicant will leave by the end of his stay.

Examination at Port of Entry

As noted in Chapter 3, obtaining a TRV does not guarantee admission to Canada. All people seeking to come to Canada, including temporary residents, must be examined by an officer in accordance with section 18 of the IRPA. Therefore, when the applicant arrives at a Canadian port of entry seeking admission, an officer from the Canada Border Services Agency (CBSA) decides whether or not to allow entry. A change in an applicant's circumstances between the time that he acquired a TRV and the time of his arrival in Canada, or additional information that has come to light about the applicant, could result in his being refused entry. In other words, a TRV allows a person to travel to a Canadian port of entry in order to visit, work, or study in Canada, but it does not in itself grant that person admission to Canada to carry out those activities.

A temporary resident's passport or travel document will be stamped at the port of entry to show the date that she entered and the date that she must leave Canada. Other terms and conditions may be included, depending on the class of temporary resident.

The officer at the port of entry authorizes the foreign national's entry as a temporary resident and will remind her of the conditions of her stay. If the officer has any doubts about her intention to live up to the terms and conditions of admission, a security deposit may be imposed (for further details, see Chapter 14).

No Right of Appeal

There is no right to appeal the refusal of an application for a TRV, study permit, or work permit to the IRB. The applicant may seek leave for judicial review at the Federal Court. If an applicant who was refused admission believes that the refusal was discriminatory and without bona fide justification, she may file a complaint under the *Canadian Human Rights Act*.

TRV Conditions

Temporary residents must comply with any conditions imposed under section 183 of the IRPR. There are general conditions that are automatically imposed on all TRVs issued, such as the requirement

- to leave by the end of the authorized period of stay, and
- not to study or work without the appropriate permit.

Status Change or Extension of a Temporary Resident Visa

After entry has been granted, a temporary resident may not change status without permission. Doing so would be a violation of the IRPA, causing the temporary resident to become inadmissible, and could result in his removal. For example, under sections 186 and 187 of the IRPR, a temporary resident holding a TRV issued under the visitor class is not allowed to work in Canada without a work permit. Under sections 188 and 189, a temporary resident generally may not study without a study permit. A temporary worker may not change jobs, and some international students may not change their approved type of educational institution without first applying to have the conditions amended.

Foreign nationals who wish to change their type of visa or a condition on their visa must first apply to CIC while still in status, at least 30 days before the visa expires. An online application option is available. The following is a sample application package:

- a completed Application to Change Conditions, Extend My Stay or Remain in Canada as a Visitor or Temporary Resident Permit Holder (IMM 5708), for applicants in Canada who wish to change their type of visa or to change the conditions imposed upon entry;
- Statutory Declaration of Common-Law Union (IMM 5409), if applicable;
- Use of a Representative (IMM 5476), if applicable;
- Document Checklist (IMM 5558); and
- Fee Receipt (IMM 5401), indicating that the cost-recovery processing fee of $100 has been paid to an approved financial institution, unless the fee is being paid online.

(Note that processing procedures regularly change, so it is prudent to verify on the CIC website that these forms have not changed.) Processing may take 30 days or more, in some cases.

The applicant should also provide the following:

- an explanation of why he wishes to stay in Canada longer;
- proof of identity;
- proof of current status in Canada (a valid and current visa);
- evidence of how he will support himself and any dependants in Canada; and
- a purchased ticket or funds set aside to prove an intention to leave Canada, and any other details, including date and type of transportation.

Under section 183(5) of the IRPR, if the temporary resident applies to extend his status, he must do so before it expires, and he will retain this status until a decision is rendered on the application: during this period, the temporary resident has implied status.[7] Similarly, if the applicant has a study or work visa and applies to extend the visa before it expires, he has the right to continue to study or work in Canada under the same conditions until a decision is rendered.

Loss and Restoration of Temporary Resident Status

A temporary resident may lose temporary resident status under section 47 of the IRPA. This can happen in a situation where a temporary resident becomes inadmissible—for example, by exceeding the authorized period of her stay. If found to be inadmissible, the temporary resident loses that status and may be removed from Canada. (The enforcement and removal process is discussed in Chapter 14.)

When a foreign national visitor, worker, or student loses status or if her temporary resident status expires and she has not left Canada, she may apply within 90 days of the loss or expiry to have her status restored. If 90 days have passed, she must leave Canada.

A **restoration of status** may be granted only in cases where the temporary resident has continued to comply with the initial requirements for her stay in Canada but has failed to comply with one or more of the subsequent requirements by

- remaining in Canada longer than the period authorized for her stay, but no longer than 90 days;
- changing the conditions of her studies—for example their type, their location, or their times and periods—without applying to change them on her study permit, if they were specified on her study permit as conditions; or
- changing employers, type of work, or location of work, without applying to change the conditions, if they were specified on her work permit.

Therefore, a temporary resident whose temporary resident status has expired is not eligible to apply for an extension but may apply for restoration of status, provided that the 90-day period has not passed. There is no guarantee that the application for restoration of status will be approved, because every application is assessed on its

restoration of status
restoration of a temporary resident's lost status as a visitor, student, or worker has expired; applied for in accordance with R182 on form IMM 1249E

---

7 Citizenship and Immigration Canada, "Temporary Resident: Implied Status (Extending a Stay)," online: <http://www.cic.gc.ca/english/resources/tools/temp/visa/validity/implied.asp>.

own merits. Therefore, the submissions should include an explanation for the failure to comply with the requirements of the TRV, with as much supporting evidence as possible.

Additionally, a foreign national may not apply for restoration of status if the loss of status resulted from non-compliance with conditions for which a six-month ban may be imposed.

Section 200(3)(e)(i) of the IRPR provides that

> (3) An officer shall not issue a work permit to a foreign worker if ...
>
> (e) the foreign national has engaged in unauthorized study or work in Canada or has failed to comply with a condition of a previous permit or authorization unless
>
> (i) a period of six months has elapsed since the cessation of the unauthorized work or study or failure to comply with a condition.

Consider the following scenario:

> Robert is working in Canada with a work permit and he is seeking an extension. Robert's work permit expired three weeks ago but he has continued to work in Canada. He did not intend to violate any conditions imposed on his work permit—he thought that he would be receiving a reminder from CIC regarding the renewal.
>
> To which case processing centre (CPC) should Robert send his application? What will Robert's status be if the CPC contacts Robert's employer and discovers that he was working after the work permit expired?

According to the IRPR, Robert may not be issued a new work permit unless a period of six months has elapsed since the cessation of the unauthorized work—in other words, he must not have worked for six months.

Furthermore, under section 306 of the IRPR, Robert must submit a completed application and the appropriate restoration fee of $200. The documents that must be submitted are the same as those listed above.

Visitor Class

The visitor class is the most straightforward of the temporary resident classes. It includes travellers, tourists, vacationers, and people who are visiting friends and family for short periods of time. Visitors contribute significantly to the Canadian economy, and it is important to welcome them with a minimum of red tape while ensuring the security and safety of Canadians.

A foreign national applying for temporary residence must satisfy the officer that he will comply with all the restrictions imposed by the visitor visa. Generally, visitors are not allowed to work or study in Canada unless they are authorized to do so under the IRPR.

There are exceptions to this rule. For example, certain categories of workers (such as business workers under NAFTA) do not require work permits to work in Canada and, in certain circumstances visitors are allowed to study in Canada without first obtaining a study permit (for example, if they are taking an English class that is less than six months in duration).

Guidelines regarding processing times suggest that foreign nationals should apply for a **visitor visa** at least one month before their intended arrival date. However, it is important to check the CIC website for the most up-to-date processing times. There are four types of visas:

1. **Single-entry visa (SEV).** An SEV will be issued when the foreign national's purpose of entry is limited (for example, an official visit); when entry is for the purpose of participating in a one-time event (for example, the 2015 Pan American Games); or when the minister has issued country-specific instructions. As of February 2014, the fee for a single-entry temporary resident visa was increased from $75 to $100. (Check the CIC website for the current fee.)

2. **Multiple-entry visa (MEV).** As of February 6, 2014, visitors to Canada are automatically considered for the MEV. The maximum validity period for an MEV is matched to the maximum validity of the length of the passport and can be up to ten years, minus one month. As of February 2014, the fee for an MEV was reduced from $150 to $100. (Check the CIC website for the current fee.)

3. **Transit visa.** A transit visa is generally required for travel through Canada to another country by anyone who would need a TRV to enter Canada. The foreign national is required to show travel tickets. We find exceptions to this requirement, too; the government has created programs that exempt certain qualified foreign nationals from certain countries from the requirement for a transit visa (for example, members of the Transit Without Visa Program).

4. **Super Visa.** Since December 1, 2011, foreign nationals who are the parents or grandparents of a Canadian citizen or a permanent resident can apply for the Parent and Grandparent Super Visa (also referred to simply as a Super Visa).

Processing Fees

The following visitor class applicants are exempt from paying the processing fee (IRPR, s 296):

- foreign nationals applying for transit visas;
- persons who are issued courtesy visas, provided that the person is listed in section 296(2) of the IRPR;
- diplomats, who are always fee-exempt, regardless of whether the purpose of their visit is official;
- members of the armed forces who comply with the *Visiting Forces Act*;
- members of the clergy and religious groups who are visiting for certain religious purposes;

visitor visa
a term commonly used in place of temporary resident visa

single-entry visa
a document that allows a foreign national to enter Canada only once, usually for no more than six months

multiple-entry visa (MEV)
a document that allows a foreign national to enter Canada from another country multiple times during the validity of the visa, for up to six months at a time

transit visa
a document that allows travel through Canada to another country by anyone who would need a temporary resident visa to enter Canada and whose flight will stop here for less than 48 hours

Super Visa
a document that allows a foreign national who is the parent or grandparent of a Canadian citizen or a permanent resident to stay in Canada for up to two years and re-enter over a ten-year period without the need to renew the visa; also called a Parent and Grandparent Super Visa

- competitors, coaches, judges, team officials, medical staff, or members of a national or international sports organizing body who are participating in the Pan American Games, or performers participating in a festival associated with the games;

- applicants who are applying at the same time and place for a work permit or a study permit;

- participants who are attending meetings hosted by the Government of Canada, an organization of the United Nations, or the Organization of American States, as representatives of the Organization of American States or the Caribbean Development Bank, or at the invitation of the Government of Canada; and

- travellers who are in transit for a period of less than 48 hours to a destination other than Canada, or who are travelling through or stopping over in Canada for refuelling.

Letter of Invitation

letter of invitation
a letter from a Canadian citizen or permanent resident in Canada on behalf of a friend or family member who wants to visit, setting out how the host plans to support the visitor and whether she has the financial means to support the visitor during a longer visit

In many cases, a **letter of invitation** will be required in order to satisfy the officer that the foreign national intends only to visit temporarily and to leave at the end of the authorized period. A letter of invitation is always required for Super Visa applicants.

A letter of invitation from the host—a Canadian citizen or permanent resident—is helpful to the person applying for temporary residence. The letter should set out important information about the host—such as her name, date of birth, contact information, status in Canada, occupation, and the number of persons residing in her household—along with a promise to support the temporary resident during his stay. The letter must also include similar information about the person being invited, including his name and contact information, his relationship to the host, the expected length of the visit, and arrangements for accommodation while in Canada. The letter may be notarized, but it does not need to be.

The person's application for a TRV is assessed along with the letter of invitation to determine the ability of the host or family member to provide support to the applicant. The following documents and evidence may be enclosed in support of the application:

- a letter of invitation from the host or family member in Canada that includes a description of the financial assistance offered, such as accommodation, transportation costs, and medical costs;

- proof of the host or family member's income—either the last two Canada Revenue Agency notices of assessment, or a letter from the host's employer indicating the host's job position, the date the employment commenced, and her annual earnings; and

- evidence of the size of the host's or family member's family in Canada, so that the officer can determine whether sufficient income, known as the minimum necessary income, is available to support all dependants (the minimum necessary income is determined by reference to an annual Statistics Canada measure called the low-income cut-off; see below).

Parent and Grandparent Super Visa

The Parent and Grandparent Super Visa was created to replace the lengthy sponsorship processing for permanent residence, so that family members may be reunited more quickly (the family class sponsorship program is discussed in Chapter 7, Family Class). With a Super Visa, the foreign national is allowed to stay for up to two years at a time without the need to renew her visa, and may re-enter as many times as she wishes over a ten-year period (the time period for which a Super Visa is valid). The applicant may include her spouse or common law partner under the Super Visa, but may not include dependants (which would be allowed if she was applying for sponsorship as a permanent resident).

Specific to the Super Visa is the requirement that all applicants undergo a medical examination and purchase Canadian medical insurance for a period of at least one year that provides a minimum coverage of $100,000 for health care, hospitalization, and repatriation and that is valid for re-entry and available for review by the officer at the port of entry. Applicants must also provide proof of the parent, or grandparent, relationship to the Canadian citizen or permanent resident (for example, birth certificate, baptismal certificate, or another official document that names the applicant as a parent or grandparent).

The child or grandchild in Canada—a Canadian citizen or permanent resident—must provide a written commitment of financial support, including a letter of invitation that sets out the living arrangements, care, and support for the duration of the parent's or grandparent's stay in Canada. The child or grandchild must establish that he meets a minimum income threshold according to the low-income cut-off (LICO) table. Therefore, the letter of invitation must include details regarding the number of members in the family unit (the "sponsoring" child or grandchild, his spouse and dependants, and the visiting parents and/or grandparents) and the number of people residing in the household, including current sponsorships.

Consider the following scenario:

> Michele, a Canadian permanent resident, and her husband, John, a Canadian citizen, have two young children, Kara and Matthew. Michele and John both work full-time and spend long hours away from their children. Michele wishes her parents could move to Canada to live with them to help care for the children. Michele's parents, Teresa and Enrique, are healthy and energetic and like the idea of being able to spend time with their grandchildren and to help out, but they are not sure they want to move permanently from their home in Mexico. The Super Visa would allow Teresa and Enrique to visit for up to two years at a time for the next ten years.

Michele, as their Canadian citizen daughter, needs to prepare a letter of invitation that proves that she can provide care and support for her parents in addition to for her Canadian family. She must show that she meets or exceeds the minimum income threshold as set out in the current LICO table (see below). In order to determine the minimum required income, calculate the number of Michele's dependants once her parents are living with her (including Michele herself), then use the LICO table:

Calculate the size of Michele's family		
Michele, John, Kara & Matthew 4	Teresa & Enrique + 2	Total # of persons = 6
Use the LICO table to determine the minimum necessary income for 6 persons		
Minimum necessary income: $56,718		

Michele will also have to provide supporting documentation to prove that she has sufficient financial resources, such as a copy of her most recent notice of assessment, the Option C printout from her latest tax return from the Canada Revenue Agency, or a copy of her most recent T1 or T4.

The LICO table is updated each year. The following table was effective from January 1 to December 31, 2015:

Size of family unit	Minimum necessary income
1 person	$23,861
2 persons	$29,706
3 persons	$36,520
4 persons	$44,340
5 persons	$50,290
6 persons	$56,718
7 persons	$63,147
For each additional person more than 7	$6,429

Source: Citizenship and Immigration Canada, "Applying for Visitor Visa (Temporary Resident Visa—IMM 5256): Income Table," online: <http://www.cic.gc.ca/english/information/applications/guides/5256ETOC.asp#incometables>.

Permit Holder Class

In exceptional circumstances, a foreign national may be issued a temporary resident permit (TRP), formerly known as a "minister's permit." This may be necessary when, for example, the foreign national is generally barred from entering Canada as a temporary resident (either because of inadmissibility or because of a failure to meet the requirements of the IRPA), or when a foreign national who is already in Canada does not meet the requirements under other programs. With a TRP, it is sometimes still possible to enter or remain in Canada despite not meeting requirements. TRPs provide flexibility to address exceptional circumstances. They are issued for a limited period of time and may be cancelled at any time.

It is important that a foreign national explore all other options for temporary entry before applying for a TRP. In a case of inadmissibility because of criminality, for example, the applicant should not apply for a TRP without first determining whether he has been deemed rehabilitated or pardoned and has therefore become admissible.

The granting of a TRP may be appropriate in connection with the following:

1. *Medical treatment.* If a foreign national wishes to come to Canada for pre-arranged medical treatment but is inadmissible on health grounds, an officer may consider such factors as whether the treatment is available in the applicant's home country, the cost of the treatment, and how the medical costs will be covered. A TRP may be issued in such a case, unless the foreigner is suffering from a communicable or contagious disease and precautions cannot be taken to guarantee that her illness will not be transmitted to anyone while she is en route to or in Canada.

2. *Minor crimes.* If a foreign national wishes to come to Canada as a visitor but is inadmissible on the grounds of criminality, a TRP may nonetheless be issued if the following are true: the offence was minor (that is, did not involve drugs, physical violence, or damage to property); there are no more than two convictions; there is no pattern of criminal behaviour; the individual has completed all sentences; and there is a high probability that the individual will successfully settle in Canada without committing further offences. However, even if the offence was minor and all the other conditions are met, the foreign national will need to demonstrate a compelling need for admission to Canada—for example, to visit a dying parent.

3. *Victims of human trafficking.* Since May 2006, immigration officers have been authorized to issue TRPs to foreign nationals who may be victims of this crime, to provide them with a period of time to remain in Canada and consider their options. In 2013, immigration officers issued 14 TRPs to victims of human trafficking.[8]

Examples of foreign nationals who may not warrant favourable consideration for a TRP include

- an inadmissible sponsored parent needing medical treatment who has other children or family members in the home country who can provide care, and
- a criminally inadmissible spouse with a risk of violence or repeat offences.

Foreign nationals who are not eligible for restoration of status as a temporary resident (visitor), worker, or student and who wish to remain in Canada may apply for a TRP.

---

8 *Supra* note 1 at 18.

Application Criteria

Under section 24(1) of the IRPA, a foreign national who is inadmissible or who does not meet the requirements of the IRPA may be eligible for a TRP if an officer is of the opinion that admission is justified in the circumstances. Whether to grant the TRP is at the discretion of the officer, who measures the risk posed by the foreign national to Canadians and Canadian society against the foreign national's need for admission (or, in some situations, the need to remain in Canada, if previously admitted). The foreign national's circumstances must be compelling and sufficient to overcome inadmissibility.

The TRP may be cancelled at any time. However, it is important to note that it remains valid until any one of the following events occurs (IRPR, s 63):

- the permit is cancelled under section 24(1) of the IRPA;
- the permit holder leaves Canada without obtaining prior authorization to re-enter Canada;
- the period of validity specified on the permit expires; or
- a period of three years elapses from the permit's date of validity.

A TRP carries privileges greater than those accorded to visitors, students, and workers. For example, foreign workers holding a TRP are allowed to submit applications inland (that is, from within Canada) for a work or study permit, and they may have access to health care or other social services.

Additionally, TRP holders may be eligible for permanent residence provided that they remain continuously in Canada on a permit for at least three years and do not become inadmissible on other grounds. Because a break in continuity may affect their eligibility for permanent residence, permit holders must be cautious in this regard. A break in continuity occurs when a permit holder leaves Canada without authorization for re-entry or neglects her responsibility to seek an extension of her status prior to the expiry of the permit. It is therefore recommended that permit holders not leave Canada unless their TRP specifically authorizes re-entry, and that they apply for an extension of their status at least 30 days before the permit expires.

Place of Application

TRPs are issued at both Canadian ports of entry and CIC inland offices, whereas temporary resident extensions are only issued inland.

A foreign national outside Canada wishing to apply for a TRP is best off doing so at the visa office. The visa office will assess the application and refuse or approve it. If approved, the TRP will be issued at the port of entry when the approved person arrives in Canada. The visa office does not issue the TRP itself.

A foreign national coming from outside Canada may apply for a TRP at the port of entry upon arrival rather than at the visa office, and the officer at the port of entry may agree to consider this type of application, but port-of-entry applications are generally not advisable; an officer always reserves the right to refuse entry and may require the person to leave immediately. Although processing times at a visa office can take several months, this route is safest.

If the officer approves the TRP, the duration of the permit will be determined on the basis of the facts and circumstances presented by the applicant. For example, a person seeking to enter Canada for a short business trip will be issued a TRP that is valid for the duration of that trip and no longer.

Consider the following scenario, in which the applicant was admitted lawfully and then her status as a temporary resident expired:

> Cecilia is seeking an extension of her work permit. She continues to work, even though her work permit expired a week ago. Unfortunately, Cecilia forgot to send the application for renewing her work permit to a case processing centre before it expired. An inadmissibility finding is made against Cecilia on the basis of her violating Canadian immigration laws by working without a valid work permit.
>
> What does Cecilia have to do to obtain a new work permit?

When there has been an inadmissibility finding against a foreign national, she requires a TRP to enter or stay in Canada, no matter what type of inadmissibility has been found (IRPA, s 24(1)). Note that Cecilia should not apply for an extension because her work permit has already expired. Furthermore, Cecilia is not eligible to apply for restoration of status because she has been found inadmissible. Thus, the fact that 90 days have not passed since the expiration of her work permit is irrelevant (IRPR, s 182).

Designated Foreign Nationals

To curtail abuse of and limit access to Canada's immigration and refugee systems, Bill C-31 (*Protecting Canada's Immigration System Act*) amended the IRPA with provisions that differentiate between those who follow the appropriate application procedures and those who do not. The latter category includes **designated foreign nationals**.

The IRPA restricts the application for a TRP by a designated foreign national until five years after he becomes designated (IRPA, s 24(5)) or five years after the final determination regarding his refugee claim or application for protection. Moreover, an application can be refused by an officer if the designated foreign national failed to comply with conditions.

designated foreign national
a person (generally, a refugee claimant) who was part of a group of persons smuggled into Canada whom the minister has designated as an irregular arrival (see IRPA, s 20.1)

APPENDIX

The following table provides a reference list of important definitions and topics that relate to temporary entry to Canada.

Provision	IRPA and IRPR
Examination	IRPA, ss 16, 18, 20
Definition, application	IRPA, s 22
Obligations—general	IRPA, ss 20, 29
Temporary resident authorization (visa)	IRPA, s 22; IRPR, ss 179 to 187
Temporary resident permit	IRPA, s 24
Loss of status	IRPA, s 47
General entry requirements	IRPR, s 7
Place of application	IRPR, s 11(2)
Medical examinations	IRPR, s 30
Deposit or guarantee	IRPR, s 45
Passport and visa exemptions	IRPR, ss 52, 190
TRV exemptions	IRPR, s 190

KEY TERMS

designated foreign national, 119

dual intent, 106

letter of acceptance, 102

letter of invitation, 114

multiple-entry visa (MEV), 113

restoration of status, 111

single-entry visa, 113

Super Visa, 113

temporary resident (TR), 97

temporary resident permit (TRP), 97

temporary resident visa (TRV), 98

transit visa, 113

visitor record, 98

visitor visa, 113

REVIEW QUESTIONS

1. What kind of documents can an applicant who wants to visit Canada provide to prove that she intends to leave at the end of the authorized stay?

2. What is a TRV?

3. Name the different types of Canadian authorizations and briefly describe their use.

4. What are the application procedures that a foreign national must take to satisfy the visa officer that he is eligible for a TRV and admissible?

5. Under what conditions can temporary residents lose their status and privilege?

6. What must temporary residents do to change the terms and conditions of their authorization or extend their stay?

7. What are the application requirements for a foreign national who is applying for a Super Visa?

CASE STUDY

Sara, a citizen of Iran, is married with three children. Her husband, an engineer, supports the family on an annual salary that is equivalent to Cdn $98,000. Sara would like to come to Canada with her children to visit her brother Payem and his family, who live in Vancouver, for six weeks. Neither Sara nor her family members have criminal records, and they are all in good health.

1. Is Sara required to apply for a temporary resident visa to enter Canada? You may check the CIC website for the answer, but you should also provide the appropriate section(s) of the IRPR to address the requirements.

2. Where is Sara required to submit her application for a temporary resident visa?

3. What requirements must Sara fulfill to qualify for a temporary resident visa?

4. What conditions will be imposed on Sara's temporary resident visa?

5. Is Sara permitted to enroll in a seven-day course during her visit to Canada? Explain. (See IRPR, s 188(1)(c).)

Temporary Residence: Students and Workers

LEARNING OUTCOMES

After reading this chapter, you should be able to:

- Summarize the general application processes for the student and worker classes of temporary residence.

- Explain when a foreign national does not need a study permit.

- Explain when an international student needs to obtain a work permit.

- Describe the purpose of the Temporary Foreign Worker Program.

- Explain the rights and obligations of Canadian employers in relation to temporary workers.

- Explain when a temporary worker needs a work permit.

- Describe the Caregiver Program, including the responsibilities of Canadian employers under the program.

- Have a general understanding of the international agreements that apply to the temporary entry of business workers.

Student Class

Consider the value of international students who bring with them new ideas and a global perspective. One reason that studying in Canada may be an attractive option for a foreign student is the possibility of future permanent residence. For example, under the federal skilled worker class of permanent residence (discussed in Chapter 8), an applicant receives credit for Canadian post-secondary education under the point system. In 2008, Canada created the Canadian Experience Class (CEC) as a way to retain Canadian-educated foreign students and absorb them into the Canadian workforce; the program has since evolved and now allows some foreign students to gain work experience that may lead to permanent residence.

Under the *Immigration and Refugee Protection Regulations* (IRPR), international students are a prescribed class of persons who may obtain temporary resident status and who have been issued study permits as members of the student class (IRPR, s 210).

In June 2014, the government introduced new rules, removed the definitions for "study" and "student" from the regulations, and renamed the program the International Student Program. Under this program, a study permit is a written authorization issued to a foreign national that authorizes her to engage in academic, professional, vocational, or other education or training that is more than six months in duration at a **designated learning institution (DLI)** in Canada. A foreign national with a study permit needs to demonstrate that she is "actively pursuing studies," which means that she must remain enrolled and show that she progressing toward the completion of her degree or diploma; otherwise, she risks being removed from Canada. The DLI is required to report international students' continued enrollment and academic status to CIC.

The criteria for a DLI are set out in section 211.1 of the IRPR; generally, it is a post-secondary institution that is confirmed by the institution's provincial or territorial ministry of education to meet minimum CIC standards. Each designated learning institution is issued a DLI number. When applying to study in Canada, a foreign national must verify that the post-secondary institution has been designated as a DLI. CIC maintains an up-to-date list of DLIs and DLI numbers on its website.

All primary and secondary schools in Canada are automatically designated and therefore do not appear on the DLI list. Applicants for primary and secondary schools do not need a DLI number on their application form.

> **designated learning institution (DLI)**
>
> generally, a post-secondary institution that is confirmed by the institution's provincial or territorial ministry of education to meet minimum CIC standards, all primary and secondary schools in Canada are automatically designated

Process for Obtaining a Study Permit

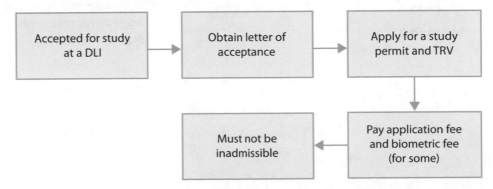

In approving a study permit, a visa officer will verify that the applicant's college or university has a valid DLI number.

The criteria for a study permit and the application process for foreign students are discussed below.

Criteria for a Study Permit

The regulations define "study permit" as "a written authorization to engage in academic, professional, vocational or other education or training in Canada that is issued by an officer to a foreign national" (IRPR, s 2). The regulations also set out who needs or does not need a study permit, and the application processes. Because these rules are set out in the regulations, they can be more easily amended to respond to Canada's changing needs.

Generally, a foreign national who wishes to study in Canada must obtain a study permit *before* entering Canada (IRPR, s 213), although there are exceptions to this rule. Some foreign nationals may apply *upon entry* (IRPR, s 214) and others may apply *after entry*, as in the case of an accompanying family member (IRPR, s 215). Some foreign nationals are exempt from the requirement to obtain a study permit; for example, a study permit is not required for a program of study that is six months or less.

Consider the following scenario:

> Liam and Fiona are Irish nationals and married to each other. Liam applied for and obtained a temporary work permit before coming to Canada. After arrival, Fiona decided to enroll in a two-year college diploma program.
>
> As the spouse of a temporary foreign worker, does Fiona need to apply for a study permit?

As an accompanying family member, Fiona is exempt from the requirement of applying for a study permit *before* she comes to Canada (IRPR, s 215(2)); however, as a temporary resident, she is required to apply for a study permit because the program of study exceeds six months.

According to section 216(1) of the IRPR, an international student may be issued a study permit if an examination establishes that he meets the basic criteria applicable to all temporary resident applicants as well as the criteria specific to students.

Visa officers look at many factors before deciding whether an applicant qualifies for a study permit. In addition to presenting the application form and basic documents that must be provided in support of all TRV applications—such as passport and travel documents (unless exempt), proof of immigration status, passport-size photos, and processing and biometric (if applicable) fees—applicants must also

- present a letter of acceptance from the educational institution where they intend to study;
- be able to pay the tuition fees for the course or program that they intend to pursue;

WEBLINK

Designated Learning Institution List
Check to see if your institution is on the list! What is your college or university's DLI number? The list can be found at <www.cic.gc.ca/english/study/study-institutions-list.asp>.

- be able to financially support themselves and any family members who will be with them during their period of study;
- be able to cover the transportation costs for themselves and any family members to and from Canada;
- pass the CIC medical examination, if required;[1] and
- receive a *certificat d'acceptation du Québec* (Quebec Certificate of Acceptance, or CAQ), if they intend to study in Quebec.

Not everybody is required to obtain a letter of acceptance from an educational institution. For example, under section 219(2)(a) of the IRPR, accompanying family members of a foreign national student or worker are exempt from obtaining a letter of acceptance if the applicant received written approval before entering Canada.

All applicants for study permits who intend to attend a Quebec educational institution at the primary, secondary, college, or university level must obtain a CAQ issued by the Ministère de l'Immigration, de la Diversité et de l'Inclusion (MIDI) before being eligible for a study permit, even for part-time courses or for courses delivered by private institutions.

A study permit will not be issued for preschool, kindergarten, courses of general interest or self-improvement, distance learning courses, or audited courses attended without credit.

letter of acceptance
a document that indicates that a foreign student has been accepted into a Canadian educational institution

Letter of Acceptance

The **letter of acceptance** is a key document that must be included in the application for a study permit. The following items, although not mandatory, should be included in the letter to increase the application's chances of approval:

- the full name, date of birth, and mailing address of the student;
- the course of study for which the student was accepted;
- the name of the institution and official contact;
- the institution's DLI number;
- the telephone, fax, website, and email information for the institution;
- the type of school or institution (for example, private or public, or if the institution is publicly funded but not a university, whether the institution is a post-secondary college, post-secondary community college, or post-secondary technical college);
- the field or program of study, level, and year of study into which the student was accepted;
- the estimated duration or date of completion of the course;
- the date on which the course of study begins;

---

1 Foreign students must meet the same medical requirements that apply to all temporary residents to Canada.

- the last date on which a student may register for a selected course;
- the academic year of study that the student will be entering;
- whether the course of study is full-time or part-time;
- the tuition fee;
- scholarships and other financial aid (if applicable);
- an expiry date indicating the date until which the letter of acceptance is valid;
- any conditions related to the acceptance or registration, such as academic prerequisites, completion of a previous degree, and proof of language competence;
- for study in Quebec, the CAQ; and
- when applicable, licensing information for private institutions, usually confirmed through letterhead.[2]

Study Permit Exemptions

Not everyone is required to obtain a study permit in order to study in Canada. Foreign nationals are exempt from the requirement of a study permit if they fall into one of the following categories:

- family members and members of the private staff of diplomats or foreign accredited representatives (IRPR, s 188(1)(a));
- members of the armed forces of a country designated for the purposes of the *Visiting Forces Act*, even if they intend to study for more than six months (IRPR, s 188(1)(b));
- persons seeking to enroll in a short-term program of study of six months or less that will be completed within the period of their temporary resident visa (IRPR, s 188(1)(c)); or
- persons who are registered Indians.

Consider the following scenario:

Carlos, a Mexican priest, has been granted temporary resident status for a period of one year for the purpose of assisting a congregation. During this time, Carlos would like to enroll in a four-month language training course and, once he completes that course, in a four-month religious studies course.

Does Carlos require a study permit?

---

2   Citizenship and Immigration Canada, "Study Permits: Letters of Acceptance" (16 September 2014), online: <http://www.cic.gc.ca/english/resources/tools/temp/students/letter.asp>.

Carlos may complete the two courses without a study permit because each course of study is less than six months long and can be completed within one year, the original period of stay authorized upon entry.

However, if Carlos wants to enroll in another short-term course of four months, he would exceed the period of temporary resident status authorized upon entry. In that case, Carlos must apply for an extension of his temporary resident status. However, his reason for requesting an extension must be to continue assisting the congregation, not to complete the course. Carlos would likely be granted an extension of his temporary resident status and could then enroll in the short-term course without a study permit.

Minors

In some cases, minor children do not need a study permit to study in Canada. These cases include the following:

- minor children attending kindergarten;
- minor children who are refugees or refugee claimants, or whose parents are refugees or refugee claimants; and
- minor children who are already in Canada with parents who are allowed to work or study in Canada, and who want to attend preschool, primary, or secondary school (*Immigration and Refugee Protection Act* [IRPA], s 30(2)).

When minor children studying in Canada without a permit reach the age of majority (18 or 19, depending on the province or territory), they must apply for a permit if they want to continue studying.

In some cases, parents may choose to send their child to Canada on his own for the purpose of studying. When minors are travelling alone, they must apply for a study permit, and the length of time for which a study permit is valid is as follows:

- Minor children in grades 1 through 8: the study permit is normally valid for one year.
- Minor children in grades 9 through 12, or attending a post-secondary institution: the study permit is normally valid for the length of time of the studies, plus 90 days.
- Minor children studying in Quebec: the study permit is valid for the same length of time as the CAQ.

If a minor child is with parents who have long-term study or work permits, the child's study permit should be valid for the same length of time as:

- the parents' permits;
- the child's passport, if it expires before the parents' permits; or
- the CAQ, if studying in Quebec.

Application for a Study Permit

The Instruction Guide (IMM 5269) and application forms are available on the CIC website.

The application package generally includes the following key forms:

- Application for a Study Permit Made Outside of Canada (IMM 1294);
- Schedule 1: Application for Temporary Resident Visa (IMM 5257);
- Use of a Representative (IMM 5476), if applicable; and
- Document Checklist for a Study Permit (IMM 5483).

Other forms must be completed as applicable: Statutory Declaration of Common-Law Union (IMM 5409), Family Information (IMM 5645), and the Custodianship Declaration—Custodian for Minors Studying in Canada (IMM 5646).

Generally, processing times can range from a few weeks to several months, depending on the visa office.

Post-secondary international students may transfer between institutions, programs of study, fields of study, and levels of study (for example, from a bachelor level to a master's level) without applying for a change to the conditions of their study permit.

Consider the following scenario:

> Claudia, from Bahamas, wishes to attend the University of Toronto to obtain a BSc in mathematics. Claudia wants to ensure that she has the required documents and information to accompany her application for a study permit.
>
> What must Claudia submit in support of her application?

The documents that must accompany Claudia's application are proof of acceptance into the BSc program at the University of Toronto, which is a DLI; her passport, because Bahamas is not on the list of visa-exempt countries; the results of her medical examination; proof of funds to pay for the program of study and to support herself while in Canada; and proof of return transportation to Bahamas.

> Claudia changes her mind after completing the first semester of her studies at the University of Toronto. She now wants to conclude her degree in mathematics at the University of British Columbia (UBC) but doesn't know whether she needs to apply for a change to the conditions of her study permit.
>
> Does Claudia need to submit an Application to Change Conditions, Extend My Stay or Remain in Canada as a Student (IMM 5709)?

Claudia may continue studying without applying for a change to her study permit conditions because she will study at another post-secondary DLI. However, she must notify CIC that she is transferring from one DLI to another, and demonstrate that she is actively pursuing her degree. She may be required by CIC to provide evidence of her continued enrollment and academic status at UBC.

Place of Application

Although most international students apply for their study permit before arrival, some foreign nationals may apply for a student visa at a Canadian port of entry (POE). Such persons include US nationals or persons who have been lawfully admitted to the United States for permanent residence, and residents of Greenland and St. Pierre and Miquelon (IRPR, s 214). Nevertheless, these foreign nationals must comply with the requirements applicable to the student class, pursuant to section 216(1) of the IRPR. CIC has modernized its services to include online applications; some applicants can now submit their applications for study permits online (see the CIC website for further details).

Processing Fees

The government processing fee for a study permit is $150. There is also a biometric processing fee of $85 for some applicants.

Section 300 of the IRPR establishes the application fee for a study permit, as well as the exceptions that exempt some applicants from paying the fee. The following persons are not required to pay the fee:

- foreign nationals who have been determined to be Convention refugees or members of a designated class prior to their arrival in Canada, and their family members;

- foreign nationals in Canada whose claims to be Convention refugees have been deemed admissible but have not yet been decided by the Refugee Protection Division (RPD), and their family members;

- diplomats accredited to Canada or another country, consular officers, representatives or officials of a foreign country, and their family members (for example, a dependent son of an accredited diplomat posted in Morocco who intends to study in Canada);

- students seeking renewal of their study permits who have become temporarily destitute through circumstances beyond their control and the control of any person on whom they are dependent for financial resources;

- foreign nationals who are in Canada or who are coming into Canada under an agreement between Canada and a foreign country or an arrangement entered into with a foreign country by the government of Canada that provides for reciprocal educational opportunities (for example, participants in the Canada–US Fulbright Program);

- an officer of the US Immigration and Naturalization Service or of US Customs who works in Canada carrying out pre-inspection duties, as an American member of the International Joint Commission, or as a US grain inspector, and their family members; and

- US government officials in possession of an official US government passport who are assigned to a temporary posting in Canada, and their family members.

Decision on Application

A foreign national whose application has been approved will receive a **letter of introduction**, which must be shown to the port-of-entry officer upon arrival in Canada.

If the application is refused, the applicant will receive a refusal letter setting out the reasons for the refusal (for example, there is insufficient proof that the applicant has enough funds to support himself and any family members; the officer is not satisfied of a genuine intent on the part of the applicant to study or that the applicant will leave; or the applicant is inadmissible).

letter of introduction
a document provided by a visa office to confirm approval of a study permit or work permit, or extended stay for a parent or grandparent from a country that does not require visas (the Super Visa program), for presentation to an officer upon arrival in Canada

Duration of Study Permit

Study permits issued after June 1, 2014 become invalid 90 days after the international student has completed her study program, which occurs when the student receives her degree, diploma, or certificate or when an official transcript or letter is received from the institution.

Study Permit Extensions

An international student may apply for the renewal of her study permit if the following conditions are met:

- the renewal application was made before the expiry of the current study permit (processing time guidelines suggest that the application for renewal should be made at least 30 days before the expiry of the current study permit);
- all conditions imposed on entry into Canada have been complied with;
- the student is in good standing at the educational institution, in accordance with section 217(1) of the IRPR; and
- the student is in compliance with the eligibility criteria for a study permit pursuant to section 216 of the IRPR.

Because it may take some time to process a renewal, an international student is allowed to continue studying in Canada with an expired study permit if the following conditions are met:

- the renewal application was made before the expiry of the current study permit;
- the student has remained in Canada since the expiry of the study permit; and
- the student continues to comply with the conditions, other than the expiry date, set out on the expired study permit, in accordance with section 189 of the IRPR.

Consider the following scenario:

Lara is an international student attending Algonquin College in Ottawa. She applied for the renewal of her TRV and study permit two weeks before they expired.

Unfortunately, Lara has not yet received a decision regarding her application for renewal and her student visa has expired.

Will Lara be in trouble with immigration if she continues to study with an expired TRV and study permit? What would you advise her to do?

Lara has *implied status* and, therefore, has the right to continue studying under the same conditions as long as she remains in Canada. Consequently, her original study permit continues to be valid until a decision is made and Lara is notified (IRPR, s 183(5)).

Study Permit Restrictions

A study permit may be subject to certain restrictions. An officer may impose, vary, or cancel conditions on the study permit. Conditions are set out in section 185 of the IRPR and may include one or more of the following:

- type of studies or course that the foreign national may take;
- educational institution that the foreign national may attend;
- location of studies;
- time and period of studies;
- the area within which the foreign national is permitted to travel or is prohibited from travelling in Canada;
- time and place at which the foreign national shall report for medical examination or observation;
- time and place at which the foreign national shall report for the presentation of evidence in compliance with applicable conditions; or
- duration of stay in Canada.

Work for Foreign Students

Although CIC requires international students to arrive in Canada with sufficient funding to cover the duration of their study period, in reality many students will need to earn extra income. This need is recognized in the IRPA and IRPR, which provide that foreign students may work while pursuing post-secondary education in Canada in certain circumstances. In some cases, a work permit is not required, as in the case of a student who works on campus. In others, a permit is required, as in the case of a student who works off campus or who is enrolled in postgraduate studies or a co-op program. Each of these situations is discussed below. An international student will need to obtain a social insurance number (SIN) to work in Canada.

On-Campus Work: No Permit

An international student in Canada on a valid study permit is authorized to work on campus *without a work permit*, provided that the student is enrolled full-time at a post-secondary DLI and maintains full-time status at the institution (IRPR, s 186(f)).

"On campus" is defined as the employment facilities within the boundaries of the campus. A student may work only on the campus of the educational institution at which she is registered. In the event that the school has more than one campus, the student may work at a different campus, provided that it is within the same municipality; the student may not work at campuses outside the municipality. The employer can be the institution, a faculty member, a student organization or a self-employed student, a private business, or a private contractor providing services to the institution on the campus.

Students working as graduate assistants, teaching assistants, or research assistants are considered to be within the scope of "on-campus" employment.

Consider the following case scenario:

> Sara has obtained a temporary resident visa and will visit Canada in September. Upon arriving, Sara wants to enroll in a five-month, full-time, postgraduate linguistics certificate program offered by Humber College. Sara also intends to work on campus to further assimilate into Canadian culture.
>
> Does Sara need a study permit? Does she need a work permit?

Recall that section 188(1)(c) of the IRPR states that a foreign national may study in Canada without a study permit if the duration of the program is six months or less. However, this exemption does not apply to a foreign national who plans to work on campus. In the present case, Sara should be advised that although she does not need a study permit to study in the five-month course at Humber College, she does need a study permit to work on campus.

Off-Campus Work: No Permit

An international student in Canada must have a valid study permit to be authorized to work off campus *without a work permit*, provided that the student is enrolled full-time in a post-secondary academic, vocational, or professional training program, or a vocational training program at the secondary level offered in Quebec, that is at least six months long and leads to a degree, diploma, or certificate at a DLI. The student must maintain full-time status at the institution (IRPR, s 186(v)). A student on an exchange program or who is taking an English or French as a second language (ESL/FSL) course would not meet the requirements to work off campus without a work permit.

Section 186(v) of the IRPR also stipulates that international students may work off campus for a maximum of 20 hours per week during their regular academic sessions, but may work full-time during scheduled breaks (for example, winter/summer holidays, reading week) as well as during the transition period to a post-graduation work permit (if applicable). Students may work on campus in addition to working the maximum 20 hours per week off campus.[3]

---

3   Citizenship and Immigration Canada, "Temporary Residents: Students" (17 October 2014), online: <http://www.cic.gc.ca/english/resources/tools/temp/students/index.asp>.

Work Requiring a Permit

According to section 208 of the IRPR, students may apply for a work permit if, by reason of circumstances beyond their control, they become temporarily destitute. Such circumstances may include war, upheaval, or collapse of the banking system in the home country.

open work permit
a document that enables a foreign national to work for any employer for a specific time period

These students may be granted an **open work permit**, which allows a student to work for any employer for a specific period of time. Usually, the time period coincides with the duration of the current term of study, rather than with the duration of the entire program or with the duration of the study permit. The student must reapply for a new permit to cover subsequent terms, if necessary.

Consider the following scenarios:

> Tara is an international student in a four-year science and technology degree program at Capilano University in British Columbia. Tara is interested in working off campus during the summer break to gain some Canadian experience but is unsure whether she is allowed to work. Tara began full-time studies in September and continued through the end of April (with the exception of the December break and reading week in February). During this time, she attended her classes regularly and has maintained good grades.
>
> Is Tara allowed to work without a work permit during the summer between semesters? What would you tell her?

Tara is allowed to work without a work permit because she has been enrolled in full-time studies in a program that will lead to a degree at a DLI, from September to April; she can show that her intent is to pursue her studies on a full-time basis as she continues to be enrolled; and she has maintained satisfactory academic standing. Tara can work on a full-time basis without a work permit during her summer break, and no more than 20 hours per week during the academic year when her classes resume in September.

> Tara's friend Geoff, a fellow international student at the university, is also interested in working while he is studying. He would like to know if he can work at the university bookstore on campus, which is managed by a private company. Geoff is also enrolled in full-time studies, but his first semester was from January until the end of April. He took four months off for summer break and resumed full-time studies in September.
>
> Is Geoff allowed to work without a work permit on campus during the school term? What would you tell him?

Geoff will not need to apply for a work permit: he is allowed to work on campus, even if his employer is a private company, as he is enrolled in full-time studies.

Post-Graduation Work Permit Program

Foreign nationals currently in possession of a valid study permit and who are about to graduate from a post-secondary institution may apply for a postgraduate open work permit under the Post-Graduation Work Permit Program (PGWPP). An open work permit enables the foreign national to seek and accept employment, and to work for any employer for a specified period of time. An open work permit also exempts the foreign national's employer from the requirement of obtaining a positive **labour market impact assessment (LMIA)** from Employment and Social Development Canada (ESDC), which is generally required to obtain a work permit.

A student is not eligible for this program if

- the student's program of study is less than eight months long;
- the student has previously been issued a post-graduation work permit;
- the student has received funding from the Department of Foreign Affairs, Trade and Development (DFATD);
- the student participated in the Government of Canada Awards Program funded by DFATD, an apprenticeship program, the Canada–Chile Scholars Exchanges Program, or the Organization of American States Fellowships Program;
- the student obtained an Equal Opportunity Scholarship, Canada–Chile; or
- the student completed a distance learning program or a program of study granted by a non-Canadian institution located in Canada, regardless of the student's length of stay in Canada.[4]

A foreign national seeking to obtain an open work permit under the PGWPP must meet the following criteria:

- the student must have continuously studied full-time in Canada at a post-secondary institution and graduated from a program of at least eight months' duration;
- the student must still be in possession of a valid study permit upon submission of a work permit application;
- the student must have received a written notification from the educational institution indicating that he is eligible to obtain a degree, diploma, or certificate; and
- the student must apply for the permit within 90 days of receiving written confirmation from the institution indicating that the academic program was successfully completed (for example, a transcript or notice of graduation).

labour market impact assessment (LMIA)
an ESDC document obtained by a Canadian employer in order to employ a foreign worker

---

4   Citizenship and Immigration Canada, "Study Permits: Post Graduation Work Permit Program" (12 December 2014), online: <http://www.cic.gc.ca/english/resources/tools/temp/students/post-grad.asp>.

Once granted, the post-graduation work permit may be valid for a period of time not exceeding the period during which the graduating student studied at a Canadian post-secondary institution, and may not exceed three years.

Once the post-graduation work permit expires, the student must apply for an LMIA to maintain work permit status. The LMIA is discussed further under the heading "Temporary Worker Class."

Co-op Work Permit Program/International Mobility Program

Students whose work experience is an essential and integral component of their program of study may be eligible for a work permit under a co-op or internship program. International students must provide a letter from the DLI that clearly states that the work is a normal component of the academic program that students are expected to complete in order to receive their degree, diploma, or certificate.[5]

To be eligible, the student must meet the following conditions:

- the work must be related to a research program (IRPR, ss 205(c)(i), (i.1));
- the student must be in possession of a valid study permit;
- the student's intended employment must be an essential part of a post-secondary academic, vocational, or professional training program offered by a DLI in Canada;
- the employment must be certified as part of the academic, vocational, or professional training program offered by a DLI by a responsible academic official of the institution;
- the student's co-op or internship employment may not form more than 50 percent of the total program of study; and
- the student must not be a medical intern or extern, or a resident physician (except in veterinary medicine).[6]

The work permit is issued with the academic institution listed as the employer.

Note that international students, scholars, and scientists may also be eligible to obtain work permits for work related to a research, educational, or training program. These work permits are issued under specific programs funded by the Canadian International Development Agency (CIDA), the International Development Research Centre (IDRC), Atomic Energy of Canada Ltd., the National Research Council of Canada (NRC), and the Natural Sciences and Engineering Research Council of Canada (NSERC).[7]

---

5 Citizenship and Immigration Canada, "International Mobility Program: Work Related to a Research, Educational or Training Program [R205(c)(i), (i.1) and (i.2)—Codes C31, C32 and C33]" (18 September 2014), online: <http://www.cic.gc.ca/english/resources/tools/temp/work/opinion/education.asp>.

6 Citizenship and Immigration Canada, "Guide 5580—Applying for a Work Permit—Student Guide" (22 May 2015), online: <http://www.cic.gc.ca/english/information/applications/guides/5580ETOC.asp>.

7 *Ibid.*

Temporary Worker Class

The rules for the worker class are many and complex; we find them in the IRPR, and they include the definition of "worker" in section 194, the authority for issuing work permits in section 200, and the eligibility criteria for applying for authorization in sections 203 to 209. Foreign nationals who wish to work temporarily in Canada are part of the worker class of temporary residents and are generally required to have a genuine job offer to obtain a work permit, unless they are exempt under section 186 of the IRPR. Generally, part of the process for obtaining a work permit is to first obtain a genuine job offer from a Canadian employer.

Temporary Foreign Worker Program

The Temporary Foreign Worker Program (TFWP) has attracted much attention and controversy over the past couple of years. On the one hand, supporters of the program argue that it helps to fill labour shortages in those jobs that Canadians do not want. Others, however, argue that foreign workers are taking jobs away from Canadians at a time of high unemployment and allowing companies to pay lower wages, because they are willing to work for less.

Today's foreign worker program has its roots in the Non-Immigrant Employment Authorization Program (NIEAP), which was introduced in 1973 to bring highly specialized workers such as academics, business executives, and engineers to Canada in order to meet labour shortage needs. In 2002, demand for temporary workers with

Temporary Worker Class Definitions

Generally, **temporary foreign workers (TFWs)** are engaged in paid work activity and are authorized to enter and to remain in Canada for a limited period to fill temporary labour and skill shortages when qualified Canadian citizens or permanent residents are not available (for example, in the Temporary Foreign Worker Program) or for business reasons under international agreements. In most instances, temporary residents who work in Canada require a work permit.

Work is defined in section 2 of the IRPR as "an activity for which wages are paid or commission is earned, or that is in direct competition with the activities of Canadian citizens or permanent residents in the Canadian labour market."

A **work permit** is a written authorization issued by an officer that allows a foreign national to engage in employment in Canada. It is linked to a specific job, employer, and location.

Depending on the nature of the activity in Canada and the country of origin of the foreign worker, a work permit and/or visa may not be necessary (for example, under an international trade agreement.)

An open work permit is not linked to a specific job, employer, or location. A foreign national with an open work permit may work in most jobs and may change employers without having to apply to CIC for approval. Some open permits, however, may have restrictions.

temporary foreign worker (TFW)
a foreign national engaged in paid work activity who is authorized to enter and to remain in Canada for a limited period

work
an activity for which wages are paid or commission is earned, or that is in direct competition with the activities of Canadian citizens or permanent residents in the Canadian labour market (IRPR, s 2)

work permit
a written authorization issued by an officer that allows a foreign national to engage in employment in Canada

---

IN THE NEWS

The Controversy over Temporary Foreign Workers

The Temporary Foreign Worker Program has proved to be controversial, especially in the fast food industry. Some critics have suggested that it allows Canadian businesses to replace Canadian workers with cheaper temporary workers, while others have alleged that it exploits temporary workers by offering low wages and few prospects of being able to stay in Canada. Businesses have responded by pointing to unskilled labour shortages and asserting that low-wage temporary foreign workers are necessary to ensure that Canadian businesses can remain competitive.

After an outcry in Alberta, Jason Kenney, the federal employment minister, introduced restrictions in June 2014 that would prevent employers from hiring foreign workers in regions where unemployment is high. The restrictions would also cap the number of foreign workers that an employer may hire, and introduce a more stringent application process.

Prior to the implementation of the restrictions, Alberta had the highest per-capita use of temporary foreign workers in the country. McDonald's has come under particular scrutiny: the *Edmonton Journal* reported that temporary foreign workers made up 23 percent of Alberta McDonald's employees, and the CBC reported that one particular McDonald's franchi-see had been blacklisted from using the Temporary Foreign Worker Program during the completion of a compliance audit.

The Alberta provincial government and private sector employers have pushed for the restrictions to be loosened, arguing that they will make it difficult for employers to find staff.

"Regional jobless rates mean very little to a small business owner who can't find enough interested workers to keep the doors open," said Dan Kelly, the president of the Canadian Federation of Independent Business, in a written statement.

Despite the pushback, Minister Kenney has argued that the restrictions are necessary to prevent Canadian employees from being displaced by cheaper temporary foreign workers.

"We need to encourage the unemployed and those who are no longer looking for work and we need to see permanent resident immigration increase in Alberta," said Kenney.

What do you think? How can we balance the need for unskilled labour with the allegations that the program exploits temporary foreign workers and displaces Canadian workers?

Sources: Sheila Pratt, "Debate Rages in Alberta over Who Should Get Jobs," *Edmonton Journal* (27 December 2014), online <http://www.edmontonjournal.com/stories+2014+rules+foreign+workers/10684660/story.html>; Susana Mas, "Temporary Foreign Worker Overhaul Imposes Limits, Hikes Inspections," *CBC News* (20 June 2014), online: <http://www.cbc.ca/news/politics/temporary-foreign-worker-overhaul-imposes-limits-hikes-inspections-1.2682209>.

---

lower skills, including in the food and construction industries, led to the creation of the Pilot Project for Hiring Foreign Workers in Occupations That Require Lower Levels of Formal Training. The program continued to expand in scope as the Low-Skill Pilot Project, and, in 2006, the government expanded the program to include 20 occupations and to expedite bringing in temporary workers.[8] Known today as the low-wage positions (or low-skilled occupations) stream of the Temporary Foreign

---

8   Jason Foster, "Making Temporary Permanent: The Silent Transformation of the Temporary Foreign Worker Program" (2012) 19 Just Labour: A Canadian Journal of Work and Society 25, online: <http://www.justlabour.yorku.ca/volume19/pdfs/02_foster_press.pdf>.

Worker Program, it is the fastest-growing area of the TFWP. Under it, low-skilled workers fill occupations that are classified as level C and D occupations under Canada's National Occupational Classification (NOC) system (see Appendix A).

As the Library of Parliament has noted, "Whereas Canada's immigration strategy was originally one of long-term nation building, Canada has been increasingly reliant on temporary foreign workers to address immediate labour shortages."[9] In 2014, as part of the TFWP overhaul, the government changed the language from "lower-skilled" occupations to "low-wage" occupations and allowed employers to offer a wage that is below the provincial/territorial median wage. After an outcry by labour groups and others, further changes were implemented and employers are now required to pay the prevailing wage rate identified as the median hourly wage (or annual salary as published on Job Bank) or higher for the particular occupation and work location, and must ensure that the wage offered is not below any federal or provincial/territorial minimum wage rates or wage schedules.

Current policy also limits the amount of time a low-skilled temporary foreign worker is allowed to work in Canada, which is meant to reinforce the temporariness of the assignment. Unlike permanent residents, foreign nationals who work temporarily in Canada do not benefit from the same rights and entitlements as other foreign nationals, such as family reunification, rights protection under various levels of legislation, mobility rights, and eventual access to citizenship. Only a few—who are usually filling higher-skilled occupations—have access to programs that lead to permanent residence. Depending on the nature of the activity in Canada and the country of origin, a work permit and/or TRV is usually necessary before the foreign worker is admitted to Canada. Moreover, as a condition of admission, most temporary workers are bound to one specific job, one employer, and one location, as described in the work permit.

In 2014, the government introduced a number of changes to the TFWP to ensure that employers only hire foreign workers as a last and limited resort, when Canadians and permanent residents are not available. The government also amended the IRPA and announced that it would be cracking down on employers and others who abuse the TFWP, through criminal prosecutions in the following ways:

- Anyone employing a foreign national who is not authorized to work in Canada can face fines of up to $50,000 and up to two years in prison, or both (IRPA, ss 124(1)(c), 125).

- Anyone who knowingly counsels, induces, aids, or abets or attempts to counsel, induce, aid, or abet any person to make a misrepresentation in the immigration process can face fines of up to $100,000 and up to five years in prison, or both (IRPA, ss 126, 128).

- Anyone who knowingly makes a misrepresentation in the immigration process can face fines of up to $100,000 and up to five years in prison, or both (IRPA, ss 127, 128).

---

9 Melissa Pang, *Temporary Foreign Workers*, Background Paper, Publication No 2013-11-E (Ottawa: Library of Parliament, 7 February 2013), online: Library of Parliament <http://www.parl.gc.ca/Content/LOP/ResearchPublications/2013-11-e.pdf>.

The government also announced that it would publicly disclose the names of employers who have been fined and the amount of those fines.

Generally, CIC differentiates occupations according to their skill levels (see Appendix A for National Occupational Classification). For the purpose of assessing employer applications for LMIA and LMIA-exempt occupations, however, ESDC has identified four labour market streams under the TFWP:[10]

high-wage positions
high-skilled positions in which the wage offered is at or above the provincial/territorial median wage

low-wage positions
low-skilled positions in which the wage offered is below the provincial/territorial median wage

Caregiver Program
a program for foreign caregivers who are hired to provide care, in a private residence, to children, seniors, or persons with certified medical needs; sometimes referred to as the Live-In Caregiver Program

primary agricultural stream
positions related to on-farm primary agriculture such as general farm workers, nursery and greenhouse workers, feedlot workers, and harvesting labourers, including under the SAWP

- **High-wage positions** (also called high-skilled occupations): positions in which the wage offered is at or above the provincial/territorial median wage (though new rules mean that employers will have to transition to prevailing rates). Examples of high-wage positions include management, professional, scientific, technical, or skilled trade occupations. Generally, these occupations are also considered high-skilled and can be found throughout many sectors of the economy, and as a result often have very diverse recruitment practices and regulatory requirements.

- **Low-wage positions** (also called low-skilled occupations): positions in which the wage offered is below the provincial/territorial median wage (though new rules mean that employers will have to transition to prevailing wage rates). Examples include general labourers, food counter attendants, and sales and service personnel.

- **Caregiver Program**: a program for foreign caregivers who are hired to provide care, in a private residence, to children, seniors, or persons with certified medical needs.[11]

- **Primary agricultural stream**: positions related to on-farm primary agriculture such as general farm workers, nursery and greenhouse workers, feedlot workers, and harvesting labourers, including under the Seasonal Agricultural Worker Program (SAWP) (discussed further below), which facilitates the entry of workers from Mexico and certain Caribbean countries to meet the temporary, seasonal needs of agricultural producers.

For high-wage workers, the TFWP provides an opportunity to come to Canada accompanied by family members and to gain Canadian experience, and it paves the way to permanent residence. On the other end of the spectrum, low-wage workers have limited rights, with program emphasis on short-term work, because they must leave after four years and have no chance of acquiring permanent residence.

The TFWP relies on the cooperation of three key departments, generally for the following activities:

---

10 Employment and Social Development Canada, "Overhauling the Temporary Foreign Worker Program: Restricting Access" (12 November 2014), online: <http://www.esdc.gc.ca/eng/jobs/foreign_workers/reform/restrict.shtml>.

11 Note that this program is listed as the Live-In Caregiver Program in some CIC/ESDC documents and as the Caregiver or In-Home Caregiver Program in other instances. For consistency, we will refer to it as the Caregiver Program in this text.

- ESDC, for conducting employer compliance reviews and making labour market impact assessments;
- CIC, for processing applications; and
- the Canada Border Services Agency (CBSA), for conducting port-of-entry examinations and admitting foreign nationals.

High-Wage Positions: Foreign Academics Program

The stream for high-wage positions favours the hiring of foreign workers in management, professional, scientific, technical, or trade occupations. Employers can hire skilled foreign workers to support either the workers' temporary employment or their permanent resident application (for example, under the Canadian Experience Class). Under this stream, there are special programs for the temporary hiring of workers in the film and entertainment occupations, and in academia under the Foreign Academics Program.

ESDC and CIC, in cooperation with universities, degree-granting colleges, and unions representing Canadian academics, set out the criteria for the Foreign Academics Program. It was created with the purpose of assisting degree-granting, post-secondary educational institutions in Canada to meet their staffing and teaching needs by seeking internationally the best-qualified and most suitable candidates for full-time academic staff positions. An "academic" is defined as an individual with at least one postgraduate degree (that is, a degree that is completed following a bachelor's degree) who earns the majority of his income from teaching or conducting research as an employee at a university or university college in Canada.[12] Under this program, the following foreign workers do not need a work permit or an LMIA:

- academic consultants and examiners,
- graduate assistants, and
- self-funded researchers.

Before hiring a foreign academic for a position in Canada, the institution must obtain a positive LMIA (unless that person is exempt; see below) and

- complete the Foreign Academic Recruitment Summary form, outlining the educational institution's hiring decision and providing summaries of Canadian applicants, which must be verified by the vice-president or other senior academic official of the educational institution; and
- complete a yearly summary report on recruitment practices for Canadian academics and results.[13]

---

12 Employment and Social Development Canada, "Hiring Foreign Academics" (1 May 2015), online: <http://www.esdc.gc.ca/eng/jobs/foreign_workers/higher_skilled/academics//index.shtml>.

13 *Ibid.*

The Foreign Academics Program does not extend to community colleges unless they are affiliated with a university and their students are able to obtain degrees, nor does it apply to the collèges d'enseignement général et professionnel (CEGEP) in Quebec.

The IRPA lists a variety of foreign academics who, while required to obtain a work permit, are exempt from obtaining an LMIA:

- post-doctoral fellows;
- research award recipients;
- eminent individuals, such as leaders in various fields;
- guest lecturers;
- visiting professors;
- citizens of the United States and Mexico appointed as professors under the university, college, and seminary levels of the North American Free Trade Agreement (NAFTA); and
- citizens of Chile appointed as professors under the Canada–Chile Free Trade Agreement (CCFTA).[14]

Low-Wage Positions

The general goal of the low-wage TFWP stream is to correct labour market imbalances when there is a shortage of Canadians and permanent residents. The stream for lower-skilled occupations is for temporary foreign workers in jobs that are listed in levels C and D of the NOC, which includes labourers, cleaners, cashiers, and drivers. Generally, these jobs require at most a high school diploma or a maximum of two years of job-specific training, and low wages are paid. It is with respect to these types of occupations that the government has received much criticism over its inability to identify whether the need to fill labour shortages is a short-term phenomenon or the result of longer-term changes in the economy.

Foreign workers must have at least a high school diploma or two years of job-specific training to qualify in this stream, while employers must agree to do the following in order to qualify:

- pay the full transportation costs for the foreign worker to Canada from the country of origin;
- cover all recruitment costs related to hiring the foreign worker;
- ensure that affordable and suitable accommodation is available for the foreign worker;
- provide temporary medical insurance coverage until the worker is eligible for provincial health insurance coverage;
- register the foreign worker with the provincial workers' compensation/workplace safety insurance plan;

---

14   *Ibid.*

- sign an employment contract that includes the wages, duties, and conditions related to the transportation, accommodation, and health and occupational safety of the foreign worker;

- offer wages that are equal to or higher than the prevailing wage rate paid to Canadians in the same occupation and region, including benefits, or, in a unionized organization, offer the same wage rate as that established under the collective agreement; and

- demonstrate continued efforts to recruit and train Canadian workers.[15]

There is no prohibition against spouses and dependent children accompanying a foreign worker to Canada for the 24 months of work. However, questions may be raised about the applicant's actual intention to work only temporarily and to leave at the end of the permitted time, as well as about the applicant's ability to support dependants while in Canada. Furthermore, spouses of workers admitted in the lower-skilled occupations at the skill level C or D of the NOC are not eligible for an open work permit (they must apply for their own work permit), and children may be required to pay international student rates to attend school.

Caregiver Program

Canada has had programs for the recruitment and employment of foreign caregivers for a number of decades, beginning with the Foreign Domestic Movement Program (1980–1992), which enabled caregivers—mostly women—to apply for what was then called landed immigrant status after living in their employers' houses for a minimum of two years. The program was created to address the shortage of caregivers in Canada. The program evolved into the Live-In Caregiver Program and increased the education and language requirements but maintained the requirement to "live in" the employer's home. This requirement raised concerns because it increased the chances of sexual abuse and/or labour exploitation. The attraction of the program for caregivers was permanent residence at the end of a work commitment. However, unlike most of the other TFW programs, the live-in caregiver was not allowed to be accompanied by any family members while fulfilling the program's requirements, thereby leading to family separation for a minimum period of two years (but usually more).

The Live-In Caregiver Program was replaced in November 2014 with the Caregiver Program. One of the attractions of the program for the caregiver is that she becomes eligible to apply for permanent residence once she has completed two years, or the equivalent of 3,900 hours, of work within a four-year period. The "live-in" requirement is now optional, and the caregiver may also be able to bring her family members with her if she can satisfy an immigration officer that she will have sufficient funds to support her family in Canada, and if her family members are not otherwise inadmissible.

---

15 Employment and Social Development Canada, "Stream for Low-Wage Positions" (12 May 2015), online: <http://www.esdc.gc.ca/eng/jobs/foreign_workers/high_low_wage/low_wage/index.shtml>.

Despite the change in program name and requirements, the Caregiver Program falls under the Live-In Caregiver class in the regulations (IRPR, ss 100–115). Employers can hire temporary foreign caregivers to work in their home under two streams, on either a live-in or a live-out basis:

- *caregivers for children under 18 years of age* (for example, lower-skilled occupations that fall under NOC code 4411—home childcare providers; check the CIC and ESDC websites for updates, because some online information continues to reference the 2006 NOC codes, such as 6474—babysitters, nannies, and parents' helpers, rather than the 2011 codes); and
- *caregivers for people with high medical needs*, such as elderly persons 65 years of age or over, or people with disabilities, including a chronic or terminal illness (for example, higher-skilled occupations that fall under NOC code 3012—registered nurses and registered psychiatric nurses, and NOC code 4412—home support workers, housekeepers, and related occupations; again, check the CIC and ESDC websites for updates).

It is important to distinguish the Caregiver Program from other categories of persons who may perform a domestic or caregiving function, such as the following:

- *Participants in an international youth exchange program.* This is a reciprocal exchange program that enables youth to engage in short-term work or study activities in Canada. Participants may find work as a parent's helper.
- *Diplomatic staff.* Employees of diplomatic staff, such as domestic workers, may enter Canada as accredited members of a diplomat's suite.

These categories are not part of the Caregiver Program, and therefore the persons who apply under them are not eligible to apply for permanent residence in Canada.

EMPLOYER REQUIREMENTS

The Caregiver Program encompasses both in-home caregivers, who live in the home of the person for whom they are caring, and live-out caregivers. An employer may also partner with another employer to share the responsibilities of hiring a caregiver. For example, adult siblings may hire a caregiver to look after their elderly parents. Both employers must meet the program requirements but would only submit one application. It is also possible for an in-home caregiver to work in two different locations when the caregiver will care for a child whose parents share custody. In this instance, both locations should be disclosed to ESDC.

Employers must be knowledgeable about the caregiver pathway and whether they are hiring from the higher-skilled occupation stream (in which some positions require licensing by a professional regulator, as in the case of registered nurses) or the lower-skilled occupation stream. To obtain an LMIA, an employer must apply to ESDC for an LMIA and pay a $1,000 processing fee, which the employer is not allowed to recover from the caregiver. The employer must satisfy the following requirements:

1. The employer must submit an application for an LMIA to ESDC that

    - identifies English and French as the only languages as a job requirement (IRPR, s 203(1.01)) in the LMIA application and in advertisements, unless it can be demonstrated that another language is essential for the job;

    - provides proof of the individual who requires care (for example, age and parentage for each child under 18 years of age; age for each senior 65 years and older; signed physician's note attesting to the patient's disability, or chronic or terminal illness); and

    - proposes to pay the worker at least the posted prevailing wage for the occupation and work location where the worker will be employed.

2. The employer must submit a contract (see the Weblink below), signed by both the employer and caregiver, setting out the following information:

    - the employer's responsibility for the following mandatory employer-paid benefits:

        - transportation to Canada from the caregiver's country to the residence where she will be working in Canada (only for employers who are hiring under a low-wage stream where the caregiver would generally be filling a lower-skilled occupation); records of all transportation costs paid (invoices, receipts, copies of flight itineraries, tickets, boarding passes, etc.) must be kept for a minimum of six years;

        - medical insurance coverage from the date of her arrival until she is eligible for provincial health insurance;

        - workplace safety insurance coverage (only for lower-skilled caregivers) for the duration of her employment; and

        - all recruitment fees, including any amount payable to a third-party recruiter or agents hired by the employer;

    - the caregiver's hours of work (and details about anticipated overtime);

    - the caregiver's wages;

    - holiday and sick leave entitlements;

    - terms that address termination and resignation;

    - proof of sufficient financial resources to pay the foreign worker the wages offered (that is, a copy of the notice of assessment from the Canada Revenue Agency);

    - the caregiver's job duties (details about the number and ages of children, etc.) including that the work must be in a private household to provide child care, senior home support care, or care of a disabled person without supervision; and

    - accommodation arrangements:

        - if live-in (Schedule J, Employer Supplied Bedroom Description, EMP5599), the employer must provide a furnished bedroom in the home of the person receiving care that meets the municipal building requirements and the provincial/territorial health standards, is private, with a door that has a lock and safety bolt on the inside, and is provided without charge (room and board), as per the policy under the TFWP; or

– if live-out, for low-skilled caregivers, the employer must ensure that suitable and affordable accommodation is available.

Quebec employers must apply for a CAQ from the Ministère de l'Immigration, de la Diversité et de l'Inclusion in addition to applying for an LMIA.

In the event that the temporary foreign worker changes employers, the new employer must obtain a new LMIA from ESDC, the new employer and caregiver must sign an employment contract, and the caregiver must apply for a new work permit.

CAREGIVER ELIGIBILITY CRITERIA

Anyone applying under this program after November 30, 2014 must apply for a regular work permit.[16] The criteria for caregiver applicants seeking to qualify for the program (and thus be able to apply for Canadian permanent residence) include educational, training, and language requirements (IRPR, s 112). The requirements for those who wish to work outside Quebec are as follows:[17]

1. *Educational requirement.* Applicants must demonstrate successful completion of the equivalent of Canadian secondary school. CIC's Live-In Caregiver operational manual provides the following: "For example, in the Philippines, 72 credits of post-secondary education is equivalent to the successful completion of Canadian secondary school. Fewer than 72 credits is not equivalent."[18]

2. *Training/work experience requirement.* Applicants must meet either the training requirement or the work experience requirement:

   • Training requirement—completion of six months of full-time classroom training in the field or in an occupation related to the job in question. "Full-time" is considered at least 25 to 30 hours per week of educational instruction. Note that the training must be in a classroom setting; correspondence courses are not acceptable.

   • Work experience requirement—completion of at least 12 months of full-time paid employment, including at least six months of continuous employment with one employer, in the related field or occupation (for example, in a daycare, hospital, or senior citizen home), within three

---

16 Anyone who applied prior to November 30, 2014 needed to have a Live-In Caregiver (LCP) work permit. Applications to extend or change employers continue to be accepted for the LCP work permit until this program is phased out.

17 Citizenship and Immigration Canada, *OP 14: Processing Applicants for the Live-In Caregiver Program* (2 October 2014) s 5 at 5–10, online: <http://www.cic.gc.ca/english/resources/manuals/op/op14-eng.pdf>.

18 *Ibid*, s 5.3 at 5.

years immediately prior to the day on which the person submits an application for a work permit to a visa office.

3. *Language proficiency requirement.* The ability to read, listen, and speak English or French at a level sufficient to communicate effectively in an unsupervised setting, such as responding to emergency situations by contacting emergency services, answering the door and the telephone, and administering medication. Therefore, at the time of application, an applicant must submit the results of her language test from a CIC approved agency to show that she meets the minimum language levels in one or both official languages for the job; test results must be valid within two years on the date of application.

4. *Mandatory employment contract.* The employer must forward the original employment contract to the applicant. As noted, the contract must be signed by both the employer (not by the employer's representative or another employee on behalf of the employer) and by the caregiver. The employment contract must be consistent with provincial employment standards.

Caregivers seeking to work in Quebec need only 6 months of work experience in the related occupation, in contrast to the 12 months of experience required to work elsewhere. However, the caregiver is required to obtain a CAQ before applying for the work permit, and the employer is required to facilitate access to French courses outside regular working hours.

The applicant must follow the procedures for applying for a work permit (as discussed earlier), including providing her language test results, proof of her educational credentials (the equivalent of Canadian secondary school graduation), and proof of training (diploma and transcripts), or proof of work experience (letters of reference from previous employers), and she must undergo a medical examination.

Consider the following scenario related to paid work experience:

> Maria, a Filipino national, is seeking to apply for a work permit under the Caregiver Program. Maria has obtained a job in Canada as a live-in caregiver to care for a Canadian employer's two minor children. The employer has obtained the required LMIA.
>
> Maria would like to know whether she is eligible to obtain a work permit under the Caregiver Program. Maria has 17 years of work experience as a caregiver taking care of her own three children at home. She has a high level of English proficiency and has completed a high school program.
>
> Would Maria qualify for a work permit?

Unfortunately for Maria, her work experience does not comply with the requirements set out by the Caregiver Program, because her work experience is not paid work experience. Although there may be situations where the applicant is employed as a live-in caregiver by a relative, applicants must satisfy the officer that they were actually paid for work performed.

Consider the following scenario on required documents:

Boupha, a Cambodian national, submitted her application for a work permit under the Caregiver Program to the Canadian embassy in Bangkok. She completed a college diploma in physiotherapy and then, within the past year, completed seven months of full-time training for live-in caregivers in a classroom setting.

Boupha has included in her work permit application all of the requisite documents that establish her experience in accordance with the requirements of the IRPA and the IRPR. In addition, she included the documents that the Canadian employer forwarded to her: the positive LMIA and the employment contract signed by the Canadian employer's legal representative. Boupha signed the employment contract prior to submitting her application to the Canadian embassy. Finally, she included the results of her medical exam, her identity documents, and police clearances for her and all members of her family. Boupha also provided her biometric information because she is from Cambodia.

Has Boupha gathered the key documents and information for her application?

Boupha carefully followed the instructions in the Instruction Guide (IMM 5487) and used the Document Checklist (IMM 5488), and therefore has the required documents for her application; she must also arrange to have any documents that are not in one of the official languages translated into English or French.

DURATION OF CAREGIVER WORK PERMIT

Generally, a caregiver's work permit is valid for four years plus three months, as long as the LMIA is approved for the same duration. The four-year period is a general policy by CIC to give the caregiver (1) enough time to complete the two years of full-time employment to qualify for permanent residence and (2) flexibility to compensate for periods of unemployment, illness, vacation, or maternity leave. The additional three months allow for a transition period to apply for permanent residence under the Caregiver Program.[19]

PLACE OF APPLICATION

Applicants seeking an initial work permit must submit their application to a visa office abroad. This may be a little confusing, because applicants already in Canada with a TRV are entitled to submit an application in Canada for work permits and renewals, study permits, and caregivers' applications for permanent residence in Canada. However, applicants seeking an initial work permit under the Caregiver Program must apply outside Canada, regardless of whether they are already in Canada with a TRV.

---

19   *Ibid*, s 5.9 at 8.

Consider the following scenario:

> Julie is a student completing a two-year nursing diploma program at Seneca College. Julie will graduate from this program in May 2016 and would like to submit her application for a work permit under the Caregiver Program soon after completing the program. She would also like to eventually become a permanent resident of Canada. Julie is unsure where to submit her application for a work permit.

Julie must submit her application for a work permit to the visa office that serves her country of nationality. Applicants seeking an initial work permit under the Caregiver Program must submit their applications outside Canada to qualify under the program and therefore be eligible for permanent residence in Canada. Consequently, if Julie submits her application to a case processing centre in Canada, she will not qualify under the Caregiver Program and will not be eligible for permanent residence in Canada. After Julie qualifies for the program, however, she may apply for extensions of her work permit in Canada and, once she is eligible for permanent residence, she may submit her application without having to leave Canada.

APPLYING FOR PERMANENT RESIDENCE

Generally, family members may not accompany caregivers to Canada. Even when an employer agrees that a family member may reside with the caregiver in the employer's residence, there are no guarantees that any subsequent employer would agree to the same terms.[20] However, if the applicant can satisfy the officer that she has sufficient funds to care for and support the family member(s) in Canada, that the family member(s) are not otherwise inadmissible, and that they have permission to live in the home of the person(s) for whom she will provide care (if she has a live-in arrangement with the employer), then she may be accompanied by her family members.

To mitigate the harsh consequences of this rule for caregivers who must leave their own children behind, the Caregiver Program allows caregivers to include their family members when applying for permanent residence after they have fulfilled the terms of the Caregiver Program—24 months of authorized full-time employment or a total of 3,900 hours of authorized full-time employment within four years of arriving in Canada.

Caregivers applying for permanent residence may request **parallel processing** for some or all of their family members residing in or outside Canada. Alternatively, caregivers may sponsor family members at a later date after becoming permanent residents themselves.

In addition, a caregiver who has received first-stage approval (approval in principle) of the permanent resident application is entitled to apply for an open work permit. This allows the caregiver to accept employment and to work for any employer for the time period specified on the work permit.

parallel processing
simultaneous processing of the permanent residence application of the main applicant and the applications of sponsored family members, such as is allowed under the Caregiver Program

---

20 *Ibid*, s 5.10 at 9.

Seasonal Agricultural Worker Program

Employers can hire temporary foreign agricultural workers under one of four streams: high-wage position, low-wage position, agricultural stream, and the **Seasonal Agricultural Worker Program (SAWP)**. The SAWP permits foreign nationals to work in lower- or higher-skilled occupations in specific on-farm primary agriculture commodity sectors such as fruits, vegetables, greenhouses, nurseries, apiary products, tobacco, sod, flowers, Christmas trees, and certain animal commodities. The SAWP was developed in cooperation with agricultural producers and a number of foreign countries, including Mexico and several Commonwealth Caribbean countries (Anguilla, Antigua and Barbuda, Barbados, Dominica, Grenada, Jamaica, Montserrat, St. Kitts-Nevis, St. Lucia, St. Vincent and the Grenadines, and Trinidad and Tobago).[21]

Employers can hire agricultural workers for up to eight months between January 1 and December 15 of the same year.

The SAWP currently operates in specific agricultural commodity sectors in all provinces.

Employers must complete and sign the appropriate employment contract (available on the ESDC website and entitled, for example, Agreement for the Employment in Canada of Seasonal Agricultural Workers from Mexico) and send it with the LMIA application to Service Canada. Prior to hiring a foreign worker under the SAWP, a Canadian employer must meet the following criteria:

- demonstrate efforts to advertise to and recruit Canadian agricultural workers or unemployed Canadians through ESDC and provincial employment programs;
- offer the foreign worker the same wages paid to Canadian agricultural workers doing the same work;
- pay for the foreign worker's airfare to and from Canada (a portion of this cost can be recovered through payroll deductions);
- provide free seasonal housing to the foreign worker that has been approved by the appropriate provincial/municipal body;
- pay the immigration visa application fee for the worker (this fee or a portion of this fee can be recovered through payroll deductions);
- ensure that the foreign worker is covered by workplace safety insurance coverage;
- ensure that the foreign worker is covered under private or provincial health insurance during his stay in Canada; and
- sign an employment contract outlining wages, duties, and conditions related to the transportation, accommodation, health, and occupational safety of the foreign worker.[22]

---

21   Employment and Social Development Canada, "Hiring Agricultural Workers" (24 April 2015), online: <http://www.esdc.gc.ca/eng/jobs/foreign_workers/agriculture/index.shtml>.

22   *Ibid.*

CIC will issue a work permit of no more than eight months, provided that the foreign worker meets the eligibility criteria set out in section 200 of the IRPR.

Cumulative Duration

On April 1, 2011, a regulation was introduced to establish the maximum allowable cumulative time that a temporary foreign worker can work in Canada. This rule generally applies to lower-skilled workers, because there are no provisions in low-wage programs that lead to permanent residence. The policy decision to limit the amount of time that a temporary foreign worker can work in Canada was implemented to prevent situations in which a temporary foreign worker sets down roots in Canada and loses ties with (and thus becomes reluctant to return to) his country of origin. The maximum cumulative duration is currently set at a total of four years, and generally must be followed by a period of four years during which the temporary foreign worker is not eligible to work in Canada (IRPR, s 200(3)(g)).

LMIA Exemptions

International Mobility Program

Foreign nationals generally need a work permit but are exempt from the LMIA requirement (IRPR, s 204(a)) under the International Mobility Program (IMP). The IMP includes all streams of work permit applications that are LMIA-exempt under one umbrella, including exemptions under NAFTA and other free trade agreements. Despite being exempt from the LMIA provision, a foreign national may obtain a work permit only after the prospective employer has submitted a job offer and other relevant information to CIC. This requirement allows for compliance monitoring of employers.

Significant Benefit

Consistent with sections 204 to 208 of the IRPR, senior managers, executives, and individuals with specialized knowledge may apply for a work permit without having first obtained an LMIA, provided that their presence in Canada will result or is likely to result in a **significant benefit** to Canada. "Significant" means important or notable.[23]

When assessing requests for work permits based on significant social or cultural benefits, immigration officers are required to consider the impact that the foreign worker would have on Canada's labour market and economy. If an individual's work in Canada is likely to produce a significant social or cultural benefit, then the balance of practical considerations argues for the issuance of a work permit in a time frame shorter than would be necessary to obtain an ESDC opinion.

significant benefit
a ground of exemption from the usual requirement of foreign workers to obtain a positive LMIA; the exemption applies to foreign workers whose presence in Canada is likely to result in a significant benefit to the country, and permits them to apply for a work permit without first obtaining the positive LMIA

---

23 Citizenship and Immigration Canada, "International Mobility Program: Canadian Interests—Significant Benefit General Guidelines [R205(a)—C10]" (18 September 2014), online: <http://www.cic.gc.ca/english/resources/tools/temp/work/opinion/benefit.asp>.

Officers rely on the following objective measures when assessing whether a foreign worker's presence in Canada will result in a significant social or cultural benefit:[24]

- the worker's academic record (for example, degree or diploma);
- whether the worker has significant full-time experience in the occupation sought (ten or more years of experience);
- awards and accolades conferred on the worker;
- membership in organizations requiring excellence of its members;
- whether the worker has judged or critiqued others' work in the field of specialty;
- the worker's scientific or scholarly contributions in the field;
- publications authored by the worker in academic or industry publications;
- whether the worker has been a leader in an organization with a distinguished reputation; and
- whether the worker is a francophone foreign worker entering an occupation under NOC skill type 0 (managerial occupations) or skill level A (professional occupations) or B (technical occupations or skilled trades), destined to work outside Quebec, who was recruited through Destination Canada or other employment events coordinated with the federal government and francophone minority communities.

Business Visitors and Professionals

business visitor
a foreign worker who seeks admission to Canada to engage in international business activities and whose primary source of remuneration remains outside Canada

A **business visitor** is a foreign worker who seeks to engage in international business activities in Canada without directly entering the Canadian labour market (IRPR, s 187(1)). Thus, the business visitor's primary source of remuneration is outside Canada, and the principal place of business and actual place of accrual of profits remains predominantly outside Canada. For example, a foreigner who wants to enter Canada for the purpose of purchasing Canadian goods for a foreign business is a business visitor, as is a foreigner who wants to enter Canada for the purpose of receiving training by a Canadian parent of the corporation that employs the foreign worker outside Canada. Business visitors must plan on visiting for less than six months; otherwise, they must apply for a work permit.

professional
under NAFTA, a citizen of the United States or Mexico who has pre-arranged employment with a Canadian employer and whose occupation is listed in NAFTA

In contrast, a business person is a **professional** who seeks entry through some sort of pre-arrangement—for example, as a salaried employee under a personal contract with a Canadian employer or through a contract with the professional's employer in the home country. The business person class includes foreign workers who are seeking to enter Canada under an international agreement such as NAFTA or GATS (see "International Free Trade Agreements" below).

---

24 *Ibid.*

Consider the following scenario:

> Maps & Software Inc. is a US company that manufactures marine maps and computer software. Maps & Software Inc. does not have any subsidiaries or affiliates in Canada. The company is interested in sending three of its employees to Toronto to conduct research for a new mapping software device that will assist mariners in navigating Lake Ontario. Once research is finalized, the three employees will return to the United States with their findings; once the product is manufactured, it will be available to anyone who wants to purchase it.
>
> Are the three employees required to obtain work permits?

In this case, the three employees of the US company are not required to obtain work permits for the following reasons: there is no Canadian employer contracting for their services; the US company will be the direct beneficiary of the foreign workers' efforts; and the employees' source of remuneration for the work performed remains outside Canada. Consequently, the three workers satisfy the business visitor criteria, which exempts them from having to obtain a work permit. In addition, because they are US nationals, they can apply for a business visitor visa at the port of entry.

Members of the clergy are another type of worker who are not required to obtain a work permit to work in Canada. Pursuant to section 186(l) of IRPR:

> A foreign national may work in Canada without a work permit … as a person who is responsible for assisting a congregation or group in the achievement of its spiritual goals and whose main duties are to preach doctrine, perform functions related to gatherings of the congregation or group or provide spiritual counselling.

However, members of the clergy are required to ask for a visitor record (IMM 1097) at the port of entry.

Consider the following scenario:

> Larry, a US national who lives in Utah, has recently been hired by a Canadian church to serve as its minister for the upcoming year. Larry has been given contradictory information regarding whether he needs a work permit. Some have said that everyone who works in Canada needs a work permit, and others have told him that members of the clergy may work without a work permit in Canada. Which opinion is correct?

Larry needs to request a visitor record from the port of entry reflecting the one-year duration of his clergy work in Canada. However, he will not need a work permit because clergy work as defined in section 186(l) of the IRPR is considered exempt work.

Intra-Company Transfers

intra-company transfer
an executive, senior manager, or qualified employee with specialized knowledge who is transferred within a company to work in Canada on a temporary basis

The **intra-company transfer** category is designed to assist multinational businesses in transferring executives, senior managers, and employees with specialized knowledge temporarily, when required for business purposes, without an LMIA. Intra-company transferees would not necessarily provide a significant benefit to the social, cultural, or economic threads of Canadian life, and therefore would not qualify under the significant benefit category. Exemptions for intra-company transferees are also explicitly provided for in some trade agreements to which Canada is a party, such as NAFTA and GATS.

The intra-company transfer category permits international companies to temporarily transfer qualified employees to Canada for the purpose of improving management effectiveness, expanding Canadian exports, and enhancing the competitiveness of Canadian entities in overseas markets. In other words, the admission of an intra-company transferee to Canada is subject to the relationship between the Canadian and foreign company. The intra-company transferee will be admitted for the purpose of assisting in the operations of a foreign company's Canadian parent, subsidiary, branch, or affiliate company.

To qualify as an intra-company transferee who is exempt from obtaining an LMIA, a foreign worker must meet the following criteria:

- be currently employed by a multinational company and be seeking entry to work in a parent, subsidiary, branch, or affiliate of that enterprise;
- be transferred in an executive, senior managerial, or specialized-knowledge capacity;
- have been employed in a similar full-time position for a minimum of one year in the three years prior to coming to Canada; and
- comply with all immigration requirements for temporary entry.[25]

The foreign worker must also submit the following documentation:

- confirmation of her continuous employment (full-time, not accumulated part-time) with the enterprise outside Canada for one year within the three-year period immediately preceding the date of application;
- an outline of her position in an executive or managerial capacity or one involving specialized knowledge, including title, position within the organization, and job description;
- in the case of a foreign national possessing "specialized knowledge," evidence that she has such knowledge and that the position in Canada requires it;
- an indication of her intended duration of stay; and

---

25 Citizenship and Immigration Canada, "International Mobility Program: Canadian Interests—Significant Benefit—Intra-Company Transferees—General Requirements [R205(a)] (Exemption Code C12)" (19 December 19 2014), online: <http://www.cic.gc.ca/english/resources/tools/temp/work/opinion/transferees/requirements.asp>.

- a description of the relationship between the enterprise in Canada and the enterprise in the foreign country and, on request, evidence of this, such as annual reports, articles of incorporation, financial statements, partnership agreements, and business tax returns.

The foreign executive may be from any country; there are no restrictions. Consider the following scenario:

> Ernesto, an executive with San Pelligrani, an Italian bottled-beverage company, is being transferred to run San Pelligrani's Canadian subsidiary. The company relationship qualifies San Pelligrani under the affiliate definition in the intra-company transfer category. The Canadian office employs 350 people.
>
> Ernesto has worked as an executive with San Pelligrani in Italy for the past 15 years. He is in good health and has no criminal record. What specific documentation will Ernesto be required to submit in support of his intra-company transfer work permit application?

Ernesto's application requires only a company support letter and the fees for the work permit. The letter from the foreign company is crucial because it will demonstrate that Ernesto has come from an executive position, that he will be moving into a similar role in the Canadian office, and that the corporate relationship between the foreign entity and the Canadian entity exists and complies with the IRPR.

The initial work permit is generally issued for only one year. Executives and senior managers are permitted to renew their initial intra-company transfer work permits for a period of up to seven years. Specialized knowledge workers may renew their work permits for a period of up to five years. After the maximum period is reached, the foreign worker must leave Canada and the Canadian labour market for at least one year. When the year is over, the foreign worker may reapply and begin the cycle again.

International Free Trade Agreements

According to section 204 of the IRPR, a foreign national may be issued a work permit without an LMIA to perform work in Canada pursuant to an international agreement between Canada and one or more countries. Among the international agreements to which Canada is a signatory are the North American Free Trade Agreement (NAFTA), the General Agreement on Trade in Services (GATS), the Canada–Chile Free Trade Agreement, the Canada–Peru Free Trade Agreement, and the Canada–Colombia Free Trade Agreement. We will briefly examine two of these agreements—NAFTA and GATS—in this section.

NORTH AMERICAN FREE TRADE AGREEMENT

NAFTA is arguably the most important agreement for those practising US and Canadian immigration law. It was created to facilitate trade among its three signatory countries: Canada, the United States, and Mexico. NAFTA facilitates trade as well as the movement of persons involved in the trade of goods or services. Business people covered by NAFTA are not required to obtain an LMIA and can gain quicker, easier, temporary entry into Canada.

NAFTA covers the following categories of foreign workers: business visitors, professionals, intra-company transferees (applying only to citizens of Mexico and the United States), and traders and investors. An overview of the first three categories is provided below.

A business visitor under NAFTA refers to citizens of the United States or Mexico who seek to engage in international business activities related to research and design; growth, manufacturing, and production; marketing; sales; distribution; after-sales service; and general service.[26] Because business visitors are restricted from entering the Canadian labour market and their primary source of remuneration must remain outside Canada, they are not required to obtain an LMIA or a work permit. However, business visitors must apply at the port of entry for a visitor record and must comply with the usual admissibility requirements for temporary entry.

A professional under NAFTA refers to a citizen of the United States or Mexico who has pre-arranged employment[27] with a Canadian employer and whose occupation is listed in the 60-plus occupations/professions covered by NAFTA. Such professions include accountants, computer systems analysts, engineers, management consultants, and technical writers. Professionals must be qualified to work, as evidenced by degrees, diplomas, professional licences, accreditation, or registration, and must comply with existing immigration requirements for temporary entry.

The professional must be qualified to provide professional services in Canada; therefore, both the qualifications of the individual and the position in Canada must be considered. For example, a lawyer must be seeking to enter Canada as a lawyer and not as a paralegal. Alternatively, a paralegal cannot be admitted to work as a lawyer unless the applicant is also qualified as a lawyer as indicated in the list of minimum education requirements and alternative credentials in appendix 1603.D.1 of NAFTA.

In addition, an individual must be seeking to enter Canada to work in a position for which he possesses the required qualifications. For example, a corporate executive cannot be admitted to Canada to be a physiotherapist, because physiotherapy is not his field of qualification.

On initial entry, the professional is given work permit status for a maximum of one year. Extensions may be issued in increments up to a total of three years, provided that the individual continues to comply with the requirements for professionals.

---

26   Citizenship and Immigration Canada, "International Mobility Program: North American Free Trade Agreement" (28 October 2014), online: <http://www.cic.gc.ca/english/resources/tools/temp/work/international/nafta.asp>.

27   *Ibid*. Evidence of pre-arranged employment includes a signed contract with a Canadian enterprise; evidence of an offer of employment from a Canadian employer; or a letter from the American or Mexican employer on whose behalf the service will be provided to the Canadian enterprise. Professionals seeking self-employment in Canada are excluded.

The professional category does not allow self-employment in Canada. However, responding to unsolicited inquiries about services that the professional may be able to perform, or establishing an office from which to deliver pre-arranged services to clients, does not constitute self-employment.

The intra-company transferee is the third category under NAFTA. It is different from the intra-company transfer category under the IRPA because it applies only to citizens of the United States and Mexico (whereas that category under the IRPA applies to foreign nationals from any country). However, because of the harmonization of IRPA and NAFTA provisions, there are now no differences in entry requirements and work permit durations.

Citizens of the United States or Mexico whose employment involves specialized knowledge or who are employed in an executive or managerial capacity for an enterprise in the United States or Mexico that has a parent, branch, subsidiary, or affiliate relationship with a Canadian company may qualify. The executive is required to have been continuously employed in a similar position outside Canada for one year in the previous three-year period. Like all other visitors, intra-company transferees must also comply with existing immigration requirements for temporary entry.

The category of intra-company transferees is the only NAFTA category to have a cap imposed on the total duration of employment. A person employed in an executive or managerial capacity may stay for a maximum of seven years, and a person employed in a position requiring specialized knowledge may stay for a maximum of five years.[28]

Consider the following scenario:

> Today, Ricardo, a Mexican citizen, arrives at a Canadian port of entry to apply for a work permit. On arrival, he advises the CBSA officer that he has been offered employment by the Canadian subsidiary of a Mexican company where he worked as a senior marketing manager from May 2010 until he left the company about two months ago.
>
> Can Ricardo be granted a work permit?

Ricardo may be granted a work permit because he qualifies as a NAFTA intra-company transferee pursuant to the LMIA exemption (code T24) under section 204(a) of the IRPR. If Ricardo is applying at the border today, he can show that under NAFTA, as a Mexican citizen, he has worked for the Mexican parent company in a managerial capacity for more than one year in the three-year period preceding his application, which is today's date.

Alternatively, both professionals and intra-company transferees may be admitted under the general service provision of the business visitor category if they are not seeking to enter the Canadian labour market and their primary source of remuneration remains outside Canada—in other words, if they meet the business visitor criteria.

---

28 *Ibid.*

GATS professional
a person who seeks to engage in an activity at a professional level in a designated profession, and who meets the GATS criteria

GENERAL AGREEMENT ON TRADE IN SERVICES

The General Agreement on Trade in Services (GATS) is similar to NAFTA in several respects, including the categories of business visitors, intra-company transferees, and professionals under which a foreign worker may apply, and the fact that such categories are LMIA-exempt.

Under GATS, each of the 160 member nations has made individual commitments to member signatories concerning trade in services in specific market sectors. In addition, GATS has set out unique rules for the entry of professionals.

A **GATS professional** refers to a person who seeks to engage in an activity at a professional level in a designated profession, and who meets the following criteria:

- possesses citizenship of a member nation, or the right of permanent residence in Australia or New Zealand;
- has an occupation that falls within the definition of an eligible GATS profession;
- works as part of a short-term services contract obtained by a company in another member nation; and
- has the necessary academic credentials and professional qualifications, which have been duly recognized, where appropriate, by the professional association in Canada.[29]

The list of GATS professional occupations are categorized into Group 1 occupations (engineers, agrologists, architects, forestry professionals, geomatics professionals, and land surveyors) and Group 2 occupations (foreign legal consultants, urban planners, and senior computer specialists). The requirements can be found on the CIC website.[30]

GATS professionals are not permitted to work in service sectors that relate to education, health services, culture, and sports services. Work permits are restricted to a maximum duration of 90 days within a 12-month period; extensions beyond the 90 days are not permitted under the GATS professional category.[31]

Open Work Permit

In some cases, an open work permit may be available. An open work permit has the advantage of not being job-specific; thus, a foreign national with an open work permit may work for any Canadian employer without first having an employment contract with a positive LMIA.

An officer may issue one of two types of open work permits, with or without occupational restrictions, depending on the applicant's medical status:

---

29 Citizenship and Immigration Canada, "International Mobility Program: General Agreement on Trade in Services" (28 October 2014), online: <http://www.cic.gc.ca/english/resources/tools/temp/work/international/gats.asp>.

30 *Ibid.*

31 *Ibid.*

- *Unrestricted.* It is generally issued to a foreign national who has passed a medical examination; it allows the applicant to work in any occupation, for any employer, at any location.

- *Restricted.* It is issued to a foreign national and allows the applicant to work for an unspecified employer, but the occupation is restricted for public health reasons because the applicant has not passed a medical examination, or the occupation is restricted owing to the applicant's medical condition.

The following persons may be eligible to apply for an open work permit:

- persons who are already working in Canada and whose applications for permanent residence have received a positive eligibility assessment under one of the following:
  - Federal Skilled Worker Program,
  - Canadian Experience Class,
  - Provincial Nominee Program,
  - Federal Skilled Trades Program, or
  - humanitarian and compassionate grounds;
- family members of persons whose applications for permanent resident have been approved under one of the programs above;
- in-home caregivers who have applied for permanent residence (IRPR, s 113);
- members of the spouse or common law partner in Canada class (IRPR, s 124);
- spouses or common law partners of foreign representatives and family members of military personnel;
- spouses or common law partners of foreign workers whose work falls under NOC skill type 0 (managerial occupations) or skill level A (professional occupations) or B (technical occupations and skilled trades);
- spouses or common law partners of foreign students at public post-secondary schools;
- spouses or common law partners of work permit holders who have been nominated for permanent residence by a province, irrespective of the skill level of the principal applicant's occupation;
- destitute students;
- persons who have a TRP that is valid for at least six months;
- persons who are participating in the Canada World Youth Program or the Working Holiday category of the International Experience Canada program;
- refugees whose claims have been referred to the IRB for refugee protection and who cannot pay for their basic needs without working while waiting for a decision on their claim;
- persons whose refugee claim has been rejected by the RPD, who cannot be removed from Canada due to reasons beyond their control, and who cannot pay for their basic needs without working;

- professional athletes who are working for a Canadian team and need to do other work to support themselves;
- international students who have graduated from a Canadian post-secondary institution;
- family members of a foreign representative; and
- family members of a foreign military member who is working in Canada.

If the foreign national requires a TRV to enter Canada, the open work permit will be issued for the same length of time. The application for an open work permit can be made prior to arrival to Canada, at the port of entry, or after arrival.

Work Permit Exemptions

Not everyone is required to obtain a work permit in order to work in Canada (IRPR, s 186). Some categories of workers who are exempt from needing a temporary work permit include the following:

- business visitors;
- diplomats;
- foreign athletes;
- military personnel;
- crew members;
- clergy;
- performing artists;
- public speakers;
- news reporters;
- expert witnesses, examiners, and evaluators; and
- students engaging in part-time work on campus.

Employers

All employers, whether they are hiring LMIA-exempt foreign nationals or temporary workers through the LMIA process, must demonstrate that they have made extensive efforts to find suitable Canadian or permanent resident candidates and that none are available to fill the position in question. All employers are subject to the same level of scrutiny with respect to their hiring and treatment of foreign workers.[32]

When an LMIA is not required, employers must pay an employer compliance fee ($230) and submit an offer of employment form directly to CIC. Employers who wish to hire temporary workers in occupations requiring an LMIA must submit an

---

32 Citizenship and Immigration Canada, "Notice—Changes to Strengthen Employer Accountability Under the International Mobility Program" (9 February 2015), online: <http://www.cic.gc.ca/english/department/media/notices/2015-02-09.asp>.

Comparison Chart: Temporary Foreign Worker Program and International Agreements

Temporary Foreign Worker Program	International Mobility Program
Objective: Last resort for employers to fill jobs for which qualified Canadians are not available	Objective: To advance Canada's broad economic and cultural national interest
Based on employer demand to fill specific jobs	Not based on employer demand
Unilateral and discretionary	Based largely on multilateral/bilateral agreements with other countries (e.g., NAFTA, GATS)
Employer must obtain an LMIA	No LMIA required
Lead department is ESDC	Lead department is CIC
Employer-specific work permits (TFWs tied to one employer)	Generally, open permits (participants have greater mobility)
Majority are low-skilled/low-wage (e.g., farm workers)	Majority are high-skilled/high-wage
Last and limited resort because no Canadians are available	Workers and reciprocity are deemed to be in the national economic and cultural interest
Main source countries are developing countries	Main source countries are highly developed countries

application through Service Canada for review and assessment by ESDC. ESDC assesses the employer's application to determine whether there is a need for a foreign worker because no Canadian workers are available to fill the position, and what impact the foreign worker would have on the Canadian labour market—positive, neutral, or negative. In the case of a positive assessment, ESDC/Service Canada will provide a positive LMIA (sometimes referred to as a "confirmation letter") to the prospective employer, who must then provide it, along with the employment contract, to the foreign national applicant.

Employers may hire foreign nationals with open work permits without needing to apply for an LMIA or pay a compliance fee. A foreign national with an open work permit is allowed to work for any Canadian employer.

The following sections provide an overview of the general procedure for prospective employers with respect to hiring foreign workers, and the eligibility requirements for foreign nationals who wish to work temporarily in Canada, including the process for vetting the job offer and the responsibilities of Canadian employers.

Employment Contract

Employers must complete and sign a contract before applying for an LMIA with ESDC (unless exempted by certain program streams from naming the foreign worker). The employment contract sets out the terms and conditions of employment, including the following information, as applicable to the program and stream:

- duration of the contract;
- the employer's responsibility for the costs of the applicant's transportation to and from Canada, between the applicant's country and the location of work in Canada;
- medical insurance coverage from the date of arrival until the applicant is eligible for provincial health insurance;
- workplace safety insurance coverage for the duration of the employment;
- all recruitment fees, including any amount payable to a third-party recruiter or agents hired by the employer;
- job duties;
- hours of work, with specific start and stop times, and breaks;
- wages, with specific start and stop times, and breaks;
- accommodation arrangements, if applicable (including room and board);
- holiday and sick leave entitlements; and
- termination and resignation terms.

As proof of a genuine job offer from a Canadian employer, the applicant must obtain a copy of the positive LMIA that was provided to the prospective employer by ESDC/Service Canada.

The rules for paying wages are varied and complex, and depend on the program and stream. Generally, however, employers are permitted to offer a wage that is below the provincial/territorial median hourly wage for low-wage occupations, but are then subject to a cap on the number of low-wage positions (for example, 20 percent as of July 1, 2015 and 10 percent as of July 1, 2016). Employers may also offer a wage that is at or above the provincial/territorial median hourly wage, but must complete a "transition plan for high wage positions."

Did You Know?

Employers are not allowed to hire a foreign worker without first obtaining authorization. The IRPA states that an employer who employs "a foreign national in a capacity in which the foreign national is not authorized under this Act to be employed" is liable to a fine up to $50,000 or to imprisonment for up to two years, or to both (ss 124(1)(c), 125).

Foreign workers are not permitted to work for employers who are ineligible or who employ workers who may be at risk of sexual exploitation: sections 200(3)(g.1) and (h) of the IRPR prohibit officers from granting a permit to a foreign worker who intends to work for an ineligible employer. Employers are ineligible for the TFWP when there are reasonable grounds to suspect a risk of sexual exploitation, such as work in strip clubs, escort services, and massage parlours.

Labour Market Impact Assessment

The TFWP has specific requirements for employers depending on the labour market stream of the temporary worker. A prospective employer must submit its job offer and apply to ESDC for an LMIA, which carries a processing fee of $1,000 for each position requested (this fee is subject to change). ESDC is responsible for confirming that the job offer conforms to current rules and regulations, including assessing the employment contract and conducting an employer compliance review. ESDC assesses the employer's application for the LMIA based on a number of factors, including but not limited to the following:

1. the employer is actively engaged in the business in which the worker will be employed;

2. the job offer is consistent with the needs of the employer;

3. the employer is reasonably able to fulfill the terms of the job offer; and

4. the employer has complied with federal and provincial/territorial laws regulating employment in the province/territory where the worker will be employed.[33]

An LMIA indicates to an immigration officer that there is a need for a foreign worker to fill the job and that no Canadian worker is available to do the job. Several factors are considered, such as wages; working conditions; the availability of Canadians or permanent residents for the position; and the skills, knowledge transfer, and job creation that may result from employing a foreign worker. These factors are reviewed below.

The LMIA is typically issued for a specific period of time, and any work permit issued will coincide with that period. Renewal of a work permit beyond the specified period is likely to require a new LMIA. For low-wage positions, ESDC limits the duration of work permits set out in LMIAs to a maximum of one year (previously two years). Employers of temporary foreign workers must reapply every year for an LMIA.

FACTORS

Unless an exemption applies, ESDC considers several factors when assessing an employment offer, including the following:

1. *Verification of the employment contract.* ESDC verifies whether the employment contract is genuine.

2. *Recruitment efforts.* The employer must show that it made reasonable efforts to hire Canadians or permanent residents for the position before offering it to a foreign worker. The onus is on the employer to prove that there were no Canadians available for the position, or that Canadian applicants could not be trained for the position in a reasonable amount of time. Ongoing recruitment

---

33 Employment and Social Development Canada, "New Requirements for Employer Compliance: Employer Conditions" (30 December 2013), online: <http://www.esdc.gc.ca/eng/jobs/foreign_workers/employer_compliance.shtml>.

efforts include advertising the job—in particular, to groups who are under-represented in the workforce (for example, Aboriginal peoples, youth, older workers, persons with disabilities, and newcomers) and who face barriers to employment.

3. *Union consultation.* All relevant unions and professional associations must be consulted with respect to the potential employment of a foreign worker, and letters of consent from them must be attached to the application for the LMIA. In addition, the employment of the foreign worker must not adversely affect the settlement of any labour dispute in progress or the employment of any person involved in that dispute.

4. *Job creation.* A position that is likely to help job creation or job retention for Canadian citizens or permanent residents has a greater chance of being approved.

5. *Transfer of skills.* Workers who are likely to transfer skills and knowledge for the benefit of Canadians or permanent residents are favoured.

6. *Labour shortages.* Consideration will be given to whether the worker is likely to fill a labour shortage in the Canadian market that is the result of a skills shortage.

7. *Wages and working conditions.* The wages and working conditions offered must be sufficient to attract Canadian citizens or permanent residents and retain them in that work. Temporary foreign workers have the same rights and protections as Canadian workers under applicable federal and provincial/territorial employment standards and labour laws, and they are paid at the same rate that Canadian workers would be paid for the same job. There is an exception: in April 2012, Human Resources and Skills Development Canada (HRSDC, now ESDC) announced a new wage structure that allows pay of up to 15 percent below the average wage for an occupation in a specific region, as long as an employer can demonstrate that the wage is consistent with that of Canadian workers based on Statistics Canada data. With respect to working conditions, the provinces and territories have primary responsibility for establishing and enforcing health and labour standards, such as safe working conditions, for all workers, including temporary foreign workers.

It is crucial that the employer's submissions include information regarding the above-noted factors, such as details about recruitment efforts and their results, and a detailed explanation of how the company would benefit from the foreign worker's employment with respect to profitability, employee skills, and positive spillover effects on Canadians.

MINIMUM ADVERTISING REQUIREMENTS

Employers seeking to hire workers that require an LMIA must show that they have conducted ongoing recruitment efforts—for example, that they have advertised on recognized Internet recruitment sites; in trade journals, newsletters, or national newspapers; or by consulting unions, professional associations, and groups that are underrepresented in the workforce. Alternatively, employers must show that they have advertised on the Government of Canada's national Job Bank (or the equivalent in British Columbia, Saskatchewan, Quebec, Newfoundland and Labrador, or the Northwest Territories) for a minimum amount of time (measured in days or weeks, depending on the stream), starting from the first day the ad appears and is accessible to the general public.

For employers who recruit for jobs in the low-wage stream, minimum advertising efforts may also include advertising in weekly or periodic newspapers, journals, newsletters, national/regional newspapers, ethnic newspapers/newsletters, or free local newspapers; advertising in the community (for example, posting ads in local stores, community resource centres, churches, or local regional employment centres); and advertising on Internet job sites (for example, on union, community resource, or ethnic group sites). All employers are required to keep records of their efforts for a minimum of six years, because records can be requested at any time by ESDC, which has the authority to conduct inspections to verify an employer's compliance with the conditions set out in the IRPR.

EMPLOYER COMPLIANCE REVIEW

ESDC conducts an employer compliance review (ECR) as part of the LMIA assessment process. ESDC reviews the employer's history as an employer

- to provide better protection to vulnerable temporary foreign workers against abusive employers and third-party agents;
- to increase the employer's accountability and compliance with the terms and conditions of its job offers to foreign nationals; and
- to restrict the use of temporary foreign workers to short-term situations.

The review is conducted to determine whether, over the past six years, the employer has reasonably respected the terms of past job offers, particularly with regard to wages, working conditions, and employment in the same occupation as the one listed in the offer of employment and LMIA. To demonstrate compliance and to help facilitate the process for subsequent LMIA applications, the employer should keep a record of all documentation. The employer may be asked to provide

- payroll records;
- time sheets;
- a job description;
- the temporary foreign worker's work permit;
- proof of registration with provincial/territorial workplace safety organizations; and
- proof that the workplace is free of physical, sexual, psychological, or financial abuse.

For employers of temporary foreign workers with lower levels of formal training, or those hired under the SAWP or the Caregiver Program, the following additional information is required:

- transportation costs,
- accommodation information, and
- private health insurance coverage (if applicable).

The government has the authority to conduct inspections of employer premises without a warrant, and may impose enforcement measures and penalties for employers who mistreat foreign workers. Employers are notified by ESDC about site inspections. Following the site inspection, an employer is given the opportunity to respond to any findings of non-compliance. If the employer does not pass the review, the employer's LMIA may be revoked. Effective December 1, 2015, penalties for non-compliance range from an administrative warning to a ban for one, two, five, or ten years or a permanent ban for the most serious violations; financial penalties range from $500 to $100,000 per violation, up to a maximum of $1 million over one year, per employer. Penalized employers will be named on ESDC's list of employers who have broken the rules of the TFWP. Furthermore, any pending applications will be denied and any previous LMIAs will be revoked.[34]

To contrast the roles of ESDC and CIC, consider this scenario:

> Kevin, a British national, is a specialized programmer of tool and die machines. He received a job offer under the TFWP from a Canadian company that is looking to fill a labour shortage in its workforce. The company has submitted an application to ESDC. In its application, the company has documented the labour shortage in Canada and described its employment offer, which is consistent with Canadian standards and wage rates. In addition, the company has argued that the recruitment of a foreign worker will result in the transfer of new skills and knowledge to the Canadian market and labour force, which will enable it to hire and train additional Canadian workers.
>
> Kevin is criminally inadmissible to Canada, because he was convicted of a crime two days after the employer submitted the application to ESDC.
>
> Will ESDC refuse the employer's application if the foreign worker is inadmissible?

This case scenario considers the two-step process in hiring a foreign national. First, the employer's application to ESDC will most likely be approved, provided that the employment contract meets all the LMIA requirements. Kevin would include the employment contract and the positive LMIA with his application for a work permit.

However, in assessing Kevin as a temporary foreign worker to Canada, the visa officer would find Kevin to be inadmissible on criminal grounds; consequently, CIC would refuse Kevin's application for a work permit. It is important to understand that

---

34   Employment and Social Development Canada, Web Highlight, "New Consequences for Employers That Break the Rules" (6 July 2015), online: <http://www.esdc.gc.ca/eng/jobs/foreign_workers/reform/highlights.shtml#consq>.

ESDC's role is to review the job's proposed wages and working conditions, the availability of Canadians or permanent residents to do the work in question, the skills and knowledge transfer, and the job creation for the benefit of Canadians or permanent residents that may result from confirming the employment of a foreign worker. Assessing an applicant's inadmissibility is outside the scope of ESDC's official duties.

When No Labour Market Impact Assessment Is Required

The International Mobility Program, including programs created under international agreements, exempts employers from obtaining an LMIA as prescribed in section 204 of the IRPR as follows:

(a) an international agreement between Canada and one or more countries, other than an agreement concerning seasonal agricultural workers;

(b) an agreement entered into by one or more countries and by or on behalf of one or more provinces; or

(c) an agreement entered into by the Minister with a province or group of provinces under subsection 8(1) of the Act.

Work permits may also be issued pursuant to section 205 of the IRPR with a view to satisfying Canadian interests when the work

- would create or maintain significant social, cultural, or economic benefits or opportunities for Canadian citizens or permanent residents;

- would create or maintain reciprocal employment of Canadian citizens or permanent residents of Canada in other countries;

- is designated by the minister as being work that is related to a research program, or is an essential part of a post-secondary academic, vocational, or professional training program offered by a DLI or a program at the secondary level, or is necessary for reasons of public policy relating to the competitiveness of Canada's academic institutions or economy; or

- is of a religious or charitable nature.

Although exempt from obtaining an LMIA, if the foreign national requires an employer-specific work permit, the employer must submit an Offer of Employment to a Foreign National Exempt from a Labour Market Impact Assessment (IMM 5802) to provide information about the business, and pay the employer compliance fee (currently $230) to CIC.

Foreign Workers' Rights

Regrettably, there have been instances where human traffickers exploit foreign workers by enticing them with false promises of work and permanent immigration, and with exaggerated wages and living conditions. Human trafficking operations include recruiting, transporting, harbouring, and controlling foreign nationals in other ways. It is important that foreign nationals understand their rights so that they are not exploited or abused.

> **WEBLINK**
>
> **Information Sources on Foreign Workers' Rights**
>
> "Understand Your Rights—Foreign Workers" is currently available at <www.cic.gc.ca/english/work/tfw-rights.asp>. This web page contains links to federal, provincial, and territorial employment standards and information on eligibility for employment insurance.

As discussed in Chapter 3, in the box entitled "Human Smuggling and Human Trafficking," exploitation occurs when a person induces another to provide labour or a service (for example, sexual services, any kind of work including drug trafficking, or begging) by engaging in conduct that could reasonably be expected to cause the victim to believe that her safety, or the safety of someone known to her, would be threatened if she did not provide that labour or service.[35]

Employers are not allowed to:

- prevent the foreign worker from leaving the work site after work;
- remove a passport or work permit;
- abuse the worker physically, sexually, or psychologically;
- threaten the foreign worker by saying that something bad will happen to the worker or a family member if the worker does not comply with a demand; or
- coach the worker into misleading CIC and/or other Canadian authorities.

Criteria for a Work Permit

Generally, a foreign national seeking to work in Canada is required to comply with a three-tiered process involving ESDC, CIC, and the CBSA, as follows, in this order:

1. the employer must undergo an employer compliance review and obtain a positive LMIA from ESDC/Service Canada;
2. the foreign national must apply for and obtain a work permit (and temporary visa, if applicable) from a visa officer; and
3. the foreign national must enter Canada only after an examination by a CBSA officer at the port of entry.

Applying for a Work Permit

The criteria used to determine eligibility for a work permit are based mainly on the same factors discussed earlier, which are applicable to all temporary residents—namely, intention to leave Canada at the end of the authorized temporary stay; possession of a passport; compliance with the medical examination requirements (IRPR, s 30); and not being inadmissible. In addition, under section 200 of the IRPR, the foreign national must satisfy a number of specific requirements related to the worker class, which include but are not limited to the following:

- a genuine offer to work in Canada from a Canadian employer (the criteria for a genuine offer are set out in section 200(5));
- approval of the employment offer by ESDC (unless exempt); and
- compliance with the requirements of the job in Canada, such as education, training, and experience.

---

35   Department of Justice, "What Is Human Trafficking?" (7 January 2015), online: <http://canada2 .justice.gc.ca/eng/cj-jp/tp/what-quoi.html>.

Process for Obtaining a Work Permit—Foreign National

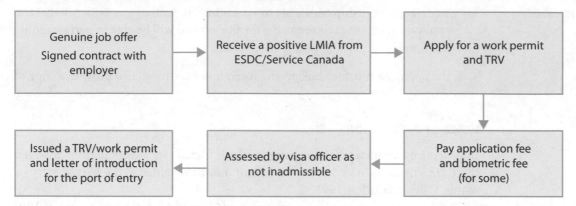

The applicant must satisfy the officer that she will be able to perform the work that is offered in the employment contract, including that she will be able to perform the work in English or French (IRPR, s 200(3)(a)).

Generally, to be eligible for a work permit, a temporary foreign worker must show that she has access to sufficient funds to cover her living expenses. Exceptions include refugee claimants subject to an unenforceable removal order; students who have become temporarily destitute; and temporary resident permit holders, as long as their permits are valid for at least six months (IRPR, s 200).

It is important to note that a work permit does not guarantee admission to Canada. The temporary foreign worker must meet the requirements for issuance of the work permit at the time the visa is issued, and must continue to meet these requirements at the time of arrival at the port of entry where the examination by a CBSA officer takes place (IRPR, s 180). Therefore, a temporary foreign worker may be refused at the port of entry if she does not comply with the requirements for issuance of the work permit (for example, if she is inadmissible on the ground of criminality), regardless of whether she has obtained a genuine job offer.

Workers are prohibited from accepting job offers from certain employers, such as

- employers in the adult entertainment industry, such as striptease, erotic dance, escort services, or erotic massages (IRPR, s 183(1)(b.1)); and
- employers whose names appear on a government list for failing to comply with conditions of employment (IRPR, ss 183(1)(b.2), 209.91(3)).

APPLICATION FORMS

In addition to the documents required to support any TRV application, an applicant must provide documents and forms specifically relevant to the worker class, including the following:

- an Application for Work Permit Made Outside Canada (IMM 1295);
- an employment contract from the prospective employer that is signed by both parties;
- a copy of the ESDC LMIA, unless the occupation or category is exempt; and

- background documents showing qualifications and experience (for example, trade/apprenticeship certificate or education credentials), as evidence that the applicant meets the requirements for the job and will be able to perform the work sought.

If the application is for Quebec, the foreign worker must also provide a copy of the CAQ.

PLACE OF APPLICATION

In general, a foreign worker must apply outside Canada for a work permit; however, there are situations in which a work permit may be obtained at the port of entry or within Canada (IRPR, s 199).

The following persons must apply *outside* Canada for a work permit (IRPR, s 198(2)):

- all persons who require a TRV;
- seasonal agricultural workers;
- live-in caregivers;
- all persons who require a medical examination, unless valid medical examination results are available at the time of entry; and
- international youth exchange program participants other than US citizens or US permanent residents, unless approved by the visa office that administers the quota granted by the DFATD abroad (CEC exemption code C21).[36]

Unless they are identified in the list of persons above who must apply outside Canada, the following persons may apply at a port of entry and have their work permit processed there (IRPR, s 198(1)):

- all nationals or permanent residents of the United States, and residents of Greenland and St. Pierre and Miquelon (contiguous territories);
- persons who are exempt from the requirement for a TRV and whose job falls within the International Mobility Program (no LMIA required);
- persons who are exempt from the requirement for a TRV, whose job falls within the TFWP (LMIA required), and who have been issued a positive LMIA by the time they arrive; and
- persons whose work permits expired while they were outside Canada, if they are otherwise eligible to apply at the port of entry pursuant to section 198 of the IRPR.[37]

---

36 Citizenship and Immigration Canada, "Temporary Foreign Worker Program and International Mobility Program: Applying at a Visa Office Before Entry" (15 September 2014), online: <http://www.cic.gc.ca/english/resources/tools/temp/work/apply.asp>.

37 Citizenship and Immigration Canada, "Temporary Foreign Worker Program and International Mobility Program: Persons Who May Apply at a Port of Entry" (16 December 2014), online: <http://www.cic.gc.ca/english/resources/tools/temp/work/port.asp>.

In addition, the following persons are eligible to apply for a work permit *within* Canada (IRPR, s 199):

- holders of valid work or study permits, and their family members;
- persons, other than business visitors, who may work in Canada without a work permit under section 186 of the IRPR, and their family members;
- students applying for postgraduate work permits;
- holders of temporary resident permits that are valid for a minimum of six months, and their family members;
- refugee claimants and persons subject to an unenforceable removal order;
- in-Canada applicants and their family members who are deemed eligible for permanent resident status (which includes live-in caregivers, spouses, and common law partners; protected persons; and persons who qualify on humanitarian and compassionate grounds);
- persons whose work permits were authorized by a visa office abroad, where the permit was not issued at a port of entry;
- Mexican citizens admitted to Canada as temporary residents, who may apply for a work permit under any NAFTA category; and
- US citizens admitted as visitors, who may apply in Canada under the professional or intra-company transferee NAFTA categories only.[38]

A foreign worker may be accompanied by a spouse or common law partner and dependent children. The family members must complete separate applications, and must be named and included either as accompanying or non-accompanying family members in the foreign worker's application. However, in the event that accompanying family members want to work in Canada, they must apply for separate work permits and must meet the same standards, including having an LMIA, if applicable. They may, however, benefit from applying for their work permit from within Canada because they will be able to meet potential employers and attend interviews in person.

Work Permit Conditions

Generally, a work permit is issued based on a specific position with a specific employer, and is subject to one or more of the following conditions:

- type of employment in which the foreign worker may work,
- employer for whom the foreign worker may work,
- location where the foreign worker may work, and
- length of time the foreign worker may work.

---

38 Citizenship and Immigration Canada, "Temporary Foreign Worker Program and International Mobility Program: Persons Who May Apply from Within Canada" (16 September 2014), online: <http://www.cic.gc.ca/english/resources/tools/temp/work/inland.asp>.

In the event that the foreign worker seeks to engage in work with a different employer, a new LMIA will be required, unless the occupation is ESDC-exempt (IRPR, s 52(1)). This is in addition to the requirement to obtain a new work permit.

Work Permit Extensions

A work permit becomes invalid when it expires or when a removal order that is made against the permit holder becomes enforceable (IRPR, s 209). As with TRVs (as described in Chapter 4), a foreign worker may apply for an extension of a work permit. The foreign worker must, however, comply with the following conditions:

- the renewal application must be made before the expiry of the current TRV and/or work permit (processing time guidelines suggest that the foreign worker should apply for a renewal at least 30 days before the expiry date); and
- the foreign worker has complied with all conditions imposed on entry into Canada.

It is important to note that the regulations allow a foreign worker to continue working in Canada under the conditions of an expired work permit if the following conditions are met:

- the renewal application was made before the original work permit expired;
- the foreign worker has remained in Canada since the expiry of the work permit; and
- the foreign worker continues to comply with the conditions, other than the expiry date, set out in the expired work permit (IRPR, ss 185(5), 186(u)).

If the foreign worker's permit expires before a decision is made, the worker is considered to have implied status as a temporary resident during that period.

APPENDIX A

National Occupational Classification

The National Occupation Classification (NOC) was developed by Human Resources and Social Development Canada (HRSDC) in partnership with Statistics Canada and is used by a variety of technicians, from economists and business analysts to career counsellors. It is a standardized system that provides formal definitions for more than 40,000 job titles in 500 occupational group descriptions. Each occupation is coded according to the type and level of skill required to perform the work. It is a tool for understanding the world of work by describing duties, skills, interests, aptitudes, educational requirements, and work settings, and it provides consistency and information about the education credentials, training, and job duties for an occupation. The NOC 2011 is used by CIC to differentiate among occupations and skill levels, and the NOC 2006 is still occasionally used by ESDC.

The NOC is organized in a matrix format to show the relationship between skill types and skill levels. There are nine skill types (coded as 1 through 9) that are listed across the top of the matrix; a tenth skill type (coded as 0) occupies the first row of the matrix. There are four skill levels (A through D) that appear on the left side of the matrix. To demonstrate how the NOC is organized, an outline of the matrix is shown below with only the skill types and skill levels included. The complete matrix is available on the NOC website.

> **WEBLINK**
>
> To view the complete NOC matrix online, including the list of occupations in each major group, visit the NOC website at <www5.hrsdc.gc.ca/NOC/English/NOC/2011/Welcome.aspx>.

NOC Matrix

	1 Business, Finance and Administration Occupations	2 Natural and Applied Sciences and Related Occupations	3 Health Occupations	4 Occupations in Education, Law and Social, Community and Government Services	5 Occupations in Art, Culture, Recreation and Sport	6 Sales and Service Occupations	7 Trades, Transport and Equipment Operators and Related Occupations	8 Natural Resources, Agriculture and Related Production Occupations	9 Occupations in Manufacturing and Utilities
0 Management Occupations (Skill Level A)									
Skill Level A									
Skill Level B									
Skill Level C									
Skill Level D									

Source: <http://www5.hrsdc.gc.ca/NOC/English/NOC/2011/Matrix.aspx>.

Higher-skilled occupations are classified as skill type 0, skill level A, and skill level B; lower-skilled occupations are classified as skill levels C and D. In addition, note the following with respect to skill types and levels:

- skill type 0 occupations require a relevant university degree, professional designation, college diploma, or other management training, and proven management experience;
- skill level A occupations require university education;
- skill level B occupations require college/technical school education or apprenticeship training;
- skill level C occupations require high school/on-the-job training; and
- skill level D occupations require short demonstration training.

APPENDIX B

The following table provides a reference list of important definitions and topics that relate to temporary entry to Canada.

Reference for Temporary Entry to Canada

Provision	IRPA and IRPR
Obligations—work, study	IRPA, s 30
Definition of "work"	IRPR, s 2
Employer requirements, offences	IRPA, ss 124, 125, 126; IRPR, ss 203(15), 209.1–209.92
Students—no permit	IRPR, ss 188, 189
Students: applications, permits, restrictions	IRPR, ss 210–222
Worker class	IRPR, ss 194–209
Workers—no permit	IRPR, ss 186, 187

KEY TERMS

business visitor, 152

Caregiver Program, 140

designated learning institution (DLI), 124

GATS professional, 158

high-wage positions, 140

intra-company transfer, 154

labour market impact assessment (LMIA), 135

letter of acceptance, 126

letter of introduction, 131

low-wage positions, 140

open work permit, 134

parallel processing, 149

primary agricultural stream, 140

professional, 152

Seasonal Agricultural Worker Program (SAWP), 150

significant benefit, 151

temporary foreign worker (TFW), 137

work, 137

work permit, 137

REVIEW QUESTIONS

1. Describe the main document that a person must submit in order to obtain a student visa.

2. What is a work permit, and what types of restrictions may it set out?

3. Some business visitors may enter Canada more easily under the provisions of trade agreements with Canada. Name two such agreements.

4. What is the maximum allowable cumulative time that a temporary foreign worker can work in Canada?

5. What is a positive LMIA and which department is responsible for its issuance?

CASE STUDY

Ikwo, a citizen of Nigeria, has been offered admission to the 24-month full-time MSc program in computer science offered at University of Ontario Institute of Technology (UOIT), a designated learning institution.

Ikwo's husband, Bako, and 3-year old son, Aren, wish to accompany her to Canada.

1. Does Ikwo need to apply for a TRV, a study permit, or both?

2. Are Bako and Aren allowed to accompany Ikwo? What requirement(s) must they meet?

3. Do Ikwo, Bako, and Aren need to provide biometric information? What about a medical examination? Explain.

4. Find the DLI number for UOIT on the CIC website.

5. What key documents must Ikwo include in her application for a study permit?

6. What would you advise Ikwo to do if she decides to continue her MSc studies at another university?

7. If Aren and Bako wish to go to school, do they need study permits to accompany Ikwo to Canada? Explain.

8. After completing her master's degree program, Ikwo would like to work in Canada. Would she qualify for an open work permit under the PGWPP? Explain.

9. With respect to applying for a postgraduate work permit, what timelines must Ikwo observe and what must she include in her application?

PART III

Permanent Immigration Programs

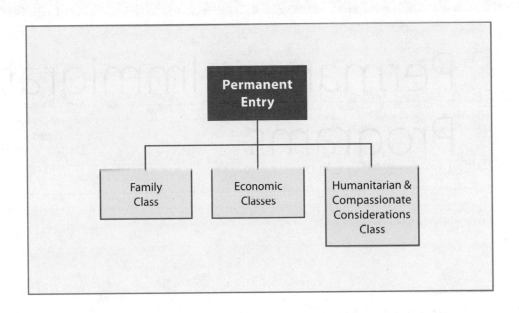

Permanent Entry: General

6

LEARNING OUTCOMES

After reading this chapter, you should be able to:

- Describe the general provisions for applying for permanent residence.

- Understand the general rights and obligations of permanent residents.

- Describe how individuals can lose their permanent resident status.

Introduction

Immigration to Canada must be beneficial to Canada. In the *2011 Annual Report to Parliament on Immigration*, the minister of citizenship and immigration reminded us that Canada is a country built by immigrants.[1] While our aging population and low birth rate mean that Canada must continue to look to immigration to fill our labour shortages, the government develops policies that favour those with certain work experience and language abilities. Moreover, because other countries are experiencing similar challenges, Canada must remain competitive in the global marketplace in order to attract workers with the right skill sets to contribute significantly to our economy.

Canada's permanent immigration policy is founded on three pillars:

- *Family reunification pillar*: policies that facilitate family reunification by permitting close family members (for example, spouses and dependent children) to immigrate with the principal applicant or to be sponsored (*Immigration and Refugee Protection Act* [IRPA], s 12(1));

- *Economic pillar*: policies that select highly skilled and experienced people who will contribute to the economic life of the country and fill labour market needs (IRPA, s 12(2)); and

- *Refugee and humanitarian and compassionate considerations pillar*: policies that aim to protect refugees and persons in refugee-like situations by fulfilling Canada's obligations as signatory to international conventions (for example, the *Convention Relating to the Status of Refugees* and the *Convention Against Torture and Other Cruel, Inhuman or Degrading Treatment or Punishment*) through an in-Canada refugee determination system and overseas programs for resettlement (IRPA, s 12(3)).

Since the 1990s, target ranges for permanent immigration have held steady at around 250,000 newcomers; however, in 2014, the minister announced an increase in the target range of 260,000 to 285,000 immigrants.[2] In the 21st century, governments have reshaped immigration policy by shifting away from the traditional pillar of family reunification toward the economic pillar, with an emphasis on the selection of the most suitable immigrants who will be able to meet immediate labour market needs—immigrants who are well educated, have some fluency in English or French or both, and are highly skilled or have business acumen. In 2013, roughly 57 percent of new permanent residents were in the economic category, compared with 32 percent in the family reunification category and just over 11 percent in the refugee and humanitarian categories.[3]

---

1   Citizenship and Immigration Canada, *2011 Annual Report to Parliament on Immigration* (Ottawa: CIC, 2011), online: <http://www.cic.gc.ca/english/pdf/pub/annual-report-2011.pdf>.

2   Citizenship and Immigration Canada, *2014 Annual Report to Parliament on Immigration* (Ottawa: CIC, 2014), online: <http://www.cic.gc.ca/english/resources/publications/annual-report-2014/index.asp>.

3   *Ibid*.

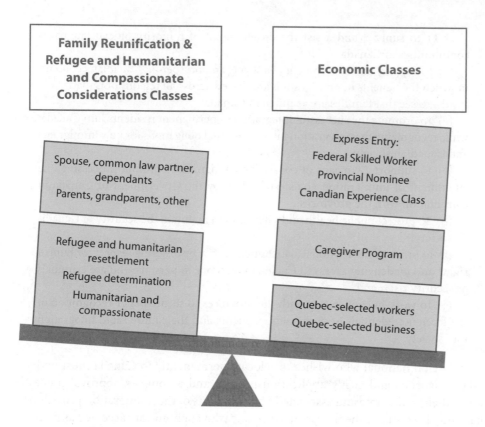

The management of immigration programs includes balancing the need to attract newcomers with the need to protect Canadians by denying access to people who pose a health, criminal, or security threat. In studying the various immigration programs, you will find examples of this balancing act. On the one hand are programs designed to attract newcomers who can contribute to Canada's population and economic growth, while on the other hand are overriding restrictions that deny access to certain individuals. The minister's power to manage permanent immigration programs was strengthened under the 2012 omnibus budget bill, the *Jobs, Growth and Long-term Prosperity Act* (Bill C-38), which included amendments to the IRPA. The amendments give the minister of CIC the power to issue instructions regarding the processing of permanent resident applications, including replacing the first-come, first-served system of application processing. This power potentially limits the number of applications to be processed, prioritizes the processing of applications of workers in certain occupations, and caps the number of applications accepted in certain categories.

The goals of permanent immigration are reflected in the following objectives in section 3(1) of the IRPA as follows:

(a) to permit Canada to pursue the maximum social, cultural and economic benefits of immigration;

(b) to enrich and strengthen the social and cultural fabric of Canadian society, while respecting the federal, bilingual and multicultural character of Canada;

(b.1) to support and assist the development of minority official languages communities in Canada;

(c) to support the development of a strong and prosperous Canadian economy, in which the benefits of immigration are shared across all regions of Canada;

(d) to see that families are reunited in Canada;

(e) to promote the successful integration of permanent residents into Canada, while recognizing that integration involves mutual obligations for new immigrants and Canadian society;

(f) to support, by means of consistent standards and prompt processing, the attainment of immigration goals established by the Government of Canada in consultation with the provinces;

(h) to protect public health and safety and to maintain the security of Canadian society;

(i) to promote international justice and security by fostering respect for human rights and by denying access to Canadian territory to persons who are criminals or security risks; and

(j) to work in cooperation with the provinces to secure better recognition of the foreign credentials of permanent residents and their more rapid integration into society.

A foreign national who wishes to relocate permanently to Canada must undertake a rigorous and costly application process and a complex approval process. Nevertheless, the time and associated financial costs of the immigration procedures have not discouraged the thousands of people who apply and are accepted as permanent residents each year.

Acquiring Canadian permanent resident status brings a foreign national a step closer to becoming a Canadian citizen. This chapter explores the general requirements and rules of eligibility that apply to all permanent resident applicants.

General Provisions

permanent resident
a person who has been granted permanent resident status in Canada and who has not subsequently lost that status under IRPA section 46; also known as a "landed immigrant" under older legislation

A foreign national who comes to Canada to live here permanently is a permanent resident. With the enactment of the IRPA in 2002, the term **permanent resident** came into use, replacing the former term, "landed immigrant." Both terms carry the same meaning. The IRPA distinguishes between permanent residents and temporary residents, including in the different rules for obtaining permanent status. After obtaining permanent status, a permanent resident has more rights than a temporary resident, but fewer rights than a Canadian citizen. The rights of permanent residents to enter and remain in Canada are solely determined by the IRPA and the *Immigration and Refugee Protection Regulations* (IRPR), which means that, under certain conditions, it is possible for a permanent resident to lose that status and be forced to leave Canada.

permanent resident status
status that permits the holder to enjoy most of the same rights guaranteed to Canadians under the *Canadian Charter of Rights and Freedoms*

Permanent Resident Visas

Before applying for Canadian citizenship, a foreign national must first obtain **permanent resident status**. A person with permanent resident status enjoys most of the same rights that Canadian citizens are guaranteed under the *Canadian Charter of Rights and Freedoms*, such as the right to live, work, and study in Canada, and must fulfill the corresponding obligations to pay taxes and respect Canadian laws. However, a permanent resident may not run for political office and may not vote: these privileges are reserved for citizens. Furthermore, although section 27 of the IRPA gives permanent residents the right to enter and remain in Canada, they must comply with statutory requirements or risk having their "permanent" status revoked, the consequence of which generally leads to their removal from Canada.

Application Made Outside Canada

For example, sponsorship of spouse, common law partner, dependent children, or family class members; economic classes; and resettled protected persons

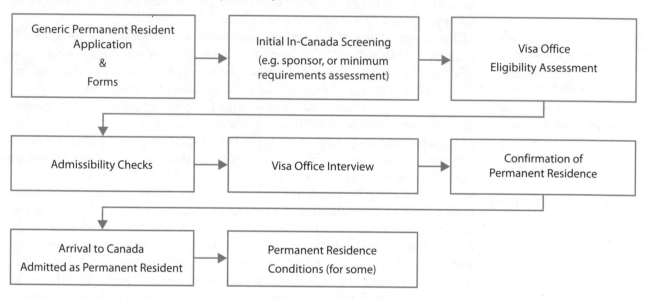

Application Made Within Canada

For example, sponsorship of spouse, common law partner, or dependent children; caregivers; and protected temporary residents (IRPR, s 72(2))

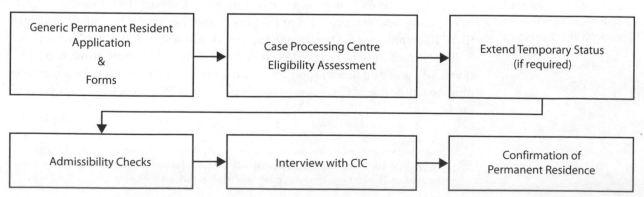

permanent resident visa
a document that allows a foreign national to travel to Canada and, after a successful examination at a port of entry, to enter Canada as a permanent resident

Under section 6 of the IRPR, all foreign nationals who wish to make Canada their permanent home must apply for and obtain a **permanent resident visa**. To obtain the visa, a foreign national must submit an application under a specific immigration program in one of three classes of permanent residence (IRPR, s 70(2)).

The regulations also require that all applications for permanent residence be made in writing; this is done by using the form provided by CIC (IRPR, s 10). Applications are available on the CIC website and must be completed by the principal applicant and include all information about her dependants. Forms can be filled out online and saved for future completion. There are forms common to all permanent residence applications, such as the Generic Application Form for Canada (IMM 0008), as well as forms related to each class of immigration.

The regulations also stipulate that counsel (anyone who assists with the application and who charges a fee for services) must provide their contact information in the application (IRPR, s 10(2); see also Chapter 16).

visa officer
a public servant working in a Canadian consulate or visa office abroad

The foreign national's application is assessed by a **visa officer** if the application is made outside Canada, or by an immigration official in Canada if the application is made within Canada. The officer assesses the application against eligibility and inadmissibility criteria, and then may issue the permanent resident visa.

confirmation of permanent residence (COPR)
a document that allows a foreign national to travel to Canada to seek entry as a permanent resident

The permanent resident visa is in the form of a document called the **confirmation of permanent residence (COPR)**, which allows the foreign national to travel to Canada to seek entry as a permanent resident. On arrival at the port of entry, the foreign national is examined by an officer who decides whether to admit her as a permanent resident. Generally, the officer examines the foreign national to confirm her intention to establish permanent residence in Canada, and to confirm that there is nothing new in her application since the time it was submitted, such as an invalid medical examination or expired permanent resident visa, that would make her or her family members inadmissible (IRPR, s 70(1)). Foreign nationals who apply from within Canada must appear for an interview with an immigration officer. Permanent resident status is acquired on the date of the foreign national's admission to Canada as a permanent resident. (Some still call this the "landing date," in reference to the former landed immigrant status.)

Permanent Resident Card

permanent resident card (PR card)
a card issued to permanent residents after their arrival in Canada showing proof of immigration status

Once in Canada, a permanent resident uses the **permanent resident card (PR card)** (see the figure below)[4] to show proof of immigration status. The PR card is a wallet-sized plastic card that is mailed to the person after her arrival in Canada, provided that CIC is informed of the person's correct address within 180 days of her arrival.

The PR card must be renewed every five years. The CIC website provides instructions and a guide on how to apply for a renewal or replacement card. The application must be sent to one of CIC's case processing centres (CPCs), together with a processing fee.

---

4 Under the former *Immigration Act* of 1976, permanent residents, known as "landed immigrants," held an IMM 1000 document in their passports as proof of status. A person who landed before June 2002 and under the former Act must now apply to CIC for a PR card.

The PR card is considered to be property of the Crown (IRPR, s 53(2)) and can be revoked if any of the following events occur (ss 59(2), 60):

Permanent Resident Card

- a new card is issued;
- the permanent resident becomes a Canadian citizen or otherwise loses permanent resident status;
- the PR card is lost, stolen, or destroyed; or
- the permanent resident dies.

Generally, a permanent resident may apply for citizenship after accumulating four years of residence in Canada. This process is fully explored in Chapter 10, Citizenship.

Source: *Confirmation of Permanent Residence*. Reproduced with permission of Citizenship and Immigration Canada.

Fees

There are a number of expenses associated with an application for permanent residence, including two fees payable to CIC:

1. *An application fee related to the specific class of permanent residence.* These fees are charged to cover the cost of assessing applications; they are non-refundable and subject to change.

2. *The right of permanent residence fee (RPRF).* This fee must be paid before a permanent resident visa is issued. The RPRF must be paid for the principal applicant and other family members. Dependent children are exempt from paying this fee. The fee is also subject to change—for example, the fee was set at $975 for a number of years before being reduced to $490 in 2006.

Because fees are subject to change, check the following sections of the IRPR for current fees: sections 295 and 301 (permanent resident fees), section 303 (RPRF), and section 308 (fees for the PR card). The CIC website also provides a current schedule of fees, as well as the list of fees contained within the instruction guides as part of application packages.

Note too that there are many expenses associated with moving permanently to Canada, and these can add up. Applicants are responsible for all fees related to having their documents translated, obtaining test results (biometric, medical, language, police checks, etc.), hiring counsel to assist with their application, moving, and travel costs. Moreover, applicants put their lives on hold while awaiting a decision from CIC. This was never more apparent than when, in 2012, with the enactment of the *Jobs, Growth and Long-term Prosperity Act*, the government terminated applications under the Federal Skilled Worker Program for anyone who applied before February 27, 2008 and had not had a decision by CIC by March 29, 2012. The new law affected roughly 100,000 applications representing 280,000 people, including dependants. Although the government agreed to return fees paid to CIC, it is not difficult to imagine how upsetting it was for applicants who had been waiting years for a decision to learn—without notice—that the government had decided arbitrarily to terminate the processing of their applications.

Loss of Permanent Resident Status

Unlike citizenship, permanent residence is technically not "permanent," because a person can lose this status. Section 2(1) of the IRPA defines a permanent resident as a person who has acquired permanent resident status and has not subsequently lost it under section 46.

Section 46 sets out the following five ways in which persons may lose their permanent resident status, other than by voluntarily renouncing it:

1. if they become Canadian citizens;
2. if they fail to comply with the residency obligations under section 28 of the IRPA;
3. if a removal order made against them comes into force;
4. if a final determination is made that they are not refugees or not entitled to protection; or
5. if the permanent resident voluntarily renounces permanent residence.

Each of these situations is discussed in more detail below.

1. Becoming a Canadian Citizen

A person who becomes a Canadian citizen is no longer a permanent resident. Citizenship includes all the rights of permanent residence, plus additional rights and obligations. Chapter 10 explains in detail the process for becoming a Canadian citizen; generally, a permanent resident must be a resident of Canada for at least four years (1,460 days) in the past six years (2,190 days). (For information on calculating days, see the box below.)

2. Residency Obligations

A person can lose permanent resident status by failing to fulfill residency obligations. Although a permanent resident is not required to spend all of his time in Canada, generally he must physically reside here for 730 days out of every five years, in accordance with section 28 of the IRPA. The permanent resident must satisfy an immigration officer that any absence from Canada was temporary. To show compliance with the residency obligation, a permanent resident can provide supporting documentation, including proof of employment, proof of attendance at school, banking activity, financial records and statements, receipt of government benefits, records of personal services, community involvement, and memberships.[5]

---

5   Citizenship and Immigration Canada, *OP 10: Permanent Residency Status Determination* (23 January 2015), online: <http://www.cic.gc.ca/ENGLISH/resources/manuals/op/op10-eng.pdf>.

There are some exceptions to the residency obligation where, in certain circumstances, time outside Canada may be counted as equivalent to days in Canada (IRPA, s 28(2)(a)). These circumstances exist where a permanent resident resides as follows:

- outside Canada while accompanying a Canadian citizen who is his spouse or common law partner or, in the case of a child, his parent;
- outside Canada while employed on a full-time basis by a Canadian business or in the federal public administration or the public service of a province; or
- outside Canada while accompanying a permanent resident who is his spouse or common law partner or, in the case of a child, his parent and who is employed on a full-time basis by a Canadian business or in the federal public administration or the public service of a province.

A person who loses permanent resident status due to failure to meet residency obligations (IRPA, s 46(1)(b)) may appeal to the Immigration Appeal Division of the Immigration and Refugee Board (IRB).[6]

Computation of Time

The *Interpretation Act* governs the computation of time in federal statutes. Section 27(2) of the Act states:

> Where there is a reference to a number of days, not expressed to be clear days, between two events, in calculating that number of days the day on which the first event happens is excluded and the day on which the second event happens is included.

In calculating the number of days required to comply with the residency obligation under section 28(2) of the IRPA, operational manual OP 10 clarifies that a "day" includes a full day or any part of a day that a permanent resident is physically present in Canada.[7]

3. Removal Order

A person who is subject to a removal order as a result of inadmissibility can lose permanent resident status. Generally, an allegation of inadmissibility is reviewed on its merits by an immigration official delegated by the minister of public safety and emergency preparedness, who, according to section 44(2) of the IRPA, decides whether to allow the person to remain in Canada or to refer the case to the Immigration Division of the IRB for a decision on admissibility and removal. The grounds of inadmissibility, such as security and criminality issues, are discussed in detail in Chapter 3; removal hearings are discussed in Chapter 14. A decision made at an admissibility hearing may be appealed to the Immigration Appeal Division (discussed in Chapter 15).

---

6   Section 63(4) of the IRPA reads: "A permanent resident may appeal to the Immigration Appeal Division against a decision made outside of Canada on the residency obligation under section 28."

7   *Supra* note 5, s 6.4 at 16.

4. Final Determination That a Person Is Not a Refugee or Is Not Entitled to Protection

A person who becomes a permanent resident following a determination that she is a Convention refugee or a person in need of protection may lose permanent resident status and be removed from Canada if her refugee claim involved fraud or misrepresentation. Misrepresentation may involve false statements and documents, as well as omissions, such as failing to disclose a relevant fact. In such situations, the minister makes an application to the Refugee Protection Division under section 109 of the IRPA to vacate the original decision because of fraud or misrepresentation. An application to vacate a decision is a request to the division to "do away with" the original decision to grant protection. The division, on a final determination, may decide to vacate the original decision for refugee protection, which consequently also leads to the loss of the person's permanent resident status.

5. Renounce Permanent Residence

A person can apply (Application to Voluntarily Renounce Permanent Resident Status, IMM 5782) to renounce his permanent residence as long as he is a citizen of another country or has legal permanent resident status in another country. A person who is under the age of 18 must have his legal guardians consent to the renunciation in writing (IRPR, s 72.6). A separate application must be made for each family member who would like to renounce their permanent resident status (IRPR, s 72.5). There is no processing fee to apply to renounce permanent residence.

CIC provides a list of reasons why an applicant may wish to voluntarily renounce his permanent residence:

- he wants to accept a diplomatic or official position with a foreign government;
- he wants to obtain citizenship or permanent resident status in another country, and that country requires the Canadian permanent resident to renounce permanent resident status in Canada;
- he no longer meets the residency obligations because he has been outside Canada for a long period of time; or
- he no longer wants to live in Canada permanently.

When an officer approves the application to renounce permanent resident status, the applicant becomes a temporary resident for a period of six months, unless he makes an application to renounce his permanent resident status at a port of entry or is not physically present in Canada on the day on which his application is approved.

Canada–Quebec Accord

Under the Canada–Quebec Accord, Quebec has the sole responsibility for the selection of permanent residents and refugees outside Canada who wish to settle there. Immigrants destined to live in Quebec must first apply to that province and meet Quebec's selection criteria. Applications from individuals who successfully meet the province's eligibility criteria are then forwarded to CIC, which tests for inadmissibility on each of the grounds that are applied to all immigrants across the country. This way, the responsibility for immigration remains with the federal government for the administrative function of processing applications and physical admission to Canada at ports of entry.

Decisions on Permanent Resident Applications

Permanent resident applications are decided by visa officers. They assess the applicant's eligibility—whether the applicant meets the requirements of the class under which he applied—and admissibility. Officers base their decision on the information provided in the application package (application form, schedules, etc.) and supporting documentation to verify, for example, the applicant's identity, the relationship to any family members listed in the application, whether they are accompanying the applicant or not, and whether the passport or travel documents are valid.

Visa officers review the application to ensure that the selection criteria are met, and that the applicant and family members are not inadmissible. If the visa officer determines that the application should be refused on the basis of the eligibility criteria, the officer issues a refusal letter with the reasons for refusal.

If the applicant meets all the requirements and his application is accepted, the visa officer issues a visa permitting the applicant to travel to Canada as a permanent resident, and the COPR. The names of non-accompanying family members are also included on the visa of the principal applicant. The principal applicant and all accompanying family members must travel before the expiry date on their visas.

Upon arrival at the port of entry, the principal applicant and all accompanying family members must present their permanent residence visas to an officer and are subject to examination. The applicant must also present two copies of a list of all personal and household items that she is bringing into the country now, and the value of each item, and two copies of a list of all items that will be arriving later, and the value of each item.

Generally, the officer counsels the new permanent residents about their rights and responsibilities as permanent residents, advises them about obtaining provincial health insurance and social insurance numbers, and officially welcomes them to Canada.

Applicants who already reside legally in Canada, such as temporary residents with legal work authorizations, are able to apply for permanent residence from within Canada. In such cases, an immigration officer in Canada assesses their application, and directs them to present themselves to a CIC location to finalize processing as permanent residents.

KEY TERMS

confirmation of permanent residence (COPR), 184

permanent resident, 182

permanent resident card (PR card), 184

permanent resident status, 182

permanent resident visa, 184

visa officer, 184

REVIEW QUESTIONS

1. Identify the three pillars of immigration and match each to the objectives set out in section 3 of the IRPA.

2. Permanent residence is not really permanent. Identify the four ways in which a permanent resident may lose his status.

3. What is a COPR?

CASE STUDY

Major Charles Brossard, a Canadian citizen, is a senior officer in the Royal Canadian Air Force. He met Selma while on a tour of duty in Asia. Charles married Selma and then sponsored her as his spouse so that she could live with him in Canada. Selma only recently obtained her permanent resident status and has been in Canada for only six months (183 days). Charles has just received an assignment to work in Casteau, Belgium for the next three years and will be moving there in one month. Should Selma be concerned about losing her permanent resident status when she moves to Belgium with Charles?

Family Class

7

LEARNING OUTCOMES

After reading this chapter, you should be able to:

- Describe who is eligible to be sponsored.

- Describe the general provisions for applying as a sponsor.

- Describe the application requirements for a permanent resident applicant under the family class.

- Understand the mutual rights and obligations that accompany an undertaking.

- Calculate the duration period of an undertaking.

- Calculate the minimum LICO necessary for a sponsorship.

- Describe the general requirements for sponsoring parents and grandparents.

- Describe the sponsorship process for adoption.

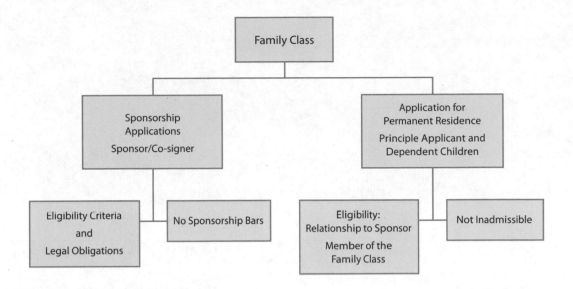

Introduction

The family reunification pillar of immigration facilitates family reunification by permitting Canadian citizens and permanent residents to sponsor close family members (*Immigration and Refugee Protection Act* [IRPA], s 12(2)). Features of the sponsorship program include:

- a modern definition of "family" that includes common law and same-sex partners;
- the ability to sponsor a relative at as young an age as 18;
- a new definition of "dependent child" that includes children under 19 years of age;
- a new sponsorship stream for parents and grandparents;
- a provision for adoption—keeping with the principle of the "best interests of the child"—that leads directly to citizenship for the adoptee;
- the length of a sponsorship requirement, which ranges from 3 to 20 years, depending on the relationship of the foreign national to the sponsor;
- an exemption for spouses and dependent children under 19 from the medical grounds of inadmissibility (for example, those grounds related to a medical condition placing excessive demand on health and social services); and
- no right to appeal in cases where a family member is found inadmissible for reasons of security, human or international rights violations, serious criminality, or organized criminality.

Who May Be Sponsored?

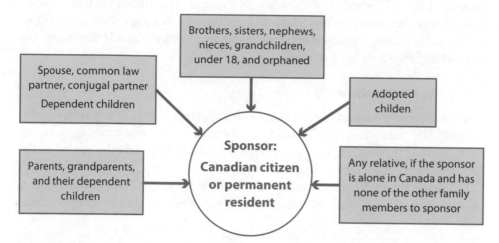

One of the stated objectives of Canadian immigration policy is to facilitate family reunification (IRPA, s 3(1)(d)). Under the family class program, the selection of permanent resident applicants is based on the relationship of applicants to their sponsors, who are either Canadian citizens or Canadian permanent residents. The list of persons who may be sponsored includes the following:

- spouses, common law partners, and conjugal partners;
- dependent children;
- children intended for adoption;
- parents, grandparents, and their dependent children;
- brothers, sisters, nephews, nieces, and grandchildren who are orphaned, who are under 18, and who are not a spouse or common law partner; and
- any relative, if the sponsor is alone in Canada and has none of the above family members to sponsor.

Relationship to the Sponsor

Spousal Relationships

Spousal relationships under the *Immigration and Refugee Protection Regulations* (IRPR) include a married spouse, **common law partner**, and **conjugal partner** (s 117.1). Under previous immigration law, a person could sponsor another person to which he or she was engaged to be married. However, it was difficult to assess whether the engagement would actually result in a marriage. Consequently, when the current IRPA came into force in 2002, this ground for sponsorship was eliminated. If an applicant for permanent residence is engaged to be married, he or she must wait until after the marriage to apply as a spouse, or may apply as a common law partner if the couple has lived together continuously for at least 12 months.

common law partner
also known as a common law spouse; a person who is cohabiting with the person in a conjugal relationship and has done so for at least one year; applicable to both opposite-sex and same-sex relationships (IRPR, s 1)

conjugal partner
in relation to a sponsor, a person outside Canada who has had a binding relationship with the sponsor for at least one year but who could not live with him or her; refers to both opposite-sex and same-sex relationships; not defined in the IRPA or IRPR

Spouses or common law partners in Canada and their dependent children who have legal temporary status in Canada—for example, as a visitor, student, or business worker—are another class who may be sponsored as a prescribed class (IRPR, s 123). An application package for sponsorship from within Canada is available for spouses and common law partners.

CONJUGAL RELATIONSHIPS

The existence of a conjugal relationship is an important feature of any spousal relationship. The term "conjugal" is traditionally used to describe marriage and, for immigration purposes, extends to marriage-like relationships (see the box below for features of a conjugal relationship).

"Conjugal" is not defined in the IRPA or the IRPR; however, CIC provides direction to visa officers in assessing the conjugal nature of a relationship in its operational

---

IN THE NEWS

The Stress of Sponsoring Family

Reunification is a primary goal of family sponsorship, but staying together can be just as difficult and stressful for families who apply from within Canada. Processing times are often longer, and the waiting period can put significant financial strain on families. The *Ottawa Citizen* reported on one family's struggle for reunification. Eduardo Vazquez and his wife, Julie Vazquez, live with their two young children in Ottawa. Eduardo is from Mexico, and Julie is Canadian. The article explains:

> Eduardo applied for permanent residency under the spousal sponsorship program … 10 months before his temporary work permit was going to expire. He studied at Algonquin College and was hoping to keep his job as a chef.

With 10,000 applications on backlog at CIC, applicants have protested that the wait is delaying their ability to find work, obtain health care, and put down roots in Canada. After Eduardo's temporary work permit expired, he was forced to live on the family's savings, but they had only budgeted for him to be out of work for a few months. At the time of the article's writing, it had been nearly a year since Eduardo had been able to work.

CIC responded to petitions to expedite applications by stating that permanent resident applicants are not required to stay in Canada; they may leave Canada and support themselves elsewhere while their applications are processed. Alternatively, CIC said, applicants have the option of applying through the Express Entry program, which processes applications more quickly.

> But Eric Laine, an active petitioner, doesn't agree … :
> "[M]ost inland families have waited for so long, it makes no sense for us to scrap spousal sponsorship and try to legalize status as skilled workers."

While he is waiting, Eduardo has applied to a CIC pilot project that permits some applicants to work temporarily, until their applications are processed, but that application has not been processed yet either. Until then, the family says, they may need to sell their home or move in with Julie's parents.

Consider that family reunification is one of the goals of Canada's immigration process. Does this process facilitate that goal and reflect the objectives of the IRPA? Why or why not?

Source: Emanuela Campanella, "Long Immigration Process 'Tearing Us Apart,' Ottawa Couple Says," *Ottawa Citizen* (23 February 2015), online: <http://ottawacitizen.com/news/local-news/long-immigration-process-tearing-us-apart-ottawa-couple-says>.

manuals. A conjugal relationship must be similar to a marriage-like relationship; the couple should be able to demonstrate that, over time, they have had exclusive and emotional ties to one another and have made a commitment to each other.

CIC's operational manual *OP 2: Processing Members of the Family Class* provides a more detailed examination of the characteristics and assessment of conjugal relationships. Visa officers are directed on how to assess whether a couple may be considered to be in a conjugal relationship. They are also cautioned to assess each case separately, taking into account cultural differences and whether local laws or customs might discourage parties from freely admitting the existence of the relationship. Officers must look beyond the presence of a physical relationship and consider the following features:

- a significant degree of attachment, both physical and emotional;
- a mutual and continuing commitment to a shared life together; and
- emotional and financial interdependency.[1]

In considering conjugal partnerships, visa officers consider

- whether the relationship is monogamous;
- whether the relationship is of some permanence—namely, a minimum duration of one year; and
- whether mutual interdependence exists between the partners.

What follows is a general discussion of each category of spouses who may be sponsored, and some of the particular considerations that apply to establishing the relationship to the sponsor in each case.

Characteristics of All Conjugal Married and Unmarried Relationships

- Mutual commitment to a shared life
- Exclusive—people cannot be in more than one conjugal relationship at a time
- Intimate—commitment to sexual exclusivity
- Interdependent—physically, emotionally, financially, and socially
- Permanent—long-term, genuine, and continuing
- Present themselves as a couple ("Here's my other half!")
- Are regarded by others as a couple
- Care for children together (if there are children)

---

1   Citizenship and Immigration Canada, *OP 2: Processing Members of the Family Class* (Ottawa: CIC, 14 November 2006) [OP 2] s 5.25 at 19–20, online: <http://www.cic.gc.ca/english/resources/manuals/op/op02-eng.pdf>.

SPOUSE

According to section 117(9) of the IRPR, to qualify for sponsorship a spouse must be at least 16 years of age, legally married, and not otherwise married to someone else. A marriage that takes place outside Canada must be legal in the country where it took place and also conform to Canadian law (IRPR, s 2). The onus of proving the marriage's validity rests on the applicant (IRPA, s 16(1)).

A same-sex spouse who is a Canadian citizen or a permanent resident qualifies to be a sponsor, provided that the marriage is legally recognized both in the country where it took place and under Canadian law, and that a marriage certificate was issued by a province or territory as of a certain date. The date varies depending on the province or territory in which the marriage occurred. For example, in Ontario, the marriage certificate must have been issued on or after June 10, 2003, and in British Columbia, on or after July 8, 2003.[2]

Telephone marriages (in which one member of the couple is not physically present but participates by telephone), proxy marriages (in which one member of the couple is not present and has named another person to represent him or her as proxy at the ceremony), and similar marriages in which one or both spouses were not physically present at the ceremony are not legal marriages for immigration purposes; the only exception to this is for Canadian Forces members (IRPR, s 5(c)).

COMMON LAW PARTNER

A common law partner is defined in section 1 of the IRPR as, "in relation to a person, an individual who is cohabiting with the person in a conjugal relationship, having so cohabited for a period of at least one year." Temporary absences aside, in order for the person in the common law relationship to qualify for sponsorship, the year of cohabiting must be a continuous 12-month period; it cannot be intermittent periods that add up to one year.

Common law relationships may be either opposite-sex or same-sex relationships. The relationship must be genuine and not for the purpose of acquiring immigration status. The applicant must have a valid passport or travel document, and must generally satisfy admissibility requirements.

The common law partner must have been separated from any spouse or previous common law partner for at least one year, and must be able to prove this.

One of the key issues that arises in determining whether a relationship meets the common law definition is whether the relationship is conjugal. (See the defining features of a conjugal relationship in the box above.)

Applicants for permanent residence must provide documentation with their application to show that they are known as a couple—that they have combined their

---

2 *Ibid*, s 5.40 at 29. The dates for the other provinces and territories are: Quebec, March 19, 2004; Yukon, July 14, 2004; Manitoba, September 16, 2004; Nova Scotia, September 24, 2004; Saskatchewan, November 5, 2004; Newfoundland and Labrador, December 21, 2004; New Brunswick, July 4, 2005; and all other provinces or territories, July 20, 2005.

affairs and set up their household together. Such documentation could include the following:

- joint bank accounts or credit cards;
- joint ownership of a home;
- joint residential leases;
- joint rental receipts;
- joint utilities (electricity, gas, and telephone);
- joint management of household expenses;
- proof of joint purchases, especially for household items; and
- correspondence addressed to either person or both people at the same address.

CONJUGAL PARTNER

Section 2 of the IRPR defines a "conjugal partner" as, "in relation to a sponsor, a foreign national residing outside Canada who is in a conjugal relationship with the sponsor and has been in that relationship for a period of at least one year." As with the definitions for spouse and common law partners, conjugal partners may be opposite-sex or same-sex partners. The conjugal partner category was created for those who might have applied as common law partners but who did not live together continuously for one year, usually because of legal or social obstacles. These obstacles include the following:

- an immigration barrier, such as where the applicant and/or sponsor were denied long-term stays in each other's countries;
- a person's marital status, such as where one partner is married to someone else and living in a country where divorce is not possible; or
- a person's sexual orientation, where the partners are in a same-sex relationship but same-sex marriage is not permitted in the country of the applicant.

Canadian immigration policy on conjugal partners assumes that if a Canadian and a foreign national could legally marry or could live together and thereby establish a common law relationship, they would have done so before submitting the sponsorship and immigration applications. In other words, this category is considered an exception that applies only when marriage or common law partnership was not an option in the particular circumstances.

Although no legal document (such as a marriage certificate) exists in these cases, the conjugal partners should be able to provide other types of evidence of their significant commitment to each other, such as the following:

- insurance policies or estates showing that they have named each other as beneficiaries,
- documents showing that they hold joint ownership of possessions, and
- documents showing that they hold joint expenses or share income.

EXCLUDED RELATIONSHIPS

An applicant for permanent residence applying as the sponsor's spouse, common law partner, or conjugal partner is excluded as a member of the family class under sections 5 and 117(9) of the IRPR if any of the following circumstances exist:

1. the applicant is under 16 years of age;
2. the sponsor is already sponsoring a spouse, common law partner, or conjugal partner, and the undertaking has not ended;
3. the sponsor is the spouse of another person;
4. the sponsor is a spouse who has lived separate and apart from the applicant for at least one year and either
    a. the sponsor is the common law partner of another person or the conjugal partner of another foreign national, or
    b. the applicant is the common law partner of another person or the conjugal partner of another sponsor; or
5. the applicant was a non-accompanying family member of the sponsor and was not examined when the sponsor previously applied to Canada as a permanent resident.

BAD-FAITH RELATIONSHIPS

The sponsorship of a spouse, common law partner, or conjugal partner is barred when the relationship between the sponsor and the applicant exists only for immigration purposes.

A "relationship of convenience," described as a "bad-faith" relationship in section 4 of the IRPR, is a relationship that is entered into primarily for the purpose of obtaining a status or privilege related to immigration (for example, permanent residence). A bad-faith relationship may be a new relationship, or a relationship formed after a previous relationship was dissolved for the purpose of entering into the relationship of convenience.

With respect to new relationships, case law[3] has held that there are two elements that must be present to bar sponsorship. In other words, the applicant only needs to disprove or negate one of them. The two elements are as follows:

- the applicant must have gone into the marriage primarily for the purpose of coming to Canada as a family class member (IRPR, s 4(1)(a)), and
- the relationship is not genuine (IRPR, s 4(1)(b)).

---

3   *Sharma v Canada (Citizenship and Immigration)*, 2009 FC 1131; *Kaur v Canada (Citizenship and Immigration)*, 2010 FC 417; *Gill v Canada (Citizenship and Immigration)*, 2012 FC 1522.

Consider the following scenario:

> Donna, a 53-year-old divorced Canadian citizen, goes on vacation to Cuba with her girlfriends and meets Grant, a 30-year-old resort manager. She spends most of her time during the next two weeks with Grant and learns all about how difficult life is for him in Cuba because of the strict government controls and general lack of opportunity. He asks for her help to immigrate to Canada, and promises to love and care for her for the rest of their lives. Donna had "the best time of her life" while on vacation and has fallen madly in love with the handsome young man. She doesn't know anything about immigration to Canada, but agrees to have an "island wedding" and marry Grant so that he can come to Canada as her spouse. They marry on the eve of Donna's return to Canada, surrounded by Donna's girl-friends and Grant's parents and friends.

In assessing Grant's application for permanent residence under the family class, the visa officer will consider a number of issues.[4] How would you answer the following questions in the case of Donna and Grant?

- Was there a wedding? Officers may need to closely examine evidence that a marriage took place. Photographs or other documents used as evidence of a marriage may have been altered. Marriage certificates and other documents may be fraudulent.

- Are they cohabiting? In some instances, home visits may be used to establish cohabitation in the case of a marriage or common law relationship (after arrival in the case of Donna and Grant).

Some factors that may be considered and that are common to marriages, common law relationships, and conjugal partner relationships are as follows:

- Do the spouses, or common law or conjugal partners, have a good knowledge of each other's personal circumstances, background, and family situations?

- What is the immigration status of the applicant and the timing of the marriage, common law relationship, or conjugal partner relationship?

- Is there evidence that both parties have planned their immigration, or the immigration of the foreign-born spouse, common law partner, or conjugal partner, jointly and over a period of time?

- Does either spouse or partner have a history of multiple marriages, divorces, common law relationships, or conjugal partner relationships?

---

4   These factors originally appeared in section 12 of OP 2, *supra* note 1, and have since been removed from the updated manual. However, it is worth noting these factors here because CIC states only that officers are trained to "recognize real immigration applications" and have "ways to spot marriage fraud" through document checks, home visits, and interviews, but there is no information about the factors that officers take into consideration when assessing spousal applications. Also see Citizenship and Immigration Canada, "Marriage Fraud" (8 April 2014), online: <http://www.cic.gc.ca/english/information/protection/fraud/marriage.asp>.

- Have previous relationships clearly ended and does the period of separation seem reasonable in the circumstances?
- Do the applicants speak a common language?

In cases where the new relationship is not genuine, the sponsor and applicant may not share a common language and may have no plans to reside together, or one may have made some kind of payment to the other for the inconvenience associated with marrying. Although Donna and Grant have a valid and legal marriage, their age difference, their quick marriage, their lack of knowledge of each other's personal circumstances, and their inability to communicate fluently in each other's language would certainly raise a red flag and be questioned by the immigration officer.

CONDITIONAL PERMANENT RESIDENCE

To deter marriages of convenience under the family class program, the government created new conditions for permanent residence in 2012. Section 72.1 of the IRPR places a condition on acquiring permanent residence status for a foreign national who is a sponsored spouse or partner when the relationship has existed for two years or less, and when there are no children from the relationship. In such cases, subject to certain exceptions (for example, abuse or neglect), the sponsored permanent resident must cohabit in a conjugal relationship with the sponsor for a continuous period of two years from the date of becoming a permanent resident. If the condition is not met, permanent residence status may be revoked from the foreign national and lead to his removal from Canada. As a further deterrence to marriage fraud or fraudulent common law relationships, the regulations also include the possibility of criminal charges against the sponsored person.

There are two exceptions to this rule that will remove the obligation:

- if the sponsor dies, or
- if the sponsored permanent resident can show that he or she was subjected to abuse or neglect during that period by the sponsor.

Suppose that in the case scenario of Donna and Grant, Donna's sponsorship was allowed. Grant's status as a permanent resident would be conditional: he must cohabit in a conjugal relationship with Donna for a period of two years after the day on which he became a permanent resident. This is required because of the length of Grant and Donna's relationship (less than two years), and because they have no children together.

Dependent Children

One of the major changes brought in by the IRPA in 2002 was that the age for a dependent child was raised from 19 to 22. On August 1, 2014, the regulations amended the rules for dependency by lowering the age from under 22 to under 19, and removing exceptions for students. The current definition (as of August 2014) of a dependent child in section 2 of the IRPR is technical and should be read carefully. In summary, a "dependent child" means a biological child (provided that the child was not adopted by a person other than the spouse or common law partner of the parent), or an adopted child of the parent, when the child is in one of the following situations of dependency:

- is under age 19 and single (has no spouse or common law partner), or
- has been financially dependent on a parent since before age 19 and is unable to be financially self-supporting due to a physical or mental disability.

Dependants over the age of 19 who are substantially dependent on their parents for financial support and have a physical or mental disability must provide evidence, such as medical records, to prove their dependency. In assessing applications, visa officers are encouraged to raise questions about the degree of dependence.

> As of August 1, 2014, children of applicants who are 19 or over but are financially dependent on their parents and are enrolled in full-time studies are no longer eligible to be processed as dependent children. Those applications that were already in process at the time of the change are being processed under the former definition of dependent child.

The lock-in age is the dependant's age on the day that the case processing centre (CPC) receives the sponsor's sponsorship application and the required processing fees. The sponsorship process can be lengthy, so the ages of dependent children will be "frozen in time" for the full duration of the time that it takes to process the sponsorship and applications for permanent residence, starting on the day the sponsor submits the sponsorship application in Canada and ending on the date of the issuance of the permanent resident visas by the visa office at the port of entry.

Specified Orphaned Relatives

Siblings, including half and step siblings, nephews, nieces, and grandchildren, may also be admitted as sponsored relatives if they meet all the following criteria (IRPR, s 117(1)(f)):

- they are orphaned,
- they are not a spouse or common law partner, and
- they are under 18.

Generally, the sponsorship for orphaned relatives who are under 18 years of age follows the same procedures as those for adopted children under 18 years of age, provided that they are unmarried and not in a common law relationship. As in adoption cases (described below), a visa officer must obtain the written consent of the appropriate authorities in the child's country of residence before the child may be removed from that country. Written consent of any legal guardians must also be obtained.

Officers are directed to counsel sponsors to obtain legal guardianship of the child upon the child's arrival in the province of residence, to ensure that the sponsor has legal obligations toward the sponsored child.[5]

Under the provisions of the former *Immigration Act*, the Federal Court of Appeal held that a visa officer did not have to consider whether or not the biological father was alive if he was not married to the mother and there had been no declaration of parentage.[6]

Adopted Children

Under the family class provisions of the regulations, a child must be related to the sponsor by a blood relationship or by adoption. The regulations provide for the adoption abroad of children both under 18 years of age and 18 years of age or older (if they also meet the definition of a dependent child).

In all cases of adoption, the genuine and informed consent of the biological parents must be provided. If both parents are alive, both should give consent. In the event that only one parent gives consent to an adoption, visa officers must be satisfied that the second parent has no legal rights with respect to the child.

Adoptions of children under 18 years of age must be in the *best interests of the child*, according to section 117(2) of the IRPR. If the foreign adoption was not in the best interests of the child, the child shall not be considered a member of the family class. To meet the "best interests" test, the following requirements (IRPR, s 117(3)) must be met:

- a competent authority has conducted or approved a home study of the adoptive parents;
- before the adoption, the child's parents gave their free and informed consent to the child's adoption;
- the adoption created a genuine parent–child relationship, and not a relationship of convenience for immigration purposes;
- the adoption was in accordance with the laws of the place where the adoption took place;
- the adoption was in accordance with the laws of the sponsor's country of residence;
- if the sponsor lived in Canada at the time the adoption took place, the competent authority of the child's province of intended destination has stated in writing that it does not object to the adoption;
- if the adoption was subject to the *Hague Convention on Protection of Children and Co-operation in Respect of Inter-Country Adoption* (the Hague Convention on Adoption), the competent authorities of both the country where the adoption

---

5 Citizenship and Immigration Canada, *OP 3: Adoptions* (Ottawa: CIC, 3 April 2009), online: <http://www.cic.gc.ca/english/resources/manuals/op/op03-eng.pdf>.

6 *Lindo v Canada (Minister of Employment & Immigration)*, [1988] 2 FC 396, 91 NR 75 (CA).

took place and the province of destination have stated in writing that they approved the adoption as conforming to the Convention; and

- if the adoption was not subject to the Hague Convention on Adoption, there is no evidence that the adoption is for the purpose of child trafficking or undue gain within the meaning of the Convention.

By definition, an adoption severs a child's legal relationship to the biological parents (IRPR, s 3(2)). Severance from the biological parents means that an adopted child may not sponsor the biological parents or grandparents in the future.

The "Best Interests of the Child" Principle

The "best interests of the child" principle is recognized by the international community as a fundamental human right of every child, and is also entrenched in article 3 of the United Nations *Convention on the Rights of the Child*. Article 1 of the Convention defines a "child" as any person under the age of 18, unless an earlier age of majority is recognized by a country's laws.

Article 3 elaborates on the meaning of "best interests" and provides that signatory states, including Canada, must ensure such protection and care as is necessary for a child's well-being, taking into account the rights and duties of parents, legal guardians, or other individuals who are legally responsible for the child, and take all appropriate legislative and administrative measures to this end.

ADOPTIONS OF CHILDREN 18 YEARS OF AGE OR OLDER

An adopted child 18 years of age or older must be considered a dependant as defined in the IRPR. In order for an adopted child 18 years of age or older to be considered a member of the family class, the following circumstances must exist (IRPR, s 117(4)):

- the adoption must have been in accordance with the laws of the place where the adoption took place and, if the sponsor resided in Canada at the time of the adoption, the adoption must have been in accordance with the laws of the province where the sponsor then resided, if any, that applied in respect of the adoption of a child 18 years of age or older;
- a genuine parent–child relationship must have existed at the time of the adoption and before the child reached the age of 18; and
- the adoption must not have been primarily for the purpose of acquiring a status or privilege under the IRPA.

Regardless of whether the adoption occurred outside or inside Canada, or if the adoptee is older than 18 years, a visa officer must be satisfied that the adoption creates a genuine parent–child relationship, and not a relationship of convenience entered into primarily for the purpose of acquiring any status or privilege under the IRPA, such as permanent residence. Section 4 of the IRPR refers to this kind of relationship as a bad-faith relationship, and excludes adoption when the relationship between the sponsor and the adopted child exists only for immigration purposes. The sponsorship will not be approved if a visa officer concludes that the purpose of the adoption is to gain admission to Canada.

Guardianship

The guardianship provisions of the IRPR were intended to provide a mechanism for individuals to sponsor an orphaned or abandoned child who would not otherwise meet the criteria as a "member of the family class," and who lived in a country where adoption is unavailable.

However, the provisions were not implemented when the IRPR came into force in June 2002, but were delayed in order to allow the provinces and territories time to conduct feasibility studies. The provinces and territories subsequently informed CIC that they would not participate in the implementation of the provisions, which made their implementation impossible.

The regulations relating to guardianship were repealed in 2005. CIC continues to deal with cases where children in need of care are brought into families through guardianships. Officers examine these situations case by case and, where humanitarian and compassionate reasons exist, use their discretion to allow these children into Canada.[7]

Other Relationships

Sponsors who do not have a closely related family member who is either a Canadian citizen or a permanent resident, or a relative who could be sponsored as a member of the family class, may sponsor one distant relative regardless of age or relationship. Unlisted relatives include independent children, uncles, aunts, nephews, nieces, and cousins. This does not work in reverse—that is, if a relative is the only one living abroad and all his relatives are in Canada, but he does not meet the definition of a member of the family class, he cannot be sponsored.

Application Processes

The sponsor and the foreign national must apply separately, as follows:

1. *The sponsor's application:* A sponsor is a person in Canada who wants to reunite with a family member. There is a separate application and approval process for becoming a sponsor. According to section 13(1) of the IRPA, a sponsor must be a Canadian citizen or permanent resident, and must meet other criteria such as financial requirements. Sponsorship kits can be obtained online from the CIC website or from a CIC call centre. All kits come with extensive guides that describe the forms in each kit, the supporting documentation that must be submitted, and the addresses for mailing. There are specific sponsoring kits that are tailored to different family

---

7   *Regulations Amending the Immigration and Refugee Protection Regulations* (8 January 2005) 139:2 C Gaz I, 62.

situations, so it is important to select the appropriate application package. The following key forms will be discussed in this text:

- IMM 1344, Application to Sponsor, Sponsorship Agreement and Under-taking (the same for all categories);
- a financial evaluation form;
- a questionnaire about the sponsor's relationship to a spouse or a common law or conjugal partner; and
- a document checklist.

2. *The permanent residence application:* Section 12(1) of the IRPA provides for an application based on the relationship of the foreign national to a Canadian citizen or permanent resident. A person applying to be sponsored for permanent residence is called the "principal applicant." To qualify for permanent residence, the principal applicant must either be the spouse, common law partner, child, or parent of the sponsor, or meet the regulatory definition of a "member of the family class" as well as specific eligibility and admissibility criteria. Application and approval are separate but related processes. All packages contain the Generic Application Form for Canada (IMM 0008, the permanent residence application form), an instruction guide, proof of payment receipt, Schedule A—Background Declaration form, and, for sponsoring a spouse or common law partner, a questionnaire about the relationship and other forms. The permanent resident's application package also contains region-specific instructions (for example, for submitting police certificates, photographs, and other details).

Both the sponsor's and the foreign national's applications must be successfully approved before the foreign national may become a permanent resident under the family class. Consider the following case scenario:

Gary is a 48-year-old Canadian citizen who lives in Toronto, Ontario. He has been divorced for several years and shares custody of his two children: Thomas, 9, and Samantha, 7. Ellie is a 45-year-old US citizen with two daughters: Amanda, 17, and Martha, 12. Ellie's husband, Paul, died when Martha was a baby.

Gary met Ellie through Paul years ago, when they were all undergraduates at Cornell University in New York. After Ellie and Paul were married, they remained close friends with Gary, who moved back to Canada after graduation. Gary's job required him to travel frequently to the United States, so it was easy to maintain his friendship with Ellie throughout the years, even after Paul died. After Gary divorced, his relationship with Ellie became intimate, leading to a marriage proposal and a legal marriage. Even though Gary could seek a job transfer to the United States through his company, he doesn't want to relocate there because he would lose joint custody of his two school-aged children. Ellie, however, is more flexible about where she can live and welcomes the chance to start a new life with Gary in Canada. Together, they decided that Gary should sponsor Ellie and the girls as permanent residents, so that they can all live together as a family in Canada.

Does Gary meet the legal requirements to sponsor Ellie and her children? Do Ellie and her dependent children, Amanda and Martha, qualify for sponsorship?

To answer these questions, we will examine the various elements of the family class program, including provisions of the IRPA and its regulations. We will learn about the two separate but interrelated processes for sponsoring a person to Canada and for applying as a permanent resident under the family class.

Throughout the text, we refer to "immigration officers" and "visa officers." The sponsor's application will be processed in Canada by an **immigration officer**, who is a public servant working at a CPC. The sponsored person's application for permanent residence will be processed abroad by a **visa officer**.

For the sake of simplicity, we will focus on the sponsorship of a spouse and dependent children, as in our scenario. However, where the requirements for sponsoring other members of the family class are different, we will explain them.

immigration officer
a public servant working in Canada at a case processing centre or other immigration office

visa officer
a public servant working in a Canadian consulate or visa office abroad

Applying to Sponsor Under the Family Class

Family class immigration involves sponsorship by a qualifying individual—the sponsor. A successful sponsorship includes many elements, but hinges on the relationship of the permanent resident applicant to the sponsor. In agreeing to enter into a sponsorship relationship, the sponsor makes a legal commitment to provide the basic living expenses of the family member being sponsored—called an undertaking—for a prescribed period of time. Sponsors must complete IMM 1344, Application to Sponsor, Sponsorship Agreement and Undertaking, which contains basic information about the sponsor (used to assess eligibility for sponsorship), the sponsor's legal obligations for sponsorship, and the agreement for sponsorship between the sponsor and the permanent resident applicant.

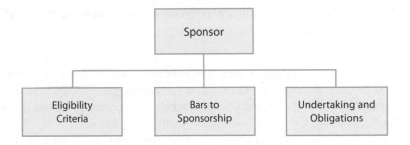

Eligibility Criteria

The process of sponsoring a person for permanent residence begins with the sponsor—in our scenario, Gary. The framework is found in section 13(1) of the IRPA, and further details are provided in section 130(1) of the IRPR. The sponsor must

- be either a Canadian citizen or a permanent resident,
- be at least 18 years old,
- reside in Canada (see the exception below), and
- file an application to sponsor a member of the family class.

RESIDE IN CANADA

Generally, the sponsor must reside in Canada. An exception is made (IRPR, s 130(2) when a Canadian citizen residing outside Canada satisfies immigration officials that he will resume residence in Canada when the sponsored person becomes a permanent resident. This allows a Canadian citizen whose work may require him to live outside Canada for a period of time to begin the sponsorship process. However, permanent residents, while living abroad, may not sponsor.

Bars to Sponsorship

Gary meets the age, status, and residence requirements of the definition of a sponsor. However, he must meet other conditions to satisfy immigration officials that he will be able to carry out his obligations as a sponsor.

Just as a bank will conduct a credit check to determine the likelihood that an individual will be able to repay a loan, the government wants to limit the risk of a sponsor defaulting on his obligations. Sponsorship requires Gary to provide the basic living expenses for Ellie and her children; therefore, he must prove that there is nothing that would prevent him from fulfilling this commitment. The immigration officer who processes Gary's application must be satisfied that nothing in Gary's history, including certain criminal offences, would make him a risk for sponsorship.

Certain activities, set out in section 133 of the IRPR, would bar Gary from sponsorship. A person may not sponsor or be a co-signer[8] (see the discussion below) if any of the following bars to sponsorship exist:

- *The person is subject to a removal order.* The IRPA requires permanent resident sponsors to reside in Canada. A person subject to a removal order is at risk of not being able to fulfill this obligation.

- *The person is detained in any penitentiary, jail, reformatory, or prison.* Such a person has no ability to provide financial support.

- *The person has been previously convicted of a specified offence.* These offences include a sexual offence (or an attempt or threat to commit such an offence), either in Canada or abroad, against anyone, or an offence resulting in bodily harm (including a threat or an attempt to commit such an offence) against a relative. This bar addresses concerns that a sponsored family member could be at risk of sexual abuse or family violence.[9] A history of such offences within five years of the sponsorship application bars the sponsor, unless he

---

8 For the purpose of sponsorship, a co-signer can only be the spouse or common law partner of the sponsor to help meet income requirements of sponsoring members other than the spouse or common law or conjugal partner by pooling resources; if the co-signer is a common law partner, the relationship must have existed for at least one year to qualify.

9 For a list of applicable sexual offences and applicable offences that equate to family violence, see Citizenship and Immigration Canada, *IP 2: Processing Applications to Sponsor Members of the Family Class* (Ottawa: CIC, 28 February 2011) appendix E at 62, online: <http://www.cic.gc.ca/english/resources/manuals/ip/ip02-eng.pdf>.

was pardoned or acquitted. For convictions outside Canada, the sponsor must show evidence of rehabilitation or acquittal.

- *The person is in default of spousal or child support payments ordered by a court in or outside Canada.* A sponsor who is in default of a court-ordered or court-registered support obligation must first resolve this matter with the local provincial or territorial authorities to remove this bar.

- *The person is in default of a debt[10] owed under the IRPA.* Sponsorship includes signing a legally binding contract with the minister of citizenship and immigration. As long as there is an unpaid debt, the minister will not enter into another legal contract with a person who is in default of payment.

- *The person is an undischarged bankrupt under the Bankruptcy and Insolvency Act.* A bankrupt person is considered a poor financial risk.

- *The person is in receipt of social assistance other than for reasons of disability.* A sponsor who receives social assistance cannot provide for his own basic necessities, let alone those of others. Only under exceptional circumstances may this bar be waived under humanitarian and compassionate grounds.

- *The person is in default of a previous sponsorship undertaking.* Such a person is considered to be a poor risk because he has not previously honoured a legal, financial obligation with the minister of citizenship and immigration.

- *Five-year requirement.* A permanent resident or a naturalized Canadian citizen who has previously sponsored a spouse or a common law or conjugal partner under section 13(1) of the IRPA may not sponsor a new spouse or partner for a five-year period after becoming a permanent resident. This bar is intended to curb abuse of the spouse/partner sponsorship program by foreign nationals who enter into relationships of convenience for immigration purposes (IRPR, s 130(3)).[11]

Gary has read about all the conditions he must meet to be a sponsor and has determined that there is nothing that would bar him from sponsoring Ellie. When Gary signs his completed application form, he will be consenting to specific obligations: an undertaking with the minister of citizenship and immigration, and a sponsorship agreement with Ellie.

Undertaking

According to the IRPR, a sponsor must make a formal commitment to become financially responsible for the family members. The duration of the commitment can vary—from 3 to 20 years—depending on the sponsorship relationship and the age

---

10   Such debts include transportation, adjustment assistance, admissibility or right of permanent residence fee loan, a deposit or guarantee of performance of an obligation, and removal costs of a foreign national.

11   Citizenship and Immigration Canada, "Five-Year Sponsorship Bar for Persons Who Were Sponsored to Come to Canada as a Spouse or Partner," *Operational Bulletin* 386 (2 March 2012), online: <http://www.cic.gc.ca/english/resources/manuals/bulletins/2012/ob386.asp>.

of the family members being sponsored. This commitment is called an undertaking and is included in the sponsor's application package (in form IMM 1344). The undertaking is a legally binding contract between the sponsor and the minister of citizenship and immigration.[12] The undertaking sets out the obligations of the sponsor, the duration of the undertaking, and the consequences of default.

OBLIGATIONS OF THE SPONSOR

The obligations of the sponsor are twofold. First, the sponsor agrees to ensure that family members receive the support they need in order to establish themselves in Canada, so that they will not require social assistance and become a financial burden on the community. Second, the sponsor agrees to repay the Canadian government for any social assistance payments made to the sponsored family members. The undertaking is unconditional and may not be terminated.

By signing the undertaking, Gary agrees to provide Ellie, the sponsored person, and Amanda and Martha, Ellie's dependent children, with basic necessities, including food, clothing, shelter, dental care, eye care, and other health needs not covered by public health services, from the day they enter Canada until the end of the specified period of the undertaking. As the sponsor, Gary remains obligated to provide the basic requirements regardless of any change in circumstances, such as a marital breakdown, unemployment, or even the death of Ellie.

DURATION OF THE UNDERTAKING

The undertaking takes effect either on the day the foreign national enters Canada with a temporary resident permit (following an application to remain in Canada as a permanent resident) or on the day the foreign national is admitted to Canada as a permanent resident. Generally, an undertaking is for a period of 10 years, but the duration of the undertaking can vary depending on the age of the person being sponsored (for a dependent child) and the relationship of the person to the sponsor, as follows:

- 3 years for a spouse or common law or conjugal partner of the sponsor;
- 10 years or age 22, whichever comes first, for a dependent child who is less than 19 years of age and is the child of the sponsor, or the sponsor's spouse or common law or conjugal partner;
- 3 years for a dependent child who is 19 years of age or older and is the child of the sponsor, or the sponsor's spouse or common law or conjugal partner;
- 20 years for the sponsor's parent or grandparent, and an accompanying dependent child; and
- 10 years for anyone else.

---

12 For a discussion about debts owed to government on default of the undertaking, see *Canada (Attorney General) v Mavi*, 2011 SCC 30, [2011] 2 SCR 504.

The duration of Gary's undertaking to sponsor Ellie and each of her daughters is as follows:

- Ellie is Gary's spouse; therefore, the duration of the undertaking for Ellie is three years from the date she arrives in Canada as a permanent resident.

Gary's obligations toward Amanda and Martha (the dependent children of his spouse, Ellie) are tied to their economic dependency and their ages, and therefore are longer in duration. Suppose both girls will be under 19 years of age on the date they become permanent residents. Gary would calculate his undertaking to be 10 years or when the girls reach the age of 22, whichever comes first, as follows:

- Amanda is 17 years old. If she is 17 when she becomes a permanent resident, the duration of Gary's undertaking will be 5 years: 22 years old − 17 years old = 5-year undertaking.
- Martha is 12 years old. If she is 12 when she becomes a permanent resident, the duration of Gary's undertaking will be the full 10 years: 22 years old − 12 years old = 10-year undertaking.

Duration of Undertakings

Person sponsored	Term of undertaking
Spouse, common law partner, or conjugal partner	**3 years** from date of becoming a permanent resident
Dependent child of sponsor or of sponsor's spouse, common law partner, or conjugal partner, if less than 19 years of age at the date of becoming a permanent resident	**10 years or age 22**, whichever comes first from date of becoming a permanent resident
Dependent child of sponsor or of sponsor's spouse, common law partner, or conjugal partner, if 19 years of age or over at the date of becoming a permanent resident	**3 years** from date of becoming a permanent resident
Parent or grandparent	**20 years** from date of becoming a permanent resident
Any other person	**10 years** from date of becoming a permanent resident

CONSEQUENCES OF DEFAULT

What happens to the sponsorship undertaking if, say, Gary becomes unemployed and can no longer afford to pay the basic necessities for Ellie and her daughters? Or if Gary and Ellie divorce, and Gary is unwilling to continue supporting Ellie, Amanda, and Martha? If Ellie and her daughters start to collect social assistance, Gary, the sponsor, is deemed to have defaulted on his undertaking, and the government may recover from him the cost of providing social assistance. Gary is liable for the sponsorship debt and will not be allowed to enter into any other sponsorship until he has repaid to the federal or provincial government all of the social assistance payments made to sponsored family members during the term of the undertaking (IRPR, s 132).

The undertaking is binding notwithstanding any change in the sponsor's personal circumstances, even if the permanent resident becomes estranged from the sponsor for any reason, including marriage fraud. Until recently, there was no protection for a Canadian citizen or a permanent resident who was duped into a marriage in exchange for permanent residence by a foreign national who had no intent of living in a relationship with the sponsor. In 2012, the government introduced a new regulation to address marriage fraud. Now, subject to certain exceptions (for example, abuse or neglect), section 72.1 of the IRPR requires a permanent resident to cohabit in a conjugal relationship with her sponsor for a continuous period of two years after the day on which she became a permanent resident (see the discussion above about conditional permanent residence).

Sponsorship Agreement

In addition to the undertaking with the minister of citizenship and immigration, Gary must enter into an agreement with Ellie. The agreement, contained in IMM 1344, sets out the mutual obligations and rights of the sponsor and the sponsored person. Both the sponsor and the sponsored person must sign the form.

After Gary signs the IMM 1344, he sends it to Ellie so that she has the opportunity to read it and understand her rights and responsibilities. The document makes it clear that the undertaking remains in effect notwithstanding events such as the granting of citizenship or a change in circumstances, such as marital breakdown.

Unfortunately, not all sponsored persons are aware of their rights. Some, especially women—for reasons such as poor language skills, poor education, and cultural norms—are vulnerable to a range of domestic abuses, including physical and financial control, isolation, and violence. A woman may stay in a relationship under threat of deportation because she is unaware of her rights and believes that she must remain in an abusive relationship or face deportation. This is false.

To address this issue, IMM 1344 includes the following statement:

> Sponsored persons and/or their family members who are being abused or assaulted by their sponsors should seek safety away from their sponsors even if this means they will have to apply for social assistance benefits. A sponsor cannot force Citizenship and Immigration Canada to remove you from Canada.

Let's suppose that Gary and Ellie separate or divorce. If this happens within three years of the start of his undertaking, Gary would continue to be financially responsible for Ellie and for the girls for the duration of his undertaking. Ellie and her children would not be forced to leave Canada, as some sponsored persons are led to believe; they would have the right to remain in Canada because they are permanent residents.

A sponsor and the principal applicant for permanent residence must sign the sponsorship agreement part of the sponsor's application form, so Gary (the sponsor) and Ellie (the spouse) will both sign the application. Amanda and Martha are both under the age of 19 and therefore will not sign the document. Ellie will have the opportunity to learn of Gary's undertaking obligations when she signs that part of the form. The agreement, however, also sets out the obligations that sponsored persons have, such as the obligation to make reasonable efforts to provide necessities for themselves and their children.

Financial Requirements

Generally, sponsors must show that they have the financial means to provide for all their family members, including those already residing in Canada and those they intend to sponsor. The minimum necessary income requirement is published annually by Statistics Canada in **low income cut-off (LICO)** levels. The general rule is that sponsors must prove that they can meet the minimum "LICO test" in order to be eligible to sponsor members of the family class. The financial evaluation forms are part of the sponsor's application package and are tailored to assess the sponsor according to his sponsorship obligations in the following circumstances:

low income cut-off (LICO)
the minimum income requirement for sponsors of permanent residents

- to sponsor a spouse, common law partner, or dependent child, whether in Canada or from abroad, unless the sponsored person has dependent children: IMM 5481, Sponsorship Evaluation;
- to sponsor a parent or grandparent: IMM 5768, Financial Evaluation for Parents and Grandparents Sponsorship; and
- to sponsor "other relatives": IMM 1283, Financial Evaluation.

Note: Sponsors living in Quebec or currently outside Canada but who intend to reside in Quebec upon their return must only complete IMM 1344, Application to Sponsor, Sponsorship Agreement and Undertaking, and IMM 5540, Sponsor Questionnaire, and provide the required documents. Sponsored persons who intend to reside with their sponsor in Quebec are not required to sign IMM 1344, because there is a separate undertaking kit provided by the Quebec Ministère de l'Immigration, de la Diversité et de l'Inclusion (MIDI).

EXCEPTIONS

The LICO financial obligations do not apply to all relatives. Excepted persons are listed in section 133(4) of the IRPR as follows:

- a spouse, common law partner, or conjugal partner who has no dependent children;
- a spouse, common law partner, or conjugal partner who has a dependent child who has no dependent children;
- a dependent child of the sponsor who has no dependent children of her own; or
- a child under the age of 18 whom the sponsor intends to adopt in Canada.

Although the sponsor is not required to meet the LICO test for these cases, he must still complete IMM 5481, Sponsorship Evaluation, so that CIC may assess the sponsorship. Gary must provide information about his sources of income and his current and past undertakings, and show that he meets the residency requirement.

In our scenario, Gary is exempt from the LICO test because he is sponsoring his spouse and her dependants.

CO-SIGNER

When a sponsor does not have the necessary financial means to be a sponsor, she may take on a **co-signer** to make up the difference financially. Consequently, the co-signer must also sign the sponsor's application form (IMM 1344), which includes the undertaking and sponsorship agreement. A co-signer must

- be either the spouse or common law partner of the sponsor,
- meet the same eligibility requirements as the sponsor, and
- assume the same obligations as the sponsor.

Together, the sponsor and co-signer become **jointly and severally liable** if there is a default. This means that either one of them may be required to pay the full amount if the other lacks funds to contribute—the obligation is not divided in half.

LOW INCOME CUT-OFF TEST

Operational manual IP 2 states that "the applicable LICO level is based on urban areas of 500,000 inhabitants or more, regardless of where the sponsor lives."[13] The sponsor's income must generally come from Canadian sources, with two exceptions:

- sponsors who commute from Canada to work in the United States may use their US employment income, provided that it is declared as income on their Canadian income tax return; and
- sponsors living in Canada who declare income from foreign sources on their Canadian income tax returns may use this foreign income to meet the financial requirements for sponsorship.

Sponsors, including those who are exempt from LICO, must provide their latest notice of assessment (option C printout) from the Canada Revenue Agency to report total income, as referenced in section 134(1)(a) of the IRPR and shown on line 150 of the notice of assessment. The following rules apply to the different categories of sponsorship:

- *Sponsoring spouse, common law partner, or dependent children:* A sponsor is exempt from the LICO test.

co-signer
a spouse or common law partner of a sponsor who co-signs with a sponsor who does not have the necessary financial means to be an approved sponsor

joint and several liability
liability for a financial obligation shared by two partners in a relationship such that either partner may be required to pay the full amount of the obligation—e.g., where a sponsor takes on a co-signer, both may be liable for the full amount in the event of a default

---

13 *Supra* note 9, s 5.32 at 22.

- *Sponsoring "other relatives"*: A sponsor must have a total income that is at least equal to the minimum necessary income.
- *Sponsoring parents or grandparents*: A sponsor must have a total income that is at least equal to the minimum necessary income, plus 30 percent, for each of the three consecutive taxation years immediately preceding the date of filing of the sponsorship application.

Quebec has its own financial capacity evaluation and criteria for the purposes of calculating undertaking requirements.[14]

HOW TO CALCULATE LICO

The LICO level is determined on the basis of the total number of family members. In sponsorship situations, the number of family members includes all members of a sponsor's own family and all sponsored persons and their family members, including family members listed as non-accompanying.

Generally, the LICO tables are updated each year, so look for the effective dates of the table. The annual tables can be found on the CIC website or within the instruction guides in the sponsor's application package.

The sample LICO table reproduced below is effective until December 31, 2015 and is used for sponsoring adopted children and other relatives (except in Quebec).

Sponsoring Adopted Children and Other Relatives: Low Income Cut-Off (LICO) Table for 2015

Size of family unit	Minimum necessary Income
1 person (Michele)	$23,861
2 persons	$29,706
3 persons	$36,520
4 persons	$44,340
5 persons	$50,290
6 persons	$56,718
7 persons	$63,147
More than 7 persons, for each additional person, add	$6,429

Source: Citizenship and Immigration Canada, "Income Table" (10 June 2015), online: <http://www.cic.gc.ca/english/information/applications/guides/5256ETOC.asp#incometables>.

---

14 Quebec, Immigration, Diversité et Inclusion, "Financial Capacity Evaluation" (30 December 2014), online: <http://www.immigration-quebec.gouv.qc.ca/en/immigrate-settle/sponsors-sponsored/requirements-sponsor/specific-requirements/financial-standards/>.

Consider the following case scenario:

> Tom, a Canadian citizen, and Ming, a Canadian permanent resident, are married with four children under the age of 12, living in Vancouver, British Columbia. Ming wants to sponsor her 15-year-old brother, Edward. Ming's parents died and Edward is considered orphaned. Because Edward is an orphaned sibling, Ming will be required to pass the LICO test.
>
> What is the size of Ming's family unit for LICO purposes, and what must Ming's minimum annual income be?

The size of Ming's family unit is equal to 7, as follows:

- Ming must count herself (1),
- her four children (4),
- her spouse, Tom (1), and
- the number of people being sponsored—Ming's brother, Edward (1).

The total number of persons to be included in the family unit is 7.

If we use the sample LICO table, Ming must show that she has an annual income of at least $63,147. Any income Ming earns in Canada is reported in her notice of assessment (option C printout) from her income tax return for the past 12 months; this is how she proves that she meets the minimum to qualify on financial grounds to sponsor her brother. If Ming has not earned enough money, she can ask Tom to act as a co-signer to make up the financial gap, provided that their pooled resources meet the minimum income requirement of $63,147. In this situation, both Ming and Tom become jointly responsible for the undertaking and sponsorship of Edward.

The sample LICO table reproduced below is effective until December 31, 2015 and is used for sponsoring parents and grandparents destined for a province other than Quebec.

The Parent and Grandparent Super Visa is a temporary option to reunite family members; however, for those who wish to pursue a more permanent solution, there is sponsorship for permanent residence, and applicants may include their dependants. The rules for sponsoring parents and grandparents are different from the rules for other categories of the family class. The length of undertaking for sponsorship of parents, grandparents, and their accompanying dependants is 20 years, and so sponsors are required to show a longer pattern of financial ability. The minimum necessary income required for each of the three years preceding the date of the sponsorship application must be equal to LICO plus 30 percent.

Consider the following case scenario about Gary and Ellie:

> Suppose that Ellie was successfully sponsored by Gary. Recall that Gary is a Canadian citizen and Ellie is now a Canadian permanent resident; they are married with four children between them and live in Toronto, Ontario. Ellie wants to sponsor her mother, Faye, who is widowed. Ellie is eligible to sponsor Faye, and she will be required to pass the LICO test.

**Sponsoring Parents and Grandparents:
Low Income Cut-Off (LICO) Table for 2015**

Size of family unit	Minimum income 2013	Minimum income 2012	Minimum income 2011
2 persons	$37,708	$36,637	$35,976
3 persons	$46,354	$45,040	$44,229
4 persons	$56,280	$54,685	$53,699
5 persons	$63,833	$62,023	$60,905
6 persons	$71,991	$69,950	$68,689
7 persons	$80,153	$77,879	$76,475
If more than 7 persons, for each additional person, add	$8,148	$7,929	$7,786

Source: Citizenship and Immigration Canada, "Guide 5772—Application to Sponsor Parents and Grandparents" (16 January 2015), online: <http://www.cic.gc.ca/english/information/applications/guides/5772ETOC.asp#apply>.

The size of Ellie's family unit is equal to 7, as follows:

- Ellie must count herself (1),
- her two children (2), and
- her spouse, Gary (1), and
- Gary's two children (2), and
- the number of people being sponsored—Ellie's mother, Faye (1).

The total number of persons to be included in the family unit is 7—the same as Ming's family. However, because she is sponsoring her parent, Ellie must show that she has an annual income of at least $80,153 for the taxation year of 2013. If Ellie was applying in 2015, she must provide her notice of assessment (option C printout) for the taxation years 2013, 2012, and 2011. If Gary is the co-signer, he must also provide his proof of income and would have to include all of his current undertakings (that is Ellie, Amanda, and Martha) in his calculations. You can see that, together, Ellie and Gary must show substantial earnings in order to sponsor Ellie's mother.

Proof of Relationship

Canadian immigration policy places the onus on the applicant to establish the nature of the relationship to the sponsor, as defined in the IRPR. Sponsors may only sponsor members of the family class, and therefore proof of the relationship must be provided at the time of application.

For relationships such as marriages, common law partnerships, and conjugal partnerships, a person must show that the relationship between the sponsor and the principal applicant is genuine and includes the existence of a conjugal relationship. Visa officers are trained to look for relationships of convenience or "bad-faith relationships" and, according to sections 4 and 4.1 of the IRPR, can refuse an application if they have evidence that an applicant entered into a relationship for the purpose of immigrating to Canada. The following forms are used to provide a detailed account of the relationship:

- IMM 5540, Sponsor Questionnaire: for sponsoring a spouse, common law partner, or conjugal partner outside Canada; or
- IMM 5285, Spouse/Common-Law Partner Questionnaire: for sponsoring from within Canada.

Document Checklist

It is important to know the kind and variety of documentation one must provide to establish the bona fides of a relationship. In the case of biological relatives, such as parents, grandparents, siblings, and children, if no documentary evidence exists to support the relationship, applicants may be required to produce DNA evidence. Applicants for sponsorship must provide proof of their identity, age, marital status (past and present), and immigration status by providing documents including their birth certificates and identity documents, proof of income, and others. The document checklist contains a list of all forms that must be submitted and is adapted to each type of sponsorship, with a list of the minimum number and type of documents to include for a sponsorship.

Permanent Residence Application as a Member of the Family Class

Permanent Residence Chart

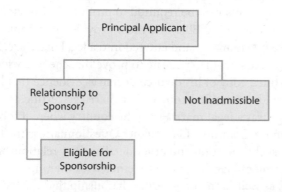

Foreign nationals who are sponsored as members of the family class are not assessed on their ability to support themselves. They obtain their permanent residence status on the sole basis of being in a familial relationship with a sponsor; they are not required to meet the financial or other selection requirements that are imposed on other classes of immigrants. It is therefore important for the sponsor and the applicant to show that a bone fide relationship exists between them. One of the eligibility requirements of sponsorship is to demonstrate that the sponsored person and her dependants are members of the family class as defined in the IRPR. Note that a "member of the family class" is not the same as a "family member." How you would define your family may not fit with the definitions in the regulations.

In our scenario, Ellie is seeking to come to Canada as a permanent resident along with her dependent children, Amanda and Martha. In order to do so, she and her daughters must meet the definition of "members of the family class" as set out in the IRPR. As discussed earlier in this chapter, a spouse (Ellie) and the dependent children of a sponsored spouse (Amanda and Martha) are considered to be members of the family class.

A person who applies for permanent residence under a family class program must have an eligible sponsor and also fulfill other requirements, as follows:

- be able to prove identity, age, and relationship to the sponsor and other family members, whether those family members are accompanying or not;
- be admissible to Canada (including family members, whether they are accompanying or not); and
- have a valid and subsisting passport or travel document.

Proof of Relationship to the Sponsor

Applicants for permanent residence must provide proof of their age and identity by providing birth certificates and identity documents. Canadian immigration policy also places the onus on the applicant to establish the nature of her relationship to the sponsor, as defined in the IRPR.

Just as the sponsor must show that his relationship to the applicant is genuine, so must the applicant provide documents and information that establish the bona fides of her relationship to the sponsor. In the case of biological relatives, such as parents, grandparents, siblings, and children, if no documentary evidence exists to support the relationship, applicants may be required to produce DNA evidence.

In our scenario concerning Ellie, she must provide documentary evidence that she and Gary were free to marry and entered into a legal marriage. She will provide a certified copy of Paul's death certificate to prove that she was widowed, and Gary will provide a certified copy of his divorce decree as evidence that he was divorced. Ellie will also provide a certified copy of her marriage certificate to Gary to show that their marriage was a legal marriage in the country where it took place.

IMM 5490, Spouse/Common-Law Partner Questionnaire is the form Ellie would complete to discuss the duration and other details of her relationship with Gary. By looking at the timing of Gary's divorce together with the timing of his subsequent marriage to Ellie, as well as the long-term relationship that existed before the marriage, the officer would likely determine that the motive to marry was not purely for immigration purposes.

Dependent Children

Both of Ellie's daughters, Amanda (17) and Martha (12), meet the regulatory definition of a dependent child. The lock-in age is on the day that the CPC receives Gary's sponsorship application and the required processing fees. The sponsorship process can be lengthy, so the ages of Martha and Amanda will be "frozen in time" for the full duration of the time that it takes to process the sponsorship and applications for permanent residence, starting on the day that Gary submits his sponsorship application in Canada and ending on the date of the issuance of the permanent resident visas by the visa office at the port of entry.

Calculating Immigration Fees

There are a number of expenses associated with an application for permanent residence. These fees do not cover the cost of medical examinations, or any criminal or background checks required. In the case of a sponsorship application, the fees payable to CIC include the following:

- sponsor's application fee—because the sponsor must be assessed for his eligibility to sponsor (approximately $75);
- application for permanent residence fee (approximately $475 for applicants over 22 years of age, and significantly less for children); and
- right of permanent residence fee (RPRF) ($490 for adults; dependent children of the applicant are exempt).

The current fee schedule is included in the sponsor's instruction guide. In our scenario involving Gary and Ellie, the processing fees in 2015 add up to $850, as shown below:

Sponsorship Application Fees

Person	Type of application	Fee
Gary—sponsor	Sponsorship application	$75
Ellie—principal applicant	Permanent residence application	$475
Amanda—accompanying family member (under 22 years of age, not married or in a common law relationship)	Permanent residence application	$150
Martha—accompanying family member (under 22 years of age, not married or in a common law relationship)	Permanent residence application	$150
Total application fees		$850

For Ellie to sponsor her mother, the processing fees in 2015 add up to $550, as shown below:

Person	Type of application	Fee
Ellie (and co-signer Gary)—sponsor	Sponsorship application	$75
Faye (Ellie's mother)—principal applicant	Permanent residence application	$475
Total application fees		$550

For Ming to sponsor her orphaned brother, the processing fees in 2015 add up to $150, as shown in the table below:

Person	Type of application	Fee
Ming—sponsor	Sponsorship application	$75
Edward (Ming's brother)—the principal applicant, who is under 19 and does not have a spouse or common law partner	Permanent residence application	$75
Total application fees		$150

For each of the scenarios above, the RPRF is $490, as shown below:

Right of Permanent Resident Fee

Person	Right of permanent residence fee
Ellie and Faye—adults	$490
Amanda, Martha, and Edward—dependent/orphaned children	$0

- Gary and Ellie's application and RPRF fees total $1,340 ($850 + $490) for Gary, Ellie, and Ellie's daughters, Amanda and Martha.
- Ellie's application and RPRF fees to sponsor her mother, Faye, total $1,040 ($550 + $490).
- Ming's application and RPRF fees to sponsor her brother, Edward, total $150 ($150 + $0).

Decisions on Applications Under the Family Class

The possible outcomes of CIC decisions with respect to both sponsorship applications and permanent resident applications, and the rights of appeal of sponsors and applicants, are described in this section. The outcomes of adoption processes are discussed in the following section.

Decision—Sponsor Applications

In our scenario, Gary sent his Application to Sponsor, Sponsorship Agreement and Undertaking (IMM 1344) to Ellie to sign and return it to him, along with her application for permanent residence package and all her supporting documents. After all his forms are completed and signed and he has gathered all his supporting documentation, Gary will send both completed packages to a centralized CPC in Mississauga, Ontario for processing. A Canadian immigration officer will assess Gary's sponsorship application to verify that Gary meets all the requirements, as follows:

- the sponsor meets the regulatory definition and is eligible to sponsor;
- the applicants for permanent residence are members of the family class; and
- the application for permanent residence is complete, including fees.

The immigration officer's decision will result in one of a number of possible outcomes, as follows:

1. *Sponsor is ineligible—elect to end processing.* If the immigration officer finds that Gary is an ineligible sponsor, and Gary has chosen to end the process (when he checked the option in box 1 of IMM 1344 to "Withdraw your sponsorship"), all processing fees (less $75) will be repaid. The immigration officer will close the file. Ellie's application will not be assessed. Gary has no right to appeal the immigration officer's decision.

2. *Sponsor is ineligible—elect to pursue application.* If the immigration officer finds that Gary is an ineligible sponsor, and Gary has chosen to pursue the matter at the next level (when he checked the option in box 1 of IMM 1344 to "Proceed with the application for permanent residence"), the immigration officer will then transfer the application for permanent residence and the negative decision (that is, the officer's finding of ineligibility) to the visa office nearest to where Ellie, the principal applicant, resides. Gary would have the right to appeal the ineligibility decision to the Immigration Appeal Division (IAD) of the Immigration and Refugee Board (IRB).

3. *Sponsor is ineligible because sponsored person is not a member of the family class.* If the immigration officer finds that Gary is ineligible because Ellie, the principal applicant, is not a member of the family class, Gary may accept this finding and elect to discontinue processing. However, if Gary does not accept the finding and elects to pursue the matter, the officer will send her decision to the visa office. Gary's right to appeal to the IAD is maintained.

4. *Sponsor is eligible.* Finally, if the immigration officer finds that Gary is eligible, the immigration officer's written decision and Ellie's application for permanent residence are forwarded to the appropriate visa office to process Ellie's application for permanent residence.

Decision—Permanent Residence Application

In processing applications under the family class program, a visa officer reviews the application for permanent residence to ensure that the applicants (Ellie and her daughters, for example) do indeed meet the regulatory definition as members of the family class and that they have an eligible sponsor. The visa officer does the following:

- examines the supporting documents to ascertain the applicants' identity, age, and relationship to the sponsor and other family members (whether or not those family members are accompanying them to Canada);
- examines their passports or travel documents to determine whether they are valid; and
- determines whether the applicants are inadmissible (including family members, whether or not they are accompanying them to Canada), according to any of the grounds of inadmissibility, described in Chapter 3.

Ellie might be called to appear for an interview with a visa officer. However, although visa officers have the authority to interview applicants, they generally waive interviews unless there is a need to confirm the applicant's identity or her relationship to the sponsor or to her dependants, or to address questions related to admissibility.

After reviewing the application, the visa officer will make one of the following two decisions:

1. *Applicant is eligible.* If all the requirements are met, the visa officer issues a confirmation of permanent residence (COPR) document and permanent resident visa to allow the applicant to travel to Canada as a permanent resident. The names of non-accompanying family members are included on the visa of the principal applicant. (In our scenario, Ellie does not have any other dependants.) Ellie and her daughters must travel to Canada before the expiry date on their visas, where they will be examined at the port of entry.

2. *Application is refused.* If one or more of the requirements are not met and Ellie's application for permanent residence is refused by the visa officer, a **refusal letter** will be sent to her setting out the grounds for the refusal—that is, the reasons why her application for permanent residence was rejected. This written record can then be used as the basis of an appeal. The visa office mails a copy of the refusal letter, together with a notice of appeal, to Gary, the sponsor. The notice informs the sponsor of his right to appeal under section 63 of the IRPA.

refusal letter
a document sent to a permanent resident applicant outlining the reasons for the application's refusal

Right to Appeal

Appeal procedures are discussed in Chapter 15, Appeals. Below is a brief explanation of when sponsorship appeals are permitted.

APPEALS PERMITTED FOR SPONSOR

A sponsor who is found to be ineligible to sponsor may appeal to the IAD. Sometimes, a sponsor may be ineligible because he does not meet the eligibility criteria—

for example, something bars him from sponsorship or he does not meet the financial criteria. The sponsor may also appeal the decision of the visa officer if the applicant for permanent residence (the person being sponsored) is not eligible. For example, a visa officer may find that the relationship is one of convenience or that the family member is inadmissible.

APPEALS NOT PERMITTED FOR SPONSOR

Sponsorship appeals are not permitted in the following cases:

1. *Ineligible sponsor—spouse or common law partner in Canada.* Appeal rights for "in-Canada" applications are different from those for appeals of sponsorship cases abroad. When a sponsor does not meet the requirements of the "spouse or common-law partner in Canada class," as defined in section 130(1) of the IRPR, it follows that the applicant for permanent residence does not have an eligible sponsor. The application for permanent residence is therefore refused, and the applicant for permanent residence is advised by the CPC of the reasons for the refusal and directed to leave Canada or risk removal action.

   In this case, neither the sponsor nor the applicant for permanent residence has a right to appeal to the IAD. However, the applicant for permanent residence may apply for a judicial review within 30 days after the date of refusal.

2. *Inadmissible applicant.* There are no appeal rights for applicants for permanent residence if they are found inadmissible on the most serious grounds of inadmissibility. Section 64 of the IRPA prohibits the right to appeal when a family member applicant is found to be inadmissible on the grounds of security, violating human or international rights, serious criminality, or organized criminality. (For a full description of these grounds, see Chapter 3.)

Adoption

To sponsor an adopted child for permanent residence, there are two processes to complete:

- the adoption process, and
- the sponsorship process for the immigration or citizenship process.

The sponsorship process must be used

- if the adoptive parents were not Canadian citizens when the adoption took place;
- the adoption took place before January 1, 1947; or
- the adoptive parents were both permanent residents at the time of adoption.

For adoptive parents where at least one parent is a Canadian citizen, there is a direct grant of citizenship and a separate citizenship process, discussed below. There are also separate adoption processes and conditions depending on whether the sponsor is adopting a child from outside or from within Canada, and whether the child is over age 18.

Adoption Process Outside Canada

International adoption is complex because of social welfare laws, immigration laws, and the laws of the child's country.

The *Hague Convention on Protection of Children and Co-operation in Respect of Intercountry Adoption* (the Hague Convention on Adoption), referenced in the IRPR, provides minimum standards and procedures for adoptions between countries. It is intended to end unethical adoption practices and promote cooperation between countries. The Convention puts in place procedures that minimize the chance of exploitation of children, birth parents, or adoptive parents during the adoption process.

The Hague Convention on Adoption requires the central adoption authority in both the child's destination country and the country of current residence to agree to the child's adoption. Canada and all provinces and territories follow the requirements of the Convention. If the child to be adopted is from a signatory state to the Convention, the adoption must follow the Convention's rules. In other words, no private adoptions may take place for a child from a signatory state. In Canada, a CIC officer must approve the sponsorship before the adoption is completed.

The Hague Convention on Adoption requires that the authorities in the child's country of origin ensure that

- the child is legally free for adoption,
- the birth parents have consented to the adoption in the child's best interests and understand the consequences for their parental rights, and
- the decision to place a child for adoption is not motivated by any financial gain.

The Hague Convention on Adoption requires that the authorities in Canada ensure the following:

- the adoptive parents are eligible and suitable to adopt, and
- the appropriate authorities have decided that the child will be allowed to enter and live permanently in Canada.

The CIC website provide a list of countries that restrict adoptions by Canadians: Rwanda (intercountry adoption suspended in July 2012 in order to implement the Convention), Russia, Democratic Republic of Congo, and Benin (intercountry adoption suspended in July 2014 in order to implement the Convention).

The ESDC website also directs sponsors/adoptive parents to links to access a list of countries that are parties to the Hague Convention on Adoption, and provinces and territories in Canada that have implemented the Convention. Canadian adoptive parents must also obtain the approval of the province in which they live. For example,

Canadian provinces and territories have suspended adoptions from Cambodia (except Quebec), Georgia, Guatemala, Liberia, Nepal, and Haiti (suspension by Nova Scotia, Prince Edward Island, and Saskatchewan).

There are several specific requirements that must be successfully met by prospective adoptive parents, as follows:

1. **Home study**. A home study is an assessment of the prospective parents with respect to their suitability to adopt. It is undertaken by provincial or territorial authorities, and is generally carried out by an accredited social worker. The home study is comprehensive and is an important precondition to an adoption. It is also required for immigration purposes under section 117(3)(a) of the IRPR.

2. **Letter of no-involvement**. A letter of no-involvement may be accepted instead of a home study when a private adoption takes place outside Canada and in a state that is not a signatory to the Convention. It may also be accepted in cases where an adoption is finalized abroad prior to the adopted child's arrival in Canada. The purpose of the letter of no-involvement is to inform the visa office that an adoption order that is in accordance with the laws of the jurisdiction in which the adoption took place will be recognized by the adopting parents' province or territory of residence.[15]

3. **Letter of no-objection**. A letter of no-objection is a written statement from the province or territory where the child will live, stating that the province or territory does not object to the adoption (IRPR, ss 117(1)(g)(iii)(B), 117(3)(e)).

4. **Letter (or notice) of agreement**. A letter or notice of agreement is required in Convention adoption cases, indicating that the province and adoptive parents agree to the adoption (IRPR, ss 117(1)(g)(ii), 117(3)(f), (g)). It is sent by the receiving provincial or territorial authorities to the visa office, with a copy to the central authority of the adopted child's country of residence.

Adoption Process Inside Canada

For in-Canada adoptions, section 117(1)(g) of the IRPR sets out the following conditions for membership in the family class:

- the child must be under the age of 18;
- there must be no evidence that the adoption is for the purpose of acquiring any privileges or status under the IRPA;
- if the adoption was subject to the Hague Convention on Adoption, the competent authority of the country in which the child lives and the province of destination of that child must have stated in writing that they approve the adoption as conforming to the Convention; and

home study
an assessment of the prospective adoptive parents with respect to their suitability to adopt

letter of no-involvement
a letter that may be accepted instead of a home study where a private adoption takes place outside Canada and in a state that is not a signatory to the Hague Convention on Adoption

letter of no-objection
a written statement from the province or territory where an adopted child will live, stating that the province or territory does not object to the adoption

letter (or notice) of agreement
a letter or notice of agreement, required in Hague Convention adoption cases, indicating that the province or territory where the adopted child will live and the adoptive parents agree to the adoption; sent by the province or territory to the visa office, with a copy to the central authority of the adopted child's country of residence

15 Citizenship and Immigration Canada, *OP 3: Adoptions* (3 April 2009) [OP 3] s 5.5 at 6, online: <http://www.cic.gc.ca/english/resources/manuals/op/op03-eng.pdf>.

- if the adoption was not subject to the Convention, the child must have been placed for adoption in the country in which he or she lives or is legally available for adoption and there must be no evidence that the adoption is for the purpose of child trafficking or undue gain within the meaning of the Convention, and the competent authority of the child's province of intended destination must have stated in writing that it does not object to the adoption.

Sponsorship for Permanent Residence

Adoptive parents may apply to sponsor their child for permanent residence if

- the adopted child is coming to Canada to live right after the adoption takes place, or
- one or both parents are Canadian citizens or permanent residents.

The adopted person does not meet the requirements for the immigration process if

- the adopted person is not going to Canada to live right after the adoption takes place, or
- the adopted person is an adult adoptee living outside Canada and not returning to Canada to live right after the application is approved.

Section 118 of the IRPA requires adoptive parents to provide a statement in writing confirming knowledge of information regarding any medical condition of the adopted child, the Medical Condition Statement form that is part of the sponsor's application package serves this purpose. Ensuring that the adoptive parents are fully aware of the health of the adopted child is intended to safeguard against the abandonment of the child by prospective parents by ensuring that they are equipped to deal with any pre-existing health or medical conditions before the adoption is complete and the child is issued a COPR document to travel to Canada.

Adoption Process: Citizenship Process

Until recently, a child adopted by Canadian citizens did not automatically become a Canadian citizen, but instead arrived in Canada with a permanent resident visa and was admitted as a permanent resident. The parents then had to apply for citizenship on behalf of the child.

However, since December 23, 2007, an adopted child may apply for Canadian citizenship without first becoming a permanent resident if the adoption was by a Canadian citizen after February 14, 1977. Adoptive parents may apply for citizenship on behalf of their adopted child. Officers consider the following factors in assessing grants of citizenship for adopted children:[16]

---

16 Citizenship and Immigration Canada, *CP 14 Adoption: Grant of Canadian Citizenship for Persons Adopted by Canadian Citizens on or After January 1, 1947* (19 June 2014), online: <http://www.cic .gc.ca/english/resources/manuals/cp/cp14-eng.pdf>.

- at least one adoptive parent is or was a Canadian citizen when the adoption took place,
- the adoption severs or severed all ties with the adopted person's legal parents, and
- the adoption was or will be completed outside Canada (except for Quebec).

The adopted person does not meet the requirements for the citizenship process if any of the following factors exist:

- neither parent was a Canadian citizen when the adoption took place;
- the adoption took place before February 15, 1977;
- the adoption did not fully sever all ties with the child's legal parents;
- the adoption will be completed in Canada; or
- a probationary period is to be completed in Canada before a final adoption order is issued from the child's birth country.

APPENDIX

Reference for Family Class

Provision	IRPA/IRPR
Objective relating to family reunification	IRPA, s 3(1)(d)
Sponsor does not meet requirements	IRPA, s 11(2)
Selection of members of family class	IRPA, s 12(1)
Rights and obligations to sponsor a family member	IRPA, s 13(1)
Inadmissible family member	IRPA, s 42
Right to appeal family class refusal	IRPA, ss 63(1), 64
Exception to excessive demand	IRPA, s 38(2); IRPR, s 24
Definitions	IRPR, ss 1, 2
Relationships of convenience	IRPR, s 4
Definition of a member of the family class	IRPR, s 117
Adoptions	IRPR, s 117
Who may sponsor	IRPR, s 130
Sponsorship criteria	IRPR, s 133

KEY TERMS

common law partner, 193

conjugal partner, 193

co-signer, 213

home study, 225

immigration officer, 206

joint and several liability, 213

letter of no-involvement, 225

letter of no-objection, 225

letter (or notice) of agreement, 225

low income cut-off (LICO), 212

refusal letter, 222

visa officer, 206

REVIEW QUESTIONS

1. Canadians believe that people who immigrate to Canada will establish themselves more easily if their family in Canada supports them. List the three objectives of the family class program as stated in the IRPA.

2. Define the following terms found in the IRPA and IRPR:

   - family member

   - common law partner

   - dependent child

   - marriage

   - conjugal partner

3. Where is the definition of a sponsor found, and who may be a sponsor?

4. What are the obligations of sponsors?

5. Find the current fees for sponsorship on the CIC website for the following: sponsor, principal applicant for permanent residence, and dependent children under 19 years of age.

6. What is an undertaking?

7. What does the sponsorship agreement set out, and who signs it?

8. List five conditions or situations that would bar a person from being a sponsor or co-signer.

9. What does the acronym LICO stand for?

10. Who is exempt from the minimum income test?

Economic Classes

LEARNING OUTCOMES

After reading this chapter, you should be able to:

- Describe the general provisions for applying under the Express Entry system.

- Be able to differentiate between the economic classes of permanent residence.

- Use the National Occupational Classification system and be able to find the code for an occupation.

- Understand how to use a point system to calculate points.

- Describe the federal skilled worker requirements.

- Describe the requirements of federal skilled trades.

- Understand who is eligible to apply under the Business Immigration Program.

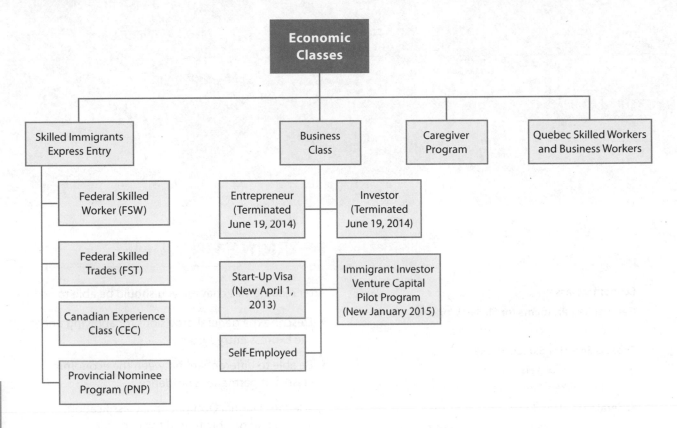

Economic Classes

Immigration under the economic classes fulfills one of the stated objectives of Canada's immigration policy: to "permit Canada to pursue the maximum social, cultural and economic benefits of immigration" (*Immigration and Refugee Protection Act* [IRPA], s 3(1)(a)). Section 12(2) of the IRPA provides that the legal basis for selecting foreign nationals as members of the economic class is their ability to become economically established in Canada. Foreign nationals who acquire permanent residence under an economic class category have traditionally contributed to the Canadian economy by filling shortages in the labour market with skills, knowledge, expertise, and other assets. Over the past eight years, the Canadian government has made significant changes to the immigration system, including expanding the economic classes by introducing new categories, such as the federal skilled workers class, as well as new application processes, such as an electronic application management system called Express Entry.[1]

According to the Annual Report, permanent immigration in the economic streams made up 57 percent of the total permanent immigration to Canada (148,181

---

1 Citizenship and Immigration Canada, "Section 1: Making Immigration Work for Canada" in *2014 Annual Report to Parliament on Immigration* (Ottawa: CIC, 2014) [Annual Report], online: <http://www.cic.gc.ca/english/resources/publications/annual-report-2014/index.asp#sec-1>.

Economic Classes 2013

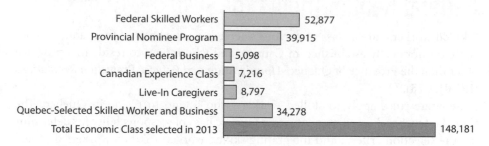

Source: Citizenship and Immigration Canada, "Section 2: Managing Permanent Immigration and Temporary Migration—Permanent Residents" in *2014 Annual Report to Parliament on Immigration* (Ottawa: CIC, 2014) table 2, online: <http://www.cic.gc.ca/english/resources/publications/annual-report-2014/index.asp#sec-2-1>.

out of 258,953 persons, including spouses and dependants). The economic class includes: skilled workers, business people, provincial or territorial nominees, the Canadian Experience Class, caregivers, and Quebec-selected workers. Within this group, the majority were admitted as federal skilled workers (36 percent or 52,877).[2]

Amendments to the IRPA made by the *Jobs, Growth and Long-term Prosperity Act* (Bill C-38) in June 2008 created new statutory powers for the minister to issue instructions without going through the parliamentary process of debate regarding the processing of applications for permanent residence. These instructions include limiting the number of applications to be processed, prioritizing the processing of applications of workers in certain occupations, and capping the number of permanent residence applications accepted by category.

The government was quick to use the statutory powers to issue instructions. For example, in 2010, the minister imposed mandatory language testing for principal applicants in the Federal Skilled Worker (FSW) stream and placed caps on the number of new applications to be processed. In 2012, the minister returned unprocessed applications submitted on or after July 1, 2012. Note that, owing to legislative amendments and/or ministerial instructions, the eligibility criteria and processing procedures in all economic classes are subject to change.

The chart at the beginning of this chapter shows the different categories of permanent immigration created under the economic stream. Each category has its own eligibility requirements and application processing procedures, both of which may change, either through an amendment to the regulations or as a result of ministerial instructions. This chapter will describe the application processes under the Express Entry system and the general eligibility requirements for the streams within the economic class.

---

2   *Ibid*, table 2.

General Requirements for Skilled Workers

"Skilled workers" are a class of persons selected "on the basis of their ability to become economically established in Canada, and who intend to reside in a province other than the Province of Quebec" (*Immigration and Refugee Protection Regulations* [IRPR], s 75).

Separate rules apply to skilled workers who intend to reside in Quebec. The Canada–Quebec Accord mandates that Quebec has sole responsibility for determining the selection criteria and integrating skilled workers. Skilled workers destined for Quebec must obtain a *certificat de sélection du Québec* (Quebec Certificate of Selection) from that province. However, issues of inadmissibility and issuance of the permanent resident visa remain federal responsibilities.

For the Canadian Experience Class (CEC) and the Caregiver Program, permanent residence status is acquired by first meeting the eligibility requirements as a temporary resident; these programs were discussed in Chapter 5 (Temporary Residence: Students and Workers).

The provisions for applying as a permanent resident are generally relevant. A person wishing to become a permanent resident is called the "principal applicant," and in addition to meeting the eligibility criteria, she must not be inadmissible. The principal applicant may include family members in her application for permanent residence as long as the visa officer is satisfied that the family members are in fact family members, and that they too are not inadmissible.

National Occupational Classification

WEBLINK

To view the complete NOC matrix online, including the list of occupations in each major group, visit the NOC website at <www5.hrsdc.gc.ca/ NOC/English/NOC/2011/ Welcome.aspx>.

Applicants for permanent residence under the federal worker classes should refer to Canada's National Occupational Classification (NOC) system. The NOC provides consistency and information about the educational credentials, training, and job duties for various occupations. The NOC 2011 is used by employers in making job offers, by applicants in assessing their work experience, and by Citizenship and Immigration Canada (CIC) to differentiate between occupations and skill levels with respect to prospective immigrants in the skilled worker and skilled trades classes.

The NOC was developed by Human Resources and Skills Development Canada (HRSDC; now Employment and Social Development Canada [ESDC]) in partnership with Statistics Canada, and is used by a variety of professionals, from economists and business analysts to career counsellors. It is a standardized system that provides formal definitions for more than 40,000 job titles in 500 occupational group descriptions. Each occupation is coded according to the type and level of skill required to perform the work. It's a tool for understanding types of employment by describing duties, skills, interests, aptitudes, educational requirements, and work settings.

The NOC is organized as a matrix to show the relationship between skill types and levels. There are nine skill types (coded by the digits 1 through 9) that are listed across the top of the matrix; a tenth skill type (coded with 0) occupies the first row of the matrix. There are four skill levels (A through D) that appear on the left side of the matrix. An outline of the matrix is shown below with only the skill types and levels included. To see the complete matrix, go to <www5.hrsdc.gc.ca/NOC/English/NOC/2011/Matrix.aspx>.

Occupations in skill type 0 require a relevant university degree, professional designation, college diploma, or other management training, as well as proven management experience.

The four skill levels refer to the type of education or training needed to perform the work:

- skill level A: university education;
- skill level B: college/technical school education or apprenticeship training;
- skill level C: high school education/occupation-specific training; and
- skill level D: short demonstration training or on-the-job training.

Generally, each matrix cell is called a major group, and consists of a list of specific occupations. Under the skilled worker class, applicants for permanent residence must have at least one year within the past ten years of continuous, full-time, paid work experience that is either in skill type 0 or in skill level A or B.

NOC Matrix

	1 Business, Finance and Administration Occupations	2 Natural and Applied Sciences and Related Occupations	3 Health Occupations	4 Occupations in Education, Law and Social, Community and Government Services	5 Occupations in Art, Culture, Recreation and Sport	6 Sales and Service Occupations	7 Trades, Transport and Equipment Operators and Related Occupations	8 Natural Resources, Agriculture and Related Production Occupations	9 Occupations in Manufacturing and Utilities
0 Management Occupations (Skill Level A)									
1—Skill Level A									
2—Skill Level B									
3—Skill Level C									
4—Skill Level D									

Source: <http://www5.hrsdc.gc.ca/NOC/English/NOC/2011/html/Matrix.html>.

To help applicants find their occupation in the NOC, CIC refers them to the ESDC website, where they can view the complete NOC matrix and descriptions of specific occupations.

For example, consider Paralegal and Related Occupations. This field is found within major group 42 in the matrix and coded in the NOC as 4211. For Paralegal and Related Occupations, the NOC describes the work performed, provides sample job titles (independent paralegal, law clerk, legal assistant, and legal researcher) and sample job duties, and sets out employment requirements.

Let's take a closer look at the NOC code. The first digit of an occupational code designates the skill type. Skill type refers to the type of work performed and the field of training or experience normally required for entry into the occupation, including the educational area of study and employment. The skill type is intended to identify employment sectors on the basis of the ten broad occupational areas from 0 through 9.

In our example of code 4211, the first digit in the code is 4, corresponding to skill type 4—Occupations in Education, Law and Social, Community and Government Services.

The second digit of the occupational code indicates the skill level: 1 corresponds to skill level A; 2 corresponds to skill level B, and so on.

If a skilled worker applicant has work experience in the category of skill level A, this means that he has experience in a professional occupation requiring a relevant university degree, professional designation, or a two-year college diploma, and several years of directly related experience.

If a skilled trades applicant has work experience in the category of skill level B, this means that he has experience as a technician or technologist. Occupations at skill level B typically require two to five years of apprenticeship training and apprenticeship or trades certification, and several years of directly related work experience.

In our example of code 4211, the second digit in the code is 2, corresponding to skill level B, which requires college/technical school or apprenticeship training.

Express Entry for Skilled Workers

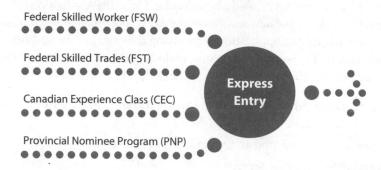

Categories Eligible for Express Entry Pool

Federal Skilled Worker (FSW)

Federal Skilled Trades (FST)

Canadian Experience Class (CEC)

Provincial Nominee Program (PNP)

Express
Entry

Express Entry is an electronic application management system. It was introduced on January 1, 2015 and replaces the former first-come, first-served system of application processing for permanent residence applications in the following subclasses and programs:

- FSW selection is based on the applicant's ability to settle in Canada and contribute to the Canadian economy;
- Federal Skilled Trades (FST) selection is based on the applicant's qualification in a skilled trade;
- CEC is a pathway for temporary residents in the student and worker classes to transition to permanent residence; and
- the Provincial Nominee Program (PNP) is for applicants who have been selected by the provinces or territories to fill their regional labour shortages; applying through Express Entry is optional.

The objective of Express Entry "is to create efficiencies by making the submission of electronic applications for permanent residence under this system mandatory and to provide exemptions to this mandatory requirement for people with physical or mental disabilities who are unable to submit an application online."[3] Furthermore, Express Entry allows employers, provinces, and territories to recruit and select skilled immigrants from a pool of candidates. The pool is created by requiring foreign nationals to first qualify for and obtain an **invitation to apply (ITA)** before submitting an application for permanent residence. Candidates compete with each other through the **Comprehensive Ranking System (CRS)**, which is used to rank candidates "with scores that reflect their human capital and ability to succeed in the Canadian economy."[4] In

invitation to apply (ITA)
under the Express Entry system, an invitation by CIC to foreign nationals who are qualified candidates to apply for permanent residence

Comprehensive Ranking System (CRS)
a point-based system that assesses and scores potential skilled worker candidates on their skills, work experience, language ability, education, and other factors, such as a job offer or a nomination by a province or territory

---

3 *Regulations Amending the Immigration and Refugee Protection Regulations*, PC 2014-1246 (6 November 2014) 148:24 C Gaz I, Regulatory Impact Analysis Statement, online: <http://gazette.gc.ca/rp-pr/p2/2014/2014-11-19/html/sor-dors256-eng.php>.

4 *Ibid.*

this way, the government is better able to control the number of applications from qualified candidates and has committed to processing them within six months.

The legislative framework for the Express Entry system was established in the government's *Economic Action Plan 2013 Act, No 2*, which received royal assent on December 12, 2013. This Act created a new division to the IRPA—division 0.1, including sections 10.1 to 10.4. The new sections of the Act set out broad provisions outlining the process for submitting applications and giving the minister the authority to determine the criteria for issuing invitations, including the number of invitations for any specified period. The minister also has the authority to determine:[5]

- which economic immigration programs are included in Express Entry and the eligibility criteria for applying;
- the process for submitting an Express Entry profile;
- the candidate ranking system;
- the system for resolving invitation-to-apply draws;
- how long candidates can be in the Express Entry pool and, if invited, time limits for submitting an application for permanent residence;
- how and what candidate information can be shared with third parties; and
- the method of notification to candidates about their expression of interest.

To control the number of applications and qualifying criteria, the minister announces regular rounds of invitations by way of instructions. The first set of instructions issued within the first month in January 2015 was for 779 invitations to be issued to candidates who were ranked a total of 886 points or more under the CRS; subsequent rounds may increase or decrease the number of invitations, the time frame, and the ranking (for example, 1,637 invitations within a one-day period between February 27, 2015 and February 28, 2015 were issued for candidates with 808 points).

After an applicant receives his ITA, the application process is no longer paper-based, and instead occurs by means of an electronic system (IRPA, s 14(5)).

There is no fee to complete and submit a profile in the Express Entry system. An applicant only pays a processing fee once he has received an ITA and submits an application for permanent residence.

Canadian Employers

Canadian employers have a direct role in recruiting economic immigrants to fill vacancies on a permanent basis when there are no suitable Canadian or permanent residents who can do so. Employers register with the Job Bank (<www.jobbank.gc.ca>) and can use private sector job boards and the PNP in their province to post job vacancies. Job postings can be viewed by foreign nationals who have prequalified to be in the pool of Express Entry candidates. By late 2015, the Job Bank will have a matching

---

5   Citizenship and Immigration Canada, "Ministerial Instructions for the Express Entry Application Management System" (26 June 2015), online: <http://www.cic.gc.ca/english/department/mi/>.

function that will connect eligible employers with Express Entry candidates so that employers can make a valid job offer or a provincial/territorial nomination. To help facilitate this, the government has committed to processing permanent residence applications in 80 percent of cases from receipt of complete application to final decision in six months or less.

Valid Job Offer

The Express Entry system has specific requirements for prospective employers. A prospective employer must provide a job offer supported by a labour market impact assessment (LMIA) by ESDC. There is no processing fee for an LMIA for Express Entry. ESDC provides an application form for employers to use for applying for an LMIA to support a permanent residence visa application for an Express Entry candidate. ESDC is responsible for ensuring that the job offer conforms to current rules and regulations by assessing the employment contract and conducting an employer compliance review. The assessment of the employer's application for the LMIA is based on a number of factors (see Chapter 5 for a discussion of the LMIA).

The LMIA serves as an opinion that allows an immigration officer to assess the effect that a permanent job offer to a foreign worker will have on Canada's economy (positive, negative, or neutral). Several factors are considered, such as wages, working conditions, the availability of Canadians or permanent residents to do the work, and the skills and knowledge transfer and job creation that may result from employing a foreign worker. For each class of economic immigrant, there are specific requirements for job offers that are supported by a positive LMIA:

1. A job offer in the FSW class:
   - must be permanent, non-seasonal, and full-time; and
   - must be skill type 0 (managerial occupations) or skill level A (professional occupations) or B (technical occupations and skilled trades) on the NOC list.

2. A job offer in the FST program:
   - must be for at least one year of full-time work;
   - must be skill level B (technical occupations and skilled trades) in one of the eligible occupations;
   - must have wages and working conditions comparable to those offered to Canadians working in the occupation; and
   - can be made by up to two employers.

3. A job offer in the CEC class:
   - must be permanent, non-seasonal, and full time; and
   - must be skill type 0 (managerial occupations) or skill level A (professional occupations) or B (technical occupations and skilled trades) on the NOC list.

4. A permanent job offer to a foreign national already working under the Temporary Foreign Worker Program in Canada:

- requires a new LMIA if the position or person was previously exempt from an LMIA; and

- does not require a new LMIA if the employer already has an LMIA for the position and now wishes to extend a permanent job offer to the candidate.

Skilled Workers: Pre-Application Stage

Pre-Application Stage

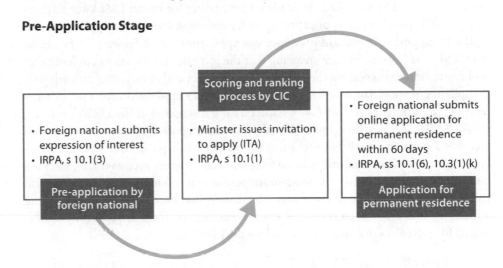

Pre-application by foreign national
- Foreign national submits expression of interest
- IRPA, s 10.1(3)

Scoring and ranking process by CIC
- Minister issues invitation to apply (ITA)
- IRPA, s 10.1(1)

Application for permanent residence
- Foreign national submits online application for permanent residence within 60 days
- IRPA, ss 10.1(6), 10.3(1)(k)

expression of interest
under the Express Entry system, the initial submission about skills, work experience, and other attributes that prospective immigrants make to indicate their interest in coming to Canada

Foreign nationals who wish to apply for permanent residence under certain classes within the economic stream must first create an online Express Entry profile on MyCIC at <www.cic.gc.ca/english/e-services/mycic.asp> to determine whether they have the necessary points to continue with the process. After creating a profile, they can submit an **expression of interest** through the CIC website (unless they are barred from doing so because they were previously found to be inadmissible for misrepresentation), where they are scored and ranked against the pool of applicants. Successful candidates—those who are selected from the pool of candidates with rankings that meet the criteria for each round of invitations—receive an ITA for permanent residence, and must submit an application for permanent residence online within 60 days. Applicants who do not wish to apply immediately remain in the system for up to 12 months.

If candidates have a sufficient number of points, they will be able to connect with employers to obtain immediate job offers. Applicants who do not have a job offer when they submit their expression of interest may register with the Canada Job Bank so that they can connect with Canadian employers seeking their specific skill set.

Comprehensive Ranking System

The CRS is a point-based system that assesses and scores a potential candidate based on skills, work experience, language ability, education, and other factors, such as a job offer or a nomination by a province or territory. The breakdown of points is not the same as that required for FSW or FST programs. Instead, as candidates progress in the pre-screening process, they are given a score out of 1,200 and ranked in the Express Entry pool. The specific calculation of points is complex and automated through the electronic system. The CRS ranks four different factors: (1) core human capital factors, (2) spouse or common law partner factors, (3) skills transferability factors, and (4) the valid job offer or a nomination from a province or territory factor. The CIC website provides a breakdown of the current scoring system (<www.cic.gc.ca/english/express-entry/grid-crs.asp>). Although a detailed discussion of the scoring system is beyond the scope of this text, what follows is an overview of the four parts of the calculation.

1. Core human capital factors: skills and experience factors—maximum 500 points for single candidates; 460 points for candidates with a spouse or common law partner.

Core Human Capital Factors

Factors	Points per factor with a spouse or common law partner	Points per factor without a spouse or common law partner
Age	100	110
Level of education	140	150
Official language proficiency	150	160
Canadian work experience	70	80
Total	460	500

2. Spouse or common law partner factors: maximum 40 points; only for candidates with a spouse or common law partner.

Spouse or Common Law Partner Factors

Factors	Points per factor (Maximum 40 points)
Level of education	10
Official language proficiency	20
Canadian work experience	10

3. Skills transferability: maximum 100 points.

Skill Transferability Factors—Maximum 100 Points

Education	Points per factor
	(Maximum 50 points)
With good/strong official language proficiency **and** a post-secondary degree	50
With Canadian work experience **and** a post-secondary degree	50
Foreign work experience	**Points per factor**
	(Maximum 50 points)
With good/strong official language proficiency (Canadian Language Benchmark (CLB) level 7 or higher) **and** foreign work experience	50
With Canadian work experience **and** foreign work experience	50
Certificate of qualification (for people in trade occupations)	**Points per factor**
	(Maximum 50 points)
With good/strong official language proficiency and a certificate of qualification	50

4. Valid job offer or a nomination from a province or territory: maximum 600 points.

Additional Points—Maximum 600 Points

Factor	Points per factor
Arranged employment (positive LMIA required)	600
PN nomination	600

To see how points are calculated, you can work through the case study at the end of the chapter. "A Tale of Two Brothers" sets out a table of factors for two different situations (with or without spouse, and with or without Canadian work experience).

Federal Skilled Workers

Even after receiving the ITA, foreign nationals who apply for permanent residence in the FSW class are assessed on a number of eligibility criteria including education, skills, work experience, language ability, and other qualifications needed to contribute to the Canadian labour market.

New regulations to the FSW program that modified the "points grid" were introduced in 2013. The following scenario demonstrates how points are assessed for permanent residence as a skilled worker.

Gautem Patel was born in Ahmedabad, Gujarat, on the west coast of India in 1982. His native language is Gujarati. He learned English at school and speaks, understands, reads, and writes fluently. He was briefly exposed to the French language as a young boy when his parents worked in the kitchen at a French consulate, but he only knows basic phrases such as "Je m'appelle Gautem."

Gautem attended primary school at the Municipal School Harda from 1987 to 1995, then attended Sadhana Higher Secondary School from 1995 to 1999. He worked in various health and yoga centres until 2003, then decided to go back to school to become a dietitian. In 2007, he graduated from a four-year degree program with a bachelor's degree in nutritional science (BSc) from the Gujarat Institute of Nutrition and Biochemistry. He has worked for the same company—Good Planet Children's Nutrition Institute of Research—in food and nutrition research as a clinical dietitian since June 2007, analyzing scientific nutritional studies and conducting research into and evaluating program effectiveness to improve the nutritional value, taste, appearance, and preparation of food for infants. In 2009, he married Diya. Diya completed a four-year bachelor's degree in 2008 and worked as an English teacher until the birth of their son, Sanjit, in 2010. Two years later, Priya, their daughter, was born. Diya has not returned to work.

In October 2015, Gautem attended an international health conference about childhood obesity hosted by the International Coalition of Child and Youth Nutritionists in Vancouver, British Columbia. Gautem met several health professionals during the conference, and was greatly inspired by the healthy lifestyle in Vancouver.

Rita, the director of the Vancouver Institute for Child Health and Nutrition, was impressed with Gautem's experience and invited him to tour the clinic. She told Gautem that she is looking to put together a highly qualified team of experts for the new clinic, but that it has been difficult to recruit and attract Canadians with Gautem's background and experience. She wants to offer him the position of chief of research and nutrition, where he would have the opportunity to advance new technologies and methodologies in childhood healthy food strategies. Gautem loves the cosmopolitan city of Vancouver and sees this as a once-in-a-lifetime opportunity to make a real impact in his field, and provide a good life for his family.

Gautem knows nothing about immigrating to Canada, but thinks he would have to apply under the FSW class. Diya is excited at the possibility of moving to Vancouver and reconnecting with her mother's sister and family. Gautem created his profile on the CIC website and applied using the Express Entry system. He received his ITA and now has 60 days to apply for permanent residence.

Is Gautem Patel a good candidate for immigrating as a permanent resident under the FSW class with his family? We consider this question in the sections below.

Requirements for Federal Skilled Workers

In our scenario, Gautem Patel is destined for Vancouver, British Columbia. To be successful in his application for permanent residence, Gautem, as the principal applicant, must first meet the minimal work experience, language, and education requirements for the FSW class, pursuant to section 75(2) of the IRPR, as follows:

1. Work experience
   - Gautem has accumulated, over a continuous period, at least one year of full-time work experience, or the equivalent in part-time work, in the occupation identified in his application as his primary occupation, that is listed in skill type 0 or skill level A or B of the NOC.
   - His occupation is not considered a restricted occupation.
   - He performed the actions described in the lead statement of the NOC for the occupation and performed a substantial number of the main duties for the occupation, including all of the essential duties set out in the occupational description of the NOC.

In British Columbia, dietitians are regulated by the College of Dietitians of British Columbia. If Gautem is going to work as a dietitian, he will be required to take steps to become licensed in that province. Rita is offering Gautem a position as chief of research and nutrition, and is likely to know whether a person in this occupation requires licensing and how to become licensed.

2. Language ability
   - Gautem must submit the results of his language test at the time of completing the Express Entry profile to show that he has met or exceeded the language threshold set by the minister, including competency in speaking, listening, reading, and writing in one or both official languages.
   - Test results must be less than two years old on the date of application to be valid.

3. Education
   - At the time of completing the Express Entry profile, Gautem must submit his Canadian secondary (high school) or post-secondary certificate, diploma, or degree, or an educational credential assessment (ECA) report from a CIC-approved agency that shows that the foreign education credential is equal to Canadian educational standards.
   - The ECA must be less than five years old on the date of application.

For some professions, the minister will designate specific institutions to carry out the assessment of the foreign diploma, certificate, or credential to ensure that it is relevant to the occupation and that it is equivalent to the Canadian educational credential required to practise in that occupation.

Gautem's application will be further assessed by a visa officer to ensure that he meets selection criteria specific to the FSW class, to show that he will be able to become economically established in Canada. Specifically (IRPR, s 76(1)),

- he must have enough points to meet or exceed the pass mark under the point system (discussed below); and
- he must be self-supporting upon arrival (that is, have a job offer) or be able to show that he has sufficient settlement funds.

Finally, Gautem and his family members must not be inadmissible (as discussed in Chapter 3, Admissibility).

Point System

Canada has used a point-based system to assess skilled workers since 1976. Under the *Immigration Act* of 1976, skilled workers were known as "independent applicants," because they were not financially reliant on sponsors or the government for their settlement.

The point system was designed to improve consistency and fairness by reducing discretion and the potential for discrimination in selecting immigrants. Under the point system, immigration officers assign points up to a fixed maximum in each of several categories. The minister is authorized to set the pass mark, or "minimum number of points required of a skilled worker," under section 76(2) of the IRPR. Such authority in the regulations allows the minister to increase or decrease the pass mark without having the standard debated in the House of Commons when there are changes in the Canadian economic and social landscape, or when there are changing demands for prospective immigrants. The pass mark is the minimum required total out of a possible 100 points for six selection factors. At the time of writing, the pass mark was set at 67 points.

In 2013, there were major changes to the point system. The point system now

- gives higher priority to younger workers;
- places emphasis on fluency in official languages, with the requirement to attain a minimum official language proficiency;
- awards points for Canadian work experience; and
- awards points for an applicant whose spouse has fluency in official languages and/or Canadian work experience.

After meeting the minimal requirements in section 75(2) of the IRPR, the principal applicant will be further assessed against the point system and must achieve a passing score on the selection grid.

When the regulations were introduced in 2002, 70 out of 100 possible points were spread over only three factors—education, language skills, and work experience—to show the importance of these factors in the selection of skilled workers. A decade later, the point system has been updated to offset the barriers that well-educated newcomers face in becoming economically established. There is now a greater emphasis on the selection of foreign nationals who are younger and have Canadian work experience, although education and fluency in Canada's official languages remain important factors.

The six selection factors for federal skilled workers are set out in sections 78 to 83 of the IRPR as follows:

1. education,
2. language proficiency in English and French,
3. work experience,
4. age,
5. arranged employment, and
6. adaptability.

Points are allocated to the principal applicant with a view to selecting applicants who possess attributes that will lead to their becoming economically established.

The current selection factors and points are as follows:

Selection factor (IRPR)	Maximum number of points
Education (s 78)	25
Proficiency in official languages (s 79)	28
Work experience (s 80)	15
Age (s 81)	12
Arranged employment (s 82)	10
Adaptability (s 83)	10
Total	100
Current pass mark	67

Each of the selection factors is briefly described below.

A worksheet for calculating points under the Federal Skilled Worker Program is included in Appendix A.

Education Factor

The visa officer awards up to 25 points for education. This is generally based, first, on the number of years of completed full-time or full-time-equivalent studies and, second, on the applicant's educational credentials.

The term "Canadian educational credential" is defined in section 73(1) of the IRPR as

> any diploma, certificate or credential, issued on the completion of a Canadian program of study or training at an educational or training institution that is

recognized by the provincial authorities responsible for registering, accrediting, supervising and regulating such institutions.

Section 78 of the IRPR sets out the education selection factor as follows:

Education Factor—Maximum 25 Points

Credential	Points
Secondary school educational credential (e.g. diploma)	5
One-year post-secondary credential	15
Two-year post-secondary credential	19
Three-year or longer post-secondary credential	21
Two or more post-secondary credentials, one of which is a three-year or longer post-secondary credential	22
Master's level or professional degree or an entry-to-practice professional degree for an occupation listed in the NOC matrix at skill level A for which licensing by a provincial regulatory body is required	23
Doctoral level	25

Educational credentials are measured on the basis of the **Canadian educational credentials** or **equivalency assessments** submitted in support of an application for a permanent resident visa that result in the highest number of points.

How many points would Gautem Patel score for education? This is a summary of Gautem's studies:

Canadian educational credential
any diploma, certificate, or credential, issued on the completion of a Canadian program of study or training at a registered/accredited educational or training institution (IRPR, s 73(1))

equivalency assessment
a determination by a designated organization or institution that a foreign diploma, certificate, or credential is equivalent to a Canadian educational credential and an assessment of the authenticity of the foreign diploma, certificate, or credential (IRPR, s 73(1))

Overview of Gautem Patel's Education

From	To	Institution	City/country	Degree/diploma held
2003	2007	Gujarat Institute of Nutrition and Biochemistry	Surat, India	Bachelor's degree in nutritional science
1995	1999	Sadhana Higher Secondary School	Mumbai, India	Secondary school diploma
1987	1995	Municipal School Harda	Harda, Madhya Pradesh, India	Primary school

Gautem has a four-year university degree, which matches the category "Three-year or longer post-secondary credential." He exceeds the requirement for a post-secondary credential. He does not have a second credential or a master's degree, so he cannot receive more points. Gautem would therefore receive 21 points.

Language Proficiency

The ability to secure employment in Canada is often predicated on a person's ability to communicate proficiently in one or more of Canada's official languages. Therefore, there is a greater emphasis placed on an applicant's fluency. This is why applicants receive credit both in the pre-application stage of Express Entry and under the specific class of permanent residence.

As of June 26, 2010, all applicants in the FSW class are required to submit the results of a language proficiency test (that is, the International English Language Testing System [IELTS] and the Canadian English Language Proficiency Index Program [CELPIP] for English, and the Test d'Evaluation du Français [TEF] for French), even if the applicant is from an English- or French-speaking country. The total number that may be awarded for this factor is a combined 28 points for both official languages. The principal applicant should consider which of the two languages, English or French, she is most proficient in and select it as her first Canadian official language on the application form.

Visa officers do not assess language proficiency, they award points based on language test results. Under section 79(2) of the IRPR, language test scores are compared to the benchmarks referred to in the Canadian Language Benchmarks (CLB) for English and *Niveaux de compétence linguistique canadiens* for French. These benchmarks assess four **language skill areas**: speaking, oral comprehension (listening), reading, and writing. The benchmarks achieved are then scored for points.

It is important for the applicant to make the distinction between "first" and "second" official language, because more points are awarded for proficiency in the first official language. The language selection factor is measured as follows:

language skill area
speaking, oral comprehension, reading, or writing (IRPR, s 73(1))

First Official Language Ability—Maximum 24 Points

Proficiency	CLB	Speak	Listen	Read	Write
High	9	6	6	6	6
Moderate	8	5	5	5	5
Basic	7	4	4	4	4

Returning to our scenario, how many points would Gautem Patel score for language proficiency? Gautem selected English as his first official language, because his English skills are stronger than his French skills. He is proficient in all four abilities with respect to English, and his score is therefore the highest possible: 24 points.

Where an applicant has language abilities in a second official language, only 4 points are awarded if his proficiency meets or exceeds CLB benchmark 5 in each of the four language skill areas.

Second Official Language Ability—Maximum 4 Points

Proficiency	CLB	Speak	Listen	Read	Write
Minimum level 5 in all skills	5	1	1	1	1

Proficiency	CLB	Speak	Listen	Read	Write
No points	4 or lower	0	0	0	0

Gautem can only speak simple phrases in French, and it seems unlikely that he would have the ability to understand and speak at an intermediate level, so he probably would not bother to undergo testing in a second official language.

Therefore, Gautem's total language score would be measured at 24 points.

Work Experience

The visa officer awards points based on the principal applicant's **full-time work** experience or the equivalent in part-time work that occurred within the past ten years of the date of the application for permanent residence.

full-time work
at least 30 hours of work over a period of one week (IRPR, s 73(1))

One year of full-time work is calculated as 30 hours per week for 12 months (for a total of 1,560 hours) at one or more jobs, or 15 hours per week for 24 months (for a total of 1,560 hours).

The applicant must show past performance of the main and essential duties of the occupation as described in the NOC to meet the regulatory definition of work experience. Furthermore, that work experience must be in the category of skill type 0, or skill level A or B, according to the NOC. Therefore, the principal applicant must provide the four-digit NOC code that corresponds to the occupation indicated on her application form.

Recalling our scenario, would Gautem Patel meet the minimum work experience requirements of having at least one year of continuous full-time paid work experience within the past ten years of the date of application in the category of skill type 0, or skill level A or B, according to the NOC?

Gautem would have to consult the NOC to find the code for his occupation as a clinical dietitian. The code for "dietitians and nutritionists" is 3132, which is skill type "3—Health occupations"; the description of the duties for jobs in these fields is included there. Gautem's job title is listed and the duties described are a match with the work he performed. We know from the scenario that he has been working full-time since 2007. He therefore exceeds the minimum requirement of work experience in an occupation that is listed in the NOC.

The visa officer awards up to a maximum of 15 points, as follows (IRPR, s 80(1)):

Years of Experience Within the Ten Years Preceding the Date of Application

	Less than one year	One year	Two to three years	Four to five years	Six or more years
Points	0	9	11	13	15

Finally, the work experience may not be in an occupation considered a **restricted occupation**. Under section 73 of the IRPR, the minister has the authority to restrict an occupation on the basis of labour market demands and consultations with ESDC,

restricted occupation
an occupation designated by the minister, taking into account labour market activity on both an area and a national basis, following consultation with ESDC, provincial governments, and any other relevant organizations or institutions

the provinces, and other organizations. At the time of writing, there are currently no designated restricted occupations.

How many points would Gautem Patel score for work experience? He would have to provide a detailed account of his work history, setting out the from-and-to dates, the employers, locations, and the title of the positions held along with the classification of the occupation according to the NOC, and the number of hours worked. On the basis of the case scenario, we know the following:

Assessment of Work Experience—Maximum 15 Points

From	To	Employer	City/Country	Position	NOC code	Hours per year
2007	Current	Good Planet Children's Nutrition Institute of Research	India	Clinical dietitian	3132	1,560 hours per year since 2007

Gautem has performed the duties of clinical dietitian (code 3132) on a full-time basis since 2007. This amounts to more than six years of experience. Therefore, he would be awarded the full 15 points.

Age

Points based on age are awarded as set out in section 81 of the IRPR.

The visa officer awards a maximum of 12 points to a principal applicant who is 18 years of age but less than 36 years of age. For every year that an applicant is older than 36, one point is subtracted, as follows:

Assessment of Age—Maximum 12 Points

Years of age	Points
18 or older but less than 36	12
36	11
37	10
38	9
39	8
40	7
41	6
42	5
43	4
44	3
45	2
46	1
Under 18 years of age or 47 years of age or older	0

How many points would Gautem Patel score for age? He was born in 1982. If he submits his application before 2019, he will fall within the range for maximum points and would score the full 12 points because he will still be under 36.

Arranged Employment

"Arranged employment" is a current offer of employment in Canada (made within two years of the date of the application for permanent residence) for an indeterminate term (meaning that the job must be open-ended and not for a fixed term), and the job must be non-seasonal. The visa officer may award 10 points if the principal applicant provides proof of an approved offer of employment, in accordance with section 82 of the IRPR. However, the occupation must be listed in skill type 0 or skill level A or B of the NOC matrix. Furthermore, the officer will assess whether the applicant is able to perform the duties, and is likely to accept and carry out the employment.

Proof of a job offer is obtained from ESDC. The full 10 points are awarded if the applicant satisfies one of the following four conditions:

1. The applicant is already in Canada as a temporary resident, holds a valid work visa based on a positive LMIA, is currently working in the job, and has a valid job offer for an indeterminate period for that same job if the applicant is accepted as a skilled worker.

2. The applicant is already in Canada as a temporary visitor under one of the international treaties for business visitors (such as NAFTA) and is exempt from the LMIA requirement, is working in the job, and has a valid job offer for an indeterminate period for that same job if the applicant is accepted as a skilled worker.

3. The applicant does not intend to work in Canada before becoming a permanent resident and has an approved job offer for an indeterminate period if the applicant is selected as a skilled worker.

4. The applicant is already in Canada as a temporary resident, holds a valid work visa or is a temporary visitor under one of the international treaties for business visitors, and has a valid job offer for an indeterminate period for another job if the applicant is accepted as a skilled worker.

How many points would Gautem Patel score for arranged employment? If Rita, the director of the Vancouver Institute for Child Health and Nutrition, follows through with her job offer, she must apply for the LMIA from ESDC. When assessing a job offer, ESDC will consider the following:

- that the category of the occupation matches the majority of duties in the NOC;
- the wages and working conditions;
- the genuineness of the offer and the employer's history; and
- that the offer is for a full-time, permanent job that is non-seasonal.

If the approval is obtained, Gautem will be assessed as having arranged employment and awarded a total of 10 points. Without a job offer, no points will be awarded.

Adaptability

Adaptability encompasses a variety of factors that are likely to benefit the applicant's chances of successful integration into Canadian society. These may include language proficiency, education, previous work or study in Canada, and arranged work, as they relate to both the applicant and the applicant's spouse or common law partner. The rationale for this is that if the applicant's partner is likely to integrate well into Canadian life, this will assist the applicant to do so as well. Other support networks, such as relatives in Canada, can also increase the applicant's chances of successful integration.

The elements for which the applicant may accumulate (in combination) up to a maximum of 10 points, as set out in section 83 of the IRPR, are as follows:

Assessment of Adaptability—Maximum 10 Points

Element	Description	Points
1. Language proficiency of spouse or common law partner	Proficiency of at least benchmark level 4 in either official language for all four language skill areas	5
2. Previous study in Canada by the principal applicant	Full-time study of at least two academic years in a program of at least two years in duration, whether or not the skilled worker has obtained an educational credential	5
3. Previous study in Canada by the spouse or common law partner	Full-time study in Canada of at least two academic years in a program of at least two years in duration, whether or not the accompanying spouse or common law partner obtained an educational credential for completing a program	5
4. Previous work in Canada by the principal applicant	For any previous period of full-time work under a work permit or under s 186 of the IRPR of at least one year in Canada in an occupation that is listed in skill type 0—Management Occupations or skill level A or B	10
5. Previous work in Canada by the spouse or common law partner	For any previous period of full-time work by the spouse under a work permit or under s 186 of the IRPR of at least one year in Canada in an occupation that is listed in skill type 0—Management Occupations or skill level A or B	5
6. Family relationships in Canada	The principal applicant or his accompanying spouse or common law partner is related to a Canadian citizen or permanent resident who is 18 years or older and a parent, grandparent, child, grandchild, child of a parent, child of a grandparent, or grandchild of a parent	5
7. Arranged employment	The principal applicant was awarded points under the arranged employment factor	5

How many points would Gautem Patel score for adaptability? He will be awarded points as a result of Diya's language proficiency. We can assume that as an English teacher, Diya is likely to meet and exceed benchmark level 4 in all four language skill areas; Gautem would therefore likely receive 5 points under adaptability. Neither Gautem nor Diya previously studied or worked in Canada, so Gautem cannot be awarded points on that basis; however, Diya has an aunt in Vancouver, which is a family relationship that would be counted for an additional 5 points for adaptability.

With Gautem's job offer, he could also be credited 5 points for having arranged employment. However, Gautem cannot acquire more than 10 points for adaptability. The total number of points earned by Gautem for adaptability would be 10 points.

Gautem Patel's overall total number of points for all factors exceeds the pass mark of 67:

Assessment of Points for Gautem Patel

Education	21
Official languages	24
Experience	15
Age	12
Arranged employment	10
Adaptability	10
Total	92
Pass Mark	67

Settlement Funds

According to section 76(b) of the IRPR, the applicant must show proof of sufficient settlement funds, unless employment has been arranged. The settlement funds must be enough to support the applicant and any dependants, and are assessed according to the applicant's family size using 50 percent of Statistics Canada's most current low income cut-off (LICO) for urban areas with populations of 500,000 or more. (See Chapter 7 for a discussion of LICO.)

If Gautem Patel has a valid job offer, he would be exempt from the requirement of settlement funds. Without a job offer, Gautem may not receive a sufficiently high ranking in the Express Entry system. However, if he were to receive the ITA without a job offer, he would have to calculate the amount of settlement funds required for his family of four (himself, his wife, and their two children), find the matching minimum amount from the LICO table, and divide it in half (which represents the amount of settlement funds for six months). The CIC website provides a table for settlement funds, which appears as follows at the time of writing:

	Number of family members	Funds required (Cdn $)
Gautem	1	$11,931
+ Diya	2	$14,853
+ Sanjit	3	$18,260
+ Priya	**4**	**$22,170**
	5	$25,145
	6	$28,359
	7 or more	$31,574

Source: Citizenship and Immigration Canada, "Proof of Funds—Skilled Immigrants (Express Entry)" (28 January 2015), online: <http://www.cic.gc.ca/english/immigrate/skilled/funds.asp>.

"Invitation to Apply" Procedures for Federal Skilled Immigrants

As of January 2015, foreign nationals interested in applying as skilled immigrants must apply through the Express Entry system. Upon receiving the ITA, applicants are provided with a document checklist. Using this checklist, they must submit clearly scanned documentation in support of their permanent residence applications online. Instructions are also provided for medical examinations and police checks. Examples of documents include copies of the following:

- passport or travel documents;
- language test results;
- ECA reports;
- a written job offer from a Canadian employer or provincial nomination, or proof of funds to support the applicant and accompanying family members;
- results of the medical exam from a panel physician; and
- police checks/clearances and certificates.

Federal Skilled Trades

Unlike foreign nationals who apply under the FSW class, foreign nationals who apply for permanent residence under the FST program are not assessed on a point system. However, there are many similarities to qualifying for permanent resident status.

skilled trade occupation
an occupation listed in skill level B of the NOC matrix as major group 72, 73, 82, or 92 or as minor group 632 or 633 (IRPR, s 87.2)

A **skilled trade occupation** (IRPR, s 87.2(1)) is defined as

an occupation, unless the occupation has been designated a restricted occupation by the Minister, in the following categories listed in Skill Level B of the *National Occupational Classification* matrix:

(a) Major Group 72, industrial, electrical and construction trades;

(b) Major Group 73, maintenance and equipment operation trades;

(c) Major Group 82, supervisors and technical occupations in natural resources, agriculture and related production;

(d) Major Group 92, processing, manufacturing and utilities supervisors and central control operators;

(e) Minor Group 632, chefs and cooks; and

(f) Minor Group 633, butchers and bakers.

Eligibility Requirements for Federal Skilled Trades

The following scenario demonstrates how a foreign national may be selected as a FST.

Kayleigh is a single, 29-year-old citizen of Ireland who is applying under the FST class. She studied at the School of Culinary Arts and Food Technology at the Dublin Institute of Technology in Ireland, where she earned a three-year BSc (baking and pastry arts management) level 7 degree. For the last five years, she has worked full-time as a certified master baker (NOC code 6332) for one of the large commercial bakeries in Cork. She has performed both the duties in the lead statement and the main duties that appear in the NOC. Her duties included a broad range of complex, technical, and professional activities that are involved in managing the production area of an in-store commercial bakery to produce high-quality baked goods, including being responsible for sanitation, management, retail sales, merchandising, and training. Although she is from an English-speaking country, Kayleigh had to take a language test to qualify under Express Entry, obtaining level 9 on the CLB in each of the competency areas of speaking, listening, reading, and writing in English.

What requirements must Kayleigh meet to succeed in an application for permanent residence?

To be successful in her application for permanent residence, Kayleigh, as the principal applicant, must meet the following language, work experience, and education requirements under the IRPR for foreign nationals:

1. *Language (IRPR, s 87.2(3)(a))*: "[F]ollowing an evaluation by an organization or institution designated under subsection 74(3), they meet the threshold fixed by the Minister under subsection 74(1) for proficiency in either English or French for each of the four language skill areas." The minimum language requirements are CLB 5 for speaking and listening, and CLB 4 for reading and writing.

   With a score of 9 in all language competency areas, Kayleigh meets and exceeds the language requirements.

2. *Work experience (IRPR, s 87.2(3)(b))*: During the five years before an application is submitted, applicants must have acquired at least two years of full-time work experience, or the equivalent in part-time work, in their skilled trade occupation, and must have performed both the actions described in the lead statement and a substantial number of the main duties listed in the NOC description of the occupation.

   Kayleigh has worked as a certified master baker for the last five years, so she meets and exceeds the work experience requirement.

3. *Relevant employment requirements (IRPR, s 87.2(3)(c))*: There are a number of different scenarios for determining whether a foreign national has the relevant employment experience, which may be either trade certification or Canadian work experience, in order to be eligible under this class. The foreign national must meet the relevant employment requirements of the skilled trade occupation specified in the application as set out in the NOC, except for the requirement to obtain a certificate of qualification issued by a competent provincial authority.

   As a certified master baker (NOC code 6332), Kayleigh has performed the main duties in the lead statement and the duties that appear in the NOC. The regulations (at s 87.2(3)(d)) provide the details for determining when a foreign national may qualify as a member of the FST class in different situations, such as when the applicant acquires her experience as a temporary worker with a work permit in Canada. For example, Kayleigh would have to have either certification or an offer of employment for her trade in Canada. Whether she will need certification will depend on where she intends to reside. For example, in Ontario, trade certification is voluntary, but in British Columbia, bakers require "Red Seal" certification or a certificate of apprenticeship, or may write a challenge test with the Industry Training Authority. Applicants who do not have a certification may acquire experience as temporary workers on valid work permits, or they need a job offer. Given that Kayleigh has not previously worked in Canada, she will need offers of employment from up to two employers in Canada, and the offers must be to work for at least one year in her trade as a baker.

4. *Education*: There is no education requirement for this class. However, to earn points under Express Entry, Kayleigh needs either a Canadian post-secondary certificate, diploma, or degree, or an ECA report produced by an agency approved by CIC, such as the International Credential Assessment Service of Canada (ICAS), to show that her education is equal to Canadian educational standards.

Canadian Experience Class

The CEC is another prescribed class of persons who are selected on the basis of their ability to become economically established in Canada, their experience in Canada, and their intention to reside in a province other than Quebec (which has its own program, Quebec Experience Program). International students who are graduates of a Canadian post-secondary institution and who possess professional, managerial, or skilled Canadian work experience may apply for permanent residence under the CEC. Certain temporary foreign workers (TFWs) may also apply for permanent residence through this program. Changes to the IRPR created the CEC in 2008, allowing graduates from post-secondary institutions and TFWs with Canadian experience to transition to permanent resident status.

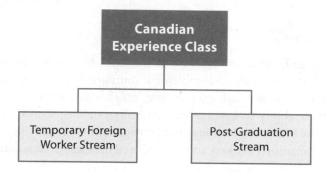

To qualify for permanent residence, a temporary foreign resident must meet the criteria set out in section 87.1(2) of the IRPR to prove that she has gained the following required work experience:

- at least 12 months of full-time work (or an equal amount in part-time work);
- in one or more occupations that are listed in skill type 0 or skill level A or B of the NOC matrix;
- within the past 36 months;
- that included the performance of the actions described in the lead statement for the occupation as set out in the occupational descriptions of the NOC matrix; and
- that included the performance of a substantial number of the main duties of the occupation as set out in the occupational descriptions of the NOC matrix, including all of the essential duties.

Applicants must take a language test to show proficiency in one of Canada's official languages, and the test results must be less than two years old on the date of application to be valid. The IRPR (s 87.1(2)(d)) requires the applicant to show a language proficiency that corresponds to the Canadian Language Benchmarks 2000 for the English language or the *Niveaux de compétence linguistique canadiens 2006* for the French language. The specific benchmarks are set out according to the applicant's work experience.

Provincial Nominees

Provincial Nominees

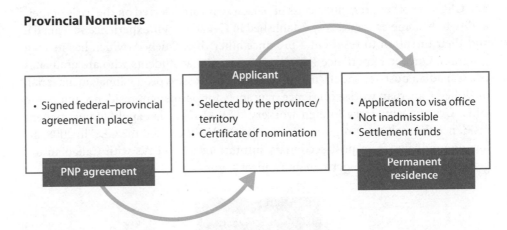

The minister is authorized by section 8 of the IRPA to sign agreements with the provinces, and to coordinate and implement immigration policies and programs. Individuals who are nominated by a province "may become permanent residents on the basis of their ability to become economically established in Canada" (IRPR, ss 87(1), (2)). The **Provincial Nominee Program** can generally provide quicker entry into Canada for qualified workers and experienced business professionals who wish to settle as permanent residents in a particular province.

The PNP provides the provinces with the benefits of targeted recruiting and the selection of foreign nationals who can help meet the local labour market and economic needs of each province, such as filling a skills shortage or attracting specialized occupational skills. Unlike the FSW and FST programs, the PNP may include the selection of semi- or low-skilled professions, and those applicants do not have to be assessed against selection factors (unless the province makes this a requirement).

The province must first enter into an agreement with the federal government to establish a PNP, because the responsibilities are shared between the two levels of government. The agreements allow the provinces to conduct their own recruiting and selection of foreign nationals, who are nominated and must then undergo an inadmissibility assessment by the federal government.

Provincial agreements and nominee programs are outlined in Appendix C.

Provincial Nominee Program

a program that allows provinces and territories to nominate foreign nationals to apply for permanent residence in Canada

Application Procedures for a Provincial Nominee Program

As with other classes of skilled workers, foreign nationals who wish to apply under a PNP must take a language test. As of July 2013, applicants in the PNP category who are applying for jobs in semi- or low-skilled professions (NOC level C and D occupations) are required to submit the results of a language proficiency test (that is, the IELTS and CELPIP for English, or the TEF for French) even if they are from an English- or French-speaking country. The ability to communicate proficiently in one or more of Canada's official languages is highly valued in the selection of new immigrants.

There are two application processes for foreign nationals who apply to be nominated under this program:

- an application to the province for nomination, and
- an application to a federal visa officer for permanent residence.

The criteria for nomination vary from province to province. Each province has its own categories or streams of occupations with the corresponding application package, which must be submitted with related documentation and appropriate fees. The province nominates the individual, together with any spouse or common law partner and dependent children, for permanent residence on the basis of that person's ability to contribute knowledge and skills and become economically established in the province.

An applicant who meets the province's selection criteria is notified by letter, so that she may begin the second stage of the application process. The province also issues a certificate of nomination and notifies CIC officials at the appropriate visa office.

Each province has a time frame for submission of the application for permanent residence to the visa office. Generally, the nominated applicant submits the application package together with the certificate of nomination and the appropriate fees to the Canadian immigration office (CIO) in Canada.

The application kit consists of a guide, several forms, and other information that is changed from time to time, so it is important to check for updates. Key federal forms include:

- Application for Permanent Residence: Guide for Provincial Nominees Instruction Guide (IMM P7000);
- Generic Application Form for Canada (IMM 0008);
- Schedule A: Background/Declaration (IMM 5669);
- Schedule 4: Economic Classes—Provincial Nominees (IMM 0008 Schedule 4);
- Schedule 4A: Economic Classes: Provincial Nominees—Business Nominees (IMM 0008 Schedule 4A);
- Additional Family Information (IMM 5406);
- Use of a Representative (IMM 5476), if the applicant uses a representative to complete the application; and
- Document Checklist (IMM 5690).

The certificate of nomination is required for the visa officer's assessment, along with the applicant's forms and other supporting documentation, including status and marriage documents, language test results, medical examination results, and police checks. A nomination by the province does not guarantee that the applicant will be granted permanent residence—the final decision rests solely with CIC.

Decisions

Applications for permanent residence by members of the provincial nominee class are decided by visa officers. The officer evaluates the nominated applicant's ability to become economically established in Canada, according to sections 87(1) and (2) of the IRPR, and ensures that the foreign national has a nomination certificate and intends to reside in the province that has nominated her; the officer also assesses inadmissibility.

If all the requirements are met and the application is accepted, the visa officer issues a visa allowing the applicant to travel to Canada as a permanent resident, and a confirmation of permanent residence document (COPR) and permanent resident visa. The names of both accompanying and non-accompanying family members are included on the visa of the principal applicant. The principal applicant and all accompanying family members must travel before the expiry date on their visas.

Business Immigration Program

The second stream of permanent residence immigration in the economic class is business immigration. Business immigrant applicants are selected primarily on the basis of their ability to create jobs for themselves and other Canadians. Requirements vary depending on the subcategory. The business immigrant program allows for the immigration of experienced business persons who can stimulate national and regional economic development in Canada with their financial capital and business knowledge. Business immigration represents only a small part of overall immigration: in 2013, only 5,098 persons were admitted as permanent residents under the federal business class, representing 3.5 percent of the total number in the economic classes and just under 2 percent of the total of new permanent residents (including their spouses and dependants).[6]

The regulations provide for three categories of business immigration:

- entrepreneurs,
- investors, and
- self-employed persons.

On June 19, 2014, however, applications that were in the backlog of the federal Immigrant Investor Program (IIP) and the Entrepreneur Program were terminated. The government replaced the IIP with the Immigrant Investor Venture Capital (IIVC) Pilot Program in December 2014 for people with high net worth who are able to invest in the Immigrant Investor Venture Capital Fund, but only accepted applications for two brief rounds in early 2015. The Entrepreneur Program was replaced with the Start-Up Visa program, aimed at "innovative immigrant entrepreneurs

---

6   Annual Report, *supra* note 1 at table 2, online: <http://www.cic.gc.ca/english/resources/publications/annual-report-2014/index.asp#sec-2-1>.

who will create new jobs and spur economic growth."[7] The one category that has undergone little change is the Self-Employed Persons Program.

A general overview of the eligibility requirements for the Start-Up Visa and Self-Employed Persons programs is provided below. As with all immigrants, the admissibility requirements apply to business immigration applicants and their family members.

Applications

Applicants in the Business Immigration Program do not apply through Express Entry. Application kits for each type of business immigration are available on the CIC website, and consist of a guide, generic forms, forms specific to the immigration program, and other instructions.

Applicants mail their completed packages to a CIO (for example, self-employed persons submit their applications to Sydney, Nova Scotia), which controls the number of applications processed and checks for completeness.

If the application is deemed complete, it is sent for processing to the visa office, which sends the applicant a letter of receipt with the visa office file number so that the applicant can track the progress of the case online.

Visa officers examine the application to ensure the applicant meets the statutory requirements and selection criteria: they examine business and financial background, evaluate the soundness of business plans in Canada, and ensure that the applicant's wealth was not obtained illegally—for example, certain applicants in the IIVC Pilot Program were required to submit due diligence reports from independent consultants to confirm that their wealth was obtained legally through private sector business or investment activity.

Settlement Funds

Business immigrant applicants must show that they have sufficient funds to support themselves and their family members for at least one year after arriving in Canada, because they do not receive any financial support from the Canadian government. Generally, the net worth requirements ensure that applicants will be able to support themselves.

Start-Up Visa Program

The purpose of the Start-Up Visa Program is to link immigrant entrepreneurs with private Canadian angel investor groups or venture capital fund organizations that have experience working with start-ups and can provide essential resources. A maximum of 2,750 applications will be processed per year under the Start-Up Business

---

7 Citizenship and Immigration Canada, News Release, "Historic New Immigration Program to Attract Job Creators to Canada" (24 January 2013), online: <http://news.gc.ca/web/article-en.do ?nid=717119>.

Class. Applicants do not have to invest their own money. A start-up business must be a new business intended to be operated in Canada that meets the criteria of a qualifying business and that has received support from a designated business organization, such as a business incubator.

The "Ministerial Instructions Respecting the Start-Up Business Class, 2014" define a qualifying business as follows:

> [A] corporation that is incorporated in and carrying on business in Canada is a qualifying business if, at the time the commitment is made,
> (a) the applicant holds 10% or more of the voting rights attached to all shares of the corporation outstanding at that time; and
> (b) no persons or entities, other than qualified participants, hold 50% or more of the total amount of the voting rights attached to all shares of the corporation outstanding at that time.[8]

If the applicant is accepted into a Canadian business incubator program, no investment is required. Otherwise, applicants must secure the following:

- a minimum investment of $200,000, if the investment comes from one or more designated Canadian venture capital funds; or

- a minimum investment of $75,000, if the investment comes from two or more designated Canadian angel investor groups.

Eligibility

Eligibility criteria for the Start-Up Visa Program are as follows:

letter of support
under the Business Start-Up Program, a written commitment by a designated organization to an applicant confirming the organization's support of the applicant's business idea; the letter must be included with the application for permanent residence

- The applicant must provide a **letter of support** stating that the business venture or idea is supported by a designated organization (for example, designated venture capital funds, designated angel investor groups, or designated business incubators). The designated organization must also send a commitment certificate directly to CIC. Both the letter of support and the commitment certificate are used to assess the application.

- The applicant must meet the language requirements by showing proficiency in either English or French for each of the four language skill areas. The minimum language requirements are CLB 5 in all four language competency areas (speaking, reading, writing, and listening).

- The applicant must have sufficient settlement funds, assessed using 50 percent of Statistics Canada's current LICO for urban areas with populations of 500,000 or more.

---

8 Citizenship and Immigration Canada, "Ministerial Instructions Respecting the Start-Up Business Class, 2014" (22 November 2014) s 7(1), online: <http://gazette.gc.ca/rp-pr/p1/2014/2014-11-22/html/notice-avis-eng.php>.

> **IN THE NEWS**
>
> ## How Practical Is the Start-Up Visa?
>
> Canada is not the only country to offer a visa tailored to attract entrepreneurs and business start-ups, but while these programs often enjoy public approval, they may not always suit the needs of entrepreneurs and investors. The following Canadian news story details the difficulties faced by Nat Cartwright and Jake Tyler in obtaining a Start-Up Visa. The two co-founded a peer-to-peer mobile payments business while studying for their MBAs in Madrid, Spain. After graduation, the Spanish government offered them one-year Entrepreneur's Visas, and they were accepted into a business accelerator. However, Ms. Cartwright wanted to build the business in her home city of Vancouver.
>
> They had hired a full-time technical lead away from IBM, invested $20,000, and attracted the attention of several potential investors; however, they were unable to bring the business to Vancouver until Mr. Tyler, an Australian citizen, could obtain a visa. The long wait— up to two years from application to decision—may scuttle the start-up before it can get off the ground.
>
> "In one year, this is going to [be] out there whether it's our company doing it or someone else's," Ms. Cartwright said.
>
> These long waits have proved to be a problem for others in the start-up community. In addition, the program is only a pilot program, and Start-Up Visa holders cannot be sure the program will be maintained past March 2018.
>
> Betsy R. Kane, an Ottawa-based senior practitioner in Canadian immigration law at Capelle Kane Immigration Lawyers, said, "This is not rocket science. They had a cap of 2,750 and in two years they've had five people. Why can't there be more uptake?"
>
> The article identifies a number of particular problems with the Start-Up Visa Program:
>
> - The program is not common knowledge among international start-ups.
> - It may be less trouble for international start-ups to simply raise venture capital rather than to apply for a Start-Up Visa.
> - Third-party investors may not be interested in vetting foreign business plans for the government.
>
> With no Start-Up Visa on the horizon, Ms. Cartwright and Mr. Tyler may have to return to Spain, where their entrepreneur visas are good for a year. But they aren't giving up: "We're going to fight really hard and we're going to use every resource we can to make it work in Canada," Ms. Cartwright said.
>
> What do you think? How might this program be modified to meet the needs of both entrepreneurs and Canada's immigration system?
>
> Source: Joseph Czikk, "Five Visas in 20 Months. Is Canada's Startup Visa Program Achieving What It Set Out to Do?" *Financial Post* (28 December 2014), online: <http://business.financialpost.com/entrepreneur/fp-startups/five-visas-in-20-months-is-canadas -startup-visa-program-achieving-what-it-set-out-to-do>.

Self-Employed Persons Program

Eligibility Requirements

To be eligible for the Self-Employed Persons Program, applicants must satisfy the definition of "self-employed person" set out in section 88(1) of the IRPR. Applicants must generally have relevant experience and the intention and ability to be self-employed and to make a significant contribution to specified economic activities in Canada. Applicants must also meet selection criteria according to a point system.

Relevant Experience

"Relevant experience" is defined under section 88(1) of the IRPR as a minimum two years of experience, during the period beginning five years before the date of application for a permanent resident visa in one of the following:

- in respect of cultural activities, two one-year periods of experience in self-employment in cultural activities, two one-year periods of experience in participation at a world-class level in cultural activities, or a combination of a one-year period of experience in self-employment in cultural activities and a one-year period of experience at a world-class level in cultural activities;
- in respect of athletics, two one-year periods of experience in self-employment in athletics, two one-year periods of experience in participation at a world-class level in athletics, or a combination of a one-year period of experience in self-employment in athletics and a one-year period of experience at a world-class level in athletics; or
- in respect of the purchase and management of a farm, two one-year periods of experience in the management of a farm.

Examples of cultural activities and athletics include the following occupations: music teachers, painters, illustrators, filmmakers, freelance journalists, choreographers, set designers, and coaches and trainers. Management experience includes theatrical or musical directors and impresarios.[9]

Intention and Ability

The self-employed applicant must demonstrate the intention and ability to establish a business that will, at a minimum, create employment for herself and that will make a significant contribution to the Canadian economy.

Selection Criteria—Points

The point system for self-employed immigrants is a modified version of the point system for FSWs and includes only five selection factors (IRPR, s 102):

- age,
- education,
- language proficiency in English and French,
- experience, and
- adaptability.

---

9 Citizenship and Immigration Canada, *OP 8: Entrepreneur and Self-Employed* (7 August 2008) s 11.3, online: <http://www.cic.gc.ca/english/resources/manuals/op/op08-eng.pdf>.

Business Immigration: Self-Employed Persons Point System

Selection factor	Maximum points
Age	10
Education	25
Language	24
Business experience 5 years: 35 points 4 years: 30 points 3 years: 25 points 2 years: 20 points	35

Adaptability
Education of spouse or common law partner: 3 to 5 points
Previous work in Canada—Applicant or spouse—One year
   full-time work in Canada: 5 points (self-employed)
Previous study in Canada—Applicant or spouse—Two years
   full-time post-secondary studies in Canada: 5 points
   (self-employed)
Family member in Canada: 5 points (self-employed)
	6

Currently, self-employed applicants must achieve a score of at least 35 points out of 100.

APPENDIX A

Worksheet for Calculating Points—Federal Skilled Worker

Selection factor	Maximum number of points	Your reason for assessment				Points awarded
Education						
Official languages	1st official language	S	L	R	W	
	2nd official language	S	L	R	W	
Experience						
Age						
Arranged employment						
Adaptability						
					Total	
					Meet or exceed pass mark?	

APPENDIX B

The boxes below summarize the relevant provisions in the IRPA and IRPR for the three main classes of permanent residents discussed in this chapter.

Reference for Skilled Worker and Business Classes

Provision	IRPA and IRPR
Economic class	IRPA, s 12(2)
Federal Skilled Worker class	IRPR, part 6, division 1
Minimal requirements	IRPR, s 75(2)
Minimum points required	IRPR, s 76(2)
Selection grid for skilled workers	IRPR, ss 78–83
Settlement funds requirement	IRPR, s 76(1)(b)(i)
Canadian Experience Class	IRPR, s 87.1
Federal Skilled Trades Class	IRPR, s 87.2
Provincial Nominee Class	IRPR, s 87
Business Immigration	IRPR, part 6, division 2
Start-Up Visa Program	*Ministerial Instructions Respecting the Start-Up Business Class, 2014*
Definitions Self-employed person Self-employed person selection criteria	IRPR, s 88(1) IRPR, ss 100–101, 102–102.3, 103(2), 108

APPENDIX C

Provincial/Territorial Nominee Agreements and Programs

Province/Territory	Agreement	Nominee program
Alberta	Agreement for Canada–Alberta Cooperation on Immigration May 11, 2007 to indefinite	Alberta Immigrant Nominee Program (AINP)
British Columbia	Canada–British Columbia Immigration Agreement Original signed in May 1998; current agreement in force from April 7, 2015 to April 7, 2020	British Columbia Provincial Nominee Program (BCPNP)
Manitoba	Canada–Manitoba Immigration Agreement Original signed in October 1996; current agreement in force from June 6, 2003 to indefinite	Manitoba Provincial Nominee Program (MPNP)
New Brunswick	Canada–New Brunswick Agreement on Provincial Nominees Original signed in February 1999; current agreement in force from March 29, 2005 to indefinite	New Brunswick Provincial Nominee Program (NBPNP)
Newfoundland and Labrador	Canada–Newfoundland and Labrador Agreement on Provincial Nominees Original signed on September 1, 1999; current agreement in force from November 22, 2006 to indefinite	Newfoundland and Labrador Provincial Nominee Program (NLPNP)
Northwest Territories	Canada–Northwest Territories Agreement on Provincial Nominees Original signed on August 5, 2009; current agreement in force from September 26, 2013 to September 26, 2018	Northwest Territories Nominee Program (NTNP)
Nova Scotia	Agreement for Canada–Nova Scotia Co-operation on Immigration September 19, 2007 to indefinite	Nova Scotia Nominee Program (NSNP)
Ontario	Canada–Ontario Immigration Agreement November 21, 2005 to November 21, 2010; one-year extension of the agreement expired March 31, 2011. Provincial Nominee Program authority extended to May 31, 2015; Temporary Foreign Workers Annex continues indefinitely	Provincial Nominee Program (PNP)

Province/Territory	Agreement	Nominee program
Prince Edward Island	Agreement for Canada–Prince Edward Island Co-operation on Immigration Original signed on March 29, 2001; current agreement in force from June 13, 2008 to indefinite	Prince Edward Island Provincial Nominee Program (PEI PNP)
Saskatchewan	Canada–Saskatchewan Immigration Agreement Original signed in March 1998; current agreement in force from May 7, 2005 to indefinite	Saskatchewan Immigrant Nominee Program (SINP)
Yukon	Agreement for Canada–Yukon Co-operation on Immigration Original signed April 2, 2001; current agreement in force from February 12, 2008 to indefinite	Yukon Provincial Nominee Program (YNP)

Source: Adapted from Citizenship and Immigration Canada, *2014 Annual Report to Parliament on Immigration* (Ottawa: CIC, 2014) table 6, Federal–Provincial/Territorial Agreements Currently in Force, online: <http://www.cic.gc.ca/english/resources/publications/annual-report-2014/index.asp#sec-3>.

KEY TERMS

Canadian educational credential, 247

Comprehensive Ranking System (CRS), 237

equivalency assessment, 247

expression of interest, 240

full-time work, 249

invitation to apply (ITA), 237

language skill area, 248

letter of support, 262

Provincial Nominee Program, 258

restricted occupation, 249

skilled trade occupation, 254

REVIEW QUESTIONS

Sohaila and Farzoneh are sisters who each obtained a bachelor of science degree at Tehran University. Their family sent them to France to further their studies.

Sohaila studied pharmacology and obtained a master's degree at the Université Paris Sud. She then worked full-time for two years as a hospital pharmacist in Paris, where she compounded and dispensed doctor-prescribed pharmaceuticals.

After obtaining a master's degree in health and society, Farzoneh also found full-time work at a Paris hospital, as a nurse's aide. There she performed duties such as shaving, bathing, dressing, and grooming patients; serving meal trays and feeding patients; lifting and turning patients; and other duties related to patient care and comfort.

Now back in Iran, they see there are few job prospects for women, despite their education. They are thinking about immigrating either to Canada or the United States, where they have an uncle. To help them decide, they are investigating the steps it takes to become Canadian permanent residents. Sohaila is 28 years old and Farzoneh is 26; they are fluent in Farsi and French. They have never travelled to Canada.

1. Use the National Occupational Classification system (2011) to look up the occupation codes for pharmacist and nurse's aide. What skill level is each occupation?

2. Sohaila and Farzoneh are highly educated and have high proficiency in one of Canada's official languages as well as work experience, so they think they can apply as skilled immigrants. Briefly describe the basic requirements to apply in the Federal Skilled Worker Program and the Federal Skilled Trades Program.

3. Under which of these classes should Sohaila and Farzoneh apply?

4. Describe the general steps to apply for permanent residence using the Express Entry system.

5. What is considered to be a valid job offer by a Canadian employer to an applicant in the federal skilled worker class?

6. What is considered to be a valid job offer by a Canadian employer to an applicant in the federal skilled trades class?

7. What is the rationale behind business class immigration, from Canada's point of view?

8. Nick has owned and operated a small café with his wife on a Greek island for the last ten years. Would Nick's experience as a self-employed café owner qualify as relevant experience in his application for permanent residence as a business class applicant in the self-employed persons' category?

EXERCISE

Go to the CIC website and look up the current ministerial instructions respecting invitations to apply for permanent residence under the Express Entry system. What number of invitations may be issued during the most recent round? For what period? Compare this with the sets of instructions issued since the beginning of this course.

CASE STUDY

A Tale of Two Brothers

It was the best of times, it was the worst of times … . (*A Tale of Two Cities*, Charles Dickens, 1859)

Eduardo and Fernando are 34-year-old twin brothers who are citizens of Mexico. Their lives and profiles are very similar, but for the fact that Eduardo is married to Rosa, who accompanied him to Canada. The brothers first came to Canada as temporary workers and have both been working legally in Canada with a work permit for three years under the International Mobility Program, and have performed the main duties on the lead statement as well as the duties as they appear in the NOC. They wish to immigrate to Canada permanently under the economic class as skilled workers. They must apply through the Express Entry system. The fact that Eduardo is married means that he will accumulate additional points for Rosa, who worked in Canada on an open work permit as an accompanying spouse.

To prepare their applications, the brothers must be tested for their language abilities. They both wrote the CELPIP-General 2014 in English to support their applications. After they received their test scores, they used the CRS language calculator tool (<www.cic.gc.ca/english/immigrate/skilled/language-tool.asp>) to determine the average score they can use for their Express Entry application. Eduardo and Fernando scored highly on their language test in each of the reading, writing, speaking, and listening skills. Their average score for their application is 8. Rosa scored 7 in all skills.

Eduardo has a four-year university bachelor's degree in business administration and Fernando has a four-year university bachelor's degree in economics. They both obtained their degrees in Mexico, and therefore obtained the ECA from a designated Canadian institution to verify that their foreign degrees are valid and equal to a Canadian one. Rosa, too, has a bachelor's degree, in business administration, which has also been verified by a designated Canadian institution.

Eduardo and Fernando submitted their expressions of interest through the CIC website. Their applications were scored and ranked against the pool of applicants, including against each other. Who would have a higher score?

Let's consider how their applications would be scored through the Express Entry system—see the CIC website for the detailed points breakdown for each of the four categories.

1. What points would you calculate for Eduardo and Fernando if they have valid job offers from their current employer? Who has the higher score?

Current Employer (with LMIA) Makes Permanent Job Offer

	FACTORS	EDUARDO (w/ SPOUSE)	FERNANDO (UNMARRIED)
Core Human Capital		Max. points: 460	Max. points: 500
	Age		
	Education		
	First language		
	Second language		
	Canadian work experience		
Subtotal			
Core Human Capital w/ Spouse		Max. points: 40	Max. points: 0
	Education		
	First language		
	Canadian work experience		
Subtotal			
Skill Transferability		Max. points: 100	Max. points: 100
	Education and language		
	Education and Canadian work		
	Foreign work and language		
	Foreign work and Canadian work		
Subtotal			
Valid Job Offer		Max. points: 600	Max. points: 600
	Employment job offer		
Subtotal			
Total			

2. What points would you calculate for Eduardo and Fernando if they (including Rosa) did not have any Canadian work experience but did have valid job offers from a Canadian employer? Who has the higher score?

No Canadian Work Experience with Permanent Job Offer

	FACTORS	EDUARDO (w/ SPOUSE)	FERNANDO (UNMARRIED)
Core Human Capital		Max. points: 460	Max. points: 500
	Age		
	Education		
	First language		
	Second language		
	Canadian work experience		
Subtotal			
Core Human Capital w/ Spouse		Max. points: 40	Max. points: 0
	Education		
	First language		
	Canadian work experience		
Subtotal			
Skill Transferability		Max. points: 100	Max. points: 100
	Education and language		
	Education and Canadian work		
	Foreign work and language		
	Foreign work and Canadian work		
Subtotal			
Valid Job Offer		Max. points: 600	Max. points: 600
	Employment job offer		
Subtotal			
Total			

Humanitarian and Compassionate Considerations Class

9

LEARNING OUTCOMES

After reading this chapter, you should be able to:

- Have a general understanding of the humanitarian and compassionate (H&C) considerations class.

- Explain how H&C factors may be applied against both inadmissibility and eligibility issues for those who do not qualify for immigration.

- Understand the factors related to the "best interests of the child" in relation to an application for H&C considerations.

Introduction

Most applicants for permanent residence fall within the family reunification, economic, or refugee classes. Some applicants, however, fall outside these classes yet still present compelling cases for permanent residence. These exceptional cases may be considered under the humanitarian and compassionate (H&C) considerations class. The H&C class provides the minister (or delegated immigration officer) with the discretion to grant permanent residence to applicants who would otherwise not be able to meet statutory and regulatory criteria.

Applicants may apply under the H&C class from outside as well as from within Canada. Generally, those who apply from within Canada are doing so in a final attempt to remain here, often after having made an unsuccessful attempt to gain refugee status. Such applicants may also include foreign nationals who would normally apply under either the spouse or common law partner in Canada class or the live-in caregiver class, as protected persons or Convention refugees, or for a temporary resident permit.

The Canadian Council for Refugees (CCR), a non-profit organization that advocates for the rights of vulnerable immigrants and refugees, claims that many of the H&C applicants for permanent residence fall into the following categories:[1]

- refugees who were refused status because of flaws in the determination system;
- survivors of human trafficking;
- family members of refugees or permanent residents;
- stateless persons;
- victims of domestic violence who left a family sponsorship because of the violence;
- persons whose removal from Canada would involve a serious rights violation, such as lack of treatment for a serious medical condition;
- persons from countries to which Canada generally does not deport because of a situation of generalized risk (moratorium countries);[2]
- persons who have been continuously into Canada for several years;
- persons who have integrated into Canada, socially, culturally, and with family; and
- persons who have worked for some time as part of temporary worker programs, such as seasonal agricultural workers.

H&C applications are one of the more subjective processes in immigration matters. Decision-making is based solely on documentation submitted by the applicant,

---

1   Canadian Council for Refugees, "Issues for H&C Roundtable, 27–28 March 2006" [nd], online: <http://ccrweb.ca/H&CMarch2006.html>.

2   Canadian Council for Refugees, "Fact Sheet for Nationals of Moratoria Countries Without Permanent Status in Canada" (July 2007, revised August 2009), online: <http://ccrweb.ca/documents/infosheetmoratoria.pdf>.

and the decision-maker has broad discretion when considering the reasons for and circumstances of the application. The onus is on the applicant to prove that she would face hardship if she were required to leave Canada. Generally, the hardship must be a hardship that is undeserved and is beyond the applicant's control; having to leave an established life in Canada and move elsewhere in order to apply for permanent residence in the normal manner is not considered a hardship. There are no definitions in the *Immigration and Refugee Protection Act* (IRPA) or its regulations for the terms "humanitarian" and "compassionate," so the minister or delegated officer must use discretion in deciding applications.

Under the IPRA, officers have the authority to exempt an applicant for particular inadmissibility matters, such as financial/economic reasons (s 39), misrepresentation (s 40), non-compliance with the IRPA (s 41), and inadmissible family members (s 42), except for reasons of health, security, human rights violations, serious criminality, and organized criminality (s 25(1)). These discretionary provisions are intended to allow for the approval of deserving cases that were not specifically anticipated when the IRPA was drafted.

H&C applications are not meant as an alternative means of immigration; they are intended only for extraordinary cases. The processing of applications is a lengthy process and the success rate is low. Permanent residence applications made under H&C considerations are approved on an exceptional basis and their acceptance rate is low compared with other types of permanent residence applications. For example, only 1.1 percent (2,875) of the total permanent residents admitted to Canada in 2013 were H&C applicants.[3] It may take years before a decision is made, and there is no right of appeal from an unsuccessful H&C application.

Bearing in mind that H&C cases are generally unique, complex, and favourably decided only on an exceptional basis, the purpose of this section is to provide a general overview of H&C cases. The examples provided are not conclusive as successful types of cases; they are merely examples used to help explain the information.

Section 25 Criteria

The H&C criteria as set out in section 25 of the IRPA infuse a degree of flexibility into an otherwise rigid and bureaucratic system. Section 25 offers an opportunity to those whose failure to qualify under any other class is causing significant distress because of individual circumstances. This section gives the minister or delegated officer the discretion to grant status to foreign nationals where there are strong humanitarian and compassionate reasons for doing so. This may apply both to those who wish to come to Canada and to those who wish to remain here, but who are inadmissible for technical, medical, or criminal reasons.

Specifically, section 25(1) of the IRPA provides that on the request of a foreign national in Canada who applies for permanent resident status and who is inadmissible or does not meet the requirements of the Act, the minister must examine the circumstances concerning the foreign national and may grant him permanent resident

---

3   Citizenship and Immigration Canada, *Facts and Figures 2013: Immigration Overview—Permanent Residents* (22 April 2015), online: <http://www.cic.gc.ca/english/resources/statistics/facts2013/>.

status or an exemption from any applicable IRPA criteria or obligations if the minister believes that doing so "is justified by humanitarian and compassionate considerations relating to the foreign national, taking into account the best interests of a child directly affected."

The minister may also do so in the case of a request by a foreign national outside Canada who applies for a permanent resident visa.

Furthermore, section 25.1(1) grants the minister the authority, on the minister's own initiative, to examine the circumstances concerning a foreign national who is inadmissible or does not meet the IRPA criteria, and grant permanent resident status or an exemption from applicable IRPA criteria or obligations if the minister believes that doing so is justified by H&C considerations, taking into account the best interests of a child directly affected.

IN THE NEWS

Humanitarian and Compassionate Considerations for a Temporary Foreign Worker

As we have already learned, H&C considerations can include a wide variety of situations. One story that has captured national news attention is that of Maria Victoria Venancio, a temporary foreign worker who came to work in Edmonton. Shortly after her arrival, she was involved in a car accident that left her quadriplegic.

Since she is unable to work, she is in Canada illegally. In April, the Alberta government denied her request for health care coverage, so her physiotherapy is paid for as part of a research project.

"I'm always scared," said Venancio. "I'm always conscious about everything—what I eat, what I do—because I don't want to get sick."

Ms. Venancio would like to stay in Edmonton for further treatment and hopefully begin working again there someday. However, she is at risk for deportation, but if she returns to her home in the Philippines, she would be located in a relatively rural area. No infrastructure exists there to meet her needs, and she would have to travel three hours to receive health care in the nearest urban area. Her lawyer is hopeful that she will be allowed to stay in Canada while her application for permanent residence is processed.

MLA Sarah Hoffman, who was appointed health minister after the May 2015 provincial election in Alberta, has stated that she is in favour of extending health benefits to temporary foreign workers, but no changes have been made yet to the legislation that would permit this.

Former MLA Thomas Lukaszuk pointed out that Ms. Venancio's case raises questions about how the Canadian immigration system deals with injured temporary foreign workers, who are particularly vulnerable.

"Do we simply just discard them because they can't work anymore, they're of no use to us, or do we take care of them?"

What do you think? How does this case fit within the criteria discussed in this chapter?

Sources: CTVNews.ca Staff, "Quadriplegic Temporary Foreign Worker Fights to Remain in Canada," *CTV News* (17 February 2015), online: <http://www.ctvnews.ca/canada/quadriplegic-temporary-foreign-worker-fights-to-remain-in-canada-1.2239700>; Andrea Huncar, "Alberta Health Minister Denies Coverage to Temporary Foreign Worker," *CBC News* (2 April 2015), online: CBC <http://www.cbc.ca/news/canada/edmonton/alberta-health-minister-denies-coverage-to-temporary-foreign-worker-1.3019954>; Jibril Yassin, "Health Minister in Favour of Injured Temporary Foreign Workers Receiving Support," *Edmonton Journal* (1 June 2015), online: <http://www.edmontonjournal.com/Health+minister+favour+injured+temporary+foreign+workers+receiving+support/11099818/story.html>.

Section 25.2(1) of the IRPA provides that the minister may grant permanent resident status or an exemption if the minister is of the opinion that it is justified by public policy considerations.

Consider the following examples in which normal eligibility requirements for permanent residence are not met, and in which a foreign national might ask to be considered for H&C reasons:[4]

- excluded family members, under section 117(9)(d) of the *Immigration and Refugee Protection Regulations* (IRPR);
- non-biological children who are separated from their only family, who is in Canada;
- parents and siblings of child refugees in Canada; and
- other family members of persons in Canada in situations in which there are specific humanitarian concerns (for example, a situation of generalized risk).

Two criteria specifically requiring consideration in the determination of an H&C application, according to section 25, are the best interests of a child directly affected by the decision and public policy considerations. Both are examined briefly below. It is important to keep in mind that it is the responsibility of the applicant to satisfy the officer that sufficient factors exist to warrant an exemption from the regular admission criteria. Officers will not return the application to ask for further information, so it is very important that all relevant evidence to support one or both of the two criteria be submitted initially.

Best Interests of the Child Considerations

Under section 25(1) of the IRPA, the minister must consider the best interests of any child who is directly affected by the decision because of the child's relationship to the applicant. In determining the child's best interests, the minister must consider the following issues:

- the child's emotional, social, cultural, and physical welfare;
- the child's age;
- the child's level of dependency on the applicant;
- the degree of the child's establishment in Canada;
- the child's links to the country in relation to which the H&C assessment is being considered;
- the conditions of that country and the potential impact on the child;
- the child's medical issues or special needs;
- the impact on the child's education; and
- matters related to the child's gender.[5]

---

4 *Supra* note 1.

5 Citizenship and Immigration Canada, "The Humanitarian and Compassionate Assessment: Best Interests of a Child—Factors to Consider" (24 July 2014), online: <http://www.cic.gc.ca/english/resources/tools/perm/hc/processing/child.asp>.

This provision applies regardless of whether the child is a Canadian citizen or a foreign national. In other words, the best interests of a child who has no right to be in Canada must also be considered, if the child is directly affected by the decision regarding the applicant. For example, how is it in the best interests of the child to remain in Canada as opposed to being removed to her home country? Are there family members in the home country to return to, or will the child be separated from relatives remaining in Canada? Are the living conditions, educational opportunities, and health care better or worse in the home country of the applicant?

Public Policy Considerations

The minister has the authority to respond to public demands through the creation of new categories for permanent residence or "public policy" cases. Consider the following examples:

1. *A temporary public policy for nationals of Haiti and Zimbabwe who were affected by the lifting of the temporary suspension of removals (TSRs)*: A policy dated November 2014 allowed officers to give consideration to nationals of Haiti and Zimbabwe who were subject to a removal order (including conditional removal orders) or who benefited from the Haiti Special Measures. "When a country has been subject to a TSR for a number of years (since 2004 for Haiti and since 2002 for Zimbabwe), an officer may consider that the applicant's continued presence in Canada may be due to circumstances beyond their control. When the decision-maker concludes that the individual's prolonged stay in Canada as a result of the TSR has led to their establishment, positive consideration may be warranted."[6]

2. *Resumption of Canadian citizenship*: The resumption of Canadian citizenship was established as a class of permanent residence specifically for former Canadian citizens who inadvertently lost their Canadian citizenship when they were minors because a parent lost his or her citizenship.

3. *Vietnamese living in the Philippines*: A number of Vietnamese persons who had been living in the Philippines without status since the mid-1970s, following the fall of Saigon, and who had close family members in Canada were admitted to Canada. In March 2008, the minister of citizenship and immigration explained that applications by members of this group that were received by December 31, 2007 would be considered on a priority basis. Immigration officers examined each application on its own merits to decide whether the applicants warranted exemption from the statutory requirements and qualified for humanitarian and compassionate considerations.[7]

---

6 Citizenship and Immigration Canada, "Procedures for Applications for Permanent Residence on Humanitarian and Compassionate Grounds as a Result of Lifting the Temporary Suspension of Removals on Haiti and Zimbabwe," *Operational Bulletin* 600 (23 January 2015), online: <http://www.cic.gc.ca/english/resources/manuals/bulletins/2015/ob600.asp>.

7 Diane Finley, "Government of Canada Welcomes Vietnamese People Living Without Status in the Philippines" (7 March 2008), online: Government of Canada <http://news.gc.ca>.

Public policy cases differ from other H&C cases because once a new category is created, all cases that fit the category are likely to be accepted (for example, all individuals who fall into one of the three categories above).

Request Under the Humanitarian and Compassionate Class

The H&C class is not intended as a parallel process to refugee determination. Refugee claimants (both in Canada and overseas) may not submit an application for permanent residence for H&C considerations while their refugee claims are still in process.

An application is assessed on its own merits: officers weigh the humanitarian and compassionate considerations for each application on the basis of the applicant's personal circumstances.

A written request for an H&C exemption must accompany either an application to remain in Canada as a permanent resident or, in the case of a foreign national outside Canada, an application for a permanent resident visa (IRPR, s 66). The request must be made by the principal applicant and, when applicable, by the following family members:

- the applicant's spouse or common law partner (if that person is in Canada and is not a permanent resident or a Canadian citizen); and

- any dependent children who are 18 years of age or older and who are not permanent residents or Canadian citizens.

A person who has a removal order against him may apply for permanent residence for humanitarian and compassionate considerations, but the application will not delay his removal from Canada. The applicant must leave on or before the date stated in the removal order, while the application is in process.

The application guide provided by Citizenship and Immigration Canada (CIC) cautions that an application in the H&C category can take as long as several years to process. The onus is on the applicant to satisfy the decision-maker that there are grounds for an exemption. The guide therefore comes with a warning that CIC will not ask for additional information, because the onus is on the applicant to list any and all factors that the applicant wishes to have considered at the time the application is submitted.

Bars

Under section 25(1.03), failed refugee claimants are barred for 12 months from applying for H&C considerations following a negative decision by the Refugee Protection Division (RPD) or the Refugee Appeal Division (RAD), or a final decision that the claimant withdrew his claim. This bar does not apply to refugee claimants who have children under 18 who would be adversely affected by the claimant's removal, or to claimants or their dependants who have a life-threatening medical condition that could not be treated in their home country.

Designated foreign national refugee claimants (see Chapter 13) may not apply for H&C considerations for at least five years after the day of their designation or a final determination by the RPD, or if there has been a negative decision on an application for a pre-removal risk assessment.

Place of Application

Like other applications for permanent residence, most public policy H&C applications must be made from outside Canada—for example, applications from those who are seeking an exemption for themselves or family members who are found to be inadmissible.[8] Generally, a foreign national does not have the right to apply for permanent residence from within Canada. However, in Canada applications are allowed by exemption under section 25 of the IRPA if the applicant lives in Canada and would experience unusual and undeserved or disproportionate hardship if he were required to leave.[9] Note that having to leave an established life in Canada and move elsewhere in order to apply for permanent residence in the normal manner is not considered an unusual and undeserved hardship. According to department policy, an "unusual and undeserved hardship" is a situation unanticipated by the IRPA or the regulations that results from circumstances beyond the applicant's control.[10]

"Disproportionate hardship" is defined as hardship that has an "unreasonable impact on the applicant due to their personal circumstances."[11] This may be the case, for example, if there is no home or support system the applicant can return to in his country of origin.

Applications

Generally, applications made from outside Canada do not require specific forms. The foreign national applies for a permanent resident visa under one of the existing classes of permanent residence and submits a written request for consideration on humanitarian and compassionate grounds. If the visa officer determines that the applicant does not meet the requirements of the class of permanent residence, the officer makes an H&C determination.

An exception is the public policy to facilitate immigration to Canada of certain groups, such as members of the Vietnamese community in the Philippines, who do not have permanent resident status but have close family members in Canada. Forms for applicants and sponsors relating to this public policy are available from CIC.

---

8   Unless the applicants are members of the live-in caregiver class, the spouse or common law partner in Canada class, or the protected temporary residents class in accordance with section 72(2) of the IRPR.

9   Citizenship and Immigration Canada, "The Humanitarian and Compassionate Assessment: Requirement to Apply for Permanent Residence from Outside Canada" (24 July 2014), online <http://www.cic.gc.ca/english/resources/tools/perm/hc/processing/out-canada.asp>.

10 Citizenship and Immigration Canada, "The Humanitarian and Compassionate Assessment: Hardship and the H&C Assessment" (24 July 2014), online <http://www.cic.gc.ca/english/resources/tools/perm/hc/processing/hardship.asp>.

11 *Ibid.*

Applications made from inside Canada require substantially more paperwork, because the applicant has the additional burden of proving that unusual and undeserved or disproportionate hardship would result if he were forced to leave Canada in order to apply. An application kit can be obtained online from the CIC website or from a CIC call centre, and it includes the Generic Application Form for Canada (IMM 0008) and other forms, including:

- Humanitarian and Compassionate Considerations Instruction Guide (IMM 5291);
- Supplementary Information—Humanitarian and Compassionate Considerations (IMM 5283); and
- Document Checklist: Humanitarian and Compassionate Considerations (IMM 5280).

The guide describes the required forms and supporting documentation that must be submitted for in-Canada applications. The key document for setting out humanitarian and compassionate grounds is the Supplementary Information form (IMM 5283). It is essential that this form be completed with as much detail as possible. The immigration officer will rely on this form in deciding whether there are grounds for exempting the applicant.

The following sections provide an overview of the relevant boxes in the Supplementary Information form, together with examples borrowed from MOSAIC.[12]

BOX 7: "EXPLAIN THE HUMANITARIAN AND COMPASSIONATE REASONS THAT PREVENT YOU FROM LEAVING CANADA."

The applicant must provide as much detail as possible to demonstrate that she would suffer unusual and undeserved or disproportionate hardship if forced to leave Canada and return to her country of origin. Supporting written arguments and other documents, such as letters and medical reports, can be attached.

Examples of hardship that would prevent the applicant from returning to the country of origin include:

- the government of the country of origin does not recognize the applicant as one of its citizens;
- there is a complete breakdown of the infrastructure in the country of origin and there is no government in charge;
- the applicant or a family member would suffer medical hardship and might die because medical treatment is not available in the home country; or
- in the case of a female applicant, she would face specific difficulties such as gender-related persecution or sexual violence.

The cost and inconvenience of applying for permanent residence outside Canada is not considered a hardship.

---

12 MOSAIC is a multilingual non-profit organization that addresses issues affecting immigrants and refugees. The following examples are taken from "A Guide to Humanitarian and Compassionate Applications (H & C)" (November 2008), online: <http://www.mosaicbc.com/sites/all/files/18/A Guide to Humanitarian and Compassionate Applications.pdf>.

BOX 8: "[C]LEARLY INDICATE IN YOUR APPLICATION THE SPECIFIC EXEMPTION(S) YOU ARE REQUESTING; AND ... PROVIDE ALL DETAILS RELATED TO THIS REQUEST, INCLUDING THE REASONS WHY YOU SHOULD BE GRANTED AN EXEMPTION ON HUMANITARIAN AND COMPASSIONATE GROUNDS."

When an applicant or family member is inadmissible—for example, because of criminality, misrepresentation, health, or financial reasons—the applicant must state the specific exemption sought. Note that CIC will not ask for this information.

BOX 9: "IF APPLICABLE, DESCRIBE THE CIRCUMSTANCES OF YOUR FAMILY AND OTHER RELATIONSHIPS THAT WOULD SUPPORT YOUR HUMANITARIAN AND COMPASSIONATE APPLICATION."

In addition to other factors, CIC considers the willingness of a family member or close relative in Canada to sign an undertaking of assistance to support the applicant's application for permanent residence. This type of sponsorship may be an important consideration when the applicant is not self-sufficient in Canada.

In such cases, the applicant must also submit the following sponsorship forms with the application:

- Application to Sponsor, Sponsorship Agreement and Undertaking (IMM 1344); and
- Document Checklist—Sponsor (IMM 5287).

BOX 10: "IF APPLICABLE, CONSIDERING THE BEST INTEREST OF THE CHILD, PROVIDE INFORMATION ON ANY CHILD AFFECTED BY THIS DECISION."

The immigration officer must consider whether the applicant's child or children would face hardship if they were to return to the applicant's home country. The child's ties to Canada will be considered, such as whether the child was born in Canada, attends school here, or has ever been to the applicant's home country.

The applicant can submit evidence in the form of an opinion letter to demonstrate how the child or children would be affected by having to leave Canada. Opinion letters about the negative mental or physical effects on children from experts such as school counsellors, health workers, physicians, social workers, or psychologists can help support the application for humanitarian and compassionate considerations.

BOX 11: "HOW HAVE YOU ESTABLISHED YOURSELF IN CANADA?"

CIC officials consider the following examples as evidence of establishment in Canada:

- the amount of time lived in Canada;
- language skills in English and/or French, and efforts to improve them;
- efforts to improve education and skills while in Canada;
- the number of family members and relatives legally in Canada;
- the amount of contact with family in Canada;

- marriage to a permanent resident or a Canadian citizen;
- Canadian-born children;
- contacts other than family in Canada; and
- community involvement (religious or non-religious) and volunteer work performed.

Evidence that does not show establishment in Canada, and that might instead demonstrate the opposite, includes the following:

- the length of time spent on welfare;
- the amount of contact with family in the applicant's home country (having many close relatives in the applicant's home country suggests no hardship on return);
- assets abroad; and
- children still living in the applicant's home country.

BOX 12: "HOW DO YOU SUPPORT YOURSELF FINANCIALLY IN CANADA?"

Evidence that the applicant is financially self-supporting in Canada may include documents such as letters from past and present employers, pay stubs, income tax assessments, mortgage statements, and bank statements. The evidence should support the existence of a reliable income stream and all assets owned.

BOX 13: "INDICATE ANY OTHER INFORMATION YOU WANT TO HAVE CONSIDERED IN YOUR APPLICATION."

The applicant may provide positive reference letters, affirming her integrity and responsibility, from employers, schools, volunteer organizations, the religious community, and others.

All applications for permanent residence made from within Canada based on H&C grounds, along with supporting documentation, may be submitted electronically or sent to a case processing centre in Canada (for example, the Backlog Reduction Office, Vancouver).

Expenses and Fees

The expenses and fees for an application for a permanent resident visa on H&C grounds are the same as those for a normal application for permanent residence. Expenses include the cost of medical examinations, legal fees, fees for police certificates, and fees to obtain documents. The two fees payable to CIC are the application or processing fee, which is non-refundable, and the right of permanent residence fee (IPRA, s 25(1.1)). However, the minister may exempt a foreign national from paying the fees (IRPA, ss 25.1(2), 25.2(2)).

Loans may be available for the right of permanent residence fee, but not for the application fee, and the applicant must show an ability to repay the loan. Fees payable to CIC can be paid online or at a designated financial institution, and the fees receipt (IMM 5401) must accompany the application forms (IRPR, s 295). Fees are subject to change, so check the CIC website regularly to keep up to date.

Decisions on Humanitarian and Compassionate Applications

For applications made outside Canada, a visa officer assesses the eligibility and admissibility of the applicant under the permanent resident category (for example, family class sponsorship) in which he applied. If the applicant does not meet the requirements of the category, the officer must decide whether to exempt the applicant from those requirements on H&C grounds. For example, if an applicant's family member is inadmissible *and* the applicant submits a written request for H&C considerations, the visa officer could waive inadmissibility (except for reasons related to security, human or international rights violations, and organized criminality) and review the case to decide whether there are grounds to exempt the applicant from this requirement.[13]

If an applicant provides sufficient evidence of H&C considerations to satisfy a visa officer, she may be exempted from the normal application requirements. However, before the permanent resident visa may be issued, the officer must be satisfied that the applicant is not inadmissible. If the applicant or any family member is inadmissible, the application must be rejected.

This may result in a Catch-22: an applicant seeks H&C consideration because he would not otherwise be able to obtain a permanent resident visa, and although the application is accepted on the basis of H&C considerations, the application may ultimately be rejected because of inadmissibility. This explains, in part, why H&C applications take so long to process and why so few are successful.

Although the officer may exempt the applicant from eligibility criteria, the officer does not have the authority to waive inadmissibility on the most serious grounds. Only the minister may waive inadmissibility on grounds related to security, human or international rights violations, and organized criminality.

For in-Canada applications, an immigration officer determines whether there are sufficient H&C grounds to justify granting the requested exemption(s).

Reasons for a refusal are not automatically provided, because there is no statutory obligation to do so. However, an applicant may write to CIC to request reasons.

Applicants have no right to appeal the refusal of applications for permanent residence on humanitarian and compassionate grounds. However, an application for leave for judicial review may be filed with the Federal Court within 30 days of the date of refusal.

---

13 As noted in former Overseas Processing operational manual OP 4: Citizenship and Immigration Canada, *OP 4: Processing of Applications Under Section 25 of the IRPA* (Ottawa: CIC, 28 July 2008), online: <http://overseastudent.ca/migratetocanada/IMMGuide/CICManual/op/op04-eng.pdf>.

APPENDIX

The relevant provisions in the IRPA and IRPR for the three main classes of permanent residents discussed in the chapter are summarized below.

Reference for Humanitarian and Compassionate Classes

Provision	IRPA and IRPR
H&C considerations	IRPA, ss 25, 25.1
Best interests of the child	IRPA, s 25
Public policy	IRPA, s 25.2
Application in writing	IRPR, s 66
Application outside Canada	IRPR, s 67
Application in Canada	IRPR, s 68
Accompanying family members	IRPR, s 69

REVIEW QUESTION

Considering the questions on the Supplementary Information form (IMM 5283), discuss examples of the following H&C factors and how they might support an application.

- "Suffer unusual and undeserved or disproportionate hardship"
- "Exemptions from grounds of inadmissibility"
- "Family and other relationships"
- "The best interests of a child"
- "Factors demonstrating that the applicant is established in Canada"
- "Factors indicating that the applicant has failed to demonstrate he is established in Canada"

CASE STUDY

A Jamaican woman applied for permanent residence on "humanitarian and compassionate considerations" in 1993. The following is a summary of the notes made by an officer and forwarded to his supervisor in considering the application of the person concerned (PC):

> PC is unemployed—on Welfare. No income shown—no assets. Has four Cdn.-born children—four other children in Jamaica—HAS A TOTAL OF EIGHT CHILDREN
>
> Says only two children are in her "direct custody". (No info on who has ghe [*sic*] other two).
>
> There is nothing for her in Jamaica—hasn't been there in a long time—no longer close to her children there—no jobs there—she has no skills other than as a domestic—children would suffer—can't take them with her and can't leave them with anyone here. Says has suffered from a mental disorder since '81—is now an outpatient and is improving. If sent back will have a relapse.
>
> Letter from Children's Aid—they say PC has been diagnosed as a paranoid schizophrenic.—children would suffer if returned—
>
> Letter of Aug. '93 from psychiatrist from Ont. Govm't.
>
> Says PC had post-partum psychosis and had a brief episode of psychosis in Jam. when was 25 yrs. old. Is now an out-patient and is doing relatively well—deportation would be an extremely stressful experience.

> Lawyer says PS [*sic*] is sole caregiver and single parent of two Cdn born children. Pc's mental condition would suffer a setback if she is deported etc.
>
> This case is a catastrophy [*sic*]. It is also an indictment of our "system" that the client came as a visitor in Aug. '81, was not ordered deported until Dec. '92 and in APRIL '94 IS STILL HERE!
>
> The PC is a paranoid schizophrenic and on welfare. She has no qualifications other than as a domestic. She has FOUR CHILDREN IN JAMAICA AND ANOTHER FOUR BORN HERE. She will, of course, be a tremendous strain on our social welfare systems for (probably) the rest of her life. There are no H&C factors other than her FOUR CANADIAN-BORN CHILDREN. Do we let her stay because of that? I am of the opinion that Canada can no longer afford this type of generosity. However, because of the circumstances involved, there is a potential for adverse publicity. I recommend refusal but you may wish to clear this with someone at Region.
>
> There is also a potential for violence—see charge of "assault with a weapon"

[Capitalization in original.]

1. Write an objective summary of the facts of this case.

2. In light of the facts, discuss the grounds for considering the H&C application.

3. Does the officer appear to consider the relevant factors? Explain.

4. Do the officer's notes raise any red flags for you? Explain.

PART IV

Citizenship

Citizenship

10

LEARNING OUTCOMES

After reading this chapter, you should be able to:

- Identify decision-making roles within the Citizenship Commission.

- Understand the rights and responsibilities of Canadian citizenship.

- Describe how to become a Canadian citizen.

- Understand the eligibility requirements and the process of naturalization of permanent residents for Canadian citizenship.

- Understand how Canadian citizenship may be renounced, revoked, and restored.

Introduction

Citizenship is an important element in the makeup and identity of Canadian society. The rules of citizenship are designed to make sure that all people recognized as citizens, and granted citizenship, have significant ties to Canada. There has been some debate about whether Canada is too generous or too tough when it comes to granting citizenship. The government responded to this debate by introducing a number of changes to citizenship legislation in Bill C-24, the *Strengthening Canadian Citizenship Act* (royal assent June 19, 2014).

Many Canadians are citizens because they were born here. Others are citizens because one of their parents is a Canadian citizen. Most of this chapter is about a third category of Canadians—those who were formerly foreign nationals, but have since acquired permanent resident status and applied to become Canadian citizens through a process called **naturalization**. In 2014, Citizenship and Immigration Canada (CIC) accepted more than 260,000 new Canadian citizens.[1]

A person is not a citizen of Canada merely because he has lived here for an extended period of time. For example, a person born outside Canada to parents who were not Canadian citizens could enter Canada—legally or illegally—as a two-year-old child, spend an entire lifetime in Canada, and yet not be a Canadian citizen. To become a Canadian citizen, a foreign national must first be admitted to Canada as a permanent resident, spend several years in Canada, and then qualify to apply to become a citizen.

This chapter describes how citizenship is conferred by place of birth or parent age, as well as how it may be actively sought by a foreign national. The process of acquiring citizenship is described in some detail. The chapter also discusses the process of renouncing citizenship and the situations in which citizenship may be revoked.

naturalization
the process by which a foreign national, after being admitted to Canada as a permanent resident, applies for and obtains Canadian citizenship

Are You a Canadian Citizen?

Probably if ...

- you were born in Canada;

- you were naturalized (that is, applied for and received Canadian citizenship);

- you were a minor when your parent was naturalized and were included in your parent's application;

- you were born outside Canada after April 17, 2009 and at least one of your parents was born in Canada;

---

1   Citizenship and Immigration Canada, News Release, "Record Number of New Citizens Welcomed in 2014" (23 December 2014), online: <http://news.gc.ca/web/article-en.do?nid=916869&_ga =1.230882911.1579089948.1434396744>.

- you were born outside Canada after April 17, 2009 and at least one of your parents was naturalized in Canada before your birth; or
- you were a "lost Canadian" and became a citizen because of changes to the *Citizenship Act*.

Probably not if ...

- you renounced Canadian citizenship and never applied to get it back;
- your citizenship was revoked by the Government of Canada; or
- you were born in Canada to foreign diplomats.

Not automatically if ...

- you are married to a Canadian citizen;
- you were adopted by a Canadian citizen;
- your refugee claim is accepted;
- you have lived in Canada as a permanent resident for many years; or
- you were born outside Canada to Canadian parent(s) on or after April 17, 2009 but neither of your parents was born or naturalized in Canada.

Source: Citizenship and Immigration Canada, "'Am I Canadian?' See if You Are Already a Citizen" (11 June 2015), online: <http://www.cic.gc.ca/english/citizenship/rules/>.

International Law

International law gives a sovereign country, such as Canada, the power to decide whom to recognize as citizens and whom as nationals. "National" is a broader term than "citizen." It may include persons who are not citizens but who have rights and obligations such as those given to Canadian permanent residents. International law also permits countries to establish rules and requirements regarding how citizenship may be acquired by **foreign nationals**.[2] **Citizenship** endows a person "with the full political and civil rights in the body politic of the state."[3] These may include the right to vote and hold political office. Citizenship may also carry potential obligations, such as military service.

In Canada, permanent residents have a right to enter and remain in Canada as long as they fulfill their obligations and maintain their permanent resident status. Unlike Canadian citizens, however, they are not permitted to vote or hold political office.

foreign national
a person who is neither a Canadian citizen nor a permanent resident in Canada

citizenship
the full political and civil rights in the body politic of the state

---

2 See general texts on public international law such as JG Castel, *International Law* (Toronto: Butterworths, 1976) and I Brownlie, *Principles of Public International Law*, 6th ed (Oxford: Oxford University Press, 2003).

3 GH Hackworth, *Digest of International Law* (Washington, DC: US Government Printing Office, 1942) vol 3 at 1, cited in Castel, *supra* note 2 at 431.

stateless person
a person who is not recognized by any nation as a citizen and has no residency rights in any country

A **stateless person** is not recognized by any nation as being its national; such a person therefore has no residency rights in any country. Statelessness is addressed in article 15 of the United Nations' *Universal Declaration of Human Rights*, as follows:

1. Everyone has the right to a nationality.
2. No one shall be arbitrarily deprived of his nationality nor denied the right to change his nationality.

The objective of article 15 is to encourage nations to take responsibility for their people, thus reducing statelessness.

Special rights of entry are accorded to anyone registered as an Indian under the *Indian Act*. Such a person may enter Canada, even if she is not a citizen or permanent resident, according to section 19(1) of the *Immigration and Refugee Protection Act* (IRPA). This special status is granted in recognition of the fact that the traditional homelands of some North American First Peoples groups straddle the border between the United States and Canada, and to protect the right of First Peoples to move freely on these traditional homelands.

Legislative History

Canada's *Citizenship Act* (1977) defines who is deemed a citizen at birth and prescribes how foreign nationals may acquire citizenship through the naturalization process. A person is a citizen if she is born in Canada or, in some cases, if she is born outside Canada to a parent who is a Canadian citizen.

Prior to 1947, Canada did not have its own citizenship act; it followed British law instead. There was legally no such thing as Canadian citizenship. Both native-born and naturalized citizens were British subjects. The rules determining who was a British subject also applied in Canada to determine the equivalent of citizenship for Canadians. Since 1947, the law has evolved through a series of Canadian citizenship statutes.

In Canada, there are three time periods of importance with respect to citizenship:

- pre-1947: British law applied;
- 1947–1977: *Canadian Citizenship Act* in force;[4] and
- 1977–2014: *Citizenship Act* (1977) in force, replacing the *Canadian Citizenship Act*.

Two major changes to the *Citizenship Act* took effect on April 17, 2009:

- Bill C-14, *An Act to amend the Citizenship Act (adoption)* (royal assent June 22, 2007), addressed the procedures for acquiring citizenship for foreign adopted children; and

---

4   This Act provided that persons born outside Canada to Canadian fathers were Canadian citizens, but persons born outside Canada to Canadian mothers had to naturalize. The overt sexism of this provision was overturned by the Supreme Court of Canada in *Benner v Canada (Secretary of State)*, [1997] 1 SCR 358.

- Bill C-37, *An Act to amend the Citizenship Act* (royal assent April 17, 2008), restored or gave Canadian citizenship to certain classes of individuals who had lost or who had never had Canadian citizenship, including to some born before 1947 as a result of outdated provisions in existing and former legislation. However, a small number of "lost Canadians," such as some first-generation children born abroad to war brides and servicemen, were still not eligible for Canadian citizenship.

At the time of writing, the most recent amendments to the *Citizenship Act* are the result of Bill C-24, the *Strengthening Canadian Citizenship Act* (see "Amendments" below).

Canada's first citizenship act, the *Canadian Citizenship Act*, came into force on January 1, 1947, and thus Canadian rather than British law applied for applications after this date. When the Canadian citizenship law changed, the new rules did not have retroactive effect; they applied only to prospective citizens. As an unintended result, some people lost or were never eligible for citizenship. For example, under the 1947 *Canadian Citizenship Act*, Canadian citizens who were not "natural-born" lost their citizenship if they resided outside Canada for a period of six consecutive years. ("Natural-born" Canadian citizens include those who are born either in Canada or outside Canada if, at the time of birth, one parent was a Canadian citizen.) This period was increased to ten years during the 1950s, and the provision was repealed altogether in 1967. However, some people had already lost their Canadian citizenship, in many cases unknowingly.[5] Amendments to the current *Citizenship Act* (see below) provide a remedy for such situations by restoring citizenship to people considered to be "lost Canadians."

The *Canadian Citizenship Act* was replaced, effective February 14, 1977, with a new *Citizenship Act*, which continues to govern citizenship applications. This new Act introduced several major changes, including the recognition of dual citizenship for Canadians and a reduction of the residency period needed to apply for citizenship.

Amendments

Policy decisions to amend immigration law rules, including rules relating to citizenship, are often controversial. Decisions regarding who will be recognized as a citizen of Canada involve fundamental policy choices about the nature of Canada. There have been a number of controversial issues with respect to the recognition of citizenship, including the treatment of foreign children adopted by Canadian parents, and the government's authority to revoke citizenship.

Amendments to the *Citizenship Act* as a result of Bill C-24, the *Strengthening Canadian Citizenship Act*, included the following changes:

- the granting of retroactive citizenship to most of the remaining "lost Canadians" dating to January 1, 1947 (or April 1, 1949, in the case of Newfoundland);

---

5   Penny Becklumb, Law and Government Division, Parliament of Canada, "Legislative Summary: Bill C-37: An Act to Amend the Citizenship Act" (9 January 2008), online: <http://www.parl.gc.ca/Content/LOP/LegislativeSummaries/39/2/c37-e.pdf>.

- citizenship was extended to "lost Canadians" who were born before the *Canadian Citizenship Act* took effect in 1947, as well as to their children who were born outside Canada in the first generation;
- fast-track citizenship was provided for permanent residents who are members of the Canadian Armed Forces (CAF);
- the first-generation limit on citizenship was clarified for those born abroad;
- the exception to the first-generation limit was extended to ensure that the children of Crown servants can pass on citizenship to their children;
- new decision-making authority for discretionary citizenship was granted to the minister of CIC;
- new residence requirements;
- new "intent to reside" requirement;
- expanded age requirements for language and knowledge testing;
- requirement to demonstrate knowledge of Canada in an official language;
- strengthened offences and penalties for fraud;
- prohibitions for foreign criminality and activities against national interests;
- new authority to designate a regulatory body for citizenship consultants;
- improved information-sharing authorities;
- a new revocation model; and
- new grounds to revoke citizenship from dual nationals who are convicted of serious crimes, or who take up arms against Canada.

Some of the amendments to the *Citizenship Act* resulting from the passage of Bill C-24 (which received royal assent on June 19, 2014) came into force immediately, while others came into effect on June 11, 2015.

The chart on the following page sets out the changes in detail.

Citizenship Commission

citizenship judges
quasi-judicial
decision-makers who
have the authority
to decide citizenship
applications

The Citizenship Commission is a quasi-judicial administrative body that consists of **citizenship judges** who are located across Canada. The Citizenship Commission is led by a senior citizenship judge, who reports to the minister of CIC and is responsible for ensuring the proper administration of the law. The senior citizenship judge also assumes responsibility for managing the administrative and professional services that the commission offers to judges. CIC provides the Citizenship Commission with administrative, financial, and human resources services; however, it maintains an arm's-length relationship on decision-making matters related to citizenship in order to ensure the independence of citizenship judges.

Citizenship judges are responsible for the following functions:

- assessing referred citizenship applications for compliance with residency requirements;
- administering the oath of citizenship and stating the rights and responsibilities of Canadian citizenship to new citizens;

Bill C-24 Amendments to the Citizenship Act

	Citizenship Act	*Strengthening Canadian Citizenship Act*
Residency requirements	Eligible to apply if living in Canada: **3 out of 4 years (1,095 days)**. No requirement in Act to be physically present in Canada. Time spent as a legal temporary resident counts as half day up to one year toward residency calculation. No requirement to prove "intent to reside" in Canada.	Eligible to apply if living in Canada: **4 years (1,460 days) out of 6 years**. Must be physically present in Canada for **minimum 183 days per year in 4 out of 6 years**. **Only time spent as a permanent resident can be used** for residency calculation. Must show **"intent to reside"** in Canada.
Language and knowledge requirements	Citizenship applicants aged **18–54**: • Must meet language requirements and pass knowledge test. • Upper age limit of 54 established by policy. • May use an interpreter to meet the knowledge requirement.	Citizenship applicants aged **14–64**: • Must meet language requirements and pass citizenship test. • Upper age limit of 64 established by legislation. • Citizenship test in official languages—English or French; **may not use an interpreter** to pass test.
Eligibility	No requirement to file Canadian income taxes to be eligible for citizenship. Not eligible if domestic criminal charges and convictions.	Applicants **must file Canadian income taxes** to be eligible for citizenship. Not eligible if **domestic or foreign** criminal charges and convictions.
Application process and procedures	The Act does not define what a complete citizenship application is.	The amended Act **defines** what a complete citizenship application is, including what **evidence** must be provided when applying.
Members of the Canadian Armed Forces (CAF)	**No fast-track** citizenship process.	Permanent residents serving with, or on exchange with, the CAF can apply for a **fast-track process**.
Decision-making process	**Three-step** decision-making process to decide citizenship applications: • review by a citizenship officer, then to two citizenship judges, and then three citizenship officers.	**One-step** decision-making process to decide citizenship applications: • applications reviewed and decided by one citizenship officer.
Discretionary decision-making	The governor in council (GiC) makes the final decision to grant citizenship.	The **minister of CIC** can decide to grant citizenship on a discretionary basis.
Lost Canadians (those not granted citizenship due to changes in 2009)	Some may (or may not) have had citizenship restored in 2009.	Lost Canadians born before 1947, and their first-generation children born abroad, will be granted Canadian citizenship.

Continued on the next page.

	Citizenship Act	*Strengthening Canadian Citizenship Act*
Revocation	No provision to revoke citizenship for acts against Canada's national interest.	Citizenship can be revoked or denied for a person with dual citizenship or a Canadian permanent resident who: • as a member of an armed force or an organized armed group, **engaged in armed conflict with Canada**; and/or • was **convicted** of terrorism, high treason, treason, or spying offences, depending on the sentence received.
Immigration consultants	**No requirement** to be registered or regulated to represent people in citizenship matters. **Few repercussions** to deter "consultants" from fraud. Fines and penalties for fraud are a **maximum of $1,000** and/or **one year in prison**.	The amended Act defines who is an **authorized representative** and provides for the development of regulations to designate a **regulatory body** of authorized consultants in citizenship matters. Prospective representatives who have been **convicted of fraud may not be authorized** to serve as consultants. Fines and penalties for fraud are a **maximum of $100,000** and/or **five years in prison**.

• maintaining the integrity of the citizenship process; and
• promoting citizenship by working with school boards, service clubs, multicultural groups, and other community organizations.

Citizenship judges' authorities and responsibilities are derived from the *Citizenship Act* and the *Citizenship Regulations*. Under the *Strengthening Canadian Citizenship Act*, the role of citizenship judges is more limited than before and over time will become mostly ceremonial.[6] Citizenship judges are independent, quasi-judicial decision makers who have the authority to decide citizenship applications upon referral from the minister only when the minister is not satisfied that the citizenship applicant's residency requirements are met. The minister and citizenship applicants may apply for leave to the Federal Court for judicial review of a decision made by a citizenship judge.

According to the *Citizenship Act*, the minister has the authority to decide the following applications:

• citizenship, involving the conferral of citizenship on a non-citizen (s 5(1));
• renunciations, involving the termination of citizenship (s 9(1)); and
• resumptions, involving the recommencement of a terminated citizenship (s 11(1)).

Most of these applications are decided by on the basis of a file review by officers.

---

6   Citizenship and Immigration Canada, "Graphic: Canada's Citizenship Decision-Making Process—June 2015" (5 June 2015), online <http://news.gc.ca/web/article-en.do?nid=985239>; and new section 14(1) of the *Citizenship Act*, introduced by Bill C-24.

Attributes of Citizenship

This section will examine four attributes of Canadian citizenship: the right to enter and remain in Canada, multiple citizenships, rights of Canadian citizenship, and responsibilities of Canadian citizenships.

Right to Enter and Remain in Canada

Every citizen has a right to enter and remain in Canada, according to section 19 of the IRPA and section 6 of the *Canadian Charter of Rights and Freedoms*. This means that a Canadian border services officer may not refuse a person admission to Canada at a port of entry if the officer is satisfied that the person is a Canadian citizen. Also, a Canadian citizen generally cannot be subject to removal or deportation from Canada.

These rights of citizenship are subject to reasonable limits, such as the power of an officer to detain a Canadian citizen subject to an arrest warrant. Similarly, although Canada may not banish or exile citizens, it may apprehend and extradite a citizen to face criminal charges in another country, according to the *Extradition Act*.

The Supreme Court examined the process of extradition in the case of *United States of America v Cotroni*[7] and confirmed that the process is in compliance with section 6(1) of the Charter. However, the court provided the following caution:

> Of course, the authorities must give due weight to the constitutional right of a citizen to remain in Canada. They must in good faith direct their minds to whether prosecution would be equally effective in Canada, given the existing domestic laws and international cooperative arrangements. They have an obligation flowing from s. 6(1) to assure themselves that prosecution in Canada is not a realistic option.

Extradition powers are important to prevent Canada from becoming an attractive place for fugitives.

Also, although Canada may not order citizens to leave the country, it may revoke Canadian citizenship that was obtained by fraud, misrepresentation, or concealment of important facts. Once citizenship is revoked, removal from Canada may be ordered (*Citizenship Act*, ss 10(1), (2)).

Multiple Citizenships

Canada has permitted **multiple citizenships** since the *Citizenship Act* was enacted in 1977. Canada allows a person who becomes a citizen of Canada to retain any previous citizenship. This is subject to the law of the other country, which may choose to revoke the citizenship of those who obtain citizenship elsewhere. Examples of countries that do not generally permit multiple citizenships (also called "multiple nationalities" or "dual citizenship") are Austria, China, India, Japan, and Norway.

multiple citizenships
a situation in which a person holds more than one citizenship

---

7 *United States of America v Cotroni; United States of America v El Zein*, [1989] 1 SCR 1469.

Rights of Canadian Citizenship

The rights of every person physically present in Canada are protected under the Charter. However, only Canadian citizens have the constitutional right to vote in provincial and federal elections, and to be qualified to be a member of Parliament or the provincial Parliament, according to section 3 of the Charter. Other rights under the Charter include language rights, equality rights, legal rights, mobility rights, the right to freedom of religion and of expression, and the right to freely assemble and associate. Like all Charter rights and freedoms, these rights are also subject to reasonable limits, such as minimum voting age requirements.

Canadian citizens also have the right to apply for a Canadian passport, which allows a citizen to return to Canada at any time after travelling or living abroad. Neither the Charter nor the *Citizenship Act* makes any distinction between persons who are born citizens and persons who acquire citizenship through naturalization. A naturalized citizen has all the same rights as a citizen who was born in Canada or born to Canadian parents. Section 6 of the *Citizenship Act* reads:

> A citizen, whether or not born in Canada, is entitled to all rights, powers and privileges and is subject to all obligations, duties and liabilities to which a person who is a citizen under paragraph 3(1)(a) is entitled or subject and has a like status to that of such person.

However, not all countries extend full political rights to naturalized citizens. For example, a naturalized citizen of the United States is prohibited from becoming president—only natural-born citizens of the United States may become president.

Responsibilities of Canadian Citizenship

Part of the naturalization process includes learning about the responsibilities of Canadian citizenship. These include obeying the law, taking responsibility for oneself, serving on a jury, voting in elections, helping others in the community, and protecting and enjoying our heritage and environment.[8]

Becoming a Citizen

The two most common principles of acquiring citizenship are the following:

jus soli
citizenship based on
the land of birth

jus sanguinis
citizenship based
on blood ties

- **Jus soli**: *Jus soli* is citizenship based on the land of birth. Under *jus soli*, at birth, a person is automatically granted citizenship of the country in which he was born.

- **Jus sanguinis**: *Jus sanguinis* is citizenship based on blood ties. Under *jus sanguinis*, at birth, a person is automatically granted citizenship of the country

---

8   Citizenship and Immigration Canada, "Rights and Responsibilities of Citizenship" in *Discover Canada: The Rights and Responsibilities of Citizenship* (Ottawa: CIC, 2012), online: <http://www.cic.gc.ca/english/resources/publications/discover/section-04.asp>.

of which one of his parents is a citizen. If the parents are citizens of separate or multiple countries, the child is granted citizenship of both or all of those countries.

Countries tend to adopt one or both of these principles, or some variation, as the basis for conferring citizenship. Other approaches used by some nations are to grant citizenship to foreign nationals who marry one of their citizens (*jure matrimonii*) or citizenship by adoption.[9] In addition, most countries allow immigrants to apply for citizenship through the process of naturalization.

The Canadian *Citizenship Act* allows for four methods of becoming a citizen—namely, being born in Canada, being born outside Canada to a Canadian citizen, being born outside Canada and adopted by at least one parent who is a Canadian citizen, and naturalization. Each method is described below.

Being Born in Canada

Generally, any person born in Canada is automatically a Canadian citizen. This is according to section 3(1) of the *Citizenship Act* and follows the principle of *jus soli*, or citizenship by soil. The rule applies even if neither parent is a Canadian citizen, and even if one or both parents are in Canada illegally.

Some locations outside Canada are deemed to be in Canada for the operation of the rule, including Canadian ships and aircraft registered in Canada. Persons born on these vessels are Canadian citizens (*Citizenship Act*, s 2(2)).

There is an exception to the rule that birth in Canada confers Canadian citizenship: a person who, at the time of birth, is the child of a foreign national who is in Canada as the representative of a foreign government or an international agency does not acquire citizenship (*Citizenship Act*, s 3(2)).

Being Born Outside Canada to a Canadian Citizen

A person born outside Canada is a Canadian citizen if one of her parents is a Canadian citizen at the time of her birth. This follows the principle of *jus sanguinis*, or citizenship by blood. The rule applies even if the baby's only connection with Canada is having a parent who is a Canadian citizen and even if the baby never resides in or even visits Canada. Often, such a baby is automatically a citizen of her country of birth as well. Canadian law allows such a person to retain Canadian citizenship unless she takes steps to renounce it.

This raises an issue with respect to the continuation of citizenship for second and subsequent generations born outside Canada. Canadian citizenship could potentially be passed on for generations, even when connection with Canada is non-existent. Canada would be obliged to admit these persons to Canada automatically, and to offer them the assistance of Canadian overseas services, such as embassies and consulates.

---

9   See Patrick Weil, "Access to Citizenship: A Comparison of Twenty Five Nationality Laws" (Presentation delivered at Metropolis Presents, 28 October 2002), online: Metropolis Canada <http://canada.metropolis.net/events/metropolis_presents/eu_speakers/weil2_e.htm>.

IN THE NEWS

Citizenship and Children of Diplomats

The story of the son of a Saudi Arabian diplomat made the news in 2007 when he found out that he was mistakenly issued a Quebec birth certificate and a Canadian passport despite not being eligible for citizenship. He discovered the mistake after submitting an application for a replacement passport, which was denied.

Ahmad Saeed Abdullah Al-Ghamdi was born in Canada and was formally told that he was a Canadian citizen, so the discovery came as a shock to him.

"I always thought of myself as a Canadian citizen and still consider myself to be one," Al-Ghamdi said in an affidavit filed in the Federal Court of Canada.

However, the Federal Court of Canada confirmed that, pursuant to section 3(2) of the *Citizenship Act*, he is not a citizen. In explaining the rationale, the court stated: "It is precisely because of the vast array of privileges accorded to diplomats and their families, which are by their very nature inconsistent with the obligations of citizenship, that a person who enjoys diplomatic status cannot acquire citizenship."

What do you think? How do situations like this fit within the Canadian conceptualization of citizenship?

Source: Based on Canwest News Service, "Children of Diplomats Have No Right to Canadian Passport, Court Says" (1 June 2007), online: Canada.com <http://www.canada.com/story_print.html?id=ae35ede6-01d0-4098-97a3-769da92c5bb2>.

People born before April 17, 2009 who are second- or subsequent-generation Canadians born abroad retain their existing Canadian citizenship (*Citizenship Act*, s 3(4)). They must still apply for a citizenship certificate because they are subject to the retention requirement. CIC notifies these individuals by letter advising them of the steps to take before their 28th birthday in order to retain Canadian citizenship.

The rule limiting citizenship by descent to one generation came into effect on April 17, 2009. This means that a child born abroad after April 17, 2009 to a parent who derived her citizenship from a Canadian parent who was also born abroad will no longer automatically become a Canadian citizen, according to section 3(3) of the *Citizenship Act*.[10] Children born to Canadian parents in the first generation outside Canada will be Canadian at birth only if

- one parent was born in Canada, or
- one parent became a Canadian citizen by immigrating to Canada and was later granted citizenship through naturalization.

An exception is provided for

people who are born to a Canadian parent working abroad in or with the Canadian Armed Forces, the federal public administration or the public service of a province, unless the parent is a locally engaged person (new section 3(5)). For such people, citizenship is automatic at birth even though the person is a second- or subsequent generation Canadian born abroad.[11]

---

10 *Supra* note 5.

11 *Ibid* at 10.

Cutting off citizenship by descent after the first generation of Canadians born abroad will result in some children of Canadians born abroad in the future being stateless. Therefore, section 5(5) of the *Citizenship Act* provides for a mandatory grant of citizenship to a person who was born outside Canada, after the provision came into force, to a parent who was Canadian at the time of the person's birth if, at the time that the person applies for Canadian citizenship, the person

- is less than 23 years old;
- has resided in Canada for at least three years during the four years immediately before the date of the application for citizenship;
- has always been stateless; and
- has not been convicted of various listed national security offences.[12]

Finally, a remaining small number of people who had lost or never received Canadian citizenship and who were still considered to be "lost Canadians" (for example, some first-generation children born abroad to war brides and service men) automatically retroactively became citizens on June 5, 2015, owing to changes provided for under the *Strengthening Canadian Citizenship Act*.[13]

Retaining Citizenship for Second- and Subsequent-Generation Canadians Born Outside Canada

John Smith was born in Calgary, Alberta in 1958. He moved to Australia in 1978 because of a job, and lived the rest of his life there. His son, Bob Smith, born in Australia in 1979, is a Canadian citizen by descent because his father was a Canadian citizen. Bob Smith lived his entire life in Australia, and had no connection with Canada. Bob's son, Roger Smith, was born in Australia in 2010.

Before the changes to the *Citizenship Act*, second- and subsequent-generation Canadians born outside Canada on or after February 15, 1977 to a Canadian parent who was also born outside Canada were allowed to apply to retain Canadian citizenship before age 28; otherwise, the "chain" would be broken and Canadian citizenship would be lost. Citizenship is now limited to only the first generation for children born outside Canada on or after April 17, 2009. Consequently, Roger Smith does not have Canadian citizenship through *jus sanguinis*.

Being Born Outside Canada: Citizenship by Adoption

The *Citizenship Act* treats foreign-born children adopted by Canadian citizens the same as biological children born abroad to Canadian citizens. Sections 3(1)(c.1) and 5.1 of the *Citizenship Act* allow for a grant of citizenship to a minor child adopted by a Canadian citizen after January 1, 1947 without first obtaining permanent residency, provided that the adoption

---

12   *Ibid* at 10–11.

13   Citizenship and Immigration Canada, Backgrounder, "Welcome Home: Extending Citizenship to More 'Lost Canadians'" (6 June 2015), online: <http://news.gc.ca/web/article-en.do?nid=985209>.

- was in the best interests of the child;
- created a genuine parent–child relationship;
- was in accordance with the laws of the place where the adoption took place and the laws of the country of residence of the adopting citizen;
- did not occur in a manner that circumvented the legal requirements for international adoptions; and
- was not primarily for the purpose of acquiring citizenship or immigration status.

These rules apply in the case of the legal adoption of a person 18 years of age or older, provided that a parent–child relationship was established prior to the child becoming 18 and that the adoption was not entered into primarily for the purpose of acquiring a status or privilege in relation to immigration or citizenship.

The *Citizenship Act* empowers the governor in council (GiC) to make regulations providing for the factors to be considered in determining whether these requirements have been met. Under section 5.1 of the *Citizenship Regulations*, these factors include: where the adoption took place (inside or outside Canada), whether the child lived in a country that was a party to the Hague Convention on Adoption, whether the Canadian provincial authority does not object to the adoption, and whether there was a pre-existing legal parent–child relationship that was permanently severed by the adoption.

There is also a special provision (s 5.1(3)) for adoptions that are under the jurisdiction of Quebec. Adoptions in Quebec are considered finalized when the child is physically in Quebec and residing with the adoptive parents. Under Quebec law, the authority responsible for international adoptions must confirm in writing that the adoption complies with Quebec law, so that Canadian citizenship can be granted to children adopted abroad before the adoption is officially approved by the Court of Quebec.

Adoption is also discussed in Chapter 7, Family Class.

Naturalization

Naturalization is the legal process that transforms a permanent resident into a Canadian citizen. In order to be naturalized, the permanent resident must apply for citizenship. Most of these applications are decided by judges on the basis of a file review. However, when a judge finds that more information is required to make a decision, the applicant must attend a hearing before that judge.

Permanent residents who wish to obtain a grant of Canadian citizenship must meet certain criteria. They must

- be admitted to Canada as a permanent resident;
- be at least 18 years old or be included with the application of a parent who is over 18 years old;
- make an application for citizenship;
- pay fees;

- provide photos;
- meet the residency requirements;
- not be under a removal order or declared to be a threat to security or a member of an organized crime group;
- show an adequate knowledge of English or French;
- demonstrate an understanding of the responsibilities of a citizen and pass the citizenship test; and
- take the citizenship oath.

An applicant who is physically or mentally unable to comply may, for compassionate reasons, have the requirements waived for language competence, the citizenship test, and the citizenship oath. Instead, the applicant must submit a medical opinion provided by his physician attesting to the fact that he is unable to meet the requirements by reason of the medical condition or disability (*Citizenship Act*, s 5(3)).

Grant of Citizenship Process

Numerous steps must be taken when applying for Canadian citizenship. Some steps, such as the payment of fees, are relatively straightforward. However, many applicants require advice and assistance with other steps in the naturalization process. For example, documents must be provided to support the application and, if the originals are not in English or French, they must be translated into one of those official languages and the translator must swear an affidavit stating that the translation is a true one.[14]

Other steps, such as demonstrating sufficient time spent residing in Canada, may be complex and require legal advice and guidance from counsel. The requirements for a grant of citizenship are found in section 5 of the *Citizenship Act*.

Application Documents

The applicant must submit a number of forms and documents that support the citizenship application. The application forms and supporting documentation include the following:

- a completed application package, including Application for Citizenship—Adults (CIT 0002) or Application for Canadian Citizenship—Minors (CIT 0003) and How to Calculate Physical Presence (CIT 0407);
- proof of Canadian permanent residence, including Record of Landing (IMM 1000) or Confirmation of Permanent Residence (IMM 5292 or IMM 5688), and a photocopy of both sides of the applicant's permanent resident card;

---

14 Citizenship and Immigration Canada, "Application for Canadian Citizenship Under Subsection 5(1)—Adults 18 Years of Age and Older (CIT 0002)," online: <http://www.cic.gc.ca/english/information/applications/guides/CIT0002ETOC.asp>.

- for applicants 14 to 64 years of age, proof of an adequate knowledge of one of Canada's two official languages;
  - Applicants must be able to carry out simple everyday conversations and basic activities, such as shopping, banking, and taking public transit, in either English or French. Citizenship officers will make note of how well applicants are able to communicate with them.
  - Applicants can use language test results from another immigration application (for example, permanent residence application) to show the equivalent of Canadian Language Benchmark/Niveaux de compétence linguistique canadiens (CLB/NCLC) level 4 or other approved tests, or to provide proof of completion of a secondary or post-secondary program conducted in French or English, either in Canada or abroad.
- photocopies of the biographical pages (containing the applicant's name, photo, passport/travel document number, issue date, and expiration date) of all passports and/or travel documents (valid and cancelled) for the relevant four-year period immediately preceding the date of application, including any renewal pages of the passport(s)/travel document(s);
- photocopies of all official education records; and
- proof of identity and age: applicants must present two identity documents (one of which must include the applicant's photo), such as a passport, health insurance card, or Canadian driver's licence, and must establish age by filing a birth certificate or other evidence that shows their date and place of birth.

Applicants must also disclose any other versions of their names that have been used. It is not unusual for permanent residents to use Canadianized versions of their names, and these names must be reported on the application.

Applicants must submit two citizenship photos that conform to the size and other requirements specified by regulation. Photos must be signed on the back by both the photographer and the applicant. The applicant's signature on the photograph must match the signature on the application. Head coverings must be removed for the photo unless the head covering is worn for the purpose of religious observance. If a head covering is worn, the applicant's full face must be visible.

Application Fees

WEBLINK

The fees required for a citizenship application can be found on the CIC website at <www.cic.gc.ca/english/information/fees/fees.asp>.

An applicant must pay the fees specified by regulation. Application fees vary depending on whether the applicant is an adult or a minor. For example, the application fee for an adult grant of citizenship was only $100 in 2013 but was increased to $530 in 2014, while the application fee for a minor remained at $100. There are also fees to process applications for retention, resumption, and renunciation of citizenship. Fees and exemptions are established in the *Citizenship Regulations* and are thus subject to change. The fees for processing applications are non-refundable.

A $100 right of citizenship fee is also payable at the time of application if the applicant is 18 years or older. This fee is refundable if the application is rejected.

Proof of Residency

According to section 5(1) of the *Citizenship Act*, to satisfy the residency requirement, the applicant must meet three conditions of residency:

1. *Lawful admittance to Canada as a permanent resident.* The applicant must file her Canadian immigration record/paper, such as the Record of Landing (IMM 1000) and Confirmation of Permanent Residence (IMM 5292), which was obtained from CIC when permanent residency was granted, and a copy of both sides of the permanent resident card. This shows entitlement to enter Canada. (It is also important to establish accumulation of the required residency period in Canada.)

2. *No loss of permanent residency.* The applicant's permanent residency must not be invalidated by a failure to maintain the connection with Canada or by an order to leave Canada. A connection with Canada is not maintained if the person is not resident in Canada for two years out of every five-year period (loss of permanent resident status is discussed in Chapter 6). Permanent resident status is also lost if a removal order is made because the person has become inadmissible and the appeals of that order have been exhausted (IRPA, s 28). This could occur if, for example, the permanent resident engaged in criminal activity.

3. *Residence in Canada.* Under sections 5(1)(c) to (e) of the *Citizenship Act*, as amended by Bill C-24, the applicant must be a permanent resident of Canada. The applicant must prove residency in Canada for at least four years (1,460 days) out of the past six years, and the applicant must be physically present in Canada for minimum 183 days per year in four out of six years. Only days spent as a permanent resident are considered for purposes of the residency calculation. Section 5(1)(c)(iii) obliges applicants to meet the requirements of the *Income Tax Act* "to file a return of income in respect of four taxation years that are fully or partially within the six years immediately before the date of his or her application." Furthermore, under section 5(1)(c.1), the applicant must show an "intent to reside" in Canada.

Before Bill C-24's residency requirements came into force, the requirement of residence in Canada had not been clear, because the *Citizenship Act* did not specify whether actual physical presence in Canada was required or whether it would be sufficient to establish a life in Canada and to treat Canada as a home base while spending time outside the country. Case law had been divided as to whether actual physical presence in Canada was required. In many cases, judges held that once a person was resident in Canada, he could be absent from Canada for periods of time, provided that the pattern and length of absences were not significant enough to show that Canadian residence had been abandoned. This allowed time spent outside Canada for a vacation or business trip to count toward the requirement. Other judges reviewing appeals of citizenship application cases, however, took the position that actual physical presence in Canada was required and that the applicant had to show that he had been physically present in Canada for at least 1,095 days during the past four years.

When calculating time in Canada, the following rules apply:

- each day spent in Canada after the applicant became a permanent resident counts as one day; and
- generally, time spent serving a sentence for an offence in Canada is not counted.

In cases where an applicant has fewer than the required number of days of physical presence in Canada, only a citizenship judge may determine whether residency requirements have been met.

Prohibited Persons

Under sections 20 and 22 of the *Citizenship Act*, certain applicants are prohibited from acquiring Canadian citizenship:

- a permanent resident who is under a probation order, a paroled inmate, or an inmate who is serving a sentence in a penitentiary, jail, reformatory, or prison;
- an applicant who is under a removal order;
- an applicant who is a declared threat to security or a member of an organized crime group;
- an applicant who directly or indirectly misrepresents or withholds material circumstances relating to a relevant matter, which induces or could induce an error in the administration of the *Citizenship Act*;
- a person who was prohibited from being granted citizenship or taking the oath of citizenship within five years immediately before the person's application;
- a person who ceased to be a citizen within the ten years immediately before the person's application; and
- a person whose citizenship has been revoked.

If applicable, any such ground of inadmissibility must be disclosed. However, the minister has discretion to grant citizenship in the face of these problems, according to section 5(4) of the *Citizenship Act*:

Despite any other provision of this Act, the Minister may, in his or her discretion, grant citizenship to any person to alleviate cases of special and unusual hardship or to reward services of an exceptional value to Canada.

Canada's Citizenship Week

In 2006, CIC launched the first Citizenship Week to promote citizenship. Citizenship Week is an annual event celebrating the value of citizenship, and promoting the privileges and responsibilities of being a Canadian citizen. Canada celebrated the 65th anniversary of Canadian citizenship in 2012. For more information about Citizenship Week, as well as other ways to celebrate Canada, visit the CIC website and search for "Celebrate being Canadian." From <www.cic.gc.ca/english/celebrate/> you will find a menu of options such as "Take part in our citizenship."

Citizenship Test

Changes to the *Citizenship Regulations* in 2010 set out procedures for an updated citizenship test. CIC revised the citizenship test as "part of overall efforts at CIC to strengthen the value of citizenship and to emphasize the integrity of the testing process."[15] The citizenship test focuses on building awareness of Canadian values and history, institutions that shape Canada, and the rights and responsibilities associated with Canadian citizenship.

The applicant for citizenship must display civic literacy through an adequate knowledge of Canada, and of the rights and responsibilities of Canadian citizenship, as outlined in section 15 of the *Citizenship Regulations*. Applicants are required to take a citizenship test measuring their knowledge of Canada's national symbols and a general understanding in the following areas:

- the chief characteristics of Canadian political and military history;
- the chief characteristics of Canadian social and cultural history;
- the chief characteristics of Canadian physical and political geography;
- the chief characteristics of the Canadian system of government as a constitutional monarchy; and
- other characteristics of Canada.

Applicants must also have a general understanding of the following:

- participation in the Canadian democratic process;
- participation in Canadian society, including volunteerism, respect for the environment, and the protection of Canada's natural, cultural, and architectural heritage;
- respect for the rights, freedoms, and obligations set out in the laws governing Canada; and
- other responsibilities and privileges of citizenship.

The test is waived for applicants over age 64 or under the age of 14.

To assist with preparations for the test, CIC provides the citizenship study guide online, called *Discover Canada: The Rights and Responsibilities of Citizenship*. Information about the test and sample study questions are available on the CIC website.

Applicants receive a notice to appear for a citizenship test, indicating the date, time, and place of the test. Testing takes place at local CIC offices. Applicants have 30 minutes to complete the multiple-choice test. To receive a passing mark, they must correctly answer at least 15 questions out of 20. Applicants who fail the test will be given another date to take the test a second time. If they fail the second test but meet all the other requirements, they must appear for an interview with a citizenship officer.

WEBLINK

To learn more about the citizenship test and to see more sample questions, visit the CIC website at <www.cic.gc.ca/english/citizenship/cit-test.asp>.

---

15 Citizenship and Immigration Canada, "Operational Bulletin 244B—February 25, 2011" (25 February 2011), online: <http://www.cic.gc.ca/english/resources/manuals/bulletins/2011/ob244B.asp>.

Citizenship Oath

Applicants who meet the basic requirements for citizenship and who have passed both the language and citizenship tests receive a notice to appear to take the oath of citizenship. All applicants over the age of 14 must take the oath. The oath is administered at a special ceremony presided over by a citizenship judge.

The oath of citizenship as set out in the schedule to the *Citizenship Act* reads as follows:

> I swear (*or* affirm) that I will be faithful and bear true allegiance to Her Majesty Queen Elizabeth the Second, Queen of Canada, Her Heirs and Successors, and that I will faithfully observe the laws of Canada and fulfil my duties as a Canadian citizen.

Historically, applicants would hold a Bible while swearing the oath. In recognition of the rights of religious freedom enshrined in our legal system, this is no longer required. Applicants with a religious or other objection to swearing an oath are given the option of affirming rather than swearing the oath. Applicants who swear the oath may hold a holy book of their choosing when taking the oath. Furthermore, all applicants must be seen taking the oath.[16]

Applications for Minors

According to section 5(2) of the *Citizenship Act*, a citizenship application for a minor may be completed by the child's parents (biological or adoptive), legal guardians, or other persons legally entitled to have custody of the child. A minor is a person who is not yet 18. A minor child between 14 and 18 years of age is expected to sign the application, unless he has a mental disability. In addition to the information provided in the application that accompanies an adult's application, the following additional items must be provided:

- Evidence establishing that the minor child is the child of a citizen. Acceptable documents include birth certificates showing the names of the parents, adoption orders, parents' passports showing the names of the children, and IMM 1000 or Confirmation of Permanent Residence forms listing parents' names for children who entered Canada as refugees.

- If the applicant is not a birth or adoptive parent of a citizen, evidence establishing that the applicant has legal custody of the child. Acceptable documents include a court order or written agreement.

---

16 Citizenship and Immigration Canada, "Oath of Citizenship" (11 June 2015), online: <http://www.cic.gc.ca/english/resources/tools/cit/ceremony/oath.asp>.

Steps After Application Submitted

Once the applicant has completed the application for citizenship, she must mail it to the Case Processing Centre (CPC) in Sydney, Nova Scotia, where the following steps occur:[17]

Step 1: A citizenship officer reviews the application to ensure that the applicant meets the criteria to become a Canadian citizen, including that the application is complete, the fee is paid, and all information is included.

Step 2: The citizenship officer reviews the documents submitted with the application—for example, the Confirmation of Permanent Residence (or the Record of Landing (IMM 1000)).

Step 3: The CPC directs the applicant to the CIC website to study *Discover Canada: The Rights and Responsibilities of Citizenship*.

Step 4: The CPC forwards the application to the following for background checks to ensure admissibility: CIC, to check for an immigration record; the RCMP, to check for a criminal record; and the Canadian Security and Intelligence Service (CSIS), to check for a security record.

Step 5: The citizenship officer prepares and sends a package of information to the CIC office nearest to the applicant.

Step 6: The CIC office sends the applicant a notice to appear for an interview/hearing with a citizenship officer and to take the citizenship test.

If the citizenship officer is not satisfied that the applicant meets the residence requirement for citizenship, the officer may refer the matter to a citizenship judge.

Step 7: If necessary, an interview with a citizenship judge is arranged to review residency issues. The *Citizenship Act* requires that judges render a decision, setting out the reasons for their decision, without delay. If the citizenship judge approves citizenship, the applicant is invited to a citizenship ceremony by way of a notice to appear to take the oath of citizenship.

If the citizenship judge refuses the application, either the applicant may reapply or the decision may be appealed by way of judicial review, but only with leave from the Federal Court of Canada. Either a non-approved applicant or the minister of CIC can file an application for judicial review. Note that only a lawyer, not an immigration consultant, may represent an applicant at the Federal Court.

If the citizen judge approves the application, the applicant is invited to a citizenship ceremony by way of a notice to appear to take the oath of citizenship.

---

17 The process outlined is based on Citizenship and Immigration Canada, *CP 12: Documents* (Ottawa: CIC, 16 June 2008), which is no longer available, and on Citizenship and Immigration Canada, "Citizenship Grants: Adult" (11 June 2015), online: <http://www.cic.gc.ca/english/resources/tools/cit/grant/adult.asp>.

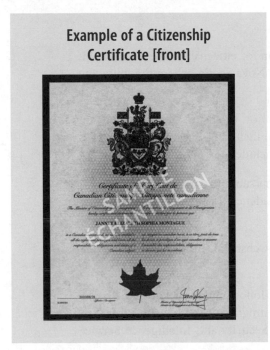

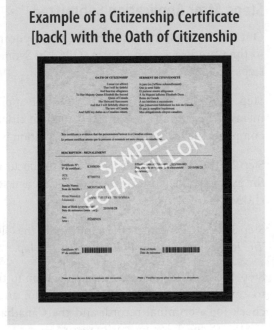

Source: *Canadian Citizenship Certificate*. Reproduced with the permission of the Minister of Public Works and Government Services Canada, 2012.

Step 8: A citizenship ceremony is held, during which the applicant takes the oath of citizenship. As of February 1, 2012, the plastic, wallet-sized citizenship certificate that was previously issued was replaced with a letter-sized paper citizenship certificate. This new certificate (see above) is a legal status document issued to new citizens and anyone applying for their proof of citizenship; although it does not include a photo of the Canadian citizen, it does contain a unique number and basic information (that is, name, date of birth, and gender) that allows the government to electronically validate the certificate in order to reduce instances of fraud. New citizens must wait at least two business days after their ceremony to apply for a Canadian passport. (Any citizen of Canada may apply for a certificate of citizenship as proof of his Canadian citizenship, according to section 12 of the *Citizenship Act*.)

Step 9: The applicant's completed file is microfilmed and stored.

Resuming Citizenship

An individual who wishes to resume Canadian citizenship must apply and be eligible to do so by meeting the following requirements:

- have been a Canadian citizen;
- have become a permanent resident of Canada after losing Canadian citizenship; and
- have lived in Canada as a permanent resident for at least one year immediately before applying.

Individuals are not eligible if:

- their Canadian citizenship was revoked;
- they were convicted of an indictable offence or an offence under the *Citizenship Act* in the three years before application;
- they are currently charged with an indictable offence or an offence under the *Citizenship Act*;
- they are in prison, on parole, or on probation;
- they are under a removal order; or
- they are under investigation for, are charged with, or have been convicted of a war crime or a crime against humanity.

Application packages to resume citizenship are available on the CIC website. Applications to resume citizenship are decided by the senior citizenship judge.

Restoration of Citizenship

Under former legislation, there were several ways that people could either lose their citizenship or never be recognized as Canadian citizens. Bill C-37, *An Act to amend the Citizenship Act*, addressed these situations by

- permitting certain persons who lost their Canadian citizenship for specified reasons to have their citizenship restored from the time it was lost;
- permitting certain persons who, born outside Canada to a Canadian parent, did not acquire Canadian citizenship for specified reasons to become Canadian citizens from the time of their birth;
- providing that certain persons born outside Canada to a Canadian parent who was himself or herself born outside Canada *do not* acquire Canadian citizenship; and
- providing for a grant of citizenship, on application, to persons who have always been stateless and who meet other specified conditions.

Bill C-37 also addressed the issue of "lost Canadians." Lost Canadians are individuals who have resided most of their lives in Canada and have a reasonable but mistaken belief they are Canadian citizens. They either ceased to be citizens at some point or never were Canadian citizens. Generally, lost Canadians only discover they are not Canadian citizens when they apply for a certificate of Canadian citizenship or other document. In the past, a person who lost Canadian citizenship had to apply for a resumption of citizenship. Amendments to the *Citizenship Act* under Bill C-37, however, allowed for citizenship to be granted or restored retroactively to most, but not all, lost Canadians.

The amendments to the *Citizenship Act* give citizenship to the following kinds of lost Canadians:

- people naturalized to Canada who subsequently lived outside the country for more than ten years prior to 1967 and lost their citizenship; and

- people born abroad to a Canadian parent before the current *Citizenship Act* came into effect on February 15, 1977.

The amendments also give citizenship to "former lost Canadians":

- people who lost their citizenship between January 1, 1947 and February 14, 1977 because they or one of their parents acquired the nationality or citizenship of another country; and
- second- and subsequent-generation Canadians born abroad since the current *Citizenship Act* came into effect on February 15, 1977.

Relief is provided for the anticipated situations where these amendments will result in some offspring of Canadians born abroad being stateless.

Finally, Bill C-24 restored citizenship to any lost Canadians born before 1947, and their first-generation children born abroad who were not granted citizenship in 2009.

Renouncing and Revoking Citizenship

Citizenship may be lost only for the reasons specified in sections 9 and 10 of the *Citizenship Act*—namely, renunciation and revocation. For administrative efficiency, applications to renounce and revoke citizenship are decided by the senior citizenship judge.

Renouncing Citizenship

Renouncing citizenship means that a citizen actively takes steps to terminate citizenship. A Canadian citizen who is no longer resident in Canada may renounce her Canadian citizenship. A person may be motivated to do this if Canadian citizenship prevents entitlement to an advantage or benefit in another country.

For example, the Canadian-born newspaper magnate Conrad Black, when he had the opportunity to become a British peer and sit in the British House of Lords, actively sought to renounce his Canadian citizenship. Black wanted to be granted a peerage by the Queen of England, an honour that has been bestowed on other wealthy Canadian newspaper owners in the past. A constitutional convention prevented the Queen from granting such a peerage to a Canadian citizen without the approval of the prime minister of Canada. The prime minister refused permission, and his refusal was upheld by the Ontario Court of Appeal in *Black v Canada (Prime Minister)*.[18] However, Black, as a resident of England, was allowed to renounce his Canadian citizenship so that the Queen could grant the peerage, and Black ceased to be a Canadian citizen in 2001.

The decision to renounce his Canadian citizenship created an unusual problem for Black. In 2007, he was convicted of three counts of fraud and one count of obstruction of justice in a US court. After having served a 42-month sentence, Black wanted to return to Canada, but could not do so because he no longer had any right

---

18 *Black v Canada (Prime Minister)*, 2001 CanLII 8537, 54 OR (3d) 215 (CA).

to enter Canada; he had to apply for a temporary resident permit as a foreign national. Black has stated that he intends to apply for Canadian citizenship in the future; however, he will have to first apply to become a permanent resident.

A person may also need to renounce his Canadian citizenship if he wishes to become a citizen of another country that does not allow dual citizenship.

Revoking Citizenship

Revoking citizenship means that the Canadian government takes steps to remove a person's citizenship. Revocation is done by Cabinet through an order in council.

Revocation proceedings may be applied to citizenship granted by any method under the Act, if it comes to light that either the person's admission to Canada for the prerequisite period of residence or the citizenship application itself involved at least one of the following:

- fraud,

- false representation (misrepresentation), or

- knowing concealment of material circumstances.

A person who has his citizenship revoked under these grounds must wait ten years from the date of revocation before applying for citizenship.

New grounds for revocation of citizenship were created under Bill C-24 and came into effect on May 28, 2015 for Canadians with dual citizenship who:

- were convicted of terrorism, high treason, treason, or spying offences, depending on the sentence received; or

- served as a member of an armed force of a country or as a member of an organized armed group and that country or group was engaged in armed conflict with Canada.

The minister must have reasonable grounds to believe that the person is a citizen of another country before pursuing revocation under these grounds. The onus rests with the Canadian citizen to prove, on a balance of probabilities, that he is not a citizen of another country (*Citizenship Act*, s 10.4(2)).

A person who has his citizenship revoked under these grounds is permanently barred from being granted Canadian citizenship.

In September 2012, the minister announced that, following investigations, steps had begun to revoke the citizenship of up to 3,100 citizens who obtained it fraudulently.[19]

For example, if it can be shown that a person's documents indicating place of birth or parentage were falsified in order to claim citizenship by place of birth, or through a birth parent, then the citizenship of that person could be revoked. Likewise,

WEBLINK

The Canadian government provides a fraud tip line in Canada at 1-888-242-2100 or online at <www.cic.gc.ca/english/information/protection/fraud/report.asp> to report cases involving false representation, fraud, or knowingly concealing material in the citizenship process.

---

19   Citizenship and Immigration Canada, News Release, "Canadian Citizenship Not for Sale: Minister Kenney Provides Update on Residence Fraud Investigations" (10 September 2012), online: <http://news.gc.ca/web/article-en.do?nid=694369>.

a person who applies to retain citizenship on the basis of having a substantial connection with Canada and who files false documents showing educational time spent in Canada could have her citizenship revoked.

Often, the cases dealing with revocation of citizenship do not clearly define which of the three reasons is the basis for the revocation. This is because the facts that give rise to revocation may be described as fraudulent, a false representation, and a knowing concealment of material circumstances.

The operation of these provisions was illustrated in the case of Helmut Oberlander, who, when he immigrated to Canada in 1954, failed to disclose that he had worked as a translator for a Nazi police unit that killed 23,000 persons in Ukraine from 1941 to 1943. Although there was no evidence that Mr. Oberlander took part in the killings, his connection to the Nazi regime was a material issue, because Canada was not admitting persons suspected of involvement in atrocities during the Second World War. In 2001, the government revoked Mr. Oberlander's citizenship following a court decision that found he had obtained his citizenship by false representation or by knowingly concealing material circumstances. Appeals have been ongoing since, and the Federal Court recently denied Mr. Oberlander's attempt to get his citizenship back.[20]

An example of citizenship being revoked because of fraud would be a case in which an applicant with a criminal record forges documents to support the application. The applicant could obtain and try to use forged certificates showing he had no criminal record.

The evidentiary requirements for proving fraud are stricter than those for proving false representation or knowing concealment of material circumstances, as was illustrated in *Canada (Citizenship and Immigration) v Odynsky*.[21] In order to establish fraud, it is not sufficient to simply show that a person did an action, such as making a false statement—it must be shown that there was some mental element involved in the activity, such as an intention to get around the restrictions in the system.

In the *Odynsky* case, the government could not prove fraud but was able to show both knowing concealment of a material circumstance and the making of a false representation. Odynsky was forced to act as a guard in a concentration camp during the Second World War. He did not reveal this fact when he applied to come to Canada in 1949, and he became a Canadian citizen in 1955. It was not proven that Canadian officials asked about his actions during the war when he made his application; therefore, his omission was not fraudulent. However, by omitting this fact, he rendered his application untrue, and thus it was a false representation. In addition, the circumstances were material because Canada would not have admitted him if he had stated he was a concentration camp guard, and he knew he was not fully revealing this information.

Note that to prove knowing concealment of a material circumstance, it does not have to be shown that the person knew the circumstances were material. Furthermore, the person does not have to know about the criteria being applied by the Canadian authorities in assessing his application.

---

20 *Oberlander v Canada (Attorney General)*, 2015 FC 46.

21 *Canada (Citizenship and Immigration) v Odynsky*, 2001 FCT 138, 14 Imm LR (3d) 3.

The mere fact of making a false representation is sufficient, even without the presence of a mental element. Thus, in the *Odynsky* case, the government did not have to prove that Mr. Odynsky intentionally did not reveal his service during the war in order to circumvent the application process. Once it showed that the statement was false, this was sufficient.

Finally, the courts have indicated that the false statement cannot be merely a technical or minor error in order to result in the revocation of citizenship.[22]

---

22 *Canada (Minister of Multiculturalism and Citizenship) v Minhas* (1993), 66 FTR 155, 21 Imm LR (2d) 31 (FCTD).

KEY TERMS

citizenship, 293

citizenship judges, 296

foreign national, 293

jus sanguinis, 300

jus soli, 300

multiple citizenships, 299

naturalization, 292

stateless person, 294

REVIEW QUESTIONS

1. List the four basic methods by which a person may become a Canadian citizen.

2. List and describe the requirements that must be satisfied for a person to become a citizen of Canada through the process of naturalization.

3. List and describe the reasons why a person may lose Canadian citizenship.

4. What are the functions of a citizenship judge?

5. In what situation will time spent in Canada not be counted toward satisfying the residency requirement for citizenship?

CASE STUDY

Vijay, who is originally from India, is a 62-year-old man who has been a permanent resident of Canada for nine years. He had never thought about naturalization until recently. Now, he is considering some of the advantages and disadvantages of Canadian citizenship.

1. What are the advantages or disadvantages of the process of renewing his permanent resident (PR) card compared with the process of getting Canadian citizenship?

2. Does Vijay have to give up his Indian citizenship to become a Canadian citizen? Why or why not?

3. Vijay would like to volunteer for a candidate in the upcoming municipal election and is thinking about a possible future run for a councillor's seat. As a permanent resident, how could Vijay become involved in politics?

4. If Vijay, as a permanent resident, is charged or convicted of a serious crime, will he automatically be deported? How would this affect his application for citizenship?

PART V

Refugee Law

Refugees and Protected Persons

11

LEARNING OUTCOMES

After reading this chapter, you should be able to:

- Understand who a refugee or a person in need of protection is.

- Identify relevant international treaties relating to the determination of refugees and protected persons.

- Describe the role of the Office of the United Nations High Commissioner for Refugees with regard to refugee protection.

- Understand the inclusion, exclusion, and cessation elements for determining protection.

- Understand Canada's obligations toward refugee claimants.

- Understand the rights and responsibilities of refugee claimants.

- Identify relevant sections of the *Immigration and Refugee Protection Act* as they relate to refugees and persons in need of protection.

Introduction

Millions of people around the world leave their homes each year, driven by war, political or religious oppression, natural disaster, environmental destruction, and poverty. Are they all refugees? Would they all receive Canada's protection? Does Canada treat people fleeing from humanitarian crises, such as the 1994 genocide in Rwanda, the same as victims of natural disasters, such as those who were left homeless in South Asia by the tsunami that struck in December 2004?

Although it is commonplace to categorize these people as "refugees," under international and Canadian law the label "refugee" has a precise meaning. The legal definition distinguishes those who are genuine or bona fide refugees from those who are economic migrants—that is, people in search of better living and economic conditions. This chapter examines the international agreements that are the legal basis for Canada's granting refugee status and providing protection, introduces the principle of *non-refoulement*, and provides a general overview of Canada's legal obligations with regard to refugee protection. By the end of this chapter, you will understand the meanings of the terms "Convention refugee" and "person in need of protection." Chapter 12 will explore the processes for selecting refugees for resettlement, and Chapter 13 will explore the refugee determination system in Canada, answering the question, "How does Canada provide protection to refugees?"

Some Terminology

- **Refugee**: a person who is forced to flee from persecution and who is outside his home country.

- **Convention refugee**: a person who meets the refugee definition in the 1951 *Geneva Convention Relating to the Status of Refugees*.

- **Refugee claimant or asylum seeker**: a person who has fled his country and is *asking for protection in another country*. Generally, we do not know whether a claimant is a refugee until his case has been decided. Refugee claimants receive a decision on whether they are refugees *after they arrive* in Canada.

---

refugee
a person who is forced to flee from persecution (as opposed to an immigrant, who chooses to move)

Convention refugee
a person who has been granted protection under the refugee definition in the 1951 *Convention Relating to the Status of Refugees*

refugee claimant
a person who has made a refugee protection claim where the decision is yet to be made; this term is used in Canada and is equivalent to "asylum seeker"

The following terms have no meaning in Canadian law: political refugee, economic refugee, and environmental refugee.

Refugees

In 2014, the Office of the United Nations High Commissioner for Refugees (UNHCR) sounded the alarm when it reported that for the first time since the Second World War, the number of refugees worldwide exceeded 50 million people: 51.2 million refugees, asylum seekers, and internally displaced people were forcibly displaced due to conflict, persecution, generalized violence, and human rights violations.[1]

---

1   UNHCR, "World Refugee Day: Global Forced Displacement Tops 50 Million for First Time in Post-World War II Era" (20 June 2014), online: <http://www.unhcr.org/53a155bc6.html>.

According to the Office of the UNHCR, the top three source countries of refugees in 2014 (Syrian Arab Republic, Afghanistan, and Somalia) accounted for 52 percent of the total number of refugees.[2] And, given that people fleeing conflict and human rights violations generally seek refuge in a neighbouring country, two-thirds of the world's refugees in 2014 ended up residing in countries neighbouring their country of origin. While Canada is not geographically close to any refugee-producing countries or easily accessible from them—and, therefore, does not have many refugees—the Middle East and North Africa have become the two regions hosting the largest number of refugees, as a result of the crisis in Syria. António Guterres, the commissioner of the UNHCR, warned, "The economic, social and human cost of caring for refugees and the internally displaced is being borne mostly by poor communities, those who are least able to afford it. Enhanced international solidarity is a must if we want to avoid the risk of more and more vulnerable people being left without proper support."[3]

According to UNHCR's global report for 2013, 86 percent of the world's refugees were hosted by developing countries because of their geographic proximity to refugee crisis. However, many are not signatories to any international refugee protection agreements and, consequently, do not have legal obligations to protect refugees, but bear the burden of sheltering them.[4] Although international law recognizes the right to seek asylum, it does not oblige countries to provide asylum, so while countries may offer "temporary protection," there is no guarantee of permanent protection. For example, article 31 of the 1951 *Convention Relating to the Status of Refugees* states that refugees should not be penalized for having entered a country illegally if they have come directly from a place where they were in danger and have made themselves known to the authorities. Therefore, asylum seekers should not be detained for being in possession of forged identity papers or for destroying identity or travel documents. A second important protection is the prohibition against forced return of a refugee (the principle of *non-refoulement*; see below). Therefore, to reach countries that will provide them with legal protection, many refugees turn to human smugglers for help in reaching European, and sometimes Canadian, shores by sea, in overcrowded and dangerous conditions. It is big business for human smugglers, who prey on human desperation to finance their criminal and terrorist enterprises.

Article 14 of the *Universal Declaration of Human Rights* states, "Everyone has the right to seek and to enjoy in other countries asylum from persecution."[5] Therefore, Canada's immigration and refugee policies must strike a balance between allowing the country to achieve its humanitarian and legal commitments to protect refugees and protecting Canadians by denying access to individuals who pose a criminal or security threat. Section 3(2) of the *Immigration and Refugee Protection Act* (IRPA) sets out the objectives of Canada's refugee system as follows:

---

2   UNHCR, *Mid-Year Trends 2014* (Geneva: UNHCR, 7 January 2015) at 5, online: <http://unhcr.org/54aa91d89.html#_ga=1.55761067.1611155960.1426969760>.

3   UNHCR, Press Release, "UNHCR Report Shows Further Growth in Forced Displacement in First Half 2014" (7 January 2015), online: <http://www.unhcr.org/54abe0e66.html>.

4   UNHCR, *UNHCR Global Trends 2013* (Geneva: UNHCR, 2014) at 2, online: <http://www.unhcr.org/5399a14f9.html>.

5   *Universal Declaration of Human Rights*, GA Res 217A (III), UNGAOR, 3rd Sess, Supp No 13, UN Doc A/810 (1948) 71, online: <http://www.un.org/Overview/rights.html>.

(a) to recognize that the refugee program is in the first instance about saving lives and offering protection to the displaced and persecuted;

(b) to fulfil Canada's international legal obligations with respect to refugees and affirm Canada's commitment to international efforts to provide assistance to those in need of resettlement;

(c) to grant, as a fundamental expression of Canada's humanitarian ideals, fair consideration to those who come to Canada claiming persecution;

(d) to offer safe haven to persons with a well-founded fear of persecution based on race, religion, nationality, political opinion or membership in a particular social group, as well as those at risk of torture or cruel and unusual treatment or punishment;

(e) to establish fair and efficient procedures that will maintain the integrity of the Canadian refugee protection system, while upholding Canada's respect for the human rights and fundamental freedoms of all human beings;

(f) to support the self-sufficiency and the social and economic well-being of refugees by facilitating reunification with their family members in Canada;

(g) to protect the health and safety of Canadians and to maintain the security of Canadian society; and

(h) to promote international justice and security by denying access to Canadian territory to persons, including refugee claimants, who are security risks or serious criminals.

International Conventions

convention
an agreement that obliges countries under international law to conform to its provisions

ratification
a confirmation to abide by an international agreement

A **convention**, "covenant," or "treaty" is an agreement that obliges countries under international law to conform to its provisions. Countries bind themselves through **ratification**, or by signing the agreement, which is a confirmation of the commitment to abide by the agreement. When a country ratifies or accedes to an agreement, that country becomes known as a "state party" to the agreement and is thereafter legally bound to the obligations imposed by the agreement.

Generally, United Nations (UN) agreements include provisions for independent monitoring bodies to supervise the implementation of the convention and to monitor compliance with the obligations and responsibilities by state parties. The relevant international conventions and their related monitoring bodies are described below.

In Canada, the basis in law for determining refugee status is found in the following UN refugee treaties:

- the 1951 *Convention Relating to the Status of Refugees*, and
- the 1967 *Protocol Relating to the Status of Refugees*.

Canada is also a state party to treaties respecting human rights. The following UN international agreements provide the basis in law for granting human rights protection:

- the 1984 *Convention Against Torture and Other Cruel, Inhuman or Degrading Treatment or Punishment*; and
- the 1966 *International Covenant on Civil and Political Rights*.

> **IN THE NEWS**
>
> ## Inside Aksaray, Istanbul's Human Smuggling Hub
>
> Istanbul's Aksaray neighbourhood is a magnet for newcomers looking for quick work and what used to be cheap housing.
>
> The square here and its large fountain right outside the metro station are now a critical connection point in what is estimated to be a multi-billion-dollar human smuggling industry here, fuelled by the desperation of refugees—mainly from Syria. ...
>
> Naim Lezieh used to live in Aleppo, Syria. He is now in limbo in Istanbul, stuck here for more than half a year now. His wife and children are scattered across Europe.
>
> Smugglers swindled them out of a total of 32,000 euros ($43,350 Cdn) during several attempts to leave Turkey.
>
> "You're looking for a light of hope and they say 'we're going to save you, we can do anything,'" Lezieh says, explaining how the smugglers gained their trust. ...
>
> "They took us to Marmaris and from there with a yacht, they were supposedly going to take us to a Greek island. We went, we paid the money and they ran away. They left us there."
>
> Lezieh and his family were spotted by police but they managed to avoid arrest and returned to Istanbul.
>
> The second attempt was more successful—but far from a happy ending. Lezieh didn't have enough money left for everyone, so he sent his wife and children and he stayed behind. ...
>
> Lezieh's third attempt to join them failed. "Again, the money was lost," he says.
>
> If you don't have money, he says, the smugglers have another solution. They offer refugees work, promising to pay them 50 euros ($67.50 Cdn) for every refugee they can convince to sign on with a smuggler.
>
> Like Lezieh, the majority of Syrian refugees are looking to land in European Union countries. ...
>
> "Compared to Europe, Canada is lower on the list. But there are still people who want to go to Canada," [Turkish print journalist Sefik] Dinç says the smuggler told him.
>
> The complete, all-inclusive package from a fake passport and other documents for a flight to Canada—$15,000. ...
>
> Dinç says some smugglers believe they are doing good deeds and feel they are legitimate businessmen. "The guy says 'actually, the government should give us a break, turn a blind eye. In a way, I see myself as a [legitimate] exporter.'"
>
> Lezieh now knows there was nothing legitimate about the smugglers he was robbed by, but he knew he was taking a risk.
>
> Why would he so willingly put so much at risk?
>
> His eyes barely dry from remembering everything they left behind in Syria, and what it took to get here, he answers, "We're already dead."
>
> **Do you think it makes a difference to a refugee claimant's claim whether he paid a smuggler to get to Canada or travelled by legitimate means?**
>
> Source: Nil Köksal, "Inside Aksaray, Istanbul's Human Smuggling Hub" (11 May 2015), *CBC News*, online: <http://www.cbc.ca/news/world/inside-aksaray-istanbul-s-human-smuggling-hub-1.3066443>.

The Office of the United Nations High Commissioner for Refugees

The Office of the United Nations High Commissioner for Refugees was created in 1950 by the UN General Assembly to ensure the protection of refugees and provide legal assistance to them. The UNHCR (also referred to as the UN Refugee Agency, in some literature) was created as an international agency responsible for supervising the refugee status determination process and safeguarding the rights of refugees. In addition to providing international legal protection for refugees, the UNHCR was to promote international refugee agreements, and provide programs and funding to assist refugees with the following:

voluntary repatriation
in the context of refugee law, the return of a refugee to her country of origin, of her own free will

resettlement
in the context of refugee law, the relocation of a protected refugee from a host state to another country where he can permanently reside; an option that is used when there is no other durable solution such as voluntary repatriation or local integration

- **voluntary repatriation** (that is, the voluntary return of a refugee to his home country, if conditions improve there);
- integration into the country of refuge; or
- **resettlement** in a third country (if, for example, the country of refuge cannot accommodate the refugee and another country agrees to do so).

Today, the UNHCR still maintains its mandate to supervise the refugee status determination process, although it has no legal power. Besides this responsibility, in 2001, the UNHCR was given another mandate by the UN to monitor and protect stateless persons. In addition, the UNHCR is a key player in working with other agencies in humanitarian efforts that help internally displaced people.[6] Also, because of its operational expertise, the UNHCR has played a role in providing international relief operations to help victims of natural disasters (for example, the 2004 Indian Ocean tsunami, the 2005 Pakistan earthquake, China's 2008 Sichuan earthquake, the 2013 Philippines typhoon, and the 2015 Nepal earthquakes).

UNHCR in Canada

In Canada, the UNHCR has a branch office located in Ottawa and employs legal officers in cities throughout the country to monitor compliance with international refugee law, to ensure that refugee claimants' rights are protected. Some practical examples of the UNHCR's work in Canada include observing refugee protection hearings and making recommendations to the Canadian government on refugee issues.

The Refugee Convention

The Refugee Convention, formally known as the 1951 *Convention Relating to the Status of Refugees*, is the major legal foundation on which the UNHCR's work is based. It was originally created to help the hundreds of thousands of people displaced in Europe after the Second World War and to help future refugees—but for a limited period of time. It was adopted by a Conference of Plenipotentiaries of the United Nations on July 28, 1951 and came into force on April 21, 1954. The framers of the 1951 Convention limited its scope to those refugee situations that existed at that time, and did not foresee that refugee issues would become a major international problem on an ongoing basis;[7] consequently, the UNHCR was only given a three-year mandate

WEBLINK

For more information about the UNHCR, and about refugees around the world, see <www.unhcr.org>. The website for UNHCR in Canada is <www.unhcr.ca>.

---

6   UNHCR, *Protecting Refugees and the Role of UNHCR* (Geneva: UNHCR, October 2014), online: <http://www.unhcr.org/509a836e9.html>.

7   UNHCR, *Handbook and Guidelines on Procedures and Criteria for Determining Refugee Status Under the 1951 Convention and the 1967 Protocol Relating to the Status of Refugees*, HCR/1P/4/ENG/REV.3 (Geneva: UNHCR, 1979, reissued December 2011) [*Handbook and Guidelines*] at 5, online: <http://www.unhcr.org/3d58e13b4.html>.

to help the post–Second World War refugees. It was hoped that it would then cease operations.

Instead, the refugee crisis spread—from Europe in the 1950s to Africa in the 1960s, and then to Asia. In 1967, the UN General Assembly adopted the 1967 *Protocol Relating to the Status of Refugees* to strengthen the 1951 Convention so that it would continue to operate to the benefit of future waves of refugees. The 1967 Protocol came into force on October 4, 1967 and removed the earlier time limit and the geographical restrictions that had limited the Refugee Convention's mandate to re-settling European refugees uprooted by the Second World War.

The Refugee Convention and its Protocol provide the framework for Canada's refugee determination system. These instruments define a "Convention refugee"; describe Canada's legal obligations toward refugees; set out the basic procedures for refugee determination; and describe the basic entitlements and obligations of refugees, as well as the role and authority of the monitoring body—the UNHCR.

The core principles of the Refugee Convention include non-discrimination, *non-refoulement*, non-penalization for illegal entry or stay, and the acquisition of rights over time.[8]

The UNHCR *Handbook and Guidelines* sets out the rights to which individuals are entitled after they have been recognized as Convention refugees in articles 12 through 30, as follows:[9]

- Refugees must be granted identity papers and travel documents that allow them to travel outside the country.

- Refugees must receive the same treatment as nationals of the receiving country with regard to the following rights:
    - free exercise of religion and religious education;
    - free access to the courts, including legal assistance;
    - access to elementary education;
    - access to public relief and assistance;
    - protection provided by social security;
    - protection of intellectual property such as inventions and trade names;
    - protection of literary, artistic, and scientific work; and
    - equal treatment by taxing authorities.

- Refugees must receive the most favourable treatment provided to nationals of a foreign country with regard to the following rights:
    - the right to belong to trade unions;
    - the right to belong to other non-political non-profit organizations; and
    - the right to engage in wage-earning employment.

---

8 *Ibid* at 1.

9 *Ibid* at 5.

- Refugees must receive the most favourable treatment possible, which must be at least as favourable to that accorded to aliens generally in the same circumstances, with regard to the following rights:
    - the right to own property;
    - the right to practise a profession;
    - the right to self-employment;
    - access to housing; and
    - access to higher education.
- Refugees must receive the same treatment as that accorded to aliens generally with regard to the following rights:
    - the right to choose their place of residence;
    - the right to move freely within the country;
    - free exercise of religion and religious education;
    - free access to the courts, including legal assistance;
    - access to elementary education;
    - access to public relief and assistance;
    - protection provided by social security;
    - protection of intellectual property such as inventions and trade names;
    - protection of literary, artistic, and scientific work; and
    - equal treatment by taxing authorities.

In 1969, Canada ratified the 1951 Convention and the related 1967 Protocol, thus cementing its obligation to establish a refugee status determination system and upholding the principle of *non-refoulement* (see below). This is notable because, prior to 1969, Canada had no legal process in place for protecting refugees. After ratifying the Refugee Convention, however, Canada began accepting refugees under a number of special programs, but it wasn't until the passage of the 1976 *Immigration Act* that Canada could legally fulfill its international obligations by distinguishing between the immigrant and refugee classes, and implementing a process to determine refugee status.

Principle of Non-Refoulement

As mentioned above, the **principle of *non-refoulement***, which is reflected in the way in which Canada manages refugee claims made in Canada, is an important principle of refugee law. Translated, *non-refoulement* means "no return." The principle of *non-refoulement* is a rule of international law that obliges countries to provide protection to refugees against return to the country where they face a risk of persecution, or where their life or freedom would be threatened because of their race, religion, nationality, membership in a particular social group, or political opinion.[10]

principle of non-refoulement

a rule of international law that obliges countries to provide protection to refugees against return to the country where they face a risk of persecution, or where their life or freedom would be threatened because of their race, religion, nationality, membership in a particular social group, or political opinion

---

10   *Convention Relating to the Status of Refugees*, 22 April 1954, 189 UNTS 150, art 33(1).

Canada is committed to the principle of not returning a refugee to the country of origin. Thus, Canada does not expel refugee claimants while their claims are being processed—they are allowed to remain in Canada until their claims are settled. The protection against *refoulement* applies in situations where an individual's life or human rights are threatened, unless an exclusion under international law applies (discussed later in this chapter under the heading "Exclusion").

Protection against *refoulement* occurs when:

- a foreign national makes a claim and is granted an automatic stay of removal with the issuance of a "conditional removal order" pending the outcome of his claim, including any post-determination proceedings;
- a foreign national has refugee status or is a protected person, and his permanent resident status is pending;
- a permanent resident has refugee status or is a protected person; or
- a foreign national is under a deportation order.

Exceptions to the right to *non-refoulement* are made in situations where the refugee claimant is inadmissible on the most serious grounds: security risk, human or international rights violations, or serious criminality. It should be noted that while a claimant may not be allowed to pursue his claim, he may be removed to a country other than his country of origin to satisfy the principle of *non-refoulement*.

Burden of Proof

An important legal principle in refugee determination is the principle that the burden of proof lies with the refugee claimant to substantiate statements with documentary and other evidence. In the *Handbook and Guidelines on Procedures and Criteria for Determining Refugee Status Under the 1951 Convention and the 1967 Protocol Relating to the Status of Refugees*, the UNHCR points out that refuge claimants who flee persecution may have little or no personal documentation with them, and, therefore, the duty to ascertain and evaluate facts falls to the decision-maker. As the UNHCR notes, if the claimant's statements appear credible, the claimant should be given the benefit of the doubt.[11]

Under domestic law, the refugee claimant must prove that her claim is eligible to be referred to the Immigration and Refugee Board (IRB). Section 100(1.1) of the IRPA states:

The burden of proving that a claim is eligible to be referred to the Refugee Protection Division rests on the claimant, who must answer truthfully all questions put to them.

And section 100(4) states:

A person who makes a claim for refugee protection inside Canada at a port of entry and whose claim is referred to the Refugee Protection Division must provide

---

11 *Supra* note 7 at 38, para 196.

the Division, within the time limits provided for in the regulations, with the documents and information—including in respect of the basis for the claim—required by the rules of the Board, in accordance with those rules.

Refugee claimants must prove their identity, because this is often tied to the claimant's credibility. Section 106 of the IRPA makes this a requirement:[12]

The Refugee Protection Division must take into account, with respect to the credibility of a claimant, whether the claimant possesses acceptable documentation establishing identity, and if not, whether they have provided a reasonable explanation for the lack of documentation or have taken reasonable steps to obtain the documentation.

Definition of a Convention Refugee

The definition of a Convention refugee describes who is a refugee, who is not, and when protection is no longer needed. With the modernization of the language, Canada has adopted in the IRPA the three parts of the 1951 Convention refugee definition almost verbatim, with the following three clauses:

1. *Inclusion clause*: defines the criteria for who is a refugee, such as people who have a well-founded fear of persecution by reason of religion (s 96).
2. *Exclusion clause*: defines who is not a refugee, such as people who commit war crimes (s 98 and Schedule).
3. *Cessation clause*: defines when a person no longer enjoys the protection of the Convention—that is, when refugee protection ceases (s 108).

Inclusion

Section 96 of the IRPA defines a Convention refugee as follows:

A Convention refugee is a person who, by reason of a well-founded fear of persecution for reasons of race, religion, nationality, membership in a particular social group or political opinion,
    (a) is outside each of their countries of nationality and is unable or, by reason of that fear, unwilling to avail themself of the protection of each of those countries; or
    (b) not having a country of nationality, is outside the country of their former habitual residence and is unable or, by reason of that fear, unwilling to return to that country.

A refugee claimant who meets all the inclusion elements of the definition will be granted refugee status as a Convention refugee. Therefore, it is important to identify each of the elements of the definition to understand how they are used in the decision-making process. There are four elements that form the positive basis for meeting the criteria of inclusion, as follows:

---

12 See Krista Daley, *Assessment of Credibility in Claims for Refugee Protection* (Ottawa: Immigration and Refugee Board of Canada, 31 January 2004) s 2.4.5.1, online: IRB <http://www.irb-cisr.gc.ca/Eng/BoaCom/references/LegJur/Pages/Credib.aspx#n2451>.

1. alienage;

2. a well-founded fear;

3. persecution; and

4. the nexus—that is, persecution under one of the five grounds in the IRPA.

A refugee claimant must meet all of the elements of inclusion in order for her claim to be accepted. What follows is a basic explanation of the four inclusion elements.

1. ALIENAGE

Generally, citizens have an expectation of protection from their government, and it is only when their government is either unable or unwilling to protect them that they need to seek protection from another country. Under the Refugee Convention, claimants must be outside their country or countries of nationality or place of habitual residence to have their claims assessed. In establishing the **alienage** element of the definition, refugee claimants must be unable or unwilling to avail themselves of the protection of their country of nationality, or, if they do not have a country of nationality (that is, if they are stateless), be unable or, by reason of that fear, unwilling to return to their former place of habitual residence. Claimants may make a claim only against their country or countries of nationality or former habitual residence.

Consider the following scenario:

Ariana is a citizen of the fictitious nation of Bovoria, an impoverished country with no universities and few prospects for women. Ariana's father is a prominent businessman in Bovoria who wants to give his daughter every opportunity to be self-sufficient, so he decides to send her outside Bovoria to study. Ariana pursues a degree in political science at the National University of Vonburg in the neighbouring country of Furtania. She is outspoken about student rights and is a regular contributor of cartoons to the student newspaper. She is detained by Furtanian authorities for three days for participating in an anti-government rally and is subsequently harassed for the publication of her cartoons, which have been deemed too political. When her cartoons are denounced by the government-run Furtanian press, Ariana fears for her life and flees the country without completing her degree, and travels to Canada where she wishes to make a refugee claim.

Would Ariana satisfy the alienage requirement of the refugee definition?

One of the first elements that Ariana must establish in making her refugee claim in Canada is the element of alienage. In seeking protection, Ariana must prove that she cannot avail herself of the protection of any of her countries of nationality (or former habitual residence, if she did not have a nationality). Ariana, like all other refugee claimants, must provide documentary evidence of her citizenship (or multiple citizenships), usually by providing a birth certificate, national identity card, or passport.

Ariana has Bovorian citizenship, so Furtania does not qualify as "a former habitual residence," despite the time she spent there. Furthermore, Ariana is not a citizen of

WEBLINK

The UNHCR's *Handbook and Guidelines on Procedures and Criteria for Determining Refugee Status* (1979, reissued December 2011) is recommended reading for an in-depth study of these elements: <www.unhcr.org/3d58e13b4.html>.

alienage

one of the four inclusion elements of the refugee definition; a refugee must be outside his country of nationality or, if stateless, his country of former habitual residence and, owing to a fear of persecution, must be unable or unwilling to avail himself of the protection of that country

Furtania and she enjoys the protection of her country of nationality, Bovoria, so she is not able to claim protection against Furtania. Moreover, she did not suffer persecution or have any reason to fear future persecution in Bovoria. The element of alienage cannot be established, and Ariana's claim would be rejected.

2. WELL-FOUNDED FEAR

In considering each refugee claim, a member of the Refugee Protection Division (RPD) will assess whether the refugee claimant's fear is well founded. There is both an objective and a subjective component to this test. The objective component considers whether the fear is reasonable in the circumstances, and considers the circumstance in which the fear arises, such as the conditions in the claimant's country of origin. The subjective component considers the personal perspective of the claimant—does the claimant actually experience fear? The following scenario sets out two cases to show how the element of **well-founded fear** must be individualized.

well-founded fear
one of the four inclusion elements of the refugee definition; the refugee claimant must establish both objective and subjective components of fear of persecution

> Kairat and Ravil are male, 30 years of age, and citizens of the fictitious nation of Zarkhanistan, a country where young males between the ages of 18 and 33 have been arbitrarily arrested and detained in the context of the "war on terror." Some detainees have disappeared, and others have been sentenced to death and executed.
>
> Kairat arrived in Canada directly from Zarkhanistan six months ago, just after a raid in his neighbouring village that resulted in a total sweep of young, unmarried males. One of Kairat's relatives has been missing since the raid. Ravil arrived in Canada around the same time as Kairat; however, he left Zarkhanistan 12 years ago to work on a cruise ship, having experienced no particular problems at the time. Ravil's contract has now expired and he wants to settle down, but he is concerned about the unstable situation in his home country.

In this scenario, both Kairat and Ravil will make refugee claims, and despite the fact that their claims may share certain similarities, the decisions in their cases will be made on the basis of their independent accounts, experiences, and circumstances. It is possible that one claim may be accepted, while the other is rejected. This is because each claim will be decided on its own merits. The outcomes may be different because each claimant, who will have the opportunity to present his own story both orally and in writing, will submit separate and individualized evidence to a member of the RPD. Furthermore, their cases will be heard by members who are independent of each other, and who will each consider both the objective and subjective basis of the claims separately. The outcomes will depend on the merits of each case, including whether the information that the claimants provide is credible and trustworthy.

Objective Component

To establish that a claim is well founded, there must be an objective component—a valid reason for the fear, such as known human rights violations and other pertinent background information. Therefore, a claimant should support his allegations with documentary evidence of the prevailing country conditions, as reported in reliable country-of-origin reports, human rights reports, newspaper articles, medical reports, and other personal documentation, and as testified to by witnesses. Claimants should use caution when using Internet sources such as Wikipedia, as any person can edit and modify the encyclopedia at any time. Other Internet sources are equally problematic if the authors of information are not known and their expertise cannot be ascertained.

In our example, Kairat and Ravil would likely present similar objective evidence about their country of origin, Zarkhanistan. The objective component requires that each claim be assessed in the context of the prevailing conditions in the country of origin. This kind of generalized information can be obtained by researching current and credible sources (for example, Amnesty International, Human Rights Watch, and the UNHCR) for information about the country, typically including:

- whether the country is in the midst of political upheaval, war, or generally unsettled conditions;
- the country's human rights record;
- whether the country has a functioning judicial system and mechanisms for seeking redress; and
- the government's ability and willingness to protect its citizens.

It is generally accepted that if a claimant has suffered persecution in the past, he continues to be at risk and, therefore, needs the protection of the Refugee Convention. However, it is not necessary for a claimant to have suffered past harm to fear the risk of it in the future. That is why the definition is forward-looking—the decision-maker must look to the future to consider whether there is a serious possibility of risk in returning the claimant to his country of origin. The decision-maker should consider asking the following questions: Is there a serious possibility that the claimant would risk persecution if he returned today or in the near future? Have the conditions in the claimant's country changed since he left? Is the risk widespread or localized? If local, is an **internal flight alternative (IFA)** a preferred solution to protection from another state? Would Ravil, who has been out of Zarkhanistan for many years, face persecution if he were to return there? Does he fit the government's profile of a potential terrorist? Is he likely to be perceived to be a threat?

internal flight alternative (IFA)
a safe place within one's own country where there is no serious risk of persecution and where a claimaint can seek refuge, instead of seeking protection in another country

Subjective Component

The subjective component of a well-founded fear considers the claimant's individual state of mind and fearfulness. The subjective basis will depend on the claimant's own background and experiences, as well as those of family and close associates. To support the subjective basis for a refugee claim, the claimant must make a credible case for future risk, and should provide evidence of past persecution, if any, by submitting documentary evidence such as medical or psychological reports. In practice, it is not always possible to provide independent evidence; most often, it is the claimant's written and verbal statements that provide insight into his state of mind.

The subjective component, therefore, is unique to each claimant. Let's suppose that Kairat's claim was accepted and Ravil's claim was rejected, even though the prevailing country conditions—the objective component—are the same. Why might the outcomes be different? The difference in their claims may be due in part to the subjective component of their alleged fear.

The RPD member will also assess whether the claimant's fear is valid, and will be interested in the chronology of events that led the claimant to make a claim for protection. Did the claimant delay leaving his country of origin when the fear arose? Did he delay making a claim or did he make a claim at the first possible opportunity? In our scenario, Kairat shows evidence of a compelling fear: he lived next to a village where men like him were arrested, one of his relatives "disappeared," and he left and sought refuge immediately when danger was imminent. Ravil, on the other hand, left the country 12 years ago for economic reasons, and in all his travels, he neither needed nor sought protection until after his contract expired. This may raise a suspicion that he is not genuinely fearful, but instead is seeking better economic conditions. Then again, he may be able to make the case that he is a "refugee *sur place*" (see the discussion below).

Human Rights Organizations

- **Amnesty International** An international organization whose mission is to conduct research and promote action to prevent human rights abuses. Online: <www.amnesty.org>.

- **Canadian Council for Refugees** A non-profit umbrella organization that promotes the rights and protection of refugees, both in Canada and internationally. Composed of organizations that aid in the settlement, sponsorship, and protection of refugees and immigrants. Online: <http://ccrweb.ca>.

- **Human Rights Watch** An organization dedicated to protecting the human rights of people around the world and investigating human rights violations. Online: <www.hrw.org>.

3. PERSECUTION

persecution
one of the four inclusion elements of the refugee definition, but not defined in the definition or in the IRPA; a serious harm that is sustained and a systematic violation of basic human rights

A refugee claimant's well-founded fear must relate to persecution. The term **persecution** is not defined in the 1951 Convention or in the IRPA; however, Canadian courts provide some parameters for defining it. Generally, to qualify as persecution, an act or series of acts must present a serious harm—a threat to life or physical freedom, or other persistent and serious violations of human rights.

Under the 1951 Convention, a refugee claimant is not entitled to protection from legitimate prosecution by his country of origin. However, for the prosecution to be legitimate, the laws and the legal processes must not violate fundamental human rights. Someone who has fled her country to avoid a trial and punishment for having committed a criminal act such as robbery or murder is not "persecuted," provided that she would receive a fair trial and fair treatment.

However, if a claimant faces prosecution for committing an act that is protected by international human rights standards—for example, the practice of her religion—this may be tantamount to persecution. In this case, the "crime" is the exercise of a fundamental right; therefore, the claimant is fleeing persecution. Even if the crime is legitimate, issues of persecution could be raised if the claimant was not given access to a fair and impartial trial, or if the punishment was unduly severe—such as torture, or execution for a minor offence.

In some cases, the refugee claimant's fear is based on acts of discrimination or harassment. Although an individual act of discrimination or harassment on its own would usually not substantiate a case for persecution, a series of acts, taken cumulatively, may amount to persecution. This could be the case if the acts are perpetrated by the government or by government agents, or if the acts are perpetrated by individuals outside the government and the government takes no steps to provide protection against them. Consider the following scenario, where discrimination and harassment occurred repeatedly and persistently:

Khalid is a 35-year-old gay man in a country that criminalizes homosexual acts. For much of his life, he has been the victim of attacks. His teachers discouraged him and verbally abused him as a child, and he had difficulty finding employment—all because of his sexual orientation. He worked in a factory for a short time, but endured physical attacks by co-workers. His employer was not interested in Khalid's problems and fired him. The police refused to investigate and press charges. On one occasion, Khalid was chased out of the police station and threatened with a beating. He joined a gay rights organization that worked to change social attitudes; this organization, however, was perceived by the authorities as a threat to local peace, and some of its members have been imprisoned under the country's sodomy laws.

The mainstream media is increasingly openly hostile toward gay people, and the government has repeatedly tried to introduce stricter penalties and new laws to ban the "promotion of homosexuality." Since joining the organization, Khalid has frequently been stopped by the police on his way home from meetings, taken into detention, beaten, and released. The detentions have become more frequent and longer, and the beatings more severe, requiring hospitalization. The authorities are not interested in stopping the violence and are sometimes the perpetrators. Other members of the gay community have suffered similarly.

Is the element of persecution made out in this case?

To determine whether the element of persecution exists, the claimant must connect the "act" of violation of human rights or criminal acts to the government or those perceived to be acting in its interest. Agents of persecution are those who carry out the acts of persecution with impunity, and include both state and non-state agents. Authorities of the claimant's country of origin, such as the police or members of the military, are **state agents**, and their acts are generally sanctioned or authorized by the government or by legislation. Discrimination and harassment by state agents amounts to persecution if these actions are persistent and serious.

Members of the militia who violate human rights, or members of the majority ethnic or religious groups, rebels, guerrillas, drug lords, or warlords, who commit serious acts of discrimination or other targeted harmful acts are known as **non-state agents**. When persecution is carried out by non-state agents, the claimant must prove that the government knowingly tolerates the acts, or is unwilling or unable to provide effective protection from those acts.

state agent
persecutors of the refugee claimant whose acts are sanctioned by the government of the claimant's country of origin—e.g., police and members of the military

non-state agent
persons or entities who perpetuate acts of persecution from which the government may be unwilling or unable to provide protection—e.g., warlords, guerilla organizations, and anti- or pro-government paramilitary groups

In the case of Khalid, the agents of persecution were both state agents (the police) and non-state agents (for example, teachers, co-workers, and the media). The police refused to assist Khalid when he reported physical assaults, and often perpetuated the physical violence with impunity. Khalid can likely make the case that, taken cumulatively, the assaults amounted to persecution.

4. THE NEXUS: PERSECUTION UNDER ONE OF THE FIVE GROUNDS IN THE IRPA

Much like Canadian human rights legislation prohibits discrimination based on prohibited grounds, the IRPA sets out five grounds of persecution. The five grounds, enumerated in the definition of a Convention refugee, are as follows:

a. race,
b. religion,
c. nationality,
d. membership in a particular social group, and
e. political opinion.

To determine whether the persecution falls under one of the enumerated grounds, the RPD considers the following questions: Does the persecutor perceive the claimant to be a member of a certain race, nationality, religion, or particular social group, or to hold a certain political opinion? Is there a reasonable chance of persecution because of that perception? It is not necessary that the perception be accurate, only that the persecutor may act on it. Therefore, it is important for the claimant to provide as much information as possible about the context of the persecution.

a. Race

A claimant may have a well-founded fear of persecution on the basis of his race, which is understood in the broadest sense to include all ethnic groups that are referred to as races. Examples of persecution include discriminatory hiring practices by government, exclusion from public education, segregation, and discriminatory taxation. The claimant must establish that he suffered persecution as a result of his race. Evidence should include examples of how the claimant was targeted, what harm he suffered, whether his race is a minority group, and how the members of that group are generally treated.

b. Religion

Claimants may be persecuted on the basis of religion because they are members of a religious minority or sect. The laws of the country may prohibit joining or worshipping in a particular religious community. In that case, the claimant must establish that he is a member of the particular religious group by detailing factors such as whether he is a practising or non-practising member, whether his religious group is legally recognized in his country, and how members of that religious group are generally treated.

Alternatively, a country may prohibit the practice of any religion, and ban any religious instruction or practice. In that case, even members of a majority religion may be persecuted.

c. Nationality

Nationality encompasses not only a person's citizenship or lack thereof (that is, statelessness), but also a person's ethnic or linguistic group, and so may sometimes overlap with race. Examples of persecution based on nationality include genocide, torture, rape, and discrimination against members of a minority or low-caste clan.

d. Membership in a Particular Social Group

According to the UNHCR, a particular social group "normally comprises persons of similar background, habits or social status."[13] The Supreme Court of Canada in *Canada (Attorney General) v Ward*[14] classified "particular social group" as consisting of three distinct categories of groups:

1. "groups defined by an innate, unchangeable characteristic" (which might include claims based on a person's gender, linguistic background, sexual orientation, family, or caste);

2. groups "whose members voluntarily associate for reasons so fundamental to their human dignity that they should not be forced to forsake the association" (which might include claims from members of human rights organizations or trade union activists); and

3. groups "associated by a former voluntary status, unalterable due to its historical permanence" (which expresses the idea that "one's past is an immutable part of the person," such as in the case of Vietnam veterans).

Some examples of persons suffering persecution on the basis of membership in a particular social group include women who face rape or other forms of violence by government agents, women who face female genital mutilation or forced marriage, homosexuals who face violence, and members of trade unions who face violence.

e. Political Opinion

A person may express a political opinion by words or actions—for example, by participating in anti-government demonstrations, distributing literature, or speaking out in public. However, a person who does not articulate a political opinion may still be identified by the government as an opponent—for example, by failing to attend pro-government rallies or join a government party. To prove the case, the claimant has to explain the significance of his actions or inactions, whether he was identified by the government, and how the government would likely react if he were returned to his country of origin. In assessing the claim, the RPD member asks: "Does the government consider the claimant's actions to be political?"

If a claimant belongs to a political party or group, it is important that he provide evidence of how his membership, activities, and opinions brought him to the attention of authorities or are the basis of a future risk. The claimant should be able to explain why the government would perceive the failure to do something, such as

> **nationality**
> refers to a person's citizenship and ethnic or linguistic group; may sometimes overlap with race

---

13   *Supra* note 7 at 17, para 77.

14   *Canada (Attorney General) v Ward*, [1993] 2 SCR 689 at 692 and 739, 103 DLR (4th) 1.

join a political party, as a political act. Documentary proof such as membership cards may also be useful.

Refugee Sur Place

What is a **refugee *sur place***? A refugee *sur place* is someone who did not flee her country with a well-founded fear of persecution when she first left, but later requires legal protection. In this situation, the person becomes a refugee while in a foreign country as a result of a change in government while the person is away from home, or some other change in circumstance. International law—specifically, the Refugee Convention—does not require that a person be a refugee at the time of leaving the country of origin. If an occurrence in the home country gives rise to a well-founded fear of persecution while the person is in another country, the person may be deemed a refugee *sur place*.

Consider the following scenario:

> Mona is an international student. After her arrival in Canada, there was a coup d'état in her country of nationality, and the new government introduced a series of repressive policies that severely limit a number of rights and freedoms for women. Human rights reports have documented cases where breaches of the new laws have led to detentions, whippings, and even public executions. Mona is not able to return to her country for fear that she will be persecuted for being "westernized." In presenting her refugee claim, Mona would make the case that she did not flee persecution, but instead has become a refugee "*sur place*."

Exclusion

Section 98 of the IRPA provides for instances where refugee protection must not be conferred: this is known as "exclusion." These exclusions apply to refugee claimants under both sections 96 and 97 of the IRPA, as provided in section 98, which states that under Canadian law, when a person is found to meet the criteria described in section E or F of article 1 of the Refugee Convention, he will not be granted Convention refugee status or protections as a person in need of protection.

Even where a refugee claimant meets all the elements of the refugee definition (IRPA, s 96) or all the elements of a person in need of protection (IRPA, s 97), he may nevertheless be returned to his country of origin if any of the following exclusions apply:

- the claimant has protection elsewhere;
- the claimant is likely guilty of persecuting others;
- the claimant is likely guilty of a serious non-political crime; or
- the claimant is likely guilty of acts contrary to the purposes and principles of the United Nations.

These exclusions are set out in sections E and F of article 1 of the Refugee Convention, and are included in the schedule to the IRPA. The sections are reproduced below:

> E. This Convention shall not apply to a person who is recognized by the competent authorities of the country in which he has taken residence as having the rights and obligations which are attached to the possession of the nationality of that country.
>
> F. The provisions of this Convention shall not apply to any person with respect to whom there are serious reasons for considering that:
>
>> (a) he has committed a crime against peace, a war crime, or a crime against humanity, as defined in the international instruments drawn up to make provision in respect of such crimes;
>>
>> (b) he has committed a serious non-political crime outside the country of refuge prior to his admission to that country as a refugee;
>>
>> (c) he has been guilty of acts contrary to the purposes and principles of the United Nations.

Claims for refugee status are to be made only as a last resort, by those who have no other options and by those who are innocent victims. Drafters of the Refugee Convention, and of the IRPA, were mindful of the potential for misuse of refugee laws by those who wish to emigrate for economic or personal reasons. Drafters also wanted to prevent refugee laws from offering protection to those who actually perpetrated acts of persecution against others. Under some circumstances, such as civil war, atrocities are often committed by individuals on each side of the conflict. Refugee laws are not intended to offer asylum to anyone guilty of such acts.

PROTECTION OF ANOTHER COUNTRY

Article E of the exclusion clause refers to a refugee claimant who has taken residence in another country or territory and has the protection of that country or territory. In that case, the claimant is not in need of Canada's protection. If a claimant has the option of living safely elsewhere, even if it is economically difficult and not the claimant's preference, she is expected to do so.

WAR CRIMES AND CRIMES AGAINST HUMANITY

Article 1F(a) of the Refugee Convention refers to a refugee claimant for whom there are serious reasons to believe that he has committed war crimes or **crimes against humanity**, such as crimes relating to genocide, slavery, torture, apartheid, or terrorist activities. Such a person is considered undeserving of the protection of the Refugee Convention and should be tried in an international court for the alleged crimes, not awarded safe asylum in a host country such as Canada. There are also practical concerns with respect to how such a person might behave in Canada, and whether he would facilitate or perpetrate those crimes within Canadian borders.

In *Ezokola v Canada (Citizenship and Immigration)*, the Supreme Court of Canada clarified that for a finding of complicity in war crimes and crimes against humanity, it is not enough for a claimant to simply belong to a group that commits

crimes against humanity
any inhumane acts or omissions that are committed against any civilian population or any identifiable group

criminal offences; it is necessary for the claimant to voluntarily and knowingly make a significant contribution to those crimes: "To exclude a claimant from the definition of 'refugee' by virtue of art. 1F(a), there must be serious reasons for considering that the claimant has voluntarily made a significant and knowing contribution to the organization's crime or criminal purpose."[15]

SERIOUS NON-POLITICAL CRIME

non-political crimes
acts committed for personal gain with no political end or motive involved

Article 1F(b) of the Refugee Convention refers to a refugee claimant for whom there are serious reasons to believe that she has committed serious **non-political crimes**. Again, such a person is considered undeserving of the protection of the Refugee Convention, and admitting her would raise practical concerns about criminal behaviour in Canada that could endanger Canadians. Although there is no list of serious crimes in the Refugee Convention, a serious non-political crime is understood to be an act committed for personal reasons or gain with no political end or motive involved. Generally, this would encompass the more serious crimes included in the Canadian *Criminal Code*, such as assault, murder, theft, and fraud. Petty crimes such as shoplifting and trespassing would likely not qualify as "serious" enough to justify the exclusion of an otherwise legitimate refugee claim.

ACTS CONTRARY TO UNITED NATIONS PRINCIPLES

Article 1F(c) of the Refugee Convention refers to a refugee claimant for whom there are serious reasons to believe that he is guilty of committing acts that breach the purposes and principles of the United Nations. Such a person is considered undeserving of the protection of the Refugee Convention. The *Charter of the United Nations* lists the four purposes of that organization[16] as follows:

1. to maintain international peace and security;

2. to develop friendly relations among nations based on respect for the principle of equal rights and self-determination;

3. to achieve international cooperation in solving international socio-economic and cultural problems; and

4. to harmonize the actions of nations in the attainment of these common ends.

For example, a refugee claimant who engages in acts of international terrorism that constitute a threat to international peace and security would be excluded from *non-refoulement* protection under article 1F(c) because such acts are contrary to the purposes and principles of the United Nations. The UNHCR, in its *Guidelines on International Protection No 5: Application of the Exclusion Clauses—Article 1F of the 1951 Convention Relating to the Status of Refugees*, cautions the following:

---

15 *Ezokola v Canada (Citizenship and Immigration)*, 2013 SCC 40 at para 84, [2013] 2 SCR 678.

16 See *Charter of the United Nations*, 26 June 1945, UNTS XVI, Can TS 1945 No 7, ch I, art 1 for the full text of these purposes.

Given the broad, general terms of the purposes and principles of the United Nations, the scope of this category is rather unclear and should therefore be read narrowly. Indeed, it is rarely applied and, in many cases, Article 1F(a) or 1F(b) are anyway likely to apply. Article 1F(c) is only triggered in extreme circumstances by activity which attacks the very basis of the international community's coexistence. Such activity must have an international dimension. Crimes capable of affecting international peace, security and peaceful relations between States, as well as serious and sustained violations of human rights, would fall under this category. … [I]t would appear that in principle only persons who have been in positions of power in a State or State-like entity would appear capable of committing such acts. In cases involving a terrorist act, a correct application of Article 1F(c) involves an assessment as to the extent to which the act impinges on the international plane—in terms of its gravity, international impact, and implications for international peace and security.[17]

Cessation of Protection

Refugee protection is not intended to be permanent. Article 1C of the Refugee Convention includes a **cessation clause**. This clause provides the framework for when protection may lawfully cease under section 108 of the IRPA.

Section 108 provides that a claim for refugee protection will generally be rejected, and a person will not be considered a Convention refugee or a person in need of protection where that person has done any of the following:

cessation clause
a clause that provides the framework for when protection may lawfully cease under section 108 of the IRPA

- voluntarily "reavailed" herself of the protection of the country of nationality—for example, by returning to live there;
- voluntarily reacquired her nationality—for example, by applying for a passport;
- acquired a new nationality and is enjoying the protection of the country of that new nationality; or
- voluntarily re-established herself in the country of former habitual residence on which the claim to refugee protection was based (where the refugee has no country of citizenship).

The cessation clause also provides that a person is not a refugee if the reasons for the claim in the first place have ceased to exist, such as when the conditions in the country of origin have stabilized. However, section 108 does provide one exception to this, in the rare cases where a refugee has been so traumatized by her experiences that she refuses to trust the protection of the country of origin when it is offered. To satisfy this exception to the cessation criteria, the refugee must establish compelling reasons arising out of previous persecution, torture, ill treatment, or punishment for refusing to return home after conditions have improved.

17 UNHCR, *Guidelines on International Protection No 5: Application of the Exclusion Clauses—Article 1F of the 1951 Convention Relating to the Status of Refugees*, HCR/GIP/03/05 (Geneva: UNHCR, 4 September 2003) para 17, online: <http://www.unhcr.org/3f7d48514.html>.

You may be wondering how the cessation clause is important to Canadian immigration law. A person with Convention refugee status, for example, is allowed to remain in Canada and can apply for permanent resident status. In cases where a removal order is issued against a permanent resident, the minister can execute the order; however, if that permanent resident also has Canada's protection, then because of the principle of *non-refoulement*, that person cannot be removed to his country of origin. Thus, where refugee status has previously been granted, the burden of proof is on the minister to show that the protection should cease. Under the *Refugee Protection Division Rules*, the minister must apply in writing to the RPD to hold a cessation hearing, and must disclose any evidence to the refugee. If the RPD makes an order for cessation of refugee status or protection, then the principle of *non-refoulement* would no longer apply. Note, however, that very few applications for cessation were made by the minister prior to 2012, and only for serious cases to strip a permanent resident of his status.

Since the changes to the IRPA in 2012 that redesigned the refugee determination system in Canada, the number of cessation applications has been on the rise, and not for inadmissibility reasons (for example, as a result of misrepresentation). According to the Canadian Council for Refugees (CCR), the government is targeting permanent residents with refugee status who have reavailed themselves of the protection of their country of origin if they meet the following criteria:[18]

- they travelled to their country of origin (even for a short visit, possibly many years ago);
- they applied to their country of origin for a passport (in some cases, simply in order to comply with Canadian government instructions to applicants for permanent residence); or
- they used their passport from the country of origin to travel to a third country.

The CCR raised concerns that the government's scrutiny of the reavailment provision of the cessation clause is holding up Canadian citizenship applications and indeed flagging cases when applicants disclose periods in which they have been out of the country. The government appears to be misinterpreting the UNHCR's guidelines for assessing reavailment, which must consider voluntariness, intention, and the fact that protection has actually been obtained.

Under the new rules, when protection ceases, permanent resident status is automatically revoked. There is no right to an appeal of a decision for cessation before the Refugee Appeal Division (RAD), and no right to appeal loss of permanent resident status to the Immigration Appeal Division. The person becomes inadmissible, without any rights in Canada, and faces immediate removal from Canada.

---

18 Canadian Council for Refugees, "Cessation: Stripping Refugees of Their Status in Canada" (May 2014), online: <http://ccrweb.ca/en/cessation-report>.

Human Rights Conventions

The *Immigration Act* of 1976 created the legal basis for a refugee determination system in Canada. Prior to the enactment of the IRPA in June 2002, however, refugee claims were assessed only within the scope of the Refugee Convention's technical definition of a refugee. Decision-makers at the tribunal had no jurisdiction to assess claims beyond that definition. Consequently, a claim could be rejected if the person did not fit the limited definition of a Convention refugee, even if the person faced a threat or risk of threat to life or freedom. Instead, failed refugee claimants could be considered for protection under an administrative process managed by Citizenship and Immigration Canada (CIC) called the Post-Determination Refugee Claimants in Canada class (PDRCC).

The IRPA significantly broadened the scope of refugee protection and filled in gaps for protection. The new statute did not eliminate the importance of the definition of a Convention refugee but, rather, expanded Canada's protection to foreign nationals by adding new grounds for protection—the danger of torture ground (IRPA, s 97(1)(a)) and the risk to life and risk of cruel and unusual treatment or punishment ground (IRPA, s 97(1)(b))—to allow a claimant to be determined to be a "person in need of protection."[19]

Let's first take a look at the human rights conventions that provide the basis for considering the refugee claims of **persons in need of protection**.

Convention Against Torture

Torture is an extreme human rights violation. The 1984 *Convention Against Torture and Other Cruel, Inhuman or Degrading Treatment or Punishment* (CAT) provides a definition of torture, bans torture, and makes torture illegal under all circumstances, including those of state emergency and external threats.

Signatories to the CAT agree to exercise the principle of *non-refoulement*: a host country may not expel, return, or extradite a person to another country where there are substantial grounds for believing that a person in need of protection would be in danger of being subjected to torture. As a signing state to the CAT, Canada has also agreed to take into account the human rights record of the person's country when deciding whether or not to return him.

The CAT consists of 33 articles, which became effective in June 1987; Canada was one of the original 20 states to ratify the CAT. To monitor the implementation of and compliance with the CAT, a ten-member Committee Against Torture was created. States that are party to the Convention must report to the committee within

person in need of protection
a person who has been granted refugee protection under the IRPA because of a danger of torture or because of a risk to life or a risk of cruel and unusual treatment or punishment; used when the refugee claim does not fall within the scope of the Refugee Convention

---

19 For a discussion, see Immigration and Refugee Board of Canada, "Consolidated Grounds in the Immigration and Refugee Protection Act: Persons in Need of Protection—Danger of Torture" (15 May 2002, revised 24 July 2015), online: <http://www.irb-cisr.gc.ca/Eng/BoaCom/references/LegJur/Pages/ProtectTorture.aspx>; Immigration and Refugee Board of Canada, "Consolidated Grounds in the Immigration and Refugee Protection Act: Persons in Need of Protection—Risk to Life or Risk of Cruel and Unusual Treatment or Punishment" (15 May 2002, revised 24 July 2015), online: <http://www.irb-cisr.gc.ca/Eng/BoaCom/references/LegJur/Pages/ProtectLifVie.aspx>.

one year after becoming signatories, and must submit a report to the committee every four years thereafter for review and recommendation.

International Covenant on Civil and Political Rights

non-derogable rights
a person's core human rights, which must be respected and cannot be taken away or suspended for any reason

derogable rights
human rights that can be temporarily suspended by a state in a time of public emergency

The 1966 *International Covenant on Civil and Political Rights* (ICCPR) serves to codify a person's core human rights, which are non-derogable. **Non-derogable rights** are rights that must be respected and cannot be taken away from an individual or suspended for any reason, even in a time of crisis. These include the right to life and freedom from torture.

By contrast, **derogable rights** are those that may be temporarily suspended, as by a state during emergencies. For example, freedom of movement may be restricted during war or a natural disaster. The ICCPR permits a state to temporarily suspend derogable rights in cases of public emergency; however, it must not discriminate between groups. For example, Canada's internship of Japanese Canadians during the Second World War would not be permitted under this exception, because it singled out Canadians of Japanese descent.

The ICCPR provides for the inherent right to life; the right to recognition everywhere as a person before the law; and the right to freedom of thought, conscience, and religion, including freedom to have or to adopt a religion or belief of one's choice. It forbids torture or cruel, inhuman, or degrading treatment or punishment; involuntary servitude; and arbitrary arrest or detention.

The ICCPR is based on the *Universal Declaration of Human Rights* (UDHR), the first international statement to use the term "human rights." The ICCPR, the UDHR, and another international legal instrument, the *International Covenant on Economic, Social and Cultural Rights* (ICESCR), are known collectively as the International Bill of Rights. In March 1976, the ICCPR became international law. Two months later, it was ratified by Canada. The UN Human Rights Committee was established to monitor ICCPR compliance.

Canada also became a party to the *Second Optional Protocol to the International Covenant on Civil and Political Rights, Aiming at the Abolition of the Death Penalty* in November 2005. The Second Optional Protocol has the objective of protecting the right to life through abolition of the death penalty, and obliges state parties to take all necessary measures to abolish the death penalty within their jurisdictions.

Persons in Need of Protection

The IRPA extends the scope of protection beyond the definition of a Convention refugee to include persons in need of protection who face individualized risk of death, torture, or cruel and unusual treatment or punishment.

A refugee claimant who is found to be a person in need of protection enjoys the same rights as those claimants who are granted protection under the Refugee Convention, including the right to apply for permanent residence; both the exclusion and cessation provisions may be applied to claims made under section 97 of the IRPA.

The definition of "person in need of protection" in section 97 confirms Canada's international obligation to protect refugees under the CAT and the ICCPR. Section 97 reads as follows:

(1) A person in need of protection is a person in Canada whose removal to their country or countries of nationality or, if they do not have a country of nationality, their country of former habitual residence, would subject them personally

(a) to a danger, believed on substantial grounds to exist, of torture within the meaning of Article 1 of the Convention Against Torture; or

(b) to a risk to their life or to a risk of cruel and unusual treatment or punishment if

(i) the person is unable or, because of that risk, unwilling to avail themself of the protection of that country,

(ii) the risk would be faced by the person in every part of that country and is not faced generally by other individuals in or from that country,

(iii) the risk is not inherent or incidental to lawful sanctions, unless imposed in disregard of accepted international standards, and

(iv) the risk is not caused by the inability of that country to provide adequate health or medical care.

(2) A person in Canada who is a member of a class of persons prescribed by the regulations as being in need of protection is also a person in need of protection.

The elements of this definition are considered in more detail below.

Country of Nationality or of Former Habitual Residence

Similar to the concept of alienage under the definition of a Convention refugee, it is generally accepted that nationality refers to citizenship. A refugee claimant must prove that there is a risk of torture (or risk to life or cruel and unusual treatment or punishment) upon return to his country of citizenship. If the claimant has more than one nationality, the claimant must prove that there is a risk of torture upon return to any of those countries of citizenship. If the claimant does not have a country of citizenship, then a claim must be established against the country of former habitual residence.

Personal Risk

Even if there is current and credible information to establish that torture is practised in the refugee claimant's country of origin, the refugee claimant must nevertheless demonstrate that, on a **balance of probabilities**,[20] she would be personally subjected to a danger of torture if returned. In order to avoid being denied refugee status, the claimant must present evidence of this personal risk—it will not be enough to establish that widespread torture occurs in the country.

The claimant may also be denied refugee status under the IRPA under the following conditions:

- there is an internal flight alternative within the claimant's country of origin;
- the risk is part of lawful sanctions, such as punishment for a crime; or
- the risk is a result of inadequate health or medical care.

balance of probabilities
the standard of proof in civil matters, determined on the basis of whether a claim or a fact as alleged is more probably true than not true; this is a much lower standard of proof than that required in criminal court, where the evidence must establish "beyond a reasonable doubt" that an accused is guilty

---

20 See *Li v Canada (Minister of Citizenship and Immigration)*, 2005 FCA 1, 249 DLR (4th) 306.

Generally, refugee protection is intended for the truly desperate; therefore, claimants who are able to find safe haven in pockets of their own country are expected to go there. The IRPA will deny refugee protection in circumstances where the floodgates would open up to large populations—for example, where all citizens of a country are at risk of torture, or where poverty on a national scale precludes health or medical care. Under those conditions, other types of interventions—such as diplomatic, military, and humanitarian aid—are considered more appropriate.

Grounds

The two grounds for claiming to be a person in need of protection are danger of torture (IRPA, s 97(1)(a)) and risk to life or risk of cruel and unusual treatment or punishment (IRPA, s 97(1)(b)). These are discussed below.

DANGER OF TORTURE

torture
the infliction of severe physical or mental pain or suffering as a punishment or means of interrogation or intimidation

Torture is considered an extreme violation of human rights. A major principle articulated in article 5 of the UDHR is that people should be free from torture or cruel, inhuman, or degrading treatment or punishment.

Article 1 of the CAT sets out the definition of torture as follows:

> For the purposes of this Convention, the term "torture" means any act by which severe pain or suffering, whether physical or mental, is intentionally inflicted on a person for such purposes as obtaining from him or a third person information or a confession, punishing him for an act he or a third person has committed or is suspected of having committed, or intimidating or coercing him or a third person, or for any reason based on discrimination of any kind, when such pain or suffering is inflicted by or at the instigation of or with the consent or acquiescence of a public official or other person acting in an official capacity. It does not include pain or suffering arising only from, inherent in or incidental to lawful sanctions.

There are three essential elements to this legal definition of torture,[21] which answer the questions "what," "who," and "why," as follows:

- *What was done?* Did the act result in severe physical or psychological pain or suffering?

- *Who did it?* Was the act intentionally inflicted by a state agent or public official, such as state police or secret security forces?

- *Why was it done?* Was the act carried out for the purpose of intimidation, deterrence, coercion, control, revenge, punishment, or information gathering?

The refugee claimant must prove, on a balance of probabilities, all three of these elements. For example, if a claimant could prove that physical pain was inflicted for the purpose of intimidation, but could not prove that the government was behind it

WEBLINK

You can find an in-depth discussion of torture and some examples in *The Torture Reporting Handbook* at <www.essex.ac.uk/torturehandbook>.

---

21 Camille Giffard, *The Torture Reporting Handbook* (Colchester, UK: Human Rights Centre, University of Essex, 2000) s 3.3.3.1, online: <http://www.essex.ac.uk/torturehandbook/handbook>.

or turned a blind eye to it, the claimant would be denied refugee status on the basis of torture. Consider the following scenario:

> Winfreda was a journalist for a national newspaper and wrote a critical piece about election fraud that exposed the criminal activities of top elected officials. She was arrested by the secret police shortly after her story was released. Winfreda was detained in a darkened cell, placed in metal restraints, and subjected to beatings and electric shock treatment during prolonged periods of interrogation about her sources, which she refused to name. She was extremely weakened by the time her interrogators dumped her by the roadside one night with a warning to stick to "fashion and entertainment reporting" or her children would "disappear." Shortly afterward, Winfreda, her husband, and her children fled the country. She continues to suffer from her physical injuries and post-traumatic stress disorder. She is making a refugee claim under section 97 on the basis of having been tortured and the future risk to her life and the lives of her family.

Under the Convention definition of torture, all three elements of torture were met: Winfreda suffered severe physical and psychological pain as a result of the incident, it was intentionally inflicted by state agents, and the purpose was punishment and intimidation.

The Canadian Centre for Victims of Torture

The Canadian Centre for Victims of Torture (CCVT) provides services to immigrants and refugees who have experienced torture. These services include language training, job search assistance, referrals to other professionals and agencies, translation, and counselling. The CCVT is a non-profit, registered charitable organization and is considered a pioneer in the rehabilitation of survivors of torture. Based in Toronto, the centre works with the community to help survivors integrate into Canadian society and to raise awareness of the continuing effects of torture and war.

For more information, visit the CCVT website at <www.ccvt.org>.

RISK TO LIFE OR RISK OF CRUEL AND UNUSUAL TREATMENT OR PUNISHMENT

The terms **risk to life** and **risk of cruel and unusual treatment or punishment** are not defined in the IRPA. However, these terms are customarily understood to refer to ill-treatment causing suffering that is less severe than torture. These acts must be intentional and intended to cause significant physical, mental, and psychological pain or suffering. Consider the following scenario:

> Zoran was a journalist for a major independent newspaper in his home country. He was investigating a story about international monetary transactions and uncovered a corruption scheme by senior government officials. On several occasions

risk to life
a personal risk that is generally not faced by other individuals in the country

risk of cruel and unusual treatment or punishment
the risk of ill-treatment that would cause suffering that is less severe than torture

(for example, on his way home from work; on his way to the market; and on his way to a friend's house, within a block from his home), Zoran was attacked and threatened by thugs wearing masks. He claims they are members of the national intelligence service, which he says is attempting to censor him. It is well documented that journalists, some of whom were Zoran's colleagues, have been unlawfully detained for their criticisms of corrupt government officials. The attacks against newspaper publishers and journalists have started to escalate. Zoran believes that even if he were to move to another city or the countryside, there would still be a risk to his life or a risk of cruel and unusual treatment or punishment, so he has fled his country.

Is a claim under section 97(1) of the IRPA appropriate in Zoran's case?

Zoran was the victim of acts that were intentional and intended to cause significant physical and mental suffering, so a claim under section 97(1)(b) of the IRPA on the basis of risk to life or risk of cruel and unusual treatment or punishment is appropriate. Note, however, that the harm suffered by Zoran was less severe than that suffered by Winfreda, and that it is less clear whether the masked thugs were state agents or acting in compliance with the state, so a claim under section 97(1)(a) may be less likely to succeed.

Summary of International Conventions

The table below summarizes and compares the international conventions we have discussed in the chapter.[22]

International Conventions

Legal instrument	Key feature	Supervised by	Year ratified by Canada	Refugee status	Protected persons
1951 *Convention Relating to the Status of Refugees*	Defines a Convention refugee	UNHCR	1969	✔	
1967 *Protocol Relating to the Status of Refugees*	Removes timelines and geographical limitations of 1951 Convention	UNHCR	1969	✔	
1984 *Convention Against Torture and Other Cruel, Inhuman or Degrading Treatment or Punishment* (CAT)	Defines torture and makes it illegal under all circumstances	Committee Against Torture	1984		✔

---

22 Also see Human Rights Web, "A Summary of United Nations Agreements on Human Rights" (8 July 1994, revised 25 January 1997), online: <http://www.hrweb.org/legal/undocs.html>.

Legal instrument	Key feature	Supervised by	Year ratified by Canada	Refugee status	Protected persons
1966 *International Covenant on Civil and Political Rights* (ICCPR)	Codifies non-derogable and derogable human rights	UN Human Rights Committee	1976		✔
Second Optional Protocol to the International Covenant on Civil and Political Rights, Aiming at the Abolition of the Death Penalty	Obliges state parties to take all necessary measures to abolish the death penalty in their jurisdictions	UN Human Rights Committee	2005		✔

Canada's Scope of Protection

Canada offers protection to the world's displaced people through three programs, which are described briefly below and more thoroughly in Chapters 12 and 13. The authority to provide refugee protection comes from section 95 of the IRPA in three distinct ways:

1. abroad, through the selection of foreign nationals who apply for permanent or temporary residence when they have already been determined to be a Convention refugee or a person in similar circumstances (s 95(a));

2. in Canada, through the determination by the RPD of the Immigration and Refugee Board that a foreign national is a Convention refugee or a person in need of protection (s 95(b)); or

3. in Canada, through an administrative decision on an application in certain cases prior to removal (pre-risk removal assessment).

From this authority, the grant of protection is carried out under three programs.

Protection Programs

In previous chapters, you learned about how individuals are selected to come to Canada as permanent residents—that is, the rigorous criteria they must meet and the complicated, expensive, and time-consuming application processes they must go through in order to meet statutory requirements. Canada's immigration programs are managed so as to control the flow of immigration through such means as established immigration levels, application criteria, enforcement procedures, and admissibility criteria. Generally, we know who is coming to Canada before they arrive, because they have had to seek prior approval from the Canadian government. However, this is not always the case for refugees. Although the government selects some refugees through the Refugee and Humanitarian Resettlement Program, Canada must also manage spontaneous arrivals, of which only some are considered to be genuinely in need of protection.

The Refugee Challenge: Spontaneous Arrivals and Overstayers

Unlike immigrants, refugees are not selected; they arrive at Canada's borders without having been subject to any immigration assessment processes and without prior approval, and they are considered to be spontaneous arrivals. Generally, these people would be turned away but for the fact they are asking for Canada's protection by seeking asylum here. Given that the criteria for a successful refugee claim does not include any of the usual criteria for immigrating (that is, ability to speak English or French, ability for self-sufficiency, future contribution to the economy, ability to integrate, or family ties), there can be much suspicion as to the individual's motivation for arriving here.

If we apply a strict immigration lens to the refugee challenge, then refugees are portrayed as illegal migrants and abusers of the immigration process; criticized for using the back door to gain entry, especially if they come from democratic countries, which can create the perception that refugees are queue jumpers with "bogus claims"; and viewed as a burden on Canada's social support systems. No doubt there is some abuse of the system by illegal migrants and the human smugglers who help them get to Canada, and some foreign nationals who do not otherwise qualify for temporary or permanent residence do try to manipulate the refugee system to their advantage. However, if we shift the conversation to refugee law, we must remember that the core principles of the Refugee Convention include non-discrimination, *non-refoulement*, non-penalization for illegal entry or stay, and the acquisition of rights over time.

For those who genuinely need protection, their motivation or intent is rooted in suffering, rather than a desire for economic betterment. Unlike immigrants, who make a considered decision to leave their homelands, refugees do not have a choice; they are forced to flee because of some serious risk to their life or because they are victims of human rights abuses, and they cannot safely return home. Therefore, in keeping with its legal obligation, Canada generally allows strangers who ask for legal protection to enter the country, then extends basic civil and legal rights to them, and will not return them to their home countries until it is determined whether they need longer-term protection. A failed refugee claim does not necessarily mean that the claim was false; it could be that the decision-maker made an error. Some claimants who are refused refugee status or protection can exercise a right to apply through other processes (for example, an appeal to the RAD, a pre-removal risk assessment, or a judicial review to the Federal Court).

Another part of Canada's formal commitment to identifying and protecting refugees is Canada's legal obligation to respect the basic rights of refugee claimants by enabling them to live normal lives. Consequently, refugee claimants have traditionally been provided with work authorizations and access to financial, legal, and medical assistance, although the government has attempted to deny basic rights to deter "bogus claimants" and to save tax dollars (see "Health Care" below).

The challenge is that we do not know whether that person knocking on Canada's door is indeed a refugee in need of protection until her case has been decided by a member of the RPD who has the specialized knowledge and training to make that determination.

Since 2008, the government has been reforming the refugee determination system with legislative amendments and new policies and procedures, with the goals of reducing the cost of refugee determination and deterring people who would use the system for immigration purposes. Reforms included giving the minister of CIC the power to identify certain countries that the government considers to be non-refugee-producing as "designated countries of origin" (DCOs); restricting access to health care for some refugee claimants; mandating early hearing dates; restricting access to post-determination rights such as appeals; and enforcing early removal from Canada. The government views these reforms as successful because "the provinces and territories are expected to save in the range of $1.6 billion over five years in welfare, education and health-care costs."[23] Refugee advocates, concerned that the reforms violated the *Canadian Charter of Rights and Freedoms* and the principles of refugee determination, have successfully challenged some of the reforms in court. At the time of writing, the Federal Court has struck down two of the government's initiatives as unconstitutional: the restrictions on access to health care[24] and the designation of DCOs and the restrictions placed on claimants from those countries.[25] These tensions demonstrate the delicate balance that must be struck between protecting Canadian interests through immigration and refugee policies and meeting Canada's international humanitarian and legal commitments to protect refugees.

Refugee and Humanitarian Resettlement Program

Canadian officials from missions abroad work with the UNHCR and various non-governmental organizations (NGOs) to identify refugees and persons in refugee-like situations from abroad who are in need of resettlement. CIC is the federal department responsible for this program. Refugees who arrive in Canada under this program arrive as permanent residents, and they are either given financial assistance by the government or are assisted through private sponsorship. The program is described in detail in Chapter 12.

Refugee Determination System in Canada

The process for deciding who is and who is not a genuine refugee is complex and can be lengthy, because each case must be decided individually and on its own merits. While the entire process includes the involvement of CIC and the Canada Border Services Agency (CBSA), the mandate to decide refugee claims rests exclusively with the RPD and the RAD. The participation, role, and mandate of each of these organizations are very specific, and this partially explains why the process is so complex and often misunderstood. The refugee determination system is discussed in greater detail in Chapter 13.

---

23 Citizenship and Immigration Canada, Backgrounder, "Canada's Fast and Fair Asylum System—One Year Later" (22 January 2014) [Archived], online: <http://news.gc.ca>.

24 See *Canadian Doctors for Refugee Care v Canada (Attorney General)*, 2014 FC 651.

25 See *YZ v Canada (Citizenship and Immigration)*, 2015 FC 892.

Pre-Removal Risk Assessment Program

Claimants in Canada who are unsuccessful in arguing their case for refugee status, and other foreign nationals who claim to face a risk if they are returned to their country of origin, may apply to have that risk assessed. CIC is responsible for this program, although legislative changes, which have not yet come into force, will transfer the authority of evaluating the risk of return and deciding applications to the RPD. This program is discussed further in Chapter 13.

Other Government Programs

Immigration Loans

Immigration Loans Program (ILP)
a federal fund available to qualifying indigent refugees and immigrants; provides loans to cover some costs of immigrating to and settling in Canada

The **Immigration Loans Program (ILP)** is a special federal fund available to indigent refugees and immigrants who qualify by demonstrating both the need for the loan as well as the potential to repay it after arrival in Canada. Under the ILP, loans may be available to cover the cost of transportation to Canada, travel documents, immigration medical examinations, the right of permanent residence fee, and assistance loans to cover expenses such as housing rentals and utilities for refugees being resettled as permanent residents.

Interest is charged at a rate set by the Department of Finance each January. However, members of the Convention refugees abroad and humanitarian-protected persons abroad classes may have a period of one to three years during which they will not be charged interest on their ILP loans. Also, under certain circumstances, loan repayment may be deferred for up to two years, and special needs refugees (urgent protection, vulnerable cases, and women at risk) may be granted financial assistance in the form of a contribution that does not have to be repaid.

Health Care

Interim Federal Health Program (IFHP)
health care coverage that is offered by the federal government on a temporary basis to resettled refugees, refugees and protected persons, refugee claimants, rejected refugee claimants, and certain persons detained under the IRPA

Resettled refugees and refugee claimants are eligible for provincial health coverage generally within 90 days of arrival, depending on the waiting period in the province or territory in which they reside. In the interim, the federal government has traditionally provided essential and emergency health care coverage that is similar to what is available to people on provincial social assistance plans through the **Interim Federal Health Program (IFHP)**. The IFHP provides health care coverage, public health or public safety health care coverage, or coverage of the immigration medical examination, on a temporary basis, to resettled refugees, refugees and protected persons, refugee claimants, rejected refugee claimants, and certain persons detained under the IRPA. Health care coverage is provided in Canada only if it is deemed to be of an urgent (that is, for an injury or illness that poses an immediate threat to a person's life, limb, or a bodily function) or essential (for example, illness, injury, or labour and delivery) nature. Health care may include:

- hospitalization;
- services by a medical professional (for example, a physician or a registered nurse);

- laboratory, diagnostic, and ambulance services; and
- immunization and medication (only if required to prevent or treat a disease that poses a risk to public health or to public safety).

On June 30, 2012, the federal government made deep cuts to the IFHP by eliminating coverage for some refugee claimants (for example, DCO refugee claimants, pre-removal risk assessment applicants) and reducing medical coverage for other refugee claimants (for example, for medical issues of public health and public security concerns). This was done both as a cost savings policy and to serve as a deterrence to future refugee claimants. The government's action led the public to believe that refugees receive health care that is superior to that received by others in Canada. This created much confusion within the health care and medical professions, and drew criticism and outrage from a broad range of people, from refugee advocates and physicians who joined the Canadian Doctors for Refugee Care (CDRC) national days of protest to public figures such as actors and writers.

The CDRC, together with the Canadian Association of Refugee Lawyers (CARL), Justice for Children and Youth, and Daniel Garcia Rodriques and Hanif Ayubi (two refugees whose health care was affected by the cuts), challenged the government's decision in the Federal Court, arguing that the government had breached Canada's obligations under the Refugee Convention and the *Convention on the Rights of the Child*, and that the changes to the IFHP violated sections of the *Canadian Charter of Rights and Freedoms*.[26]

The Federal Court held that the individuals who were affected by the government's actions (that is, the cuts) were being subjected to "treatment" as contemplated by section 12 of the Charter (which provides protection against cruel and unusual treatment or punishment), and that the government made the changes "for the express purpose of inflicting predictable and preventable physical and psychological suffering on many of those seeking the protection of Canada."[27] The court ruled that the cuts were unconstitutional and that they constituted "cruel and unusual treatment"[28] as defined by the Charter. Mactavish J wrote that the government

> intentionally set out to make the lives of these disadvantaged individuals even more difficult than they already are. It has done this in an effort to force those who have sought the protection of this country to leave Canada more quickly, and to deter others from coming here to seek protection.[29]

The court also noted that the distinction the government made for refugee claimants from DCO countries put

---

26 *Canadian Doctors for Refugee Care v Canada (Attorney General)*, *supra* note 24.

27 *Ibid* at para 587.

28 *Ibid* at para 1080.

29 *Ibid* at para 1079.

their lives at risk, and perpetuates the stereotypical view that they are cheats, that their refugee claims are "bogus," and that they have come to Canada to abuse the generosity of Canadians.[30]

Mactavish J concluded that the 2012 changes to the IFHP provided

a lesser level of health insurance coverage to refugee claimants from DCO countries in comparison to that provided to refugee claimants from non-DCO countries. This distinction is based entirely upon the national origin of the refugee claimants, and does not form part of an ameliorative program.[31]

Following the court's ruling, the government said it would appeal the decision to the Federal Court of Appeal. Health care coverage was temporarily restored for some refugees pending the outcome of an appeal,[32] but the government has been criticized for ignoring the rule of law by continuing to deny health care benefits to a select group of refugees.[33]

30 *Ibid* at para 1082.

31 *Ibid* at para 1081.

32 Susana Mas, "Refugee Health Care Temporarily Restored in Most Categories" (4 November 2014), online: CBC News <http://www.cbc.ca/news/politics/refugee-health-care-temporarily-restored-in-most-categories-1.2823265>.

33 See Jennifer Bond, "Ottawa Ignores Rule of Law in Refugee Health Cuts Case" (11 November 2014), online: TheStar.com <http://www.thestar.com/opinion/commentary/2014/11/11/ottawa_ignores_rule_of_law_in_refugee_health_cuts_case.html>.

KEY TERMS

alienage, 331

balance of probabilities, 345

cessation clause, 341

convention, 324

Convention refugee, 322

crimes against humanity, 339

derogable rights, 344

Immigration Loans Program
  (ILP), 352

Interim Federal Health
  Program (IFHP), 352

internal flight alternative (IFA), 333

nationality, 337

non-derogable rights, 344

non-political crimes, 340

non-state agent, 335

persecution, 334

person in need of protection, 343

principle of *non-refoulement*, 328

ratification, 324

refugee, 322

refugee claimant, 322

refugee *sur place*, 338

resettlement, 326

risk of cruel and unusual treatment
  or punishment, 347

risk to life, 347

state agent, 335

torture, 346

voluntary repatriation, 326

well-founded fear, 332

REVIEW QUESTIONS

1. What is the fundamental difference between an immigrant and a refugee?

2. Describe in your own words the principle of *non-refoulement*.

3. What is a refugee *sur place*?

4. Name the two international instruments that are the basis for determining refugee status in Canada.

5. Name the two international human rights instruments that are the basis for protecting persons in need of protection in Canada.

6. List the ways that the UNHCR, as the main agency offering international legal protection for refugees, helps the world's uprooted peoples.

7. List the three programs through which Canada provides protection to refugees.

8. What is the name of the IRB division that has exclusive jurisdiction to hear and decide refugee claims in Canada?

9. What are the three clauses of the Convention refugee definition that have been adopted in the IRPA?

10. What are the five grounds of persecution contained in the definition of a Convention refugee?

11. Under what section(s) of the IRPA can a refugee claimant ask for protection when the Refugee Convention definition does not fit the claimant's situation?

12. On what grounds may a person be excluded from *non-refoulement* protection?

13. In what situations does refugee protection cease to apply under the IRPA?

DISCUSSION QUESTIONS

1. Discuss why refugee protection is not intended to be a permanent status.

2. A refugee claimant whose claim is rejected by the RPD is sometimes considered to be a "bogus" claimant and a person who is solely in Canada to take advantage of social assistance programs. What situations should we consider when thinking about refugee claimants whose claims have been rejected?

Refugee and Humanitarian Resettlement Program

LEARNING OUTCOMES

After reading this chapter, you should be able to:

- Understand Canada's role in the resettlement of refugees.

- Identify the organizations involved in refugee resettlement.

- Define the different classes of refugees under the resettlement program.

- Describe the eligibility criteria for applying for resettlement.

- Describe the inadmissibility assessment that forms part of the resettlement application process.

- Understand the roles and obligations of different types of sponsors of refugees.

Introduction

Canada offers protection to the world's displaced people through the Refugee and Humanitarian Resettlement Program. The program, which is managed by Citizenship and Immigration Canada (CIC), is intended to protect refugees and people in refugee-like situations for the following purposes:

- to address humanitarian needs;
- to meet international responsibilities; and
- to respond to international crises.

This chapter provides an overview of Canada's Refugee and Humanitarian Resettlement Program, including the various types of sponsorship and settlement assistance available.

The Refugee and Humanitarian Resettlement Program applies only to those refugees who are located outside Canada, such as those who have sought temporary refuge in camps across the border from their war-torn countries. Canadian officials from missions abroad work with the United Nations High Commissioner for Refugees (UNHCR) and various non-governmental organizations (NGOs) to identify refugees and persons in refugee-like situations who are in need of resettlement.

Note that the Refugee and Humanitarian Resettlement Program does not apply to refugee claimants seeking a status determination while already inside Canada. Refugee claimants who have found their own way here are subject to different procedures, which are examined in Chapter 13.

The program is part of a broader international effort led by the UNHCR to find durable solutions for refugees. A **durable solution** is a lasting solution, and in the context of refugee law generally means one of the following:

durable solution
a lasting solution to a refugee's temporary status: local integration in the country of asylum, voluntary return to the refugee's home country (repatriation), or resettlement in another country

- *voluntary repatriation*: voluntary return of the refugee to his home country because it is safe to do so;
- *local integration*: integration in the country of refuge; or
- *resettlement*: resettlement in a third country, such as Canada, where a participating state provides legal and physical protection that should eventually lead to citizenship.

Consider the following scenario:

Dumo Akuak's husband was killed a year ago by a land mine, and she was left with five young children to support. One night, she was awakened by the screams of neighbours. She smelled fire and could make out flames in the dark. Was the village under attack by soldiers? Or rebels? Dumo was not sure because both sides had been involved in a conflict in this region of Solaria for the past year. Dumo shouted out to her children and together they fled into the night, wearing only light sleepwear. The family hid in the bush and waited until dawn. There was nothing left of their home. Dumo tried to shield her children's eyes from the hacked-up bodies that lay on the side of the road. The family set out for the border of a neighbouring country, hoping to find safety. They walked for days, and along the way met other people who had lost their homes, parents, spouses, and children.

By the time they reached the border, Dumo and her family had not eaten in days; the children were so weak they could not even cry. Somehow, Dumo found her way to a temporary camp, but it soon filled up. She waited in line for hours to register for shelter; life had become one long line-up for water, food rations, and news. The family lived in limbo, with no status in the new country; they could not work legally and the children were not allowed to attend school. Life was on hold as they spent the next year living in a temporary tent city as refugees. The family waited for the day when they could safely return home.

When a refugee does not have the option, in the foreseeable future, of either returning home or integrating into the country to which she has fled, the only durable solution for a safe and viable new life is resettlement in a third country. Resettlement offers protection to those who need it, and Canada shares in the responsibility of resettling refugees for whom resettlement is the appropriate durable solution.

Canada has been providing humanitarian assistance to people fleeing conflicts and persecution in their homeland since the end of the Second World War. Currently, only a small number of states participate in the UNHCR's resettlement program: 26 states including Canada that have regular resettlement programs, and 6 with ad hoc/special resettlement programs.[1] Canada has traditionally ranked among the top three countries participating in the program in terms of the total number of refugees resettled, and has a history of accepting large numbers of persecuted and displaced persons. This has included refugees from the following countries at the following times:

- Hungary, in the 1950s;
- Czechoslovakia, in the 1960s;
- Chile, Uganda, and Vietnam, in the 1970s (including 5,608 Vietnamese immigrants between 1975 and 1976, and another 50,000 people from Vietnam—refugees who later became known as the "Boat People"—in 1979 and 1980);
- the former Yugoslavia, in the late 1990s;
- Sudan and Somalia, in 2003;
- Myanmar (the Karen refugees), in 2006;
- Tibet, in 1972 and the 2010s (including the resettlement of 230 Tibetans from Northern India under the Tibetan Refugee Program in 1972, and 1,000 Tibetans from the state of Arunachal Pradesh in India, over a period of five years beginning in 2010);
- Afghanistan, in the late 2000s (including the resettlement of over 550 Afghan nationals, which began in 2009 under a special immigration measures program for those who supported the Canadian mission to Kandahar and faced extraordinary and individualized risk as a result of that work);

---

1 UNHCR, *UNHCR Projected Global Resettlement Needs, 2015*, 20th Annual Tripartite Consultations on Resettlement, Geneva, 24–26 June 2014, online: <http://www.unhcr.org/543408c4fda.html>.

WEBLINK

For this year's resettlement targets, consult the *Annual Report to Parliament on Immigration*, found on the CIC website at <www.cic.gc.ca/english/resources/publications/>. Under "Other Publications," choose "About the Department."

- Bhutan (more than 6,000 Bhutanese refugees from Nepal), between 2008 and 2014;
- Iraq (more than 20,000 Iraqi refugees), as of December 2014; and
- Syria (a commitment to resettle 11,300 Syrian refugees), by the end of 2017.[2]

Refugees who resettle in Canada need a lot of support to adapt to their new home and become self-sufficient. A significant feature of the Refugee and Humanitarian Resettlement Program is that it allows private groups to sponsor refugees. Sponsorship is an important feature of the program, which provides financial and other resources to refugees. Generally, refugees who are re-settled in Canada become permanent residents upon their arrival, and this may lead to citizenship.

immigration resettlement plan
a plan tabled by the CIC minister each year that includes the number and types of foreign nationals who can come to Canada as permanent residents

The minister of CIC reports on the number of refugees who have resettled in the prior year in the annual **immigration resettlement plan**. As we learned in Chapter 2, the minister tables this plan every year, and includes the number and types of for-eign nationals who can come to Canada as permanent residents. Included in this plan are Canada's targets for resettlement by class of refugee.

These targets are established through consultations both within CIC and between CIC and the provincial governments, Canadian NGOs, and the UNHCR. Funding is then allocated to visa offices on the basis of projected resettlement needs.

Under the government's plan to reform immigration and refugee policies, the government announced that it will continue the tradition of resettling refugees.

Referral for Resettlement

A foreign national has one of two options for being identified as in need of resettle-ment:

1. *Sponsor-referred cases.* The refugee has a sponsor from contacts with rela-tives, friends, or religious and community organizations in Canada, and can name or identify the sponsor to CIC. For this reason, sponsor-referred cases are also known as **named cases**.

   named cases
   sponsor-referred refugee cases

   Sponsor-referred sponsorships are meant to promote and facilitate family reunification where refugee applicants meet the eligibility criteria of one of the refugee classes. Applicants must include their sponsor's application at the same time as their own application for resettlement (*Immigration and Refugee Protection Regulations* [IRPR], s 140.2(1)).

2. *Visa office-referred cases.* The refugee does not have a sponsor, or, conversely, private sponsors may not know a refugee or a refugee family. These cases

---

2 Citizenship and Immigration Canada, "The Refugee System in Canada" (12 June 2015), online: <http://www.cic.gc.ca/english/refugees/canada.asp>; Citizenship and Immigration Canada, "Canada: A History of Refuge" (10 October 2012), online: <http://www.cic.gc.ca/english/refugees/timeline.asp>.

are matched up by the visa office. For this reason, visa office-referred cases are also known as **unnamed cases**. Instead of identifying a specific refugee, the sponsor submits to CIC a Request for a Refugee Profile form, and CIC refers the request to the CIC Matching Centre. CIC then sends the sponsor information that includes a description and profile about the refugee's family, community affiliation, language, and work skills, and any special needs to determine whether the match is suitable for the sponsor. Generally, this process is used when the UNHCR identifies a refugee in need of resettlement (IRPR, s 140.3). The Blended Visa Office-Referred (BVOR) Program uses the matching process for sponsorship agreement holders (and their constituent groups—see "Sponsorship Agreement Holders and Their Constituent Groups" later in this chapter).

unnamed cases
refugee sponsorship requests referred to the CIC Matching Centre, which attempts to find a suitable match for a would-be sponsor

Important Organizations

There are many organizations, agencies, and people who assist refugees in their quest for a durable solution. Three of the most important organizations are described below.

The UNHCR

If a person seeking to apply to resettle in Canada does not have a sponsor, he must provide a referral from a recognized referral organization (IRPR, s 140.3(1)). Currently, the only referral organization recognized by the Canadian government is the UNHCR. The UNHCR's responsibilities include finding solutions to refugee problems, including resettling refugees in Canada. The UNHCR selects refugees—often those involved in protracted situations—when local integration in the host country is not a viable or feasible solution. The role of the UNHCR is to assess each refugee's situation and identify to CIC those cases for which resettlement is the only durable solution—typically, those where the UNHCR deems there are risks to the refugee's life, liberty, safety, health, or fundamental human rights in the country of refuge. The UNHCR electronically submits to a Canadian visa office a "refugee referral form," which serves as documentary proof of the referral, and contains the refugee claim and information about the claimant and the claimant's family.

Citizenship and Immigration Canada

CIC is the federal department responsible for the selection process for refugees and persons in refugee-like situations coming to Canada from abroad (note that Quebec has its own resettlement process under the Canada–Quebec Accord). Visa officers receive referrals from the UNHCR or named referrals from private sponsors, as well as applications for resettlement from those in need. They assess, evaluate, and decide the outcome of the permanent resident applications on the basis of whether the applicant for resettlement meets Canadian eligibility and admissibility requirements.

In assessing permanent resident applications for resettlement, visa officers place emphasis on the following principles, which are articulated in the objectives of section 3(2) of the *Immigration and Refugee Protection Act* (IRPA):

- to recognize that Canada's refugee program is about saving lives and offering protection to persecuted and displaced persons;
- to facilitate rapid refugee family reunification;
- to develop relationships with partners, such as sponsors; and
- to accelerate the processing of urgent and vulnerable protection cases.

CIC works with the International Organization for Migration to coordinate the refugee's travel and resettlement arrangements.

International Organization for Migration

International Organization for Migration (IOM)
an intergovernmental organization that works with partners in the international community to assist in meeting the operational challenges of migration, advance understanding of migration issues, encourage social and economic development through migration, and uphold the human dignity and well-being of migrants

Established in 1951, the **International Organization for Migration (IOM)** is an intergovernmental organization that assists in the resettlement of displaced persons, refugees, and migrants and works closely with governmental, intergovernmental, and non-governmental partners. Canada is a founding member and a full member of the IOM, and works with the organization in resettlement cases.

The IOM organizes and makes arrangements for the transfer of refugees, displaced persons, and other individuals in need of international migration services to receiving countries. It also arranges counselling and performs medical examinations or screens medical documents for refugees. In several locations around the world, the IOM assists refugees in language training, reception, and the integration process before they arrive in Canada through an in-depth Canadian Orientation Abroad (COA) Program, which serves to "reduce their level of anxiety while increasing the overall chances of successful integration, and empowering them to adapt more rapidly to the day-to-day demands of their new life."[3]

General Eligibility Requirements

In order for refugees seeking resettlement to Canada to be issued a permanent resident visa, they must meet the general requirements set out in the IRPR. According to section 139, a refugee must:

- be outside Canada;
- submit a completed application for a permanent resident visa that includes the names of all family members, whether they are accompanying or not;
- be seeking to come to Canada to establish permanent residence;

---

3 International Organization for Migration, "Benefits and Outcomes," online: <https://www.iom.int/benefits-and-outcomes>. For further information about the IOM, see International Organization for Migration, "Canadian Orientation Abroad: Helping Future Immigrants Adapt to Life in Canada," online: <https://www.iom.int/about-coa>.

- be in need of a durable solution;
- be a member of either the Convention refugees abroad class or the humanitarian-protected persons abroad class;
- have an eligible private sponsor, or, if a member of the Convention refugees abroad class, be in receipt of financial assistance from a governmental resettlement assistance program, or be self-supporting;
- demonstrate the ability to become successfully established in Canada, taking into account the following factors (vulnerable or in urgent need of protection are excepted):
  - resourcefulness and other similar qualities that assist in integration in a new society,
  - presence of relatives in the expected community of resettlement,
  - potential for employment in Canada based on education, work experience and skills, and
  - ability to learn to communicate in one of the official languages;
- if intending to reside in Quebec, be able to meet that province's selection criteria; and
- not be inadmissible (there is an exemption for health grounds based on excessive demand on health or social services).

Classes of Refugees for Resettlement

There are two main classes of refugees under the Refugee and Humanitarian Resettlement Program: the Convention refugees abroad class and the humanitarian-protected persons abroad class.[4] The country of asylum class is a prescribed subclass of the humanitarian-protected persons abroad class. Refugees under the Convention refugees abroad class and the humanitarian-protected persons abroad class (including the country of asylum class) arrive in Canada with a permanent resident visa, unless they are expedited as a special needs case, in which case they arrive with a temporary permit pending their permanent resident status. The definitions and specific criteria for each class are provided in the IRPR.

Convention Refugees Abroad Class

As the name suggests, refugees under the Convention refugees abroad class must first be granted that status under the Convention by a visa officer (IRPR, s 145). Refugees, however, must apply for resettlement *outside* Canada (this process is different from the one for those arriving in Canada, as discussed in Chapter 13), and it

---

4 Under refugee policy reform, the government repealed the sections of the regulations that prescribed the subclass "source country" (IRPR, ss 148, 149) on October 7, 2011. The source country class and the accompanying list of prescribed countries were for individuals who were in refugee-like situations, but who remained in their country of nationality.

must be established that no other durable solution (such as voluntary repatriation or integration in the host country of refuge) other than resettlement is viable.

To qualify for resettlement as members of the Convention refugees abroad class, individuals must possess the necessary financial resources to resettle. Many, however, do not have such resources, so part of the qualifying criteria requires that financial assistance be available to them to support themselves and their dependants through government assistance or private sponsorship (described later in this chapter.)

Humanitarian-Protected Persons Abroad Class

The humanitarian-protected persons abroad class includes persons who are not Convention refugees but who are in circumstances similar to those of a Convention refugee (IRPR, s 146).

Country of Asylum Class

The country of asylum class includes individuals who are in refugee-like situations—that is, they are outside their countries and can show, as required under section 147 of the IRPR, that they "have been, and continue to be, seriously and personally affected by civil war, armed conflict or massive violation of human rights." In this context, "seriously and personally affected" refers to a sustained and effective denial of basic human rights.

Applicants for resettlement under this class must have a private sponsor or have their own financial means to support themselves and their dependants. In certain situations, they may qualify for a joint assistance sponsorship if they also qualify as a special needs case (described below).

Special Needs Cases

urgent need of protection
a term that describes, in respect of a member of the Convention refugees abroad class and the country of asylum class, a person whose life, liberty, or physical safety is under immediate threat and who, if not protected, is likely to be (a) killed; (b) subjected to violence, torture, sexual assault, or arbitrary imprisonment; or (c) returned to her country of nationality or former habitual residence (IRPR, s 138)

All special needs refugees must be members of either the Convention refugees abroad class or the humanitarian-protected persons abroad class. A refugee with "special needs" is defined in the regulations as "a person [who] has greater need of settlement assistance than other applicants for protection abroad owing to personal circumstances," such as a large number of family members, trauma resulting from violence or torture, medical disabilities, and the effects of systemic discrimination (IRPR, s 157(2)). Special consideration is given to these cases, including priority processing and a deviation from the routine assessment eligibility criteria. Two categories of special needs cases are defined in section 138 of the IRPR: vulnerable persons cases and urgent need of protection cases. These cases are given special consideration because they involve refugees in greater need of protection or in more immediate danger.

A person in **urgent need of protection** is defined in section 138 of the IRPR as a member of the Convention refugees abroad or the country of asylum class whose life, liberty, or physical safety is under immediate threat and who is likely to be

(a) killed, (b) subjected to violence, torture, sexual assault, or arbitrary imprisonment, or (c) returned to her country of nationality or former habitual residence. The term "**vulnerable**" is defined in section 138 of the IRPR as a Convention refugee or a person in similar circumstances who has a greater need of protection than other applicants for protection abroad because the person's particular circumstances give rise to a heightened risk to their physical safety.

For example, a visa officer may identify as vulnerable a female refugee who is at risk of rape or sexual abuse because she does not have the protection of a family or support network. Similarly, victims of torture who are in need of medical treatment may be deemed vulnerable.

In assessing applications for special needs cases, the visa officer gives more weight to the need for protection than to the refugee's ability to settle in Canada. In these cases, the criteria are not applied as strictly, and individuals may be accepted despite having limited settlement prospects, because the overriding concern is their safety. All special needs cases are exempt from the requirement under section 139(1)(g) of the IRPR to successfully establish themselves in Canada.

Furthermore, although inadmissibility on the grounds of security risk, violating human or international rights, serious criminality, and organized criminality is still assessed, there are policies and procedures in place that allow visa officers to assess these grounds less stringently in cases involving refugees. For example, in the assessment of inadmissibility on criminality grounds, it is a matter of policy that officers do not require refugees to submit police certificates or certificates of no criminal conviction from their home country, so as not to risk alerting authorities in the country of alleged persecution. Instead, officers may request police certificates from countries of temporary asylum. As well, under section 38(2)(b) of the IRPA, special needs cases are exempt from inadmissibility on the ground of creating excessive demand on Canada's health care system.

Special needs cases usually require expedited processing. The visa officer issues a temporary resident visa in situations like these, to allow the refugee to travel to Canada prior to the completion of the admissibility assessment process. The admissibility assessment (regarding medical, security, and criminality concerns, as discussed in Chapter 3) is completed after the refugee has arrived in Canada. While awaiting the finalization of her application, the refugee holds status in Canada as a protected temporary resident, which is a prescribed class under the IRPR (s 151.1). When the applicant passes the assessment, she may then apply for permanent residence from within Canada.

There are two programs that address special needs cases: the Urgent Protection Program and Women At Risk Program. They are discussed below.

Urgent Protection Program

When the UNHCR notifies a visa office of an emergency case where a refugee is in need of urgent protection because of immediate threats, the Urgent Protection Program (UPP) allows Canada to respond. CIC's *Private Sponsorship of Refugees Program* provides the following examples of urgent protection cases:

vulnerable
a term describing Convention refugees or persons in similar circumstances who have a greater need of protection than other applicants for protection abroad because their particular circumstances give rise to a heightened risk to their physical safety (IRPR, s 138)

- those who are under threat of refoulement, expulsion, prolonged arbitrary detention or extra-judicial execution; or
- those who are facing a real, direct threat to their physical safety, which could result in their being killed or subjected to abduction, rape, sexual abuse, violence or torture.[5]

Resettlement in urgent protection cases is undertaken as a priority where there is no other way to guarantee the security of the person concerned. The UPP program allows sponsorship agreement holders and their constituent groups (private sponsors) to share the sponsorship with the government through the blended visa office referral (see "Joint Assistance Sponsorship" later in this chapter).

Women at Risk Program

The **Women at Risk Program (AWR)** is designed to offer resettlement to women who are members of the Convention refugees abroad or humanitarian-protected persons abroad class so that they may be admitted to Canada even if they do not meet the normal regulatory standard of "ability to establish" themselves.[6]

In times of conflict, it is often civilian women and girls who suffer violence, abuse, and exploitation solely on the basis of their gender. According to the UNHCR, one of the defining characteristics of armed conflict is sexual and gender-based violence (SGBV), including rape, forced impregnation, forced abortion, trafficking, sexual slavery, and the intentional spread of sexually transmitted infections, including HIV/AIDS.[7] Women in these circumstances generally require additional assistance re-establishing themselves. They often are unable to meet the eligibility requirement of having the potential to become self-sufficient in the short or medium term. Women refugees face special, gender-based problems and can be at risk for a multitude of reasons, including the following:

- *They are alone.* A woman may have lost her husband and/or may not have the protection of a male relative or family members. She may therefore face increased risks to her safety and security, and threats to her physical protection, as a result of her gender.
- *They are isolated.* A woman may be isolated because of the stigma of being raped or abused, and may therefore face circumstances of severe hardship resulting in exposure to exploitation and abuse.
- *They lack basic skills.* A woman may be illiterate as a result of a lack of schooling for women and girls, owing to their status in society because of religion,

---

5   Citizenship and Immigration Canada, *Private Sponsorship of Refugees Program* (Ottawa: Citizenship and Immigration Canada, 2015) s 3.5, online: <http://www.cic.gc.ca/english/pdf/pub/ref-sponsor.pdf>.

6   *Ibid* at s 3.4.

7   UNHCR, *UNHCR Handbook for the Protection of Women and Girls* (Geneva: UNHCR, 1 January 2008) ch 1, "Introduction to Protecting Women and Girls," online: <http://www.unhcr.org/47cfab342.html>.

culture, and/or poverty; or may lack basic skills to manage the needs of her family owing to her youth and inexperience, as in the case of a female adolescent who suddenly becomes the head of her household and therefore is particularly at risk of violations and marginalization.

- *They face health concerns.* A woman and her children may face exacerbated health problems as a result of living in refugee camps (which are often located in insecure areas and are subject to cross-border attacks) and as a result of conflict, famine, war-related injuries, or lack of medical attention.

- *They are vulnerable.* A woman and her children may be vulnerable to violence, sexual abuse, and sexual exploitation, and may have experienced harassment by local authorities or even by members of their own community.

- *They face barriers to resettlement.* A woman may have a minimal level of education, limited job skills, or heavy child-care responsibilities.

A woman who has been identified as "at risk" requires help in starting a new life. Generally, a woman who is resettled under this program requires a joint assistance sponsorship, described below, and needs a longer period to become integrated and established in Canada.

WEBLINK

For more information about the risks and challenges faced by refugee women and girls, see the *UNHCR Handbook for the Protection of Women and Girls* at <www.unhcr.org/47cfab342.html>.

Application Requirements for Refugee Resettlement

Refugees in need of resettlement must apply for permanent residence under the program at a Canadian high commission, embassy, or consulate outside their home country. The Canadian government sponsors some refugees and works closely with NGOs—such as refugee groups, religious communities, and ethnic associations—in sponsoring refugees for resettlement in Canada.

Applicants must meet the general criteria for permanent residence discussed above, although exemptions are made in special needs cases (discussed above under the heading "Special Needs Cases").

An application for refugee resettlement must be accompanied by a referral from the UNHCR or by an undertaking for private sponsorship. Refugees destined for Quebec require a *certificat de sélection du Québec*,[8] along with the required documentation. Copies of documents must be translated and certified. In situations where the refugee applicant cannot provide all the necessary documentation, such as when the documents are not available from her homeland or when the documents do not exist, an explanation is required. Failure to explain why documents are missing will result in rejection of the application as incomplete.

There are no application or processing fees for refugees applying for permanent residence under this program, and the refugee applicant receives a letter of confirmation with a file number once the visa office receives the application.

---

8 This certificate is issued to an applicant who meets Quebec's provincial selection criteria.

The refugee applicant must meet the statutory requirements for admissibility to Canada, which apply to almost all new immigrants, and the regulatory requirements for eligibility under the Refugee and Humanitarian Resettlement Program. The procedures manual for visa officers acknowledges that the capacity to process and finalize applications is based on the available resources of the visa office. A pre-screening process helps to identify special needs cases for priority processing; however, it appears that backlogs occur for other applications and, consequently, processing may take years.

Eligibility

The refugee applicant must be eligible for resettlement under the Refugee and Humanitarian Resettlement Program, which means that he must already have a sponsor (IRPR, s 140.2) or

1. be referred by the UNHCR (IRPA, s 140.3(1)(a)), or as a result of an arrangement between the minister and a foreign government, or an agreement between the Canadian government and an international organization or foreign government (IRPR, ss 140.3(1)(b), (c)), or through direct access (IRPR, ss 140.3(2), (3));[9] and

2. meet the regulatory definition of one of the following:
   - a member of the Convention refugees abroad class, or
   - a member of the humanitarian-protected persons abroad class.

A Canadian visa officer decides whether the applicant falls into one of the classes of refugees and is eligible under the program by assessing whether the applicant meets selection criteria and is not inadmissible. A visa officer generally holds an interview to supplement the refugee's application and supporting documentation. If the applicant is found to be ineligible, the application is rejected. If the refugee is found to be eligible, then she must undergo further screening for admissibility.

An applicant is not eligible if there is a reasonable prospect of a durable solution other than resettlement, meaning that the applicant

- already has the protection of another country and is allowed to live in that country,
- has integrated into the host country, or
- can safely return home.

Individuals whose applications have previously been rejected may not reapply unless they can show that their circumstances have changed or that they have new information that was not available in their previous application.

---

9   Under sections 140.3(2) and (3) of the IRPR, there are exemptions for a foreign national to have direct access through self-referral, when the minister has identified a geographic area as having a large number of refugees and has granted it direct access. For example, recent programs include the resettlement of Karen refugees living in remote camps in Thailand beginning in 2006, and the resettlement of up to 5,000 Bhutanese refugees beginning in 2008. At the time of writing, there are currently no geographic areas that have been granted direct access.

Admissibility

Just like any applicant for permanent residence, there are a number of checks that a refugee applicant must pass to establish that she is "not inadmissible." (Inadmissibility is described in detail in Chapter 3.) The visa officer considers the information along with the documents provided in the application and the interview, and determines whether the refugee applicant is inadmissible. Some refugee applicants do not have to meet the normal requirement for being self-sufficient, because they are exempted from financial inadmissibility by section 139(3) of the IRPR.

The following is a very brief overview of four of the grounds of inadmissibility as they relate to this program:

1. *Medical inadmissibility.* Canada normally bars individuals who are inadmissible for health reasons due to a health condition that is likely to be a danger to public health, a health condition that is likely to be a danger to public safety, or a health condition that might reasonably be expected to cause excessive demand on health or social services. Refugee applicants, however, are exempted from the "excessive demand" grounds by section 139(4) of the IRPR. Nevertheless, all refugee applicants and their dependants must undergo medical examinations for health and public safety reasons. They must pass a medical examination to ensure that there is no medical condition that is likely to be a danger to Canadian public health or safety. The examination is carried out by a **panel physician** (a local physician), who is authorized to perform a medical examination by the Canadian government.

   If a refugee applicant cannot afford to pay for the medical examination, he may be issued a loan under the provisions of the Immigration Loans Program (see Chapter 11).When the IOM is arranging travel for the refugees, the IOM may also arrange and prepay for medical examinations. The IOM usually covers the cost of medical examinations for those refugees who are referred by the UNHCR. Canada later reimburses the IOM for costs incurred on behalf of refugees resettled to Canada.

2. and 3. *Serious criminality grounds* and *criminal checks.* The refugee applicant is not required to submit a police certificate from the country from which he has fled, and Canada does not contact organizations or individuals that could place the refugee applicant or his family members in danger. However, a police certificate may be requested from any host country that granted the applicant temporary asylum.

4. *Security or violation of human or international rights.* A refugee applicant can be inadmissible on security grounds because of his own activities or those of an organization to which he belongs outside Canada where the activities are related to espionage, subversion, and terrorism, or are considered to be a danger to the security of Canada or which might endanger the lives or safety of persons in Canada. An applicant can also be found inadmissible if he has been convicted of or has committed crimes against humanity (for example, extermination, enslavement, imprisonment, torture, sexual violence, or persecution committed against any civilian population), genocide, or war crimes. Applicants who held positions within the government

panel physician
a local physician, authorized by the Canadian government; formerly known as a "designated medical practitioner"

or military regimes that participated in war crimes or crimes against humanity are inadmissible as a risk to security. Likewise, individuals who belong to organizations that espouse violence, such as terrorist groups, are also inadmissible.

If an applicant is found inadmissible, his application is rejected.

Selection Factors and the Admissibility Interview

Refugees who seek protection when already in Canada cannot be subjected to immigration selection criteria unless they are first sent back to their country of nationality or former habitual residence. Obviously, this would not be an appropriate response to those claiming to have fled persecution and violence. However, applicants for permanent residence under the Refugee and Humanitarian Resettlement Program are not yet in Canada, and a process of selection is necessary to ensure that the number of refugees admitted does not exceed the resources available for their absorption in Canada.

There are a number of methods of selection, such as by order of application ("first come, first served"), by need, or by ability to become self-sufficient. The Refugee and Humanitarian Resettlement Program first emphasizes need and the ability to become self-sufficient, although once applicants are in the system, they are processed in the order received. Need may take priority over other considerations when an applicant falls within one of the special needs categories of urgent protection, vulnerable cases, or women at risk. For example, the selection factors with respect to self-sufficiency are not applied as strictly in cases identified by a visa officer as special needs because the overriding concern is the applicant's protection.

Applicants are assessed on the basis of their ability to become self-sufficient within 12 months of their arrival in Canada, although support may be extended for up to two years for refugees with special needs. To determine the likelihood of the applicant attaining self-sufficiency, the visa officer considers a modified version of the factors measured by the formal point system of skills and adaptability that is applied to skilled workers in the economic class. Refugees are interviewed as part of the selection process, and the following factors are considered (IRPR, ss 139(1)(g)(i)–(iv)):

> (i) their resourcefulness and other similar qualities that assist in integration in a new society,
>
> (ii) the presence of their relatives, including the relatives of a spouse or a common-law partner, or their sponsor in the expected community of resettlement,
>
> (iii) their potential for employment in Canada, given their education, work experience and skills, and
>
> (iv) their ability to learn to communicate in one of the official languages of Canada.

Although these factors are similar to those used in the formal point system, the threshold for refugees is much less onerous. To illustrate the process by which the selection factors are evaluated, we return to our example of Dumo Akuak, a refugee from Solaria:

The UNHCR came in contact with Dumo and her family in a refugee camp located in a neighbouring country. A UNHCR protection officer assessed Dumo's situation and determined that resettlement was the only durable solution. Furthermore, because Dumo is a single woman with five children, the officer concluded that she may qualify under Canada's AWR program.

To serve as documentary proof of the UNHCR's referral, a refugee referral form would then be sent to a Canadian visa office. The form includes the refugee claim and information about the family. The family would then submit an application for permanent residence, along with the referral, to the Canadian embassy located in the capital of the host country.

In the host country, a Canadian visa officer would assess Dumo's application. In some cases, visa officers travel to camps to interview refugee applicants, and in other cases, they hold interviews at an embassy or consulate.

In Dumo's case, the interview was held in person at the visa office to determine the family's admissibility and the appropriate refugee class, and to assess Dumo's ability to become self-sufficient in Canada as a permanent resident. An interpreter was provided at the interview.

The interview is used to establish the refugee's identity, settlement plans, and her ability to be self-supporting. When assessing Dumo, the visa officer would ask many questions and consider many factors.

The visa officer determined that Dumo and her family were not personally subjected to persecution in their country of origin and therefore did not meet the regulatory definition of persons under the Convention refugees abroad class. However, because of their ethnic and religious background, there was a reasonable chance, given the genocide in their country of origin, that they were at risk should they be returned there.

The visa officer also determined that even if the Akuak family were not Convention refugees, they met the requirements for the country of asylum subclass of the humanitarian-protected persons abroad class. They had fled their country as a result of war and human rights violations. They had been seriously and personally affected—their home was destroyed and their lives threatened.

Before permitting Dumo to resettle in Canada under the Refugee and Humanitarian Resettlement Program, the visa officer would consider the following criteria:

- *No other durable solution.* The host country was not willing or able to take Dumo and her children permanently, and they would be at risk if returned to their home country. Resettlement was the only viable and durable solution.

- *Self-sufficiency.* Normally, Dumo would have had to demonstrate to the visa officer that she had the potential to become self-sufficient within three to five years and not burden Canada by depending on social assistance after that time period. To assess Dumo's earning potential, the visa officer asked about her level of education, work experience and training, language skills, and whether she had any family in Canada. Dumo had a grade 8 education, and her work experience was limited to fieldwork for a neighbouring farm and her own small garden. She spoke broken English, and had no known family in Canada. Furthermore, she would have to take care of a large family on her own. However, the visa officer was impressed by the speed with which Dumo was learning English and by her resourcefulness in taking care of her five children under such terrible circumstances.

- *Private sponsor or financial means.* Dumo had neither a private sponsor nor the financial means to support herself and her five children, but she had the required referral from UNHCR.

- *Inadmissibility.* The visa officer also found that Dumo was not inadmissible to Canada on security or criminality grounds.

Dumo had come this far, but might have been rejected by Canada. Fortunately for her, the visa officer determined that she qualified for government assistance as a special needs case. The UNHCR referral identified her for the Women at Risk Program as a woman alone, without the protection of a male relative, and particularly vulnerable because of her five young dependent children. As a result, her poor outlook for self-sufficiency within 12 months was given less weight, and her profile was entered into the matching centre database so that she could be sponsored by a sponsorship agreement holder and receive financial support through a joint assistance sponsorship. She was also able to defer medical examinations for her and the children, necessary to confirm their admissibility, until after they arrived in Canada.

Canadian Orientation Abroad (COA) Program
a one- to five-day program designed to help integrate refugees into Canadian society

Because Dumo and her family were destined to settle in a country very different from their own, the officer believed that she was a good candidate for the **Canadian Orientation Abroad (COA) Program** to help her learn about Canada and ease her integration into Canadian society. This program, conducted in partnership with the IOM, provided Dumo with learning modules that lasted from one to five days. Topics included an introduction to Canada, the settling-in period, employment, rights and responsibilities, climate, finding a place to live, living in a multicultural society, cost of living, family life, education, communications, and adaptation to Canada. Dumo attended the sessions before travelling to Canada.

Forms and Documents

An Application for Permanent Residence in Canada (IMM 0008) is the generic form used to apply for permanent residence. Each refugee applicant over 18 years of age must submit it along with other forms that the department requires. Here are examples of some of the forms that have been required in the past:

- Generic Application Form for Canada (IMM 008) and Schedule 2: Refugees Outside Canada;
- Additional Dependants/Declaration (IMM 0008DEP);
- Schedule A: Background/Declaration (IMM 5669); and
- Use of a Representative (IMM 5476).

There are many additional documents that applicants must provide with their application forms, such as the following:

1. photos of each refugee applicant;
2. identity and civil status documents for each refugee applicant:
   - copies of birth certificates,
   - copies of marriage, divorce, annulment, or separation certificates,
   - copies of death certificates of family members, and
   - children's information—copies of birth certificates, adoption papers, proof of custody papers, etc.;
3. background documents for each refugee applicant (where applicable):
   - completion of military service card and military records,
   - membership cards (for social, political, vocational, and cultural organizations),
   - educational certificates, diplomas, and school-leaving certificates,
   - trade/apprenticeship certificates, and
   - letters of reference from past employers;
4. travel documents for each refugee applicant:
   - copy of passport,
   - copy of national identity document, and
   - copy of UNHCR registration card or national refugee registration document;
5. proof of settlement funds (if self-supporting), including financial statements and proof of assets;
6. copy of the UNHCR referral or sponsorship undertaking (if privately sponsored); and
7. proof of refugee status, such as a mandate card, refugee status document, ration card, or identity card from the UNHCR or a local government authority.

Applicants may also have to submit other documents that are case or country specific. Generally, visa offices require that documents be translated into English or French.

WEBLINK

All forms are available on the CIC website and include general guidelines for completing them. Guide 6000—Convention Refugees Abroad and Humanitarian-Protected Persons Abroad can be found at <www.cic.gc.ca/english/information/applications/conref.asp>.

Decision

The final decision as to whether to accept or reject a refugee applicant for resettlement is made by the visa officer, after consideration of both the eligibility and admissibility criteria. Applicants who are accepted for resettlement are issued a confirmation of permanent residence, and at the time of arrival in Canada, they are generally granted permanent resident status. They enjoy the same rights accorded to all permanent residents, and are eligible to apply for Canadian citizenship. Applicants who are refused admission to Canada as refugees are informed of this decision and sent a letter outlining the reasons for the refusal. The IRPA does not specifically provide for a direct appeal of the visa officer's decision. However, the refused refugee applicant may seek leave for judicial review before the Federal Court of Canada.

Financial and Resettlement Support

Refugees and their families who are in need of resettlement and who do not have sufficient resources of their own may obtain support from a number of sources, as follows:

- the Canadian government, through the Government-Assisted Refugee Program;
- Canadian citizens and permanent residents, individually or in groups, through the Private Sponsorship of Refugees Program; or
- both the Canadian government and private sponsors, through the Joint Assistance Sponsorship Program.

Government-Assisted Refugee (GAR) Program
a program that applies only to the sponsorship of members of the Convention refugees abroad class, including special needs cases

The **Government-Assisted Refugee (GAR) Program** applies only to the sponsorship of members of the Convention refugees abroad class, including special needs cases. Private sponsorship applies to all categories of refugees.

Government-Assisted Refugee Program and Resettlement Assistance Program

Resettlement Assistance Program (RAP)
a program that provides financial and immediate essential services to government-assisted refugees

As the name suggests, government-assisted refugees are sponsored or supported by the Canadian or Quebec governments, generally through the **Resettlement Assistance Program (RAP)**. Immigration loans and temporary health care may also be available.

Each year, the Government of Canada plans for the resettlement of a number of refugees from abroad, and supports these refugees through the RAP. The RAP provides both financial and immediate essential services to government-assisted refugees, who require help integrating into their new community as they work toward self-sufficiency and independence. Part of the eligibility requirements for resettlement, as noted above, is the ability to be self-supporting or to become self-supporting within 12 months of arrival (that is, possess the ability to find employment based on language and skills).

Consider the following types of assistance available under the RAP:

- *Financial assistance.* The refugee's personal assets, as described in the application, are considered when the need for financial assistance is assessed. The amount of income support is guided by provincial social assistance rates for food and shelter, and covers the most basic needs for up to 12 months after arrival in Canada, or up to an additional 24 months for refugees identified as special needs cases. This money may be used for food, clothing, accommodation, basic household goods and furniture, and incidentals such as toiletries.

- *Settlement assistance.* Unlike refugees who are privately sponsored, government-assisted refugees have no integration assistance from members of the community. Settlement services are provided by immigration service provider organizations, which consist of individuals, non-profit organizations, agencies serving immigrants, community groups, businesses, provincial and municipal governments, and educational institutions that receive funding from CIC. Therefore, from the moment these refugees arrive and require assistance, they are provided with reception at the airport, transportation, temporary accommodation and meals, and winter clothing if needed. They receive assistance locating permanent housing and are provided with household furnishings and basic necessities. They receive help completing essential paperwork, such as that concerning medical insurance, social insurance numbers, and child tax benefits. Furthermore, they receive language training, employment training, and vocational training, which are usually administered by Employment and Social Development Canada.

Under the RAP, settlement officers in Canada have authority to transfer government-assisted refugees with special needs from the GAR program to the Joint Assistance Sponsorship Program after their arrival in Canada if the officers determine that it will take longer for them to adapt to resettlement and become self-sufficient.

Joint Assistance Sponsorship

There are certain types of refugees who are not likely to become independent after only 12 months of living in Canada. Consider the following examples:

- urgent need of protection cases;
- women at risk;
- refugees who are severely traumatized by torture;
- large families of refugees;
- refugees who lived in refugee camps for extended periods; and
- refugees with medical conditions.

The **Joint Assistance Sponsorship (JAS) Program** was designed to accommodate these kinds of situations. It is a hybrid of the GAR program and private sponsorship program. The JAS program extends the normal sponsorship commitment of 12 months up to 24 months for special needs refugees, or 36 months in exceptional cases, because of the extra care required for special needs cases.

Joint Assistance Sponsorship (JAS) Program
a refugee sponsorship program that involves both CIC and a private sponsor

Under the JAS program, the responsibilities for sponsorship are shared between CIC and private sponsors (specifically, sponsorship agreement holders; see the discussion of private sponsors below). CIC provides the financial assistance necessary to meet basic resettlement costs such as food, shelter, clothing, and essential household goods. The private sponsor provides personal contact in the form of ongoing guidance, orientation to the community, help with language skills and job searches, and friendship.

The IRPR also allows for private sponsorships to be extended in exceptional circumstances (for example, when the refugee needs more time to resettle). The sponsor must agree to the extension and divide the responsibilities of sponsorship with the government.

The Blended Visa Office-Referred (BVOR) Program falls under the JAS program. This is a program through which the Government of Canada will provide up to six months of income support through the RAP, while private sponsors—specifically, sponsorship agreement holders—will provide another six months of financial support and start-up costs, and up to a year of social and emotional support.

Private Sponsorship Programs

Private individuals often agree to sponsor relatives or members of their own communities. However, sometimes individuals or groups simply want to help others. Consider the following scenario:

Kim-Ly was only four years old when she, her parents, and two brothers fled the oppressive communist regime in Vietnam and arrived in Canada in 1980. She was one of 9,000 Indochinese "boat people" sponsored under Canada's newly created Private Sponsorship Program. Kim-Ly's family settled in a small town in Ontario, the same community as the local church group that had sponsored her family. They were safe and in a new land now. They were the only Vietnamese family in town, but that didn't matter to the community: people welcomed the family into their parish and their hearts.

Kim-Ly recalls that there were always people around to help the family learn the intricacies of the English language; ensure they had the proper clothes for chilling winters; and take them to local fairs, Thanksgiving dinners, and pancake breakfasts. Kim-Ly's father, a former schoolteacher, eventually opened his own vegetable and flower shop in town. He became what people consider "independent" or "self-sufficient." Kim-Ly's mother stayed home to care for Kim-Ly, her two brothers, and a sister born here. Kim-Ly started junior kindergarten shortly after her arrival; eventually, she earned a college diploma and moved to the city to pursue a career in fashion.

On one of her recent visits to her parents' home, Kim-Ly became curious about her homeland and what had led to her family's departure. Her parents had refused to speak about the atrocities they had suffered and witnessed. She doesn't have any memories of "back home"—Canada is the only home she knows. However, Kim-Ly did have frequent, horrible nightmares as a child and sometimes still wakes at night for no apparent reason. There is a great sadness behind her father's eyes that no one ever talks about. She remembers that her mother used to cry often. She probably suffered from bouts of depression from missing her relatives who were killed.

Kim-Ly knows that her life was saved by the kind people who had sponsored her family. She laments to her mother that there seem to be so many people in the world today who deserve the same help that she and her family received. Her mother peers over her glasses at Kim-Ly and says, "So why don't you sponsor a refugee? One at a time, you can make a difference, Kim-Ly." Her voice trails off. Could Kim-Ly really do that? Sponsor someone? She is excited … but where to start?

The private sponsorship of refugees is the hallmark of Canada's refugee resettlement program, because it opens the door to a greater number of refugees and helps them adapt to their new communities. Sponsorship is considered a three-way commitment between the Canadian government, the sponsor, and the refugee.

Sponsors enter into a legal contract, called an undertaking, with the Canadian government, whereby they agree to be responsible for income support and medical costs for the refugee(s) for one year after the arrival of the refugee(s) they are sponsoring, but they also help with so much more. For example, sponsors help refugees find accommodation and basic household items, help the family adjust to their new community, and orient them to resources and services available in the community. This may involve assistance with basic activities such as banking, registering children for school, taking public transportation, shopping, and searching for a job. Sponsors may also help enroll adult refugees in English- or French-language classes, and with anything else that needs to be done to promote their self-sufficiency as soon as possible within the first 12 months of arrival. Resettled refugees are free to live anywhere when they arrive; however, they will receive support from their sponsors provided that they remain in the same community as their sponsor.

Types of Private Sponsorship

Although sponsoring one refugee or an entire family can be rewarding, it requires some effort, and there is much to do before the refugee arrives. In our example, Kim-Ly may or may not know whom to sponsor or from which part of the world. She has a choice of three different types of private sponsorship in which to participate. Her choice will likely dictate whether she will be involved in sponsoring a "named case" or a refugee who is matched by a visa office.

Would-be sponsors must also determine their desired level of involvement in the sponsorship. Kim-Ly must decide whether she wants to be solely responsible for the sponsorship, or whether she would prefer to join a community group and share the responsibilities. Perhaps she would prefer to forgo responsibility altogether and simply donate money to an organization with experience in sponsoring refugees. CIC provides a Refugee Sponsorship Training Program to groups that are interested in private sponsorship of refugees in need of resettlement. The following is an overview of the three types of private sponsorship groups and their general requirements.

WEBLINK

Refugee Sponsorship Training Program

For further information about the Refugee Sponsorship Training Program, visit <www.rstp.ca>.

GROUP OF FIVE

Group of Five (G5)
a group of five or more people who join together to sponsor one or more refugees

Kim-Ly may decide to form a **Group of Five (G5)** with four or more other people she knows. Any group of five or more individuals may join together to sponsor one or more refugees, provided that each member also meets the following requirements:

- is at least 18 years of age;
- is a Canadian citizen or permanent resident;
- lives in the community where the refugees are expected to settle;
- is not in default on any other sponsorship undertaking; and
- has the necessary resources (such as financial, material, and social) to guarantee support for the full duration of the sponsorship, usually up to a 12-month period.

G5 sponsors are usually one-time sponsors who get together to respond to a special situation. In our example, Kim-Ly could form her group with friends, co-workers, and members of her family.

The five sponsors must show that they can afford to support the refugees through a financial assessment and by providing a detailed plan for the refugees' settlement in the community. The individual members of the G5 act as guarantors: they ensure that the necessary support is provided for the full duration of the sponsorship.

If Kim-Ly chooses to form a G5, she will need to assess the financial resources of each potential member of the group. Once the group is formed, it must start saving or raising funds. Kim-Ly's group must then apply to CIC using the G5 sponsorship application kit. They will then complete a Sponsor Assessment form and an Undertaking/Application to Sponsor—Group of Five form. The G5 must also research and write a settlement plan and financial plan.

COMMUNITY SPONSORS

community sponsor
an organization, association, or corporation that sponsors refugees

Community sponsorship is open to organizations, associations, and corporations that meet certain requirements. **Community sponsors** must

- demonstrate the financial capacity to fulfill the sponsorship by raising funds, if necessary;
- demonstrate the ability to provide necessary emotional and social supports, organizing members to take on various roles; and
- be based in the community where the refugee family is expected to live.

In our example, Kim-Ly may join an existing community sponsor, or she may initiate the formation of a new group interested in sponsoring refugees. Generally, these groups are formed because a person in the community knows of a refugee, such as a relative, who needs to be resettled. That person approaches a community or faith-based organization to request its participation in the sponsorship. Several groups may come together as co-sponsors to form the sponsorship group. For example, if Kim-Ly belongs to a church near her home, regularly attends the local Vietnamese cultural centre, or is a member of her college's women's alumni association, she could approach one or more of these organizations to solicit their participation.

The composition of the community sponsor group will depend on a number of factors, including the amount of money that the group can raise, how much each potential member can commit to donating, and how much each potential member can assist in the settlement of the refugees for the full duration of the sponsorship. All members of the community sponsor group are named in the undertaking with the minister of CIC; therefore, all members are held legally responsible for the sponsorship. One member, however, must be identified as the contact person. By signing the undertaking, the members are subject to any collection action by CIC, should they breach the conditions of their financial obligations.

SPONSORSHIP AGREEMENT HOLDERS AND THEIR CONSTITUENT GROUPS

In contrast to community sponsors, **sponsorship agreement holders (SAHs)** are established, incorporated organizations. They have signed a sponsorship agreement with the minister of CIC (or with the Quebec government) to facilitate the sponsorship process. There are many SAHs across Canada, ranging from religious organizations to ethno-cultural groups and other humanitarian organizations. SAHs may undertake sponsorships on an ongoing basis and are completely responsible for managing sponsorships under their agreements.

Examples of organizations that have signed sponsorship agreements with the minister of CIC include national faith-based organizations such as the United Church of Canada, the Islamic Foundation of Toronto, the Canadian Unitarian Council, and the Presbyterian Church in Canada, and ethno-cultural groups such as the Afghan Women's Counselling and Integration Community Support Organization and the Canadian International Immigrant and Refugee Support Association.

SAHs may sponsor refugees directly, or they may undertake sponsorships indirectly through a local **constituent group (CG)**, which sponsors the refugees under the SAH agreement. For example, a local congregation of a national faith-based organization may apply to its head office to become recognized as a CG so that it can sponsor a refugee.

Each SAH sets its own criteria for recognizing CGs and is responsible for managing and training any CGs belonging to it. A CG must be authorized in writing by the SAH to act on its behalf to sponsor refugees for resettlement. CGs are usually located in the community where the refugees are destined to live.

In our example, Kim-Ly might find that her local parish or congregation is already a CG, has experience sponsoring refugees, and is already in the process of sponsoring a family. Kim-Ly could therefore approach the organization and volunteer to raise funds, serve as a greeter, or provide some other ongoing assistance to the refugee after arrival in Canada.

Many universities and colleges across Canada have a Student Refugee Program (SRP) in place to sponsor a student refugee. The SRP functions as the CG, and the SAH is the World University Services of Canada (WUSC), which manages the program. WUSC participates in the BVOR program, and therefore works with CIC to review profiles of suitable refugee youth and to determine whether

sponsorship agreement holder (SAH)
an established, incorporated organization that has signed an agreement with the minister of CIC to facilitate refugee sponsorship

> **WEBLINK**
>
> For a list of sponsorship agreement holders, see the CIC website at <www.cic.gc.ca/english/refugees/sponsor/list-sponsors.asp>.

constituent group (CG)
a group authorized by a sponsorship agreement holder to sponsor refugees on its behalf

- the student refugee's ethno-cultural background is represented in the student community;
- campus housing or other suitable accommodation is available in the student community;
- the university/college community has the necessary support services such as medical facilities, trauma counselling, and language training in place; and
- there is a suitable program of study in the university or college community and the cost of tuition is covered for post-secondary studies.

The local SRP is responsible for arranging funds to cover the refugee's tuition, accommodation, books and supplies, and general living expenses. After WUSC is satisfied that the local SRP has the necessary funds and can manage the sponsorship, it will arrange the resettlement with CIC.

Does your university or college have a student refugee program in place?

Obligations of Refugee Sponsorship

Refugees are responsible for becoming self-sufficient in 12 months or less from the date of arrival. This is a relatively short span of time, considering that many refugees come to Canada with limited ability to speak, read, or write in English or French; minimal education; and psychological issues as a result of trauma suffered in refugee camps and their homeland. In exceptional circumstances, the length of the sponsorship may be extended to up to 24 months, but only with the consent of the sponsor.

The obligations of sponsors are also onerous. The sponsorship application, together with the sponsorship undertaking, is a legally binding contract between the sponsor and the minister of CIC. The minister can collect the financial obligation should the signees default in their undertaking, and may refuse any future applications for sponsorship. Sponsoring groups undertake to work alongside refugees in order to ensure that they have the necessary support to integrate into life in Canada and to become independent. Consider the following examples of the responsibilities of sponsors:

- *Reception services.* Meeting the refugee upon arrival in the community and orienting him to the community and life in Canada, which includes providing information about public transit, community resources, libraries, and volunteer and settlement agencies.
- *Accommodation.* Locating suitable accommodation, basic furniture, and other household essentials.
- *Access to education.* Arranging language training such as that provided by the Language Instruction for Newcomers to Canada program, or other basic training, and enrolling children in school or daycare.
- *Employment.* Assisting with resumé writing, skills training, and job searches.
- *Financial orientation.* Explaining where and how to shop, bank, and budget.
- *Financial support.* Arranging for payment of rent, utilities, telephone, groceries, local transportation, clothes, and household supplies.

- *Assistance and support.* Completing forms, such as health insurance, social insurance, and child tax benefits forms; helping the refugee understand the rights and responsibilities of being a permanent resident; explaining local laws; helping the refugee find a physician and dentist; and providing ongoing friendship and emotional support.

The commitment to sponsor a refugee may be substantial in terms of both financial resources and time and energy. Fortunately, potential sponsors may choose from the several options described above, depending on what they have to give—money or time—and the degree of commitment they are comfortable making.

SETTLEMENT PLAN

A **settlement plan** details the sponsor's commitment to provide the sponsored refugee with the following:

- basic financial support, such as money for lodging and food; and
- care, such as showing the refugee how to register their children in school or daycare and providing a network of support and orientation.

The settlement plan is the framework for facilitating the newcomer's independence. It serves as a guide to members of the sponsoring group, and allocates responsibilities for each of the many tasks involved. The settlement plan must be submitted with the sponsor's application.

settlement plan
the details of a refugee sponsor's commitment to provide basic financial support and care for a sponsored refugee

Sponsorship Application Process

Anyone interested in becoming a sponsor should begin by reading the *Private Sponsorship of Refugees Program* guide, available on the CIC website. The guide provides information about sponsorship opportunities and processes.

If the sponsor does not have a particular refugee in mind, she may request a match form from CIC.

There is a separate sponsorship application kit for each type of private sponsorship—namely, G5, community sponsor, and SAH/CG. Generally, the sponsoring group must submit the application, an undertaking, and a financial and settlement plan to its local CIC branch. The sponsorship kits for all categories of private sponsorship can be found on the CIC website, and include the guide, the application and undertaking, the requirements for a settlement plan, financial assessment forms, and document checklist. The case processing centre in Winnipeg is responsible for processing sponsorship applications.

CIC assesses the sponsorship application to determine whether the applicant meets the eligibility criteria and to ensure that there is no bar to the applicant becoming a sponsor. Bars to application include being in default of a child support obligation, or involvement in certain criminal offences and immigration violations, as described in section 156(1) of the IRPR. If the applicant for sponsorship is approved, CIC sends an approval letter to the sponsor and provides information about how long it will take to process the refugee's application.

The refugee's application is then processed by the appropriate visa office. As explained earlier, this begins with an assessment by a visa officer, which involves an interview, medical examination, and criminal and security checks. If the refugee's application for resettlement is approved, the refugee receives a visa to travel to Canada as a permanent resident. Travel arrangements are generally made through the IOM. Meanwhile, the sponsor receives a **notice of arrival** with information about the refugee's arrival in Canada.

notice of arrival
notice of a refugee's arrival into Canada that is sent to the sponsor

After attending a Refugee Sponsorship Training Program session, Kim-Ly decided to participate in a local group's sponsorship, which already had a sponsorship agreement in place. She participated in some local fundraisers on behalf of the CG, and collected clothes and furniture in preparation for a refugee family's arrival. The CG sponsored Dumo and her children. Kim-Ly was so excited when Dumo and her children were confirmed to arrive that she volunteered to meet the family at the airport. She told her mother that this was finally her chance to make a difference in someone's life and that she looked forward to helping Dumo and her children settle into their new home and community, just as so many kind people had done for her own family so many years ago.

APPENDIX

Reference for Refugee and Humanitarian Resettlement Program

Provision	IRPA and IRPR
Inadmissibility exemptions	IRPA, ss 38, 39
Definitions	IRPR, s 138
General application requirements	IRPR, s 139
Convention refugees abroad class	IRPR, ss 144, 145
Humanitarian-protected persons abroad	IRPR, s 146
Referral	IRPR, s 140
Applications	IRPR, ss 140, 140.1, 140.2, 140.3, 140.4
Sponsorship	IRPR, ss 152–156
Special needs cases	IRPR, s 157

KEY TERMS

REVIEW QUESTIONS

1. What is the role of the UNHCR in refugee resettlement to Canada?

2. Briefly describe the Convention refugees abroad class.

3. Briefly describe the country of asylum class.

4. What are the general requirements for applying as a refugee for resettlement?

5. Refugee applicants for resettlement are exempt from some grounds of inadmissibility. What are those grounds?

6. Describe the three ways an applicant for permanent residence may be referred for sponsorship under the Refugee and Humanitarian Resettlement Program.

7. The Government-Assisted Refugee Program is for special needs refugees. Briefly describe the types of special needs cases that qualify, and describe the features of the program.

8. Briefly list the categories of private sponsorship.

9. Briefly describe the process to sponsor a refugee, and identify the sponsor's responsibilities.

10. Who is responsible for sponsoring refugees for resettlement under the Blended Visa Office-Referred (BVOR) Program, and what are their specific responsibilities?

Refugee Determination System in Canada

13

LEARNING OUTCOMES

After reading this chapter, you should be able to:

- Identify the main federal organizations involved in the in-Canada refugee determination process.

- Describe front-end stage processing and the eligibility criteria.

- Summarize the main activities of the Refugee Protection Division in processing claims.

- Identify important timelines in the refugee determination process.

- Understand the importance of the Basis of Claim Form.

- Explain a refugee claimant's rights and responsibilities.

- Explain the role and responsibilities of participants in the refugee hearing process.

- Describe post-determination options available to the refugee claimant.

Introduction

In Chapter 1, we learned how the *Canadian Charter of Rights and Freedoms* is part of the legal framework for refugee law in Canada. We also learned about a significant Supreme Court decision in Canadian refugee law—the 1985 *Singh* decision[1]—which is notable for establishing standards of procedural fairness for the adjudication of refugee status claims.

The core of refugee determination is found in the 1951 *Convention Relating to the Status of Refugees* and its protocol (Refugee Convention), which was discussed in Chapter 11. In that chapter, we learned that Canada, as a signatory to the Convention and its protocol, cannot return Convention refugees to territories where they face persecution on the basis of their race, religion, nationality, membership in a particular social group, or their political opinions, and that the 1984 *Convention Against Torture and Other Cruel, Inhuman or Degrading Treatment or Punishment* (Convention Against Torture) is also embedded in domestic law to provide protection to "persons in need of protection" who face an individualized risk of death, torture, or cruel and unusual treatment. The statutory and regulatory provisions of the *Immigration and Refugee Protection Act* (IRPA) provide a basic legal framework for refugee determination. In this chapter, we explore the processes involved in determining refugee status.

Refugee law and Canada's determination system are complex. Imagine the challenge decision-makers face in attempting to distinguish between someone who made a choice to leave her homeland and someone who was forced to flee, especially when the country conditions are such that there is conflict, violence, or poverty. Recall that everyone who presents themselves at a port of entry (POE) must have legal permission to enter Canada, so when a person who does not have status as a Canadian citizen, a permanent resident, or a temporary resident arrives at the border, she would normally not be allowed to enter. But what if that person asks not to be returned to her country because she faces a risk, and asks for Canada's protection? Such a request triggers processes that are often in conflict with routine immigration procedures.

Refugee claimants who arrive spontaneously have not gone through the regular immigration assessment processes and may not have prior approval from Canadian authorities for admission; protection is granted *later* by an administrative tribunal without regard to the refugee's origin, ability to speak English or French, ability for self-sufficiency, future contribution to the economy, ability to integrate, or family ties. We could say that such cases go against the grain, because refugees select Canada (instead of the other way around) and, by doing so, immigration officials must employ exceptions in immigration law and procedures. Generally, a finding that a person is a protected person leads to permanent residence and citizenship. Consequently, refugees are oftentimes portrayed as illegal migrants who abuse the immigration

---

1 *Singh v Minister of Employment and Immigration*, [1985] 1 SCR 177.

process, and they are criticized for the illegal ways in which they use "back-door strategies" to gain entry. While some refugee claimants have used the refugee determination system improperly to their advantage, the motivation or intent of a person who is genuinely in need of protection is rooted in an overriding desire to escape human rights violations and to seek safety and protection, rather than economic betterment. The fundamental difference, therefore, between an "illegal migrant," "immigrant," or "economic migrant" and a refugee is that a refugee *needs* protection. Recall, too, that the core principles of refugee law (non-discrimination, *non-refoulement*, non-penalization for illegal entry or stay, and the acquisition of rights over time) are often at odds with immigration laws.

We should note here, too, that we should not be too quick to judge a "failed" refugee claimant. He is not automatically a person who is trying to cheat the Canadian system. He may have left his country to escape generalized violence and poverty; however, his personal situation and individual experiences may not have met the legal requirements for acquiring refugee status and Canada's protection, or the decision-maker may have erred in the determination. For some claimants, there may be options available through other administrative mechanisms, such as a pre-removal risk assessment.

Legislative Reforms

Bill C-11, the *Balanced Refugee Reform Act* (BRRA), received royal assent on June 29, 2010, with major amendments to the refugee determination system that were scheduled to come into force on June 29, 2012. However, before these changes could be fully implemented, the government introduced Bill C-31, the *Protecting Canada's Immigration System Act* (PCISA), which received royal assent on June 28, 2012, resulting in amendments to both the IRPA and the BRRA. Most of the changes that affected the in-Canada refugee determination system came into force on December 15, 2012; this chapter provides an overview of this "new" refugee determination system. Any refugee claim made prior to this date is considered a "legacy case" and is processed under the former rules; an overview is provided in Appendix C.

In this chapter, we consider the general process for making a claim for refugee protection and examine the major steps leading up to the decision, as well as the claimant's post-determination options. This process involves the following three main organizations:

- Citizenship and Immigration Canada (CIC) and its officials, whose role in the process primarily relates to immigration;
- the Canada Border Services Agency (CBSA), whose role in the process primarily relates to enforcement and security functions; and
- the Immigration and Refugee Board (IRB)—specifically, the Refugee Protection Division (RPD), which processes the refugee claims and makes the determination about refugee status, and the Refugee Appeal Division (RAD), to which refugee appeals are made and which is examined in Chapter 15.

Refugee Determination System

As we learn about the refugee determination system, we will no doubt recall cases we heard or read about where failed refugee claimants continue to oppose their removal years later or where some refugees have waited a long time to learn about the outcome of their claims. According to the minister of CIC, changes to the refugee system were necessary to deter "fake asylum claims coming particularly from the democratic European Union" to "enroll in Canada's generous welfare social income, health care, subsidized housing and other social support programs," and "to stop them from clogging up the system."[2] Reforms are intended to create a faster system; decisions for claimants who are "found not to be in need of our protection ... will be made quickly and they'll be removed quickly."[3]

Some people argue that the negative characterization of refugees by the government is unfair. For example, refugee advocates such as the Canadian Council for Refugees (CCR) oppose the changes to the refugee determination system on the basis that the new law—which provides the minister with the authority to designate countries of origin, to limit rights for some refugee claimants, and to impose mandatory detention—"creates a two-tier system of refugee protection" where refugee protection is "vulnerable to political considerations, rather than ensuring a fair and independent decision about who is a refugee."[4] Advocates criticized the new time frames for hearing claims as unrealistic and argued that they "will particularly disadvantage the most vulnerable refugees, including survivors of torture and rape, women with claims based on gender persecution, and refugees fleeing persecution on the basis of their sexual orientation."[5]

In this chapter, we set out the process and procedures that are generally expected to be carried out; in some instances, we will point out some of the controversial issues related to the new refugee determination system. To simplify the process, we have organized the system into the following three stages of assessment and processing:

1. the front-end stage, which includes the initial application for a refugee claim and the assessment of the claimant's eligibility (CIC, CBSA);

2. the refugee determination stage, where the claim is heard and refugee status is decided before the tribunal (RPD); and

3. the post-determination stage, which sets out the next steps for successful and unsuccessful claimants (CIC, RAD, Federal Court).

---

2   Jason Kenney, "Speaking Notes for The Honourable Jason Kenney, P.C., M.P. Minister of Citizenship, Immigration and Multiculturalism: At a News Conference to Announce Royal Assent of the *Protecting Canada's Immigration System Act*" (29 June 2012), online: Citizenship and Immigration Canada <http://www.cic.gc.ca/english/department/media/speeches/2012/2012-06-29.asp>.

3   *Ibid.*

4   Canadian Council for Refugees, "Media Release: New Bill Further Undermines Refugees" (16 February 2012), online: <http://ccrweb.ca/en/bulletin/12/02/16>.

5   Canadian Council for Refugees, "Concerns About Changes to the Refugee Determination System" (December 2012), online: <http://ccrweb.ca/en/concerns-changes-refugee-determination-system>.

Stages of the Refugee System

| Front-End (CIC, CBSA) | Determination (RPD) | Post-Determination (CIC, RAD, Federal Court) |

Case Differentiation

People who make refugee claims in Canada have different motivations for doing so: there are those who are genuinely in need of protection from persecution, war, and civil conflict; those who wish to improve their living conditions for themselves and their family members (because of poverty, war, or civil conflict); and still others who knowingly circumvent legal immigration processes. The aim of legislative amendments to the IRPA by the BRRA and the PCISA was to address these differences, primarily as a policy decision to deter individuals who would use the refugee determination system for immigration rather than for protection purposes, but also as a government cost-cutting measure (fewer claims and quicker removals would reduce the overall cost of the refugee system and the related costs of medical, educational, and social assistance). Consequently, amendments to the statute and its regulations set out different timelines for processing claims, limit the right to appeal to certain claimants, and, in some cases, impose restrictions for applying for permanent residence even if a claimant is successful in having his refugee claim accepted.

Designated Country of Origin

Among the amendments to the IRPA was the enactment of section 109.1, which provides the minister of CIC the authority to create a list of "designated countries of origin" (DCOs). See Appendix A for the list of DCOs. Generally, DCOs will be those countries that have a high number of claims and low acceptance rates, or high withdrawal and abandonment rates. In designating a country, the minister is required to take the following criteria into consideration:

- the human rights record of the country in question as it relates to the factors found in the definitions of a Convention refugee and a person in need of protection, and in other international human rights instruments;
- the availability of mechanisms in the country in question for seeking protection and redress;
- the number of refugee claims made by claimants from the country in question;
- the acceptance rate by the RPD and the rate of appeals allowed by the RAD; and
- any other criteria set out in the regulations.

A DCO claim must be processed according to separate and faster timelines set out in the *Immigration and Refugee Protection Regulations* (IRPR). As a matter of policy, the quicker processing times serve to deter other individuals who are considering using Canada's refugee determination process for immigration rather than for protection purposes, and provide for earlier removal of failed refugee claimants. A DCO claimant is not allowed to apply for a work permit until after his claim has succeeded. The timelines for a first hearing date for a claimant, depending on the circumstances of his claim, are shown below.

30 days	DCO claims initiated at CIC in-land office
45 days	DCO claims initiated at POE
60 days	All non-DCO claims

A failed DCO claimant did not originally have the right to appeal the decision to the RAD. He is also not eligible to apply for a pre-removal risk assessment (PRRA) until 36 months have passed since the negative determination of his claim. He can, however, apply for a judicial review in the Federal Court, but he will face immediate deportation as there is no stay of his conditional removal order.

Refugee advocates have criticized the policy of designating countries of origin as being unfair because the policy discriminates between refugees on the basis of their country of origin.[6] In *YZ v Canada (Citizenship and Immigration)*, the applicants asked the court to look at the short timelines for DCO claimants. On July 23, 2015, the court ruled that timelines are not relevant in this case and also ruled that denying DCO claimants the right to appeal decisions of the RAD is a violation of the *Canadian Charter of Rights and Freedoms*.[7]

Designated Foreign National

designated irregular arrival
a group (generally, of refugee claimants) that the minister has reasonable grounds to believe was part of a human smuggling operation and is so designated in the public interest

designated foreign national (DFN)
a person (generally, a refugee claimant) who was part of a group of persons smuggled into Canada that the minister has designated as an irregular arrival (see IRPA, s 20.1)

Refugees sometimes arrive as part of a smuggled group of people. While some of the smuggled individuals are legitimate refugees, others are economic migrants who do not qualify either for Canada's immigration programs or under Canada's refugee protection laws, or, worse, are inadmissible for security reasons.

The minister of public safety has the discretion to confer the status of **designated irregular arrival** on a group (two or more individuals). Unless a foreign national can prove he has the appropriate visa—which most refugee claimants do not—a foreign national who is part of a designated irregular arrival group will also be designated and known as a **designated foreign national (DFN)** (IRPA, s 20.1(2)).

Section 20.1(1) of the IRPA gives the minister the authority in the public interest to designate a group of persons as irregular arrivals if the minister:

(a) is of the opinion that examinations of the persons in the group, particularly for the purpose of establishing identity or determining inadmissibility—and any investigations concerning persons in the group—cannot be conducted in a timely manner; or

---

6 Canadian Council for Refugees, Media Release, "New Bill Further Undermines Refugees" (16 February 2012), online: <http://ccrweb.ca/en/bulletin/12/02/16>.

7 *YZ v Canada (Citizenship and Immigration)*, 2015 FC 892.

(b) has reasonable grounds to suspect that, in relation to the arrival in Canada of the group, there has been, or will be, a contravention of subsection 117(1) for profit, or for the benefit of, at the direction of or in association with a criminal organization or terrorist group.

A DFN is subject to automatic detention upon arrival, and detention is mandatory for a refugee claimant over the age of 16 years (IRPA, s 55(3.1)). Briefly, a foreign national with a DFN designation will be held in detention until her refugee claim is finalized or she is released by order of the Immigration Division (IRPA, s 58) or by order of the minister (under IRPA, s 58.1). The review of the reason for the detention (and, consequently, the release from detention) is also subject to case differentiation (see Chapter 14), as the initial review of the detention only has to take place within 14 days of the detention, and a second and any subsequent reviews only have to take place every six months until a final determination is made.

The designation may also be made retroactively to March 31, 2009.[8] In recent years, two groups of refugee claimants arrived by boat: one aboard the *Ocean Lady*, in October 2009, and the other aboard the *Sun Sea*, in August 2010. Refugee claimants who arrived on these boats may be affected should the government decide in the future to retroactively designate these two groups as designated irregular arrivals.

A DFN whose claim is determined positively will need to wait five years before being able to apply for permanent residence and will not be able to sponsor her family members until after she acquires her permanent resident status. If a DFN's refugee claim is rejected by the RPD, she has no right to appeal to the RAD. Although a DFN may apply to the Federal Court for a judicial review, there will be no stay of her conditional removal order, so she will be vulnerable to deportation while her application is being processed.

Safe Third Country Agreement

A **safe third country** is a country other than Canada or a refugee claimant's country of persecution in which the refugee claimant should make a claim for refugee protection. The criteria for designating a country as a safe third country are found at section 102 of the IRPA. Unlike other refugee claimants, those who arrive directly or indirectly from a safe third country are not allowed to enter Canada to pursue their claims for refugee protection (IRPA, s 101(1)(e)).

The United States is the only country to date to be designated as a safe third country for the purposes of section 102 of the IRPA. This is because Canada and the United States signed the *Agreement Between the Government of Canada and the Government of the United States of America for Cooperation in the Examination of Refugee Status Claims from Nationals of Third Countries* on December 5, 2002

safe third country
a country in which an individual, in passing through that country, should have made a claim for refugee protection if that country can provide legal protection against *refoulement*; to date, the United States is the only country that is designated as a safe third country under the IRPA

---

8 Julie Béchard & Sandra Elgersma, "Legislative Summary of Bill C-31: An Act to amend the Immigration and Refugee Protection Act, the Balanced Refugee Reform Act, the Marine Transportation Security Act and the Department of Citizenship and Immigration Act," Publication No 41-1-C31E (29 February 2012, revised 16 May 2012) s 2.2.2.1.2, online: Parliament of Canada <http://www.parl.gc.ca/About/Parliament/LegislativeSummaries/bills_ls.asp?ls=c31&Parl=41&Ses=1#a20>.

(commonly referred to as the Safe Third Country Agreement). Final Canadian regulations relating to this agreement were published in part II of the *Canada Gazette* on November 3, 2004.

The Safe Third Country Agreement predates the recent legislative amendments but is discussed here because refugee claimants arriving from the United States by land will not be allowed to enter Canada to pursue a claim for refugee protection, unless they qualify for an exception to the agreement.[9]

The agreement covers refugee claimants who are seeking entry to Canada from the United States at Canada–US land border crossings by train or at airports (for example, if the person is a failed refugee claimant in the United States and is in transit through Canada after being deported from the United States). As a result, most refugee claimants who pass through the United States on their way to Canada are not eligible to make a claim in Canada. Instead, they must make their refugee claim in the United States. CBSA officers who examine such claimants at the POE are obliged to carry out the provisions of the agreement.

On November 29, 2007, the Federal Court ruled that the December 2004 Safe Third Country Agreement between Canada and the United States violated refugee rights, and made an order quashing the designation of the United States as a safe third country. However, on June 27, 2008, the Federal Court of Appeal reversed the decision, and on February 5, 2009, the Supreme Court of Canada declined to hear an appeal.

Front-End Stage

Consider the following scenario:

> Mr. M arrives by air at one of Canada's international airports on a cold day in February. He hasn't slept in 48 hours—he is too nervous, too afraid he will be sent back. From his window in the airplane, he can see that the ground is covered in white, but it isn't sand like back home; the ground staff wear ear muffs and large mitts—he can see their breath. He is confident he knows what he's doing; leaving was the only way to save his life. Soon, he hopes he can send for his wife and children. He practised for hours the only words he knows in English: "Please give me asylum. I am a refugee." Mr. M follows the passengers off the plane, finally arriving in a large room where line-ups form in front of officials in booths. Mr. M suddenly feels weak and begins perspiring. He clutches the passport he bought from "an uncle," some man named Mak, who got it from someone else; it cost nearly a month's wages.
>
> When it is his turn at the booth, he hands the passport, the customs declaration card, and his ticket stub to the official, a woman in a dark uniform. The woman looks at Mr. M then back at the photo; she doesn't smile; she says something but

---

9 Exceptions are outlined in section 159.5 of the IRPR and, generally, safeguard the principles of family reunification, the best interests of the child, and no return to a country where a person faces the death penalty.

Mr. M doesn't understand. *A woman*, he thinks. *What does she know? I need to talk to a man.* The officer is staring at him coldly now, so Mr. M moves in closer and quietly says, "Please, asylum, refugee." The woman is talking again; she doesn't smile. Mr. M just shakes his head, not understanding; he wonders whether he should give her some money; he has a little. Then he notices that she is directing him to another official. He is escorted to a bright, windowless room: secondary inspection. Mr. M. knows he broke some rules to get to Canada—but isn't that how it's done? How else was he supposed to escape safely?

Consider a refugee like Mr. M who flees his homeland because his life is at risk. Somehow he chooses Canada: refugee claimants might have relatives or friends in Canada, might have heard that it is a safe haven, or might have paid a smuggler; some arrive as temporary residents and then, because of a change in their country's conditions, become refugees *sur place*.

POE officials do not decide the legitimacy of a refugee claim, but they have the authority to manage access to Canada, and, therefore, access to the refugee determination system.

Not every person is allowed to make a claim for protection in Canada. The front-end stage serves to screen people early in the determination process as a means to control who may have a claim heard by the RPD and who will be denied access; furthermore, it serves to filter out potential security risks and criminal cases. Officers assess admissibility and eligibility and decide who should have access to the RPD. In addition, security screening is initiated at the time that a claim is made because most refugee claimants have not undergone background checks before arrival. CBSA officials work with the Canadian Security Intelligence Service (CSIS) to conduct security screenings and criminality checks.

The diagram below summarizes how the process of making a refugee claim begins. Each of the three stages is discussed further in the following sections.

Front-End Stage

Claimant Initiates Application	**Officer Examination**	**Eligibility Interview**

• Orally or in writing:
  – port of entry (CBSA) or
  – inland office (CIC)
	• Assesses admissibility (section 44 report)
	• Issues conditional removal order
	• Initiates background security checks; biometric information
		• Decide if eligible under IRPA s 101 within 3 days or claim is deemed referred under s 100(3)
		• Issue notice of eligibility/ notice of referral
		• Basis of Claim Form

Initial Application

In all cases, the process of making a refugee claim begins with an initial application submitted to an officer. Unlike many of CIC's application processes, which are done electronically or through mail-in services, the refugee claim must be initiated in person. Refugee claimants apply at a POE or at an inland office to provide information to an officer

- orally, in an interview; or
- through a combination of oral interview and written application form.

To prevent the refugee system from being used by non-refugees as a last-ditch effort to avoid removal, a refugee claim may not be initiated after a removal order is enforceable. However, a claim may be made at any point in the process while the claimant is in Canada up to the time that a removal order is made. The manner in which refugee claims are processed varies slightly according to whether the claim is made

- at a POE—for example, land border or airport (CBSA); or
- by notifying an immigration officer at an inland immigration office (CIC).

Generally, at the POE, the application process commences at the time an officer conducts the immigration examination (oral interview). The purpose of the oral application is to provide "tombstone" information about the claimant, such as his name, date of birth, country of origin, telephone number, address, language spoken, and other background information that can help establish his identity. Refugee claimants are provided with the Generic Application Form for Canada (IMM 0008) for permanent residence at this stage.

If the claimant does not speak English or French, the officer will attempt to find an interpreter so that the refugee claimant will be able to communicate during the officer's examination. Generally, refugee claimants are not represented by counsel[10] at this stage of the process.

In the scenario above, Mr. M made an oral application at a POE—an airport. After all his information has been taken by the officer, his application will be considered complete. The process starts when the "application" is received by the officer (IRPA, s 99(3)).

The process is different at an inland office: a person may be a legal temporary resident or may be without any legal status when she appears at the CIC office to make a claim for protection. Generally, the refugee claimant will be provided with two key documents: the Generic Application Form for Canada (IMM 0008) and a Basis of Claim Form. The claimant will also be given a date and time to return with the completed forms for her eligibility interview with an officer.

---

10 Immigration examinations at the POE are conducted without representation. Generally, claimants who appear at an inland office for their eligibility interview to initiate their claim may do so with "counsel." Counsel may be either legal counsel (a member of a law society or of the Chambre des notaires du Québec) or lay counsel; however, if a non-lawyer is representing the refugee claimant for a fee, counsel must be a licensed member in good standing of the Immigration Consultants of Canada Regulatory Council.

Examination

Refugee claimants must undergo an examination by the officer to determine the following:

- identity,
- inadmissibility, and
- eligibility.

The officer creates a file and assigns a client identification number, which the claimant must use when communicating with CIC about any matter related to the file.

Generally, at the POE examination and during the interview, the officer considers both inadmissibility and eligibility at the same time. The claimant, such as Mr. M, is photographed and fingerprinted. The officer conducts a search in various databases for information (for example, previous immigration file and outstanding warrants for arrest) as a part of the preliminary background and criminality checking processes. Mr. M must surrender all identity documents, including passport and travel documents. He will receive certified copies if his documents are legitimate. Otherwise, the documents are seized and may become the subject of a forensic analysis.

Inadmissibility Report and Order

Typically, when a refugee claimant makes a claim at a POE, he is considered inadmissible because he came to Canada with the intent of remaining in Canada without obtaining a visa. An inadmissibility report (section 44(1) report) is prepared and a **conditional removal order** is issued (for more information about inadmissibility, see Chapter 3).

A conditional removal order comes into effect in any of the following circumstances:

- the claim is refused and all further steps have been exhausted,[11]
- the claimant abandons the claim, or
- the claimant withdraws the claim.

The conditional removal order may also specify terms and conditions (such as a requirement to report a change of address or to appear for all hearings and other matters, or a prohibition against working). The removal order is "conditional" upon the outcome of the claim for protection. When the refugee claimant is granted protected status, the conditional removal order has no force or effect. Should the claimant be refused refugee protection, the removal takes effect and the claimant must leave Canada (provided that he does not have rights to appeal, for a judicial review, or a PRRA).

conditional removal order
a departure order with conditions attached; issued pending the outcome of a refugee claim

---

11 In certain cases, after a claim is refused by the RPD, the claimant may not be immediately removed should he appeal to the RAD or apply for a judicial review or a PRRA. The removal order comes into effect only after the claimant has exhausted all legal options available to him.

When a claim is made inland, however, the officer must consider whether the claimant is inadmissible or still *in status*, meaning that the refugee claimant may be in Canada as a temporary resident. Generally, the temporary status will not be extended after it expires.

According to section 103 of the IRPA, if there are allegations that a refugee claimant is inadmissible because of criminality or a security risk, the case is "suspended," either because the allegations need to be argued before a member of the Immigration Division (ID) or because the officer considers it necessary to await a decision of a court. (See Chapter 14 for further details about the ID hearing process.)

Detention

The officer may also consider detention in the following circumstances:

- there are reasonable grounds to believe that the refugee claimant is a danger to the public or is unlikely to appear for examination, an admissibility hearing, or removal from Canada (IRPA, s 55(2)(a));
- the refugee claimant does not have any identity documents (IRPA, s 55(2)(b));
- it is necessary to do so in order for the examination to be completed (IRPA, s 55(3)(a)); or
- there are "reasonable grounds to believe" that the claimant is inadmissible because of security reasons, violating human or international rights, serious criminality, criminality, or organized criminality (IRPA, s 55(3)(b)).

For DFN claims, detention is automatic, and the rules for reviewing the reasons for detention by the ID are different.

A refugee claimant who is detained must be advised of the right to counsel. If the officer decides to detain Mr. M—for example, because the officer believes that his passport is not legitimate or his identity is in question—it is at this point that he would be informed of his right to counsel.

Eligibility Interview

Eligibility is not the same thing as admissibility. The officer's determination of eligibility answers the questions, "Will this claim be referred to the RPD for consideration?" and "Is there some reason to bar the claimant from a refugee determination hearing?" under section 101 of the IRPA. It is not a decision about whether the claim is valid or whether the claimant is in need of protection; the IRPA does not give such decision-making powers to officers of CIC or the CBSA. The officer has authority to decide only whether the claimant may seek a hearing before the RPD. As in all immigration matters, the refugee claimant is duty-bound to answer all questions truthfully and produce all documents and information as requested (IRPA, ss 16, 100(4)). The burden of proof is on the claimant to show that he should have access to the RPD (see Chapter 11 for a discussion of burden of proof).

Mr. M's claim will be referred to the RPD if the officer finds that he is "not ineligible" for a refugee hearing. Under section 100(1) of the IRPA, officers have three working days to make their eligibility decision; otherwise, the claim is deemed to be referred to the RPD. This does not, however, preclude a later finding of ineligibility.

Occasionally, after the claim has been referred to the RPD, CIC will become aware of information that would have made the claimant ineligible to proceed with the claim—for example, the claim was referred as a result of the claimant directly or indirectly misrepresenting or withholding material facts relating to a relevant matter and was not otherwise eligible to be referred to the RPD (IRPA, s 104(1)(c)) or was not the first claim that was received by an officer in respect of the claimant (IRPA, s 104(1)(d)). In such cases, proceedings before the RPD are terminated or, if a determination has already been made, nullified (IRPA, s 104(2)).

Ineligible Claims

Claims that are ineligible to be referred to the RPD fall under one of the following criteria listed in section 101 of the IRPA:

- the claimant made a previous refugee claim in Canada and that claim was either accepted, rejected, deemed ineligible, withdrawn, or abandoned;
- the claimant has been recognized as a refugee under the 1951 Refugee Convention (that is, he is a Convention refugee) by a country other than Canada and can be sent or returned to that country;
- the claimant has been determined to be inadmissible on grounds of security, violating human or international rights, serious criminality, or organized criminality; or
- the claimant came to Canada through a third country designated by the regulations as a "safe third country."

Refugee claimants whose claims are ineligible will not be referred to the RPD. For example, if Mr. M is found to be inadmissible on grounds of security, violating human or international rights, serious criminality, or organized criminality, this would preclude him from eligibility according to the criteria above, and he would not be permitted to take his case for refugee status to the RPD.

When a claimant is found to be ineligible, the immigration officer issues an *ineligibility notice* and the removal order is enforceable. Some claimants will be provided an opportunity to make an application for a PRRA at this stage.

Although few refugee claimants exercise this right, in some circumstances, claimants may apply to the Federal Court to seek leave for judicial review of an unfavourable eligibility decision on the basis of procedural unfairness.

Referral to the Refugee Protection Division

Refugee claimants who are found eligible (or are automatically referred because of the deeming provision of three working days) are referred to the RPD. Returning to our scenario, suppose Mr. M is found to be eligible—in that case, he would be referred to the RPD to have his case for refugee status heard. The immigration officer would then issue the "eligibility notice" and provide him with a notice of hearing setting out the date and time for a first hearing. The following documents are also given to refugee claimants:

- a copy of the admissibility report (section 44(1) report);
- a copy of the removal order, along with any conditions;
- a copy of the officer's notes relating to personal information about the claimant;
- certified copies of any travel or identity documents that were seized and a "seizure" form;
- medical forms and instructions (to complete medical examinations);
- an interim federal health letter and instructions;[12]
- a list of immigrant and community services; and
- a list of non-governmental organizations (NGOs) that assist refugee claimants (may be available in English, French, or selected foreign languages).

Basis of Claim (BOC) Form

a form used to present a refugee protection claim to the RPD; includes information about the claimant and a detailed account of the basis for her claim

Rule 3 of the *Refugee Protection Division Rules* (RPD Rules) sets out the requirements for providing the claimant with the **Basis of Claim (BOC) Form**, in English or French,

- if the claim was made at a POE—with instructions to complete and send the form to the RPD within 15 days; or
- if the claim was initiated at an inland office—with instructions to complete and provide the form to the CBSA or CIC officer, who will submit it directly to the RPD along with the referral.

Basis of Claim Form

Port of entry	• Officer provides BOC Form at eligibility interview • Claimant submits BOC Form directly to RPD (e.g., within 15 days)
Inland	• Claimant completes and submits BOC Form to officer at eligibility interview • CBSA/CIC submits BOC Form to RPD

The officer must also provide information about the claimant to the RPD, as set out in Schedule 2 of the RPD Rules, including the following:

- basic information about the claimant (for example, name, gender, date of birth, and contact information);
- contact information for the claimant's counsel, if any;
- the official language chosen by the claimant as the language of proceedings before the RPD;
- whether the claimant needs an interpreter, and for what language;
- the country or countries in which the claimant fears persecution, torture, a risk to his life, or a risk of cruel and unusual treatment or punishment;

---

12 The interim federal health letter provides coverage of emergency health services until the refugee claimant is eligible for provincial health coverage.

- if a claim of the claimant's spouse, common law partner, or relative has been referred to the RPD, the name and CIC identification numbers of each of those persons;
- whether the claim was initiated at the POE or inland; and
- any other information about the claimant that the officer considers to be relevant to the claim.

At the time of referral, an officer of the CBSA (or CIC) will also schedule the first hearing date with the RPD. When scheduling the hearing, the officer will identify DCO claims for earlier hearing dates. The first date of hearing must be no later than the following:

- 30 days after the DCO claim was referred from an inland office;
- 45 days after the DCO claim was referred from a POE; or
- 60 days after the claim was referred, for all non-DCO claimants.

Security Screening

Generally, refugee claimants have not undergone background checks before arrival. Security screening is therefore conducted for all refugee claimants. Front-end security screening is used to identify people who pose potential security and criminal risks to Canada, and to restrict their access to the refugee determination system. In our example, Mr. M will be fingerprinted and photographed, and his travel and other identity documents will be seized; this is part of the security screening process.

Security screenings are conducted in partnership with the CBSA and CSIS. The CBSA is responsible for coordinating and informing the RPD when security screenings are completed. The RPD will, as a matter of policy, delay the hearing pending the results of the security checks.

Accommodation, Work, and Study

Mr. M's next step while awaiting his hearing date is to find accommodation. If he does not have a place to live with relatives, friends, or community members, the officer will make a referral to local social service agencies. Refugees without funds are entitled to social assistance, although DCO and DFN cases will generally not be entitled to the same level of assistance.

Most refugee claimants want to work because they arrive with little or no funds; however, to be authorized to work they must be in need of a job—that is, they must not be economically self-sufficient and must otherwise be in need of social assistance—and they must meet the following criteria:

- complete and pass medical examinations;
- comply with all notices; and
- apply for authorization to work, as described in Chapter 5, and apply for a social insurance number.

Access to social assistance, however, could become problematic for refugee claimants in the future. Bill C-43, the government's omnibus budget bill (which received royal assent on December 16, 2014), allows the government to make amendments to the *Federal–Provincial Fiscal Arrangements Act* (FPFAA), which governs federal transfer payments. Prior to the amendments, the FPFAA provided a national standard so that no province receiving a transfer of federal money through the Canada Social Transfer could impose a minimum residency period as a pre-requisite for receiving social assistance, except for Canadian citizens, permanent residents, victims of human trafficking who hold a temporary resident permit, and protected persons.

Following the amendments, however, provinces can now impose waiting times for refugee claimants, as they are no longer held to that national standard. Consequently, if a province were to impose a minimum residency requirement, refugee claimants would be denied social assistance for the first months after arriving in Canada, or after moving from another province. Not-for-profit community, cultural, and religious organizations are increasingly taking on the burden of sheltering and assisting refugees.

Refugee claimants who wish to study must apply for a student authorization; they are not exempt from the obligation to have a study permit, even for a short-term course or program of study. To secure a study authorization, the claimant must obtain a letter of acceptance from a designated learning institution and apply for a permit just like any other temporary resident, as described in Chapter 5. Note, however, that refugee claimants do not have to pay processing fees to CIC.

Refugee claimants from DCO countries, however, will not be allowed to work or apply for benefits until their claim is accepted or their refugee claim has been in the system for more than 180 days with no decision.

Health Care

Refugee claimants are traditionally entitled to basic medical care, emergency dental care, and vision care under the Interim Federal Health Program (IFHP), similar to what is available to people on provincial social assistance plans. See Chapter 11 for a description of services covered.

Determination Stage and the Refugee Protection Division

The RPD has jurisdiction to hear and decide refugee claims when it receives a notice of eligibility (or notice of referral) from the CBSA or CIC. (A notice of eligibility indicates that the officer made the determination. If no decision was made within three days, a notice of referral deems the determination to have been made.) This referral starts the clock for counting the number of days that the claim is with the RPD. In our scenario, the RPD must also wait for notification from the CBSA that Mr. M has been cleared by the front-end security screening process before it can proceed with his hearing.

Determination Stage

Referral to RPD		RPD		Inquisitorial Hearing
Notice of eligibility/referral Tribunal record Receipt of BOC Form: • from claimant within 15 days (if from POE) • from officer with notice of eligibility (for inland claims)		BOC review and case preparation: • Identify issues • Research Hearings scheduled: • 30 days for inland DCO • 45 days for POE DCO • 60 days for all other claims		Presentation of case by claimant Intervention by minister (in some cases) Hearing and decision by member Notice of decision Reasons

The registrar creates a file and issues a file identification number that is unique to the claimant. The RPD file number is the reference to be used in all communications with the RPD about matters related to the case. Note that the RPD file number is *not* the same as the client identification number issued by the CBSA/CIC. Legal professionals should always use the appropriate case file number when communicating with the CBSA/CIC or the RPD on behalf of the refugee claimant.

Know and Follow the Division Rules and Policies

As noted in Chapter 2, the chairperson has the authority, under section 161 of the IRPA, to make rules relating to the RPD's activities, practices, and procedures, in consultation with the deputy chairperson, and subject to the approval of the governor in council. These rules are binding, and it is important to know them well. Failure to comply with the rules may have severe consequences for claimants and their counsel.

When circumstances that are not addressed by the IRPA, its regulations, or the RPD Rules arise, the board and its chairperson have authority under the IRPA to address these gaps through policy instruments. Moreover, the division has found that where a claimant may not be able to comply with a rule for valid reasons, sometimes a flexible, non-binding approach to following procedures is more appropriate than rigid rules that must be followed in all circumstances. There are various policy instruments that guide RPD procedures, including chairperson's guidelines, policies, chairperson's instructions, policy notes, jurisprudential guides, and identified persuasive decisions; all policy instruments are available on the IRB website. Some policy instruments are general in application, while others are specific to the RPD. Familiarity with policy instruments will provide legal professionals with confidence when navigating RPD processes. For an overview of the IRB's policy instruments, see Chapter 1. In order to serve their clients more efficiently and effectively, legal professionals should familiarize themselves with these policy instruments, despite their non-binding nature.

> **WEBLINK**
>
> There are several ways to find the RPD Rules, including searching on the CanLII website at <www.canlii.org>, searching on the IRB website at <www.irb-cisr.gc.ca> under the Refugee Claims tab, or searching in the Table of Contents of the IRPA at <laws-lois.justice.gc.ca/eng/acts/I-2.5/>.

Refugee Protection Division Rules

The RPD Rules set out roles and responsibilities, and govern practices and procedures, in matters brought before the RPD. The RPD Rules are a "how to" for adjudicating a claim, from the time of referral to the resolution and closing of the file. For example, the rules require that applications and most communications be made in writing and within specific time limits, and that the claimant be copied.

Legal professionals who represent claimants in RPD proceedings must have a thorough knowledge of the rules, in addition to knowing the provisions of the IRPA that set out the jurisdictions of the IRB and the RPD to hear and decide cases for refugee protection. A legal professional who is unsure about the meaning or application of a particular rule may direct questions and requests for clarification to the tribunal's registrar at the nearest business office of the IRB.

Compliance with the RPD Rules by everyone involved is intended to lead to the fair and consistent resolution of matters before the RPD.

Before examining the RPD Rules, note that it is not possible to predict every possible scenario that might arise in the future, so there is a general rule (usually found under general provisions) that provides the RPD with the necessary flexibility to address new concerns, to change the requirement of a rule, or to excuse a person from the requirement of a rule. Consider the following examples:

- in the absence of a provision in the RPD Rules, the RPD may do "whatever is necessary" to deal with a matter (r 69);
- members of the RPD may act on their own initiative to change a rule, to excuse a person from a rule, or to extend or shorten time limits (r 70); and
- failure to follow a rule in a proceeding does not, in itself, make the proceeding invalid (r 71).

In this way, the rules attempt to strike a balance between the value of predictability and consistency, and the need to make adjustments to meet the particular needs of individual cases. The tribunal expects the legal professional to know and follow current rules before advising and representing a claimant before the RPD. What follows is an overview of some of the key procedures.

Definitions

Important key terms are defined in rule 1 of the RPD Rules. Legal professionals—referred to as "counsel" by the IRB—demonstrate professionalism by understanding and using relevant and appropriate terminology while presenting refugee claims. For example, counsel must understand that a "proceeding" may refer to a claim that is decided with or without a hearing, a conference, or an application. The refugee claimant may need to participate in one or more of the following proceedings:

- *Conference.* At a conference, the claimant (and/or counsel) meets with the RPD member before the hearing to discuss issues, relevant facts, and any other matter for the purpose of making the hearing more fair and efficient.

- *Application.* On an application before the RPD, prior to or during the main hearing, the claimant (or counsel) asks the RPD to make a decision on a specific matter—for example, on a request for additional time for some compelling reason—or to change the date or time of a hearing.
- *Hearing.* At a hearing, the claimant appears in person before a member of the division (with or without counsel) to present evidence and testimony and to answer questions related to his claim.

Scheduling a First Hearing

Tribunals do not generally wish to fix a date on their calendar if a case is not going to proceed. However, under the new rules for processing claims, the date, time, and location are fixed by the officer referring the claimant for a first hearing date (r 3): hearings would be held within 30 days for DCO claimants who make their claims inland; 45 days for DCO claimants who make their claims at ports of entry; and 60 days for all non-DCO claimants (IRPR, ss 159.8, 159.9).

In the event that the claimant and his counsel need additional time to gather information and prepare for the hearing, they may need to ask for a postponement or file an application to change the date or time of a proceeding, and the rules serve to assist with this.

Claimant Information

The RPD Rules define "contact information" as a person's name, postal address, telephone number, fax number, and email address, if any (r 1). Contact information for both the claimant and counsel must be provided to the RPD so that the division can serve notices about proceedings and other matters (r 4). If the claimant does not receive the RPD's notices, such as a notice to appear, because the RPD does not have the proper address, the claimant might fail to appear at the proceeding, resulting in a final determination that the claim has been abandoned. If there are changes to the claimant's information, the claimant must notify the RPD immediately.

The RPD Rules also require the claimant to provide documents that establish his identity, including a copy of identity and travel documents, genuine or not, and a copy of any other relevant documents in the claimant's possession. Identity is especially problematic for the RPD, because many claimants use fraudulent documents to gain entry to Canada (see the "In the News" feature in Chapter 11, page 325, for a discussion of the cost of these documents).

Counsel of Record Information

Rule 4(4) of the RPD Rules requires a claimant who is represented by counsel to provide the counsel's contact information in writing to the RPD and the minister without delay, and notify them of any limitations on the retainer. If the information changes, the client must notify the RPD and the minister in writing without delay.

Unrepresented claimants who wish to be represented are expected to retain counsel without delay. If the claimant has already agreed to a hearing date, a counsel who is available to appear on that date should be chosen. It is a matter of professional ethics for an authorized representative—such as a member of the Immigration Consultants of Canada Regulatory Council (ICCRC)—not to undertake representation unless he has the ability and capacity to deal adequately with the matters to be undertaken. This includes being available on an agreed-upon hearing date.

In some cases, counsel may wish to be removed from the record—for example, if the claimant refuses to pay, is very difficult, or informs counsel that he has not been truthful about certain aspects of his claim. In the latter case, counsel is bound by professional ethics to advise the client that he is under a duty to tell the truth. The claimant has a duty before the tribunal not to misrepresent, and, therefore, counsel has a responsibility to the claimant not to allow him to be party to a fraud. Counsel should try his best to establish the claim with an explanation as to the claimant's change in story. However, if the claimant is reluctant to acknowledge the misrepresentation, then counsel has no choice but to withdraw without prejudicing his client. Counsel is guided by his regulator's rules of professional conduct (for example, a law society or the ICCRC). The rules direct counsel to seek permission from the RPD to withdraw from a case. If, on the other hand, the claimant wishes to remove counsel, the claimant must generally provide written notice to the RPD and to the minister (if the minister is a party to the proceeding) (r 15). The regulator of immigration consultants—the ICCRC—also has rules about the circumstances and steps that a licensed immigration consultant must adhere to when withdrawing from representation (see article 14 of the *Code of Professional Ethics* in the appendix to Chapter 16).

Counsel must complete and submit the Counsel Contact Information form (IRB/CISR 101.02 (12/2012))[13] to the IRB. This includes providing her membership identification number for either the ICCRC or the provincial law society to which she belongs.

Any counsel who represents a client and is not charging a fee should use the Notice of Representation Without a Fee or Other Consideration form (IRB/CISR 101.03 (12/2012)).[14]

Notice to Appear

The RPD is responsible for notifying the claimant and the minister of the date, time, and location of a proceeding in accordance with rule 25 of the RPD Rules. This communication is usually done in writing in a notice to appear. The RPD must also provide the claimant with a copy of any notice or information that the division provides to the minister (for example, notice of possible exclusion issue at a hearing, or notice of minister's intervention).

---

13   This form is available on the IRB website at <http://www.irb-cisr.gc.ca/Eng/res/form/Documents/IrbCisr10102_e.pdf>.

14   This form is available on the IRB website at <http://www.irb-cisr.gc.ca/Eng/res/form/Documents/IrbCisr10103_e.pdf>.

Communicating with the Decision-Maker

The claimant and counsel must never communicate directly with members of the tribunal, but rather must direct all communication through the division's registry or business office (r 2). This applies to all communication, both oral and written, including questions about the process, documents, and a particular proceeding. A list of registries may be found in Appendix B at the end of this chapter.

Communicating through a registry is an important procedure to follow, as it prevents suspicions of bias or influence. All parties must be aware of all information being passed on to the decision-maker, so that they have the opportunity to respond. Applications and other communications must be made in writing within prescribed time limits.

Interpreters

Generally, the claimant must choose a language of record, either English or French (r 17) and report on the BOC, the language and dialect required for the claimant's hearing (r 19(1)). If counsel later becomes aware that the refugee claimant's language and dialect are different from what was originally reported to the RPD, counsel must notify the RPD in writing no later than 10 days before the hearing (r 19(2)). The rules require that the RPD be notified if an interpreter will be required to enable a witness to testify on behalf of the claimant (r 19(4)).

At the time the claim is referred to the RPD, the claimant will be directed to community organizations, such as community legal clinics, and settlement and newcomer agencies, which provide referrals, advice, and language assistance. Many community organizations have interpreters on staff or as volunteers to assist with the variety of linguistic skills required by refugee claimants.

Most refugee claimants do not speak English or French, so unless counsel speaks the claimant's language, counsel should conduct business with the claimant through an interpreter. It is preferable not to use family members or friends for this purpose because they are not likely to understand the legal terminology or the consequences of omitting or embellishing information, and they may paraphrase or put their own spin on the claimant's statements. Furthermore, in cases where the claimant has experienced a traumatic event such as rape or torture, the presence of family members or friends may inhibit the claimant from describing the event. It is also important to reassure the refugee claimant that information (on the BOC Form or in documents for filing) will be kept confidential; that her case, including the file and hearing, are closed to the public; and that the RPD will not share the information with representatives of her country of nationality.

When meeting with the refugee claimant, the legal professional should ensure that the interpreter is not providing information to the claimant, but rather accurately translating only the information that is spoken or written. When an interpreter is used to help translate the BOC Form or other documents for the refugee claimant, the interpreter is required to sign and date the "interpreter's declaration."

For confidentiality and competency reasons, note that only **accredited interpreters** are used by the IRB for hearings in any division. IRB-accredited interpreters have

accredited interpreter
an interpreter used in an IRB proceeding who has undergone a security check and has passed a language exam

undergone security checks, passed a language exam, and attended an orientation and training period. IRB-accredited interpreters are not employees of the IRB; rather, they have a personal services contract with the board and are hired on a case-by-case basis. They are permanently bound by their promise to interpret accurately once they take an oath or make a solemn affirmation to do so.

Generally, before the beginning of a proceeding, the interpreter will use a standardized script to confirm that she and the party, or witness, understand each other. At the beginning of a proceeding, the interpreter must take an oath or make a solemn affirmation to interpret the proceedings accurately and in accordance with the rules. The interpreter may not guide, provide advice, or offer an opinion.

Documents

There are several kinds of documents relevant to refugee claim proceedings. These documents include identity documents and medical reports. Documents are important evidence at refugee proceedings, and the rules for filing documents are similar for all of the board's divisions. Because of the importance of documents to a fair resolution of the claim, the RPD Rules cover preparation and filing of documents (r 31) and disclosure (rr 33 and 34), to ensure that everyone has a copy of the documents well before the hearing. They also specify timelines for filing and replying to disclosed documents.

The legal professional must use appropriate forms and adhere to the following general rules:

- all documents provided to the RPD must be provided to the division registry, and
- any document provided to the minister must be provided to the claimant.

Counsel should provide organized and professional-looking documents. All documents intended for use at a proceeding must comply with the rules. The requirements for handling documents are similar for each of the board's divisions:

- *Format (rule 31)*. Documents must be typewritten in a type not smaller than 12 point, on one or both sides of 216 mm by 279 mm (8½ inches × 11 inches) paper, with pages consecutively numbered. If the document is a photocopy, it must be clear and legible. If there is more than one document, a numbered list of all documents must also be filed.
- *Language (rule 32)*. Documents must be submitted in either English or French, which may require translation.
- *Method of service (rules 39 and 40)*. Documents may be provided by a number of methods: by hand, by regular or registered mail, by courier, by fax (for documents no more than 20 pages long), and sometimes by electronic mail. Otherwise, a request for permission must be made to the division to provide it in an alternative format (or not at all).
- *Computation of time (rule 41)*. A document is considered received by the division on the day that the document is date stamped. When a document is

delivered to the claimant or the minister by regular mail, it is considered to be received seven days after the day that it was mailed. If day 7 falls on a Saturday, Sunday, or statutory holiday, then the document is considered received on the next working day.

General Procedures for Applications

There are many issues that may require resolution before a refugee hearing can even begin. Such issues include a change to the date or location of the hearing, reinstatement of a claim, or cancellation of a summons to witness. If counsel wants a decision on such a matter, the general procedures for making applications are set out in rules 49 to 52 of the RPD Rules. In general, counsel must make an application in the following manner:

- in writing (although oral applications are sometimes accepted) and without delay;
- stating the outcome sought;
- providing the reasons for the request;
- stating (if known) whether the other party agrees to the application (in the case where the minister intervenes);
- including any evidence that the party wants considered, in an affidavit or statutory declaration; and
- with a statement of how and when a copy of the application was sent to the other party.

If the minister is intervening, then the minister and the refugee claimant—as parties to the proceedings—are given an opportunity to respond within specified time limits (generally, within five days of receiving a copy of the application). The response to the written application must be provided in the following manner:

- in writing;
- stating the outcome sought;
- providing the reasons for seeking that outcome;
- including any evidence that the party wants considered, in an affidavit or statutory declaration; and
- providing a statement of how and when a copy of the written response was sent to the other party.

The applicant then has an opportunity to reply to the response. Generally, the applicant must do so within three days after receiving a copy of the written response.

Changing the Location

A request to change the location of a proceeding as specified in the notice to appear may be made by application to the RPD. This situation may arise if the claimant wishes to transfer the case to another office. The application must follow the general application procedures. Generally, such a request must be made no later than 20 days before the proceeding. If the application is not allowed, the claimant is expected to appear for the proceeding at the location fixed by the RPD.

The RPD will consider the factors set out in rule 53(4) of the RPD Rules when deciding an application to change the location of a proceeding, including the following:

- whether the claimant is living in the same location as the proceeding;
- whether a change of location would allow the proceeding to be full and proper;
- whether a change would likely delay the proceeding;
- how a change of location would affect the division's operation;
- how a change of location would affect the parties;
- whether a change of location is necessary to accommodate a vulnerable person; and
- whether a hearing may be conducted by a means of live telecommunication with the claimant or protected person.

Requesting a Public Hearing

Proceedings in the RPD are generally private and closed to the public. However, from time to time, someone may wish to make the proceeding open to the public. This typically occurs when there is media interest in a claim.

In accordance with rule 57 of the RPD Rules, any person may make an application to have the hearing held in public. Such an application must include

- a request for a public hearing,
- reasons why the RPD should agree to a public hearing, and
- any evidence that the applicant wants the RPD to consider in deciding the application.

The original application and two copies must be provided to the RPD, and the RPD will provide a copy of the application to the parties (that is, the claimant and the minister).

Before the Proceeding

The RPD Rules require that certain activities occur within certain time limits. Before taking on a refugee case, counsel must first consider both the time requirements of the RPD and the time necessary to go over the client's information thoroughly and carefully. For example, Mr. M's counsel must consider his caseload together with the specific needs of Mr. M's case, such as communication barriers, the time needed to gather documents and information related to Mr. M's claim, and even Mr. M's ability to relive events, before deciding whether or not to take on Mr. M's case.

Basis of Claim Form

> When Mr. M met with his counsel, he was resentful and impatient about having to provide such personal details. He couldn't understand why the people at the refugee board wanted to have so much information about him, including some of the same information he'd already given the other officials at CIC. He was also worried about what the Canadian government officials would do with the information. Would it be shared with officials of his country?

The BOC Form is the key document that provides the RPD with the first glimpse of the claimant's case. The RPD uses the information in the BOC Form to achieve the following objectives:

- identify the key issues in the case to prepare for the hearing, and
- prepare research and information about the claimant's country conditions for the hearing.

For refugee claims made at a POE, claimants must provide the BOC Form and documentation to the RPD within 15 days. For claims made at an inland office in Canada, refugee claimants must provide the BOC Form and documentation to an immigration officer at their eligibility interview. The officer forwards the BOC Form at the time of referral to the RPD. It is essential for counsel to learn about where and when their clients made their refugee claim in order to comply with the deadlines. (See the Basis of Claim Form table on page 398.)

Two copies of all supporting documents (for example, passport and identity, travel, medical, psychological, or police documents) must be provided with the BOC Form. Documents must be certified translations in English or French at the claimant's expense.

Any travel or identity documents that the claimant obtains after submitting the BOC Form must be received by the IRB and by the minister of CIC, if the minister is a party, at least ten days before the hearing. Also, any information or documents required must be disclosed to the minister.

The BOC Form must be completed by the claimant to provide information about the claimant's reasons for seeking refugee protection. Its use streamlines the collection of information about the claimant and focuses on specific aspects of the claim for protection. Much of the content of the BOC Form will not duplicate other information collected, such as personal information solicited in the Generic Application for Canada (IMM 0008) for permanent residence and any accompanying forms required by the CBSA or CIC. The content of the BOC Form is set out in Schedule 1 to the RPD Rules. In our example, Mr. M is required to complete the BOC Form and file it with the RPD before he can apply for a work or student authorization. The short deadline to complete it means that if Mr. M plans to seek assistance in completing the form (for example, at a legal clinic, at an NGO, or through his own representative), he must do so right away.

The BOC Form is used by the RPD together with the officer's notes as part of the RPD's early review of the claim to gain a better understanding of the reasons why a refugee is making a claim, to detect discrepancies (and thereby assess the refugee's credibility), and to provide any instructions to tribunal personnel and the minister as may be required.

The BOC Form also provides information that the RPD may use to invite the minister to intervene in the claim. The RPD would notify the minister before a hearing begins that there may be issues that give rise to exclusion, integrity, inadmissibility, or ineligibility, so that the minister has an opportunity to intervene (RPD Rules, rr 26–28). The claimant would receive a copy of the notice.

The Record

The RPD opens a claimant's file with the notice of referral and adds the BOC Form and the officer's interview notes. Documents are added to the file as they are received by the RPD and comprise the record. The record may include any or all of the following documents:

- BOC Form;
- Notification of Client Contact Information form;
- change of address notifications, if any;
- Counsel Contact Information form (from counsel);
- Notice of Representation Without a Fee or Other Consideration form;
- List of Claimant's Documents form;
- List of Minister's Documents form (from the minister's representative, if the minister is intervening in the case);
- copies of any notices sent by the CBSA, CIC, and the RPD;
- copies of any other correspondence; and
- any documents disclosed.

Like Mr. M, many refugee applicants do not communicate well in English or French, and need help to understand the numerous forms and documents. One of the important roles of counsel is to take the time to explain the purpose and importance of the various documents and forms, especially the BOC Form—the most important one.

It is also counsel's role to identify those documents required as evidence to support the claims made, and to verify facts to the extent possible, to ensure that they support the claims made. Mr. M's counsel therefore has an important role in assisting Mr. M to develop a complete background for his BOC Form (including family history, education, employment, and military service) and a logical and chronological history of events that gave rise to his fear and flight (such as dates of activities, arrests, travel history within the country, departure, and travel outside the country).

Refugee claimants already face language and cultural barriers, and they are not expected to be experts on refugee law; knowing what information to provide in the BOC Form can therefore be confusing for them. Consequently, the assistance counsel provides in assisting refugee claimants in completing these and other important documents is invaluable.

Refugee claimants will not necessarily understand that the RPD is separate and independent from other government departments and officials. For this reason, it is equally important for counsel to reassure clients about the confidentiality of the process, at least with regard to sharing information with officials from the claimant's country of origin.

Types of Documents

Consider the following types of documents, which are important in order to establish the facts of the case and to support the testimony of witnesses:

1. **Identity documents**. It is important that the refugee claimant provide acceptable documents to establish his identity and other elements of the claim, or provide a credible explanation as to why such documents are not available and what steps were taken to attempt to obtain them. Identity documents may include the following:

   - birth certificate;
   - passport or national identity card;
   - marriage certificate;
   - divorce certificate;
   - voter registration card;
   - driver's licence;
   - professional or religious membership card;
   - military documents;
   - police records; and
   - school certificates or university transcripts.

   The existence of these kinds of documents bolsters the claimant's credibility and helps to establish the claimant's identity.

   identity documents
   lawfully obtained documents designed to prove the identity of the person carrying them (for example, a passport or birth certificate)

2. **Corroborative documents**. Documents that corroborate a claimant's allegations are a boost to his credibility, and may replace the need to relive traumatic events at the hearing. For example, if the claimant has been tortured, there may be medical or psychiatric reports to corroborate the claim. Examples of useful corroborative evidence that may be filed include

   - references to the claimant or associates of the claimant in any high-profile human rights reports;
   - newspaper references to the claimant's involvement in incidents or activities, such as demonstrations;
   - evidence of the claimant's membership in a political party or social or religious group; and
   - objective evidence, including background research.

   corroborative documents
   documents that corroborate a claimant's allegations

country information
for a refugee claimant,
information on the country
of reference, such as
country-of-origin information, as provided by the RPD

3. **Country information.** Information on the country of reference, such as country-of-origin information, is provided by the RPD. This means that every case will have some basic documentary evidence, which becomes part of the exhibit list used at the hearing. Counsel may already be familiar with the country conditions and human rights violations in the country of origin if they have represented other clients from the same place. Counsel should review the country information with the claimant to address any inconsistencies with the claimant's own personal experience.

Country-Specific Sources for Research Purposes

This is a small selection of credible sources where you can begin your research on background country conditions.

- Amnesty International. For country reports and special studies.
  Online: <http://www.amnesty.org>.
- Human Rights Watch Reports.
  Online: <http://www.hrw.org/publications>.
- Immigration and Refugee Board. Check out the "Research Program" link on the IRB website; the research database contains papers on a variety of countries.
  Online: <http://www.irb-cisr.gc.ca/Eng/ResRec/>.
- Journal of Refugee Studies.
  Online: Oxford Journals <http://jrs.oxfordjournals.org/content/by/year>.
- US Department of State Country Reports on Human Rights Practices.
  Online: <http://www.state.gov/j/drl/rls/hrrpt/humanrightsreport/>.

In our scenario, Mr. M's counsel should review the copies of the identity documents that Mr. M provided to the officer at the front-end stage. In preparing for Mr. M's hearing, counsel should ask whether the claimant can obtain legitimate identity documents such as a passport, birth certificate, voter registration card, or domicile registration card, without putting relatives at risk, because Mr. M had used fraudulent documents to get to Canada. If documents cannot be safely obtained, are there any witnesses who can testify as to the claimant's identity?

Counsel should make a list of any evidence needed to confirm the facts of Mr. M's allegations. It is crucial that counsel be prepared to deal with discrepancies between information given at the eligibility interview, in the BOC Form, and during Mr. M's hearing. Too many discrepancies may lead to a finding of "no credible basis," or to a finding that the allegations are fraudulent or are "manifestly unfounded."

FILING DOCUMENTS

Counsel must use appropriate forms and follow the rules for filing documents. Generally, the rules concerning documents can be applied to any document, notice, or request. Counsel should provide organized and professional-looking documents to the RPD. All documents intended for use at the hearing must comply with the rules.

If the claimant files more than one document to be included in the record, a numbered list of all such documents must also be filed. The List of Claimant's Documents form (RPD.12.08)[15] should be used for this purpose.

DISCLOSURE AND PROVISION OF DOCUMENTS

Documents are exchanged before the hearing to ensure that all participants have an opportunity to review them in preparation for the hearing and to respond, if necessary. To ensure that this happens, the RPD Rules require **disclosure** of documents to the RPD and to the minister (if the minister is intervening), and impose requirements for providing copies of the documents to those entitled to have them.

disclosure
the release of documents
to the opposing side
in a proceeding

Consider the following general criteria regarding disclosure:

- Observe time limits for disclosing documents so that they are received before a proceeding.
- Disclose any documentary evidence to be used in support of a client's claim to the RPD by listing the documents on the List of Claimant's Documents form, filed within the time limits set out in the RPD Rules (at least ten days before the hearing, under Rule 34).
- The RPD may refuse to use or allow documents that are not produced within the time limits.
- Consider the progress of the claim because, generally, if the hearing has already started, the member can consider whether to allow admission of the documents on the basis of the document's relevance and probative value, what new evidence the document brings to the hearing, and whether there was a reasonable effort made to provide the document on time. It would be perceived as unfair and inefficient if documents were withheld until the last minute.

Hearings

Hearing Preparation

Prior to a hearing, counsel must be familiar with the RPD Rules that relate to matters such as document disclosure, and with the relevant legislation and case law. Counsel must also have a clear understanding of the legal issues in the particular case. Common legal issues that frequently require hearings to resolve include the following:

- identity/nationality;
- existence of other claims;
- delay in making the claim;
- credibility assessment;
- nexus to the grounds (which grounds apply);

---

15 This form is available on the IRB website at <http://www.irb-cisr.gc.ca/Eng/res/form/Documents/RpdSpr1208_e.pdf>.

- the agents of persecution;
- objective evidence to support the claim; and
- what the claimant fears if he were to be returned.

In addition, counsel must be aware of all the pertinent facts of the case, and what to expect from witness testimony. Finally, counsel must be able to apply the facts to the law, and formulate persuasive arguments to make at the hearing. For further information, see "Chairperson Guideline 7: Concerning Preparation and Conduct of a Hearing in the Refugee Protection Division."[16]

Hearings are usually held in private, and are conducted in an informal and non-adversarial manner. In a limited number of cases, the minister, represented by counsel, may intervene to argue against the claim—arguing, for example, that the claimant should be excluded from protection or that there are issues of integrity, that the claimant may be inadmissible on the most serious grounds, or that the claimant ought to have been found ineligible to make a claim. The hearing may be conducted publicly in rare cases where the media takes an interest, but only after an application for the hearing to be held in public has been brought and approved.

Generally, the different offices of the IRB may employ their own scheduling initiatives in managing their claim loads. Typically, the RPD attempts to hold hearings as follows:

1. *Fast-track hearings.* Fast-track hearings are claims scheduled as short duration hearings because, based on the information in the BOC Form, they are straightforward and appear to be either manifestly founded or manifestly unfounded.

2. *Regular hearings.* Claims scheduled as regular, full hearings usually involve more than two issues and require about a half day of hearing time.

3. *Complex hearings.* Complex hearings are held for claims that have multiple issues, and which may include issues about the claimant's identity, credibility, or other serious matters where the minister will be a party to the proceeding because he would intervene in the claim. When the minister intervenes, the hearing becomes adversarial and generally requires more hearing time. These cases may be scheduled for a half day or longer.

Ministerial Intervention

The minister may choose to intervene at the refugee protection hearing rather than suspend it. When the minister intervenes, he is represented by "minister's counsel"—a public servant from the CBSA. The refugee hearing becomes adversarial because the minister's counsel will argue against the claim in the following areas:

---

16 Guideline 7, one of the Chairperson's Guidelines that provide guidance for decision-makers in adjudicating cases, changes the order of questioning by having the RPD leading the inquiry at the refugee hearing. This guideline is available on the IRB website at <http://www.irb-cisr.gc.ca/Eng/BoaCom/references/pol/GuiDir/Pages/GuideDir07.aspx>.

- credibility (issues about the honesty and accuracy of the claimant's statements and/or authenticity of documents);

- exclusion under section 98 of the IRPA (for example, to exclude a refugee claimant because she already has protection according to article 1E of the Refugee Convention or article F of the Convention, which excludes those who have been in the role of persecutor from later being granted protection);[17]

- inadmissibility (on grounds of security, violating human or international rights, serious criminality, or organized criminality, or on the ground that there is an outstanding charge against the refugee claimant); or

- ineligibility (when the minister receives information after the claim has been referred and now wishes to argue that the claimant is ineligible according to the criteria provided in section 101 of the IRPA, that there is misrepresentation according to section 104(1)(c), or that the claim is not a first claim, as provided in section 104(1)(d)).

Note that refugee hearings are normally non-adversarial. However, cases involving credibility issues or the exclusion clause of the Convention refugee definition raise serious concerns that are better suited to a ministerial intervention, in which an adversarial process can be used to argue against the claimant's inclusion under the Convention.

It is important that the RPD provide the claimant with a copy of the minister's notice of intervention and any accompanying information that was provided to the tribunal. Should the minister decide to intervene in a case, either as a result of the RPD's notice or acting on the minister's own information, the RPD Rules require the minister to give the RPD notice of the minister's intention to intervene in a claim. The notice sets out how the minister will intervene, the minister's counsel contact information, and proof of notifying the refugee claimant. The notice must be given to the RPD, generally no later than 20 days before the hearing. The minister must also serve the refugee claimant with a written copy of the notice of the minister's intention to intervene.

Presenting the Refugee Claim

Consider Mr. M's experience when he appears for his hearing and interacts with his counsel, his interpreter, and the RPD member:

> Mr. M received a notice to appear for a hearing. On the day of his hearing, Mr. M arrives half an hour early to meet his counsel and go over last-minute details. His counsel warned him not to be late because if the member is kept waiting for more

---

17   Exclusions are set out in sections E and F of article 1 of the UN *Convention Relating to the Status of Refugees* (located in the Schedule to the IRPA), and essentially bar a refugee claimant from refugee protection if the claimant engaged in alleged war crimes, crimes against humanity, serious non-political crimes, or acts contrary to the United Nations principles. (Exclusion is more fully discussed in Chapter 11.)

than 15 minutes, she might conclude that Mr. M has abandoned his claim. Because he is early, this also gives him time to meet with the interpreter for his hearing; she asks him some questions to establish that they can understand each other. Mr. M is wearing a suit that he bought at a second-hand store for this day and he is very nervous. It has been so hard living in this new country, he has had difficulty making new friends, and he misses his family. He reminds himself that this is his only chance to convince the decision-maker that he cannot return home, and that he needs to get his family out of that country. There is a television screen in the waiting area indicating the hearing room in which his claim will be heard and the start time.

When it is time to begin the hearing, Mr. M's counsel leads him down a hall and they stop at a hearing room. He recognizes the Canadian flag at the front of the room, behind an oversized desk: this is where the member sits. There are three long tables, in a horseshoe formation around the member's desk. There is a microphone on each side of the desk and one at the back of the room facing the desk. There are some chairs along the room's perimeter. Mr. M is seated next to the interpreter, facing the member. His counsel takes a seat to the side at one of the tables.

The RPD member enters from a door at the front of the room a few minutes later, turns on the recording device, and introduces herself. From this point on, everything said in the room is translated into Mr. M's language so that he can understand, and everything he says is translated by the interpreter into English. Mr. M is given the choice of taking an oath or making a solemn affirmation at the beginning of the hearing. He hesitates, wondering what would please the member the most, and then decides he needs all the help of greater powers, so he chooses to swear on his holy book. The next part is confusing; he is feeling nauseous but tries to smile and nods when the interpreter asks whether he understands. The interpreter is translating something about "the order of the proceeding" and who will start the questioning first.

Changing the Hearing Date

Under the new refugee determination process, the timelines for a first hearing are set out in the IRPR. Refugee advocates have signalled to the minister that the time frames are not sufficient to allow counsel to fully prepare a case and to properly represent a refugee claimant. However, counsel must work within the time frames. Generally, postponements for a change of date and time of a proceeding will not be granted, and there are strict rules for allowing such an application. The application must follow the general application procedures of the RPD Rules, without delay, and be filed no later than three days before the hearing. If this cannot be done in writing, counsel must appear on the scheduled date and make an oral application.

An application to change the date must provide alternate dates no later than ten days from the date fixed, and provide reasons for the request. Rule 54 states that a postponement will only be allowed in exceptional circumstances. Only a few factors may be considered by the RPD when deciding to allow an application to change the date or time of a proceeding, including the following:

- whether the claimant had counsel at the time the date was fixed by an officer;

- whether the claimant had retained counsel within five working days after the day the date was fixed by an officer;

- whether counsel is not available on the date fixed for the hearing; and

- whether the date or time change has been requested for medical reasons (a medical certificate must be provided if the claimant makes the application for medical reasons).

Persons in Attendance

There are a number of people who must be present at a hearing, such as the claimant and the RPD member. Other persons who are likely to be present include the claimant's counsel and an interpreter, as well as witnesses, a designated representative, and the minister's counsel. Occasionally, a representative of the UNHCR or other observers may also be present.

RPD MEMBER

The RPD member would have reviewed Mr. M's claim file within a few days of his claim having been referred. The panel of the RPD comprises a single decision-maker who has the authority to hear a refugee claim. The authority of the member has been extended to include the specific authority to question witnesses and the refugee claimant (IRPA, s 170). At the hearing, the member is therefore actively involved in the RPD's inquiry process and has the authority to tell the hearing participants how to present their cases.

Case law has established that the RPD has control of its own procedures.[18] The division decides and gives directions regarding how a hearing is to proceed. A member is a specialist in refugee law and is well informed about human rights abuses and other conditions and events in the country presented. Therefore, the member may inquire into anything considered relevant to establishing whether a claim is well founded. The member will study the case file prior to a proceeding, to become familiar with the issues that require resolution.

Members are not bound by the usual rules of evidence; however, they are required only to admit evidence that is determined to be "credible and trustworthy," and they may take notice of any facts that may be judicially noticed, any other generally recognized facts, and any information or opinion that is within their specialized knowledge.

Members must assess the credibility of the claimant's testimony and the veracity of his documentary evidence. The nature of the inquisitorial process permits the member to question the claimant and witnesses directly, and in as much detail as is necessary to make a determination with regard to the allegations. Members write reasons if they render a negative determination.

---

18 See *Rezaei v Canada (Minister of Citizenship and Immigration)*, 2002 FCT 1259, [2003] 3 FC 421, which refers to the powers of administrative tribunals according to *Prassad v Canada (Minister of Employment and Immigration)*, [1989] 1 SCR 560.

CLAIMANT

The claimant must be personally in attendance at the hearing.

Refugee Claimants' Rights and Responsibilities

When working with refugee clients, it is important that counsel review with them their rights and responsibilities. Clients must understand that they have the following rights:

- the right to counsel;
- the right to an interpreter;
- the right to present evidence and call witnesses; and
- the right to be present at their own case before an impartial and independent decision-maker.

Clients must also understand that they have the following responsibilities:

- the responsibility to provide credible and trustworthy information and testimony; and
- the responsibility to meet the burden of proof—that suffering persecution upon return to one's own country is probable, not merely possible.

CLAIMANT'S COUNSEL

Counsel's role is essentially to protect the claimant's interests and right to a fair hearing. Counsel has a duty to explain the process, provide advice, and present the case in an efficient manner, within the limits set by the RPD.

The refugee claimant may choose to self-represent, or to be represented either by an unpaid trusted adviser, such as a family member or clergy, or by a paid consultant or lawyer. As of 2011, the IRPR[19] requires that non-lawyers who provide immigration advice be members in good standing of the ICCRC (or "the Council") as regulated Canadian immigration consultants; members in good standing of a provincial or territorial law society, including licensed paralegals who are regulated by a provincial law society; or members of the Chambre des notaires du Québec. Any counsel who represents the claimant must provide her contact information, including her membership identification number from the relevant professional regulatory body, to the RPD and the minister in writing.

---

19 Section 91.5 of the IRPA gives authority to make regulations to designate a body; section 13.2 of the IRPR sets out the requirements that the designated body must follow. The actual designation was given by Ministerial Guideline OB 317 of June 30, 2011.

INTERPRETER

Only accredited interpreters are used for refugee hearings. At the beginning of the proceeding, the interpreter confirms that she used a standardized script to ensure that she and the refugee claimant understand each other. The interpreter may not guide, provide advice, or offer an opinion to the claimant.

WITNESSES

If counsel wishes to call a witness other than the claimant, she must comply with the RPD Rules. For example, counsel must provide to the RPD—and to the other party, if the minister is intervening—the witness's contact information, counsel's reasons for calling the witness, and an estimate of the amount of time needed for the witness's testimony at the hearing in writing within the time limits set out in rule 44 (no later than ten days before the hearing).

To reduce the risk of the witness failing to appear, it is prudent for the claimant's counsel to request the RPD to issue a summons to order a witness to testify. Under rule 45, the claimant must provide the summons to the summoned witness by hand and notify the RPD of this fact in writing. Witness fees and travel expenses are the responsibility of the claimant. Should a summoned witness fail to appear, the RPD Rules set out the process for making a request to the RPD to issue a warrant for that person's arrest.

DESIGNATED REPRESENTATIVE

There are situations in which a refugee claimant is not capable of making decisions, such as in the case of an unaccompanied minor or a person deemed mentally incompetent or unable to understand the proceedings. In these instances, the division appoints a person to act and make decisions on behalf of the claimant (IRPA, s 167(2); RPD Rules, r 20). The **designated representative** may be a relative or a professional, such as a lawyer or social worker. Counsel is permitted to take on the role of designated representative.

designated representative
a person chosen by the RPD to act and make decisions on behalf of a refugee claimant who is incapable of doing so

MINISTER'S COUNSEL

Although most refugee hearings proceed without intervention from the minister, the RPD is required to notify the minister when it has information (found in the BOC Form, for example) that might be of interest to the minister for the purpose of intervening in a case, such as the claimant's military service, which might indicate he was part of a regime that carried out human rights abuses. The RPD Rules require the RPD to give written notice to the minister when the RPD has this kind of information, and to provide the minister with the related information. When there is a minister's intervention, the hearing becomes adversarial and the minister is a party to the proceeding.

REPRESENTATIVE OF THE UNHCR

A representative of the UNHCR is entitled to observe any refugee claimant's proceeding, according to section 166(e) of the IRPA.

Evidence

Returning to our scenario, during the hearing, Mr. M must answer questions about the information he provided on the BOC Form and about any documents he provided to the RPD. He also has the opportunity to tell the member about his experiences and his fears with regard to returning to his homeland. He will explain why he is making a claim for refugee protection and provide details about his persecution or cruel treatment along with the facts that support his allegations. He will be expected to describe the actions he took to seek protection in his country of nationality, including steps to move to another part of his country.

The RPD is not bound by any legal or technical rules of evidence, but must base its decision on evidence that is considered credible or trustworthy in the circumstances, provided that the evidence is presented in the proceedings. The RPD has exclusive jurisdiction to hear and determine all questions of law and fact, including questions of jurisdiction, and must also deal with all proceedings that are before it as informally and quickly as the circumstances and requirements of fairness and natural justice permit, in accordance with section 162 of the IRPA.

judicial notice
a rule of evidence that allows a decision-maker to accept certain commonly known, indisputable, and uncontentious facts without requiring that they be proven with evidence

The RPD may take **judicial notice** of any generally recognized facts, or information or opinion within its specialized knowledge, provided that it gives notice to the refugee claimant that it is doing so, according to section 170 of the IRPA. This means that it is unnecessary to bring evidence to prove a fact that is generally known. For example, it would not be necessary to prove that student protesters in Beijing's Tiananmen Square were massacred in June 1989, because this event is now generally known.

Oral Representations

oral representation
an argument that is made orally, such as at the end of a refugee hearing

After all questioning of Mr. M and any other witnesses is complete, and the member is satisfied that all the evidence has been heard, counsel has the opportunity to deliver **oral representations**—that is, make a final statement. Representations are to be relevant, focused, and concise so that they help the member to decide the claim efficiently and make it possible for the member to give an oral decision and reasons at the end of the hearing.[20]

Deciding the Claim and Reasons

The RPD member does not decide whether Mr. M would make a good permanent resident or Canadian citizen, or whether he can remain in or must leave Canada. Rather, the member decides only whether Mr. M has established his claim under one of the following grounds:

---

20 Immigration and Refugee Board, "Chairperson Guideline 7: Concerning Preparation and Conduct of a Hearing in the Refugee Protection Division" (15 December 2006, amended 15 December 2012) s 5.9, online: <http://www.irb-cisr.gc.ca/Eng/BoaCom/references/pol/GuiDir/Pages/GuideDir07.aspx#RepC5>.

- persecution under a Convention refugee ground,
- danger of torture, or
- risk to life or risk of cruel and unusual treatment or punishment.

There are five possible outcomes, as follows:

1. the claim is allowed because the claimant is found to be a Convention refugee;
2. the claim is allowed because the claimant is found to be a person in need of protection;
3. the claim is rejected because the claimant is neither a Convention refugee nor a person in need of protection;
4. the claim is rejected because the claimant is neither a Convention refugee nor a person in need of protection, and there is no credible basis; or
5. the claim is rejected because the claimant is neither a Convention refugee nor a person in need of protection, and the claim is manifestly unfounded.

Wherever practicable, the RPD member renders the decision and reasons orally at the end of the hearing, which means that the majority of refugee claimants will know the outcome of their claim at the end of the hearing. A copy of the written reasons and the **notice of decision** will generally follow by mail.

The division is required by the RPD Rules to issue a written decision, called a notice of decision, to the claimant and to the minister, whether or not the minister intervened.

In the case of a rejected claim, written reasons for the decision must accompany the notice of decision. Furthermore, section 107(2) of the IRPA stipulates that if the claim is rejected because there was no credible or trustworthy evidence, or if the claim is a manifestly unfounded claim (MUC) (IRPA, s 107.1), the member must include this finding in the reasons for rejecting the claim. The purpose of the "no credible basis" and the "manifestly unfounded claim" labels is to identify these cases to immigration officials (because the conditional removal order must be executed). This is an immigration policy that is intended to discourage frivolous and non-genuine claimants by restricting their access to post-determination processes such as appeals, thereby providing for their speedier removal.

If the claim is successful, the claimant or the minister may request written reasons, as long as the request is in writing and is made within ten days of notification of the decision, in accordance with the RPD Rules and section 169 of the IRPA.

notice of decision
a written decision by the decision-maker, issued to those involved in the case

No Credible Basis

A refugee claim that is rejected and found to have *no credible basis* is a claim where the member determined there was no credible or trustworthy evidence on which the claim could have been accepted (IRPA, s 107(2)). Such a finding is stated in the member's reasons for a negative determination decision. In accordance with the IRPR, the failed refugee claimant does not have the right to appeal the decision to the RAD and may be subject to other restrictions on any future applications to remain in Canada.

Manifestly Unfounded Claim

The MUC label is for refugee claims that were rejected by the RPD because the member was of the opinion that the claimant was clearly fraudulent and states so in his reasons for the negative determination decision (IRPA, s 107.1). According to the IRPR, an MUC finding means that the failed refugee claimant does not have the right to appeal the decision to the RAD and is subject to other restrictions on any future applications to remain in Canada.

Post-Determination Stage

Claim Accepted

If Mr. M's claim is allowed, the conditional removal order issued by the CBSA officer during the front-end process does not take effect. As a successful claimant, Mr. M's next step, whether as a Convention refugee or as a person in need of protection, is to apply for permanent resident status for himself and for his spouse and dependent children, who are abroad.

Application information will normally accompany the notice of decision from the IRB. In the application for permanent residence, the protected applicant may include family members who in Canada or abroad. There is no time frame to apply for permanent residence stipulated in the regulations. In our scenario, application for Mr. M is processed in Canada at the Case Processing Centre in Vegreville, Alberta by an immigration officer and for his family by a visa office. Although there are processing fees for the application process, the right of permanent residence fee is waived for protected persons. In the interim, CIC issues a "protected person status document" to confirm the successful refugee claimant's status in Canada.

Mr. M may have to undergo security screening and medical examinations again if the initial security checks and medical examinations have expired.

Claim Accepted

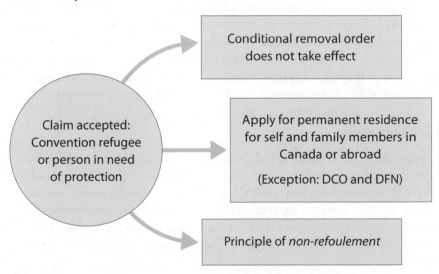

- Claim accepted: Convention refugee or person in need of protection
  - Conditional removal order does not take effect
  - Apply for permanent residence for self and family members in Canada or abroad (Exception: DCO and DFN)
  - Principle of *non-refoulement*

Designated Foreign National

If Mr. M had arrived as part of a group that was designated as an irregular arrival—for example, on a boat whose passage was arranged by human smugglers—then he would not be able to apply for permanent residence for five years after receipt of his determination by the RPD. Instead, Mr. M would be allowed to remain in Canada on a temporary resident permit, and the consequence of this is that he would not have any right to sponsor his family members. Mr. M's family would therefore not be able to join him in Canada as permanent residents during that time.

Not Eligible for Permanent Residence

Under the IRPA, a successful refugee claimant is not eligible to apply for permanent residence in any of the following examples:

- *Protection has ceased.* There is no further need to protect the refugee claimant—for example, as a result of a newly elected government in the claimant's country of origin (s 108(2)).
- *Protection has been vacated.* For example, an application by the minister is allowed by the RPD because the original decision for protection was obtained as a result of directly or indirectly misrepresenting or withholding material facts relating to a relevant matter. The RPD will **vacate** its original decision and the refugee's claim is nullified.

vacate
to nullify or to void

For each of the above situations, the minister must apply to the RPD to request a hearing into the matter to argue cessation or vacation.

CESSATION

The cessation clause of the refugee definition is embedded in the IRPA at section 108. As noted in Chapter 11, the provision exists so that the RPD may terminate refugee status when protection is no longer needed (if the refugee has signalled he no longer fears persecution by renewing his passport and/or voluntarily returning to the country where he originally feared persecution for extended visits; if he obtained citizenship from a country other than his country of nationality; or if the country conditions that gave rise to his fear of persecution have changed). The process of applying for cessation requires the minister to file an application for cessation in accordance with the RPD Rules. Although the provision has existed in Canadian immigration law for a long time, it was rarely used by the minister until recently.

Claim Rejected

If Mr. M's claim is rejected, the removal order will come into effect. However, before removal takes place, the unsuccessful refugee claimant may have the following options:

- voluntary departure;
- appeal of the RPD determination to the RAD;

- application for leave for judicial review by the Federal Court, during which the removal order may be stayed; or
- application to CIC for a PRRA within 15 days from the date of the notice of decision (unless there was a "no credible basis" or "MUC" stipulation).

Instructions for applying for leave for judicial review, and for a PRRA, are sent to the rejected claimant by the RPD with the notice of decision.

Claim Rejected

Claim rejected: Neither a Convention refugee nor a person in need of protection

Conditional removal order may take effect

15 days to apply to the RAD or for judicial review

Exception: DCO, DFN, no credible basis, MUC claims

15 days to apply for a PRRA

36-month wait for DCO claimants

Voluntary departure

Appeal to the Refugee Appeal Division

There is limited access to the RAD. Only claimants who made claims after December 15, 2012, under the new refugee determination system may appeal their decision. Furthermore, an appeal to the RAD restricts access for a number of unsuccessful claimants if they were rejected and are designated as DFN claims or were found to have MUC or no credible basis claims (as discussed in Chapter 15).

There are advantages to appealing to the RAD (for those claimants who are permitted to do so) over "appealing" to the Federal Court. First, an application to the Federal Court is for a judicial review, and a person must first apply for leave (ask permission). A judicial review focuses on the legality of the RPD's process and decision-making, not the merits of the case. Furthermore, new evidence is not permitted, and remedies are generally limited to referring the matter back for redetermination. See Chapter 15 for a broader discussion of the RAD and the refugee appeal process.

Judicial Review by the Federal Court

Some failed refugee claimants who have no right to appeal to the RAD may apply for a judicial review by the Federal Court. An applicant for judicial review must first seek leave of the Federal Court, requesting the court to hear the case. This must occur within 15 days of either the notice of the decision or the issuance of written reasons by the RPD, whichever is later. The application requirements (such as the use of Form IR-1) and the procedures for applying for leave are set out in the *Federal Courts Citizenship, Immigration and Refugee Protection Rules*. The claimant's application for leave must also be served on the minister, who may decide to oppose it.

In our example, the effect of Mr. M's application is that there will be a stay of the conditional removal order that was issued against him, allowing him to remain in Canada pending the decision on his application for leave (in accordance with the IRPR). However, if Mr. M's claim was rejected with a finding of "no credible basis" or if it was a "manifestly unfounded claim," then he would not be entitled to a stay of removal.

If the Federal Court grants leave, the stay of the removal will be extended to allow Mr. M to remain in Canada until the judicial review is decided.

A judicial review is not an appeal on the merits of a claim or a rehearing of the claim. There are six grounds, set out in section 18.1(4) of the *Federal Courts Act*, on which a judge may grant a judicial review, such as if there was an error of law or of fact in the decision of the RPD, or if there was a failure to observe a principle of natural justice. If an application for judicial review is allowed, the Federal Court will normally set aside the decision of the RPD and send the case back to the IRB to be reconsidered.

Pre-Removal Risk Assessment

The PRRA program is another example of Canada's commitment to the principle of *non-refoulement*. However, it is important to remember that the PRRA is not an appeal or a review of a negative decision by the RPD. The PRRA is a program intended for people (not just failed refugee claimants) who are about to be removed from Canada and who are desperate to stay because one of the following circumstances exists:

- a well-founded fear of persecution, according to the Convention refugee definition; or
- a risk of torture, risk to life, or risk of cruel and unusual treatment or punishment, according to the Convention Against Torture.

The PRRA program is managed by CIC, but was expected to be transferred to the RPD two years after all other changes to the refugee determination system came into force on December 15, 2012. However, at the time of writing, CIC continues to process PRRA applications.

Generally, a successful PRRA applicant will be granted refugee protection, will not be removed, and may apply for permanent residence. However, a negative decision on the application means that removal arrangements will proceed, and the applicant must leave Canada.

WHO MAY APPLY

The PRRA is for people who are **removal ready**, meaning that they are subject to a removal order that is in force or that a security certificate has been issued against them

removal ready
refers to people who are subject to a removal order that is in force or to a security certificate that has been issued against them

(IRPA, s 112(1)), and they are in possession of a valid passport or travel document. There are several circumstances under which an applicant may generally not apply for a PRRA, pursuant to section 112(2) of the IRPA:

- the person is subject to extradition under section 15 of the *Extradition Act*;
- the person's claim for refugee protection was determined ineligible because she came directly or indirectly from a designated country, other than a country of her nationality or former habitual residence;
- less than 12 months—or, in the case of a person from a DCO, less than 36 months—have passed since the person's refugee claim in Canada was rejected, withdrawn, or abandoned by the RPD or the RAD;[21] or
- the claim was rejected because it was vacated or falls under the exclusion provisions (that is, was rejected on the basis of section E or F of article 1 of the Refugee Convention).

In assessing the application, the PRRA officer must take into account whether the applicant is a danger to the public in Canada. Section 112(3) stipulates that protection may not be granted to a PRRA applicant if the applicant

- is determined to be inadmissible on grounds of security, the violation of human or international rights, or organized criminality;
- is determined to be inadmissible on grounds of serious criminality with respect to a conviction in Canada punishable by a term of imprisonment of at least ten years or with respect to a conviction outside Canada for an offence that, if committed in Canada, would constitute an offence under an Act of Parliament punishable by a maximum term of imprisonment of at least ten years;
- made a claim for refugee protection that was rejected on the basis of section F of article 1 of the Refugee Convention (individuals who have been in the role of persecutor are excluded from later being granted protection); or
- is named in a **security certificate** referred to in section 77(1) of the IRPA.[22]

security certificate
a document providing for a removal hearing in the absence of the person named, where information must be protected for reasons of public safety

Applicants for a PRRA who fall under the section 112(3) restrictions are still entitled to have their applications considered for a risk assessment on the grounds of the Convention Against Torture, but they will not be assessed against the Refugee Convention. They will not be granted refugee status in keeping with the principle of the definition's exclusion clauses, and they will not be able to apply for permanent residence.

---

21 In the case of a failed DCO refugee claimant, the person cannot apply for 36 months; however, the minister has the discretion to exempt claimants from that bar if there is a sudden change in country conditions that could lead to a personal risk if the clamant were returned to his country of origin. A DCO claimant whose claim was rejected on the basis of an exclusion—section E or F of article 1 of the Refugee Convention—is not eligible to apply.

22 A security certificate is issued in exceptional circumstances where a person is deemed inadmissible for reasons of national security, for violating human or international rights, or for involvement in organized or serious crimes.

EVIDENCE CONSIDERED

A person who has been permitted to apply for a PRRA is allowed to remain in Canada until such time as the circumstances change—for example, there is a change in country conditions (IRPA, s 114(1)(b)). Such changes would prompt the minister to re-examine the grounds on which the application was allowed, and may lead to a cancellation of a stay and the execution of a removal order. Until this happens, the applicant is allowed to remain in Canada in a kind of legal limbo: she cannot apply to sponsor family members; if she leaves Canada, she most likely will not be able to return; and although she is allowed to work, her work permit is issued for a short period of time.

The PRRA is an administrative process conducted by officers with specialized knowledge, called PRRA officers. Generally, applications are decided without a hearing, although there are exceptions. PRRA officers process applications through a paper review of the application, consider documentary evidence and written submissions from the applicant and the minister, and assess whether there are any new facts or evidence that would help them decide whether there is a risk in removing and returning a person subject to a removal order.

Applicants Under Removal Order

Applicants under a removal order may present only evidence that arose after the rejection of their claim or evidence that the applicant could not reasonably have been expected in the circumstances to have presented at the time of the rejection—for example, information that the applicant was not aware of at the time of his claim. This evidence could relate to the individual or it could be evidence of a deterioration or change in the country conditions of the person's country of origin. PRRA officers have the statutory authority to decide whether an oral hearing is warranted in exceptional cases. In rendering their decisions, PRRA officers assess applications against the requirements of the Refugee Convention (for the granting of refugee status) or assess whether there is a risk of torture under the Convention Against Torture (for the granting of protection as "a person in need of protection").

Failed Refugee Claimants

Eligible applicants whose refugee claims were rejected may give new evidence only—that is, evidence that could not reasonably or possibly have been provided at the refugee hearing. An example is a change in the applicant's country conditions that puts the applicant at risk, such as a new political party coming to power, the passage of a new law that seriously violates the applicant's human rights, or the outbreak of a civil war. Evidence may also include documentation that was not available at the hearing.

TIMELINES

A person who has an enforceable removal order issued against him (that is, a person found ineligible by the CBSA/CIC to make a refugee claim at the front-end stage, or a foreign national who is inadmissible) will be notified in an "advanced information notice" that he has 15 days to decide to apply for a PRRA; in the interim, the removal order is suspended. In the case of a failed refugee claimant, the clock starts ticking on the date of the notice of decision of a negative determination by the RPD; the failed refugee claimant is notified by the RPD whether he is entitled to this option at the time of receiving the notice of decision.

Upon receipt of either the "advanced information notice" or the "notice of decision," the applicant has 15 days to complete the PRRA application form and return it to CIC. Once the application is submitted, the claimant cannot be removed until the PRRA officer makes a decision on the application. There is also a 15-day extension available for submitting evidence to support the application. Failure to submit the PRRA application by the 15-day deadline can result in the removal of the PRRA applicant.

DECISION

If the PRRA application is accepted, the applicant is usually granted status as a protected person (IRPA, s 114(1)(a)). Such applicants may then apply for permanent residence.

PRRA applicants who are successful in their request not to be removed but who were found to be ineligible for refugee determination (because of inadmissibility on grounds of security, violating human or international rights, or serious or organized criminality, or because they are named in a security certificate further to section 77(1) of the IRPA) may not apply for permanent residence. Instead, the successful outcome of the PRRA application has the effect of a stay of the execution of the removal order, and the applicant is not removed from Canada. The person is allowed to remain in Canada under a temporary resident permit until such time as the circumstances change—for example, there is a change in country conditions. Such changes would trigger the minister's re-examination of the grounds on which the applicant was allowed to stay in Canada, and may lead to a cancellation of a stay of the removal order and its subsequent execution.

PRRA applicants who are rejected must generally be removed from Canada. There is, however, the possibility of applying to CIC to remain in Canada on humanitarian and compassionate grounds (see Chapter 9).

APPENDIX A

Designated Countries of Origin

December 15, 2012	February 15, 2013	May 31, 2013	October 2014
Austria	Mexico	Chile	Andorra
Belgium	Israel (excluding Gaza and the West Bank)	South Korea	Liechtenstein
Croatia	Japan		Monaco
Cyprus	Norway		Romania
Czech Republic	Iceland		San Marino
Denmark	New Zealand		
Estonia	Australia		
Finland	Switzerland		
France			
Germany			
Greece			
Hungary			
Ireland			
Italy			
Latvia			
Lithuania			
Luxembourg			
Malta			
Netherlands			
Poland			
Portugal			
Slovak Republic			
Slovenia			
Spain			
Sweden			
United Kingdom			
United States of America			

APPENDIX B

Immigration and Refugee Board Regional Offices

The following are the business offices, also known as the "registries," for the purpose of contacting the Immigration and Refugee Board. All communication (oral or written) with the board's divisions must be made through a registry.

Eastern and Central Regions

Eastern Region: Montreal	Central Region: Toronto
Registrar	Registrar
Immigration and Refugee Board of Canada	Immigration and Refugee Board of Canada
Guy Favreau Complex	74 Victoria Street, Suite 400
200 René-Lévesque Boulevard West	Toronto, ON M5C 3C7
East Tower, Room 102	Tel.: (416) 954-1000
Montreal, QC H2Z 1X4	Fax: (416) 954-1165
Tel.: (514) 283-7733	
Fax: (514) 283-0164	

Western Region

Western Region: Vancouver	Western Region: Calgary
Registrar	225 Manning Rd NE, 2nd Floor
Immigration and Refugee Board of Canada	Calgary, AB T2E 2P5
Library Square	Telephone: (403) 292-6620 or 1-855-6764
300 West Georgia Street, Suite 1600	Fax: (403) 292-6131
Vancouver, BC V6B 6C9	
Tel.: (604) 666-5946	
Fax: (604) 666-3043	

APPENDIX C

Legacy Claims

All claims made prior to December 15, 2012 are considered legacy cases and continue to be processed under the former rules; however, because legacy cases are not subject to the regulatory time limits of the new system, the RPD continues to hear and decide as many legacy claims as possible using its existing resources. The following is a general overview of the process.

Previously, claimants who were found eligible completed a Personal Information Form (PIF), which was a much longer form than the Basis of Claim Form. All claimants were given 28 days to complete and submit the original form along with two copies to the RPD. The PIF was used together with the port-of-entry notes or the officer's notes.

Role of the Refugee Protection Officer

The role of the refugee protection officer (RPO) was eliminated by legislative amendments to the IRPA as of December 2012. However, it is a role that is worth noting for its uniqueness within a tribunal system. The role was created at the inception of the IRB in 1989, when officers (career public servants known under such titles as refugee hearing officers, refugee protection officers, or tribunal officers) performed various critical functions within the non-adversarial refugee determination system. The RPO worked alongside members at the pre-hearing stage to identify issues in a refugee claim, to make recommendations for claim-specific research, and to prepare the claim with the requisite research (country and claim-specific) in time for the hearing. The officer conducted interviews and made recommendations for the positive determination in a number of claims—this was not only expeditious for the claimant, but also an efficient case-management strategy to deal with manifestly founded claims. Refugee hearings are inquisitorial in nature, so the officer played a unique "neutral" role in the hearing room by ensuring that all evidence was presented and evaluated by the member. The officer could also question a claimant and other witnesses "vigorously," which was especially important when there were issues of credibility. Officers were equally talented in focusing on relevant issues when the minister intervened and the hearing became adversarial. The officer's role was built into the RPD Rules and included a provision to "do any other thing that is necessary to ensure a full and proper examination of a claim or other matter" (former RPD Rules, r 16(g)).

Hearing Process

Claims under the former refugee determination system were screened and streamed into different hearing streams; hearing dates were fixed by an IRB official (instead of by CIC or the CBSA). The RPD had flexibility to schedule cases into an expedited process for an interview with the RPO, or a fast-track, regular, or complex hearing process. Claims were heard and decided by members who were appointed by the governor in council (GiC), not public servants. Legacy claims might be heard and decided either by a GiC-appointed RPD member whose mandate had not expired and who was authorized by the chairperson to hear legacy claims, or by a public servant RPD member.

The expedited process was a shorter process used to quickly decide *manifestly founded* claims. The claimant was interviewed by the RPO when the claimant's identity was established; there were no issues of credibility arising from the PIF or POE notes; there were no minister's interventions; and the evidence for the case could be supported by known occurrences of human rights violations in the reference country. No member was present for the interview; instead the member based the decision on the officer's interview notes and recommendations. In this way, the RPD was able to finalize many cases each day and expend fewer resources. With the final positive determination, claimants had their claims decided relatively early compared with those who were scheduled into the hearing process. If the officer or the member decided that the claim could not be determined positively, then a hearing was scheduled, and the elements of natural justice were preserved.

KEY TERMS

accredited interpreter, 405

Basis of Claim (BOC) Form, 398

conditional removal order, 395

corroborative documents, 411

country information, 412

designated foreign national (DFN), 390

designated irregular arrival, 390

designated representative, 419

disclosure, 413

identity documents, 411

judicial notice, 420

notice of decision, 421

oral representation, 420

removal ready, 425

safe third country, 391

security certificate, 426

vacate, 423

REVIEW QUESTIONS

1. What is a spontaneous arrival?

2. List the government organizations that are involved in the refugee protection claim process in Canada.

3. Under what circumstances is a refugee claim ineligible to be referred to the RPD?

4. Name the key document that is relevant to a refugee claim. Outline the requirements for submitting this document for review by the RPD.

5. As counsel, you should be able to explain the refugee determination process in full and prepare your client for a refugee hearing. Answer the following questions for your client:

    a. Prior to a hearing, what information, forms, and documents must be provided to the RPD, and according to what timelines?

    b. What is the nature of the proceedings?

    c. What are a refugee claimant's rights and responsibilities at a proceeding before the RPD?

    d. Who is present at a typical regular refugee hearing in which the minister is not intervening? What are the roles of each person present?

    e. What are all of the possible determinations that an RPD member can make?

6. Explain the residency options available to the refugee claimant if his claim is accepted.

7. Explain the options available to the refugee claimant if his claim is rejected.

DISCUSSION QUESTION

Refugee claimants are duty-bound to answer all questions truthfully and produce all documents and information as requested.

Imagine someone who has fled for her safety, who is fearful of government officials, and who cannot understand or speak either of our official languages. What factors might affect such a person's trust in the immigration officer in an interview and her willingness to answer all questions truthfully? Discuss.

EXERCISES

1. Find out what resources exist in your community to assist newcomer immigrants and refugees. Together with your classmates, compile a list of agencies and the services that they provide.

2. The refugee claimant will be nervous on the day of the interview or hearing. Counsel can make the event more comfortable by managing the claimant's expectations. With a partner, assume the roles of counsel and client. As counsel, describe and explain to your client the following:

    • the physical layout of a hearing or interview room, and the fact that counsel may not be sitting next to the claimant;

    • the fact that the proceedings are private (generally closed to the public to protect the confidentiality of the claimant);

    • the fact that the proceedings will be recorded;

    • the fact that the proceedings will be held in English or French, although an interpreter will be provided;

- the type of proceeding—will it be an interview (expedited), a pre-hearing conference, or a hearing?—as well as what to expect during the proceeding;

- who will be present and what their roles are;

- the fact that the proceedings will be non-adversarial unless the minister's representative is intervening; and

- the order of questioning.

PART VI

Enforcement

CHAPTER 14 Immigration Hearings and Detentions

Immigration Hearings and Detentions

14

LEARNING OUTCOMES

After reading this chapter, you should be able to:

- Describe general control and enforcement activities.

- Describe the grounds for detaining a foreign national or permanent resident under the *Immigration and Refugee Protection Act*.

- Explain the process for initiating an immigration hearing before the Immigration Division.

- Summarize the main activities of the Immigration Division.

- Identify important timelines for detention reviews.

- Describe the role of participants at Immigration Division proceedings.

- Distinguish among the various removal orders.

- Find your way around the *Immigration Division Rules*.

Introduction

We learned in previous chapters that a foreign national must apply for a visa before being given permission to enter Canada. Everyone who arrives at a port of entry (POE) must submit to an examination by an officer, who decides whether to admit the person, such as in the case of Canadian citizens. The officer will also decide whether to impose conditions on or deny entry to permanent and temporary foreign residents. But what happens to permanent and temporary residents if they become inadmissible after they've been admitted? This chapter will explore how officers enforce the *Immigration and Refugee Protection Act* (IRPA) and its regulations when someone becomes inadmissible after arrival, including general removal procedures. It will also provide an overview of the role of the Immigration Division (ID) of the Immigration and Refugee Board (IRB) in hearing and presiding over immigration hearings and detention reviews. The examples of successful and unsuccessful cases in this chapter are examples only, and are not intended to guarantee a particular outcome in similar situations.

Allegation of Inadmissibility Steps at a Glance

Allegation	Allegation that a foreign national or permanent resident has breached the IRPA Officer writes inadmissibility report (s 44(1))

⬇

Minister's Delegate Reviews Report	Issues removal order or referral to the ID

⬇

ID Hearing	Admissibility hearing held to determine whether minister's allegation is true

⬇

Decision	Decision to allow a person to enter, to remain, or to be removed

Enforcement Activities

Recall that the Canada Border Services Agency (CBSA) reports to the minister of public safety and is responsible for border management and enforcement activities; it is the agency that is primarily responsible for carrying out the enforcement provisions of the IRPA.

After being admitted to Canada, neither temporary nor permanent residents have any absolute right to remain in Canada. A person who violates a Canadian law, such as the *Criminal Code* or the IRPA or its regulations, may become inadmissible, triggering enforcement activities such as being reported to the minister, arrest and

Stages in Immigration Enforcement Matters

Enforcement	**Immigration Division Hearings**	**Execution of Order**
Inadmissibility Report & Referral and/or Detention of Foreign Nationals and Permanent Residents	Admissibility Hearing Detention Review	CBSA / CIC Admission or Removal Release or Detain

detention, and even removal from Canada. The general process is initiated when the minister's representative (an officer who has the delegated authority) submits a report of an allegation that a foreign national or permanent resident has violated immigration laws; this is followed by a process that may lead to removal. The process we will examine requires a referral to the tribunal for a decision about admissibility and potentially a **removal order**. Both the CBSA and the ID may detain a person under the IRPA for reasons discussed later in this chapter.

Key immigration enforcement and control activities of the CBSA include the following:[1]

- carrying out **interdiction** functions, or control activities that prevent illegal travellers and criminals from reaching Canada;
- conducting background checks and other observations before visas are issued;
- gathering information on activities such as human smuggling and illegal migration;
- gathering intelligence on activities such as the creation, use, and distribution of fraudulent documents;
- cooperating with other enforcement agencies, both domestic and international;
- performing examinations abroad and at ports of entry;
- conducting investigations and appearing at admissibility hearings;
- issuing removal and exclusion orders;
- creating and implementing measures to deal with dangerous criminals, security and safety risks, and war criminals;
- arresting and detaining foreign nationals who pose a security or safety risk;
- enforcing penalties for illegal activities; and
- removing any person who has been issued a removal order for violating the IRPA or its regulations.

This chapter examines the general enforcement activities that lead to the admissibility hearing and a detention review before the ID.

removal order
a legal document issued either after an examination or at an admissibility hearing ordering a person to leave Canada

interdiction
control activity that prevents illegal travellers from reaching Canada

---

1   This information is from the Office of the Auditor General of Canada, "Chapter 5: Citizenship and Immigration Canada—Control and Enforcement," in *2003 April Report of the Auditor General of Canada* (2003), online: <http://www.oag-bvg.gc.ca/internet/English/parl_oag_200304 _05_e_12911.html>.

Inadmissibility Reports

Section 33 of the IRPA provides that "[t]he facts that constitute inadmissibility under sections 34 to 37 include facts arising from omissions and, unless otherwise provided, include facts for which there are reasonable grounds to believe that they have occurred, are occurring or may occur." (See Chapter 3 for a discussion about the grounds of inadmissibility in sections 34 to 42 of the IRPA).

When an officer is of the opinion that a foreign national or permanent resident who is seeking entry into Canada or who is already in Canada is inadmissible, the officer writes an **inadmissibility report** (also known as a "**section 44(1) report**"). The report sets out the grounds of inadmissibility on which the person is alleged to have violated the IRPA, with a brief description of the relevant facts in narrative form. Depending on the seriousness of the ground of inadmissibility, the officer may also detain the person under the IRPA pending the admissibility hearing. The officer forwards the report to the minister's delegate, who has the authority to either issue a removal order or refer the matter to the ID.

inadmissibility report (section 44(1) report) an officer's report under section 44(1) of the IRPA that sets out the grounds of inadmissibility for which the person is alleged to have violated, including a brief description of the relevant facts in narrative form

Port of Entry

All persons (that is, Canadian citizens, registered Indians, permanent residents, permanent resident visa holders, temporary resident visa holders, and foreign nationals) seeking entry to Canada are subject to an examination at a POE (IRPA, s 18(1)) to determine whether they have a right to enter Canada. In most cases, people will be subject to a brief primary examination by a border security officer (BSO) of the CBSA. However, where the officer is not satisfied that the person should be allowed entry, the officer refers the person for a more in-depth secondary examination. The purpose of the secondary interview is to confirm the identity of the traveller, verify documents such as passports and permits, and gather information about the person's purpose for entering Canada to make an informed decision regarding admissibility.

An officer who believes that it may be contrary to the IRPA and its regulations to admit a person may take any of the following actions:

- inform the person that she is inadmissible and is allowed to leave Canada voluntarily (*Immigration and Refugee Protection Regulations* [IRPR], s 37(c))—the person will be given an Allowed to Leave Canada form (IMM 1282B);
- write the section 44(1) report and detain the person pending an admissibility hearing; or
- write the section 44(1) report and allow the person to enter temporarily to attend an admissibility hearing.

In certain situations, the minister's delegate, after reviewing the section 44(1) report, may issue the removal order.[2]

---

2   Citizenship and Immigration Canada, *ENF 4: Port of Entry Examinations* (17 June 2013) s 5, online: <http://www.cic.gc.ca/english/resources/manuals/enf/enf04-eng.pdf>.

After Admission

An officer who believes that a permanent resident or foreign national who is already in Canada has become inadmissible may prepare a report setting out the relevant facts to be reviewed by the minister, in accordance with section 44(1) of the IRPA.

Authority to Write Report

Generally, it is Citizenship and Immigration Canada (CIC) officers who have the authority to write inadmissibility reports. However, if the grounds of inadmissibility include security, violations of human or international rights, or organized criminality, the cases are managed by the CBSA.[3]

Discretion to Write Report

In some cases, writing the report is at the discretion of the officer. However, when an officer believes that a permanent resident has failed to comply with residency obligations and has lost permanent resident status as a result, the officer *must* write an inadmissibility report.

When the matter involves the more serious reasons for a finding of inadmissibility (that is, security, violations of human or international rights, serious criminality, or organized criminality), an officer will write an inadmissibility report and transmit it to the minister's delegate, who will review the report and may refer the case to the ID, which initiates the hearing and removal process.

For matters involving less serious, non-criminal matters, an officer at a POE examination considers a number of options. For example, the officer may either allow the person to withdraw her application and leave Canada immediately (IRPR, s 37(c) or s 42(1)), report the person (IRPR, s 44(1)), or authorize the person to enter Canada for the purpose of further examination or an admissibility hearing (IRPA, s 23; IRPR, ss 43, 44).

CIC's operational manual *Writing 44(1) Reports* lists several factors that officers may consider when deciding whether to write a report:[4]

- the length of time the person has been in Canada and her status;
- the grounds of inadmissibility;
- whether the person is already the subject of a removal order;
- whether the person is already the subject of a separate inadmissibility report incorporating allegations that will likely result in a removal order;
- whether the officer is satisfied that the person is, or soon will be, leaving Canada, and, if so, whether the imposition of a future requirement to obtain consent to return is warranted;

3   Citizenship and Immigration Canada, *ENF 5: Writing 44(1) Reports* (20 May 2011, updated 20 August 2013) s 4, online: <http://www.cic.gc.ca/english/resources/manuals/enf/enf05-eng.pdf>.

4   *Ibid*, s 8.

- whether there is a record of the person having previously contravened immigration legislation;
- whether the person was cooperative;
- whether a temporary resident permit was authorized;
- how long the person has been a permanent resident (for example, since childhood);
- whether the person was cooperative and forthcoming in providing information; and
- whether the person accepts responsibility and is remorseful.

Consider the following scenario:

Eunice is a 22-year-old citizen of Jamaica. Eunice applied for and obtained a temporary resident visa as a visitor so she could visit her older sister, Nadine, and Nadine's family in Toronto. Eunice had not seen Nadine since Nadine left for Canada over ten years ago. She was happy to get reacquainted with her older sister and to become acquainted with Nadine's two school-aged children and husband. Eunice was provided with her own room in Nadine's home, shown around the city, and given new clothes (so she could face the Canadian cold). Eunice adored her niece and nephew and played with them often. This caught the attention of a next-door neighbour, who asked if Eunice could watch over her children one day while she went shopping. One of the neighbour's children was knocked down while playing with Eunice's nephew and got a bump on the head. This upset the neighbour, who thought Eunice too lenient about the ordeal. She also suspected that Eunice was an "illegal," seeing as she had been living next door for almost a year now.

The neighbour—jealous about Nadine having the extra hands at home and offended by Eunice's attitude—decided to call the police and falsely accused Eunice of hitting her child. After investigating the incident, the police determined that none of the children had been abused and did not charge Eunice. However, they informed immigration authorities. It turns out the neighbour was right about one thing: Eunice overstayed her temporary resident visa.

In this scenario, Eunice will be interviewed about her immigration status by an immigration investigator at the local immigration office. If the officer has reasonable grounds to believe that Eunice is inadmissible because her temporary resident visa expired and, consequently, no longer has authorization to be in Canada, the officer has no discretion and must write an inadmissibility report.

Contents of Report

The officer must complete the section 44(1) report in writing and include the following information:

- the date of the report and place of issue;
- basic information about the person (for example, full and correct name, date of birth, marital status, contact information, and immigration status);

- information about when the temporary resident visa was issued and when it expired;
- the allegation (in Eunice's case, that she failed to leave Canada by the end of the authorized period of stay);
- the exact section of the IRPA invoked (in Eunice's case, section 41(a)—non-compliance with the Act); and
- the facts in the narrative of the report that constitute reasonable grounds for the officer's belief that the person is inadmissible (in Eunice's case, the address where she is staying, the date and place her visa was issued, the date and place where she was admitted to Canada, the date her temporary visa expired, and any other details to support the allegation).

In our scenario, there is no information to support the neighbour's allegation that Eunice committed a crime, so the officer does not include this information in her report or base her finding of inadmissibility on criminal grounds.

The officer must sign the report and address it to the minister for review.

Review and Referral

The minister is authorized under section 44(2) of the IRPA to take one of the following actions:

- allow the person to stay in Canada, if the minister concludes that the report is not well founded;
- issue a removal order, if the minister concludes that the report is well founded and that it falls within the jurisdiction of the officer who wrote the report; or
- refer the case to the ID of the IRB, if the minister concludes that the report is well founded but does not fall within the jurisdiction of the officer who wrote it.

If the minister (in practice, it is the officer's supervisor who is the officer with the delegated authority) is of the opinion that the report is well founded, the minister may issue a removal order of the foreign national in certain cases (IRPR, s 228).

Alternatively, depending on the grounds of inadmissibility, the minister may refer the report to the ID for a hearing. In Eunice's case, the minister will refer the matter to the ID for a hearing because Eunice was already legally admitted to, and living in, Canada.[5]

The officer will tell Eunice at the time of the interview that she is not under arrest and that there is no reason to detain her; she is free to return to Nadine's home to await her admissibility hearing. The officer will explain that Eunice will be sent a notice of admissibility hearing by mail, that she must attend that hearing, and that

---

5   In situations involving unaccompanied minor children, and cases where the person is unable to appreciate the nature of the proceedings and is not accompanied by a parent or adult who is legally responsible for that person, the minister's delegate *must* refer the section 44(1) report to the ID for an admissibility hearing (IRPR, ss 228(4)(a), (b)).

she may make her case for staying in Canada. However, if the ID member finds that Eunice is inadmissible, an exclusion order will be issued and she will be required to leave Canada.

Onus of Proof

The onus of proof is the burden of proving facts, such as proving inadmissibility. In a criminal trial, the onus is on the prosecution to prove guilt. In a civil trial, the onus is generally on the plaintiff to prove that the defendant caused harm or breached a contract.

At an admissibility hearing, the onus of proof depends on whether the person concerned (PC) has legal status in Canada. If the PC was denied the right to enter Canada, and therefore has no legal status, the onus is on the PC to prove that she is not inadmissible. However, if the PC was allowed to enter Canada and is alleged at a later time to have become inadmissible, then the onus is on the hearings officer to prove those allegations.

Standard of Proof

The standard of proof is the degree of proof necessary to satisfy the onus of proof. At an admissibility hearing, this means the degree or amount of proof necessary to make a decision on inadmissibility. It also applies to the decisions of a visa officer abroad or a CBSA officer at a POE.

Reasonable Grounds

The standard of proof varies depending on the ground of inadmissibility at issue. However, in most cases the decision-maker must have reasonable grounds for believing that some act has taken place, is taking place, or may take place in order to reach the conclusion of inadmissibility.

Reasonable grounds involve more than a mere suspicion that a person is inadmissible; rather, there must be an objective basis for the allegation. The decision-maker must have credible information that is sufficiently specific and reliable to support the allegation that a person is inadmissible.

Consider the following scenario relating to the minister's authority to make decisions that could lead to a foreign national's removal from Canada (as in the previous scenario, the minister's authority has been delegated to officers who carry out the immigration functions):

> Jose Rodriguez came to Canada as a temporary resident to visit his uncle Juan, who owns a small restaurant called Mama Rosa's. Jose has been living with Juan, his wife Maribella, and their two young children in a small apartment over the restaurant. All of the signature dishes are based on Maribella's grandmother Rosa's recipes, and she does most of the cooking and looks after their two young children while Juan manages the restaurant. One of Juan's employees quit suddenly, so he asked Jose to help him out until he could find a replacement. Jose agreed and, over a

period of several weeks, pitched in as a waiter and bus boy, and even helped his aunt in the kitchen to give her a break. Jose was having fun learning about running a restaurant. One slow day at the restaurant, Uncle Juan gave Jose the day off and gave him some cash to "go have some fun" in the city.

Jose came to the attention of immigration officials when officers conducted a raid of restaurants in the neighbourhood. Jose was allowed entry to Canada as a temporary visitor but had no authorization to work. The officer alleges that Jose was working illegally, and wrote an inadmissibility report for failing to comply with the IRPA—namely, not being in possession of a work authorization (see s 41). The way the officer sees it, there are too many illegals working in the restaurant district, and this is just another example of a foreign national who violated the terms of his visitor visa and has become inadmissible.

In Jose's case, the minister's delegate will review the officer's admissibility report to ensure there are sufficient details to establish a case against Jose, and make a decision that will also lead to an admissibility hearing and the potential order for Jose to leave Canada. What do you think? Does the officer have reasonable grounds to believe that Jose was working illegally? Who has the onus of proof at Jose's admissibility hearing: Jose or the minister?

Probable Grounds

The standard of proof with respect to serious criminal acts under section 36 of the IRPA is higher than that for other grounds of inadmissibility.

For these cases, the decision-maker must have probable grounds for believing that some act has taken place, is taking place, or may take place to reach a finding of inadmissibility. In other words, the facts must be proven on a balance of probabilities. This means that the decision-maker must believe that the allegations are more probable than not. In practice, the officer would attempt to obtain evidence such as the record of conviction; however, it is not always possible to do so.

Arrest and Detention

The CBSA has the authority under the IRPA to arrest and detain permanent residents and foreign nationals at a POE, or after they are in Canada. Detention may also be ordered by a member of the ID at an admissibility hearing following submissions by an officer. Depending on the risk posed by the person in detention, he may be held at a provincial correctional facility, or a CBSA immigration holding centre (there are three: Toronto, Laval, and Vancouver).[6]

When a person is arrested or detained, the *Canadian Charter of Rights and Freedoms* requires the officer to inform that person of his rights, including:

---

6 Canada Border Services Agency, "Information for People Detained Under the Immigration and Refugee Protection Act," BSF5012 (E) Rev 13, online: <http://www.cbsa-asfc.gc.ca/publications/pub/bsf5012-eng.pdf>.

- the right to know the reason for the arrest and detention;
- the right to counsel; and
- the right to notify his government representative of the arrest or detention.

At a Port of Entry

At the POE, an officer may arrest and detain a permanent resident or foreign national to ensure that the person will be available for examination (IRPA, s 55(3)(a)). The officer may also arrest and detain a permanent resident or foreign national at a POE if the officer has reasonable grounds to believe that the person is inadmissible on any of the most serious grounds of inadmissibility, such as a threat to security, violation of human or international rights, serious criminality, or organized criminality (IRPA, s 55(3)(b)). The officer must notify the ID so that a detention review can be held within 48 hours.

Within Canada

An officer may arrest and detain a permanent resident or foreign national after the person has been admitted to Canada. Generally, an officer is required to issue an immigration warrant for arrest and detention when the person is a permanent resident or a foreign national and there are reasonable grounds to believe that the permanent resident or foreign national is a danger to the public or is unlikely to appear for examination, for an admissibility hearing, for removal from Canada, or at a proceeding that could lead to that person's removal from Canada because of a removal order issued by the minister (IRPA, s 55(1)).

Within 48 hours of a detention, an officer may review the reasons for the detention and may exercise her authority under section 56(1) of the IRPA to release the person if the reason for detention no longer exists. Otherwise, the officer must notify the ID about the detention without delay, so that the ID may hold a review hearing into the reasons for the detention (IRPA, s 55(4)). There are exceptions to this procedure if the foreign national is a designated foreign national (see "Detention Reviews" later in this chapter).

Admissibility Hearings

A person appearing at an admissibility hearing may already be in detention, or may be detained at the end of the hearing (for example, as a result of a submission made by a hearings officer to the ID member requesting the member to order the detention of the person). This will be discussed in more detail below.

Detention of Children

According to section 60 of the IRPA, children under 18 should be detained only "as a measure of last resort." The best interests of the child must be taken into account generally when considering detention, as well as the following specific criteria from section 249 of the IRPR:

Detention of Designated Foreign Nationals

On June 29, 2012, Bill C-31, *Protecting Canada's Immigration System Act*, received royal assent and amended the IRPA. These amendments give the minister the authority to confer the status of **designated foreign national (DFN)** on a person who arrives in Canada as part of a group of smuggled persons who were also conferred special legal status as **designated irregular arrivals**.

The minister has the authority

■ to designate a group of persons as irregular arrivals;

■ to prosecute human smugglers and impose minimum mandatory prison sentences (see Chapter 3); and

■ to hold ship owners and operators to account for allowing the use of their vessels to smuggle human beings.

Unless a foreign national can prove he has the appropriate visa, a foreign national who is part of a group that is a designated irregular arrival will be designated and known as a DFN under section 20.1(2) of the IRPA, and subject to automatic detention if he is 16 years of age or older (s 56(2)). As a consequence of being designated, the foreign national is subject to specific rules for the timing of detention reviews, and, upon release, he is subject to rules for in-person reporting to immigration officials that are different from those for other foreign nationals.

designated foreign national (DFN)
a person (generally, a refugee claimant) who was part of a group of persons smuggled into Canada whom the minister has designated as an irregular arrival (see IRPA, s 20.1)

designated irregular arrival
a group (generally, of refugee claimants) that the minister has reasonable grounds to believe was part of a human smuggling operation and is so designated in the public interest

• the availability of alternative arrangements with local childcare agencies;

• the anticipated length of detention;

• where human smugglers brought the children to Canada, the risk of continued control by those smugglers;

• the type and the conditions of the detention facility that would be used;

• the possibility of segregation of the children from adults in detention; and

• the availability of educational, counselling, and recreational services for the children in detention.

The Immigration Division

The ID functions as an independent decision-making body with the jurisdiction to hear and decide immigration cases referred to it by the minister, and to decide whether a person is inadmissible (and, consequently, should be removed from Canada); it also holds review hearings into the reasons for the detention under the IRPA. The two types of these proceedings are as follows:

• **Admissibility hearings**. The ID has the authority under section 45 of the IRPA to hear and decide whether permanent residents and foreign nationals alleged to have contravened the IRPA should be allowed to enter or remain in Canada, or should be ordered removed.

admissibility hearing
an adversarial hearing to determine whether or not an applicant is inadmissible; held at the ID when a person allegedly breaches Canadian immigration laws pursuant to IRPA section 44(1), where an officer is of the opinion that a permanent resident or foreign national is inadmissible

detention review
a hearing before the
ID for the purpose of
reviewing the reasons
for a foreign national or
permanent resident's
detention under the IRPA

• **Detention reviews.** The ID has the authority under section 54 of the IRPA to review the reasons for the immigration detention of permanent residents, foreign nationals, and DFNs to decide whether to release them or whether there are sufficient reasons to continue the detention.

Proceedings Before the ID

Hearings before an ID member are quasi-judicial proceedings and are adversarial. The ID member is expected to hear and decide cases in an impartial and unbiased manner. As explained in Chapter 2, according to section 173 of the IRPA, the ID is not bound by any legal or technical rules of evidence. Under section 162(2), it may deal with matters more informally and efficiently than a court within the principles of natural justice.

Given the seriousness of the outcome of an immigration matter—namely, that the client can be removed—the client may have a high level of anxiety. To reduce the risk that this may interfere with the client's ability to answer questions clearly and credibly, it is important for counsel to prepare the client for the hearing by describing and explaining what will happen and answering any questions that the client may have. The following is a list of typical questions that clients may ask (or may want to know the answers to, even if they do not ask), organized by topic. Sample answers are provided in parentheses.

• *Type of hearing.* What can the client expect during the hearing? What are the time frames? Is it possible that the client will be removed immediately after the admissibility hearing? (No, this will not happen immediately.) What happens if the client is not released from detention? Is the matter expected to take all day? (We must arrange for alternatives to detention. Do you have someone who can post a bond?)

• *Hearing room.* What is the physical layout of the hearing room? Will the proceeding be held via videoconferencing—for example, if the client is being held in a local jail or immigration holding centre? In that case, where will counsel be? (Counsel will be with the client.)

• *Public or private hearing.* Will the hearing be open to the public? (The proceedings are public, which means there could be observers. However, there are some exceptions—for example, if a refugee claimant or protected person is involved.)

• *Recording of hearing.* Will the hearing be recorded? (Yes. A transcript of the proceeding can be produced for appeal purposes, for example.)

• *Language.* In what language will the hearing be held? (The hearing will be held in English or French, and an interpreter will be provided if requested.)

• *Nature of the proceeding.* Will the hearing be adversarial? (Yes, the nature of the hearing is adversarial and involves the minister's counsel, who will question the client and any witnesses, and argue that the client should be removed and/or detained, depending on the type of hearing.)

• *Consequences for family members.* If the client is ordered to be removed, will her family members be removed as well? (Family members who are included in the inadmissibility report may be subject to the same removal order, if one is made.)

- *Participants.* Who will be present and what is the role of each person? (The ID member, the hearings officer, counsel, the client, and possibly witnesses will be present).

Clients who are being detained will have many questions about getting released or moved to a more comfortable facility, such as an immigration holding facility rather than a jail. It is also important to explain the difference between a criminal incarceration and an immigration detention.

Persons in Attendance

There are a number of people who must be present at an ID hearing, including the PC, the minister's counsel, and the ID member. Other persons, such as the claimant's counsel, are likely to be present. Still others, such as witnesses, may be present.

ID MEMBER

Each case is heard by only one member of the ID, who is a public servant. The member has the authority to hear and decide immigration matters of inadmissibility and reasons for detention. The member will also hear and decide any applications that are made orally at the hearing.

PERSON CONCERNED

The PC must be personally in attendance at the hearing. This means being present either physically or by videoconference, for example.

MINISTER'S COUNSEL

Minister's counsel is a public servant who works for the CBSA with the title of hearings officer. A hearings officer represents the minister of public safety and emergency preparedness at ID proceedings. Prior to the hearing, the hearings officer reviews the report and prepares the case. At the hearing, the hearings officer examines and cross-examines witnesses and presents evidence.

COUNSEL

The legal professional who has the role of counsel is present to protect the interests and right to a fair hearing of the PC. Counsel explains the process, provides advice, and presents the case in an efficient manner, within the limits set by the ID member.

The PC may choose to be represented by either an unpaid, trusted adviser, such as a family member or clergy, or a paid, legal professional. An unpaid adviser who represents a client and is not charging a fee should use the Notice of Representation Without a Fee or Other Consideration form (IRB/CISR 101.03).[7]

---

7 This form is available on the IRB website at <http://www.irb-cisr.gc.ca/Eng/res/form/Documents/IrbCisr10103_e.pdf>.

All paid counsel must be members in good standing of the Immigration Consultants of Canada Regulatory Council (ICCRC) or a provincial or territorial law society (including licensed paralegals), or of the Chambre des notaires du Québec. Counsel who represent a PC for a fee must provide their contact information and membership identification number to the ID in writing; otherwise, the ID may consider the client as unrepresented. If counsel is charging a fee, the appropriate form to complete is the Counsel Contact Information form (IRB/CISR 101.02).[8]

According to rule 13 the *Immigration Division Rules* (ID Rules), counsel is deemed to be counsel of record once a date for a proceeding is set. In some cases, counsel may wish to be removed from the record—for example, if the client refuses to pay or is very difficult. Rule 14 provides that counsel must notify the ID and the minister to withdraw as counsel of record, and rule 15 provides that the client may remove the representative as counsel of record, also by notifying the ID and the minister.

INTERPRETER

Only interpreters accredited by the IRB are used for hearings; this means they have undergone security checks and passed a language examination. They are not employees of the ID but are contracted for on a case-by-case basis. They are permanently bound by their promise to interpret accurately once they take an oath or make a solemn affirmation to do so. At the beginning of the proceeding, the interpreter confirms that she has used a standardized script to ensure that the interpreter and PC understand each other. The interpreter may not guide, provide advice, or offer an opinion to the PC.

The ID Rules require that if a client or witness requires an interpreter, counsel must notify the ID in writing and specify the language and dialect needed before the hearing.

WITNESSES

If counsel wishes to call a witness other than his client, he must fulfill the requirements of rule 32 of the ID Rules. Information such as the reason for calling the witness, the party's relationship to the witness, the amount of time required at the hearing for the witness's testimony, and whether the testimony will be provided by videoconference or telephone must be provided in writing to the ID and copied to the other party. The timelines are set out in the ID Rules.

To reduce the risk of the witness failing to appear, it is prudent to request the ID to issue a summons to order a witness to testify, in accordance with rule 33, either in writing or orally at a proceeding. The party is responsible for providing the summons to the summoned person by hand, for notifying the ID in writing of this, and for paying witness fees and travel expenses. In the request, counsel must set out the factors to be considered in issuing the summons, such as the importance of the witness's testimony and the witness's ability to provide the testimony.

---

8 This form is available on the IRB website at <http://www.irb-cisr.gc.ca/Eng/res/form/Documents/IrbCisr10102_e.pdf>.

A witness may apply to the ID to cancel the summons. If the witness is unsuccessful with the application and subsequently fails to appear, the party who requested the summons may ask the ID to issue a warrant for her arrest, pursuant to rule 35.

The hearings officer may request that witnesses be excluded from the hearing room during the PC's testimony. A witness is not allowed to share any testimony given at the hearing with any other witness.

DESIGNATED REPRESENTATIVE

Occasionally, there are situations where the PC is not capable of making decisions, such as in the case of an unaccompanied minor or a person deemed unable to understand the proceedings (IRPA, s 167(2)). In these instances, the ID Rules provide that the ID will appoint a person to act and make decisions on behalf of the person. Where counsel for either party believes that a designated representative is required, counsel must notify the ID without delay. The designated representative may be a relative or a professional, such as a lawyer or social worker. Alternatively, counsel may choose to take on the role of designated representative.

Know and Follow the Division Rules

Legal professionals who represent persons who are subject to a proceeding in the ID must have a thorough knowledge of the ID Rules and the provisions of the IRPA that set out the jurisdiction of the IRB and the ID to hear and decide matters. The ID Rules are discussed further in Appendix A to this chapter.

Chairperson's Guidelines

The Chairperson's Guidelines pertaining to ID procedures provide counsel with additional information to help them navigate the ID processes competently.

Although the majority of the Chairperson's Guidelines apply to the Refugee Protection Division (RPD), there are guidelines that have a general application to all divisions, including the ID:

- Guideline 2—Detention—deals specifically with detention issues, including long-term detention, danger to the public, alternatives to detention, and evidence and procedure;
- Guideline 6—Scheduling and Changing the Date or Time of a Proceeding; and
- Guideline 8—Concerning Procedures with Respect to Vulnerable Persons Appearing Before the Immigration and Refugee Board of Canada.

As explained in Chapter 1, the guidelines are not binding, and members are not specifically directed to follow them; however, they are a source of guiding principles. This is important in order to preserve the independent nature of the member's role in making decisions while balancing the need for consistency in the treatment of particular issues.[9]

---

9 The Chairperson's Guidelines can be accessed on the IRB website at <http://www.irb-cisr.gc.ca/Eng/BoaCom/references/pol/GuiDir/Pages/index.aspx>.

Admissibility Hearings

Whereas reports regarding admissibility are called "inadmissibility reports," hearings on the same subject are referred to as "admissibility hearings." The inadmissibility report is used as the basis of the minister's allegations against the PC and is filed as part of the record at the admissibility hearing.

The minister's referral under section 44(2) of the IRPA gives the ID jurisdiction to hold an admissibility hearing. In addition to providing the inadmissibility report to the ID, as required by section 44(1), the minister is compelled by rule 3 of the ID Rules to provide other specific information, such as basic data about the PC (including name, contact information, date of birth, immigration status, and marital status), language of record, language of the interpreter (if required), and other details. The form used for this is the Request for Admissibility Hearing/Detention Review Pursuant to the Immigration Division Rules (BSF 524).[10]

The minister's representative—the hearings officer—presents a case for the inadmissibility of the PC whose admissibility is in question. The PC may be represented at the hearing by a member in good standing of the ICCRC or of a provincial or territorial law society (as discussed above and in Chapter 16). A member of the ID conducts the hearing, listens to both sides, and renders a decision.

Hearing Procedures

The ID member begins by making an opening statement. Then, the member has the parties and their counsel identify themselves for the record, and confirms that the PC can understand the interpreter (if one is required), swears in the interpreter, and deals with other matters such as witnesses.

The hearings officer reads the inadmissibility report into the record and asks to file it as the minister's evidence. The member then explains the possible outcomes of the hearing to the PC.

Generally, the hearings officer then calls the PC, who is sworn in and examined. The hearings officer files evidence and calls any other witnesses with information that supports the case for inadmissibility.

The PC (or her counsel, if represented) may then examine witnesses and file evidence. She may argue that the inadmissibility report is incorrect for technical, legal, or factual reasons. For example, she may argue that dates and names are wrong, that signatures are missing, that the grounds of inadmissibility do not apply, or that the facts are inaccurate.

After all the evidence has been heard, counsel must be prepared to make a final oral statement, called "representations," at the end of the hearing.

Consider the following scenario:

---

10   This form is available on the CBSA website at <http://www.cbsa-asfc.gc.ca/publications/forms
      -formulaires/bsf524.pdf>.

Frederico came to Canada on a temporary resident visa from Colombia to take an ESL summer course. Shortly after his arrival, he discovered a print shop, not far from his apartment off campus, which was owned by Antonio and Maria. Antonio was an old friend of Frederico's father from Colombia, and Frederico often visited the print shop for his photocopying needs, to visit, and to get a "taste of home." When Antonio asked Frederico if he could help out a little on weekends, informing him that he would be paid cash "under the table," Frederico was happy to help, even though he already had enough money to pay for his course, books, accommodation, and food expenses. However, an ex-girlfriend of Frederico's spotted him working there. Upset over their recent breakup, she informed immigration officials that Frederico was working in the print shop illegally.

Frederico's case would not be easy for a hearings officer to prove at an admissibility hearing. Are there reasonable grounds for believing that Frederico "worked" without authorization and was therefore in non-compliance with the IRPA? What credible information is available to support the allegation? Would testimony from an ex-girlfriend who was angry with him be credible?

The officer would have to prove that Frederico was working, and would apply the IRPR's legal definition of "work" (s 2). The onus would be on the officer to prove that Frederico engaged in "an activity for which wages are paid or commission is earned, or that is in direct competition with the activities of Canadian citizens or permanent residents in the Canadian labour market." Were wages paid? How could you prove this? In this case, would you like to be Frederico's representative or the officer, and how would you argue your side of the case?

At the end of the admissibility hearing, the ID member will ask the hearings officer to make a recommendation about any aggravating circumstances that the ID ought to consider, because section 229(3) of the IRPR directs that a deportation order instead of the prescribed removal order be made against a person if the PC meets any of the following criteria:

- the person was previously subject to a removal order and is now inadmissible on the same grounds as in that order;
- the person failed to comply with any condition or obligation imposed under the IRPA or prior legislation, unless the failure is the basis for the removal order; or
- the person was convicted in Canada of an offence under an Act of Parliament punishable by way of indictment or of two offences under any Act of Parliament not arising out of a single occurrence, unless the conviction or convictions are the grounds for the removal order.

Decision on Admissibility

Generally, following recommendations and oral representations, the ID member delivers the decision orally at the end of the hearing. A decision rendered orally takes effect at the time that it is stated (IRPA, s 169; ID Rules, r 11(3)). If the hearing is adjourned for a decision to be made in writing, the decision takes effect on the date that the member signs and dates the decision.

In accordance with section 45 of the IRPA, the ID member may make any of the following decisions:

- recognize the right of the person to enter Canada where the person is a Canadian citizen within the meaning of the *Citizenship Act*, a person registered as an Indian under the *Indian Act*, or a permanent resident;

- grant permanent or temporary resident status to a foreign national if the member is satisfied that the foreign national meets the requirements of the IRPA;

- authorize a permanent resident or a foreign national, with or without conditions, to enter Canada for further examination; or

- make the applicable removal order (a) against a foreign national who has not been authorized to enter Canada, if the member is not satisfied that the foreign national is not inadmissible, or (b) against a foreign national who has been authorized to enter Canada or a permanent resident, if the member is satisfied that the foreign national or the permanent resident is inadmissible.

If the decision is favourable to the PC, the member signs and dates a notice of decision and provides the minister's counsel with a copy. In accordance with rule 7(2) of the ID Rules, if the decision is unfavourable to the PC, the member must do the following:

- sign and date an notice of decision and provide a copy to the parties; and/or

- sign and date a removal order and provide a copy to the parties (see the discussion of removal orders later in this chapter); and

- advise the parties of their right to an appeal before the Immigration Appeal Division (IAD) or of a judicial review by the Federal Court (in cases where the PC does not have appeal rights).

Counsel may make an oral request for written reasons at the end of the hearing, or later, in writing, in accordance with rule 7(4) of the ID Rules, provided that the request is made within ten days of the date of the decision.

The type of removal order made against a PC depends on which of the ground(s) of inadmissibility are found to have been violated. The ID member can issue one of three types of removal orders, each of which carries a different degree of penalty for the PC (these details are discussed under the heading "Removal" later in this chapter). The three types of removal orders are as follows:

- **departure orders** (IRPR, s 224);
- **exclusion orders** (IRPR, s 225); and
- **deportation orders** (IRPR, s 226).

departure order
a type of removal order that generally provides a person with 30 days in which to leave Canada

exclusion order
a type of removal order that includes a one-year or five-year ban from re-entering Canada

deportation order
a type of removal order that bars re-entry to Canada indefinitely

Inadmissibility on Serious Grounds

The most stringent rules and procedures apply to the entry of persons who are inadmissible based on the most serious grounds, as follows:

- security;
- the violation of human or international rights;
- serious criminality; or
- organized criminality.

Where there is a finding of inadmissibility on one or more of these grounds, the PC has fewer rights. For example, there is no right to appeal the member's decision (IRPA, s 64(1)), and no right to make a refugee claim.

Refugee Claimants

According to section 101(f) of the IRPA, a person who is found inadmissible on any of the most serious grounds is barred from making a refugee claim. However, there is a strict time frame provision to process refugee claimants soon after a person asks to make a claim. As a result, it is not always possible to obtain the results of the security and background checks within this time frame. Consequently, the deeming provisions to refer claimants take effect, and refugee claims that otherwise should have been stopped may slip through and proceed to a refugee hearing (as discussed in Chapter 13).

Where information that the claimant is ineligible is received by the minister too late—that is, after a claim was referred to the RPD—the minister may choose to deal with the matter in one of two ways. The minister may suspend the refugee proceedings and hold an admissibility hearing, where issues of inadmissibility will be fully examined. (In this case, the RPD hearing will be held only if the claimant is successful at the admissibility hearing.) Alternatively, the minister may intervene and make arguments at the RPD hearing.

SUSPENSION

According to section 103 of the IRPA, the minister may serve notice to suspend a refugee claim at the RPD. The matter of inadmissibility is then argued by a hearings officer at an admissibility hearing before a member of the ID. If the member finds the claimant inadmissible on security grounds, the claimant is consequently ineligible to make the refugee claim. Under section 104 of the IRPA, the proceedings at the RPD are then terminated.

When opting to suspend refugee proceedings and hold an admissibility hearing, officers must consider the alleged grounds of inadmissibility, according to CIC's operational manual ENF 24 on ministerial interventions.[11] For example, cases

---

11 Citizenship and Immigration Canada, *ENF 24: Ministerial Interventions* (2 December 2005) s 5.4, online: <http://www.cic.gc.ca/english/resources/manuals/enf/enf24-eng.pdf>.

involving security, criminality, or new trends in the movement of refugees (such as fraud and trafficking) are better suited to an admissibility hearing before the ID than to ministerial intervention at an RPD hearing. This is because the ID member can issue the appropriate removal order at the end of the proceeding and then consider the issue of detention, both of which are immigration matters, not refugee matters.

Right to Appeal a Removal Order

Where there is a finding of inadmissibility on any of the most serious grounds, there is no right to appeal. This may result in earlier removal because, in theory, there will be no delay in awaiting the outcome of further immigration processes. In practice, however, removal is not as easy or timely as it sounds.

Note that for a foreign national who has been classified as a DFN, there is no right of appeal to the Refugee Appeal Division (RAD).

Detention Reviews

A permanent resident or foreign national may be arrested and detained under the IRPA for a variety of reasons (for example, the person's identity cannot be confirmed or there is a risk that the person will not appear for a hearing or for removal). The detained person has a right to have the reasons for the detention reviewed. The ID is the body that has jurisdiction to review the reasons for the detention. The detention review is initiated when the ID receives a request for a detention review from the minister. The process requires that the CBSA provide the ID with a *request for detention review,* which generally contains the original grounds for detention and basic information about the PC. The ID Rules require the minister to provide the date, time, and place of detention and the type of review (for example, 48-hour review, 7-day review, or 30-day review), as well as basic information about the PC (including name, contact information, date of birth, immigration status, and marital status); the language of record and language of the interpreter, if one is required; and other details (ID Rules, r 8). Sections 57(1) and (2) and 57.1(1) and (2) of the IRPA set out specific time limits for detention reviews.

The issue of detention may also arise at the end of the admissibility hearing, after the member has issued a removal order. The minister may argue that there is a reason to place the PC in detention (for example, to ensure that the person will be available for removal after a departure order is issued). In such situations, the ID has the authority to order the detention of the PC (IRPA, s 58(2)). Counsel must be prepared to argue the issue of detention and propose alternatives, such as payment of a deposit or the posting of a guarantee for compliance with the conditions (IRPA, s 58(3)).

Timing of Detention Reviews

There is no limit to the amount of time that a person may be in immigration detention as long as there is a periodic review. This principle was upheld by the Supreme Court of Canada when it stated that "extended periods of detention" are constitutionally valid so long as they are "accompanied by a process that provides regular

IN THE NEWS

Indefinite Detention: The Man with No Name

As you have learned, foreign nationals may be held in immigration detention for extended periods of time as long as their cases are reviewed periodically. In 2005, a man with a US passport in the name of Andrea Jerome Walker arrived in Canada, and his story prompted criticism from Canadian and international observers, including the UN High Commissioner for Human Rights' Working Group on Arbitrary Detention.

Shortly after arriving in Canada, the man was charged and convicted for possessing a small amount of crack cocaine. When the CBSA attempted to deport him, it discovered that his passport and name were both false. He was detained while the government attempted to uncover his true identity, but despite tentative links to Haiti and Guinea, attempts to deport him failed. In January 2015, the *National Post* reported:

> A global fingerprint search by Interpol, the international police organization, came back with eight different identities. He repeatedly lied about his identity, offering a name and nationality until the lie was proved, then offering a different name.

Since he could not be identified, he could not be deported, and as a result he was detained in an Ontario jail for nine years. While groups called for his release, the government worried that he would simply adopt a new identity and disappear again.

Finally, in August 2015, the CBSA was able to identify him as Michael Mvogo, a Cameroonian national. Mr. Mvogo had first offered this identity in 2010, but the Cameroonian government denied having any record of him, requiring an intensive search by a CBSA officer in rural Cameroon to uncover his family ties and birth certificate. His deportation was scheduled for August 24, 2015.

What do you think? In situations such as this one, how can we strike a balance between protecting Canada's borders and avoiding indefinite detention?

Sources: Adrian Humphreys, "Man with No Name's Constitutional Bid to Gain Release After Eight Years Thwarted by Decades of Lying," *National Post* (30 January 2015), online: <http://news.nationalpost.com/news/canada/man-with-no-names-constitutional-bid-to-gain-release-after-eight-years-thwarted-by-decades-of-lying>; *Toronto Star*, "Canada Must Free 'Undeportable Man' Michael Mvogo: Editorial" (25 July 2014), online: <http://www.thestar.com/opinion/editorials/2014/07/25/canada_must_free_undeportable _man_michael_mvogo_editorial.html>; Debra Black, "After Nearly a Decade in Ontario Jail—'Man with No Name' No Longer a Mystery," *Hamilton Spectator* (24 August 2015), online: <http://www.thespec.com/news-story/5810846-after-nearly-a-decade-in -ontario-jail-man-with-no-name-no-longer-a-mystery/>.

opportunities" for "judicial review of the continued need for and justice of the ... detention."[12]

Within 48 hours of a permanent resident's or foreign national's detention, an officer must review the reasons for the detention and has the authority under section 56 of the IRPA to release the person if the reason for the detention no longer exists. The officer may release the person with or without conditions such as the payment of a deposit or the posting of a guarantee.

The purpose of a hearing before the ID is to review the reasons for a continued detention. The timing for when the ID holds a hearing into the reasons for detention is set out in sections 57(1) and (2) of the IRPA. Reviews must be conducted as follows:

---

12 *Charkaoui v Canada (Citizenship and Immigration)*, 2007 SCC 9, [2007] 1 SCR 350 at paras 110 and 123.

- *the initial review*: within 48 hours of the person's detention;
- *the second review*: at least once during the seven days following the first detention review; and
- *subsequent reviews*: at least once during each 30-day period following each of the previous reviews.

After the first review, the PC or the minister may make a written request for an early detention review, in accordance with rule 9 of the ID Rules, if evidence to be produced could lead to release.

Designated Foreign Nationals

DFNs are subject to different detention rules. In matters involving the release of a DFN, the ID may consider whether he is a danger to the public; whether he is unlikely to appear for a proceeding or removal from Canada; and whether his identity has been established. The ID must also consider whether the minister is taking necessary steps to investigate whether the foreign national is inadmissible on the most serious of grounds, such as security, violating human or international rights, serious criminality, criminality, or organized criminality (IRPA, s 58(1.1)).

Generally, the detention review process for DFNs is as follows:

- *the initial review*: review of the reasons for continued detention must be held within 14 days of the person's detention (IRPA, s 57.1(1));
- *the second and subsequent reviews*: review of the reasons for the person's continued detention must be held on the expiry of six months following the conclusion of the previous review (IRPA, s 57.1(2)).

Detention will continue until the RPD makes a final positive decision on a successful refugee claim, or the ID or the minister orders release (IRPA, s 56(2)).

These time frames are in place to give the CBSA time to determine the real identity of the DFN, and to investigate whether the DFN is inadmissible for the more serious grounds of inadmissibility, such as security, the violation of human or international rights, serious criminality, or organized criminality.

Upon release, a DFN must comply with any conditions imposed, such as in-person reporting to immigration officials, the payment of a deposit, or the posting of a guarantee for compliance.

A DFN who is under 16 years of age is excluded from the detention provisions of the IRPA.

Security Certificate

Detention reviews for permanent residents who are being held under a security certificate are conducted by the Federal Court, not the ID (IRPA, s 82). For permanent residents, the detention review process is as follows:

- *the initial detention review*: review of the reasons for continued detention must be conducted no later than 48 hours after the permanent resident is taken into detention;
- *the second and subsequent detention reviews*: review of the reasons for continued detention must be conducted at least once in the six-month period following each preceding review, and at any other times that the judge authorizes.

Detention Review Hearings

A CBSA officer must bring the detainee to the ID, or to a place specified by it, to argue and provide evidence as to why she should be released. This means that the PC might stay in the detention facility and be brought to a room with videoconferencing equipment or, alternatively, be physically transported to the ID (IRPA, s 57(3)). The location will be specified in the notice to appear.

Detention reviews before the ID are adversarial hearings. A hearings officer attends the hearing to argue why the detention should be continued or to make recommendations about conditions for release. The PC has the right to counsel, although the proceeding is not generally adjourned for this purpose. In some provinces, duty counsel may assist the PC. Where the detained PC has no counsel, the hearings officer will also provide information about the hearing process and the PC's rights.

The ID member may make an opening statement; have the parties and counsel identify themselves for the record; confirm that the PC can understand the interpreter, if one is required; swear in the interpreter; and deal with other preliminary matters. The member explains the purpose of the detention review and the possible outcomes.

The hearings officer then begins by submitting facts and arguments concerning the detention. The hearings officer will also make a recommendation to continue the detention or to release the PC with conditions. The PC, or counsel if one has been retained, also has the opportunity to provide facts and arguments for release from detention. After all the evidence has been heard, the ID member gives each party the opportunity to make a final oral statement—called oral representations—at the end of the detention review hearing.

Factors That Affect Detention

There are a number of factors that the ID member must consider when determining whether a person should be detained. The factors are set out in the IRPR, in the following four categories (s 244):

1. **flight risk**,
2. danger to the public,
3. identity not established, and
4. other factors (see ss 248 and 249).

Consider the following scenarios with respect to these factors:

flight risk
a person who is likely to fail to appear at an immigration proceeding

Shauna showed up for her admissibility hearing, but she has a history of staying in Canada after the expiry of her temporary resident visa. Five years ago, Shauna overstayed her visa and was brought before the ID; at that hearing, she cried on record, apologized, and claimed that she forgot about applying to extend her stay. She was issued a departure order and left Canada. This time, the evidence suggests that Shauna has done exactly the same thing: overstayed her status and failed to apply to extend the terms and conditions of her stay. After hearing the allegations, Shauna realizes their serious nature and asks for time to obtain counsel to assist her with her case. The hearing is adjourned; however, the officer wishes to ensure that Shauna will appear for the continuation of the proceeding. The officer is concerned that if Shauna is not detained, she may simply disappear. The officer will argue that Shauna is a flight risk and should therefore be detained.

Jerome has several convictions for assault in another country and entered Canada illegally using an alias to flee from prosecution. However, he was arrested in a drug raid by Canadian police. It was only after he was fingerprinted that Jerome's true identity, along with information about his prior foreign convictions, was discovered. Police believe that Jerome has ties to organized crime, and although the case is part of a larger, ongoing investigation, they were only able to charge him with a minor offence, for which he was convicted. As soon as Jerome was released from jail, however, he was immediately detained by the CBSA as a flight risk. While he waits for his admissibility hearing, Jerome is brought before an ID member to review the reasons for his detention. Since Jerome's last review (the seven day detention review), the officer has learned that there are outstanding warrants for Jerome's arrest in his country. The officer is waiting for confirmation of this information from foreign authorities. This is Jerome's first 30-day review and the officer asks for the detention to continue. Jerome has no family in Canada.

With these scenarios in mind, let's consider each of the prescribed factors in more detail.

FLIGHT RISK

Section 245 of the IRPR sets out the following factors that the ID will consider when determining whether a person is a flight risk:

- Is the person a fugitive from justice in another country?
- Has the person previously complied with a departure order?
- Has the person appeared for any previous immigration hearing or criminal proceeding?
- Has the person previously complied with any immigration conditions that were imposed when he was admitted to Canada, previously released from detention, or granted a stay of removal?
- Does the person have a history of avoiding examination or escaping from custody or attempting to do so?

- Does the person have any involvement in people smuggling or human trafficking?
- Does the person have strong ties to a community in Canada?

In the scenario involving Shauna, the officer would argue that Shauna is a flight risk because she did not comply with immigration conditions—for example, she did not leave Canada by the expiry of her visa, she did not extend her visa, and she has a history of overstaying. The officer could also seek alternatives to detention, such as the posting of a cash bond (see below under the heading "Release from Detention"), because although there are some factors to suggest flight risk, they are not so great as to require detention. Shauna, on the other hand, does not wish to be detained. She would remind the ID member that she has complied with a previous departure order and would promise to appear for the resumption of her hearing.

Jerome's case is more complex and more serious than Shauna's case; the officer would do everything to make the case to keep Jerome in detention, pending the outcome of Jerome's admissibility hearing. Usually when an officer asks for the detention to be continued, it is for the same reasons as the original detention. In Jerome's case, the officer would also present the latest information about Jerome's convictions. The officer would ask that the detention be continued because Jerome is a flight risk and is wanted on foreign charges. To support the latter claim, the officer would point to the following facts:

- Jerome has prior convictions and may be fleeing prosecution. The officer will inform the ID member that he is still waiting to hear from foreign authorities about whether Jerome has any outstanding charges against him because of his ties to organized crime.
- Jerome entered Canada illegally and under an alias in an effort to avoid detection.
- The only ties that Jerome appears to have with anyone in Canada are with criminal elements (possibly an organized drug ring).

DANGER TO THE PUBLIC

Being detained as a danger to the public is serious because it means that the PC has likely engaged in or will likely engage in serious criminal acts. The hearings officer will provide evidence related to the grounds of inadmissibility. A member of the ID will hear arguments from both parties when considering whether to order the detention to continue or to order release. The member considers the following factors, set out in section 246 of the IRPR:

- Is the person inadmissible on grounds of security, the violation of human or international rights, or serious criminality? Criminal convictions outside or in Canada considered to be serious crimes include sexual offences, violent offences, weapons offences, and drug trafficking.
- Is the person associated with a criminal organization?
- Has the person engaged in people smuggling or human trafficking?

- If the person has criminal convictions outside Canada, are they considered to be for serious crimes, such as drug-related offences?

IDENTITY NOT ESTABLISHED

There are a number of reasons why a person might conceal his identity from Canadian authorities. Consider the following examples:

- A person may be evading prosecution in his home country and be avoiding returning, such as in the case of Jerome.
- A person may have been previously deported from Canada.

When the PC is a foreign national whose identity is not confirmed, or when the person is uncooperative in proving his identity, the hearings officer will argue to keep the person in detention. In making a decision, the ID member will consider a number of factors set out in section 247 of the IRPR—for example, whether the person was cooperative in providing

- evidence of his identity (to determine whether his identity documents are legitimate or false or were destroyed);
- information about his date and place of birth, as well as the names of his mother and father; and
- detailed information about his travel itinerary to Canada, or in completing an application for a travel document or in assisting to obtain evidence of identity.

Note that the factors above do not have an adverse effect on special considerations for minor children.

Additional questions that are asked include the following:

- Has the person destroyed identity or travel documents, or travelled with fraudulent documents?
- Has the person lied or provided contradictory information about his identity?
- Are there any documents that contradict information provided by the person about his identity?

Obtaining truthful information from a refugee claimant may pose a challenge for immigration officers and legal professionals alike. As a result of experiences with corrupt government officials in their country of origin, many refugee claimants are averse to divulging personal information to government officials for the purpose of obtaining identity documents. They may also be reluctant to be completely candid with Canadian officials because of a general distrust of authority. Nevertheless, legal professionals should counsel their clients to cooperate in obtaining identity documents and provide all requested information that would help establish their identity so that they can be released from detention.

OTHER FACTORS

Other factors to be considered are set out in section 248 of the IRPR, and include the following:

- the reasons for detention;
- the length of time already spent in detention, in cases where the person was previously detained;
- whether there are any elements that can assist in determining the length of time that detention is likely to continue and, if so, that length of time;
- any unexplained delays or unexplained lack of diligence caused by CIC, the CBSA, or the PC; and
- the existence of alternatives to detention.

Decision on Detention Reviews

The decision at a detention review hearing is usually rendered orally at the end of the hearing, and takes effect immediately. On rare occasions, the hearing may be adjourned for a decision to be rendered in writing, in which case it takes effect on the date the ID member signs and dates the decision. The member must do one of the following, in accordance with the ID Rules:

- sign an order for release and provide a copy to the parties; or
- sign an order for detention, provide a copy to the parties, and advise the PC of her right to a judicial review by the Federal Court (in cases where the PC does not have appeal rights).

An order for release may contain conditions, such as the payment of a deposit or the posting of a guarantee for compliance with the conditions (IRPA, s 58(3)). Counsel may make an oral request for written reasons at the end of the hearing or later in writing, as long as the request is made within ten days of the date of the decision.

Release from Detention

A person may be released from detention by an officer before the first detention review by the ID if the officer is of the opinion that the reasons for the detention no longer exist. The officer may also impose conditions, such as the payment of a deposit (cash bond) or the posting of a guarantee (performance bond) for compliance with the conditions (IRPA, s 56(1)).

A member of the ID may also release a person from detention with conditions as an alternative to detention. Conditions many include the payment of a deposit or the posting of a guarantee for compliance with the conditions (IRPA, s 58(3)). The member may also consider other conditions, such as the "periodic reporting, confinement to a particular location or geographic area, the requirement to report changes of address or telephone number, and detention in a form that could be less restrictive to the individual."[13]

On request of a DFN who was 16 years of age or older on the day of her arrival, or on the minister's own initiative, the minister may order the release of the DFN from detention if there are exceptional circumstances that warrant release or if the reasons for the detention no longer exist. Alternatives to detention include imposing conditions such as the payment of a deposit or the posting of a guarantee for compliance with the conditions (IRPA, s 58.1).

Sections 45 to 49 of the IRPR set out the requirements for deposits and guarantees. The amount of a bond is based on the following:

- the person's financial resources;
- the obligations that result from the conditions imposed;
- the costs that would likely be incurred to locate, arrest, detain, and remove the person; and
- in the case of a guarantee, the costs that would likely be incurred to enforce it.

If a third person or group acts as guarantor, it must, under section 47 of the IRPR, satisfy the decision-maker of the following:

- that it is not in default of another guarantee;
- that it is a Canadian citizen or permanent resident;
- that it is physically present and residing in Canada;
- that it can ensure that the detainee obeys any conditions imposed; and
- that it has the ability to fulfill the obligation if the person fails to comply with conditions imposed (evidence of this ability must be provided).

Also, if there are reasonable grounds to believe that the guarantor's money was obtained illegally, it must be refused (IRPR, s 47(3)).

Both the detainee and guarantor must notify CIC or the CBSA, as directed, of any change of address and must appear for any matter as directed by an officer or the ID, according to section 48 of the IRPR. If any conditions are broken, the cash bond is forfeited. In the case of a guarantee, the signing person is required to pay the specified amount of money. The CBSA, and not the ID, is responsible for the administration and enforcement of cash bonds.

Consider the following additional information in the case of Eunice, who overstayed her temporary resident visa:

> When Eunice appeared for her admissibility hearing, she was not "on immigration hold." Eunice chose to have legal representation at her admissibility hearing and felt well prepared. She knew there was a possibility that she could be detained after her hearing, but her counsel was confident that he could show that Eunice

---

13   Immigration and Refugee Board, "Chairperson Guideline 2: Detention" (5 June 2013) s 3.6.3, online: <http://www.irb-cisr.gc.ca/Eng/BoaCom/references/pol/GuiDir/Pages/GuiDir02.aspx#s36>.

would not be a flight risk. Eunice did not have a criminal record outside Canada and had not committed any crimes while in Canada, so she would not be considered a danger to the public. All of Eunice's identity and travel documents were in good order, she had complied with police and immigration authorities, and her identity was not in question.

At the admissibility hearing, it was clear from the evidence presented by the hearings officer that Eunice had, in fact, overstayed her visit. The ID member found Eunice to be inadmissible for "failing to comply," and issued a departure order.

After the order was made, the hearings officer made submissions that Eunice was a flight risk because she was close to her family members in Canada and overstayed her visit to be with them. Eunice's counsel proposed, as an alternative to detention, that her older sister Nadine act as a guarantor to ensure that Eunice leaves Canada. (Before Eunice's hearing, her counsel explained these conditions and arranged for Nadine to attend the hearing just in case.)

The hearings officer recommended an appropriate sum as a deposit, which the member accepted. Nadine was able to answer questions to show that she met the regulatory requirements of a guarantor. The member imposed this as a condition so that Eunice would comply with her removal order without having to be detained. Before Eunice was free to go, Nadine posted the deposit. When Nadine paid the sum of money to a CBSA official as a guarantee, she was given a copy of a security deposit form. She and Eunice were also required to sign an acknowledgment of conditions form as proof that they both understood the conditions imposed.

Had Eunice's counsel not been adequately prepared for this situation, it is possible that Eunice would have been detained pending removal.

Removal

Canadian citizens are not generally subject to removal, even if they do something that would make a permanent resident or foreign national inadmissible (for example, commit a crime). The only situation in which a citizen may be removed from Canada is if his citizenship is first revoked. This may happen, for example, in a situation where citizenship was granted on the basis of a misrepresentation or fraud. Also, citizenship may be revoked when, after becoming a Canadian citizen who has dual citizenship, a person (a) "was convicted of terrorism, high treason, treason, or spying offences, depending on the sentence received"; or (b) "served as a member of an armed force of a country or as a member of an organized armed group and that country or group was engaged in armed conflict with Canada."[14]

Foreign nationals and permanent residents who stay in Canada lawfully generally need not be concerned about removal. However, when a non-citizen is found to be inadmissible in Canada either at the POE or after being admitted (such as in the case of Eunice), the person may be ordered removed. As noted earlier, a removal order may be made in either of the following circumstances:

---

14 These grounds took effect on May 28, 2015 under the *Strengthening Canadian Citizenship Act* (SCCA). See "Revocation of Citizenship" on CIC's website at <http://www.cic.gc.ca/english/resources/tools/cit/acquisition/revocation.asp>.

- following an examination, in the circumstances detailed in section 44(2) of the IRPA, in which case the minister issues the removal order; or
- at an admissibility hearing, in which case a member of the ID issues the removal order.

Any family members in Canada who are dependants of a person who is the subject of a removal order may also be included in the order as long as they are not Canadian citizens or permanent residents 19 years of age or over (IRPR, s 227).

Removal Orders

The regulations provide for three types of removal orders: departure orders, exclusion orders, and deportation orders. Each has a different consequence for the person against whom the order is made, as outlined in the following sections.

Departure Orders (IRPR, Section 224)

A departure order generally requires a person to leave Canada within 30 days of the departure order coming into effect, and to obtain a certificate of departure as part of the criteria for removal (IRPR, ss 240(1)(a) to (c)).

The ID must issue a departure order under section 229(1)(k) of the IRPR when a permanent resident is found to be inadmissible to Canada for failing to comply with any conditions of permanent residence or his residency obligations.

A departure order is usually issued for a less serious violation of immigration law. A person may successfully request a departure order at an admissibility hearing if voluntary compliance can be shown. As counsel, you can prepare your client by providing proof of the client's ability and willingness to leave Canada. Proof may include a valid passport or travel document, an ability to pay for travel arrangements with a return ticket, a letter of resignation from the employer, or arrangements to terminate a lease or the sale of a house.

A person who leaves Canada on a departure order may apply to return to Canada as long as a certificate of departure was obtained from CBSA officials at the POE just prior to departure. Although Canada does not have exit controls, the certificate of departure is a type of control that serves as proof that the person complied with the order by leaving for a country of destination that allowed lawful entry.

If a person fails to leave Canada within the 30-day time period, or leaves and fails to obtain a certificate of departure, the departure order is automatically deemed to be a deportation order, according to section 224(2) of the IRPR. This has serious consequences should the person ever wish to return to Canada (see "Deportation Orders (IRPR, Section 226)," below).

Additionally, if immigration officials cannot locate the person, they may issue an immigration warrant for the person's arrest. The immigration warrant can be viewed in the Canada-wide Canadian Police Information Centre (CPIC), a computerized information system that provides Canadian law enforcement agencies with information about crime and criminals. A person for whom an immigration warrant has been issued usually comes to the attention of CBSA or CIC officials after apprehension by police—for example, after being stopped by police for a minor traffic violation. When the person who has not left Canada is eventually arrested, he will likely be detained pending removal. It may then be difficult for counsel to arrange for the person's release from detention given his previous failure to appear for removal.

EXCEPTIONS TO THE 30-DAY RULE

There are several exceptions to the 30 days allowed for departure under a departure order, as follows:

1. *Conditional removal order.* A conditional removal order, or removal order with conditions, is a departure order with conditions attached. It is issued by an officer (IRPR, s 228(3)) pending the outcome of a refugee claim, for example.

2. *Stay of removal order.* A stay of removal is an order that freezes the removal order temporarily and allows the person to remain in Canada until the removal order becomes enforceable.

3. *Detention.* When a foreign national is detained within the 30-day period, such as for arrest on a criminal charge, the 30-day period is suspended until either the foreign national is released or the removal order becomes enforceable.

Exclusion Orders (IRPR, Section 225)

The exclusion order differs from the departure order in that it bars a foreign national from returning to Canada for a specified period of time—either for one year or for five years.

The one-year ban is generally issued when a foreign national has committed a minor offence, such as failing to appear for an examination. The five-year ban is reserved for more serious offences; for example, if the person engaged in misrepresentation, an exclusion order for five years must be issued (IRPR, s 225(3)).

Under the regulations, an exclusion order must be issued by the ID when a person is found to be inadmissible to Canada

- on health grounds (IRPR, s 229(1)(f));
- for financial reasons (IRPR, s 229(1)(g));
- for misrepresenting or withholding material facts, or through sponsorship by a person who is inadmissible for misrepresentation under section 40(1)(a) or (b) of the IRPA (IRPR, ss 229(1)(h), (n));
- for failing to appear for an examination (IRPR, s 229(1)(j));
- for failing to establish permanent residence (IRPR, s 229(1)(l)); or
- for failing to establish that he will leave at the end of his stay (IRPR, s 229(1)(m)).

A person against whom an exclusion order has been issued may not return to Canada for the duration of the ban without the written authorization of an officer. The person must apply for an authorization to return to Canada.

Deportation Orders (IRPR, Section 226)

The deportation order permanently bars a person from future admission to Canada unless that person obtains the written consent of the minister. The person must apply for an authorization to return to Canada.

A deportation order must be issued by the ID under the regulations in one of the following circumstances:

- the person has been found to be inadmissible to Canada
  - on grounds of security (IRPR, s 229(1)(a)),
  - for violating human or international rights (IRPR, s 229(1)(b)),
  - for serious criminality (IRPR, s 229(1)(c)),
  - for criminality (IRPR, s 229(1)(d)),
  - for organized criminality (IRPR, s 229(1)(e)), or
  - for having citizenship revoked under section 40(1)(d) of the IRPA (IRPR, s 229(1)(i)); or
- a departure order issued against the person has been turned into a deportation order (IRPR, s 224(2)).

If the deportation order is made against an accompanying family member of an individual who was found inadmissible, that family member may return to Canada without written authorization.

Types of Stays of Removal

Enforcement of a removal order may be stayed pending some other action or outcome. Specifically, there are five ways in which a removal order may be stayed:

1. by the minister,
2. by application for leave for a judicial review,
3. by application for a pre-removal risk assessment (PRRA),
4. by application for humanitarian and compassionate considerations, or
5. by appeal to the IAD.

Each of these is discussed below.

1. Minister's Stay

According to section 230(1) of the IRPR, the minister has discretion to stay a removal order in situations where the person would be sent to a country engaged in an armed conflict, a country dealing with a serious environmental disaster, or a country dealing with another situation that poses a risk to the civilian population there. The minister of public safety and emergency preparedness has the authority to impose, maintain, or lift a "temporary suspension of removal."[15] Generally, unsuccessful

---

15   Government of Canada, Backgrounder, "Temporary Suspension of Removals (TSRs)" (1 December 2014), online: <http://news.gc.ca/web/article-en.do?nid=910579>.

refugee claimants and others who are inadmissible and who would normally be removed are allowed to stay in Canada on a temporary resident permit. However, the minister's discretion is limited by the need to protect Canadian society. The minister may not issue a stay when

- the person is inadmissible on grounds of security, the violation of human or international rights, serious criminality, or organized criminality;
- the person is a refugee claimant who is ineligible because of section F of article 1 of the Refugee Convention (crimes against peace, war crimes, or crimes against humanity); or
- the person has consented in writing to her removal (IRPR, s 230(3)).

A minister's stay is cancelled when the minister is satisfied that the circumstances in the country no longer exist and the person under the removal order would not be at risk if removed to that country (IRPR, s 230(2)).

2. Stay Pending Judicial Review

An unsuccessful refugee claimant may obtain a stay of removal under section 231 of the IRPR if the claimant applied for a judicial review at the Federal Court within the permitted time limit following a determination by the RAD, except if the claim was made by a DFN.

3. Stay Pending Pre-Removal Risk Assessment

The PRRA program is available to certain persons who are considered to be "at risk" and who are about to be removed from Canada. The PRRA is a program intended for people who cannot return to their country of origin. For a person to be eligible, one of the following conditions must exist:

- the person must have a well-founded fear of persecution in the country to which he would be returned, according to the Convention refugee definition; or
- if the person were returned to that country, one of the following risks would exist: a risk of torture, a risk to life, or a risk of cruel and unusual treatment or punishment, according to the Convention Against Torture.

When a person applies for a PRRA within the appropriate time limits and in accordance with section 232 of the IRPR, the removal order is stayed pending the decision on the application.

For more information on the PRRA program, see Chapter 13.

4. Stay Pending Humanitarian and Compassionate Considerations

A removal order may be stayed if the minister is of the opinion that humanitarian and compassionate considerations or public policy considerations exist. The stay will be granted under section 233 of the IRPR until a decision whether to grant permanent resident status is made.

5. *Stay Pending Appeal*

Where the right to appeal exists, a person may appeal the removal order to the IAD. Pursuant to section 68 of the IRPA, the removal order may be stayed until the appeal is heard if the IAD member is satisfied that, taking into account the best interests of a child or humanitarian and compassionate considerations, the decision ought to be stayed.

A more detailed discussion about the IAD is provided in Chapter 15.

Timelines for Removal

Removal from Canada is an important enforcement activity that is carried out by the CBSA and authorized under the IRPA. In some cases, people leave voluntarily after being issued a removal order; in other cases, CBSA officers must enforce removal orders by physically removing those persons.

Depending on the type of removal order, the person may be allowed time to prepare and arrange for leaving. The length of time allowed may vary. Or, according to section 49 of the IRPA, a removal order may be enforceable on the latest of the following dates:

- the day the removal order is made, if the person has no right to appeal the order;
- the day the appeal period expires, if the person has a right to appeal but has not appealed the order; or
- in the event of an appeal, not until a final determination has been made by the IAD.

However, where refugee claimants and protected persons are the subject of a removal order, the removal is conditional on the outcome of the claim. This is important because the consequences of removal may be life threatening. Generally, the order takes effect as follows:

- 7 days after a person is determined ineligible;
- 15 days after the claim has been decided by the RPD and is rejected;
- 15 days after notice that the claim has been decided as withdrawn, abandoned, or terminated; or
- 15 days after notice that the claim has been decided by the RAD and has been rejected.

In some cases, a removal order may be enforceable immediately. For example, when a foreign national arrives at a POE, the CBSA may issue a removal order against him and enforce it on the same day if he waives or exhausts any legal right to remain in Canada.

However, the removal process is not often so simple. After the removal order is issued, a person may seek a judicial review of the matter before the Federal Court of Canada, and this decision may be appealed to the Federal Court of Appeal. In some cases, it may even reach the Supreme Court of Canada. The removal order takes effect when the person either does not pursue any further legal recourse or has exhausted these avenues.

Before the CBSA may carry out the removal order, however, it must attend to a number of activities which may also prolong or further delay removal, especially if the individual being removed is not cooperative. These activities include the following:

- instructing the individual for removal to ensure that he understands his responsibilities, such as the requirement to prepare for removal within the stipulated time frame and the need to report to an immigration officer before leaving;
- confirming the identity of the person (who may conceal his identity to avoid being returned);
- obtaining travel documents, such as passports and visas, from the person's country of destination (this is made more difficult if there is a situation of general unrest in the country or if the person is concealing his identity); and
- issuing an immigration warrant for the person's arrest and detention under the IRPA if the person fails to appear for removal.

For the actual removal of a person, such as boarding the person on a plane destined for another country, the CBSA may assign escorts if there is any concern that the person will not obey the removal order, that the person poses a risk of violence to himself or others, or that the person poses a threat to the health or safety of other travellers. Generally, CBSA officers or security guards contracted by the CBSA carry out removals but, in some cases, they may be assisted by the Royal Canadian Mounted Police if there are safety or security concerns, or by medical personnel if there are health-related concerns.[16] Furthermore, the airline may refuse to transport the person without an escort.

The function of removing a person from Canada is further complicated by the fact that the country of destination must be willing to allow the person to return. Generally, Canada removes persons to one of the following countries (IRPR, s 241):

- the country from which they came to Canada,
- the country in which they last permanently resided before coming to Canada,
- the country in which they are a national or citizen, or
- their country of birth.

However, if none of these countries is willing to accept the person, the minister may select another country that is willing to allow the legal entry of the person. Section 39(a) of the IRPR allows persons who are under removal orders and who leave Canada but are not granted legal permission to be in any other country and subsequently are returned to Canada, by force of circumstances, to return and enter Canada.

---

16 Canada Border Services Agency, "Arrests and Detentions" (30 September 2014), online: <http://www.cbsa-asfc.gc.ca/security-securite/arr-det-eng.html>.

Removal Costs

Removal costs may be paid by the person being removed (usually when the person leaves voluntarily), by the transporter (for example, an airline), or by the government. In cases where the foreign national arrives at an airport and is not allowed to enter Canada, the airline must cover the cost (IRPR, s 278). It is the transporter's responsibility to ensure that travellers hold the proper documentation. If the airline transported the person without proper documentation, the airline is responsible for returning the person and also incurs an administrative fee.

The government has estimated the cost for removal to be in the range of $1,500 to $15,000, but it can go as high as $300,000 if a chartered aircraft is used. Detention is estimated to cost $200 per day.[17]

A person who is removed at the expense of the government is not allowed to return to Canada until he has paid back the removal costs, as prescribed under section 243 of the IRPR.

---

17   Citizenship and Immigration Canada, "Backgrounder—Detention, Removals and the New Assisted Voluntary Returns Program" (30 March 2010), online: <http://www.cic.gc.ca/english/department/media/backgrounders/2010/2010-03-30c.asp>.

APPENDIX A

Immigration Division Rules

The ID Rules are the division's regulations, established to set out roles and responsibilities, and govern practices and procedures in proceedings before the ID.

Section 161(1) of the IRPA gives the chairperson of the IRB the authority to make rules related to the ID's activities, practices, and procedures, in consultation with the deputy chairpersons, subject to the approval of the governor in council. The Rules are part of the regulations under the IRPA. They are binding, and it is important to know them well; failure to comply with them may have severe consequences for both clients and counsel. Requests for clarification about the meaning or application of a particular rule may be made to the registrar's staff at the nearest business office of the IRB.

The Rules are divided into three parts:

- Part 1—Rules Applicable to Admissibility Hearings
- Part 2—Rules Applicable to Detention Reviews
- Part 3—Rules That Apply to Both Admissibility Hearings and Detention Reviews

> ## WEBLINK
>
> The *Immigration Division Rules* are regulations made under the IRPA, and may be accessed at various websites, including the IRB website, under the "Legal and Policy References" tab, as well as the Department of Justice website <laws-lois.justice.gc.ca/eng/regulations/SOR-2002-229/index.html> and the CanLII website <www.canlii.org/en/ca/laws/regu/sor-2002-229/latest/sor-2002-229.html>.

In addition to the binding ID Rules, there are important policy instruments that may relate to the ID's practice and procedure—namely, chairperson's guidelines and policy notes (see Chapter 1).

Rules: Before the Proceeding

Compliance with the ID Rules by everyone involved is intended to lead to a fair and consistent approach. However, when the Rules were drafted, it was not possible to predict all potential scenarios that might arise in future cases, so rule 49 provides the ID with the flexibility to "do whatever is necessary to deal with the matter" should a procedural problem arise during a proceeding. Consider the following examples:

- ID members may act on their own initiative to change a rule, to excuse a person from a rule, and to extend or shorten time limits (r 50); and
- failure to follow a rule in a proceeding does not, in itself, make the proceeding invalid (r 51).

In this way, the Rules attempt to strike a balance between the value of predictability and consistency, and the need to make adjustments to meet the particular needs of individual cases. The following is an overview of those Rules that counsel will work with most often in a proceeding before the ID. However, it is important to review and understand *all* the Rules before representing a client before the ID.

DEFINITIONS

It is very important to know the meaning of key terms, which are defined in rule 1. For example, "detention review" is defined as a "forty-eight hour review, a seven-day review and a thirty-day review," and then each of these terms is further defined. Counsel demonstrate their professionalism when they understand and use relevant and appropriate terminology while presenting immigration cases.

TIME LIMITS

The ID Rules require that certain activities occur within certain time limits. The time limits are included in the Rules for specific actions, as follows:

- holding detention reviews—rules 8(2) and 9;
- disclosing documents—rules 26(a) and (b);
- providing witness information—rule 32(2);
- making applications—rule 38(2);
- responding to applications—rule 39(3);
- responding to written responses—rule 40(3);
- making applications to conduct a proceeding in private—rule 45(4);
- making applications to conduct a proceeding in public—rule 46(4); and
- providing a notice of constitutional question—rule 47(4).

A document is considered received by the division on the day that the document is date stamped by the division, according to rule 31(1). When counsel sends a document to the minister's counsel by regular mail, it is considered received seven days after the day it was mailed, according to rule 31(2). If day seven falls on a Saturday, Sunday, or statutory holiday, the document is considered received on the next working day.

SCHEDULING A HEARING AND NOTICE TO APPEAR

According to rule 21, the ID must "fix the date for a hearing and any other proceeding relating to the hearing." The ID may "require the parties to participate in the preparation of a schedule of proceedings by appearing at a scheduling conference or otherwise providing information."

According to rule 22, the ID is responsible for notifying both the PC and the minister of the date, time, and location of a hearing. This may be done orally—for example, at a proceeding—or in writing, in a notice to appear document.

COMMUNICATING WITH THE DECISION-MAKER

The parties and their representatives must never directly communicate with the decision-maker, but rather must direct all communication through the registry, according to rule 2 of the ID Rules. This applies to all communication, both oral and written, including questions about the process, documents, or a particular proceeding.

It is very important that everyone follow rule 2 in order to avoid suspicions of bias or influence. All parties must be aware of all information being passed on to the decision-maker so that they have the opportunity to respond. Applications and other communications must be made in writing, within the time limits, and generally with proof that all parties have been served.

CONTACT INFORMATION

"Contact information" is defined in rule 1 as a person's name, postal address and telephone number, and fax number and electronic mail address, if any.

Contact information for both the PC and counsel must be provided to both the ID and the minister. This is necessary to ensure that notices of proceedings and other matters can be communicated. Rule 12 requires counsel of record to provide this information.

According to rule 4, changes to contact information must also be provided to the ID and the minister without delay, unless the person is detained. If notices, such as a notice to appear for a hearing, are not received because the ID does not have the proper address, the PC might fail to show up for the proceeding, resulting in the issue of a warrant for the person's arrest.

INTERPRETER SERVICES

According to rule 17, if the PC or any witness needs an interpreter, the party must notify the ID of this. Notice should be given as soon as possible in the case of a 48-hour or 7-day review or an admissibility hearing held at the same time, and in all other cases at least 5 days before the hearing.

DOCUMENTS

Documents are important evidence at ID proceedings. There are several kinds of documents, such as documents that confirm the identity of the client, travel documents, documents that show the client's willingness to leave Canada, court documents, and conviction records. Because of the importance of documents to a fair resolution of the case, there are rules regarding filing documents with the ID, disclosing documents to the opposing side, and ensuring that everyone has a copy of the documents well before the hearing.

The rules concerning documents apply to any document, notice, written request, or application, according to rule 27. The timing for providing documents to the registry and parties is set out in rule 26. Any document provided to a party must also be provided to the party's counsel.

All documents intended for use at the proceeding should be organized and look professional, and must comply with the following requirements:

- *Format.* According to rule 24, documents must be typewritten using only one side of 21.5 cm by 28 cm (8½" × 11") paper, with pages numbered. If the document is a photocopy, it must be clear and legible. If more than one document is filed, a numbered list of all the documents must also be filed.

- *Language.* According to rule 25, documents must be submitted in either English or French, which may require translation.
- *Method of service.* According to rule 29, documents may be provided by a number of methods: by hand, by regular or registered mail, by courier or priority post, by fax (for documents no more than 20 pages long), and sometimes by electronic mail.

Documents are exchanged before the hearing to ensure that all parties have an opportunity to review them, and respond if necessary, in preparation for the hearing. If counsel plans to provide documentary evidence at a client's hearing, the evidence must be disclosed to the opposing side before the proceeding.

The time limits for disclosing documents are set out in rule 26 as follows: as soon as possible, in the case of a 48-hour or 7-day review or an admissibility hearing held at the same time, and at least 5 days before the hearing in all other cases.

Rules: Application Procedures

There are many issues that may require resolution before the hearing can begin. If a party wants a decision on a matter, such as a change to the date or location of the hearing, an application must be brought.

The general procedures that apply to all applications are set out in rules 38 to 40. In addition, each specific type of application is governed by its own rule, as follows:

- changing the location of a hearing—rule 42;
- changing the date or time of a hearing—rule 43;
- joining or separating hearings—rule 44; and
- making oral representations—rule 48.

GENERAL PROCEDURES

According to rule 38, applications must be provided to the ID in the following manner:

- orally or in writing and as soon as possible or within the time limit in the IRPA or the ID Rules;
- stating the outcome sought;
- providing the reasons for the request;
- including any evidence that the party wants considered;
- including supporting evidence in an affidavit or statutory declaration, if the application is not specified in the Rules; and
- with a statement of how and when a copy of the application was sent to the other party.

Under rule 39, the opposing party has the opportunity to respond to the application as soon as possible in the case of a 48-hour or 7-day review or an admissibility hearing held at the same time, and, in all other cases, no later than 5 days after the party received a copy of the application. The response must be provided in the following manner:

- in writing;
- stating the outcome sought;
- providing the reasons for seeking that outcome;
- including any evidence that the party wants considered;
- including supporting evidence in an affidavit or statutory declaration, if the application is not specified in the Rules; and
- providing a statement of how and when a copy of the written response was sent to the opposing party.

According to rule 40, the applicant then has an opportunity to reply to the response.

SPECIFIC APPLICATIONS

Below is a description of the rules that apply to each type of application, in addition to the general procedures in rule 38, which also apply.

Change of Date and Time

A request to change the date and time of a proceeding as specified in the notice to appear may be made by application to the ID, according to rule 43. This situation may arise if, for example, the PC wishes to postpone or adjourn a hearing to provide for more time to gather evidence. Rule 43 also provides several factors that may be considered by the ID when deciding an application to change the date or time of a proceeding, including the following:

- when the application was made;
- whether the party was consulted about the date and time;
- the time already afforded to the party to prepare;
- the party's efforts to prepare;
- whether there have been exceptional circumstances;
- whether there have been previous delays;
- the nature and complexity of the matter to be heard;
- whether the party has counsel;
- whether the time and date fixed for the hearing was peremptory; and
- whether allowing the application would unreasonably delay the proceeding or likely cause an injustice.

It is important for counsel to address these factors when arguing for a change of date or time, because they will be considered by the ID member when she makes her decision.

Change of Venue

A request to change the location of a proceeding as specified in the notice to appear may be made by application to the ID, according to rule 42 of the ID Rules. This may arise if the client wishes to transfer the case to another IRB business office.

Rule 42 also provides several factors that may be considered by the ID when deciding an application to change the location of a proceeding, including the following:

- whether a change of venue would allow the proceeding to be full and proper;
- whether a change would delay the proceeding; and
- whether the change would endanger public safety.

If the application is not allowed, the PC is expected to appear for the proceeding at the fixed location.

Public and Private Hearings

According to section 166(a) of the IRPA, proceedings before the ID that do not concern a refugee claimant are generally required to be held in public. Proceedings that concern a refugee claimant or protected person are generally held in private. From time to time, someone may wish to make a public proceeding private, or a private proceeding public. In such a case, an application must be brought under rule 45 or rule 46, respectively.

Application for a Private Hearing

An application to make a public hearing private may be brought under rule 45 in the following circumstances (IRPA, s 166(b)):

- there is a serious possibility that the life, liberty, or security of a person will be endangered if the proceeding is held in public;
- there is a real and substantial risk to the fairness of the proceeding such that the need to prevent disclosure outweighs the societal interest in a public proceeding; or
- there is a real and substantial risk that matters of public security will be disclosed.

According to rule 45, a request to have the proceeding conducted in private must provide the following:

- a statement of the desired outcome;
- reasons why the ID should agree to make the hearing private; and
- any evidence that the applicant wants the ID to consider in deciding the application.

Application for a Public Hearing

Although proceedings before the ID are generally held in public, matters concerning a refugee claimant or a protected person are generally held in private. From time to time, someone may wish to make the private proceeding open to the public, such as when there is media interest in a claimant or protected person.

According to rule 46, any person may make an application to have the hearing held in public. The application must provide the following:

- a request for a public hearing;
- reasons why the ID should agree to a public hearing; and
- any evidence that the applicant wants the ID to consider in deciding the application.

Non-Disclosure of Information

Occasionally, the minister may have information that must remain confidential because its disclosure could be injurious to national security or endanger the safety of any person. In such circumstances, section 86 of the IRPA allows the minister to make an application for non-disclosure to exclude information from the PC.

In accordance with rule 41, before the admissibility hearing or before a detention review, the minister must make the application for non-disclosure. A member of the ID will hold a meeting with the hearings officer *ex parte*—meaning privately, in the absence of the PC and counsel—before the immigration matter has commenced.

If the minister makes the application during a hearing, rule 41(2) requires the member to exclude the PC and counsel from the hearing room before hearing the application.

According to rule 41(3), if the member decides that the minister's information is relevant to the matter and requires non-disclosure, the member writes a summary of the excluded material without disclosing it, a copy of which is provided to the PC and the minister. The member may then consider all the non-disclosed information when determining the immigration matter.

APPENDIX B

The following table provides a reference list of important topics that relate to enforcement procedures.

Reference for Enforcement Procedures

Provision	IRPA and IRPR
Removals	IRPR, part 13
Removal orders	IRPR, ss 223 to 226 and 228 to 229
Removal orders stayed	IRPR, ss 230 to 232
Removal orders—minors	IRPR, s 249
Entry requirements	IRPA, ss 11, 16
Examinations	IRPA, ss 15, 18
Right of entry	IRPA, s 19
Detention and release	IRPA, ss 54 to 61; IRPR, part 14
Inadmissibility	IRPA, ss 33 to 43
Admissibility hearings	IRPA, ss 44, 45

APPENDIX C
Decision-Making Authorities

The following tables summarize the various decisions that the minister or ID member can make regarding admissibility and detention review hearings, the provisions that grant jurisdiction, and the associated appeal rights to the Immigration Appeal Division (IAD).

Admissibility Hearings

Decision-makers and their powers	Director general (manager): authority as designated by the minister ID member: public servant, employed in accordance with *Public Service Employment Act*. The ID member has the power and authority of a commissioner (*Inquiries Act*) to • administer an oath • issue a summons (ID Rules, r 33).
Essential features of the proceeding	Held to determine whether the person is inadmissible to and removable from Canada. Inadmissibility and removal are assessed on the following grounds: • security: espionage, subversion, terrorism • violations of human or international rights: war crimes, crimes against humanity • serious criminality convictions inside or outside Canada • criminality/organized criminality • health grounds • financial reasons • misrepresentation • non-compliance with the IRPA.
Provisions granting jurisdiction	The manager must "refer" the case to the ID under section 44(2) of the IRPA. The ID member has jurisdiction to hear a matter when a referral for an admissibility hearing is received from the minister (ID Rules, r 3).
Nature of the proceeding	Quasi-judicial Adversarial Proceedings generally held in public Parties are the subject of the proceeding and include • person concerned (PC); • counsel for the PC, who may be a lawyer or member of the Canadian Society of Immigration Consultants, or other counsel if not paid; • hearings officer as the minister's counsel (PSEP/CBSA). Conducted before a single member. Not bound by any legal or technical rules of evidence. Decision based on evidence considered credible or trustworthy.

Decisions/Reasons	The ID member must give reasons for her decision.
	The decisions may be given orally or in writing.
	At the request of the PC or the minister, the ID member must provide written reasons within ten days of the notice of decision.
Possible outcomes	Recognize right to enter Canada.
	Grant permanent or temporary resident status.
	Permit entry to Canada for further examination.
	Make one of the following removal orders:
	• departure order
	• exclusion order
	• deportation order.
Appeal	If the PC has the right to appeal, he may appeal to the IAD.
	If the PC has no right of appeal, he may file an application for judicial review to the Federal Court (IRPA, s 72).
	The PC has no right to appeal to the IAD if he is inadmissible on one of the following grounds:
	• security
	• violating human or international rights
	• serious criminality (punished in Canada; imprisonment of at least two years)
	• organized criminality.

Detention Review Hearings

Decision-makers and their powers	See "Admissibility Hearings" table.
Essential features of the proceeding	Applies to most persons detained under the IRPA. Timing of detention reviews (IRPA, s 57): • within 48 hours after the person is detained; • at least once during the seven days following the first detention review; and • at least once during each 30-day period following each previous review.
Provisions granting jurisdiction	A referral for detention review from the minister (IRPA, ss 57(1), (2); ID Rules, rr 3, 8).
Nature of the proceeding	See "Admissibility Hearings" table.
Decisions/Reasons	The decision may be given orally or in writing. The ID member must give reasons for her decision. At the request of the PC or the minister, the ID member must provide written reasons within ten days of the notice of decision.
Possible outcomes	Release, with or without conditions. Continue detention on one of the following grounds: • danger to public • unlikely to appear • flight risk • identity not established • other factors.
Appeal	The PC has the right to file an application for judicial review by the Federal Court.

APPENDIX D

Removal Orders

The following chart, based on sections 228 and 229 of the IRPR, summarizes the grounds of inadmissibility and the related removal orders that can be made, by type of decision-maker. For a complete list and explanation of the exceptions listed in the footnotes to this chart, consult part 13 of the IRPR.

Removal Orders

Person against whom the removal order is made	Ground(s) of inadmissibility	Action taken by minister's delegate	Prescribed removal order
Refugee claimant	At the time the claimant makes the claim: • reasons of health • financial grounds • non-compliance	Issues removal order	Departure[a]
Foreign national	The foreign national is: • an unaccompanied minor, or • a person unable to appreciate the nature of the proceedings Any ground of inadmissibility (IRPR, s 220(4))	Refers case to ID	Order depends on ground of inadmissibility
Foreign national or permanent resident	Security risk (IRPA, s 34(1))	Refers case to ID	Deportation
Foreign national or permanent resident	Violating human or international rights (IRPA, s 35(1))	Refers case to ID	Deportation
Foreign national	Serious criminality in case where the evidence is straightforward and does not require extensive analysis or weighing (IRPA, s 36(1)(a) or 36(2)(a))	Issues removal order	Deportation
Foreign national	Serious criminality (IRPA, s 36(1)(b) or (c), or s 36(2)(a), (b), (c), or (d))	Refers case to ID	Deportation
Permanent resident	Serious criminality (IRPA, s 36(1))	Refers case to ID	Deportation
Foreign national or permanent resident	Organized criminality (IRPA, s 37(1))	Refers case to ID	Deportation

a   Exception: Departure order is stayed and is conditional upon the outcome of the matter: the claim is ineligible; has been decided by the RPD and is rejected; or is withdrawn, abandoned, or terminated.

Person against whom the removal order is made	Ground(s) of inadmissibility	Action taken by minister's delegate	Prescribed removal order
Foreign national	Health grounds (IRPA, s 38)	Refers case to ID	Exclusion[b]
Foreign national or permanent resident	Financial grounds (IRPA, s 39)	Refers case to ID	Exclusion[c]
Foreign national	Misrepresenting or withholding material facts (IRPA, s 40(1)(a)) Being sponsored by a person who is determined to be inadmissible for misrepresentation (IRPA, s 40(1)(b))	Refers case to ID	Exclusion[d]
Permanent resident	Misrepresenting or withholding material facts (IRPA, s 40(1)(a))	Refers case to ID	Exclusion
Permanent resident	Having been sponsored by a person who is determined to be inadmissible for misrepresentation (IRPA, s 40(1)(b))	Refers case to ID	Departure
Foreign national	On a final determination to vacate a decision to allow the claim for refugee protection by the permanent resident or the foreign national (IRPA, s 40(1)(c))	Issues removal order	Deportation
Foreign national or permanent resident	On ceasing to be a citizen (IRPA, s 40(1)(d); *Citizenship Act*, s 10)	Refers case to ID	Deportation
Foreign national	Non-compliance: • failing to appear for an examination or an admissibility hearing (IRPR, s 228(c)).	Issues removal order	Exclusion
Foreign national	Non-compliance: • failing to appear for examination (IRPA, s 41(a))	Refers case to ID	Exclusion[e]

b   Exception: A departure order to be issued for undecided refugee claims on health grounds, and for persons who were previously removed for the same reasons.

c   Exception: A departure order to be issued for undecided refugee claims for financial reasons and for persons who were previously removed for the same reasons.

d   Exception: A departure order to be issued for persons who were previously removed for the same reasons of misrepresentation.

e   Exception: A departure order to be issued for refugee claimants whose claims are undecided for failing to appear for an examination and for persons who were previously removed for the same reasons.

Person against whom the removal order is made	Ground(s) of inadmissibility	Action taken by minister's delegate	Prescribed removal order
Permanent resident	Non-compliance: • failing to comply with any conditions imposed under the regulations, or • failing to comply with residency obligations (IRPA, s 41(b), 27(2), or 28)	Refers case to ID	Departure
Permanent resident	Non-compliance: • failing to establish permanent residence (IRPA, s 41(a))	Refers case to ID	Exclusion[f]
Foreign national or permanent resident	Non-compliance: • failing to comply with any other section of the Act (IRPA, s 41(a))	Refers case to ID	Exclusion[g]
Foreign national	Non-compliance: • failing to leave Canada by the end of the authorized period of stay (IRPA, s 41(a))	Refers case to ID	Exclusion[h]
Foreign national	Non-compliance: • failing to obtain the authorization to return to Canada (IRPA, ss 41, 52(1))	Issues removal order	Deportation
Foreign national	Non-compliance: • failing to establish that they hold a visa (IRPA, ss 41, 20)	Issues removal order	Exclusion
Foreign national	Non-compliance: • failing to leave Canada by the end of the authorized period of stay (IRPA, ss 41, 29(2))	Issues removal order	Exclusion
Foreign national	Non-compliance: • failing to comply with any conditions on the visa (IRPA, ss 41, 29(2), 184)	Issues removal order	Exclusion

f   Exception: A departure order to be issued for persons who are inadmissible for reasons of failing to establish permanent residence if the person was previously removed for failing to establish permanent residence.

g   Exception: A departure order to be issued for refugee claimants whose claims are undecided if inadmissible for reasons of failing to comply; or for persons who are inadmissible for failing to comply with the Act if the person was previously removed for the same reasons, or the person failed to comply with conditions under the previous Act, or the person has been convicted of an indictable offence or two offences in Canada, unless the grounds for removal are the convictions.

h   Exception: A departure order to be issued for undecided refugee claims if inadmissible for reasons of overstaying a temporary visa.

Person against whom the removal order is made	Ground(s) of inadmissibility	Action taken by minister's delegate	Prescribed removal order
Permanent resident	Non-compliance: • failing to comply with a residency obligation (IRPA, ss 41, 28)	Issues removal order	Departure
Foreign national	Inadmissible family member (IRPA, s 42)	Issues removal order	Same removal order as issued to the inadmissible family member

KEY TERMS

admissibility hearing, 447

departure order, 454

deportation order, 454

designated foreign national (DFN), 447

designated irregular arrival, 447

detention review, 448

exclusion order, 454

flight risk, 459

inadmissibility report
(section 44(1) report), 440

interdiction, 439

removal order, 439

REVIEW QUESTIONS

1. What is the purpose of an admissibility hearing?

2. List and briefly describe the prescribed factors that must be considered when determining whether to detain a person.

3. List and briefly describe the three types of removal orders.

4. What are a person's rights and responsibilities at a proceeding before the ID?

5. What information must a section 44(1) report contain?

6. Compare and contrast the roles of the minister's counsel and counsel for the PC.

PART VII

Appeals

Appeals

LEARNING OUTCOMES

After reading this chapter, you should be able to:

- Describe the four types of immigration appeals.

- Understand who has the right to appeal to the Immigration Appeal Division and the Refugee Appeal Division.

- Understand the general rules for appearing at an appeal tribunal of the Immigration and Refugee Board.

- Find your way around the Immigration Appeal Division and Refugee Appeal Division rules.

- Know the contents of the memorandum to file an appeal before the Refugee Appeal Division.

- Understand the role of participants at immigration appeal proceedings.

- Describe the basic procedures for filing a judicial review of an administrative decision.

Introduction

What happens next? An application for sponsorship is denied by a visa officer; a refugee claimant's claim is rejected; a permanent resident's application for citizenship is denied: is there anything an applicant can do?

Generally, in administrative law, when an applicant is denied the right or benefit sought, she may challenge the decision. Depending on the governing statutory framework, this challenge may include the right to an appeal to an independent tribunal or a judicial review. Under the *Immigration and Refugee Protection Act* (IRPA), tribunal decisions from the Immigration Division (ID) may be appealed to the Immigration Appeal Division (IAD), as provided for in sections 62 through 71; and decisions from the Refugee Protection Division (RPD) may be appealed to the Refugee Appeal Division (RAD), as provided for in sections 110 to 111. Most administrative decisions made by the Canada Border Services Agency (CBSA), Citizenship and Immigration Canada (CIC), the IAD, and the RAD may be judicially reviewed by the Federal Court. Section 72 provides for the right to a judicial review of any decision, determination, or order relating to immigration and refugee protection matters, other than an interlocutory judgment, where no statutory right of appeal exists or those rights have been exhausted.

At the Immigration and Refugee Board (IRB), a member of the IAD hears immigration appeals and a member of the RAD hears appeals from rejected refugee claimants. Individuals who have a right to appeal at the IRB have the right to counsel, the right to an interpreter, the right to present and call witnesses, and the right to be heard—either through a written application process or by hearing—before an independent and impartial decision-maker.

As appellate bodies, the IAD and the RAD have the following in common:

- they have "sole and exclusive jurisdiction to hear and determine all questions of law and fact" in respect of the proceedings brought before them (IRPA, s 162);
- they may base their decision on any evidence adduced in the proceeding (IAD at IRPA, s 175(1)(c); RAD at IRPA, s 171(a.3));
- they are not bound by any legal or technical rules of evidence (IAD at IRPA, s 175(1)(b); RAD at IRPA, s 171(a.2));
- they may grant a remedy if they determine that the lower decision is "wrong" in law, in fact, or in mixed law and fact (IAD at IRPA, s 67(1)(a); RAD at IRPA, s 111(2)(a));
- they may set aside the lower decision and substitute their own determination (IAD at IRPA, s 67(2); RAD at IRPA, s 111(1)(b)); and
- they are not required to hold an oral hearing in every circumstance (IAD at IRPA, s 175(1)(a); RAD at IRPA, s 110(3)).[1]

---

1   See *Huruglica v Canada (Citizenship and Immigration)*, 2014 FC 799 at para 50.

Note that there is no citizenship appeal tribunal. The section of the *Citizenship Act* that provided for an appeal (s 14(5)) was repealed when Bill C-24, the *Strengthening Canadian Citizenship Act*, was passed on June 19, 2014. Decisions of a citizenship judge may be reviewed by the Federal Court only when leave is granted for a judicial review.

This chapter examines the appeal processes before the Immigration Appeal Division and the Refugee Appeal Division, and briefly examines the judicial review process for administrative decision-making.

Know and Follow the Divisional Rules

Legal professionals who represent persons who are subject to a proceeding in any of the IRB's divisions must have a thorough knowledge of that division's rules, in addition to the provisions of the IRPA that set out the jurisdiction of the IRB and the division to hear and decide matters. For example, if an appeal is filed and the division does not have jurisdiction to hear it, the appeal will not proceed, so it is important not to mislead a client into thinking that "it's worth a try."

Each division of the IRB has a distinct set of rules. The divisional rules are the division's regulations established to set out roles and responsibilities, and govern practices and procedures in proceedings before the division. Section 161 of the IRPA gives the chairperson of the IRB the authority to make rules related to each division's activities, practices, and procedures, in consultation with the deputy chairpersons, and subject to the approval of the governor in council.

The rules of each division are regulations made under the IRPA, and they are binding, so it is important to know them well. Failure to comply with the rules may have severe consequences for the client. For example, if the appeal is not "perfected"— that is, if it does not contain the required information and supporting documents because the rules were ignored—then the tribunal does not have to hear and decide it.

A legal professional who is unsure about the meaning or application of a particular rule may direct questions and requests for clarification to the tribunal's registrar at the nearest business office of the IRB.

It is important to keep apprised of amendments to the rules. The IRB's website (<www.irb-cisr.gc.ca>) is updated regularly with practice notices and information pages for appellants about the appeals processes. What follows is a general overview of the rules.

General Rules of the IAD and RAD

A number of the *Immigration Appeal Division Rules* (IAD Rules) and *Refugee Appeal Division Rules* (RAD Rules) are similar. This section provides an overview of those rules that are common to the IRB's two appeal divisions.

WEBLINK

There are several ways to find the rules for the IAD and RAD, including searching on the CanLII website at <www.canlii.org>; on the IRB website at <www.irb-cisr.gc.ca> under "Legal and Policy References"; or on the Justice Laws website at <laws-lois.justice.gc.ca>.

Definitions

Important key terms are defined in rule 1 of each division's rules. Legal professionals—referred to as "counsel" by the IRB—demonstrate professionalism by understanding and using relevant and appropriate terminology while representing their clients before an appeal. For example, legal professionals must understand that a "proceeding" may refer to an appeal that is decided with or without a hearing, a conference, an application, or an alternative dispute resolution process. It is also important for counsel to be able to distinguish the terms "appellant" and "respondent" and to understand terms such as "contact information."

The parties to an appeal are called the appellant and the respondent. The rules define "appellant" as the party requesting that the appeal be heard, and the "respondent" as the party arguing that the lower decision should stand. In most cases, the minister is the respondent.

The divisional rules define "contact information" as a person's name, postal address, telephone number, and fax number and electronic mail address (IAD Rules, r 1; RAD Rules, r 1).

The IAD Rules have an additional rule for contact information (r 13): contact information for both the appellant and counsel must be provided to the division so that the division can serve notices about proceedings and other matters.

If notices, such as a notice to appear, are not received because the division does not have the proper address, the appellant might fail to show up for the proceeding, leading to dismissal of the appeal. Changes to the appellant's or counsel's contact information must be provided to the division and the other party without delay.

Scheduling a Hearing

Tribunals do not generally wish to fix a date on their calendar if a case is not going to proceed, and so the rules serve to ensure that the parties are prepared and will be ready to proceed. Unless otherwise provided for in the *Immigration and Refugee Protection Regulations* (IRPR), appeals are scheduled when the record has been perfected and the matter is considered *ready to be heard*, meaning that the appeal record and/or the required documents have been received, documents have been exchanged pursuant to the rules of disclosure, and witnesses are available.

Generally, the parties may be required to participate in a scheduling conference. For example, the IAD may hold *assignment courts*, which are formal proceedings that are recorded and presided over by a member for the purpose of setting a hearing date pursuant to rule 22 of the IAD Rules. In the example of a scheduling conference, assignment court is held so that the parties can speak to the matter of their readiness to proceed. The parties have the opportunity to agree to a hearing date or, alternatively, to explain why they are not ready to proceed. For example, the IAD member presiding at assignment court can remind unrepresented appellants of their right to counsel, explain the hearing process, and describe what is expected of them. Where the record has not been received on time pursuant to the IAD Rules, or where there is reason to believe that one of the parties is delaying the hearing, the member may decide to proceed peremptorily by setting a date for a hearing.

Notice to Appear

The division is responsible for notifying the parties of the date, time, and location of a hearing in accordance with its rules. This may be done orally (for example, at assignment court or another proceeding before the IAD) or in writing in a notice to appear (for example, within a specific time frame, in a case before the RAD).

Counsel of Record Information

The divisions have rules that require counsel of record to provide contact information, regardless of whether counsel is considered an authorized representative or not (IAD Rules, r 13(3); RAD Rules, r 16).

Who May Be Counsel of Record Under the IRPA

Representation or advice for consideration

91(1) Subject to this section, no person shall knowingly, directly or indirectly, represent or advise a person for consideration—or offer to do so—in connection with the submission of an expression of interest under subsection 10.1(3) or a proceeding or application under this Act.

Persons who may represent or advise

(2) A person does not contravene subsection (1) if they are

(a) a lawyer who is a member in good standing of a law society of a province or a notary who is a member in good standing of the Chambre des notaires du Québec;

(b) any other member in good standing of a law society of a province or the Chambre des notaires du Québec, including a paralegal; or

(c) a member in good standing of a body designated [by the minister].

Unrepresented appellants who wish to be represented are expected to retain counsel without delay. If the appellant has already agreed to a hearing date, he should choose counsel who is available to appear on that date. (It is a matter of professional ethics that an authorized representative—that is, a member of the Immigration Consultants of Canada Regulatory Council [ICCRC]—not undertake representation unless she has the ability and capacity to deal adequately with the matters to be undertaken, which includes being available. For more about the ICCRC, see Chapter 16.

Once retained, counsel must inform the division without delay. In some cases, counsel may wish to be removed from the record—for example, if the client refuses to pay or is very difficult. The divisions have rules that direct counsel to seek permission from the division to withdraw from a case. If, on the other hand, the client wishes to remove counsel, the client must generally provide written notice to the division, to counsel, and to the minister. The regulator of immigration consultants—the ICCRC—also has rules about the circumstances and steps that a licensed immigration consultant should adhere to when withdrawing from representation (see article 14 of the *Code of Professional Ethics* in the appendix to Chapter 16).

In addition, all representatives must complete a form with their contact information. For licensed representatives, the IRB provides a Counsel Contact Information form (IRB/CISR 101.02),[2] which requires representatives to provide their membership identification number for either the ICCRC or the provincial law society to which they belong.

Any lay counsel who represents a client and is not charging a fee should use the Notice of Representation Without a Fee or Other Consideration form (IRB/CISR 101.03).[3]

Communicating with the Decision-Maker

The parties and their representatives must never communicate directly with the decision-maker; rather, they must direct all communication through the registry. This applies to all communication, both oral and written, including questions about the process, documents, or a particular proceeding.

Following this procedure is important in order to avoid suspicions of bias or influence. All parties must be aware of all information being passed on to the decision-maker, so that they have the opportunity to respond. Applications and other communications must be made in writing, within specified time limits, and generally with proof that all parties have been served.

Interpreters

The appellant must choose a language of record, either English or French, no later than 20 days after filing a notice of appeal with the IAD, pursuant to rule 17 of the IAD Rules. Appeals before the RAD are generally paper-based; however, when a hearing is held, the appellant has a right to an interpreter (RAD Rules, r 59).

Only accredited interpreters are used by the IRB for hearings in any division. IRB-accredited interpreters have undergone security checks, have passed a language exam, and have attended an orientation and training period. IRB-accredited interpreters are not employees of the IRB; rather, they have a personal services contract with the board and are hired on a case-by-case basis. They are permanently bound by their promise to interpret accurately once they take an oath or make a solemn affirmation to do so.

Generally, before the beginning of the proceeding, the interpreter will use a standardized script to confirm that she and the party, or witness, understand each other. At the beginning of a proceeding, the interpreter must take an oath or make a solemn affirmation to interpret the proceedings accurately and in accordance with the rules. The interpreter may not guide, provide advice, or offer an opinion.

---

2 This form is available on the IRB website at <http://www.irb-cisr.gc.ca/Eng/res/form/Documents/IrbCisr10102_e.pdf>.

3 This form is available on the IRB website at <http://www.irb-cisr.gc.ca/Eng/res/form/Documents/IrbCisr10103_e.pdf>.

Documents

There are several kinds of documents relevant to appeal proceedings, such as financial statements, medical reports, and documents that show the client's relationship to family members, in a sponsorship appeal, or new information, such as identity documents or country-specific information, at a refugee appeal. Documents are important evidence at appeal proceedings, and the applicable rules are similar for the IAD and the RAD. Because of the importance of documents to a fair resolution of the case, there are rules regarding filing documents, ensuring that everyone has a copy of the documents well before the hearing, and timelines.

Counsel must use appropriate forms and follow these rules for filing documents:

- all documents provided to the IAD or the RAD must be provided to the division registry;
- any document provided to the minister must be provided to the minister's counsel; and
- any document provided to a person other than the minister must be provided to that person's counsel, if the person is represented.

Counsel should provide organized and professional-looking documents. All documents intended for use at a proceeding must comply with the rules. The requirements for handling documents are similar for the IAD and the RAD, with only minor variations between the divisions, as follows:

- *Format (IAD Rules, r 28; RAD Rules, r 27).* Documents must be typewritten using only one side of 8½" × 11" paper, with pages numbered. If the document is a photocopy, it must be clear and legible. If more than one document is filed, a numbered list of all documents must also be filed.
- *Language (IAD Rules, r 29; RAD Rules, r 28).* Documents must be submitted in either English or French, which may require translation.
- *Method of service (IAD Rules, r 34; RAD Rules, r 32).* Documents may be delivered by a number of methods, including by hand, by regular or registered mail, by courier or priority post, by fax (for documents no more than 20 pages long), and, sometimes, by email or other electronic means. Otherwise, a request must be made to the division asking for permission to provide the document in an alternative format (or not at all).
- *Computation of time (IAD Rules, r 36; RAD Rules, r 35).* A document is considered received by the division on the day that the document is date-stamped.

When a document is delivered to the appellant or respondent by regular mail, it is considered to be received 7 days after the day that it was mailed. If day 7 falls on a Saturday, Sunday, or statutory holiday, then the document is considered received on the next working day.

The IAD Rules provide for situations where, if the document was mailed to or from outside Canada, it is considered received 20 days after the day that it was mailed. If day 20 falls on a Saturday, Sunday, or statutory holiday, then the document is considered received on the next working day. (See Chapter 6, page 187 for an explanation of how to compute time in accordance with the *Interpretation Act*.)

The Immigration Appeal Division

The IAD has jurisdiction to hear and decide certain types of appeals on immigration matters, pursuant to section 62 of the IRPA. This section discusses who may appeal to the IAD, the types of immigration appeals, and how to initiate an appeal. It also gives a brief overview of the related processes.

The right to appeal an immigration decision is not available in all cases, but only in the following circumstances:

- sponsorship appeals by Canadian citizens and permanent residents whose applications to sponsor close family members to Canada have been refused (IRPA, s 63(1));

- removal order appeals by permanent residents, foreign nationals with a permanent resident visa, and protected persons who have been ordered removed from Canada (IRPA, ss 63(2), (3));[4]

- loss-of-permanent-residence appeals (also called residency obligation appeals) by permanent residents who have been determined not to have fulfilled their residency obligation by an immigration officer outside Canada (IRPA, s 63(4));[5] and

- minister's appeals (IRPA, s 63(5)).

Usually—as in the first three circumstances above—the appellant is an individual, such as a sponsorship applicant, the subject of a removal order, or a failed permanent resident applicant. However, the minister of public safety, who has responsibility for the CBSA, also has a right to appeal a decision made by a member of the ID at an admissibility hearing (IRPA, s 63(5)).

According to section 64 of the IRPA, a person has no right to appeal to the IAD if he has been found inadmissible on grounds of security, violation of human or international rights, serious criminality, or organized criminality. The loss of appeal rights for reasons of serious criminality requires that the person have been sentenced in Canada to at least six months for a single sentence. Furthermore, a person has no right to appeal if found inadmissible for misrepresentation unless that person is the sponsor's spouse, common law partner, or child.

The chart below summarizes the types of appeals to the IAD.

---

4   There is no right to appeal a removal order if the person was found inadmissible on the grounds of security, violations of human or international rights, serious criminality, or organized criminality.

5   In Canada, a removal order is issued against a permanent resident who loses her permanent resident status; that person can appeal the minister's decision to issue the removal order. The difference is that outside Canada, there is no removal order made against a person who loses her status.

Right of Appeal to the IAD

Appeal	Right of appeal	No right of appeal
Sponsorship appeal of a decision by an officer (IRPA, s 63(1))	Canadian citizen Permanent resident	Persons found inadmissible because of • security, violating human or international rights, serious criminality, or organized criminality (IRPA, s 64(1)); • serious criminality that was punished by a sentence of at least six months' imprisonment or conviction of an offence outside Canada or commission of an act outside Canada that would be punishable in Canada by a maximum term of imprisonment of at least ten years (IRPA, s 64(2)); or • misrepresentation, unless the foreign national is the sponsor's spouse, common law partner, or child (IRPA, s 64(3)).
Removal order appeal of a decision by the ID in an admissibility hearing (IRPA, s 63(2))	Foreign national with permanent resident visa	Persons found inadmissible because of • security, violating human or international rights, serious criminality, or organized criminality (IRPA, s 64(1)); • serious criminality that was punished by a sentence of at least six months' imprisonment or conviction of an offence outside Canada or commission of an act outside Canada that would be punishable in Canada by a maximum term of imprisonment of at least ten years (IRPA, s 64(2)); or • foreign nationals without a permanent resident visa.
Removal order appeal of a decision by the ID in an admissibility hearing (IRPA, s 63(3))	Permanent resident Protected person	
Residency obligation appeal of a decision by an officer outside Canada (IRPA, s 63(4))	Permanent resident	N/A
Minister's appeal of a decision of the ID in an admissibility hearing (IRPA, s 63(5))	Minister	N/A

IAD Rules

The IAD Rules set out the applicable procedures first by appeal type, such as sponsorship appeals or removal order appeals, then by rules that apply to all immigration appeals. There are 60 rules in all, governing practices and procedures before the IAD.

Rule 57 of the IAD Rules provides the IAD with the flexibility to "do whatever is necessary to deal with the matter" should a procedural problem arise during a proceeding. Consider the following situations:

- According to rule 58, IAD members may act on their own initiative to change a rule, to excuse a person from a rule, and to extend or shorten time limits.
- According to rule 59, failure to follow a rule in a proceeding does not, in itself, make the proceeding invalid.

Notice of Appeal

In all cases, the appeal process begins with a notice of appeal, generally filed at the registry (IRB business office) closest to the appellant's residence. The notice of appeal must meet the following criteria:

- it must be made by a person who has the right to appeal,
- it must be filed on time, and
- it must be filed in accordance with the rules of procedure specific to the type of appeal.

The IAD must then notify either the minister or the ID of the appeal so that the record can be prepared.

Time Limits for Filing Appeals

The time requirements for filing appeals are very important. If the notice of appeal is not filed on time, the minister may dispute the appellant's appeal right and make an application to dismiss the appeal on the basis that the IAD does not have jurisdiction to hear it. Time limits may differ depending on the type of appeal, as noted below.

Time Limits for Filing Appeals

Type of appeal	Trigger for filing appeal	Time limit
Sponsorship appeal	From date of officer's reasons for refusal	30 days
Removal order appeal		
ID decision	At admissibility hearing	At end of admissibility hearing
	From date of appellant's receipt of removal order	30 days
Officer decision at examination	From date of appellant's receipt of removal order	30 days
Residency obligation appeal	From date of appellant's receipt of written decision	60 days
Minister's appeal	From date of decision	30 days

Sponsorship Appeals

A refused sponsorship application may be appealed. The appellant must provide the notice of appeal, together with the visa officer's written reasons for the refusal, to the IAD no later than 30 days after the sponsor received the written reasons for refusal, according to rule 3 of the IAD Rules.

Removal Order Appeals

Removal orders may be issued by a member of the ID at an admissibility hearing or by an officer at an examination. The person against whom a removal order is made may appeal in either situation. The time limits for appeal in each situation are discussed below.

DECISION AT ADMISSIBILITY HEARING

If the appellant is subject to a removal order made at an admissibility hearing, then rule 5 of the IAD Rules provides the following two options:

1. the appellant may provide the notice of appeal by hand at the end of the admissibility hearing to the member of the ID who made the removal order, in which case it is the ID member's responsibility to provide the notice of appeal to the IAD without delay; or

2. the appellant may provide the notice of appeal, together with the removal order, directly to the IAD no later than 30 days after the appellant received the removal order.

DECISION AT EXAMINATION

If the appellant is subject to a removal order made by an officer at an examination, rule 7 of the IAD Rules requires the person to provide the notice of appeal, together with the removal order, to the IAD no later than 30 days after receiving the removal order. In this situation, the IAD must notify the minister of the appeal with the removal order, without delay.

Residency Obligation Appeals

A permanent resident outside Canada may appeal an officer's decision that he has lost his permanent resident status. To do so, the appellant must provide the IAD with a notice of appeal along with the officer's written decision, which must be delivered to the registry closest to where the appellant last resided in Canada, within 60 days after receiving the written decision, according to rule 9 of the IAD Rules.

The longer time limit for this type of appeal (60 days rather than 30 days) is intended to account for the fact that the appellant is located outside Canada. The IAD must notify the minister of the appeal with the written decision without delay.

If the appellant wishes to be physically present in Canada for the appeal hearing, this must be indicated in the notice of appeal, and the appellant must formally make a request under rule 46 of the IAD Rules (see below under the heading "Return to Canada—Rule 46").

Minister's Appeals

The minister of public safety, as a party to the admissibility hearing, also has the right to appeal the decision of a member of the ID. To initiate the appeal, the minister must provide a notice of appeal to the respondent (the subject of the admissibility hearing), to the ID, and to the IAD, in accordance with rule 11 of the IAD rules, no later than 30 days after the ID decision was made.

The Appeal Record

After receiving a notice of appeal, the IAD verifies that it has jurisdiction to hear the matter. If the IAD is satisfied that the notice of appeal complies with all requirements, the IAD notifies the respondent (the minister or the ID, depending on the type of appeal), without delay. It is then the responsibility of the respondent to prepare and serve a group of documents, known as the appeal record, in accordance with the IAD Rules.

Time Limits for Serving the Appeal Record

The IAD may not commence a hearing until the appeal record is received. In the past, the time limitation afforded to the minister to prepare the record was problematic, generally because of operational demands such as heavy workload of visa offices and transfer of personnel. Consequently, appellants were kept waiting for lengthy periods for their appeal to be scheduled and heard. To shorten these delays, the IAD created rules to address situations where the record is not received on time. These are discussed below with respect to each type of appeal.

Time Limits for Serving Appeal Record

Type of appeal	Record prepared by	Number of days after notice of appeal served
Sponsorship appeal	CIC—Visa Office	120
Removal order appeal *ID decision*	ID	45
Officer decision at examination	CIC	45
Residency obligation appeal	CIC—Visa Office	120
Minister's appeal	ID	45

SPONSORSHIP APPEALS

According to rule 4 of the IAD Rules, the minister must prepare the record when notified of an appeal. In practice, the visa office will receive notice of a sponsorship appeal, and this triggers the preparation of the appeal record by the officer who refused the sponsorship. The record consists of the following documents:

- a table of contents,
- the application for permanent residence that was refused,

- the sponsor's application and undertaking,
- documents that were considered in the application, and
- the written reasons for refusal.

The record must be provided to both the IAD and the appellant no later than 120 days after the minister is served with the notice of appeal.

If the record is not received within the 120 days, rule 4(5) compels the minister to explain the delay and provide reasons to wait for the record, or provides the IAD with the option to start the appeal hearing with a partial record or no record.

REMOVAL ORDER APPEALS

Decision Made at an Admissibility Hearing

The ID is responsible for preparing the appeal record, which consists of the following documents in accordance with rule 6 of the IAD Rules:

- a table of contents,
- the removal order,
- the transcript of the admissibility hearing,
- documents admitted into evidence at the admissibility hearing, and
- the ID's written reasons for the removal order.

The record must be provided to the IAD, the appellant, and the minister no later than 45 days after the ID received the notice of appeal. Unlike sponsorship appeals, there is no rule dealing with non-receipt of the record because the ID is a division of the same tribunal as the IAD, and there are internal procedures in place to meet the 45-day time frame. Rule 6 is silent, however, on the issue of the ID's failure to provide the record within this time frame. The record in these situations is prepared by the registrar, who is responsible for providing support to both the ID and the IAD.

Decision Made at an Examination

For appeals relating to a decision made at an examination, the minister is responsible for preparing the appeal record no later than 45 days after the minister received the notice of appeal. In accordance with rule 8 of the IAD Rules, the record must consist of the following:

- a table of contents,
- the removal order,
- any document relevant to the removal order, and
- the written reasons for the minister's removal order.

The record must be provided to the IAD and the appellant. Rule 8(5) provides the IAD with a process for dealing with late receipt of the record: if the record is not received within the 45 days, the IAD may ask the minister to explain the delay and provide reasons to wait for the record, or it may start the appeal hearing with a partial record or no record.

RESIDENCY OBLIGATION APPEALS

The minister of CIC is responsible for preparing the appeal record, which is composed of the following documents in accordance with rule 10 of the IAD Rules:

- a table of contents,
- any document relevant to the decision on the residency obligation, and
- the visa officer's written decision and reasons.

The minister must provide the record to the IAD and the appellant no later than 120 days after the minister received the notice of appeal. Rule 10(5) provides the IAD with a process for dealing with late receipt of the record: if the record is not received within the 120 days, the IAD may ask the minister to explain the delay and provide reasons to wait for the record, or it may start the appeal hearing with a partial record or no record.

MINISTER'S APPEALS

The ID is responsible for preparing the appeal record, which consists of the following documents in accordance with rule 12 of the IAD Rules:

- a table of contents,
- the ID's decision,
- the transcript of the ID admissibility hearing,
- any document accepted into evidence at the hearing, and
- any written reasons for the ID's decision.

The ID must provide the record to the IAD, the respondent, and the minister no later than 45 days after the ID receives the notice of appeal.

Disclosure of Documents

Documents are exchanged before the hearing to ensure that all parties have an opportunity to review them, and respond if necessary, in preparation for the hearing. According to rule 30, if a party plans to provide documentary evidence, the party must disclose the evidence to the opposing side before the proceeding and, with a copy to the IAD, must provide a written statement of how and when the copy was provided to the other party. If a document is not disclosed before the hearing, the party may not use it at the hearing unless allowed by the division, according to rule 31.

Documents must be disclosed at least 20 days before the hearing, unless the documents are being disclosed in response to another document provided by the other party, in which case disclosure must occur at least 10 days before the hearing.

There is a separate rule for the disclosure of medical documents related to an appeal based on inadmissibility on health grounds: these documents must be disclosed no later than 60 days before the hearing, unless the document is in response to another medical document, in which case the time limit is 30 days before the hearing.

Application Procedures

There are many issues that may require resolution before a hearing can even begin (for example, a change to the date or location of the hearing). If a party wants a decision on such a matter, the party must bring an application. There are general procedures that apply to all applications, and other procedures that apply for each kind of application.

General Procedures

The general procedures for applications are set out in rule 42 of the IAD Rules and apply to all of the following matters:

- a request to return to Canada to appear for an appeal hearing—rule 46;
- an application to change the location of a hearing—rule 47;
- an application to change the date or time of a hearing—rule 48;
- an application to have a proceeding held in private—rule 49;
- a notification to withdraw an appeal—rule 50; and
- an application to reinstate an appeal that was withdrawn—rule 51.

Note that each type of application is also governed by its own rule, as shown above.

According to rule 43 of the IAD Rules, applications must be provided to the IAD in the following manner:

- orally or in writing, and as soon as possible or within the time limit in the IRPA or IAD Rules;
- stating the outcome sought;
- providing the reasons for the request;
- including, if known, whether the other party agrees to the application;
- including supporting evidence in an affidavit or statutory declaration, if the application is not specified in the IAD Rules; and
- with a statement of how and when a copy of the application was sent to the other party.

The opposing party has the opportunity to respond to the application under rule 44, no later than seven days after receiving the application. The response must be provided in the following manner:

- in writing (if the application was made in writing);
- stating the outcome sought;
- providing the reasons for seeking that outcome;
- including supporting evidence in an affidavit or statutory declaration, if the application is not specified in the IAD Rules; and
- providing a statement of how and when a copy of the written response was sent to the opposing party (the applicant).

The applicant then has the opportunity to reply to the response according to rule 45, no later than five days after receiving the copy of the response.

Specific Applications

Below is a description of the rules that apply, in addition to the general procedures under rule 43 of the IAD, to each type of application.

RETURN TO CANADA—RULE 46

A request to return to Canada to appear for an appeal hearing may be made to the IAD according to rule 46. This may arise if the client is appealing an officer's decision that he has lost his permanent resident status because he did not meet the residency obligation of residing in Canada for two years out of a five-year period. Documents must be provided to the IAD no later than 60 days after the notice of appeal has been filed on the IAD. If the application is accepted and the IAD orders the person to physically appear for his hearing, CIC must issue a travel document for that purpose according to section 175(2) of the IRPA.

CHANGE OF LOCATION—RULE 47

A request to change the location of a proceeding as specified in the notice to appear may be made by application to the IAD according to rule 47. This situation may arise if the client wishes to transfer the case to another office. Documents must be provided to the IAD no later than 30 days before the proceeding. If the application is not allowed, the client is expected to appear for the proceeding at the fixed location.

Rule 47 provides several factors that the ID may consider when deciding an application to change the location of a proceeding, including the following:

- whether the party is residing in the location where she wants the proceeding to take place;
- whether a change of location would allow the proceeding to be full and proper;
- whether a change of location would delay or slow the proceeding;
- how a change of location would affect the operation of the IAD; and
- how a change of location would affect the parties.

CHANGE OF DATE AND TIME—RULE 48

A request to change the date and time of a proceeding as specified in the notice to appear may be made by application to the IAD, according to rule 48. This situation may arise if, for example, the person concerned wishes to postpone a hearing to provide for more time to gather evidence. The application must be received at least two working days before the proceeding, and must include at least six alternative dates. If the application is not allowed, the client is expected to appear for the proceeding at the fixed date and time.

Rule 48 provides several factors that the IAD may consider when deciding an application to change the date or time of a proceeding, including the following:

- whether the party was consulted about the date and time;
- when the application was made;
- the time already afforded to the party to prepare;
- the party's efforts to prepare;
- in the case of a party who wants more time to obtain information, whether proceeding in the absence of such information would cause an injustice;
- the knowledge and experience of counsel representing the party;
- whether there have been previous delays, and the reasons for the delay(s);
- whether the time and date fixed for the hearing were peremptory;
- whether allowing the application would unreasonably delay the proceedings; and
- the nature and complexity of the matter to be heard.

PUBLIC VERSUS PRIVATE HEARINGS—RULE 49

The IRPA requires that proceedings before the IAD be held in public (IRPA, s 166(a)). However, from time to time someone may wish to make the proceeding private. This typically occurs when

- there is a serious possibility that the life, liberty, or security of a person will be endangered if the proceeding is held in public;
- there is a real and substantial risk to the fairness of the proceedings such that the need to prevent disclosure outweighs society's interest in a public proceeding; or
- there is a real and substantial risk that matters involving public security will be disclosed.

A request to have the proceeding conducted in private must be made no later than 20 days before the proceeding (r 49(2)). Any person may respond to the request in writing if allowed to do so by the IAD (r 49(3)).

NON-DISCLOSURE OF INFORMATION

Occasionally, the minister may have information that must remain confidential because its disclosure could be injurious to national security or endanger the safety of any person. In such circumstances, section 86 of the IRPA allows the minister to make an application for non-disclosure, to exclude information from the person concerned.

Before the hearing, the minister must make the application for non-disclosure in accordance with the general application rules. A member of the IAD will hold a meeting with the hearings officer *ex parte*, meaning in the absence of the appellant and counsel, before the appeal hearing has commenced.

If the minister makes the application at the appeal hearing, the IAD member adjourns the hearing before holding the *ex parte* meeting.

If the member decides that the minister's information is relevant to the appeal and requires non-disclosure, the member writes a summary of the information and gives it to the minister. If the minister agrees with the summary, it is provided to the appellant. The member may then consider all the non-disclosed information when deciding the appeal. Should the minister disagree with the summary, in whole or in part, the minister has the option of withdrawing the application or the information, and then the member's decision shall not take into consideration any of the information.[6]

Immigration Appeal Hearings

Jurisdiction

IAD hearings are *de novo* (Latin for "anew") and, therefore, the IAD member is not limited strictly to reviewing the evidence that led up to the refusal or removal order, but must also consider any additional facts as they exist at the time of the hearing.

The IAD has jurisdiction to hear appeals from decisions of the CBSA, CIC, or the ID, and may consider whether the decision was wrong in law, fact, or mixed law and fact, or whether there was a breach of natural justice.

Preparing for the Hearing

Counsel can prepare the client for the appeal process by describing and explaining it, and by answering any questions that the client may have. Below is a list of typical questions that clients may ask (or may want to know the answers to even if they do not ask), organized by topic. Sample answers are provided in parentheses.

- *Type of hearing.* What can the client expect during the appeal hearing? What are the time frames? Is the matter expected to take all day? (The length of the hearing depends on the number of witnesses and other factors. It is important to set out which issues will be examined and cross-examined.)

- *Hearing room.* What is the physical layout of the hearing room?

- *Public or private hearing.* Will the hearing be open to the public? (The proceedings are public, which means there could be observers.)

- *Recording of hearing.* Will the hearing be recorded? (Yes. The hearing will be recorded.)

- *Language.* In what language will the hearing be held? (The hearing will be held in English or French, and an interpreter will be provided if requested.)

- *Participants.* Who will be present and what is the role of each person? (See "Persons in Attendance," below.)

---

6 Immigration and Refugee Board, *Weighing Evidence* (31 December 2003) ch 8, Security Evidence in Appeals, online: <http://www.irb-cisr.gc.ca/Eng/BoaCom/references/LegJur/Pages/EvidPreu08.aspx>.

- *Nature of the proceeding.* Will the hearing be adversarial in nature? (Yes. The hearing is adversarial and involves the minister's counsel questioning the client and any witnesses, and arguing against the appellant's appeal.)
- *New evidence.* Can new evidence be presented during the appeal hearing? (Yes. Information that wasn't presented or available at the time that the decision was made may be presented during the appeal hearing.)

Generally, after the appellant and any witnesses are sworn in, the appellant's counsel will begin the examination, followed by the minister's counsel. Counsel should first address any preliminary issues, such as the basis of the appeal and any agreement of fact and law; identify the key issues; and indicate whether there are any witnesses.

Persons in Attendance

There are a number of people who must be present at an appeal, including the appellant, the minister's counsel, and the IAD member. Other persons who are likely to be present include the appellant's counsel and witnesses.

APPELLANT

The appellant must be in attendance at the appeal: in most cases, the appellant will be physically present, while in other cases, such as for residency obligation appeals, the appellant will attend by telephone.[7]

COUNSEL

Counsel's role is to protect the appellant's interests and right to a fair hearing. Counsel explains the process, provides advice, and presents the case in an efficient manner, within the limits set by the IAD. Counsel questions the appellant and any witnesses, and, following all testimony, makes the arguments or submissions in the case.

As noted, the appellant may choose to be represented by either an unpaid trusted adviser, such as a family member or clergy, or a paid consultant or a member in good standing of a law society, such as a lawyer or licensed paralegal, or a member of the Chambre des notaires du Québec. An unpaid adviser who represents a client and is not charging a fee should use the Notice of Representation Without a Fee or Other Consideration form (IRB/CISR 101.03).[8]

MINISTER'S COUNSEL

The minister's counsel is a public servant who works for the CBSA with the title of hearings officer. A hearings officer may represent the minister of public safety and emergency preparedness (PSEP) or the minister of CIC, depending on the decision

---

7 Immigration and Refugee Board, "Information Guide—Residency Obligation Appeal Hearings" (August 2005, revised August 2011), online: <http://www.irb-cisr.gc.ca/Eng/BoaCom/references/procedures/Pages/InfoGuideReside.aspx>.

8 *Supra* note 2.

being appealed. For example, for sponsorship appeal or residency obligation appeal hearings, a hearings officer represents the minister of CIC; for any other appeal, the hearings officer represents the minister of PSEP.

At the hearing, the hearings officer's role is generally to defend the decision against which the appeal is made, such as a visa officer's refusal of a sponsorship application or the minister's or the ID member's decision to issue a removal order. However, a hearings officer may in some cases consent to allow the appeal if she agrees with the appellant that there was an error in law or fact, or a breach of natural justice. The minister's counsel may also question the appellant and the appellant's witnesses, and may bring his own witnesses to testify.

IMMIGRATION APPEAL DIVISION MEMBER

Generally, only one decision-maker, a member of the IAD, has the authority to hear and decide appeals. The member will also hear and decide any applications that are made orally at the hearing.

INTERPRETER

If a client or witness requires an interpreter, rule 18 of the IAD Rules requires that counsel notify the IAD in writing and specify the language and dialect needed no later than 20 days before the hearing.

WITNESSES

If counsel wishes to call a witness other than her client, she must fulfill the requirements of rule 37 of the IAD Rules by informing the opposing party and the IAD in writing no later than 20 days before the hearing. The following information must be provided:

- the witness's contact information,
- the amount of time required at the hearing for the witness's testimony,
- the party's relationship to the witness,
- whether the testimony will be given by videoconference or telephone, and
- a signed report with qualifications and summary of evidence for any expert witness.

Under rule 37(4), if counsel does not make the request in writing, she faces the risk that her witness may not be allowed to testify.

To reduce the risk of the witness failing to appear, it is prudent to request that the IAD issue a summons to order a witness to testify, according to rule 38, in writing or orally at a proceeding. The party is responsible for providing the summons to the summoned person by hand, notifying the IAD in writing of this, and paying witness fees and travel expenses. In the request, counsel must set out the factors to be considered in issuing the summons, such as the importance of the witness's testimony and the witness's ability and willingness to provide such information. Under rule 39, the witness may apply to the IAD to cancel the summons.

Rule 40 sets out the process for making a request to the IAD to issue a warrant for the arrest of a summoned witness who fails to appear.

Witnesses testify following the appellant's testimony. While the appellant testifies, witnesses stay in the waiting room. A person is not allowed to share any testimony given at the hearing with any witness who was excluded from the hearing room until after the witness has testified, according to rule 41.

DESIGNATED REPRESENTATIVE—RULE 19

Sometimes, the person concerned is not capable of making decisions, as in the case of an unaccompanied minor, or a person deemed mentally incompetent or unable to understand the proceedings (IRPA, s 167(2)). If counsel for either party believes that a designated representative is required, counsel must notify the IAD without delay, according to rule 19. The IAD may then appoint a person to act and make decisions on behalf of the person concerned. The designated representative may be a relative or a professional such as a lawyer or social worker. Alternatively, counsel may be permitted to take on the role of designated representative.

Alternative Dispute Resolution

Alternative dispute resolution (ADR) in the context of immigration appeals involves mediation and negotiation, as provided by rule 20(1) of the IAD Rules. In many cases, it is an effective way to resolve the appeal quickly, without a hearing.

ADR brings the parties together in an informal meeting or conference to explore opportunities to negotiate and settle the appeal. The process for ADR is much shorter than that for a hearing, often lasting about an hour. Generally, sponsorship appeals are suited to resolution through the ADR process.

In addition to the appellant and counsel, and the minister's counsel, a dispute resolution officer (DRO) attends the conference to facilitate the process. The DRO is a specially trained tribunal officer or a member of the IAD (IAD Rules, r 20(2)). The DRO is not a party and does not decide the outcome of the appeal. Rather, the DRO is neutral and does the following:

- makes an opening statement;
- meets with the parties separately, if desired;
- asks questions about why the appeal should be allowed;
- provides an opinion about the strengths and weaknesses of the appeal;
- prepares a summary statement if the minister consents to allowing the appeal, or, if the appeal cannot be settled, prepares an objective assessment for consideration by the appellant in deciding whether to proceed to a hearing or to withdraw the appeal; and
- sets a date for a hearing, if required.

During the meeting, the parties may also ask each other questions, and provide information and evidence. The process is confidential. Possible decisions arising from the ADR conference include the following:

- *Appeal **allowed on consent***. The appeal may be allowed on consent if the minister concedes to the appellant's position.
- *Appeal **withdrawn***. The appeal may be withdrawn by the appellant if the appellant concedes to the minister's position.
- *Appeal referred to a hearing*. The appeal may be referred to a hearing if it is unresolved—that is, if neither party is willing to concede.

Even when the minister consents to an appeal, a member of the IAD must approve the settlement. A notice of decision will be issued thereafter, and, in the case of a sponsorship appeal, the minister will advise the visa office to process the sponsorship application.

If the appeal cannot be settled, the appellant maintains the right to be heard by a member at a hearing or may withdraw the appeal. Under rule 20(4), any information, statement, or document that was used at the ADR meeting generally remains confidential and does not appear on the hearing file unless it is disclosed in accordance with the IAD Rules.

Decisions

A final disposition of an appeal is communicated to the parties by way of a notice of decision, according to rule 53 of the IAD Rules. Sponsorship appeals and any decision to stay a removal order require written reasons for the decision (r 54(1)). The decision may be one of the following:

1. *Appeal allowed.* The appeal may be allowed pursuant to section 67 of the IRPA if the appellant satisfies the IAD member that the minister's decision was wrong for any of the following reasons:
   - there was an error of law,
   - there was an error of fact,
   - there was an error of mixed fact and law, or
   - there was a breach of the principles of natural justice.

   The IAD may also allow the appeal if, taking into account the best interests of a child directly affected by the decision, sufficient humanitarian and compassionate considerations warrant special relief in light of all the circumstances of the case (IRPA, s 67(1)(c)).

   If the appeal is allowed, the original decision is set aside and the IAD may substitute its own decision, such as to admit the person to Canada, or refer the matter to the appropriate decision-maker for reconsideration. For example, if the appeal of a decision in a sponsorship case is allowed, the sponsorship application will be returned for further processing and assessment.

2. *Stay of the removal order.* A stay of a removal order may be granted pursuant to section 68 of the IRPA if the appellant satisfies the member that, taking into account the best interests of a child, or humanitarian and compassionate considerations, the original decision ought to be stayed. A stay does not make the removal order go away—in a sense, it buys the person time to prove that

he can stay out of trouble and comply with the IRPA. If the member stays the removal order, he may attach conditions. Under section 68(2)(a) of the IRPA, some conditions are mandatory. For example, under section 251 of the IRPR, a person must do the following:

- provide current address information in writing;
- provide a copy of a valid passport or travel document;
- not commit any criminal offence;
- if charged with a criminal offence, immediately report to the CBSA or as instructed by the IAD in writing; and
- if convicted of a criminal offence, immediately report to the CBSA or as instructed by the IAD in writing.

The IAD also has the discretion to impose "any condition that it considers necessary" under section 68(2)(a) of the IRPA. For example, a person may be required to

- report in person to the CBSA as determined by the IAD,
- submit to drug testing,
- attend meetings of Alcoholics Anonymous, or
- attend drug or alcohol rehabilitation programs or counselling.

The IAD does not monitor compliance with stay conditions. This is the responsibility of the CBSA (for example, for criminality cases) or CIC (for example, for monitoring compliance in entrepreneurial cases).

A review of a stay of a removal order may occur if there is a concern regarding compliance with the conditions. A person who breaches any condition must appear before the IAD to speak to the matter of the breach.

The IAD may, on application by the minister or on its own initiative, reconsider the appeal, pursuant to section 68(3) of the IRPA. A *reconsideration of the appeal* is made to determine whether the person is complying with the conditions of the stay of the removal order. At the review, the IAD hears recommendations by the minister and makes a decision to do one of the following:

- maintain the stay for an additional amount of time, and maintain the conditions or issue new or additional conditions;
- cancel the stay, dismiss the appeal, and order the removal to be enforced; or
- cancel the stay, allow the appeal, and quash the removal order (this is very unlikely if conditions have been breached).

However, in cases where a person who was inadmissible on the ground of criminality is subsequently convicted of a serious offence, the stay is cancelled by operation of law and the appeal is terminated.

3. *Dismiss the appeal.* The appeal may be dismissed pursuant to section 69 of the IRPA if the appellant does not satisfy the member that the appeal ought to be allowed or a removal order ought to be stayed.

The IAD is required to provide written reasons for all decisions regarding an appeal by a sponsor and for decisions that stay a removal order. For all other decisions, the person concerned or the minister must request written reasons within ten days of the day that the person receives the decision, according to rule 54(2).

IN THE NEWS

Sponsorship Appeal Delays

The IAD hears and decides on appeals from persons whose applications to sponsor close family members have been refused. If the appeal is successful, the IAD may refer the matter back to the decision-maker for reconsideration.

However, the appeals process is lengthy, and backlogs at the IAD have resulted in multi-year waits that can present real challenges for families—in July 2015, the IAD reported that it had a backlog of over 11,000 cases waiting to be resolved. The *Toronto Star* reported on the case of a Mississauga woman, Indrani Banerjee, who has been waiting for five years after her original application to sponsor her Pakistani husband, Mazhar Elahi Khan, was refused due to suspicions that their marriage was not genuine:

> "We waited three years just to get a decision on our sponsorship. Now we have to wait for another two years just to get a hearing on our appeal," said Banerjee, an accountant whose application was rejected [in fall 2013]. "It is so frustrating."

In a similar case, Karla Piedrasanta waited for three years for her appeal to be heard after CIC refused her application to sponsor her Moroccan husband in 2008. Although the IAD decided in her favour in 2012, it meant a further multi-year wait while her application was reconsidered, and, as a result, their 19-month-old son has never met his father. *Metro News* reported:

> "It is emotionally and financially devastating," said Piedrasanta, 35, who works full time as a customs agent for a courier company while caring for Amin. "Every year we hope we will be together. We are doing everything we can to comply with the application process. My husband is missing our son growing up."

The *Toronto Star* has reported that, since 2010, the IAD has lost 12 members, reducing its ability to deal with the backlog and increasing processing times to an average of 20 months. In response to the backlog, the IAD introduced changes in July 2015 that were designed to expedite the process of declaring an appeal abandoned and to reduce the amount of time that the division spends on appeal notices that are outside its jurisdiction.

What do you think? Can you think of any changes to the appeals process that would serve to reunite families more quickly?

Sources: Nicholas Keung, "Immigration Appeal Delays Separate Couples for Years," *Toronto Star* (20 January 2014), online: <http://www.thestar.com/news/immigration/2014/01/20/immigration_appeal_delays_separate_couples_for_years.html>; Torstar News Service, "Immigration Red Tape Leaves Wife of Six Years Raising Her Son Alone in Canada," *Metro News* (4 March 2014), online: <http://metronews.ca/news/toronto/960602/immigration-red-tape-leaves-wife-of-six-years-raising-her-son-alone-in-canada/>; Immigration and Refugee Board of Canada, "Notice—The Immigration Appeal Division Introduces Administrative Changes to Appeal Process" (11 August 2015), online: <http://www.irb-cisr.gc.ca/Eng/ImmApp/Pages/NotAviAdmCha.aspx>.

The Refugee Appeal Division

Jurisdiction

When the IRPA came into force in June 2002, the sections that would have given appeal rights to refugee claimants (sections 110 and 111) were never proclaimed into law. Bill C-11, the *Balanced Refugee Reform Act* (BRRA), received royal assent on June 29, 2010 and created a new IRB structure (see Chapter 2), which included, most significantly, the board's fourth division—the RAD. The BRRA was to be implemented within two years, or on any earlier day or days that may have been fixed by order of the governor in council. However, before the provisions of the BRRA could come into force, the government introduced Bill C-31, the *Protecting Canada's Immigration System Act* (PCISA). The PCISA amended both the IRPA and the BRRA, and further delayed the implementation of the RAD. It also required a revision of the rules. The RAD became operational on December 15, 2012. However, refugee claimants who were referred to the RPD prior to this date do not have access to the RAD.

What follows is a general description of the refugee appeal process.

In most cases, appeals to the RAD are from refugee claimants whose claims were negatively determined by the RPD. However, section 110(1) of the IRPA also provides for an appeal by the minister of a decision made by a member of the RPD, stating that the minister "may satisfy any requirement respecting the manner in which an appeal is filed and perfected by submitting a notice of appeal and any supporting documents."

According to section 110(1) of the IRPA, the appeal may be made against a decision of the RPD to allow or reject a claim for refugee protection

- on a question of law,
- on a question of fact, or
- on a question of mixed law and fact.

The RAD has the authority to confirm a decision of the RPD, to substitute a determination that, in its opinion, should have been made, or to refer the matter back to the RPD for a redetermination, with directions that it considers appropriate (IRPA, s 111(1)).

Most RAD appeals are decided by a single member through a paper review, which satisfies the right to be heard; in exceptional cases, there is a right to an oral hearing. The RAD allows the refugee to introduce new evidence that was not reasonably available at the time of his hearing at the RPD; therefore, the RAD member is not strictly limited to reviewing the evidence that led to a negative determination.

As with the IRB's other tribunals, appellants before the RAD have the right to counsel, the right to present evidence, and the right to be heard—generally, through the submission of a memorandum.

Right to Appeal

Pursuant to section 110(2) of the IRPA, there are a number of claimants who will not have the right to appeal, as shown in the following table.

Right of Appeal to the RAD

Right of appeal	No right of appeal
All claimants who do not fall into one of the categories listed in column to the right	• DFN claimants (designated irregular arrival—IRPA, s 110(2)(a)) • Claimants who withdrew or abandoned their claim (IRPA, s 110(2)(b)) • Manifestly unfounded claimants (IRPA, s 110(2)(c)) • No credible basis claimants (IRPA, s 110(2)(c)) • Claims referred as exceptions to the Safe Third Country Agreement (IRPA, s 110(2)(d)(i)) (see Chapter 13) • Cessation decisions of protected person status (IRPA, s 110(2)(e)) • Vacation decisions of protected person status (IRPA, s 110(2)(f)) • Claims referred prior to December 15, 2012

Until the Federal Court's decision in *YZ v Canada (Citizenship and Immigration)*, the IRPA also barred claimants from a designated country of origin (DCO) from a right to appeal (IRPA, s 110(2)(d.1)). However, in July 2015, the Federal Court ruled that section 110(2)(d.1) of the IRPA violates section 15(1) of the *Canadian Charter of Rights and Freedoms*, because it "draws a clear and discriminatory distinction between refugee claimants from DCO-countries and those from non-DCO countries, by denying the former a right to appeal a decision of the RPD and allowing the latter to make such an appeal. This is a denial of substantive equality to claimants from DCO countries based upon the national origin of such claimants."[9]

Notice of Appeal and Time Limits

Generally, the appellant must submit three copies of the written notice of appeal no later than 15 working days after the day on which the refugee claimant or the minister receives written reasons for the decision by the RPD (IRPR, s 159.91(1)(a)). The Notice of Appeal from a Refugee Protection Division Decision form (RAD.00)[10] must be filed at the registry that is located in the same region as the RPD office where the refugee claim was originally decided, and the minister must be served with a copy.

---

9   *YZ v Canada (Citizenship and Immigration)*, 2015 FC 892 at para 130.

10   This form is available on the IRB website at <http://www.irb-cisr.gc.ca/Eng/res/form/Documents/RadSar00_e.pdf>.

The Refugee Appeal Record

The appellant has 30 working days after the day on which the refugee claimant or the minister receives written reasons for the decision by the RPD to perfect the appeal (IRPR, s 159.91(1)(b)). Rule 3 of the RAD Rules sets out the requirements for perfecting the appeal. The appellant must provide a memorandum (appellant's memorandum, and requirements of rules 3(3)(g)(ii) and 9(2)(f)(ii) of the *Refugee Appeal Division Rules* form (RAD.04.14))[11] that sets out the details of the appeal (for example, the grounds and/or errors), including whether the appellant is including new evidence, whether an oral hearing is sought, and the outcome sought, along with two copies of the record containing the following documents:

- the notice of decision, written reasons for the RPD decision, and the transcript of the RPD proceedings;
- details setting out the specific errors made by the RPD and whether these are in the reasons or in the recording or transcript of the hearing;
- any documents that were refused as evidence by the RPD; and
- any documents, law, case law, or other legal authority that the appellant wants to rely on in the appeal.

The memorandum must not be longer than 30 pages; additional requirements for format and content are set out in the RAD Rules.

The appellant is permitted to present only evidence that arose after the rejection of his claim or that was not reasonably available at the time of his RPD hearing, or that he could not reasonably have been expected in the circumstances to have presented at the time of the rejection (IRPA, s 110(4)).

If the appellant is requesting an oral hearing, he should explain why the RAD should hold a hearing.

Overview of the Refugee Appeal Process

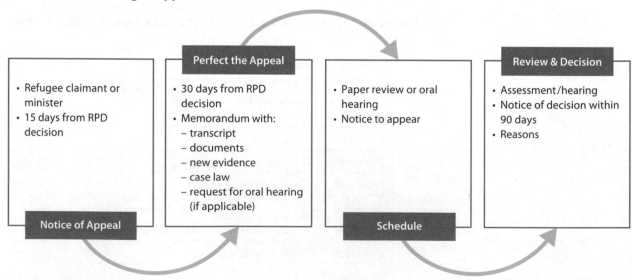

---

11   This form is available on the IRB website at <http://www.irb-cisr.gc.ca/Eng/res/form/Documents/RadSar0414_e.pdf>.

Refugee Appeal Hearings

Appeals before the RAD are intended to be paper-based. According to section 110(3) of the IRPA, the RAD must

> proceed without a hearing, on the basis of the record of the proceedings of the Refugee Protection Division, and may accept documentary evidence and written submissions from the Minister and the person who is the subject of the appeal and, in the case of a matter that is conducted before a panel of three members, written submissions from a representative or agent of the United Nations High Commissioner for Refugees and any other person described in the rules of the Board.

The RAD may hold a hearing if there is documentary evidence that

- raises a serious issue about the claimant's credibility;
- is central to the decision with respect to the refugee protection claim; and
- if accepted, would have justified allowing or rejecting the refugee protection claim (IRPA, s 110(6)).

Decisions

The government's intent in setting out timelines in the IRPA and regulations is for an appeal process that is efficient, including the decision-making process. Most decisions on appeals are expected to be made within 90 days unless an oral hearing is required (IRPA, s 111.1(e); IRPR, s 159.92(1)). Section 111(1) sets out the options for deciding appeals:

- confirmation of the determination of the RPD;
- setting aside the determination of the RPD and substituting it with the determination that should have been made; or
- referring the matter back to the RPD with directions for a redetermination.

The following table shows the breakdown, by type of decision, that the RAD may render.

RAD Final Dispositions

Disposition	Result/explanation
Allowed	Substituted decision
Allowed	Referred back
Dismissed	Lack of jurisdiction
Dismissed	Appeal not perfected
Dismissed	Confirm the decision—same reasons
Dismissed	Confirm the decision—other reasons
Dismissed	No credible basis
Withdrawn	
Abandoned	

Judicial Review in Refugee Matters

For failed refugee claimants, there is a provision to seek leave for a judicial review. However, under section 72(2)(a) of IRPA, applications for leave for a judicial review may not be made until any right of appeal under the IRPA is exhausted. For some refugee matters, this includes the right to appeal before the RAD. Both refugee claimants and the minister have the right to make an application for leave with respect to any decision of the RAD, whether or not the minister took part in the RPD or RAD proceedings (IRPA, s 73). The minister is not routinely a party to a refugee proceeding unless the minister intervenes to argue exclusion, among other things. There is no appeal of the Federal Court's decision of a leave application to the Federal Court of Appeal (IRPA, s 72(2)(e)) unless the judge certifies that a serious question of general importance is involved, and states the question (IRPA, s 74(d)).

Citizenship Appeals

As mentioned, there is no citizenship appeal tribunal. However, until the passage of Bill C-24, the *Strengthening Canadian Citizenship Act*, on June 19, 2014, both the minister and citizenship applicants had the right to appeal the decision of a citizenship judge to the Federal Court for citizenship grants and resumption applications. Amendments to the *Citizenship Act* eliminated the right to appeal (sections 14(4) to (6) are repealed); instead, applicants must now seek leave before the Federal Court for an administrative review. The Canadian Bar Association, in its review of Bill C-24, noted, "The Federal Court's ability to overturn administrative decisions on judicial review is very limited and requires a prior successful application for leave to apply for judicial review."[12] An overview of the judicial review process is provided in the following section.

Judicial Review

Federal Courts

The Federal Courts—the Federal Court and the Federal Court of Appeal—were created under section 101 of the *Constitution Act, 1867*. They derive their authority primarily from the *Federal Courts Act*, and hear and decide legal disputes in relation to federal matters. The Federal Courts have their own set of rules, general rules called the *Federal Courts Rules*, and specific rules for immigration, refugee, and citizenship matters called the *Federal Courts Citizenship, Immigration and Refugee Protection Rules*. The rules are the courts' regulations, established to set out roles and responsibilities, and govern practices and procedures in proceedings before the courts. The courts' rules set out very detailed procedures for filing and service of the notice and

---

12 Canadian Bar Association, National Immigration Law Section, *Bill C-24, Strengthening Canadian Citizenship Act* (Ottawa: CBA, April 2014) at 6, online: <http://www.cba.org/cba/submissions/pdf/14-22-eng.pdf>.

WEBLINK

There are several ways to find the *Federal Courts Rules* and the *Federal Courts Citizenship, Immigration and Refugee Protection Rules,* including searching on the CanLII website at <www.canlii.org>; the Federal Court website at <cas-ncr-nter03.cas-satj.gc.ca/portal/page/portal/fc_cf_en/Rules>; or the Department of Justice website at <laws-lois.justice.gc.ca/eng/regulations/sor-98-106> and <laws.justice.gc.ca/eng/regulations/sor-93-22>.

other documents required for the application leave process and the appeal process; they are extensive and far more complex than the rules for the IRB. Rule 119 of the *Federal Courts Rules* allows individuals to represent themselves before the Federal Courts. Regulated immigration consultants and licensed paralegals are not authorized to appear before the courts; where a person wishes to be represented, his counsel must be a lawyer, in accordance with Federal Courts Rule 119.

The parties and their representatives must never communicate with the judiciary directly, but must direct all communication through the registry of the Courts Administration Service (CAS). This applies to all communication, both oral and written, including questions about the process, documents, or a particular proceeding.

Judicial Review Under the IRPA

Section 72(1) of the IRPA provides for a judicial review by the Federal Court "with respect to any matter—a decision, determination or order made, a measure taken or a question raised," provided that the applicant has exhausted any appeal rights provided for under the IRPA (IRPA, s 72(2)). Remember that not all applicants have been provided with the right to appeal: for immigration matters that are decided outside Canada, there are no appeal rights for foreign nationals who are generally making applications to enter Canada as permanent or temporary residents. For some other immigration matters, such as in sponsorship cases, residency obligation cases, and removal order cases, we learned earlier in this chapter that there are limited appeal rights to the IAD, as provided for in sections 62 and 63 of the IRPA. As noted in relation to refugee matters, failed refugee claimants must first exhaust their right to appeal to the RAD (where the right exists) before seeking a remedy with the Federal Court.

The respondent to an application for leave in immigration matters is the minister of CIC; the minister may also make an application for leave with respect to any decision of the IAD or the RAD.

Judicial Review Under the Citizenship Act

In citizenship matters, the former appeal right to the Federal Court no longer exists, so failed applicants may now seek relief through a judicial review only. Applicants must make their application for leave within 30 days of the date that they receive notice of the decision (*Citizenship Act*, s 22.1(2)(a)). The respondent to a failed applicant's application for leave in a citizenship matter is the minister of CIC. There is no appeal of the Federal Court's decision on an application for leave to the Federal Court of Appeal (*Citizenship Act*, ss 22.1(2)(d), 22.2(2)(d)).

Application for Leave

The judicial review process commences when the applicant files an application for leave (Application for Leave and for Judicial Review form (Form IR-1))[13] with the Federal Court and serves a certified copy on the respondent[14]

- within 15 days of notification of the decision or order for a matter arising in Canada (for example, from a decision of the IAD or the RAD),
- within 30 days of notification of the decision or order for a matter arising in citizenship matters, or
- within 60 days for a matter arising outside Canada (for example, a visa officer's decision).

There is a filing fee—currently $50—set out in the rules (*Federal Courts Citizenship, Immigration and Refugee Protection Rules*, r 23). The registry will certify copies of leave applications so that they may be served on the respondent. Applicants must provide the court with proof of service on the respondent within ten days of service (*Federal Courts Citizenship, Immigration and Refugee Protection Rules*, r 7(2)). Applicants then start to gather the documents to prepare the record to perfect the application for leave, which consists of the following (*Federal Courts Citizenship, Immigration and Refugee Protection Rules*, r 10(2)):

- the decision of CIC or order of the IRB;
- the written reasons given by the tribunal, or the notice of decision;
- supporting affidavits verifying the facts relied on in support of the application;
- a memorandum of argument which set out the facts and law; and
- the relief sought, should leave be granted.

As the respondent, when the minister wishes to make representations, the minister must serve and file a notice of appearance and file proof of service with the registry within 10 days of being served with the leave application.

The record must be filed with the court within 30 days from the date of filing the leave application, together with proof of service that the applicant has served the respondent (if a notice of appearance was filed). The respondent has 30 days to respond to the application record by serving and filing a memorandum of argument and affidavits. The applicant then has 10 days to serve a reply on the respondent and file the response with the court.

---

13 This form can be found in the schedule to the *Federal Courts Citizenship, Immigration and Refugee Protection Rules*.

14 See IRPA, s 72(2)(b); *Federal Courts Citizenship, Immigration and Refugee Protection Rules*, rr 4(2), 7(1); and *Citizenship Act*, s 22.1(2)(a). Also see Court Administration Service, "Immigration and Refugee Proceedings in the Federal Court and the Federal Court of Appeal" (May 2006), online: <http://cas-ncr-nter03.cas-satj.gc.ca/fct-cf/pdf/Immigration_practice_guide_e.pdf>; and Federal Court (Canada), "How to File an Application for Judicial Review?" (23 August 2012), online: <http://cas-ncr-nter03.cas-satj.gc.ca/portal/page/portal/fc_cf_en/ApplicationJR>.

Overview of the Judicial Review Process for Decisions Made Within Canada

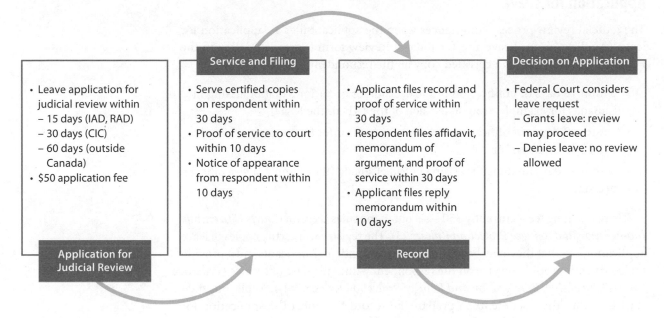

Decision on Application for Leave

There is generally no requirement for a personal appearance in court when the judge considers the application for leave. When leave is denied, the court sends a written notice of decision to both the applicant and respondent, and there is no further action for the applicant. When leave is granted, the judge issues an order that includes (*Federal Courts Citizenship, Immigration and Refugee Protection Rules*, r 15(1)) the following:

- the place, language, and date for hearing of the judicial review application;
- the time limit within which the tribunal (the IAD or the RAD) or the decision-maker (CIC) is ordered to provide a complete record;
- the time limits within which further material, if any, including affidavits, transcripts of cross-examinations, and memoranda of argument, is to be served and filed;
- the time limits within which cross-examinations on affidavits are to be completed; and
- any other matter that the judge considers necessary or expedient for the hearing of the application for judicial review.

The tribunal or decision-maker must serve the parties certified copies of, and file with the Federal Court Registry two copies of, a complete record consisting of documents, in the following sequence, on consecutively numbered pages (*Federal Courts Citizenship, Immigration and Refugee Protection Rules*, r 17):

- the decision or order and the written reasons given;
- all papers relevant to the application in possession or control of the tribunal or decision-maker;
- any affidavits or other documents filed during any hearing or application; and
- a transcript, if any, of any oral testimony given during the hearing that gave rise to the decision or order or other matter that is the subject of the application.

Hearings

The hearing of a judicial review application provides the parties with an opportunity to present oral submissions. Hearings are held in the city closest to where the applicant resides. In immigration matters, section 74 of the IRPA requires the court to hold a hearing of the judicial review application no sooner than 30 days and no later than 90 days after leave is granted, unless the parties agree to an earlier date. The same time requirements for citizenship matters are set out in section 22.1(2) of the *Citizenship Act.*

Decisions

The purpose of judicial review is to consider whether the tribunal or decision-maker in an administrative matter followed a fair procedure, understood the facts of the case, and acted within the authority of the statute in arriving at a decision. Section 18.1(4) of the *Federal Courts Act* gives the court the authority to allow an application for judicial review where it is satisfied that the federal board, commission, or other tribunal

- acted without jurisdiction, acted beyond its jurisdiction, or refused to exercise its jurisdiction;
- failed to observe a principle of natural justice, procedural fairness, or other procedure that it was required by law to observe;
- erred in law in making a decision or an order, whether or not the error appeared on the face of the record;
- based its decision or order on an erroneous finding of fact that it made in a perverse or capricious manner or without regard for the material before it;
- acted, or failed to act, by reason of fraud or perjured evidence; or
- acted in any other way that was contrary to law.

APPENDIX

Reference for the Immigration Appeal Division

Provision	IRPA and IRPR
Removal orders stayed	IRPR, ss 230 to 234
Right to appeal	IRPA, ss 62 to 64
Decision on appeals	IRPA, ss 66 to 69
Judicial review	IRPA, ss 72 to 74

Reference for the Immigration Appeal Division Rules

Provision	IAD Rules
Definitions	r 1
Communicating with the division	r 2
Sponsorship appeals	rr 3, 4
Removal order appeals	rr 5 to 8
Residency obligation appeals	rr 9, 10
Minister's appeals	rr 11, 12
Contact information	r 13
Counsel of record	rr 14 to 16
Language of appeal	rr 17, 18
Designated representative	r 19
Alternative dispute resolution	r 20
Conferences	r 21
Scheduling	rr 22, 23
Stay of removal order	rr 26, 27
Documents	rr 28 to 36
Witnesses	r 37
Applications	rr 42 to 49
Withdrawal of appeal	r 50
Decisions	rr 53 to 56
General provisions	rr 57 to 59

Reference for the Refugee Appeal Division

Provision	IRPA
Right to appeal	s 110(1)
Exceptions to the right to appeal	s 110(2)
Decision on appeals	s 111
Judicial review	ss 72 to 75

Reference for the Refugee Appeal Division Rules

Provision	RAD Rules
Definitions	r 1
Filing and perfecting an appeal	rr 2 to 7
Minister's appeal	rr 8 to 13
Communicating with the division	r 14
Counsel of record	rr 16 to 20
Language of appeal	r 22
Designated representative	r 23
Conferences	r 26
Documents	rr 27 to 35
Applications	rr 36 to 39
Withdrawal of appeal	r 47
Decisions	rr 50 to 51
General provisions	r 52
Fixing a date	r 55
Witnesses	r 61

Reference for the Citizenship Act

Provision	Citizenship Act
Judicial review	ss 22.1, 22.2

Reference for the Federal Courts Citizenship, Immigration and Refugee Protection Rules and the Federal Courts Rules

Provision	Federal Courts Citizenship, Immigration and Refugee Protection Rules
Filing and service of application for leave and for judicial review	r 7
Perfecting application for leave	rr 10(1), (2)
Grant of application for leave	r 15(1)
Tribunal record	r 17
Provision	**Federal Courts Rules**
Representation	rr 119 to 121

KEY TERMS

allowed on consent, 512
withdrawal, 512

REVIEW QUESTIONS

1. List and briefly describe the four types of immigration appeals before the Immigration Appeal Division.

2. What types of admissibility cases do not have a right to an immigration appeal?

3. Discuss the advantages and disadvantages of a scheduling conference.

4. Briefly describe hearings before the Immigration Appeal Division.

5. What are the appellant's rights at a proceeding before the Immigration Appeal Division and the Refugee Appeal Division?

6. What are the advantages of alternative dispute resolution as an immigration appeal process? What type of appeal is suited to ADR?

7. What are the grounds for appealing a decision by the Refugee Protection Division?

8. What decisions or determinations by the Refugee Protection Division may not be appealed?

9. Can a person appeal a decision on a citizenship application made by a citizenship judge? Explain.

PART VIII

Legal Professionals

CHAPTER 16 Regulating the Practice of Immigration, Refugee, and Citizenship Law

Regulating the Practice of Immigration, Refugee, and Citizenship Law

16

LEARNING OUTCOMES

After reading this chapter, you should be able to:

- Identify which level of government regulates immigration and citizenship consultants.

- Describe how a non-lawyer can be authorized to act in immigration and citizenship matters.

- Apply the Immigration Consultants of Canada Regulatory Council Code of Professional Ethics.

- Distinguish between professional misconduct and conduct unbecoming a regulated consultant.

- Apply the profession's code of ethics to the operation of a regulated consultant's practice.

- Understand the process for dealing with claims of misconduct against regulated consultants and the discipline measures that may be taken.

Introduction

This chapter provides an overview of the need to protect consumers of immigration, refugee, and citizenship services and to protect the public interest through the regulation of the practice of immigration and refugee law and citizenship law in Canada by non-lawyers who practise in these areas.

In other fields of law, non-lawyers who provide legal services are called *independent paralegals*. In the field of immigration and refugee law, non-lawyers who provide legal services are called *immigration consultants*, and, in the field of citizenship law, citizenship consultants. All are licensed to work independently and must be distinguished from *law clerks*, who also provide legal services, but are employed and supervised by lawyers.

In the past, there have been highly publicized instances of non-lawyers involved in immigration work committing fraud on their clients and the Canadian government, and engaging in shoddy work; they did so in the absence of any control over their education, their qualifications, their competence, and their probity as providers of immigration legal services. Governments use regulation as a policy tool to benefit consumers of legal services and to protect the public interest, as in the case of lawyers who are regulated by their law societies. In 2003, the federal government decided to regulate the business of immigration consulting. The *Immigration and Refugee Protection Act* (IRPA) requires non-lawyers who practise immigration law to be members in good standing of the Immigration Consultants of Canada Regulatory Council (ICCRC or the council) as Regulated Canadian Immigration Consultants (RCICs), or licensed paralegals who are regulated by a provincial law society. Similarly, recent changes to the *Citizenship Act* require non-lawyers who practise in the field of Canadian citizenship law to be members in good standing of the ICCRC as regulated Canadian citizenship consultants (RCCCs).

Background: Regulation of Immigration Consultants

Regulation of the business of immigration consulting was introduced in 2003, when the government established the Canadian Society of Immigration Consultants (CSIC) as the regulator. The CSIC was a self-regulating, professional organization that determined the requirements for entry to practise, set rules for the professional conduct of its members, and imposed discipline or other corrective measures if those rules were disregarded. Many of the unethical and prohibited activities addressed by the CSIC *Rules of Professional Conduct* were identified by the government in its reasons for regulating immigration consultants:

> Most representatives conduct their work in an ethical, professional and effective manner. However, there were persistent and credible reports that some unscrupulous immigration consultants, both in Canada and abroad, facilitate people smuggling and fabricate documents permitting foreign nationals to enter this country illegally. Certain consultants who hold themselves out as experts have no

training or experience handling complex files. Others promise the impossible and fail to deliver, and charge exorbitant fees for their services. In a number of reported cases, consultants have charged fees for an unfulfilled promise to file immigration applications, while providing bogus file reference numbers and advising clients that the Canadian government refused the application.[1]

Consider the following example of conduct engaged in by an unscrupulous immigration consultant. Gideon McGuire Augier was convicted of defrauding would-be immigrants through his bogus scheme for getting immigrants into Canada. Some of his clients lost their life savings. It is alleged that he cheated hundreds of people in Russia and Ukraine. He sold desperate families the dream of job opportunities and new lives in Canada. He collected fees, in some cases $5,000, from people abroad by promising to expedite their work permits for Canada, often without making any application. He also charged families to be sponsored under a non-existent family sponsorship scheme, and accepted consulting fees from people in Russia and Ukraine, knowing their applications to enter Canada on humanitarian and compassionate grounds could not be made from outside the country.[2]

There were many other reported instances of misconduct by immigration consultants, but it took several years for the profession to be regulated. The failure of government to legislate was a result, in part, of uncertainty as to whether the federal or provincial level of government had jurisdiction. This constitutional issue was resolved by the Supreme Court of Canada in 2001 in *Law Society of British Columbia v Mangat*.

Federal Jurisdiction: Law Society of British Columbia v Mangat

The Supreme Court of Canada, in the case of *Law Society of British Columbia v Mangat*, determined that the federal government had jurisdiction to regulate immigration consultants.[3] The *Mangat* case arose when the Law Society of British Columbia claimed that only lawyers could legally provide paid immigration services under section 26 of the BC *Legal Profession Act*, which prohibited non-lawyers from engaging in the practice of law. However, the *Immigration Act*, which was in force at the time, granted aliens the right to be represented in proceedings before the Immigration and Refugee Board (IRB) by either lawyers or "other counsel" for a fee. This was broad enough to allow non-lawyers to act on behalf of clients on immigration matters, but there were no restrictions on how immigration law was practised by non-lawyers— anyone could open up a business and call himself an "immigration consultant." This total lack of regulation led to many instances of incompetence and fraud.

---

1   Government of Canada, "Regulatory Impact Analysis Statement" (14 April 2004) C Gaz II, Extra, Vol 138, No 4 at 4, online: <http://publications.gc.ca/gazette/archives/p2/2004/2004-04-14-x/pdf/g2-138x04.pdf>.

2   See *Protsko v Angel Edward & Associates*, 2004 CanLII 2550 (Ont SC). See also Steve Buist, "Who Is the Real Gideon McGuire?" *The Hamilton Spectator* (14 December 2013), online: <http://www.thespec.com/news-story/4271989-who-is-the-real-gideon-augier-/>.

3   *Law Society of British Columbia v Mangat*, 2001 SCC 67, [2001] 3 SCR 113.

Mr. Mangat, an immigration consultant, was charged with the provincial offence of conducting an unauthorized legal practice because he was not a lawyer, yet he provided immigration services to clients for a fee. The services provided by Mr. Mangat included appearing on behalf of clients at the IRB, drafting immigration documents for clients, and giving clients advice about Canada's immigration laws.

Remember that under the *Constitution Act, 1867*, the provinces have the legislative authority to regulate the practice of law, the federal government has the authority to legislate in relation to naturalization and aliens, and immigration itself is an area of shared federal and provincial jurisdiction. Consequently, after examining the division of powers, the Supreme Court found the following:

> The subject matter of the representation of aliens by counsel before the IRB has federal and provincial aspects. Parliament and the provincial legislatures can both legislate pursuant to their respective jurisdiction and respective purpose.[4]

Since the subject matter had a "double aspect," the doctrine of paramountcy applied, and the provisions of the federal *Immigration Act* prevailed over the provisions of the provincial *Legal Profession Act*.

The *Mangat* case clarified that the federal government had the power to regulate the practice of law before the IRB. The federal government chose not to prohibit practice by non-lawyers, as the BC government had attempted to do; instead, it set up a regulatory regime to ensure the competence and integrity of immigration consultants and the quality of their services.

Legal Challenges to Regulation

In its first few years of existence, the CSIC was challenged by immigration consultants who did not wish to be regulated, and by the Law Society of Upper Canada (LSUC) in Ontario, which would have preferred to take over that regulatory role itself.

In *Chinese Business Chamber of Canada v Canada*, several organizations and some individuals challenged the power of the government to regulate and restrict immigration practice. They challenged the creation of a regulatory scheme that requires all immigration consultants to be members of the CSIC, and applied to the court for an order preventing Citizenship and Immigration Canada (CIC) and the IRB from refusing to deal with immigration consultants who were not members of the CSIC.

The court rejected these claims and stated the following:

> The immigration consultant regulations are aimed at the protection of vulnerable persons and the preservation of the integrity of the immigration process, both of which are clearly in the public interest. Indeed, all of the parties agree that regulation in this area is both necessary and long overdue.[5]

The court found that the applicants had failed to demonstrate that they would suffer irreparable harm as a result of regulation.

---

4   *Ibid* at para 47.

5   *Chinese Business Chamber of Canada v Canada*, 2005 FC 142 at para 91, aff'd 2006 FCA 178.

In *Law Society of Upper Canada v Canada (Citizenship and Immigration)*, the LSUC contested the CSIC's authority to regulate immigration consultants. The court confirmed that the CSIC did have authority: it is an independent body separate from CIC. It further found that delegation of regulatory powers to the CSIC was authorized by section 91 of the IRPA and that investigation by the CSIC of complaints against consultants employed at law firms did not pose a risk of breach of solicitor–client privilege.

In its reasons, the court reaffirmed the importance of immigration consultants and the valuable role they play in helping individuals navigate the immigration system.[6]

Bill C-35: "Cracking Down on Crooked Immigration Consultants Act"

Despite the establishment of the CSIC, there continued to be a number of complaints from the public and from within the profession that unacceptable practices by immigration consultants continued. In 2008, the House of Commons Standing Committee on Citizenship and Immigration heard representations from a wide range of stakeholders including CIC, the Canadian Bar Association, immigration practitioners, the LSUC, the RCMP, and the public. Complaints concerning the CSIC's governance and accountability framework raised concerns that immigration consultants were not adequately regulated in the public interest with respect to the provision of professional and ethical consultation, representation, and advice. Consequently, the standing committee made a number of recommendations that led to the introduction of Bill C-35, *An Act to amend the Immigration and Refugee Protection Act* (originally called the *Cracking Down on Crooked Immigration Consultants Act*). Bill C-35 was introduced June 8, 2010, received royal assent on March 23, 2011, and came into effect on June 30, 2011.

Amendments to the IRPA provide for more government oversight in order to improve the way in which immigration consultants are now regulated. Bill C-35 granted the minister the authority to make regulations to designate or revoke the designation of a body responsible for the regulation of immigration consultants under section 91(5) of the IRPA, and to provide for transitional measures, by regulation, in relation to the designation or revocation of the body responsible for regulating immigration consultants under section 91(7).

The federal government may also make regulations, in accordance with section 91 of IRPA, to license immigration consultants under a regulatory body that is accountable to the minister. The most notable change to the regulation of immigration consultants was the government's selection of a new regulatory body, the ICCRC, in 2011. Section 13.2 of the *Immigration Refugee Protection Regulations* (IRPR) sets out information requirements for the regulator.

---

6 *Law Society of Upper Canada v Canada (Minister of Citizenship and Immigration)*, 2008 FCA 243, [2009] 2 FCR 466.

IN THE NEWS

Lost in Migration

The *Toronto Star*'s "Lost in Migration" was a three-part investigative series that involved interviews with immigration consultants, lawyers, police, advocacy groups, and immigrants. It found that three years after the creation of CSIC, there were still major loopholes in the regulatory system: "Incompetent or unscrupulous consultants, registered or not, give poor advice, encourage clients to lie, and place them in the wrong immigration stream." Such unethical practice "jeopardizes a client's chance of being accepted and strains an overburdened system."

In one example, a woman facing removal paid $10,000 to an immigration consultant who claimed to have an inside contact at CIC. The consultant refused to give her a receipt for the fee and promised to make her problems disappear; he told her, "In this country, you no have to be honest." In another example, an undercover reporter posing as a temporary resident whose visitor's visa was about to expire was advised to make a refugee claim, to buy her time in Canada, and then to find a guy to marry and apply for spousal sponsorship.

The *Star* investigation noted that, in spite of "measures that were supposed to keep unqualified people out of the business, it seems anyone can still hang out a shingle as a consultant":

It's been estimated as many as 6,000 immigration consultants were operating in Canada before 2004, and untold numbers abroad and on the Web. CSIC has only 1,068 current members, down from the original 1,600—many were suspended after failing a required test or not paying dues.

CIC can refuse an application if it discovers that an immigration consultant is not a member of CSIC, but it is the clients of such consultants who lose. First, they lose their fee for bad advice. And then they may lose the chance to come to Canada. The problem of ghost consulting—unregulated consultants who charge for their services but avoid detection by not signing clients' application paperwork—goes largely unpunished. Instead, their clients are threatened with a two-year ban on coming to Canada. The RCMP gets involved only if it suspects fraud or a violation of immigration law.

CSIC has no jurisdiction over non-member consultants, recruiters, and agents who work outside Canada. And it does not "aggressively pursue members who violate the rules. It acts only on complaints—and then weakly. CSIC officials said they had received hundreds of complaints over the past three years and dealt with three-quarters of them. But it had yet to hold a single disciplinary hearing."

What do you think? Can you think of any changes to the regulation of immigration consultants that would help protect immigration, refugee, and citizenship applicants? Do you think the Canadian government can effectively protect the public from so-called ghost consultants?

Sources: Nicholas Keung & Jim Rankin, "Lost in Migration," *The Toronto Star* (16 June 2007), online: <http://www.thestar.com/news/2007/06/16/lost_in_migration.html>; Nicholas Keung, Surya Bhattacharya & Jim Rankin, "How to Stay in Canada by Cooking Up a Story," *The Toronto Star* (17 June 2007), online: <http://www.thestar.com/news/2007/06/17/how_to_stay_in_canada_by_cooking_up_a_story.html>; Nicholas Keung & Jim Rankin, "Watchdog Needs Teeth," *The Toronto Star* (18 June 2007), online: <http://www.thestar.com/news/2007/06/18/watchdog_needs_teeth.html>.

Other Amendments

In May 2012, the IRPR was amended to authorize government officials (from CIC, the CBSA, and the IRB) to disclose to the regulating body—the ICCRC or a law society—information about an immigration representative's professional or ethical conduct (IRPR, s 13.1).

Changes under Bill C-24, the *Strengthening Canadian Citizenship Act*, include a new authority for the government to develop regulations to designate a regulatory body whose members would be authorized to act as consultants in citizenship matters, and to monitor and collect information concerning citizenship consultants (*Citizenship Act*, s 21.1(5)). On June 18, 2015, the ICCRC announced that it had become the new regulator for citizenship matters under the *Citizenship Act* (and not the IRPA).[7]

Authorized Practitioners

Although individuals with an immigration, refugee, or citizenship matter can seek the help of unpaid third parties, such as family members, friends, and non-governmental or religious organizations, to act on their behalf, many choose to obtain assistance from knowledgeable and experienced representatives; regulation serves to protect the consumer of immigration, refugee, and citizenship services.

It is an offence for anyone other than a lawyer, an authorized consultant, other representative, or authorized entity to charge a fee for immigration or citizenship advice or representation *at any stage* of an application or proceeding. This includes

> representing or advising persons for consideration—or offering to do so—to all stages in connection with a proceeding or application under the *IRPA* [or the *Citizenship Act*], including before a proceeding has been commenced or an application has been made.[8]

Those who are authorized in the IRPA or the *Citizenship Act* to represent individuals for a fee include lawyers and paralegals in good standing of a provincial or territorial law society, notaries in Quebec (members of the Chambre des notaires du Québec), and authorized consultants.

---

7 ICCRC, Press Release, "ICCRC Named New Regulator for Citizenship Consultants" (18 June 2015), online: <https://www.iccrc-crcic.ca/admin/contentEngine/contentImages/file/PRESS_RELEASE_CITIZENSHIP_CONSULTANTS_ANNOUNCEMENT__18JN15.pdf>.

8 Citizenship and Immigration Canada, "Coming Into Force of Bill C-35, An Act to Amend the Immigration and Refugee Protection Act (Authorized Representatives)," OB 317 (30 June 2011), online: <http://www.cic.gc.ca/english/resources/manuals/bulletins/2011/ob317.asp>. Also see Citizenship and Immigration Canada, Backgrounder, "Strengthening Canadian Citizenship Act: Cracking Down on Citizenship Fraud" (26 June 2014), online: Government of Canada <http://news.gc.ca/web/article-en.do?mthd=tp&crtr.page=1&nid=863279&crtr.tp1D=930>.

Unauthorized Representation

A persistent but illegal practice is that of *ghost consulting*. In this practice, a person who is not authorized to practise as an immigration consultant completes the application forms on behalf of a client, but then has the forms submitted as if they were personally completed by the applicant. Fake consultants pass themselves off as legitimate immigration professionals but do not have a licence to provide assistance on any immigration matter, and are therefore unauthorized. The unauthorized person then charges a fee for the work done. Ghost consulting is a breach of the IRPA and may be subject to an investigation by the RCMP. Ghost and fake consulting also carry a risk for the client. If a client has difficulties with a non-authorized consultant, he will have no access to the complaint procedures of the ICCRC because the council has no power to deal with the practices of ghost consultants. The ICCRC will investigate the situation and, where necessary, pass the information along to the RCMP, the CBSA, a provincial or territorial law society, or any other authority.

Consider the following scenario:

Joe, originally from Mexico, is a permanent resident of Canada and works at a travel agency.

Joe is sometimes approached by visitors from Mexico—particularly, those who have a limited ability to read and write in English—for advice and assistance with regard to extending their visits. Joe wants to help his clients, so he explains Canada's immigration laws and advises them about alternatives, such as first applying as a student. Joe has even helped some of his clients to fill out immigration application forms, but he does not sign them. In return for his trouble, Joe has received free dinners, drinks, and other gifts.

Do Joe's actions constitute ghost consulting?

If dinner, drinks, and gifts qualify as a "fee," Joe may be in violation of the rule against ghost consulting. A number of industry-related professionals may find that their work may place them in a position where they wish to dabble in immigration law. The ICCRC provides a series of immigration advisories for various industries that set out the type of activities that may not be performed by unauthorized representatives. For example, travel agents, recruiters, human resource professionals, and educational representatives are not authorized to explain or provide advice about completing immigration forms, or to communicate with CIC or the CBSA on behalf of a client; recruiters may not represent employers in an arranged employment opinion or labour market opinion application; and adoption agencies are not allowed to advertise that they can provide immigration advice for compensation, or represent clients in an immigration application or proceeding.

There are penalties for unauthorized representatives who provide, or offer to provide, advice or representation for a fee, at any stage of an application or proceeding, *including the period before a proceeding begins or an application is submitted.*

The indictable offence of providing unauthorized representation carries a penalty of up to $100,000, imprisonment for a term of up to two years, or both, while a summary conviction carries a fine of up to $20,000, imprisonment for a term of up to six months, or both (IRPA, s 91(9); *Citizenship Act*, s 29.1).

A non-lawyer, such as a licensed paralegal or a regulated consultant, must be a "member in good standing" of the regulatory body to

- provide direct or indirect representation,
- advise a person for consideration, or
- offer to advise or represent a person in connection with a proceeding or application under the IRPA or the *Citizenship Act*.

This requirement applies to all matters before the following decision-makers:

- the minister of CIC,
- the minister responsible for the CBSA,
- immigration officers, and
- the IRB.

Paralegals

It appears that section 91(2)(b) of the IRPA and section 21.1(2)(b) of the *Citizenship Act* authorize paralegals to represent clients as long as they are members in good standing of a provincial or territorial law society as authorized representatives. As of July 2015, however, the only law society to regulate paralegals in Canada is the LSUC in Ontario. Under the LSUC's regulatory scheme, paralegals are required to have minimum education credentials, pass a licensing examination, and meet good character requirements (*Law Society Act*, s 27(2); LSUC Bylaw 4, s 8(1), para 3). The LSUC also accredits private and public colleges in Ontario, and is therefore responsible for determining the educational competencies for paralegals. Those educational competencies do not currently include the requirement for specialized knowledge in immigration or refugee law. However, Bylaw 4 permits a licensed paralegal only to appear "before a tribunal established ... under an Act of Parliament" (LSUC Bylaw 4, s 6).This means that licensed paralegals in Ontario may represent clients before the IRB but may not provide other legal services, such as filing temporary visas or permanent resident applications, unless they are supervised by a lawyer of the LSUC. Licensed paralegals must follow their regulator's bylaws with respect to permitted areas of practice.

Immigration Consultants of Canada Regulatory Council and Regulated Canadian Immigration Consultants

The minister revoked the CSIC's designation as regulator and, as of June 30, 2011, designated the ICCRC as the new self-regulated body. Members of ICCRC are called RCICs, to distinguish them from ghost consultants—those who are not authorized to practise.

Members in good standing of the ICCRC are listed on that organization's website.[9]

Most regulated professions require specialized education, knowledge, and skill, and usually employ a code of ethics to govern the conduct of members in their relationships with clients, employees, colleagues, and the public, as well as some system of accountability.[10] In the case of RCICs, regulation has the features of a professional organization, including licensing, which will grant an individual entry into the immigration profession. To be admitted as a member of the ICCRC, and thus be permitted to practise as an RCIC, former members of CSIC were given a transitional period of time ending on October 28, 2011 to register with the ICCRC to become members in good standing of the new regulatory body. For a new applicant to become a member of the ICCRC, she must satisfy the following criteria:

- be at least 18 years old and a Canadian citizen, permanent resident, or registered Indian under the *Indian Act*;
- have graduated from an accredited immigration practitioner's program;
- have passed an ICCRC-approved language competency test in English or French within the past two years;
- sign a statutory declaration attesting to good character and good conduct;
- pass a "full skills exam" on immigration and practice management, consisting of a three-hour set of 100 scenario-based multiple-choice questions (up to four attempts are permitted);
- be of good character, as shown by police certificates, in accordance with the requirements set by the Admissions Committee of the ICCRC, and submit sworn statements regarding countries of residence, police certificates, and criminal record; bankruptcy; suspension or expulsion from another regulatory body; and practising immigration law for a fee while unauthorized, contrary to the IRPA prior to admission; and
- provide proof of a business registration, pay membership dues, open a trust account, and obtain errors and omissions insurance.[11]

In addition to the above, a licensed paralegal who wishes to become a member of the ICCRC must not be an undischarged bankrupt or be involved in a current creditor proposal agreement.

Members of the ICCRC maintain their membership by

- fulfilling annual continuing professional development requirements;
- fulfilling mandatory practice management and education requirements;

WEBLINK

Full Skills Exam

The ICCRC provides a study guide for the full skills exam at <www.iccrc-crcic.ca/becominganRCIC/studyguide>.

---

9   See ICCRC, "Who Can Represent You?" online: <https://www.iccrc-crcic.ca/AboutUs/public/advisories.cfm>.

10   Canadian Network of National Associations of Regulators, "FAQ," online: <https://www.cnnar.ca/en/faq.html>.

11   ICCRC, Registration Guide: *Writing the Full Skills Exam and Becoming a Regulated Canadian Immigration Consultant (RCIC)*, version 2015-0001 (Burlington, Ont: ICCRC, 2015) at 2, Mandatory Requirements, online: <http://www.iccrc-crcic.ca/admin/contentEngine/contentImages/file/Registration%20Guide_FINAL_01July%202013.pdf>.

- paying membership dues and a liability insurance fee for errors and omissions insurance (visit the ICCRC website for up-to-date fees);
- on a biennial basis, providing a statutory declaration regarding criminal charges, bankruptcy, and suspension or expulsion from any other regulatory body; and
- abiding by the regulator's *Code of Professional Ethics*.

ICCRC Structure

The ICCRC is governed by an elected board of directors consisting of seven directors from which a chairperson is elected. Members are elected based on regional representation (Ontario, 4; Quebec, 2; Western Canada, 4; Other, 2), and 3 others are elected as public interest directors, for a total of 15 directors. Directors receive $2,500 per month for their services, and the chairperson is entitled to an additional $2,500 per month. In addition to usual directors' responsibilities related to their area of oversight (for example, as a director of a particular region or of finance and operations), directors are responsible for operating the council.

The ICCRC has enacted a set of bylaws to govern the operation of the organization. These bylaws include rules for the election of directors and conduct of directors' meetings, rules for the establishment of standing committees (Admissions Committee, Appeal Committee, Communications Committee, Complaints Committee, Discipline Committee, Finance and Audits Committee, Governance and Nominating Committee, Human Resources and Compensation Committee, Outreach Committee, Practice Management and Education Committee, Practice Quality Review Committee, and the Review Committee), and rules to determine the conditions that must be satisfied for entry to practise as a regulated immigration consultant.

Code of Professional Ethics

The *Code of Professional Ethics* is intended to protect the public from unprofessional, unethical, incompetent practice by ICCRC members and students (Article 1). An RCIC who fails to comply with the Code may face disciplinary measures, including the revocation of membership from the ICCRC.

The Code provides guidelines on how to run an immigration consulting practice in a proper manner. Note that minimal compliance with the strict letter of the Code may not be sufficient, because the immigration professional is expected not only to comply with the minimum set of specific situations detailed in the Code but to live up to the "spirit of the Code," especially in situations that are not specifically dealt with under it.

The Code is organized into 20 articles, as follows:

Article 1. Intention of Code

Article 2. Interpretation

Article 3. Ethical Practice

Article 4. Professionalism

Article 5. Competence

Article 6. Quality of Service

Article 7. Advising Clients

Article 8. Confidentiality

Article 9. Conflicts of Interest

Article 10. Preservation of Client Property

Article 11. ICCRC Member as Advocate

Article 12. Retainer and Fees

Article 13. Joint Retainers

Article 14. Withdrawal from Representation

Article 15. Outside Interests

Article 16. Advertising, Solicitation and Making Services Available

Article 17. Discrimination and Harassment

Article 18. Errors and Omissions

Article 19. Disciplinary Authority

Article 20. Responsibility to ICCRC and Others

These topics are explained briefly below; however, RCICs should be familiar with the *Code of Professional Ethics* in its entirety. The Code is reproduced in the appendix to this chapter, and is also available on the ICCRC website.

Conduct Unbecoming (Interpretation, Article 2)

conduct unbecoming
conduct that occurs in an immigration consultant's personal or private capacity that tends to bring discredit on the profession

Conduct unbecoming refers to improper conduct that occurs in the member's personal or private capacity and tends to bring discredit on the profession. Generally, it does not directly affect a client. The rationale behind prohibiting such conduct is that any improper conduct by a person identified with the profession might discredit the profession in the eyes of the public. This could undermine the public's confidence in the integrity of all immigration consultants.

Examples of the types of conduct that are prohibited and will likely result in discipline include the following:

- participating in criminal activity, such as fraud, that brings into question the member's integrity, honesty, trustworthiness, or fitness;
- committing a breach of the Code;
- taking improper advantage of a person in a vulnerable situation, such as a person who is young, ill, unsophisticated, poorly educated, inexperienced, or lacking in business savvy;
- engaging in conduct involving dishonesty; and
- failing to abide by a fee dispute resolution resolved by the ICCRC or a court of competent jurisdiction.

A purely private indiscretion on the part of a member that does not bring into question the consultant's integrity should not compel the ICCRC to impose discipline, but it is left to the ICCRC to determine the boundaries between conduct unbecoming and purely private conduct.

Professional Misconduct (Interpretation, Article 2)

Professional misconduct is any improper action of an immigration consultant during the course of conducting business that tends to discredit the profession. It is professional misconduct for the RCIC to

- violate or attempt to avoid or violate the bylaws, rules, regulations, Code, or policies of the ICCRC, or knowingly assist or induce another member, employee, or agent to do so;
- violate or attempt to violate any requirement of the IRPA; or
- engage in conduct that undermines the integrity of Canada's immigration system.

It is also professional misconduct for an RCIC to misappropriate or deal dishonestly with another person's money, including any of the client's money deposited with the consultant. This prohibition is so important that it is addressed again in Article 10: Preservation of Client Property and in Article 12: Retainer and Fees.

It goes without saying that an RCIC may not bribe or attempt to bribe a government official to ignore immigration rules or give preferential treatment to a client. It is also professional misconduct for an RCIC to state or imply that he is engaged in this type of activity.

Consider the following scenario:

> Lara is a licensed immigration consultant. She has been working in this field for many years and is familiar with many immigration officials and tribunal members. When a prospective client comes into her office, she promotes herself by emphasizing that she "knows everyone in this business" and "knows how to get her clients through the red tape." "It's all about who you know and keeping them happy," she says.
>
> Do Lara's statements constitute professional misconduct?

Lara's statements could be interpreted as meaning that she knows how to get preferential treatment for her clients. Even if she has never actually bribed any officials, intimating that she does constitutes professional misconduct.

Competence (Article 5) and Quality of Service (Article 6)

An RCIC must be diligent, efficient, and conscientious. Unprofessional habits, such as poor record keeping, disorganization, shoddy work, or failing to respond to phone calls and correspondence, are unacceptable. Members must have an effective

professional misconduct
any improper action of an immigration consultant during the course of conducting business that tends to discredit the profession

tickler system
a reminder system
for deadlines

tickler system in place for reminding them of deadlines. Missing a deadline for the filing of information, where the consequences to the client may be severe, is a particularly serious transgression.

The standard of competence and quality of service demanded is objective, and is based on what could be expected of a reasonably competent immigration professional in similar circumstances. The standard is not perfection—reasonable people are not perfect. However, it does not allow for personal circumstances or disability, such as addiction or depression, to excuse poor performance. Members have a responsibility to keep abreast of changing laws, regulations, and policies affecting their practice, and must continue to develop their knowledge and skills in compliance with the continuing education policies of the ICCRC.

Professional Responsibility for Agents and Staff (Article 6)

A member may hire employees to perform tasks such as record-keeping, reception, and interviewing clients. A licensed immigration consultant may also hire agents to perform functions such as delivering documents. A member may not hire any person who has previously been removed from membership or suspended by the ICCRC or any designated legal regulatory body as a result of disciplinary action. It is important that the duties of employees and agents not involve advising, consulting with, or representing clients, unless the agent or employee is also a member of the ICCRC. It is not sufficient to have an RCIC member supervise an agent or employee who is not a member of the ICCRC.

As noted above, it is professional misconduct if a member knowingly assists or induces an agent or employee to violate any of the bylaws, rules, regulations, Code, or policies of ICCRC. Thus, an RCIC member cannot try to avoid the consequences of breaching the rules of the ICCRC by having someone else carry out the improper actions on his behalf. Immigration professionals should also be aware that they may be held personally responsible for the actions of agents or employees, according to the principle of **vicarious responsibility**.

vicarious responsibility
a principle that can lead to
immigration professionals
being held personally
responsible for the actions
of agents or employees

Advising Clients (Article 7)

Immigration consultants must provide *proper advice* to their clients, meaning they must be "honest and candid." To enable the client to make appropriate decisions and give directions to the consultant, a consultant must explain the case in a manner that the client understands. If the consultant does not speak the client's language, he should use an interpreter.

The Code states that the consultant must take reasonable steps to avoid becoming "the tool or dupe of an unscrupulous" client. The consultant must be careful never to "knowingly assist in or encourage" dishonesty, the omission of relevant information, the provision of misleading information, fraud, crime, or illegal conduct. The consultant may advise a client on how to comply with immigration law and regulations, but must not advise him on how to violate the law. For example, a client sponsoring a spouse who is a resident in a foreign country should be encouraged to collect and maintain all records of contact with the spouse, such as letters and phone records, but it would be improper to encourage the client to fabricate such records.

The consultant must be very cautious in providing services, especially when dealing with clients outside the country and when providing advice and completing documents based on documents produced outside the country. The IRPA makes misrepresentation an offence, and if the consultant suspects that the client's documents are false, she should not use them.

Confidentiality (Article 8)

An immigration consultant is required to keep client information and communications confidential, and generally must obtain the client's permission before disclosing any such information, even after the termination of the retainer. However, the consultant may be compelled by a court to disclose confidential information in a legal proceeding or by order of a tribunal. For example, if a client is charged with an IRPA or *Criminal Code* offence, or there is a lawsuit against the client, the immigration consultant may be subpoenaed and be required to attend court and answer questions related to the legal proceeding.

Also, according to article 29 of ICCRC By-Law 2014-1, which repealed and replaced all prior ICCRC bylaws on December 2, 2014, in the course of an investigation, the ICCRC may demand information—including a client file—from an immigration consultant. This obligation overrides the duty of confidentiality owed to clients. By contrast, client information and communications shared in the context of a lawyer–client relationship are protected by **solicitor–client privilege**. A court may not compel the disclosure of such information against the wishes of the client, and this may be an important advantage to clients in some cases. Therefore, immigration consultants should explain their duty of confidentiality, and how it differs from solicitor–client privilege, at the time of the initial interview with the client. It is important that the clients of immigration consultants be aware that they are not protected by solicitor–client privilege, before they divulge information.

solicitor–client privilege
the protection of client information and communication shared in the context of a solicitor–client relationship

Avoiding Conflicts of Interest (Article 9)

A **conflict of interest** occurs where a consultant represents clients with incompatible interests. In other words, the best course of action for one client may harm the interests of another.

There may also arise a situation where there is a potential for a conflict, but no actual conflict. For example, a consultant may represent both an employer and a foreign worker that the employer wants to hire. In these circumstances, the consultant must inform both the employer and foreign worker of the potential for a conflict of interest. Should an actual conflict arise, such as the foreign worker obtaining a job offer from another employer, the consultant must cease representation of one or both parties.

conflict of interest
occurs where a consultant represents clients with incompatible interests

Preservation of Client Property (Article 10)

Immigration consultants must be very careful with property belonging to clients. They must keep meticulous records, and designate a trust account so that client property does not find its way into the general business account. (For details, see the discussion below.) Funds held in trust on behalf of a client should be limited to an amount reasonably necessary for payment of the consultant's fees and disbursements, any agent's fees, and CIC fees. Funds for other purposes, such as those required for entry under the investor class, should not be in the possession of the consultant.

ICCRC Member as Advocate (Article 11)

Members may appear before government officials or the IRB to advocate for clients. The duty of a member is to represent the client's interests resolutely, fearlessly raise every issue, and advance every argument to support the client's position. However, the member must do so while treating board members, the minister, and other parties with candour, courtesy, and respect. The member must act legally and ethically. For example, the member must not counsel a witness to lie or make claims that are clearly unsupported or false.

The member has an absolute duty to abide by the rules of procedure of the IRB.

Retainer and Fees (Article 12)

A member must provide a written retainer agreement or engagement letter to a client to account for funds paid in advance of services. Retainers must be deposited in a separate trust account at a financial institution, and be transferred into the business account only after services are rendered on the client's behalf and the client is billed.

The retainer agreement must indicate the reason that the member is being hired, and set out the fair and reasonable fees for services and disbursements (that is, out-of-pocket expenses, such as photocopying) that will be charged. Terms and conditions, such as a statement that interest will accrue on unpaid accounts, should also be specified. The agreement must also inform the client of how to contact the member and the ICCRC in the event of a disagreement over fees.

Withdrawal from Representation (Article 14)

Once a member has accepted a client, the member is generally obliged to maintain the relationship. There are, however, exceptions that allow the member to terminate the relationship, and a few circumstances in which the member is required to do so.

A member must withdraw her services when

- the client discharges the member,
- the client instructs the member to violate the law or contravene the *Code of Professional Ethics*, or
- the consultant will be placed in a conflict of interest by continuing to represent the client.

From time to time, there may be situations in which there is a serious loss of confidence between the ICCRC member and a client, making withdrawal optional. This may happen when the client

- deceives the member,
- fails to give adequate instructions to the member, or
- refuses to take the member's advice on a significant matter.

An ICCRC member may sever the professional relationship with the client only for a proper purpose and if doing so would not be unfair or prejudicial to the client.

The Code also provides for situations where a member may end the relationship with a client who has failed to provide funds on account of disbursements or fees.

A member who wishes to withdraw representation must ensure that the client has a sufficient opportunity to seek the assistance of new counsel in time for any upcoming hearing dates. The member must return the client's papers and information on the case; return any retainer funds held in trust (less the amount of any outstanding fees); account for fees and disbursements; cooperate with any new representative hired by the client; and inform CIC, the CBSA, and/or the IRB. Terminating the relationship for the purpose of delaying a hearing to allow the client to stay in Canada longer is an improper purpose, even if it is the client's wishes.

There are no restrictions on a client's ability to "fire" a member. The client may end the relationship at any time, without explanation. However, the client does remain responsible for payment of any outstanding fees.

It is prudent for anyone taking over a case from another ICCRC member to contact the former consultant and confirm that she is no longer handling the case.

Advertising, Solicitation, and Making Services Available (Article 16)

Advertising must be in good taste and not bring the profession, the ICCRC, or the laws of Canada into disrepute. Advertising may not be false or misleading. In particular, advertising should not guarantee results or guarantee maximum times for completing processing of applications. It also should not express or imply that the member has special access to or influence with the minister or government officials, or that the member is a lawyer. The member must be careful that any foreign credentials listed, such as a foreign law degree, do not suggest to the public that the consultant is a lawyer in Canada.

A member of the ICCRC may advertise his ICCRC designation and use the ICCRC logo. A member may use endorsements and testimonials in advertisements, as long as he has obtained consent from the client and as long as the statements are true and accurate.

Discrimination and Harassment (Article 17)

A member of the ICCRC is not permitted to discriminate against clients on the basis of age, gender, sexual orientation, same-sex partnership status, marital status, family status, national or ethnic origin, ancestry, race, colour, religion, creed, citizenship, physical or mental disability, political affiliation, record of offences, or socio-economic status. Discrimination may include charging more or refusing to represent a particular client. Consultants will often target their marketing efforts at particular groups by noting that they are able to speak certain languages, by advertising in specific community newspapers, and by obtaining referrals from contacts within a certain community. This is acceptable practice and is not considered to be discrimination. It is also possible—and is, in fact, required—for a member to refuse clients on the basis that the service requested is outside the member's area of expertise. However, it is not permissible for ICCRC members to refuse clients based on their ethnicity, or to indicate that they will represent only people of a particular religion, gender, or ethnic group.

A member of the ICCRC is not permitted to engage in sexual or other forms of harassment of a colleague, a staff member, a client, or any other person. This includes electronic harassment through unsolicited electronic messages that are abusive, offensive, intrusive, unprofessional, or unwanted.

Consider the following scenario:

Gita is a qualified ICCRC member and an immigrant herself. She has a law degree from her native country and she speaks four languages—English and three other languages from her country of birth. She is very connected to her ethnic community in Canada, and her clients are exclusively from that community. Gita writes a column in her local ethnic newspaper, where she lists her law degree and membership in the ICCRC. Gita also advertises in this newspaper and sometimes includes words of praise from well-known members of her community who were former clients.

This scenario raises a number of issues. Gita must be careful when referencing her foreign law degree. She must not misrepresent herself as a lawyer in Canada. There is nothing wrong with promoting her services to her own ethnic community, but she must be careful not to refuse to represent clients who do not belong to her ethnic group.

Errors and Omissions (Article 18)

Members of the ICCRC must purchase liability insurance, also called errors and omissions insurance. This insurance protects clients by providing funds for compensating clients for any successful professional negligence or fraud claim against a regulated immigration consultant. For example, if a member of the ICCRC defrauds a client of $100,000 by telling him that the money will be used for a qualifying investment under the Business Immigration Program, the insurer will pay the money back to the client. This is important, because the money may have disappeared and may not be retrievable.

Errors and omissions insurance also protects regulated immigration consultants—without it, a member could be forced to use personal assets, such as a family home, to pay a damages award. Consider a regulated immigration consultant who misses a deadline and thereby forces a client to spend an additional $60,000 in legal fees. The consultant would benefit from the insurer paying the amount of the damages award, rather than being required to cash in a registered retirement savings plan in order to pay it.

Disciplinary Authority (Article 19)

An unsatisfied client of a member of the ICCRC must submit a complaint in writing to the ICCRC (the specific form can be found on the ICCRC website). The member must be informed of the complaint and be given 30 days to respond to the allegations. If the complaint is groundless, no action will be taken. However, if an investigation discloses that the claim is credible, the ICCRC may negotiate a settlement, caution or admonish the member, or refer the complaint to the Discipline Committee to commence discipline procedures.

The member has a right to appeal to the Appeal Committee of the ICCRC.

Certain complaints cannot be resolved by the ICCRC, because it has authority only to discipline a member for professional misconduct or for conduct unbecoming an ICCRC member. If the investigation discloses that the complaint relates to negligence, the matter may be referred to the errors and omissions insurance company or to the civil courts. If the complaint is against an individual who is not a member of the ICCRC, the issue is referred to the police for prosecution pursuant to the IRPA (see ss 126 and 127 for offences and penalties related to counselling and misrepresentation) and the *Citizenship Act* (s 29.2). In this case, the ICCRC cannot resolve the issue; it is a matter for the courts.

If the Discipline Committee finds the member guilty of professional misconduct, it may make an order to do one or more of the following:

- revoke the member's membership;
- suspend the member's membership;
- reprimand the member;
- direct the member to refrain from using any ICCRC designation or logo, or to return her certificate of membership;
- direct the member to take any specific rehabilitative measure (for example, professional development training, counselling, or treatment); or
- direct the member to pay a fine.

The ICCRC's responsibility is limited to enforcing the Code and the bylaws, and the remedies it may impose are limited to discipline and costs.

APPENDIX

Immigration Consultants of Canada Regulatory Council
Code of Professional Ethics
June 2012

ARTICLE 1. INTENTION OF CODE

1.1 Standard of Professional Conduct
This Code establishes high standards of professional conduct for ICCRC members and provides guidance for their practice.

1.2 Primary Purpose
The primary purpose of this Code is to protect the public from unprofessional, unethical, incompetent practice by the ICCRC members and students.

1.3 Code Binding
This Code is binding on all ICCRC members and, with necessary variations, to all ICCRC students.

1.4 Following Spirit Required
ICCRC members must endeavour to follow the spirit of this Code. This Code cannot address every potential situation or impropriety, but provide principles that govern all conduct.

1.5 Discipline upon Breach
ICCRC members or students who breach this Code are subject to disciplinary proceedings.

ARTICLE 2. INTERPRETATION

2.1 Interpretation Consistent with Bylaws
This Code shall be interpreted in a manner consistent with the Bylaws of ICCRC unless the context otherwise requires.

2.2 Defined Terms
In this Code:
  2.2.1 "Agent" means a person who:
      (i) does not provide immigration advice for a fee in contravention of IRPA;
      (ii) represents an ICCRC member in furtherance of the member's practice;
      (iii) solicits or facilitates business in connection with the ICCRC member's practice;
      (iv) is registered, or required to be registered, as an Agent pursuant to ICCRC's Bylaws;
  and for greater certainty, "Agent" does not include an individual who merely refers a Client to a member but does not otherwise take any part in a proceeding or application, or potential proceeding or application, under the IRPA;

2.2.2 "Board" means the Immigration and Refugee Board and any of its staff, branches or divisions;

2.2.3 "Bylaws" mean the bylaws of ICCRC;

2.2.4 "Canadian Society of Immigration Consultants" (and the acronym "CSIC") means the body incorporated under the Canada Corporations Act and previously designated by the Minister pursuant to section 91 of the Immigration and Refugee Protection Act, S.C. 2001, c. 27, as amended, (IRPA) as a regulatory body for immigration consultants;

2.2.5 "CBSA" means Canada Border Services Agency, and any successor agency;

2.2.6 "CIC" means Citizenship and Immigration Canada;

2.2.7 "Client" means a person whose interests the ICCRC member undertakes to advance, for a fee or otherwise, regarding a proceeding or application, or potential proceeding or application, under the IRPA;

2.2.8 "Conduct Unbecoming an ICCRC member" means conduct in the member's personal or private capacity that tends to bring discredit upon the profession including, but not limited, to:

(i) committing a criminal act that reflects adversely on the member's integrity, honesty, trustworthiness, or fitness as an ICCRC member;

(ii) committing a breach of this Code;

(iii) taking improper advantage of a person's youth, age, inexperience, lack of education, lack of sophistication, ill health, or un-businesslike habits;

(iv) engaging in conduct involving dishonesty; or

(v) failing to abide by a fee dispute resolution resolved by the ICCRC or a court of competent jurisdiction.

2.2.9 "Designated Legal Regulatory Body" means a law society of a province or territory or the Chambre des notaires du Québec;

2.2.10 "Employee" means a person who is in an employee/employer relationship with an ICCRC member, excluding another ICCRC member;

2.2.11 "Firm" means a firm as defined in the Bylaws;

2.2.12 "IRPA" means the Immigration and Refugee Protection Act, S.C. 2001, c. 27, as amended, and includes all Regulations made pursuant to it;

2.2.13 "ICCRC" means Immigration Consultants of Canada Regulatory Council;

2.2.14 "ICCRC member" means a person who is a member of ICCRC;

2.2.15 "Minister" means the Minister or Ministers responsible for the administration of IRPA; namely the members of the Queen's Privy Council designated as such by the Governor-in-Council;

2.2.16 "Officer" means any person or class of person designated as Officers by the Minister to carry out any purpose or any provision of IRPA;

2.2.17 "Practice" means professional work undertaken by an ICCRC member in connection with any application or proceeding, or potential application or proceeding, under IRPA;

2.2.18 "Professional Misconduct" means conduct in the ICCRC member's practice that tends to discredit the profession including:

(i) violating or attempting to avoid or violate the Bylaws, Rules, Regulations, Codes or policies of ICCRC, or knowingly assisting or inducing another ICCRC member to do so;

(ii) violating or attempting to violate any requirement of IRPA;

(iii) knowingly assisting or inducing an Employee or Agent to engage in conduct prohibited by clause 2.2.18(i) or clause 2.2.18(ii);

(iv) engaging in conduct that undermines the integrity of Canada's immigration system;

(v) misappropriating or otherwise dealing dishonestly with money or property in connection with a member's practice;

(vi) stating or implying an ability to influence improperly any government agency or official; or

(vii) engaging in conduct prejudicial to the administration of justice.

2.2.19 "Student" means a student registered with ICCRC.

ARTICLE 3. ETHICAL PRACTICE

3.1 Serve Honourably

An ICCRC member has a duty to provide immigration services honourably, and to discharge all responsibilities to Clients, government agencies, the Board, colleagues, the public and others affected in the course of the member's practice with integrity.

3.2 Privileged Role

An ICCRC member, as an authorized representative of individuals in the immigration and refugee system, has a privileged role to play in maintaining the integrity of Canada's immigration system and the administration of justice. Despite any request or demand to the contrary received from any person, an ICCRC member must uphold the rule of law and act at all times honestly and in good faith towards immigration officials, without intent to deceive or undermine the integrity of the system, or assist others to do so.

ARTICLE 4. PROFESSIONALISM

4.1 Maintain Integrity

An ICCRC member shall act in such a way as to maintain the integrity of the profession of immigration practice.

4.2 Courtesy and Good Faith

An ICCRC member shall be courteous and civil, and shall act in good faith, in all professional dealings. An ICCRC member should avoid maligning the reputation of colleagues for personal motives.

4.3 No Offensive Communications

An ICCRC member shall not send correspondence or otherwise communicate with the ICCRC, a Client, another ICCRC member, a government official or any other person in a manner that is abusive, offensive or otherwise inconsistent with the proper tone of professional communication from an ICCRC member.

4.4 Report of Breaches of This Code

Subject to the duty of Client confidentiality, an ICCRC member should report to the appropriate authority any unprofessional, illegal or unethical conduct by colleagues or others. Wherever possible, the ICCRC member should request an explanation first from this individual to assist in determining whether there is any obligation to report the conduct.

4.5 No Misconduct or Conduct Unbecoming

An ICCRC member shall not engage in professional misconduct or conduct unbecoming an ICCRC member.

4.6 No Breach of Bylaws

An ICCRC member shall not engage in conduct that is a violation of the Bylaws.

ARTICLE 5. COMPETENCE

5.1 Nature of Competence

To be competent includes knowing and applying the relevant legal rules, policies and practices appropriate to the matter undertaken on behalf of a Client.

5.2 Duty of Competence

An ICCRC member owes duty to be competent to perform any services undertaken for a Client in connection with the member's practice.

5.3 Standard of Service

An ICCRC member shall perform any services undertaken on behalf [of] a Client to the standard of a competent ICCRC member.

5.4 Not Practice if Not Competent

An ICCRC member shall be alert to recognize any lack of competence for a particular task and the disservice that could be done to the Client by undertaking that task, and shall not undertake a matter without being competent to handle it or being able to become competent without undue delay or expense to the Client.

5.5 Obligation if Not Competent

An ICCRC member who discovers a lack of competence to complete a retainer shall either decline to act or obtain the Client's consent to retain, consult or collaborate with another person who is competent and licensed to perform that task.

5.6 Maintenance of Skills and Knowledge

An ICCRC member has a responsibility to adapt to changing laws and policies affecting professional practice, as well as requirements and policies of the ICCRC. The member must keep up-to-date on the skills and knowledge needed for competent practice and comply with the requirements and the spirit of the Continuing Education policies of ICCRC.

ARTICLE 6. QUALITY OF SERVICE

6.1 Maintenance of Quality Service

An ICCRC member must conduct all elements of practice in a conscientious, diligent and efficient manner, and provide a quality of service at least equal to that which ICCRC members generally would expect of a competent member in a similar situation. The ICCRC member must at all time use best efforts to:

6.1.1 meet all applicable deadlines;

6.1.2 conduct Client affairs in an efficient, cost-effective manner;

6.1.3 communicate with the Client at all stages of a matter in a timely and effective way;

6.1.4 engage the services of an interpreter when necessary;

6.1.5 answer reasonable Client requests in a timely and effective manner;

6.1.6 apply intellectual capacity, judgment, and deliberation to all functions;

6.1.7 pursue appropriate training and development to maintain and enhance knowledge and skills;

6.1.8 adapt to changing laws, requirements, standards, techniques and practices; and

6.1.9 comply in letter and in spirit with this Code.

6.2 Professional Responsibility for Agents and Staff

The ICCRC member is responsible for the acts or omissions of the member's Agents and Employees, and must ensure that all Agents and Employees conduct themselves in accordance with this Code.

6.3 Supervision of Agents and Staff

An ICCRC member must assume complete professional responsibility for all work entrusted to the member and adequately supervise Employees and Agents who have been assigned specific tasks.

6.4 Registration of Agents

An ICCRC member must register with ICCRC the names of all Agents, and ensure that any registered Agents are de-registered when no longer engaged. Application for registration or de-registration shall be made promptly after it occurs, but in every instance, within thirty (30) days after the event.

6.5 Prohibited Employees and Agents

Except with the written permission of ICCRC, an ICCRC member may not employ or retain in any capacity having to do with the member's practice a person whose membership or registration has been removed or suspended by ICCRC or any Designated Legal Regulatory Body as a result of a disciplinary action, or share space [with] or be a partner or associate of such a person.

6.6 Mandatory Assistance When Required

An ICCRC member should seek help from colleagues and appropriately qualified professionals for personal problems that adversely affect either professional practice or responsibilities to ICCRC.

ARTICLE 7. ADVISING CLIENTS

7.1 Honesty and Candour Required
An ICCRC member must be honest and candid when advising Clients.

7.2 Restricted to Scope of Practice
An ICCRC member shall not undertake or provide advice with respect to a matter that is outside the member's permissible scope of practice.

7.3 Avoid Corrupt Associations
An ICCRC member shall take all reasonable measures to avoid becoming the tool or dupe of an unscrupulous Client, person or persons associated with same.

7.4 Cheating Prohibited
An ICCRC member must exercise due care and not knowingly assist in or encourage:

7.4.1 any dishonesty, fraud, crime or illegal conduct,

7.4.2 the provision of misleading information,

7.4.3 the omission of any required relevant information,

7.4.4 counselling of a Client on how to violate the law or

7.4.5 counselling of a Client on how to avoid punishment, but this shall not preclude the provision of information as to mitigation of possible sentence for breach of IRPA.

7.5 Response to Illegality
When an ICCRC member is employed or retained by a person or organization to act in a matter the ICCRC member knows is dishonest, fraudulent, criminal or illegal with respect to that matter, then in addition to any obligations above, the ICCRC member shall:

7.5.1 advise the person or organization from whom the ICCRC member takes instructions that the proposed conduct would be dishonest, fraudulent, criminal or illegal, and should be stopped; and

7.5.2 if the person or organization, despite the advice, intends to pursue the proposed course of conduct, withdraw from acting in the matter in accordance with Article 14.

7.6 Translation Services Required
When advising a Client who does not speak English or French, or another language in which the ICCRC member is fluent, the ICCRC member must make a reasonable effort to engage the services of an interpreter when communicating with the Client.

7.7 Availability of ICCRC Language Services
An ICCRC member shall, where the Client speaks French but not English, inform the Client in writing in the French language of the contact information and French services of ICCRC; and reciprocally, where the Client speaks English but not French, an ICCRC member shall inform the Client in writing in the English language of the contact information and English services of ICCRC.

ARTICLE 8. CONFIDENTIALITY

8.1 Maintenance of Confidentiality

An ICCRC member has a duty to hold in strict confidence at all times all information concerning the personal and business affairs of a Client acquired during the course of practice, and should not disclose such information unless disclosure is expressly or impliedly authorized by the Client, required by law or by a tribunal of competent jurisdiction, or is otherwise permitted by this Code.

8.2 Confidentiality Survives Retainer

The duty of confidentiality under Section 8.1 continues indefinitely after the ICCRC member has ceased to act for the Client, whether or not differences have arisen between them. For greater clarity, an ICCRC member, subject to being compelled by law or legal process, shall preserve the Client confidential information even after the termination of the retainer.

8.3 Protection of Confidential Information

An ICCRC member shall take all reasonable steps to ensure the privacy and safekeeping of a Client's confidential information. The ICCRC member shall keep the Client's papers and other property out of sight, as well as out of reach, of those not entitled to see them.

8.4 Disclosure Prohibited

An ICCRC member shall not disclose the fact of having been consulted or retained by a person unless the nature of the matter requires such disclosure.

8.5 Application to Employees and Agents

An ICCRC member should ensure that their Employees and Agents maintain and preserve the Client's confidential information.

8.6 Exception When Required by Law

Notwithstanding the above, an ICCRC member may disclose confidential information when required by law or by order of a tribunal of competent jurisdiction.

8.7 Exception for Defence of Allegations

In order to defend against allegations, an ICCRC member may disclose confidential information if it is alleged that the ICCRC member or the member's Agents or Employees are:

    8.7.1 guilty of a criminal offence involving a Client's affairs;
    8.7.2 civilly liable with respect to a matter involving a Client's affairs; or
    8.7.3 guilty of a breach of this Code.

8.8 Exception for Collections

An ICCRC member may disclose confidential information in order to establish or collect professional fees or disbursements.

8.9 Limits on Exceptions

An ICCRC member shall not disclose more information than is necessary when disclosing confidential information required or permitted by Sections 8.6, 8.7 or 8.8.

ARTICLE 9. CONFLICTS OF INTEREST

9.1 Prohibition Where Conflict

An ICCRC member shall not represent parties with potentially conflicting interests in an immigration matter, unless after adequate disclosure to and with the consent of the parties, and shall not act or continue to act in a matter where there is or is likely to be a conflict of interest.

ARTICLE 10. PRESERVATION OF CLIENT PROPERTY

10.1 Safekeeping of Client Property

An ICCRC member owes a duty to the Client to ensure the safekeeping of the Client's property in accordance with the law and with the same care of such property as a careful and prudent owner would when dealing with property of like description.

10.2 Notification of Safekeeping

An ICCRC member shall promptly notify the Client of the receipt of any money or other property of the Client, unless satisfied that the Client is aware that the property has come into the member's custody.

10.3 Segregation of Client Property

An ICCRC member shall clearly label and identify the Client's property and place it in safekeeping, distinguishable from the ICCRC member's own property.

10.4 Safekeeping Records Required

An ICCRC member shall maintain such records as necessary to identify Client property that is in the ICCRC member's custody.

10.5 Accounting for and Return of Client Property

An ICCRC member shall account promptly for any Client property that is in the member's custody and shall, upon request, deliver it to the order of the Client.

ARTICLE 11. ICCRC MEMBER AS ADVOCATE

11.1 Twin Responsibilities

When representing the Client before government officials or the Board, the ICCRC member should resolutely, and honourably, within the limits of the law, represent the Client's interests while treating the Board members, the Minister, Officers and other parties with candour, courtesy and respect.

ARTICLE 12. RETAINER AND FEES

12.1 Content of Retainer Generally

The ICCRC member must provide the Client with a written retainer agreement or engagement letter that:

12.1.1 clearly states the matter and scope of services for which the ICCRC member is retained;

12.1.2 fully discloses
    (i) the fees payable, such fees to be fair and reasonable in the circumstances;
    (ii) the disbursements to be charged;
    (iii) the payment terms and conditions:
        a) by the hour or
        b) flat fee billing with payment by milestones or by predetermined date;
    (iv) schedule of payments.

12.1.3 identifies the nature but not the amount of any other remuneration, such as but not limited to a referral fee, being or to be received by the ICCRC member in connection with the matter;

12.1.4 discloses that the ICCRC member is a member of ICCRC; and

12.1.5 provides sufficient details as to how to contact ICCRC.

12.2 Specific Content of Retainer

The retainer agreement shall provide a written complaint procedure regarding Client fee disputes, the failure to respond to requests for information, and the return of Client's property. The retainer agreement shall provide that any complaint be made in writing to the ICCRC member, and that the member will address the concerns of the Client within a specified time period.

12.3 Application of Trust Money

An ICCRC member must not appropriate any money or property of a Client held in trust or otherwise under the ICCRC member's control for or on account of fees or disbursements without the express or implied authority of the Client.

12.4 Certain Prohibition

An ICCRC member may not hold Client money for the benefit of a third party except for money to pay the ICCRC member's fees, including Agent's fees, CIC fees and disbursements related thereto. For greater clarity, the prohibition on holding Client monies applies to money the Client needs to qualify for any eligibility program under the IRPA.

ARTICLE 13. JOINT RETAINERS

13.1 Initial Obligation

Before agreeing to act for more than one Client in a matter, an ICCRC member shall advise the Clients that:

13.1.1 no information received in connection with the matter from one Client can be treated as confidential so far as any of the others are concerned; and

13.1.2 if a conflict develops that cannot be resolved, the ICCRC member cannot continue to act for both or all of them and may have to withdraw completely.

13.2 Where Continuing Relationship with One

If an ICCRC member has a continuing relationship with a Client for whom he or she acts regularly, before agreeing to act for that Client and another Client in a matter or transaction, the ICCRC member shall advise the other Client of the continuing relationship and recommend that the Client obtain independent legal advice about the joint retainer.

13.3 When [to] Avoid Joint Retainer

Although all parties concerned may consent, an ICCRC member shall avoid acting for more than one Client if it is likely that an issue contentious between them will arise or their interests, rights, or obligations will diverge as the matter progresses.

ARTICLE 14. WITHDRAWAL FROM REPRESENTATION

14.1 When Withdrawal Required

Withdrawal is obligatory, and an ICCRC member shall sever the professional relationship with the Client or withdraw as the representative, if:

14.1.1 discharged by the Client;

14.1.2 instructed by the Client to do something illegal or in contravention of professional obligations or this Code;

14.1.3 the ICCRC member's continued involvement will place the ICCRC member in a conflict of interest; or

14.1.4 the ICCRC member is not competent to handle the matter.

14.2 When Withdrawal Optional

Withdrawal is optional and an ICCRC member may, but is not required to, sever the professional relationship with the Client or withdraw as representative if there has been a serious loss of confidence between the ICCRC member and Client, such as where:

14.2.1 the Client has deceived the ICCRC member;

14.2.2 the Client has refused to give adequate instructions to the ICCRC member; or

14.2.3 the Client has refused to accept and act upon the ICCRC member's advice on a significant point.

14.3 Withdrawal on Other Basis

In situations not covered by Sections 14.1 and 14.2, an ICCRC member may sever the professional relationship with the Client or withdraw as representative only if the severance or withdrawal:

14.3.1 will not be unfair to the Client; and

14.3.2 is not done for an improper purpose.

14.4 Withdrawal on Failure to Pay

Where, after reasonable notice, the Client fails to provide funds on account of disbursements or fees, an ICCRC member may withdraw for non-payment of fees or disbursements unless serious prejudice to the Client would result.

14.5 Member Action Required on Withdrawal

When an ICCRC member withdraws, the ICCRC member should try to minimize expense and avoid prejudice to the Client and should do all that can reasonably be done to facilitate the orderly transfer of the matter to a successor. Upon discharge or withdrawal, an ICCRC member should:

14.5.1 deliver to or to the order of the Client all papers and property to which the Client is entitled;

14.5.2 give the Client all information that may be required in connection with the case or matter;

14.5.3 account for all funds of the Client held or previously dealt with, and refund any funds not earned during the retainer;

14.5.4 promptly render an account for outstanding fees and disbursements;

14.5.5 co-operate with the successor so as to minimize expense and avoid prejudice to the Client; and

14.5.6 notify in writing any government agency, such as Citizenship and Immigration Canada, CBSA or the Board where the ICCRC member's name appears as representative for the Client, that the ICCRC member has withdrawn.

14.6 Obligation of Successor Member

Before agreeing to represent a Client, a successor ICCRC member should be satisfied that the former ICCRC member, or other representative authorized by law to represent the Client, has withdrawn, or has been discharged by the Client.

14.7 Where Withdrawal Threat Prohibited

An ICCRC member shall not use the threat of withdrawal as a device to force a hasty decision by the Client on a difficult question.

ARTICLE 15. OUTSIDE INTERESTS

15.1 Other Work Not to Compromise Member's Obligations

An ICCRC member who engages in another profession, business, occupation or other outside interest, or who holds public office concurrently in addition to practice, shall not allow the outside interest or public office to jeopardize the member's integrity, independence, or competence.

15.2 Maintenance of Independence

An ICCRC member shall not allow any involvement in an outside interest or public office to impair the exercise of independent judgment on behalf of a Client.

ARTICLE 16. ADVERTISING, SOLICITATION AND MAKING SERVICES AVAILABLE

16.1 Quality of Service Availability

An ICCRC member should make professional services available to the public in an efficient and convenient manner that will command respect and instil confidence, and by means that are compatible with the integrity, independence and effectiveness of the profession and the integrity of Canada's immigration program.

16.2 Quality of Holding-Out

An ICCRC member, or Employees and Agents of members, shall not engage in false or misleading advertising or representations or misrepresent or mislead a Client as to the member's qualifications, services, fees, available programs or benefits or provide false or unrealistic expectations regarding potential results, or processing times. An ICCRC member, or Employees or Agents of members, may not hold themselves out as having special access or influence with respect to the Minister, an Officer, or the Board.

16.3 Endorsements and Testimonials

An ICCRC member may use endorsements or testimonials or both in the member's advertising and promotion provided that the nature of the form and content of any such endorsement or testimonial conforms to the policies of ICCRC[;] unless and until otherwise determined by ICCRC, any such endorsements or testimonials or both shall conform to the following:

16.3.1 any such endorsement or testimonial has actually been given by a Client or former Client;

16.3.2 any such endorsement or testimonial is true and accurate; [and]

16.3.3 the Client or former Client has given to the member written permission for the exact content of any such endorsement or testimonial.

16.4 Good Taste

In all instances, advertising should be in good taste and is not such as to bring the profession, ICCRC or the laws of Canada into disrepute.

16.5 Use of ICCRC Designation and Logo

An ICCRC member shall only use the ICCRC designation and the logo of ICCRC in compliance with ICCRC's policies.

ARTICLE 17. DISCRIMINATION AND HARASSMENT

17.1 No Discrimination

An ICCRC member shall not discriminate against any person in the course of their practice on such grounds as age, gender, sexual orientation, same-sex partnership status, marital status, family status, national or ethnic origin, ancestry, race, colour, religion, creed, citizenship, physical or mental disability, political affiliation, record of offences, or socio-economic status.

17.2 Respect for All

An ICCRC member shall respect the dignity and integrity of all individuals and ensure fair and equitable treatment in all aspects of the provision of immigration services.

17.3 No Denial of Service

An ICCRC member shall ensure that no one is denied services or receives inferior service on the basis of the grounds set out in this Article 17. This does not affect the ICCRC member's right to refuse to accept a Client for legitimate reasons.

17.4 No Harassment

An ICCRC member shall not engage in sexual or other forms of harassment of a colleague, a staff member, a Client or any other person on the ground of race, ancestry, place of origin, colour, ethnic origin, citizenship, creed, sex, sexual orientation, age, record of offences, marital status, family status or disability.

17.5 Use of Electronic Medium

An ICCRC member shall not engage in electronic harassment by sending unsolicited email messages of an abusive, offensive, intrusive, unprofessional or unwanted nature to another ICCRC member or a member of the public, in particular where the recipient has expressly requested to be removed from the sender's list.

17.6 Employment Practices Included

An ICCRC member's employment practices may not offend this Article 17.

ARTICLE 18. ERRORS AND OMISSIONS

18.1 Errors and Omissions Insurance Required

Every ICCRC member shall maintain the errors and omissions insurance in the minimum amount as prescribed by ICCRC from time to time.

18.2 Required Action upon Discovery of Error or Omission

If the ICCRC member discovers, in connection with a matter for which the ICCRC member was retained, an error or omission that is or may be damaging to the Client and that cannot be rectified readily, the ICCRC member shall:

18.2.1 promptly and fully inform the Client of the error or omission, being careful not to prejudice any rights of indemnity that either of them may have under an insurance, Clients' protection or indemnity plan, or otherwise;

18.2.2 seek advice from the ICCRC's Practice Management Unit where needed;

18.2.3 recommend that the Client obtain legal advice elsewhere concerning any rights the Client may have arising from the error or omission;

18.2.4 advise the Client that in the circumstances, the ICCRC member may no longer be able to act for the Client;

18.2.5 promptly inform his or her errors and omissions insurance provider; and

18.2.6 promptly inform ICCRC that the errors and omissions insurance provider has been informed.

ARTICLE 19. DISCIPLINARY AUTHORITY

19.1 ICCRC Impose Discipline

ICCRC may discipline an ICCRC member for Professional Misconduct or Conduct Unbecoming an ICCRC member.

19.2 Location of Conduct Irrelevant

An ICCRC member is subject to the disciplinary authority of ICCRC regardless of where the conduct occurred that is alleged to be a breach of this Code, or where the person resides.

19.3 Conduct Before Becoming ICCRC Member

An ICCRC member who was a CSIC member immediately before joining ICCRC is subject to the disciplinary authority of ICCRC for conduct which occurred during the period of CSIC membership which constitutes a breach of this Code.

19.4 Liability for Costs

An ICCRC member who is subject to discipline may also be required to pay all or a portion of the costs associated with the investigation and discipline hearing.

ARTICLE 20. RESPONSIBILITY TO ICCRC AND OTHERS

20.1 Maintenance of Contact Information

An ICCRC member shall immediately notify ICCRC and Clients of any changes in contact information, including but not limited to home and business address, telephone, fax and email address.

20.2 Obligation to Respond to ICCRC

An ICCRC member shall reply promptly to any communication from ICCRC.

20.3 Restriction on Communicating with Complainant

An ICCRC member shall not communicate with a person who has made a complaint to ICCRC unless the complainant has otherwise requested.

KEY TERMS

conduct unbecoming, 542

conflict of interest, 545

professional misconduct, 543

solicitor–client privilege, 545

tickler system, 544

vicarious responsibility, 544

REVIEW QUESTIONS

1. List the steps that a person must take to become a member of the ICCRC.

2. What is the difference between a regulated immigration consultant and a law clerk?

3. Compare and contrast professional misconduct and conduct unbecoming a regulated immigration consultant.

4. What is ghost consulting and why would Canadian officials want this practice stopped?

5. Describe the types of advertising that are acceptable to the ICCRC.

6. How should a consultant deal with money paid to him in order to pay fees to CIC?

7. What is the obligation of a consultant acting as an advocate in a hearing before the IRB?

8. What organization can impose discipline on a regulated immigration consultant? What reasons will motivate that organization to impose discipline, and what forms of discipline is that organization authorized to impose?

9. If a regulated immigration consultant operates more than one business, what must the consultant do in order to avoid improper practices?

10. What is a conflict of interest? How can a regulated immigration consultant (a) avoid getting into a conflict of interest, and (b) resolve a conflict of interest if one arises?

Glossary

A

accredited interpreter an interpreter used in an IRB proceeding who has undergone a security check and has passed a language exam

acquittal a finding of not guilty

administrative tribunal a specialized governmental agency established under legislation to implement legislative policy—for example, the Immigration and Refugee Board is an administrative tribunal established under the IRPA

admissibility hearing an adversarial hearing to determine whether or not an applicant is inadmissible; held at the ID when a person allegedly breaches Canadian immigration laws pursuant to IRPA section 44(1), where an officer is of the opinion that a permanent resident or foreign national is inadmissible

alienage one of the four inclusion elements of the refugee definition; a refugee must be outside his country of nationality or, if stateless, his country of former habitual residence and, owing to a fear of persecution, must be unable or unwilling to avail himself of the protection of that country

allowed on consent an appeal that is allowed when the minister concedes to the appellant's position

arrest to take a person into legal custody

B

balance of probabilities the standard of proof in civil matters, determined on the basis of whether a claim or a fact as alleged is more probably true than not true; this is a much lower standard of proof than that required in criminal court, where the evidence must establish "beyond a reasonable doubt" that an accused is guilty

Basis of Claim (BOC) Form a form used to present a refugee protection claim to the RPD; includes information about the claimant and a detailed account of the basis for her claim

business visitor a foreign worker who seeks admission to Canada to engage in international business activities and whose primary source of remuneration remains outside Canada

C

Canadian educational credential any diploma, certificate, or credential, issued on the completion of a Canadian program of study or training at a registered/accredited educational or training institution (IRPR, s 73(1))

Canadian Orientation Abroad (COA) Program a one- to five-day program designed to help integrate refugees into Canadian society

Caregiver Program a program for foreign caregivers who are hired to provide care, in a private residence, to children, seniors, or persons with certified medical needs; sometimes referred to as the Live-In Caregiver Program

case law interpretations of statutes and regulations created by the judgments of courts and other adjudicators; case law is part of the common law

cessation clause a clause that provides the framework for when protection may lawfully cease under section 108 of the IRPA

citizen a person who has the right to live in a country by virtue of birth or by legally acquiring the right

citizenship the full political and civil rights in the body politic of the state

citizenship judges quasi-judicial decision-makers who have the authority to decide citizenship applications

co-signer a spouse or common law partner of a sponsor who co-signs with a sponsor who does not have the necessary financial means to be an approved sponsor

codified formalized and clarified in writing in the form of binding legislation

common law a body of legal principles and rules that can be traced back to Britain and that are found in court judgments

common law partner also known as a common law spouse; a person who is cohabiting with the person in a conjugal relationship and has done so for at least one year; applicable to both opposite-sex and same-sex relationships (IRPR, s 1)

community sponsor an organization, association, or corporation that sponsors refugees

Comprehensive Ranking System (CRS) a point-based system that assesses and scores potential skilled worker candidates on their skills, work experience, language ability, education, and other factors, such as a job offer or a nomination by a province or territory

conditional removal order a departure order with conditions attached; issued pending the outcome of a refugee claim

conduct unbecoming conduct that occurs in an immigration consultant's personal or private capacity that tends to bring discredit on the profession

confirmation of permanent residence (COPR) a document that allows a foreign national to travel to Canada to seek entry as a permanent resident

conflict of interest occurs where a consultant represents clients with incompatible interests

conjugal partner in relation to a sponsor, a person outside Canada who has had a binding relationship with the sponsor for at least one year but who could not live with him or her; refers to both opposite-sex and same-sex relationships; not defined in the IRPA or IRPR

constituent group (CG) a group authorized by a sponsorship agreement holder to sponsor refugees on its behalf

Constitution the basic framework within which all other laws are created, establishing the basic principles to which all other laws must conform

convention an agreement that obliges countries under international law to conform to its provisions

Convention refugee a person who has been granted protection under the refugee definition in the 1951 *Convention Relating to the Status of Refugees*

corroborative documents documents that corroborate a claimant's allegations

country information for a refugee claimant, information on the country of reference, such as country-of-origin information, as provided by the RPD

crimes against humanity any inhumane acts or omissions that are committed against any civilian population or any identifiable group

criminality domestic crime, as opposed to crimes against humanity or war crimes as proscribed by international law; the IRPA defines three categories of criminality: serious criminality under section 36(1), criminality under section 36(2), and organized criminality under section 37

customary international law international legal customs and practices that take on the force of law over time

D

deemed rehabilitated an exemption from criminal inadmissibility; a person who was convicted outside Canada and who meets the criteria under section 18(2) of the IRPR may be deemed rehabilitated and permitted to enter Canada

delegation of authority the giving of decision-making power to someone else; for example, a minister may delegate authority to an immigration officer

departure order a type of removal order that generally provides a person with 30 days in which to leave Canada

deportation order a type of removal order that bars re-entry to Canada indefinitely

derogable rights human rights that can be temporarily suspended by a state in a time of public emergency

designate choose someone for a position, duty, or responsibility

designated foreign national (DFN) a person (generally, a refugee claimant) who was part of a group of persons smuggled into Canada whom the minister has designated as an irregular arrival (see IRPA, s 20.1)

designated irregular arrival a group (generally, of refugee claimants) that the minister has reasonable grounds to believe was part of a human smuggling operation and is so designated in the public interest

designated learning institution (DLI) generally, a post-secondary institution that is confirmed by the institution's provincial or territorial ministry of education to meet minimum CIC standards; all primary and secondary schools in Canada are automatically designated

designated representative a person chosen by the RPD to act and make decisions on behalf of a refugee claimant who is incapable of doing so

detain to restrict a person's liberty in any way; in the context of immigration, to keep a person in legal custody, such as in a prison or an immigration holding centre, prior to a hearing on a matter

detention review a hearing before the ID for the purpose of reviewing the reasons for a foreign national or permanent resident's detention under the IRPA

disclosure the release of documents to the opposing side in a proceeding

dual intent an intention to become first a temporary resident and then a permanent resident

durable solution a lasting solution to a refugee's temporary status: local integration in the country of asylum, voluntary return to the refugee's home country (repatriation), or resettlement in another country

E

eligible in an immigration context, meeting the criteria set out in the IRPA or IRPR for the type of entry sought (temporary or permanent)

equivalency assessment a determination by a designated organization or institution that a foreign diploma, certificate, or credential is equivalent to a Canadian educational credential and an assessment of the authenticity of the foreign diploma, certificate, or credential (IRPR, s 73(1))

exclusion order a type of removal order that includes a one-year or five-year ban from re-entering Canada

expression of interest under the Express Entry system, the initial submission about skills, work experience, and other attributes that prospective immigrants make to indicate their interest in coming to Canada

F

federal system of government a division of law-making powers between the national (federal) and provincial governments according to subject matter

flight risk a person who is likely to fail to appear at an immigration proceeding

foreign national a person, including a stateless person, who is not a Canadian citizen or a permanent resident

full-time work at least 30 hours of work over a period of one week (IRPR, s 73(1))

G

GATS professional a person who seeks to engage in an activity at a professional level in a designated profession, and who meets the GATS criteria

genocide an act or omission committed with intent to destroy, in whole or in part, an identifiable group of persons

Government-Assisted Refugee (GAR) Program a program that applies only to the sponsorship of members of the Convention refugees abroad class, including special needs cases

governor in council the governor general acting with the advice and consent of Cabinet; formal executive authority is conferred by the statutes on the governor in council

Group of Five (G5) a group of five or more people who join together to sponsor one or more refugees

H

high-wage positions high-skilled positions in which the wage offered is at or above the provincial/territorial median wage

home study an assessment of the prospective adoptive parents with respect to their suitability to adopt

hybrid or dual procedure offences offences for which the Crown prosecutor may choose to proceed either by summary conviction or by indictment

I

identity documents lawfully obtained documents designed to prove the identity of the person carrying them (for example, a passport or birth certificate)

immigrant a person who wishes to settle (or has settled) permanently in another country

immigration the movement of non-native people into a country in order to settle there

Immigration and Refugee Board (IRB) an independent, quasi-judicial tribunal whose mission is "to make well-reasoned decisions on immigration and refugee matters, efficiently, fairly and in accordance with the law"

Immigration Loans Program (ILP) a federal fund available to qualifying indigent refugees and immigrants; provides loans to cover some costs of immigrating to and settling in Canada

immigration officer a public servant working in Canada at a case processing centre or other immigration office

immigration resettlement plan a plan tabled by the CIC minister each year that includes the number and types of foreign nationals who can come to Canada as permanent residents

inadmissibility ineligibility for entry to Canada, on grounds such as criminality

inadmissibility report (section 44(1) report) an officer's report under section 44(1) of the IRPA that sets out the grounds of inadmissibility for which the person is alleged to have violated, including a brief description of the relevant facts in narrative form

inadmissible barred from entry to Canada for reasons that include security, criminality, and health grounds

indictable offences serious offences, such as murder, with longer periods of imprisonment and more complex prosecution procedures than those for summary conviction offences

individual rehabilitation a method of removing a ground of inadmissibility (criminality, for example) that requires the applicant to apply to a visa officer, who will then consider whether certain criteria for removal have been met

interdiction control activity that prevents illegal travellers from reaching Canada

Interim Federal Health Program (IFHP) health care coverage that is offered by the federal government on a temporary basis to resettled refugees, refugees and protected persons, refugee claimants, rejected refugee claimants, and certain persons detained under the IRPA

internal flight alternative (IFA) a safe place within one's own country where there is no serious risk of persecution and where a claimaint can seek refuge, instead of seeking protection in another country

International Organization for Migration (IOM) an intergovernmental organization that works with partners in the international community to assist in meeting the operational challenges of migration, advance understanding of migration issues, encourage social and economic development through migration, and uphold the human dignity and well-being of migrants

intra-company transfer an executive, senior manager, or qualified employee with specialized knowledge who is transferred within a company to work in Canada on a temporary basis

invitation to apply (ITA) under the Express Entry system, an invitation by CIC to foreign nationals who are qualified candidates to apply for permanent residence

J

joint and several liability liability for a financial obligation shared by two partners in a relationship such that either partner may be required to pay the full amount of the obligation—e.g., where a sponsor takes on a co-signer, both may be liable for the full amount in the event of a default

Joint Assistance Sponsorship (JAS) Program a refugee sponsorship program that involves both CIC and a private sponsor

judicial notice a rule of evidence that allows a decision-maker to accept certain commonly known, indisputable, and uncontentious facts without requiring that they be proven with evidence

jus sanguinis citizenship based on blood ties

jus soli citizenship based on the land of birth

L

labour market impact assessment (LMIA) an ESDC document obtained by a Canadian employer in order to employ a foreign worker

language skill area speaking, oral comprehension, reading, or writing (IRPR, s 73(1))

letter (or notice) of agreement a letter or notice of agreement, required in Hague Convention adoption cases, indicating that the province or territory where the adopted child will live and the adoptive parents agree to the adoption; sent by the province or territory to the visa office, with a copy to the central authority of the adopted child's country of residence

letter of acceptance a document that indicates that a foreign student has been accepted into a Canadian educational institution

letter of introduction a document provided by a visa office to confirm approval of a study permit or work permit, or extended stay for a parent or grandparent from a country that does not require visas (the Super Visa program), for presentation to an officer upon arrival in Canada

letter of invitation a letter from a Canadian citizen or permanent resident in Canada on behalf of a friend or family member who wants to visit, setting out how the host plans to support the visitor and whether she has the financial means to support the visitor during a longer visit

letter of no-involvement a letter that may be accepted instead of a home study where a private adoption takes place outside Canada and in a state that is not a signatory to the Hague Convention on Adoption

letter of no-objection a written statement from the province or territory where an adopted child will live, stating that the province or territory does not object to the adoption

letter of support under the Business Start-Up Program, a written commitment by a designated organization to an applicant confirming the organization's support of the applicant's business idea; the letter must be included with the application for permanent residence

low income cut-off (LICO) the minimum income requirement for sponsors of permanent residents

low-wage positions low-skilled positions in which the wage offered is below the provincial/territorial median wage

M

medical surveillance a designation by the panel physician that provides for the monitoring of an applicant's medical condition

member the title given to a decision-maker in the Refugee Protection Division, Immigration Division, or Immigration Appeal Division of the Immigration and Refugee Board

misrepresentation a ground of inadmissibility under the IRPA that involves misstating facts or withholding information

multiple citizenships a situation in which a person holds more than one citizenship

multiple-entry visa (MEV) a document that allows a foreign national to enter Canada from another country multiple times during the validity of the visa, for up to six months at a time

N

named cases sponsor-referred refugee cases

nationality refers to a person's citizenship and ethnic or linguistic group; may sometimes overlap with race

naturalization the process by which a foreign national, after being admitted to Canada as a permanent resident, applies for and obtains Canadian citizenship

non-derogable rights a person's core human rights, which must be respected and cannot be taken away or suspended for any reason

non-political crimes acts committed for personal gain with no political end or motive involved

non-state agent persons or entities who perpetuate acts of persecution from which the government may be unwilling or unable to provide protection—e.g., warlords, guerilla organizations, and anti- or pro-government paramilitary groups

notice of arrival notice of a refugee's arrival into Canada that is sent to the sponsor

notice of decision a written decision by the decision-maker, issued to those involved in the case

O

officer under section 6(1) of the IRPA, a person or class of person designated by the minister to carry out any purpose of any provision of the IRPA and given specific powers and duties

open work permit a document that enables a foreign national to work for any employer for a specific time period

oral representation an argument that is made orally, such as at the end of a refugee hearing

orders in council administrative orders that serve notice of a decision taken by the executive arm of government

P

panel physician a local physician, authorized by the Canadian government; formerly known as a "designated medical practitioner"

parallel processing simultaneous processing of the permanent residence application of the main applicant and the applications of sponsored family members, such as is allowed under the Caregiver Program

peace officer a law enforcement officer with the power to examine people and perform searches and seizures

permanent resident card (PR card) a card issued to permanent residents after their arrival in Canada showing proof of immigration status

permanent resident status status that permits the holder to enjoy most of the same rights guaranteed to Canadians under the *Canadian Charter of Rights and Freedoms*

permanent resident visa a document that allows a foreign national to travel to Canada and, after a successful examination at a port of entry, to enter Canada as a permanent resident

permanent resident a person who has been granted permanent resident status in Canada and who has not subsequently lost that status under IRPA section 46; also known as a "landed immigrant" under older legislation

persecution one of the four inclusion elements of the refugee definition, but not defined in the defin-ition or in the IRPA; a serious harm that is sustained and a systematic violation of basic human rights

person in need of protection a person who has been granted refugee protection under the IRPA because of a danger of torture or because of a risk to life or a risk of cruel and unusual treatment or punishment; used when the refugee claim does not fall within the scope of the Refugee Convention

policy non-binding guidelines that are created by agencies to support the administration of statutes and regulations, and that reflect the government and agency's agenda

precedent a court ruling on a point of law that is binding on lower courts

prescribed senior official as referenced under section 35(1)(b) of the IRPA, a senior official in the service of a government that has been designated by the minister as a perpetrator of terrorism, human rights violations, genocide, war crimes, or crimes against humanity within the meaning of sections 6(3) to (5) of the *Crimes Against Humanity and War Crimes Act*

primary agricultural stream positions related to on-farm primary agriculture such as general farm workers, nursery and greenhouse workers, feedlot workers, and harvesting labourers, including under the SAWP

principle of *non-refoulement* a rule of international law that obliges countries to provide protection to refugees against return to the country where they face a risk of persecution, or where their life or freedom would be threatened because of their race, religion, nationality, membership in a particular social group, or political opinion

professional under NAFTA, a citizen of the United States or Mexico who has pre-arranged employment with a Canadian employer and whose occupation is listed in NAFTA

professional misconduct any improper action of an immigration consultant during the course of conducting business that tends to discredit the profession

Provincial Nominee Program a program that allows provinces and territories to nominate foreign nationals to apply for permanent residence in Canada

R

ratification a confirmation to abide by an international agreement

reasonable grounds a set of facts and circumstances that would satisfy an ordinarily cautious and prudent person and that are more than mere suspicion; a lower standard of proof than a balance of probabilities

record suspension (pardon) a grant under the *Criminal Code* resulting in an offence being deemed not to have occurred; formerly known as a pardon

refugee a person who is forced to flee from persecution (as opposed to an immigrant, who chooses to move)

refugee claimant a person who has made a refugee protection claim where the decision is yet to be made; this term is used in Canada and is equivalent to "asylum seeker"

refugee *sur place* a person who did not initially flee his home country, but while in another country became a refugee in need of protection because of changed conditions or circumstances in his home country

refusal letter a document sent to a permanent resident applicant outlining the reasons for the application's refusal

regulations detailed rules, created pursuant to a statute by the governor in council, that fill in practical details regarding the statute's administration and enforcement

removal order a legal document issued either after an examination or at an admissibility hearing ordering a person to leave Canada

removal ready refers to people who are subject to a removal order that is in force or to a security certificate that has been issued against them

resettlement in the context of refugee law, the relocation of a protected refugee from a host state to another country where he can permanently reside; an option that is used when there is no other durable solution such as voluntary repatriation or local integration

Resettlement Assistance Program (RAP) a program that provides financial and immediate essential services to government-assisted refugees

residual power power that is not otherwise delegated elsewhere; the federal government has residual power to legislate in all subject areas that are not specifically assigned to the provinces

restoration of status restoration of a temporary resident's lost status as a visitor, student, or worker has expired; applied for in accordance with R182 on form IMM 1249E

restricted occupation an occupation designated by the minister, taking into account labour market activity on both an area and a national basis, following consultation with ESDC, provincial governments, and any other relevant organizations or institutions

risk of cruel and unusual treatment or punishment the risk of ill-treatment that would cause suffering that is less severe than torture

risk to life a personal risk that is generally not faced by other individuals in the country

rules a category of regulation that has the purpose of establishing practices and procedures for the presentation of cases

S

safe third country a country in which an individual, in passing through that country, should have made a claim for refugee protection if that country can provide legal protection against *refoulement*; to date, the United States is the only country that is designated as a safe third country under the IRPA

Seasonal Agricultural Worker Program (SAWP) a program that allows the entry of foreign nationals to work in the agricultural sector in Canada

security certificate a document providing for a removal hearing in the absence of the person named, where information must be protected for reasons of public safety

settlement plan the details of a refugee sponsor's commitment to provide basic financial support and care for a sponsored refugee

significant benefit a ground of exemption from the usual requirement of foreign workers to obtain a positive LMIA; the exemption applies to foreign workers whose presence in Canada is likely to result in a significant benefit to the country, and permits them to apply for a work permit without first obtaining the positive LMIA

single-entry visa a document that allows a foreign national to enter Canada only once, usually for no more than six months

skilled trade occupation an occupation listed in skill level B of the NOC matrix as major group 72, 73, 82, or 92 or as minor group 632 or 633 (IRPR, s 87.2)

solicitor–client privilege the protection of client information and communication shared in the context of a solicitor–client relationship

special advocate a person who must be appointed to act on behalf of a person who is subject to a closed security certificate hearing process to protect his or her interests

sponsorship agreement holder (SAH) an established, incorporated organization that has signed an agreement with the minister of CIC to facilitate refugee sponsorship

state agent persecutors of the refugee claimant whose acts are sanctioned by the government of the claimant's country of origin—e.g., police and members of the military

stateless person a person who is not recognized by any nation as a citizen and has no residency rights in any country

statute law passed by Parliament or a provincial legislature; also called an "act"; often specifically provides for the authority to make regulations or to delegate this power; distinguished from subordinate legislation

summary conviction offences less serious offences that carry a maximum sentence of six months in jail, a maximum fine of $5,000, or both, and that are prosecuted using streamlined procedures

Super Visa a document that allows a foreign national who is the parent or grandparent of a Canadian citizen or a permanent resident to stay in Canada for up to two years and re-enter over a ten-year period without the need to renew the visa; also called a Parent and Grandparent Super Visa

T

temporary resident (TR) a foreign national who is legally allowed to be in Canada on a temporary basis, such as a tourist, student, worker, or business person

temporary foreign worker (TFW) a foreign national engaged in paid work activity who is authorized to enter and to remain in Canada for a limited period

temporary resident permit (TRP) a permit that may be granted in exceptional circumstances to a person who does not meet the eligibility and/or the admissibility requirements to enter or remain temporarily in Canada

temporary resident visa (TRV) a document authorizing a person to enter and remain in Canada for a period of time; it is an official counterfoil document issued by a visa officer and placed in the applicant's passport to show that the foreign national has met the eligibility and admissibility requirements for a single entry or multiple entries to Canada as a temporary resident

terrorist group as defined under section 83.01 of the *Criminal Code*, an entity or an association of entities "that has as one of its purposes or activities facilitating or carrying out any terrorist activity"

tickler system a reminder system for deadlines

torture the infliction of severe physical or mental pain or suffering as a punishment or means of interrogation or intimidation

transit visa a document that allows travel through Canada to another country by anyone who would need a temporary resident visa to enter Canada and whose flight will stop here for less than 48 hours

U

unnamed cases refugee sponsorship requests referred to the CIC Matching Centre, which attempts to find a suitable match for a would-be sponsor

urgent need of protection a term that describes, in respect of a member of the Convention refugees abroad class and the country of asylum class, a person whose life, liberty, or physical safety is under immediate threat and who, if not protected, is likely to be (a) killed; (b) subjected to violence, torture, sexual assault, or arbitrary imprisonment; or (c) returned to her country of nationality or former habitual residence (IRPR, s 138)

V

vacate to nullify or to void, such as may happen to a refugee determination that was obtained fraudulently

vicarious responsibility a principle that can lead to immigration professionals being held personally responsible for the actions of agents or employees

visa (or permit) a document that permits the holder to enter Canada for a specific purpose either temporarily or permanently

visa officer a public servant working in a Canadian consulate or visa office abroad

visitor record a record of information documented by a port-of-entry officer, stapled to the holder's passport; it outlines the conditions of admission, specifies the date by which the foreign national must leave Canada, and includes other information about the foreign national and the purpose for seeking entry to Canada

visitor visa a term commonly used in place of temporary resident visa

voluntary repatriation in the context of refugee law, the return of a refugee to her country of origin, of her own free will

vulnerable a term describing Convention refugees or persons in similar circumstances who have a greater need of protection than other applicants for protection abroad because their particular circumstances give rise to a heightened risk to their physical safety (IRPR, s 138)

W

war crime an act or omission committed during an armed conflict that violates international laws of war

well-founded fear one of the four inclusion elements of the refugee definition; the refugee claimant must establish both objective and subjective components of fear of persecution

withdrawal an appeal that is withdrawn by the appellant if she concedes to the minister's position

withholding to hold back from doing or taking an action

Women at Risk Program (AWR) a program to resettle women who are members of the Convention refugees abroad class or humanitarian-protected persons abroad class

work an activity for which wages are paid or commission is earned, or that is in direct competition with the activities of Canadian citizens or permanent residents in the Canadian labour market (IRPR, s 2)

work permit a written authorization issued by an officer that allows a foreign national to engage in employment in Canada

References

Legislation

An Act to amend the Citizenship Act, SC 2008, c 14 [Bill C-37].

An Act to amend the Citizenship Act (adoption), SC 2007, c 24 [Bill C-14].

An Act to amend the Immigration and Refugee Protection Act, SC 2011, c 8 [Bill C-35].

An Act to amend the Immigration and Refugee Protection Act (certificate and special advocate) and to make a consequential amendment to another Act, SC 2008, c 3 [Bill C-3].

Anti-terrorism Act, SC 2001, c 41.

Balanced Refugee Reform Act, SC 2010, c 8 [Bill C-11].

Bankruptcy and Insolvency Act, RSC 1985, c B-3.

Canadian Charter of Rights and Freedoms, Part I of the *Constitution Act, 1982*, being Schedule B to the *Canada Act 1982* (UK), 1982, c 11.

Canadian Human Rights Act, RSC 1985, c H-6.

Canadian Multiculturalism Act, RSC 1985, c 24 (4th Supp).

Citizenship Act, RSC 1985, c C-29.

Citizenship Regulations, SOR/93-246.

Constitution Act, 1867 (UK), 30 & 31 Vict, c 3, reprinted in RSC 1985, App II, No 5.

Constitution Act, 1982, being Schedule B to the *Canada Act 1982* (UK), 1982, c 11.

Contraventions Act, SC 1992, c 47.

Crimes Against Humanity and War Crimes Act, SC 2000, c 24.

Criminal Code, RSC 1985, c C-46.

Customs Act, RSC 1985, c 1 (2nd Supp).

Extradition Act, SC 1999, c 18.

Faster Removal of Foreign Criminals Act, SC 2013, c 16 [Bill C-43].

Federal Courts Act, RSC 1985, c F-7.

Federal Courts Citizenship, Immigration and Refugee Protection Rules, SOR/93-22.

Federal Courts Rules, SOR/98-106.

Federal–Provincial Fiscal Arrangements Act, RSC 1985, c F-8.

Immigration and Refugee Protection Act, SC 2001, c 27.

Immigration and Refugee Protection Regulations, SOR/2002-227.

Immigration Appeal Division Rules, SOR/2002-230.

Immigration Division Rules, SOR/2000-229.

Indian Act, RSC 1985, c I-5.

Inquiries Act, RSC 1985, c I-11.

Interpretation Act, RSC 1985, c I-21.

Jobs, Growth and Long-term Prosperity Act, SC 2012, c 19 [Bill C-38].

Protecting Canada's Immigration System Act, SC 2012, c 17 [Bill C-31].

Public Service Employment Act, SC 2003, c 22.

Refugee Appeal Division Rules, SOR/2012-257.

Refugee Protection Division Rules, SOR/2012-256.

Strengthening Canadian Citizenship Act, SC 2014, c 22 [Bill C-24].

Supreme Court Act, RSC 1985, c S-26.

Visiting Forces Act, RSC 1985, c V-2.

Young Offenders Act, RSC 1985, c Y-1 [repealed].

Youth Criminal Justice Act, SC 2002, c 1.

Conventions and Protocols

Charter of the United Nations, 26 June 1945, UNTS XVI, Can TS 1945 No 7.

Convention Against Torture and Other Cruel, Inhuman or Degrading Treatment or Punishment (1984), 1465 UNTS 85, Can TS 1987 No 36, online: <http://legal.un.org/avl/ha/catcidtp/catcidtp.html6-7>.

Convention on the Rights of the Child, 20 November 1989, UNTS 1577, online: <http://www.ohchr.org/en/professionalinterest/pages/crc.aspx>.

Convention Relating to the Status of Refugees, 22 April 1954, 189 UNTS 150, online: <http://www.unhcr.org/3b66c2aa10.html>.

International Covenant on Civil and Political Rights, GA Res 2200A (XXI), 21 UN GAOR Supp (No 16) at 52, UN Doc A/6316 (1966), 999 UNTS 171, entered into force 23 March 1976, online: <http://www.ohchr.org/en/professionalinterest/pages/ccpr.aspx>.

Protocol Relating to the Status of Refugees, 606 UNTS 267, entered into force 4 October 1967, online: <http://www.unhcr.org/3b66c2aa10.html>.

Universal Declaration of Human Rights, GA Res 217A (III), UN Doc A/810 at 71 (1948), online: <http://www.un.org/Overview/rights.html> and <http://www.un.org/en/documents/udhr/index.shtml>.

Cases

Andrews v Law Society of British Columbia, [1989] 1 SCR 143.

Benner v Canada (Secretary of State), [1997] 1 SCR 358.

Black v Canada (Prime Minister), 2001 CanLII 8537, 54 OR (3d) 215 (CA).

Canada (Attorney General) v Mavi, 2011 SCC 30, [2011] 2 SCR 504.

Canada (Attorney General) v Ward, [1993] 2 SCR 689, 103 DLR (4th) 1, 20 Imm LR (2d) 85.

Canada (Citizenship and Immigration) v Odynsky, 2001 FCT 138, 14 Imm LR (3d) 3.

Canada (Minister of Employment and Immigration) v Chiarelli, [1992] 1 SCR 711.

Canada (Minister of Multiculturalism and Citizenship) v Minhas (1993), 66 FTR 155 21 Imm LR (2d) 31 (FCTD).

Canada (Minister of Multiculturalism and Citizenship) v Minhas (1993), 66 FTR 155, 21 Imm LR (2d) 31 (FCTD).

Canadian Doctors for Refugee Care v Canada (Attorney General), 2014 FC 651.

Charkaoui v Canada (Citizenship and Immigration), 2007 SCC 9, [2007] 1 SCR 350.

Chinese Business Chamber of Canada v Canada, 2005 FC 142, aff'd 2006 FCA 178.

Ezokola v Canada (Citizenship and Immigration), 2013 SCC 40, [2013] 2 SCR 678.

Gill v Canada (Citizenship and Immigration), 2012 FC 1522.

Hill v Canada (Minister of Employment and Immigration) (1987), 1 Imm LR (2d) 1 (FCA).

Huruglica v Canada (Citizenship and Immigration), 2014 FC 799.

Kahlon v Canada (Minister of Employment and Immigration) (1989), 7 Imm LR (2d) 91, 97 NR 349 (FCA).

Kaur v Canada (Citizenship and Immigration), 2010 FC 417.

Law Society of British Columbia v Mangat, 2001 SCC 67, [2001] 3 SCR 113.

Law Society of Upper Canada v Canada (Minister of Citizenship and Immigration), 2008 FCA 243, [2009] 2 FCR 466.

Li v Canada (Minister of Citizenship and Immigration), 2005 FCA 1, 249 DLR (4th) 306.

Lindo v Canada (Minister of Employment & Immigration), [1988] 2 FC 396, 91 NR 75 (CA).

Oberlander v Canada (Attorney General), 2015 FC 46.

Prassad v Canada (Minister of Employment and Immigration), [1989] 1 SCR 560.

Protsko v Angel Edward & Associates, 2004 CanLII 2550 (Ont SC).

R v Appulonappa, 2013 BCSC 31, rev'd 2014 BCCA 163, leave to appeal to SCC granted, 2014 CanLII 60080 (SCC).

R v Oakes, [1986] 1 SCR 103.

Rezaei v Canada (Minister of Citizenship and Immigration), 2002 FCT 1259, [2003] 3 FC 421.

Sharma v Canada (Citizenship and Immigration), 2009 FC 1131.

Singh v Minister of Employment and Immigration, [1985] 1 SCR 177.

Suresh v Canada (Minister of Citizenship and Immigration), 2002 SCC 1, [2002] 1 SCR 3.

United States of America v Cotroni; United States of America v El Zein, [1989] 1 SCR 1469.

YZ v Canada (Citizenship and Immigration), 2015 FC 892.

Zundel v Canada, 2004 FCA 145, [2004] 3 FCR 638.

Zundel, Re, 2005 FC 295.

Human Rights Organizations

Amnesty International. An international organization whose mission is to conduct research and promote action to prevent human rights abuses.
Online: <http://www.amnesty.org>.

Canadian Centre for Victims of Torture. Based in Toronto, the CCTV is a non-profit, registered charitable organization that provides services to immigrants and refugees who have experienced torture. The CCVT is considered a pioneer in the rehabilitation of survivors of torture.
Online: <http://www.ccvt.org>.

Canadian Council for Refugees. A non-profit umbrella organization that promotes the rights and protection of refugees, both in Canada and internationally; composed of organizations that aid in the settlement, sponsorship, and protection of refugees and immigrants.
Online: <http://ccrweb.ca>.

Centre for Refugee Studies (York University). For research on refugee issues; an organized research unit of York University, founded in 1988.
Online: <http://crs.yorku.ca>.

Human Rights Watch. An organization dedicated to protecting the human rights of people around the world and investigating human rights violations.
Online: <http://www.hrw.org>.

Refugee Studies Centre (Oxford Department of International Development, University of Oxford). Founded in 1982, the centre's purpose is to build knowledge and understanding of the causes and effects of forced migration in order to help improve the lives of some of the world's most vulnerable people.
Online: <http://www.rsc.ox.ac.uk>.

United Nations High Commissioner for Refugees. Founded in 1950, the agency is mandated to lead and coordinate international action to protect refugees and resolve refugee problems worldwide.
Online: <http://unhcr.org>.
UNHCR in Canada, online: <http://unhcr.ca>.

Index